SCIENCE & SPIRIT

Why Matter Isn't All that Really Matters

Frank Blume

ISBN-10: 1500864668
ISBN-13: 978-1500864668

To
Ferdi and Babette

Acknowledgments

First and foremost, I would like to express my gratitude to John Brown University for sponsoring my work on this book with five summer grants and one sabbatical leave. I also am thankful to Simone Schroder for processing hundreds of interlibrary loan requests, to Lothar Schäfer and Preston Jones for kindly supporting my grant proposals, to Calvin Piston for teaching additional courses during my sabbatical leave in the fall of 2008, to Grace Davis for her much needed words of encouragement, to Henry Stapp for providing me with valuable information concerning a quantum-mechanical theory of consciousness, and last but not least to my wife, Li Ping, for tolerating my mental preoccupation with *Science and Spirit* for more than eight years.

Preface

Given our current cultural conflicts and partisan divides, one may expect that any book on science and religion will be centrally concerned with evolutionary theory and carefully define a pro or con position. However, the purpose of this present work is not to contribute a skirmish to a battle. Instead, my goal in writing it has been to honestly account for many years of personal experience in trying to align my spirit with my intellect.

I was brought up in a society, in what was formerly West-Germany, in which it was assumed, by way of popular philosophy, that everything that happens has a cause that human reason can discover. Reality and human rationality, so I was taught, were totally congruent. Implicit in this thought is the idea that modern science and technology have long ago made obsolete all notions of transcendence. God, the human soul, and immortality are ancient wishful fantasies that simply are not useful any longer. The problem, though, was that I found that life in absence of these fantasies was really not worth living. There is no meaning to be found in anything I do, if everything there is is energy and matter. If I am just an aggregate of electrons and quarks in mathematical relatedness, then my existence in this world is altogether pointless.

This loss of meaning, which I very strongly felt, is the unifying theme that underlies the broad array of topics that are covered in this book. Among these, the topic of evolution clearly is significant, but other topics, too, are very much important. Perhaps the most important one of all of them concerns the nature of the consciousness. For the limitations of the materialistic worldview are nowhere more starkly apparent than in the problem of establishing how a purely physical system, such as a human brain, can ever bring about an actual experience. How can an aggregate of molecules, described by quantum physics, be conscious and aware? No one knows.

So insofar as we consider this perplexity to be expressive of a fundamental flaw in matter-bound ontologies, it does seem proper to assign to evolution as a topic—relative to consciousness—a somewhat less exalted status. To be sure, questions that pertain to life's historical development are well deserving of attention. Yet more deserving still may be the question of how any form of life can ever be truly alive by being capable, to some degree, of sensory or cognitive experience. For as we come to realize that this capacity is not material in kind, we can begin to see again those spirit-filled transcendent realms that modern science and philosophy have all along conspired to conceal.

Exactly how this claim regarding the non-materiality of consciousness can be convincingly supported is for the reader to discover by plowing through the many pages of this book. But what I should perhaps explain at this point is that all my arguments concerning this or any other claim are so aligned that through them I can tell an overarching story—the story of philosophy from ancient Greek antiquity to modern Western Europe. That is to say, the history of thought provides a natural chronology that integrates the arguments presented in this work into an encompassing context. In taking this approach I hope to demonstrate that my own personal experience—my struggle for meaning—is really not just personal. There is a larger process here involved, and it is this process that *Science and Spirit* is meant to elucidate.

In order to make more readily apparent this intimate bond between the personal and the superpersonal, each section in this book (with three minor exceptions) is broken up into two parts: an expository part that establishes the general historical context and a subsequent discussion part that is written in dialogue form and is typically intended to reveal how past ideas are relevant to individual experience at present. The dialogues feature two interlocutors— *Philonous* and *Sophie*—that are largely autobiographical but not entirely so. Commonly but not always, *Philonous* argues for my current point of view, and *Sophie* expounds beliefs that I endorsed quite long ago while still a student in Berlin. Moreover, the name *Philonous* is adopted from the *Dialogues* of Bishop Berkeley so as to indicate my close affinity to Berkeley's world of thought.

Given these remarks, it should be fairly obvious that *Science and Spirit* is highly interdisciplinary in character. Indeed, in order to be fully qualified to author it I would have to hold advanced degrees in almost all the fields of human intellectual endeavor: mathematics, physics, chemistry, biology, art history, philosophy, cosmology, astronomy, ethology, psychology, linguistics, and theology—the list goes on. In other words, the question of my competence deserves to be commented on: due to my educational and professional background in mathematics and physics, I generally felt well prepared to faithfully represent the various scientific topics that I chose to discuss in this book—not because I am an expert in all the fields of science but because there is in science a common mode of thought that I am well acquainted with. Naturally, I deliberately interpreted that mode of thought in ways that are unorthodox whenever my integrative purposes compelled me to do so. But I do believe that in each of these cases a more traditional rendering would have been well within my powers to provide.

Furthermore, in approaching topics that lay outside my immediate area of competence, which happened very frequently, I always took great care to examine a variety of sources so as to distill a consensus opinion. That is to say, my attitude in this regard was very much restrained. I did not attempt to create flamboyant new theories, but rather to accurately summarize the central facts and insights that experts can agree upon.

Most probably, of course, a specialist will find some of my statements to be inadequate or lacking in precision. But as it is, I do not think that shortfalls such as these invalidate my effort as a whole. In my view, the successful completion of an interdisciplinary work like *Science and Spirit* is far more strongly dependent on the diligence applied in doing one's research than on any expert knowledge that one happens to possess. The fact, for instance, that I understand, as a mathematician, how the theorem of Pythagoras can be formulated in a highly generalized Hilbert-space setting, does not make my reference to this theorem in the section on *The Spirit of Pythagoras* any more insightful or profound. There simply is no need for higher-level expertise in reasonings that are quite elementary in kind.

Concerning the specific sources that I used, I would like to mention that, in my studies of philosophy, I did not rely merely on second-hand expository accounts but always consulted as well (with some rare exceptions) the original philosophical writings on which these accounts are based. Among the former, the ones I used most frequently were the very comprehensive nine-volume treatise on the *History of Philosophy* by Copleston, the *Kleine Weltgeschichte der Philosophie* by Störig, and *The Passion of the Western Mind* by Tarnas. Other works and influences that were especially significant to me were the *Confessions* of Leo Tolstoy and St. Augustine, the analysis of *Evil in Modern Thought* by Susan Neiman, the *Meditations* of Marcus Aurelius, the imagery of Dante's *Divine Comedy*, the exposition on the *Comedy's* metaphysics by Christian Moevs, the account given by Thomas Kuhn of *The Copernican Revolution*, the works of Kübler-Ross and other near-death researchers, the writings of Albert Schweitzer, Carl Jung, and Dietrich Bonhoeffer, *The Hiding Place* by Corrie ten Boom, and, as indicated previously, the *Dialogues* of Bishop Berkeley on immaterialist philosophy.

That said, it only remains for me to express my hope that the reader may find some positive stimulation in the fruits of my labors and kindly overlook the many imperfections that my work undoubtedly contains.

FRANK BLUME, MAY 2014.

Contents

Chapter 1

Framing the Problem

To discern the causes that brought about the great transition from the Middle Ages to the modern world is no easy task. In our time of postmodern deconstruction, the traditional answers, pointing for example to the rediscovery of ancient learning in the Renaissance, to economic shifts, or rapid advances in science and technology as catalysts for change, are seriously challenged. The very notion, in fact, that a Scientific Revolution did indeed occur has fallen out of fashion.[1] And it is fair enough: we never can set up truly objective criteria for the designation of distinct historical periods, and no feat of scholarship, no matter how broad in scope, can ever encompass the whole of human life in all its vast complexity in any bygone era. However, there also can be no doubt whatsoever that dramatic change in Western Civilization has somehow been effected. We no longer live under the direct cultural and political control of the Catholic Church, and the *Summa Theologica* of Saint Thomas Aquinas, this great medieval synthesis of Aristotelian philosophy and Christian dogma, no longer sets the standard in our intellectual discourse.

What happened in the 15th, 16th, and 17th centuries is perhaps best likened to the psychological developments that mark the passage from childhood to adolescence. Here as there, a new consciousness is born, but a precise timeline or chain of causation is difficult to ascertain.

With the advent of the Italian Renaissance, the human spirit emerged from the shadow of the Church's parental authority to assert its autonomy and test its strength. Inasmuch as this quest for intellectual emancipation was characterized by a greater appreciation for the worth and dignity of the individual or by aspirations for increased political freedom and religious tolerance, our assessment of the legacy of modernity will be unambiguously positive. With scientific methods of disease control at our command, the bubonic plague no longer ravages the nations of Europe, and the Age of Enlightenment has put an end to the witch hunts and the Inquisition. On the darker side, however, a note of caution is in order, for throughout the modern era men and women of sincere conviction have expressed their sense of unease at the parting with tradition and the uncontested rule of reason. In the days of the Copernican Revolution, for instance, John Donne voiced his discomfort at the Earth's exile from its familiar place at the center of the universe in his poem *An Anatomy of the World:*[2]

> [The] new philosophy calls all in doubt,
> The element of fire is quite put out;
> The sun is lost, and th'earth, and no man's wit
> Can well direct him where to look for it.
> And freely men confess that this world's spent,
> When in the planets, and the firmament
> They seek so many new; then see that this
> Is crumbled out again to his atomies.
> 'Tis all in pieces, all coherence gone;
> All just supply, and all relation:
> Prince, subject, father, son, are things forgot,
> For every man alone thinks he hath got
> To be a phoenix, and that then can be
> None of that kind, of which he is, but he.

Francisco Goya apparently was motivated by similar sentiments when he etched a somber vision of monsters produced by "the dream of reason."

Figure 1.1: *The Dream of Reason Produces Monsters* by Goya (1799).

On this less favorable view, it may indeed appear that "all coherence" was lost when the modern analytic mind set out to demonstrate that reality in its entirety is but an aggregate of "atomies." Driven by the underlying presumption of the comprehensive reach of the human intellect, modern thought has spread before us barren lands of fragmentary knowledge in which the human soul can find no place of rest. As our conceptual scientific understanding advanced, the world receded ever further from the immediacy of direct experience toward the realm of abstraction. Images that once were tied to deeply felt beliefs have faded into pale blue rational reflections. A mountain range no longer is the place where legends tell of dragons slain by heroes of the past. For we have learned to look at it more truthfully, or so we think, as we record the elevation of its peaks and measure its extent in degrees of latitude. Under the austere light of reason, reality is stripped bare of its metaphysical attachments, and, sensing the void, we feel unsettled.

The triumph of the scientific method has revealed a mechanistic universe that seems to leave no room for soul or spirit. It is a universe in which the grinding force of randomness is countered only by the cold efficiency of mathematical necessity. Our very existence, indeed, is but an accident. Not providence but mere historical contingency has placed us on our tiny planetary home, and nowhere in the vast expanse of empty space in which we float do our telescopes discover signs that our presence might be known.

This spiritual loss that the age of science has inflicted can often be most clearly felt in encounters with the ancient customs and beliefs of tribal cultures. A case in point here is a travel memoir in which the renowned psychologist Carl Jung recounts his thoughts and impressions during a visit to the Pueblo Indians in 1925. Back then, the people of the tribe still lived in their traditional settlements high up on the Taos plateau in New Mexico.[3] Here, on "the roof of the world,"[4] they found themselves in a position of special favor, closest to their god and father the Sun. Their apparent sense of dignity and worth derived from their belief that they, acting for all the world, were given the responsibility to prayerfully guide the Sun-god on his daily journey across the sky. Realizing the depth of religious emotion invested in this faith, Jung could not help but envy his hosts for being in possession of a myth that so closely linked experience with meaning. What he saw was a wholeness well beyond the reach of our fragmented modern minds.

We probably are well advised not to engage at this point in romantic musings concerning natural man in his presumed primordial state of bliss, but the obvious contrast to our contemporary Western disposition will surely give us pause. For in place of the unity of sense-experience and meaning, so prominent in natural mythology, there is manifest in our present state of consciousness a strict polarity between the subject and the object of perception: the interior reality of the human self stands rigidly opposed to an external objective realm that is thought to be conditioned only by the impersonal demands of material causation.

Initially, this setting-apart of the modern self was no doubt liberating.

When René Descartes proclaimed the dualism of mind and matter at the dawn of the Enlightenment, he set the stage for a fruitful critical reflection that swept aside medieval superstition and cleared the way for reason to assert itself. His method of reductionistic inquiry proved greatly beneficial, and his dispassionate detachment in the pursuit of truth was laudable indeed. But as we follow the "trajectory"[5] of modern thought from *The Revolutions* of Copernicus to Darwin's *Origin of Species* and on to Freud's *Interpretation of Dreams*, we also realize that we are heirs to a legacy that has profoundly alienated modern man from the world in which he lives, from God, and even from himself.

The Copernican vision of a heliocentric universe wherein the Earth is but a planet among planets provided the initial impetus for a seismic shift in consciousness that may be best described as the second banishment of man. The price we had to pay for exposing to our intellect the secrets of the skies and the inner workings of the cosmos was exile—not from the Garden of Eden, but from the focus of divine attention at the center of creation. The analogy indeed is striking, for the emergence of modernity, just as the Fall of Man, was intimately linked to an advance in knowledge—and, here as there, the human subject became estranged from the object of experience. In the *Book of Genesis* we are told how Eve "saw that the fruit of the tree [of knowledge] was good for food and pleasing to the eye"[6] and how she was thus misled to disobey God's command. In trusting the evidence of her senses, she caused herself and all mankind to fall from grace and to be expelled from Paradise. Instead of the original Creator-creature harmony, there suddenly was nothing left but a bitter sense of separation and an irrevocable loss of innocence.

In Christian theology, of course, the rift caused by the Fall is overcome in Christ whose atoning sacrifice at Golgotha enabled God to grant divine forgiveness. The wound of Adam's sin is healed as God descends in human form to suffer punishment in our stead. It is this doctrine of the Incarnation that is directly relevant as well to our modern disconnect between experience and meaning. For the emergence of transcendent divinity in immanent material reality inherently signifies a restoration of oneness.

What is needed, so it seems, is a vision of existence as a whole that truly reconciles the inner with the outer realm—a vision of a living universe in which the human self is more than just an accidental or even providential singularity of spirit. The rigid dualism of Descartes must be replaced with a more accommodating ontology that allows for spirit to be active. Mind and matter must not appear as isolated opposites but rather as constituents that closely interlock.[1]

---

[1]This is obviously not to say that no attempts to overcome Cartesian dualism have been made within the last 350 years. Attempts of this sort are legion, and it may well be said that strictly dualistic views have long since been discredited in many philosophical circles. Whether the same can be said, however, of many of today's practicing scientists or of the

This realignment, so we hope, will open up a more appealing vista from which all artificially dichotomized conceptions are removed. Familiar antagonisms such as science versus religion, immanence versus transcendence, or object versus subject that have defined the major fault lines of Western thought and culture for the past five hundred years are to be reconceived in more holistic terms so that connections can be emphasized and harsh divisions be replaced with separations by degree.

As a matter of course, the present exposition in itself is but a tentative approach to such a larger goal. Yet even modest efforts may here be of some worth as the stakes involved are very high indeed. Afterall, the way we view reality determines not only our spiritual and emotional well being but also the course of our actions. If the world around us is perceived as soulless matter, then as such it will be treated, and the distressing symptoms of our philosophical pathologies are therefore painfully apparent all around: from environmental pollution and global ecological degradation the list of relevant disturbances extends to medical technologies applied with no concern for mind or soul, to perversely cruel agricultural facilities of animal mass production, to hyper-competitive economic structures driven by the rapid cycles of technological innovation rather than human need, and many more besides.

It is this range of present-day concerns that constitutes the broader context of the integrative view which we intend to propagate. Not academic self-absorption but existential need is here the motivating theme. In this spirit then, we will now give our two protagonists—*Philonous* and *Sophie*—an opportunity to share with us their thoughts on what we said so far.

Sophie: Against the admonition to abstain from "romantic musings," I will admit that the idea of a living natural mythology has always been to me exceedingly attractive. If only I were able to escape for once the modern curse that demands to cast aside anything that reason cannot fathom, the world would be reborn. Living close to the earth, so I imagine, my soul would be set free to re-establish all those bonds that long ago were broken. Mountains would again be holy mountains, the water flowing in the streams and rivers would be living water, and the Sun would be restored to his rightful rank as the divine giver of life—the father of us all.

Philonous: Your longing is to let your consciousness return to that place in time from which it first emerged, but are you sure it was a place of peace?

Sophie: 'Peace' may be too strong a word to use, but I would hope to find a reassuring sense of being part of a larger whole that still is in its primal state—a sense that everything still is what it was always meant to be. It is this embeddedness, I feel, in a timeless cosmic order that is so movingly apparent, for example, in prehistoric art. The famous paintings in the

---

public at large is quite a different matter. Furthermore, one very strong tendency in modern thought has been to overcome Cartesian dualism in the direction of materialistic monism[7]—a move that hardly is conducive to achieving our goal of science-spirit integration.

Figure 1.2: paintings in the cave of Altamira, © Manuel Alvarez Alonso / Dreamstime.com

caves at Lascaux and Altamira (Figure 1.2) and some other sites convey a spirit of deep rootedness that I have always found arresting. Only a people living in synchrony with the ancient rhythms of the earth could ever have produced such wonderful depictions.

Philonous: You are forgetting, though, it seems, the purpose that these works originally served.

Sophie: Rituals of magic—if I am not mistaken.

Philonous: Indeed, the tribesmen who once gathered in those caves probably believed the drawing of an image gave them special powers. The mammoth would more readily succumb to the hunters' spears if a spell was cast upon its picture on the wall. It is the desire to gain control over nature's numerous adversities and ominous uncertainties that speaks to us from such religious practices. Only against the backdrop of the harsh realities of life in the grasslands of the Ice Age do the paintings at Lascaux assume their proper meaning.[8]

Sophie: Are you asserting then that man in his original environment was dominated by hardship and fear?

Philonous: The possibility is real.

Sophie: But what about our own, distinctly modern quest for rational scientific understanding? I sense that it as well is driven by a fundamental fear of the unknown and a corresponding need to keep in check those "numerous adversities" you speak of. That is to say, we really have no right to think of rituals of magic or natural mythologies as being characteristic of a primitive mentality that our own, supposedly advanced societies have long outgrown. All our civilized sophistries really do not constitute a gain but only serve to cover up the loss of something vital.

Philonous: If I may add to that, let me suggest that certain fruits of what we proudly call 'technological progress' are likely to inspire greater fear than the rigors of nature faced by our ancestors.

Sophie: Are we in agreement then?

Philonous: As far as your assessment is concerned that something vital has been lost we are. But what I don't believe is that a resolution can be found by going back to some imagined prior stage of man's historical development.

Sophie: Neither do I. Consciousness must be permitted to expand and regression therefore has to be avoided.

Philonous: So what do you propose?

Sophie: A proposal I don't have. But what I do have is a word that perfectly denotes the problem that we face. The word is 'disenchantment'.[9] With the rise of modern science, the sacred was removed from our sight, and the more the universe seemed comprehensible, the more it also seemed indifferent to our personal existence.[10] Where in the past people could still look at the world and deeply feel its purpose and provision, we moderns are resigned to ponder the effects of mechanistic laws on random lumps of matter.

Philonous: No doubt, we find it difficult to earnestly believe that a hot globe of gas, such as the Sun, might also be a god. But perhaps we can agree that "an invisible god"[11] has purposefully placed it in the sky. Would such a view be satisfactory?

Sophie: The idea, of course, is well familiar but, unfortunately, a fully transcendent divinity is also fully irrelevant to all explanatory schemes we commonly employ. In other words, the Sun remains a globe of gas regardless of who formed it. Similarly, we can imagine, if we wish, the rainbow to be a sign of God's covenant, but no scientific description will ever have recourse to such an outdated statement of faith. The laws of reflection and refraction are all we need to understand the rainbow as a quantifiable phenomenon.

Philonous: Your problem, briefly stated, is that immanence is bleak and transcendence even bleaker.

Sophie: Briefly stated, yes, because I very strongly sense that aspirations for transcendence deprive me of vitality. And my desire therefore is to be immersed in the world that I can see and be immediately aware of. Yet it is this very world of my direct experience that scientific insight has shown to be a void without soul or purpose.

Philonous: I think the issue we are dealing with has now been well defined. So let us carefully examine it. We were agreed, as I recall, that consciousness must not regress.

Sophie: We were indeed, that is correct.

Philonous: Is it fair then to assume that your quest for meaning can succeed only if the knowledge science has revealed can be affirmed?

Sophie: Certainly, for a regression in essential knowledge would imply a regression in consciousness as well.

Philonous: Since that is so, the goal we ought to strive for is to widen our field of vision until science can be seen in a larger context wherein its dominance is broken.

Sophie: It sounds like sensible advice. So where do we begin?

Philonous: If science is the subject, then science we must try to understand. When you remarked, for instance, that scientific insight has shown the world of your direct experience "to be a void," I could not help but think that in your estimation science must be very powerful indeed. Has really *all* the world been bleached by its reductionist abstractions?

Sophie: I am aware that there are still a few uncharted territories. But on the whole, the map of physical reality that scientists have drawn is stunningly extensive and precise. Moreover, I seriously doubt whether solving some of the remaining puzzles will significantly alter the underlying paradigm. For very probably, no 'theory of everything' will ever challenge the idea that our world is ruled by laws that are at bottom mathematical and thus entirely impersonal.

Philonous: In the light of this assessment I would like us to consider a simple everyday occurrence such as the movement of a hand. What does science have to say about it?

Sophie: The details may be intricate, but the basic outline of the process is reasonably simple: an electric impulse from the neurons in the brain is transmitted through the nerves in the arm to the muscles in the hand where it causes a contraction and thus induces motion.

Philonous: Your account sounds plausible, but how do you explain the initial activation of the neurons?

Sophie: Initially, there is of course an act of will.

Philonous: This answer is perplexing, for I do not know a single book on physics that describes how acts of will can generate or influence electric currents. The electrons that constitute these currents are subject only to electric fields, and the notion that a mental process could affect such fields is simply not within the reach of current-day scientific understanding. To be sure, it has been clearly recognized in modern quantum physics that material reality requires for its completion an accounting for the freely chosen acts of consciously observing agents.[12] But such a purely factual acknowledgment of the integral role of consciousness does not afford us any genuine insight into the nature of consciousness itself nor into its purported link to matter at the level of a more detailed 'mechanical' account. In other words, all our thoughts, all our emotions, and even the simplest acts of our will are deeply mysterious as far as their relation is concerned to what we commonly regard as 'physical reality.' [II]

[II]Authors such as Henry Stapp, Roger Penrose, and Michael Lockwood (see [Sta3], [Pen], and [Lockw]) have attempted to formulate models of mind/matter interaction that are based on the laws of quantum physics, and their efforts certainly are laudable and competent. However, the fundamental problem of genuinely capturing an actual first-person experience by means of strings of discrete symbols—the laws of quantum physics or the words these authors use—can never be resolved. It is in this regard that quantum mechanical models of

Sophie: Your conclusion is appealing but your argument is not. For the mystery that you perceive would simply disappear if it could be shown that consciousness as well is merely a material phenomenon.

Philonous: Are you saying then that mental processes may not be real as such but only as derivatives of matter?

Sophie: The idea, at least, is worth considering.

Philonous: It clearly is, but imagine for a moment that a brain could be enlarged to such a size that we could enter and examine it[13]—that we could see immediately the workings of each cell, observe the composition of each molecule, and even watch the electrons form currents (in momentary disregard of certain basic quantum laws).[III] In such a close-up view the brain would surely be revealed to be stupendously complex. But where would we detect in it a thought, an act of will, or an emotion?

Sophie: That's the problem, I agree. For science is reductionistic by its very nature and is founded on the principle that any complex system must be understood in terms of the properties and interactions of its constituent parts. Unfortunately, in any such analysis all individuality is lost. The elementary components, be they cells or molecules or atoms, are entirely devoid of personality, and it is difficult to see how any entity composed of them could possibly be more than a machine. Are we to believe that at some level of integration the physical and purposeless is suddenly made meaningful by some aberrant spirit leap? The notion is absurd.

Philonous: Yet even more absurd is the idea that all you ever have experienced, all your thoughts, your intuitions, and your sentiments of love and hate are nothing but the workings of a mechanism. Is it possible for the impersonal and purposeless to be transformed into the personal and purposeful? Absolutely! Just consider how we view a painting. Can we ever hope to grasp the meaning it conveys by studying scientifically the pigments on its surface? And did you not yourself perceive a spiritual quality in prehistoric art that cannot be reduced to mere materiality?

Sophie: I wish I could agree with you, but I also must be honest. For if, as you suggest, there is something more to life, something that science cannot capture, then how do we explain that reductionism has been so enormously successful? How could the scientific method work so well if it didn't closely correspond to the structure of reality as it really is?

Philonous: These are valid and important questions. There is no doubt that science's success has been remarkable indeed and cannot be ignored. The

---

consciousness are no less elusive than any other such models present or past.

[III]The laws of quantum physics do not allow for the continuous observation of an electron in motion, but for the sake of argument we have here chosen to ignore this fact because our intent at present is to highlight the problems inherent in a classical reductionistic view of consciousness. However, we also readily admit that quantum phenomena are conceivably of great importance for the formation of consciousness and that a mechanistic image of the brain is overly simplistic—even within an essentially materialistic paradigm.

technological devices that scientific progress has produced would have been seen as first rate miracles in any age preceding ours. However, it is this very success that has seduced us to believe that scientific reasoning is broader in its scope than the evidence permits us to infer. If even such a simple everyday occurrence as the movement of a hand is ultimately beyond our reckoning, then we probably are well advised to openly admit that our knowledge—even nowadays—is still quite limited and crude.

Sophie: There may be limits, it is true, but to concentrate on them will always be a losing strategy. Those who retreat into the realm of the unknown will often find themselves exposed when research breaches new frontiers.

Philonous: I heartily agree. Carving out a niche of ignorance in which to hide is not a promising approach. It would be a grave mistake to think that meaning always must be tied to lack of comprehension. That said, however, we also need to recognize that truthfulness demands that we acknowledge our fundamental finitude. Human cognition is limited inherently and will remain so quite regardless of how far our knowledge and our science in the future will extend. By implication, a healthy realistic attitude—an attitude conducive to this integrative quest—can only be assumed if we are really realistic, that is, if we uphold a vision of proportion: the world is larger than the reach of our minds and our senses.

Sophie: Then how do we decide which limitations are fundamental in kind and which are not?

Philonous: A final answer to this question is impossible to give. But I hope that our journey through the history of science and philosophy will offer you at least a plausible perspective. Keeping this intent in mind, we now return to where it all began—to ancient Greece and Asia Minor.

Chapter 2

The Origins of Science

The Ionian Pioneers

The time from about 800 to 200 B.C., which is commonly referred to as the Axial Period,[I] marks a turning point in the history of civilization. In this age, great personalities such as Confucius and Laotzu in China, the Buddha in India, Zarathustra in Persia, and the Old-Testament prophets in Palestine created systems of ethical and metaphysical thought that have exerted a defining influence on the religious and intellectual development of mankind ever since. "[R]adical questions"[1] were asked concerning the nature of God and man, the meaning of suffering, and the problem of knowledge. In retrospect it seems as though there was a simultaneous movement of the spirit across the known world. New and higher levels of awareness were reached as men reflected on the secrets underlying their material and ethical existence.

These centuries of transformation also witnessed the birth of natural philosophy among the people who had settled in the western coastal region of Asia Minor. Here, at the meeting-place of Orient and Occident, where the great caravan routes from the Asian continent reached the Mediterranean Sea, the Ionians had established flourishing centers of trade that facilitated contacts with the cultures of the East. It was in this environment of cultural exchange where, in the first half of the 6th century B.C., *Thales of Miletus* rose to prominence for his accomplishments in astronomy and mathematics. He is said to have predicted the solar eclipse of 585 B.C., and a geometric theorem pertaining to right triangles inscribed to semicircles still bears his name today.[II] With

---

[I]This era is sometimes also referred to as the *First* Axial Period, with our current age of globalization being regarded as the *Second* Axial Period. However, Karl Jaspers who first introduced the term 'Axial Period' strictly rejects this distinction as he considers our present age to be a time, not of spiritual renewal, but "of catastrophic descent to poverty of spirit, of humanity, love and creative energy."[2]

[II]If an arbitrary point P on a semicircle is connected with the two endpoints of the

regard to the history of philosophy, his greatest contribution was the raising of the question concerning the natural origins of the universe. Tales of origins, of course, abound in mythological traditions, but the attempt to discern the nature of all things by rational effort alone had never been made before.

Our knowledge of the philosophy of Thales is limited indeed, for no original writings of his have been preserved, and of secondary sources there are but few. According to Aristotle, Thales taught that water is the fundamental substance—the *Urstoff*—of which everything is made. This notion, which strikes us as preposterous at first, seems more convincing in the light of our everyday experience that water changes its appearance when it freezes or evaporates.[3][III] For state transitions of this kind will readily suggest to us the far more general idea that diverse phenomena can have a common, unifying cause. In this sense, it is justified to say that Thales was the first to pose the problem of "Unity in Difference,"[5] the pursuit of which in modern times has led to all the great discoveries in science. Afterall, any law of nature that scientists have ever formulated is nothing but a principle that underlies and *unifies* a certain set of *differing* material phenomena.

A significant advance over the ideas of Thales was achieved by his younger contemporary and fellow Milesian, *Anaximander*, who lived from about 611 to 549 B.C. Taking a far more abstract approach, Anaximander rejected the belief that water is the *Urstoff*[IV] of all things and proposed instead that the ground of being was indeterminate and infinite. He envisioned an eternal cosmic background, from which all things arose and to which they all returned at "the appointed time"[6] when they had made "reparation and satisfaction to one another for their injustice."[7] Implicit in this thought is the idea that physical reality is linked to purpose and even moral valuations—an indication of the fact that in the early days of natural philosophy a clear dividing line between matter and spirit had not as yet been drawn.[8]

That said, however, we also need to emphasize that the cosmological system of Anaximander differs quite decidedly from the older, mythological tradition of Hesiod and Homer. For in its emphasis on material causation it clearly is more rational in kind. The formation of the world, for instance, is described as a process whereby "something capable of begetting hot and cold [is] separated off from the eternal,"[9] and the creation of the heavenly bodies is explained from the assumption that a sphere of flames around the Earth was broken up and then "enclosed in rings."[10] At the center of these rings a cylindrical Earth was thought to be floating freely in the space surrounding it. Furthermore,

---

semicircle, then the angle formed at P is equal to $90°$.

[III]Thales himself apparently provided a slightly different argument, for he is said to have observed that "the nutriment of all things is moist... and that water is the origin of the nature of moist things."[4] However, it is highly likely that he also was aware of the phenomenon of state transitions and that he recognized its significance.

[IV]The word 'Urstoff' is German and has no direct English translation. Its meaning approximately is 'primal, primordial substance'.

with respect to the origins of life, Anaximander argued from the comparative helplessness of human infants that man could never have survived, unless, "in the beginning [he] was born from animals of different species." [11] And in another source we read that all "[l]iving creatures arose from the moist element" [12] and that man initially had been a fish. It is to explanations such as these that we trace back the roots of modern Western science. For in omitting any reference to the supernatural or to divine intervention, the world is brought within the reach of human understanding.

The last of the Milesian philosophers was *Anaximenes*, an associate of Anaximander whose teachings, though, were more akin to those of Thales.[V] He had in common with the latter the belief that physical reality at bottom was determinate and also that there had to be a fundamental substance. According to Anaximenes, however, this ultimate material was air rather than water. In support of this assertion he invoked the concepts of condensation and rarefaction, but the details of his argument need not concern us here.

The School of Miletus came to a violent end when the city was destroyed by the Persians in 494 B.C. Yet the timeless questions that those who belonged to it had asked have been with us ever since.

The Spirit of Pythagoras

The questions have been with us, but the answers have not. Modern scientists no longer think that the physical world is grounded in substance—that water or air or some other tangible stuff composes the core of existence. Instead, at the bottom of any present-day physical theory we always find an abstraction—a mathematical equation, say, or a formal axiomatic description. Some examples that come here to mind are the fundamental laws of mechanics that Newton devised, the Maxwell equations of electrodynamics, the field equations of Einstein's general relativity, and the Schrödinger equation of quantum mechanics. Ultimate reality in modern scientific representations is mathematical and therefore, in essence, relational rather than concretely material. Remarkably, though, it was not a modern physical scientist who was the first to propose this amazing idea, but rather an ancient natural philosopher by the name of *Pythagoras*.

Pythagoras was born around 570 B.C. on the island of Samos off the coast of Asia Minor. He is believed to have been a student of Thales and probably also attended the lectures of Anaximander. When he grew dissatisfied with the tyranny of Polycrates, he left his homeland and spent many years in travel, visiting Egypt, Babylon, and perhaps even India. [14] Eventually, he

---

[V] To be precise, the teachings of Anaximenes incorporated elements from the thought of both Thales *and* Anaximander, but it is the greater concreteness of the former's doctrine that seems to be the more evident influence.

settled down in Southern Italy where he established a fellowship of like-minded thinkers near the city of Crotona. The rule of this brotherhood was constituted upon certain ascetic practices and mystical beliefs that directly tied in with Pythagoras's more rational, philosophical doctrine. But it is only the latter—the philosophical doctrine—that shall be here of interest to us.

According to Aristotle, the Pythagoreans "were the first to take up mathematics" and to view "its principles" to be foundational to everything there is.[13] That is to say, reality, in Pythagorean philosophy, was thought to be derivative of abstract quantitative relations and numerical patterns. Numbers were commonly represented by geometric arrangements of pebbles or dots in the sand, and certain of these configurations assumed sacred significance. The *tetraktys*, for instance, that shows the number 10 to be the sum of 1, 2, 3, and 4 (Figure 2.1), was given the role of a quasi-divine generating entity. The num-

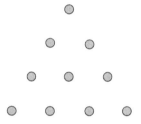

Figure 2.1: the tetraktys.

ber 1, as the most basic unit, was identified with a single point; the number 2, represented by two points, defined a line, 3 a plane, and 4 symbolized the spatial structure of a tetrahedron. In asserting further that all material objects are composed of elementary geometric building blocks, the Pythagoreans came to conclude that numbers form and organize the whole of physical existence.

To Pythagoras and his followers is also attributed the discovery of the mathematical laws underlying musical harmony. In studying tonal scales on stringed instruments, they realized, for instance, that the pitch of a vibrating string is raised by one octave if its length is cut in half. This conditioning of an individual's experience of harmonious sound by numerical relations was believed to be of great significance. For it was thought to indicate that harmony was perceived as the soul entered into a state of resonance with the abstract order of the cosmos.

Given their predisposition to search for universal truths in the ethereal realm of abstraction, it is perhaps not surprising that the Pythagoreans are generally credited with having been the first to have employed rigorous methods of deduction in mathematics. Most famously, the theorem of Pythagoras, according to which the square of the hypotenuse of any right triangle equals the sum of the squares of its sides, was shown to be valid by way of rational

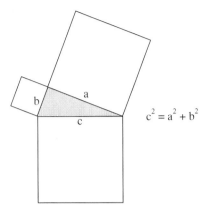

$$c^2 = a^2 + b^2$$

Figure 2.2: the theorem of Pythagoras.

argument.[1] The details of the proof have not been handed down to us, but we can speculate that it involved partitions of a square like those in Figure 2.3. Here we are shown two squares of side length $a + b$ that are broken up in different ways. Since the four shaded triangles on the left are equal in size to those on the right, it follows that the remaining non-shaded areas are equal as well. In other words, c^2 equals $a^2 + b^2$.

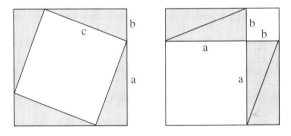

Figure 2.3: proof of the theorem of Pythagoras.

Sophie: The proof is beautiful in its simplicity. It must have left a deep impression on those who first discovered it.

Philonous: No doubt, to become aware of the force of necessity carried by such arguments is truly a remarkable experience.

Sophie: Perhaps then it was this revelation of a necessary truth that inspired the Pythagoreans to believe that mathematics forms the core of everything

---

[1]Some skepticism is here in order because the Greek sources that make this claim were all written several centuries after Pythagoras had died.[15] Moreover, the theorem itself without a proof was known already earlier in China and in Sumer.

there is. For if, as they asserted, the order of the cosmos is linked to our perception of harmony in music, then, by analogy, it also may be linked to our innate capacity for quantitative geometric thought. In other words, any lawful process that we commonly observe, such as the falling of an object when we drop it, may here appear to be endowed, as it were, with quasi-mathematical necessity.

Philonous: I never really looked at it this way, but the idea is certainly attractive. In fact, it may directly lead us to the origins of rational philosophy. For what is here at stake is our mode of knowledge acquisition: the notion that the patterns of our thought, especially in mathematical deduction, are reflective of the structure of the universe may cause us to believe that knowledge can be gained internally, in abstract reasonings, without appeal to any form of sensory perception. Amazingly, this doctrine, that mind and cosmos are homologous, has frequently been well confirmed by scientific practice.

Sophie: Your assertion is surprising, for I always thought that science by its very nature must be grounded in experiment. Can there be knowledge that is firm without an adequate empirical foundation?

Philonous: There is no doubt that science in the modern world has often been inspired by experiment. We moderns have been taught by research over centuries that empiricism and rationalism must be joined for knowledge to progress. But what is so astonishing is that the mathematical structures underlying certain laws of nature could sometimes be discovered—or created—long before experiments suggested them. That is to say, it can occur that abstract thoughts, conceived entirely apart from any observation, are later found to properly reflect material reality.

Sophie: The claim is bold. What would be an example?

Philonous: Are you familiar with *The Elements* of Euclid?

Sophie: To some extent I am. The work is famous for its axiomatic treatment of geometry.

Philonous: Indeed, in the *The Elements* Euclid formulated five postulates and five common notions from which all the geometric propositions in the text could be derived. The last of the five postulates, however, the so-called parallel postulate, was different in tone from the first four and also less self-evident. It essentially asserts that given an infinitely extended line L in a plane, and given a point P not on this line, there is exactly one infinitely extended line that passes through P and does not intersect the given line L, namely the line parallel to L (Figure 2.4).[II] Almost from the day

---

[II]The original formulation of Euclid's parallel postulate reads as follows: if a straight line falling on two straight lines makes interior angles on the same side less than two right angles, then the two straight lines, if produced indefinitely, meet on that side on which the angles are less than the two right angles.[16] It can be shown that this formulation is equivalent to the one stated above—so long as Euclid's first four postulates are assumed to be valid.

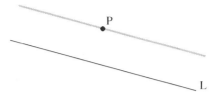

Figure 2.4: the parallel postulate.

The Elements was published, mathematicians tried to derive the parallel postulate from the first four postulates. But for more than two millennia all efforts were in vain. Complicated arguments were devised that commonly turned out to be dependent on a claim that was equivalent to the parallel postulate itself. Finally, in the first half of the 19th century, it was discovered that there are consistent geometric systems that satisfy the first four postulates but violate the last. The first to publish an article concerning such constructions was the Russian mathematician Nicolai Ivanovich Lobachevsky in 1829. At about the same time in Hungary, Janos Bolyai independently arrived at similar results, and already a decade earlier, Carl Friedrich Gauss had privately concluded that non-Euclidean geometries did indeed exist. In a parallel development Gauss also initiated the study of the local geometric properties of arbitrary curved surfaces, but seemingly without a cogent link to Lobachevsky's system.

Sophie: But only seemingly, I guess.

Philonous: That's right. The link was there and finally was found by one of Gauss's colleagues, the brilliant *Bernhard Riemann.* In 1854, three years after gaining his doctorate, Riemann was preparing to take up a position as *Privatdozent* at the University of Göttingen. In his probationary lecture to the faculty he presented a thesis entitled *Über die Hypothesen, die der Geometrie zu Grunde liegen (On the Hypotheses Underlying Geometry).* As it turned out, Riemann's work was of such visionary quality that it almost instantly assumed a legendary status—and even the great Gauss was fervently applauding. And rightly so, for Riemann had accomplished nothing less than to devise a comprehensive formalism for the study of geometric relations in generalized spatial frameworks of arbitrarily high dimension. His conception was so broad that it included both the Gaussian theory of curved surfaces and the non-Euclidean geometries of Bolyai and Lobachevsky as special cases.

Sophie: The achievement seems impressive, I admit, but could it be applied?

Philonous: It couldn't at the time, and Riemann's work might thus have easily been judged a useless outgrowth of a self-serving academia. Amazingly, though, some 60 years later, in 1916, Albert Einstein published a paper on a revolutionary new theory of gravity in which the methods Riemann had devised were vitally employed to give that theory its geometric form.[III] In other words, an abstract mathematical construct, conceived as a grand unifying theory of geometry in the mind of Bernhard Riemann, turned out to closely match the large-scale structure of the cosmos.

Sophie: And hence Pythagoras was right: the universe is ordered mathematically and thus accessible to human understanding.

Philonous: Indeed, the anticipation of Einstein's theory of relativity by Riemann's research into the foundations of geometry brings to light a deep Pythagorean correspondence between the laws of nature and the patterns of our thought. It really seems as though there is a kind of structural analogy between mind and matter that enables our intellect to freely form conceptions that describe—unwittingly at times—the actual physical world.

Sophie: In essence then you are suggesting that the universe is comprehensible *inherently:* mind comprehends matter because mind and matter somehow are alike.[17]

Philonous: At least I find it difficult to see on what alternative account we might expect the human mind to be equipped with such astounding powers of prescient abstract thought. Afterall, the evolutionary process, from which that mind supposedly emerged, did not involve selective pressures pertinent to the ability to formulate the fundamental principles of spacetime gravitation. What we must therefore ask is this: why do the intellectual faculties, which man acquired in prehistory to meet the challenge of survival, allow us to discover in advance the proper mathematical descriptors of even such a far removed phenomenon as geometric gravity?

Sophie: I don't suppose that happenstance could be a reason you accept.

Philonous: Chance, no doubt, may be importantly involved whenever evolution is at issue, but a sufficient explanation for the astounding versatility of the human intellect it is not. For only those characteristics of the human mind that are directly relevant to the problems of survival in natural environments can be within the explanatory reach of evolutionary theory. And the capacity to understand, let's say, how spacetime can be curved may therefore seem inherently mysterious.

Sophie: Unless, of course, we postulate the "structural analogy" to which you just alluded (see above).

Philonous: Unless we do, that is correct.

Sophie: So the fact that the range of our intellect far exceeds the set of tasks by which success in evolution was defined cannot be understood unless it is the case that mind and matter are intrinsically connected.

Philonous: Indeed, I do believe that our intellect's ability to represent in abstract thought the universal laws of nature is not directly due to adaptation but rather is expressive of an underlying similarity in how these two

---

[III]The only essential difference between the formalisms of Riemann and Einstein is that the metric tensor is positive definite in the former but not in the latter.

domains—mind and matter—are configured.

Sophie: You may be right, but what is here the larger implication? Are you sure that this conclusion furthers our quest?

Philonous: I see no reason why it wouldn't.

Sophie: Well, as I recall, one central goal that we set out to reach is to resolve the problem of the loss of meaning in reductionistic thought. And, more specifically, we asked in reference to this goal whether the phenomenon of consciousness is also just material in nature (p.9).

Philonous: ...because this question is of critical importance. If consciousness were strictly physical, then the totality of human life would be encapsulated by the formulas that physicists employ to specify the properties of matter. There wouldn't be a soul, there wouldn't be a purpose, and our present conversation, in particular, would also be completely void and pointless.

Sophie: If that is so, then I suggest we take a closer look at your attendant claim that mind is linked to matter by an "underlying similarity." What, if I may ask, do you propose the nature of that similarity to be?

Philonous: That, of course, remains to be determined. But let me warn you: the problem is a sticky one.

Sophie: Perhaps it isn't quite so sticky afterall, because the similarity may simply be an actual identity: mind is matter and nothing but matter, and, by implication, so is consciousness. That is to say, your argument may well be taken to support reductionistic thought because the "structural analogy," which you inferred from our mind's ability to penetrate the abstract order of the cosmos—sometimes in advance—may well be most conveniently explained from the assumption that mind is merely matter.

Philonous: Your reasoning is certainly admissible, but notice also this: the alternative assumption—matter is mind—is logically of equal plausibility because it differs from the version you proposed only in its emphasis on mind, rather than matter, as the primary reality.

Sophie: "Matter is mind"? The notion is absurd.

Philonous: ...not any more absurd, as I would say, than your idea of mind as matter.

Sophie: But how can matter be derivative of thought? Can solid substance be produced by something mental and elusive?

Philonous: The question can be easily inverted. For the contrast you perceive between the fleeting and the firm makes matter seem no less incapable of bringing forth mind than mind of bringing forth matter. That is to say, we don't gain much by granting primacy to either realm if there are no discernible connections.

Sophie: So what do you propose?

Philonous: ...to take a more coherent, unified approach: the assumption that the qualities associated with mind are incompatible with those assigned to matter is unwarranted and overly constrictive. In other words, to properly

address the problem of the comprehensibility of physical reality, we must
be open to the thought that matter also can be "mind-like."[18]

Sophie: Your logic, I admit, is not entirely unsound. But is there evidence
    in science to support it? Do any present theories suggest that mind and
    matter are alike?

Philonous: The theory that I believe corroborates this claim is modern quan-
    tum physics. However, as I said, the problem is a sticky one, and all at-
    tempts to tackle it had better be preceded by some serious reflection on the
    character and general philosophy of scientific thought. In other words, to
    adequately handle it we must be well prepared. So please be patient—part
    two will follow later (in the section on *Mind over Matter*).

The Fall, the Logos, and the Cat

Anyone who traces and examines the origins of science and philosophy in ancient Greek antiquity is liable to feel at times the optimistic spirit of a pioneering venture. The idea of asking questions never asked before creates a sense
of hope. For the answers that are found may open up the new horizon of perhaps a better world. Unfortunately, though, the facts of history, surveyed in
retrospect, are somewhat sobering. The promise proved elusive, and a "better
world" is sadly still a very distant fantasy.

The question though is "Why?" Why can we not improve the human lot
more readily and steadily by deepening our insight? Should not the search
for knowledge and for truth be leading us reliably to genuine advancement?
By instinct we incline to answer "yes," but we do well not to forget that in
the *Book of Genesis* it is the tree of *knowledge* that bears the forbidden fruit.
Man comes to *know* what good and evil are by being disobedient to God's
benevolent proscription. In consequence, the unity of being is destroyed, and
a world of harsh alternatives emerges—right and wrong, faith and fear, hope
and despair.

Seen in this light, the story of the Fall may strike us as a symbol for
the process of becoming conscious. As animal instinct gives way to human
volitional liberty, man's own nature becomes his greatest source of conflict.
For he now is free to choose. Man knows and can decide and therefore is
divided—against himself, his fellow men, and also his Creator. His knowledge
is his curse.

So are we then to say that conflict and division will occur whenever consciousness advances? Are inner strife and outer war the requisites of progress?
A man who would have answered "yes" to either of these inquiries—conceivably
and probably—was the Ionian thinker *Heraclitus* who lived in the late 6th and
early 5th century B.C.

On the surface it may seem that Heraclitus merely modified the natural
philosophies of Thales and Anaximenes. Not water or air, but rather fire

he declared to be the *Urstoff* of the universe: "All things are exchanged for
Fire, and Fire for all things, as wares are exchanged for gold and gold for
wares."[21] Yet looking deeper we can see how fire here is viewed to be an
agent of transformation—a force that always moves the world and never lets
it rest. Reality, according to Heraclitus, is an ever changing flux of state
transitions wherein opposing tendencies are constantly in conflict: "Cool things
become warm; what is warm cools; what is wet dries out; what is dry becomes
moist."[22] In one of Plato's dialogues, this doctrine of the permanence of change
is summarized as follows:

> Heraclitus... says that everything moves on and that nothing is at
> rest; and, comparing existing things to the flow of a river, he says
> that you could not step into the same river twice.[23]

Moreover, to further underscore the vital role of conflict, Heraclitus claims
explicitly that "war is universal and justice is strife, and that all things take
place in accordance with strife and necessity."[24]

In taking this approach, it will appear that any genuine advance in knowledge and awareness will always be resultant of a crisis. That is to say, the
evolution of consciousness—in this way of thinking—is a perpetual struggle
wherein any resolution of a conflict always leads to other conflicts, which then
in turn demand a resolution, and so forth *ad infinitum*. In fact, the rise of modern science in particular may easily be said to be a part of this development as
well. By implication then, we needn't be surprised to learn that science also
poses problems formerly unknown, such as the loss of purpose in reductionism.

However, as conflict follows conflict follows conflict, the question will arise
if there is overall some progress being made. Perhaps the whole charade is
just a cycle closing in upon itself. What reason is there to expect that on
the whole there will be true advancement? To view this question properly,
we need to understand that Heraclitus very crucially did not consider strife
to be synonymous with chaos. Instead he thought the interplay of opposites
to be embedded in an encompassing cosmic order that he referred to as the
Logos. "It is opposition," so he proclaimed, "that brings things together,"[25]
and "[t]he harmonious structure of the world depends upon opposite tension,
like that of the bow and the lyre."[26]

So is it then not possible that progress is induced—predictably—by Heraclitus's *Logos*? The answer is that we don't know. But Heraclitus himself would
likely have endorsed this view, and other thinkers who derived their inspiration from his pertinent ideas have echoed it as well. According to the German
philosopher *Friedrich Hegel*, for example, there is indeed discernible in history
a directed movement of the spirit to higher levels of awareness. Progress in
history, as well as in philosophical thought, occurs dialectically whenever a
polarity of thesis and antithesis is restored to unity on the higher plane of a
coherent synthesis.

For instance, the problem of the loss of meaning in reductionistic thought might here be framed as follows: reductionism is the *thesis*, and holism, that is, the belief that the whole of reality is more than the sum of its parts, is the *antithesis*. Closely related to both the thesis and the antithesis is the experiential quality that we refer to as 'meaning' because this quality is negated by the thesis and therefore implies the antithesis.[1] Initially, the thesis of reductionism as a principle of rational analysis and practical application in science appears perfectly reasonable in its own right. But as we try to grasp its essence more astutely, its limitations are revealed, and the antithesis of holism emerges. As the Hegelian dialectic thus unfolds, we strive to deepen our insight until a *synthesis* becomes manifest that not only removes the seeming contradiction between thesis and antithesis but also makes them both appear more cogent and transparent. In other words, a unity in difference is established as neither the thesis nor the antithesis is denied and as both are subsumed by a truth of higher order.

Sophie: So the Hegelian synthesis in this example is the very goal that you and I are after: the re-establishment of meaning in the face of modern science.
Philonous: In essence, yes it is.
Sophie: Then I will say this dialectic strikes me as abstract. There is no way for me to solve my personal dilemma by studying how progress in history is globally derivative of thesis-and-antithesis polarities.
Philonous: ...or so it may appear. But Hegel took a different view. For he believed that knowledge has the goal to justify the world and help us feel "at home"[27] in it. That is to say, in Hegel's thought, the subject and the object can be reconciled as comprehensive insight can be gained into the nature of latter by the former. Reality thereby can be divested "of its strangeness"[28] because the human subject's intellect is able to perceive—correctly and entirely—the Spirit that connects the multitude of facts that constitute *objectively* the flow of universal history.
Sophie: I tend to think, as I explained before (p.8), that scientific knowledge is extensive. But even so it seems to me, that Hegel's view of human rationality, as you have just described it, is vastly overconfident.
Philonous: There is a problem, I agree. For in effect what Hegel claims is nothing less than that, in principle, the mind of man can fully comprehend the Spirit of God. As Adam became god-like—"like one of us," as it says in *Genesis*—by "knowing good and evil,"[29] so Hegel makes the human intellect divine by making it the arbiter of God's activity and providence in history. In fact, I find it tempting to conclude in light of this that Hegel's grand philosophy is really just another case of breaking God's command—of eating fruit that is forbidden.

---

[1]To say that *A* negates *B*, is the same as saying that *A* implies the negation of *B*, which in turn is equivalent to the assertion that *B* implies the negation of *A*.

Sophie: You almost make it sound as though all knowledge and philosophy will always be heretical of needs.

Philonous: That would be overstating it. For knowledge has its benefits no doubt. It makes us more secure and thereby can induce in us a sense, as Hegel says, that we can be "at home." But knowledge also causes us, quite frequently, to feel impiously enamored with its reach. We like to revel in the thought how very far indeed our comprehension is extended, and our grasp of true reality in consequence is woefully reduced.

Sophie: It is reduced? What do you mean?

Philonous: The problem that I'm getting at is evident in simple form in animal behavior. My cat, for instance...

Sophie: Your cat?

Philonous: Yes—my cat. She has developed habits that are most peculiar. When I let her out into the garden, for example, she never heads directly for the door but rather nears it from the side, from underneath the dining table. More perplexing still, is her reaction when the exit way is partially blocked by, say, a bucket or a bag. Instead of simply walking past the obstacle, she always goes around the table for a second time in the apparent hope that her familiar path will somehow be unblocked (Figure 2.5). Eventually, of course, she finds her way outside, but not before she failed on two or three attempts.

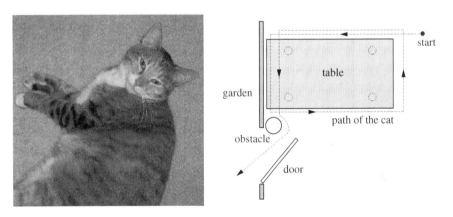

Figure 2.5: the path habits of Curry the cat.

Sophie: The significance of feline path-habits[30] in our current context is a bit obscure. Please clarify.

Philonous: If we ask ourselves why cats or other animals are prone to show such patterns of behavior, the answer is not difficult to find. In a natural environment, habitual acquaintance with a certain territory can be of great survival value. For it may facilitate the search for food and also aid a quick escape in case a predator is charging. What is required at the outset is, of course, some basic means of knowledge acquisition. Initially, a new terrain must be explored so that its features can be entered into memory. When this is done, however, the knowledge thus produced will tend to fossilize as now a habit is established. So here we have a case where flexibility is lost as knowledge is increased. My cat's reluctance, for example, to circumnavigate an obstacle, is a sign that her knowledge of my living room effectively diminishes her cognitive adaptiveness.

Sophie: And your suggestion therefore is that by analogy the same applies to human beings too.

Philonous: Indeed, I do believe that human knowledge also has at times a similarly limiting effect. If we imagine prehistoric man in his original environment, it is quite obvious how here as well a need for knowledge was directly tied to problems of survival. Afterall, knowledge clearly is a means by which we gain control, and fear is overcome in familiarity. I think that herein also lies the reason why we humans—just as animals—display a tendency to cling to that which we have learned and know. We too are creatures of habit, and traditions are important in directing our lives. By implication, we too may suffer loss of cognitive agility: as our knowledge is increased in a particular domain—as science, for example—we easily lose sight of other aspects of reality, and our field of vision thus contracts.

Sophie: I understand, all habits are inherently restrictive. But Adam's sin was clearly not to follow too inflexibly a custom or tradition. He was expelled from Eden not because he had established a routine but rather because his newfound knowledge of morality had somehow made him god-like.

Philonous: There is a difference, I agree. But as regards your personal dilemma, I *will* say that I *do* believe my argument is relevant. For when you said in our first discussion that science has shown the world of your direct experience "to be a void" (p.7), you really made it obvious thereby how very much indeed reality can shrink when knowledge of a certain kind is crudely overemphasized. It seems to me your problem is, in part at least, that scientific knowledge in your mind is simply far too dominant. Furthermore, in taking here a broader view, we also can discern a link to Adam's Fall in that the rise of science too has brought on separation. In science man attempts to recreate the world in terms of concepts that describe the flow of his perceptions. But as his cognitive abilities are limited inherently, this world that he conceives is partial and inadequate. It is an abstract mental scheme which is as such quite spiritless and barren. In other words, the mind of man cannot achieve what only God is able to accomplish: to author a reality that really is complete.

Sophie: So what you reckon is that I, by being science-minded, have limited my world and thereby made it godless.

Philonous: The paraphrase is apt.

Sophie: By implication then, religion is the remedy.

Philonous: In speaking of the Fall it may be more appropriate to say the remedy
is Jesus. It is in faith in Christ and His redeeming sacrifice that we behold
the key to re-establish oneness.

Sophie: But only if we can indeed believe that Jesus *was* the Christ. That
is to say, if we can somehow comprehend how someone could be killed by
being crucified, then rise again, and then be lifted up from earth into the
sky. But as for me a faith as this is simply not an option. I cannot see
how resurrections work scientifically, nor do I find it obvious how Jesus's
death at Golgotha could ever help me feel more wholesome and connected.
There is no link from ancient Christian fairy tales to my experience of life
in present-day realities.

Philonous: ...realities that you believe are strictly physical in kind.

Sophie: That is correct, and that is also why—most probably—religions are
inventions. They are projections that portray to us, not actual transcendent
worlds, but human wishful thinking.

Philonous: I don't agree, but I admit that such a view may readily occur to
us. In fact, already in antiquity did people criticize religious faith, along
these lines, as being just made up. A case in point in this regard are the
ideas of *Xenophanes* to whom we will turn next.

The Timeless World of Elea

Xenophanes was born around 570 B.C. in the eastern part of Asia Minor. He
was a philosophical satirist who spent much of his very long life—about 100
years—in travels across the Mediterranean world, entertaining his listeners
with poetry and song. Whether he ever visited the town of Elea, at the west
coast of Italy, is not entirely certain, but due to the nature of his thought, he
is generally regarded as the founder of the Eleatic School of philosophy.

In his poems Xenophanes criticized and ridiculed the authors of Greek
mythology for their portrayals of deities in the unflattering likeness of men:
"Homer and Hesiod have ascribed to the gods all things that are a shame and
a disgrace among men, thefts and adulteries and deception of one another."[31]
In another fragment we read:

> But if cattle, or lions, or horses had hands, just like humans; if they
> could paint with their hands, and draw and thus create pictures
> then the horses in drawing their Gods would draw horses; and
> cattle would give us pictures and statues of cattle; and therefore
> each would picture the Gods to resemble their own constitution.[32]

Against the naive anthropomorphisms of mythology, Xenophanes propa-
gated a pantheistic doctrine wherein the divine was identified with the totality

of being—the One.[I] It is this idea of an all-embracing cosmic unity in the
One that became the guiding inspiration of the philosophers of Elea and of
Parmenides, in particular, the greatest among them.

Parmenides was born about 525 B.C. and possibly received his philosophical
instruction from Xenophanes. Not very much is known about his life, but at
the advanced age of about 65 he apparently traveled to Athens where he met
the young Socrates. As it turned out, the latter was deeply impressed and later
spoke admiringly of the "glorious depth of mind"[34] which Parmenides during
his visit displayed.

In his philosophical writings Parmenides expounded an idea of the One that
directly opposed the unity in difference perceived by Heraclitus. Not conflict
and change predominate existence but perfect immobility and everlasting permanence. The One, we are told, "is uncreated and indestructible" Being that is
"alone, complete, immovable and without end."[35] Furthermore, in order to explain the absolute immutability of the One, Parmenides observes that implicit
in the notions of change and movement is the idea of coming-into-existence
which in turn presupposes *the reality* of non-existence or non-being—a contradiction in terms. In other words, if change is real, then something which is
now was not then, but that is inconceivable because that which is not cannot
give rise to that which is. Along similar lines, Parmenides also rejects the
concept of plurality as he imagines the One to be a continuous material unity
that exists in the eternal Now. Consequently, time, as change, is merely an
illusion.[II]

In order to establish doctrines such as these that completely defy the evidence of sense, Parmenides maintained a rigid distinction between "the way
of truth"[37] and "the way of opinion."[38] Only pure reason leads to the truth,
while opinion derived from sensory perception leads to error. In adopting this
strictly rational view he exerted a strong influence on the idealistic philosophy
of Plato, but it is important to understand that he himself was not an idealist. Reality, according to Parmenides, is revealed in thought but is not itself
identical with thought; the One is material rather than spiritual or mental.

Given the highly counterintuitive nature of his teachings, it scarcely is
surprising that Parmenides became the subject of scorn and derision among
his contemporaries. In consequence, his student and close associate, *Zeno*,
devised a series of logical arguments that were intended to refute the charges
of the critics. Most famously, Zeno argued for the impossibility of motion
by describing a grotesque race between Achilles and a tortoise in which the
tortoise always stays in the lead. As the race commences, the tortoise is given

[I]This characterization of the thought of Xenophanes is based on certain remarks by
Aristotle, but according to the available fragments, it also seems possible that Xenophanes
was a monotheist rather than a monist. For example, in one fragment we read: "There is one
god, the greatest among gods and men, neither in form nor thought like unto mortals."[33]

[II]In the fragment from which this conclusion is drawn Parmenides asserts that the One
never was and never will be; "for now it is, all at once, a continuous one."[36]

a small head start, but Achilles quickly tries to close the gap by moving to the place from which the tortoise had set out. The tortoise, in the meantime, moved as well and therefore stays ahead by a certain small distance. Achilles swiftly covers that distance, too, but finds himself again in second place, as the tortoise has advanced yet a little farther. Continuing in this fashion through an infinite succession of steps, Achilles realizes to his great amazement that he is getting ever closer but unable to take the lead. Thus, according to Zeno, the assumption of the reality of motion forces us to admit that a tortoise cannot be overtaken by a fast-paced runner. Since this conclusion is ridiculous, the assumption must be false, and, by implication, motion as a concept is found to be untenable.

In another argument of this sort, Zeno observes that an arrow in flight always occupies one particular position in space at any one moment. Since an object that occupies a certain position must be at rest in that position, it follows that the arrow is simultaneously in motion and at rest, which is impossible. Again the concept of motion is seen to be illogical.

To counter the Pythagorean claim that matter is composed of elementary geometric units and to thereby defend Parmenides's teaching concerning the non-existence of plurality, Zeno further asserts that inherent in the concept of a unit in the Pythagorean sense is the notion of infinite divisibility. In other words, any given unit can always be divided into smaller subunits, and the total number of such subunits must therefore be infinite. That, however, is impossible because either each subunit has magnitude zero, in which case the totality also has magnitude zero, or each subunit has a certain positive magnitude, in which case the totality has magnitude infinity. Consequently, the Pythagorean doctrine of plurality implies that all material objects are either vanishingly small or infinitely large, which is absurd.

Since the three arguments outlined above are of great importance for our understanding of mathematical modeling in science,[III] we will now examine more closely whether and how the paradoxes they entail can be resolved.

To discuss the first, concerning the race between Achilles and the tortoise, we assume (for the sake of simplicity) that the starting positions of the two contestants are 1 unit of distance apart (Figure 2.6), that Achilles is moving at a rate of 2 units of distance per unit of time, and that the tortoise is moving at exactly half that rate. Given this initial setup, common sense suggests that Achilles will overtake the tortoise after one unit of time has passed because in this amount of time Achilles will move 2 units of distance, the tortoise will move 1 unit, and the difference $2-1=1$ will equal the starting separation. But how do we reconcile this straightforward prediction with Zeno's more detailed

---

[III]The historical importance of these arguments is also attested to by the fact that Galileo Galilei—the man who pioneered the use of mathematics in modern physical science— addresses himself to a variant of Zeno's first paradox in his treatise on *The Two New Sciences*.[39]

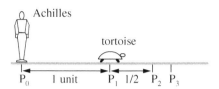

Figure 2.6: Achilles and the tortoise.

account according to which Achilles must pass through an infinite series of steps, none of which completely closes the gap? How can an infinite number of positive temporal steps add up to the finite total of merely one unit?

If we follow Zeno's approach in our present example, then Achilles will need half a unit of time in his first move to cover the one unit of distance between the starting positions P_0 and P_1. Simultaneously, the tortoise will crawl half a unit of distance from P_1 to P_2 (Figure 2.6). In his second move Achilles will advance from P_1 to P_2 in one quarter of a unit of time, while the tortoise will cover one quarter of a unit of distance in moving from P_2 to P_3. Continuing in this manner, we readily observe that the total amount of time is given by the sum

$$\frac{1}{2} + \frac{1}{4} + \frac{1}{8} + \frac{1}{16} + \ldots \textit{ ad infinitum.}$$

The value of this sum is easily determined if we represent it geometrically by infinitely subdividing a line segment of length one in the manner shown in Figure 2.7 where the rightmost subsegment is always cut in half. Since the

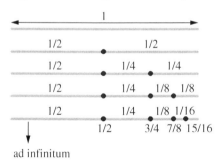

Figure 2.7: subdividing a line segment of length one.

lengths of the subsegments generated in this way are equal to the terms in the infinite sum above, it follows that the value of this sum must be equal to the total length of the line segment, that is, it must be one. Consequently, Zeno's method of breaking up the time it takes to overtake the tortoise into infinitely many subintervals yields the same result as the common sense approach that we used initially. The paradox of Achilles and the tortoise therefore finds its resolution in the realization that a sum of *infinitely* many positive terms can in fact be equal to a *finite* total value.

Turning our attention now to the second paradox concerning the arrow that is simultaneously in motion and at rest, we begin our analysis with the observation that Zeno's reference to the concept of a 'moment in time' indicates that he considers time—for the purpose of his argument—to be composed of separate individual instants. Such a conception of time is consistent with our current-day understanding because in modern physics intervals of time are commonly represented geometrically by line segments on an axis which in turn is thought to be made up of infinitely many individual points (Figure 2.8). Consequently, we may in fact agree with Zeno that the arrow is at rest at

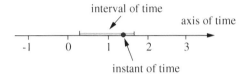

Figure 2.8: a line segment on an axis.

any given instant, because a single point is understood to be unextended. Put differently, a single point represents a time interval of length zero, and motion is impossible if no time is passing. This conclusion, however, is highly perplexing because in 'adding up' the distances traveled over all the instants that make up a certain interval of time we are, it seems, simply 'adding up' infinitely many zeros, and the total distance traveled should therefore be zero as well. Afterall, if we follow the same procedure as in the preceding example where the total sum

$$1 = \frac{1}{2} + \frac{1}{4} + \frac{1}{8} + \frac{1}{16} + \ldots \textit{ ad infinitum}$$

was geometrically approximated by the finite sums

$$\frac{3}{4} = \frac{1}{2} + \frac{1}{4}$$
$$\frac{7}{8} = \frac{1}{2} + \frac{1}{4} + \frac{1}{8}$$
$$\frac{15}{16} = \frac{1}{2} + \frac{1}{4} + \frac{1}{8} + \frac{1}{16}$$
$$\vdots$$

then it follows that the infinite sum

$$0 + 0 + 0 + 0 + \ldots \textit{ ad infinitum}$$

is equal to zero because the finite sums

$$0 + 0,$$
$$0 + 0 + 0,$$
$$0 + 0 + 0 + 0,$$
$$\vdots$$

are equal to zero as well. So our intuitive understanding that the sum of an infinite number of zeros, lined up in an infinite sequence, must equal zero is indeed correct. An insoluble contradiction would therefore arise if it were possible to list the individual points, of which an interval consists, in an infinite, *discrete* sequence because in that case, the total length represented by these points would be both equal to zero and equal to the length of the interval. We will see, however, that such a listing of points can never be produced (see the argument in the dialogue below) because, in a sense, a *continuously* drawn line contains 'more' points than an infinite *discrete* sequence, despite the fact that the number of points is infinite in both of them. In other words, infinity is not necessarily equal to infinity! And it is this issue of different orders of infinity and the related issue of *continuity* versus *discreteness* that lies at the heart of Zeno's second paradox.

Sophie: The argument is quite confusing. So I would like to re-examine it to verify that I have grasped it.

Philonous: A good idea.

Sophie: At the outset, so I understood, we represented an interval of time over which the flight of an arrow is recorded by a line segment of a certain positive length. Since such a line segment is thought to consist of individual points, we were led to conclude that the zeros representing the lengths of these points somehow 'add up' to a positive value, namely the positive length of the segment. Correct?

Philonous: Correct.

Sophie: On the other hand, if we add up one by one an infinite sequence of zeros in exactly the same manner as in the case of the infinite sum $1/2 + 1/4 + 1/8 + \ldots$, we get zero, that is, $0 + 0 + 0 + \cdots = 0$. The paradox therefore lies hidden in the fact that the zeros representing the lengths of the points in an interval 'add up' to something greater than zero while the zeros in an infinite sequence add up to zero.

Philonous: ...and in order to avoid the absurd conclusion that the length of an interval can be both greater than zero and equal to zero simultaneously, we need to demonstrate that no infinite discrete sequence can ever contain all the points of which an interval consists.

Sophie: I think, I followed what you said, but how can such a statement concerning the nonexistence of a certain sequence ever be established? It seems intractable to say the least.

Philonous: Surprisingly, the proof of nonexistence in this case can easily be given if we represent the points in an interval by numbers in decimal form.

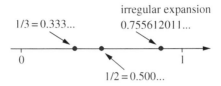

Figure 2.9: representing points by numbers.

Consider for example the interval from zero to one on the coordinate axis shown in Figure 2.9. Every point in this interval can be identified (by definition) with an infinite decimal expansion starting with a zero. Some of these expansions are repeating, such as $1/2 = 0.500\ldots$ (the zeros are repeating) or $1/3 = 0.333\ldots$, but others may be totally irregular. Given this representation of points by numbers, it remains to be shown that no infinite, discrete listing of decimal expansions can ever exhaust the entire range of values between zero and one. In other words, we need to show that for any given listing, such as

$$0.500000000\ldots$$
$$0.333333333\ldots$$
$$0.755612011\ldots$$
$$0.123218814\ldots$$
$$0.971091002\ldots$$
$$\vdots$$

there exists at least one decimal expansion of a number between zero and one that the listing does not contain. To this end we write down the expansion represented by the diagonal digits

$$0.\boxed{5}00000000\ldots$$
$$0.3\boxed{3}3333333\ldots$$
$$0.75\boxed{5}612011\ldots \longrightarrow 0.53529\ldots$$
$$0.123\boxed{2}18814\ldots$$
$$0.9710\boxed{9}1002\ldots$$
$$\vdots$$

and add or subtract 1 from each of its decimal positions depending on whether the digit in that position is less than 5 or greater than or equal to

5 (i.e., we add 1 if the digit is less than 5, and we subtract 1 if the digit is greater than or equal to 5). Thus 0.53529... is transformed into

$$0.44438...,$$

and, as desired, this resulting decimal is distinct from all the decimals in our listing because it differs from the first number in the list in its first decimal position, from the second number in its second decimal position, from the third number in its third decimal position, and so forth *ad infinitum.*

Sophie: The proof is beautiful and very clever—we take an infinite listing, extract the diagonal expansion, change it in every digit, and obtain a number that differs from all the numbers listed. The reasoning is unambiguous, and the conclusion is remarkable indeed: infinities exist in different orders.

Philonous: But what about the paradox of Zeno?

Sophie: I thought the issue had already been decided. For according to the argument we just discussed, there is nothing contradictory in the idea that an extended object, such as a straight line segment, representing a stretch of time, may be composed of unextended points. Hence it does seem plausible to think that an arrow moving in flight can also be at rest at any given instant.

Philonous: To that I can agree, but here is where the problem lies: in all of our reasonings so far we silently assumed that time is real and is in fact continuous. Unfortunately, though, this premise is impossible to verify empirically because measurements of 'time' can never be performed at an infinite degree of accuracy and in a quantity equivalent to the order of infinity associated with the totality of points in a given interval.

Sophie: So the notion of continuous time is simply an invention?

Philonous: Indeed, continuity is nothing but a mental construct, a mode of thought. It is a useful concept in mathematical modeling, and it appeals to our intuition, but verifiably intrinsic to the structure of reality it certainly is not. By implication, the alternative assumption of discreteness can also be coherently adopted.

Sophie: Discreteness of time? Are you saying, so to speak, that time is leaping past us step by step?

Philonous: ...or we are leaping past *it.*

Sophie: Your speculation is extravagant.

Philonous: ...yet plausibly consistent with the facts. For what is here at stake is not exterior reality but our inner willingness to mentally adjust. By habit we may cling to certain modes of thought, but habits can be broken. That is to say, if viable alternatives exist, we may as well be flexible and keep our options open. For our purpose ought to be to broaden our view and not to randomly restrict it. Furthermore, given such baroque complexities as higher orders of infinity, which continuity entails, it isn't really obvious why temporal discreteness, as a concept, is inherently inferior. I do not find it difficult at all to imagine, for example, that physical reality is not a seamless flux but is instead composed of states or 'pictures' that are changeless and discrete.[41] In fact, if we go one step further and assume these 'pictures' to be pre-existent, then we may, if we wish, dispose of time entirely.

Sophie: ...but only, I suppose, if notions such as these are properly compatible with all the laws of nature.

Philonous: It may surprise you, but non-temporal descriptions of material reality have been in fact quite plausibly devised.[42] Such models, to be sure, are not yet commonly accepted, but transparently false they also are not.

Sophie: I am surprised indeed, for how could any change that we observe be ever modeled and accounted for if time did not exist?

Philonous: A conclusive answer to this question is beyond the scope of our present discourse, but here is an idea: change and conscious perception of change can logically be interchanged. That is to say, a seeming change in the external world may really be and only be a change in how attention is directed. Indeed, the astrophysicist James Jeans suggests in reference to this point that our human consciousness may be akin to "that of a fly caught in a dusting-mop which is being drawn over the surface of [a] picture; the whole picture is there, but the fly can only experience the one instant of time with which it is in immediate contact."[43] Perhaps Parmenides and Zeno were right—there is just one immutable reality, pre-existent in all its possibilities. Is it not conceivable that in such a static world it is attention that creates a seeming temporality by choosing to perceive the given that is there one picture at a 'time'?

Sophie: You make it sound as though a cosmic movie was projected into our minds, image after image.

Philonous: It is an option to consider. But what I truly wish to advocate, more generally speaking, is openmindedness for the sake of intellectual integrity. Plain and simple honesty bids us to acknowledge that our physical concepts are not uniquely determined by the available empirical evidence but are instead to some extent contingent. If we say, for example, "time is an illusion" or "time is real" or "time is continuous," we do not make a claim about observable phenomena but merely voice a personal opinion. Afterall, there cannot be a physical experiment that demonstrates that time is real, because time, as all scientific concepts, is essentially a figment of our imagination. Nothing, of course, prevents us from recording, say, the different positions of the hands on a stopwatch and then proclaiming afterwards that 'time' has thus been measured. But the assumption that such an association of a set of sense perceptions with a metaphysical or linguistic construct reveals the ultimate nature of physical reality is entirely unwarranted.

Sophie: Scientific concepts are figments?

Philonous: Indeed, the concepts that we form are just that—concepts. Being in itself, Being as it really is, can never be the object of scientific inquiry. We can analyze sense perceptions by means of reason to formulate what we refer to as 'scientific theories', but any statement concerning the ground of being from which these sense perceptions arise is by necessity a statement of faith. Albert Einstein, for example, explained this point as follows:

> Physical concepts are free creations of the human mind, and are not, however it may seem, uniquely determined by the external world. In our endeavor to understand reality we are somewhat like a man trying to understand the mechanism of a closed watch. He sees the face and the moving hands, even hears the ticking, but he has no way of opening the case. If he is ingenious he may form some picture of a mechanism which could be responsible for all the things he observes, but he may never be quite sure his picture is the only one which could explain his observations. He will never be able to compare his picture with the real mechanism and he cannot even imagine the possibility or the meaning of such a comparison.[44]

Sophie: The conclusion then is inescapable—scientific knowledge is arbitrary and mostly subjective.

Philonous: Not at all. Nothing could be further from the truth, as I perceive it, than such a radically skeptical opinion.

Sophie: There is a certain pattern here emerging: whenever I believe to have grasped your meaning, you simply turn around and contradict yourself. At first we were agreed that time was continuous, then we decided that it was discrete, then it didn't exist at all, then the question of whether it did or did not exist was inessential, then again it was a figment of our imagination, then *all* concepts were figments, but that, of course, is not to say that knowledge based on figments might be arbitrary—on the contrary, it is as solid as can be.

Philonous: Your irony aside, I totally agree: scientific knowledge "is as solid as can be." It all depends of course on what we mean by 'knowledge'—and that is where the trouble lies. For the problem of knowledge is one of those eternal conundrums that can never be truly resolved and never be simply ignored. In other words, we too will have to address it.

Sophie: ...so as to get lost in the process?

Philonous: That is correct but hardly a reason not to proceed.

Sophie: So what do you propose?

Philonous: To take another look at that stopwatch to which I just alluded.

Sophie: And as we do that, what do we see?

Philonous: Exactly the same: some hands that are moving. In other words, the knowledge that we gain by recording how far a given hand advances in a given run of the stopwatch is fairly close to fully objective: it doesn't depend on any observer's subjective opinion because all observers will report it equally.

Sophie: In other words, the knowledge "is as solid as can be."

Philonous: The knowledge is solid but also *per se* completely detached from any confusing conceptions. We may of course proclaim, as I previously said, that the movement of a hand somehow signifies the passage of time, but then again we also may not. Either way our knowledge will not be affected. Furthermore, the same detachment of knowledge from any conceptual schemes still holds if we extend our little experiment to include a falling body and a yardstick. Using the latter to measure the height from which the former is dropped, and using the stopwatch to measure the 'time' that it takes for the body to fall to the ground, we naturally produce two columns of values: in the first we record a sequence of heights or initial 'positions' for successive falls of the body, and in the second we list the corresponding 'times'.

Sophie: ...and thus we find a lawful dependence.

Philonous: Indeed, as we analyze the data, we notice that there is a correlation: the values in the first column are approximately equal to (or proportional to) the squares of the values in the second. To confirm this observation, we perform additional experiments, and slowly build up sufficient confidence to inductively assert that, under the conditions we have chosen in our experimental setup, the values in the first column will *always* come out to be approximately equal to the squares of the values in the second.

Sophie: Provided that induction is a creed that we confess.

Philonous: Well, yes, but that is not the point. What matters here is not the problem of inductive inference but rather the fact that the two columns of data in conjunction with the results of our rational analysis constitute the essence of the knowledge that we gained. This essence, as I see it, is entirely independent of the physical or metaphysical interpretations that we commonly attach to it. We can say of course that the *position*-values in the first column approximately equal the squares of the *time*-values in the second, but just as well we may assert that *noitisop* approximately equals the square of *emit*.

Sophie: I beg your pardon.

Philonous: It's *position* and *time* spelled backwards.

Sophie: Is this supposed to be profound?

Philonous: Look, what I am trying to make clear is the idea that the conceptions of position and time, in the example we discussed, represent nothing more than perfectly inconsequential and insubstantial naming conventions. The labels we use—'position' and 'time' or some other compounds of letters—do not add anything *to* the data, they do not facilitate the analysis *of* the data, and they also do not make more valid or precise the law derived *from* the data—nor, for that matter, do they increase in the least this law's predictive power. Afterall, when it comes to predicting the fall of a body quantitatively, the critical issue is not to determine how a supposedly continuous change in position can be seen to be correlated with a fictional flow of a metaphysical entity, referred to as 'time', but rather to identify how an observable motion along a yardstick is matched—as predicted—by a parallel and equally observable motion of a hand on a stopwatch.

Sophie: Your reasoning is well thought out, except for the fact that no one ever designed a watch to measure *emit* and no one ever set up an experiment to explore how *noitisop* depends on it. Put differently, we simply will not gain the pertinent empirical knowledge unless we have, at the outset, some sort of a *concept* of both 'position' and 'time'.

Philonous: An excellent point, and yes, I agree.

Sophie: You do?

Philonous: Of course.

Sophie: But that's another contradiction.

Philonous: Not at all. For what I have been arguing against is not the central importance of rational conceptual thought in the development of science but merely the spurious belief that the mental constructs which we refer to as 'concepts' are part of our knowledge of exterior reality. In the case of classical Newtonian mechanics, for instance, the foundational concepts of an absolute, continuous space and an equally absolute and equally continuous time are merely made up but nonetheless useful and therefore important. From the latter part of the 17th century up until the end of the 19th the use of these concepts was wholly unquestioned and greatly advanced the endeavor called 'science'. A problem only arose when the astounding success of the Newtonian paradigm led physicists to believe that concepts as these are truly a part of the actual world—that there truly is such a thing as an absolute space in absolute time and that we somehow truly live in it. For it was precisely this false identification of a conceptual model with the reality it models that made it so difficult, at the turn of the 20th century, to adjust the classical framework to novel empirical facts and theoretical insights. In the end, it took the genius of a man like Einstein, the world's foremost scientific intellect, to scale a mental and conceptual barrier that had been reinforced by more than two hundred years of stunning successes. Einstein, in approaching the problem, decided to strictly adhere to the facts and to assume nothing but that which can be observed—and only then could a new, relativistic *conception* of space and time be finally forged.

Sophie: In other words, the moral of the story is this: concepts are fine as long as they fully align with observable facts.

Philonous: That's the kind of positivistic view that Einstein as well initially took—and it also is the view that allowed him, as I just said, to set aside some deeply ingrained misconceptions. Later in his career, however, he underwent a radical sea change and referred to this view quite bluntly as "nonsense."[45]

Sophie: He did? But why?

Philonous: Because ultimately the demand to limit oneself to concepts that are directly expressive of observable facts can never be satisfied. Speaking of 'time', for instance, we might argue naively that a mathematical variable describing it is fully aligned with observable phenomena, such as the fall of a body or the motion of a hand on a watch. But when we further ask whether that variable is to be construed as continuous or discrete, we are facing two options that observation cannot distinguish. Either way, our variable will be given an attribute—continuity or discreteness—that is wholly detached from empirical facts. Similarly, the notion of a continuously changing position in an absolute, three-dimensional space is strictly a rational fiction that no experiment will ever confirm. But it would be entirely absurd to suggest that Newton should therefore have abstained from employing it. For without that notion, the fabulous edifice of classical physics could never have been erected, and the growth of science, as a result, would have been feeble and stunted. In other words, the positivistic purist demand to only use concepts that observation fully supports is not only impossible to satisfy but also severely counterproductive.[46]

Sophie: So when it comes to concepts, we more or less do as we please—whatever works is alright.

Philonous: Indeed, concepts are human inventions whose only reason for being is to help us to muddle along. If the progress of science requires that we purify them, reduce them, bring them in line with the facts, or simply remove them, then we are at perfect liberty to do exactly that; if not, then we are free to create them, inflate them, or otherwise enhance them whenever a compelling reason to do so arises. Quoting Einstein yet again, we may say that

> the external conditions, which are set for [the scientist] by the facts of experience, do not permit him to let himself be too much restricted in the construction of his conceptual world, by the adherence to an epistemological system. He, therefore, must appear to the systematic epistemologist as a type of unscrupulous opportunist...[47]

Sophie: In other words, he is an anarchist that scientist.[48]

Philonous: ...but only on the rational, conceptual side—on the empirical side, where his knowledge of reality truly resides, he always defers, like an obedient subject, to the absolute rule of the facts.

Sophie: Or better, let's say, he ought to do so ideally.

Philonous: That's right.

Sophie: I wonder, though, if such a view can ever be consistent. For the notion that knowledge of reality is grounded solely in facts, that is, in perception, runs counter not only to the Parmenidean emphasis on reason as "the way of truth" but also contradicts directly the Pythagorean doctrine concerning the homology of mind and cosmos. Did you not yourself admit that this doctrine "has frequently been well confirmed by scientific practice" (p.16)?

Philonous: In the history of ideas the teachings of Pythagoras did indeed give rise to a school of philosophical thought according to which reason rather than sense perception is the most reliable source of knowledge—including knowledge of the exterior, physical world. Plato, for example, derived from them his high regard for mathematics as an ideal form of knowledge, and from Platonic rationalism the influence of the Pythagorean school extended further to Plotinus and Augustine, the scholastics of the Middle Ages, and implicitly even to the modern rational philosophies of Spinoza and Descartes. However, the fact that rationalism and Pythagoreanism are historically linked does not allow us to conclude that Pythagoreanism is inherently incompatible with the particular brand of empiricism that I have here been trying to put forth (without pretending to have clearly defined it).

Sophie: Maybe not from a purely logical perspective, but given that the Pythagoreans believed that mathematics is "foundational to everything there is" (p.14), we hardly can avoid to draw precisely this conclusion. Afterall, if mathematics is the essence of existence, then all conceptual mathematical knowledge may very well be thought to be descriptive of reality as such.

Philonous: Again I must object. For even the strong ontological interpretation of Pythagoreanism that you referred to in your quote is not incompatible with empiricism as long as it is recognized to be a statement of faith. I do not wish to deny anyone the right to *believe* that a certain concept or a certain theory or perhaps all of mathematics is a true representation of the world as it is—only the corresponding claim to *knowledge* I regard as inadmissible. A modern physicist, for instance, may firmly be convinced that the mathematical structure of quantum mechanics is a wholly accurate description of material reality. But he or she must never venture to proclaim that such a view is in the realm of knowledge. No rational argument and no experimental observation will ever justify such a crossing-over from faith to knowledge or, more generally, from transcendence to immanence. There is no doubt, of course, that physical reality and scientific thought are closely correspondent, but verifiably identical, in an ontological sense, they clearly are not.

Sophie: But why?

Philonous: Just consider once again the concept of temporal continuity: as a fundamental assumption that underlies just about every mainstream scientific model, present and past, this concept may safely be regarded as one of the most successful theoretical constructs in the entire history of science. By implication, it almost certainly is vitally involved whenever a scientific theory is anticipated in mathematical thought. The temporal continuity of

Einstein's general relativity, for instance, is a direct reflection of the spatial continuity in the Riemannian conception of geometry. So if ever there was a concept that deserves to be regarded as a *true* Pythagorean representation of physical reality, temporal continuity may very well be it. Yet even in this very solid case we do not really *know* that it is *true* because, as we saw earlier, viable alternatives to temporal continuity do in fact exist.

Sophie: Are you thinking here of temporal discreteness?

Philonous: ...or models that we called 'non-temporal'.

Sophie: But how do you explain that these alternatives have so far not been met with general acceptance? Is this a case of mere historical contingency, or is perhaps the standard model of continuous time objectively more adequate?

Philonous: It is more adequate by far in that it rests on well-ingrained habitual assumptions and also is much easier to work with. A discrete formulation of Newtonian physics, for example—while feasible—would be extremely cumbersome indeed. For it would cause the whole machinery of calculus, which physicists have grown accustomed to, to sputter to a halt. But as far as ultimate truth is concerned, I simply fail to see why habitual acquaintance or computational convenience should be regarded as objectively significant criteria.

Sophie: What you are lacking is that earnest faith of someone like Pythagoras. For if indeed you did believe that mind and cosmos are homologous you would pursue such arguments concerning rational efficiency and plausibility with vastly greater confidence.

Philonous: I can assure you that this doctrine of Pythagoras has always very much impressed me. The notion that the human mind is able to anticipate by logical or mathematical deduction the order of the universe is really most intriguing. And in the light of history, the Pythagorean faith in the beauty and simplicity of nature's universal laws can certainly be seen to be a very able guide to scientific truth. Moreover, I also do acknowledge, as I said, the relevance of concepts. I am acutely aware, for example, what wonderful discoveries were made—by the power of reason alone—as the generations of scientists following Newton explored the conceptual framework of his marvelous mechanics. The knowledge, however, that is gained in any such process of exploration is entirely self-referential. It is knowledge of the framework itself rather than of physical reality. As a matter of course, theoretical results will frequently be found to closely match some given observations, but no theoretical scientific investigation will ever validate its own conceptual foundation. It is for this reason that I continue to insist that scientific knowledge—restrictively construed as knowledge of material reality—is necessarily empirical.

Sophie: I still do not believe that such a rigid stance can be coherently maintained. What you apparently are trying to put forth is the idea that knowledge merely is a rationally purified extraction from a naked stream of sensory perceptions. But such a stream that is completely concept-free does simply not exist. You advertised experiments with falling bodies as prime examples of empirical investigation. But you conveniently neglected to discuss that, strictly speaking, falling bodies cannot even be observed. What we refer to as a falling body merely is a stereoscopic projection—a superimposition of two shifting color patches in a larger panoramic field. It is only the *conceptual* processing scheme of our cognitive apparatus that produces for us from this raw experience the impression of a body moving in a spatial setting. That is to say, in absence of a pre-existing frame of reference in our mind, there would be no such things as meaningful perceptions.

Philonous: In fact, I'd even go so far as to assert that the very notion of a material object in space is nothing but a theoretical construct. It is a helpful *concept* that we unconsciously impose on the empirical information available to us, but ultimate significance it probably has not.

Sophie: So you concur?

Philonous: Yes and no. 'Yes' because your criticism beautifully illustrates how careful we must be to not confuse the fictions with the facts, and 'no' because I never did confuse them—at least not blatantly. You see, it certainly is true that the human cognitive apparatus inevitably attaches to any piece of data it receives a fair amount of theory—or 'proto-theory'— by simply being able to receive it. Consequently and in the light of my general dictum that concepts are inherently fictitious, it is quite tempting to conclude that knowledge of exterior reality is simply unattainable. Afterall, if *all* knowledge is unavoidably conceptual and if no conceptual knowledge is knowledge of exterior reality, then, by implication, knowledge of the latter type can only be illusory. Such a radical view, as all radical views, can be appealing for its superior simplicity—and it also conveniently solves the problem of knowledge by aborting its object. But unfortunately, it doesn't explain why science in practice can be relied upon with so much success. There really is no doubt that quite in spite of any philosophical qualms or logical objections, we really *can* predict how far the hands on a stopwatch will move while a falling body drops a given distance. And hence it is absurd to claim that knowledge of exterior reality is wholly nonexistent.

Sophie: ...and thus we are led to conclude, as I would say, that the concepts we use are accurate, faithful descriptors of the actual physical world.

Philonous: I might say "yes" if only I knew exactly what you mean by "faithful descriptors." But this is getting too tedious. For no matter how well we define the words that we use, the problem of knowledge will ultimately always elude us. That said, however, it still is meaningful to note that in the case, for instance, of experiments concerning falling bodies the collection of the data, its numerical analysis, and the subsequent formulation of a law with predictive potential, require nothing but the data itself. For at the level of that genuine empirical knowledge of external reality from which this predictive potential derives—that is, at the level at which the power of science truly resides—the concepts of position and time contribute nothing more than a couple of naming conventions. This observation in itself, of course, does not establish a truly coherent position. Afterall, identifying sense perceptions as the source does not provide us any insight, for example, into how perceptions are created or affected at the outset by what you called a "pre-existing frame of reference." Nor does it elucidate in any way whatever how knowledge is transferred to memory or how it is conditioned socially. Exactly how are sense perceptions linked to any of the memories we have of them? Or why for that matter do we speak of 'science' as a dependable body of 'knowledge' despite the fact that we will never be able to perceive firsthand the vast multitude of physical phenomena that scientists throughout the ages have reportedly observed? What social norms and pressures are the catalysts that elevate a certain body of information to the status of 'scientific knowledge'? In the light of questions such as these and many others like them, it should be obvious indeed that a comprehensive view of knowledge, if it be at all within our reach, cannot be limited to bare accounts of sensory perceptions.

Sophie: Your attitude apparently is somewhat more accommodating than I thought. But even so I wonder still how your epistemology, which is so stringently empirical in kind, can properly facilitate the integrative quest that we have chosen to pursue. It seems that your intent is not to "broaden our view," as you not long ago suggested (p.32), but rather to reduce it down to microscopic size.

Philonous: My intent is twofold and benign: on the one hand, it is true, I did indeed attempt to argue that the physical, external world cannot be really known apart from sensory experience. But on the other hand, I also tried to show that knowledge at its core is certain and quite solid. Knowledge of material reality, as I conceive of it, is valid and reliable but also is sufficiently compact to leave us ample room for further exploration.[49] In taking this approach, I am enabled to maintain a fundamental openness without denying what is factual and true.

Sophie: So integration then occurs, it seems, within that open space—that "ample room"—that knowledge is incompetent to fill.

Philonous: In principle, that is correct. But I would like to add that knowledge also has a very crucial role to play. For insofar as integration is our goal, we must not only strive to understand what scientific knowledge *is* but also be prepared to earnestly *embrace* it. If facts are not acknowledged and accepted, all integrative efforts will be crude and ill informed. An attitude of obstinate denial will not unlock the door to faith, but only to absurdity.

Sophie: Very slowly, I admit, your view is starting to appear a little more coherent. But before I can accept it, I need to ponder it a bit.

Philonous: No problem, take your *time*—we aren't in a hurry.

Sophie: Granted the assumption, I suppose, that *time* indeed exists.
Philonous: Granted that assumption!

To wrap up our discussion of the paradoxes of Zeno, we need to add a few comments concerning Zeno's argument against the Pythagorean notion of plurality. This final paradox can be resolved, just as the second one, from the assumption of continuity. If three-dimensional space is mathematically represented as a continuum of points, then, as in the case of an extended interval of time, there is nothing inherently contradictory in the idea that an extended object in space can be composed of unextended points. However, here as there, the postulate of continuity is essentially unwarranted as other modes of 'spatial' modeling are certainly conceivable. In conclusion, then, we have to say that Zeno's paradoxes, in the final analysis, are insoluble because the ultimate nature of space and time or, more generally, of physical reality is unknowable.

Empedocles on Love and Hate

The philosophical ideas of Heraclitus and Parmenides presented us with two antithetical visions: ever-present change on the one hand and perfect permanence on the other. Underlying this ontological juxtaposition there was the epistemological problem of empiricism versus rationalism: does knowledge arise from sensory experience or rational deduction? The first to propose a plausible compromise was a statesman and physician by the name of *Empedocles*. The exact dates of his life and death are not known, but he is thought to have been born around 490 B.C. in the city of Akragas on the island of Sicily.

In the history of philosophy Empedocles left his mark not so much as a pioneer of new ideas but rather as a synthesizer who elaborated and harmonized the thoughts of others. He adopted the position of Parmenides concerning the indestructibility and materiality of Being, but also sought to account for the reality of change by depicting the world as being composed of four essential elements—water, fire, earth, and air—that were undergoing ever-recurring cycles of intermingling and separation:

> There is no coming into being of aught that perishes, nor any end for it in baneful death; but only mingling and separation of what has been mingled. Coming into being is but a name given to these by men.[50]

And in another passage we read:

> But when the elements have been mingled in the fashion of a man and come to the light of day, or in the fashion of the race of wild beasts or plants or birds, then men say that these come into being;

and when they are separated, they call that, as is the custom, woeful death. I too follow the custom and call it so myself.[51]

According to Empedocles, the four essential elements compose a timeless ground of Being that is immutable in its bare material existence but not in the arrangement of its parts. Coming-into-being therefore is illusory, but change is not. In this reconciliation of the opposing ontological positions of Parmenides and Heraclitus we easily recognize the rudiments of our own, contemporary view: the modern analogues of water, fire, earth, and air are the various fundamental particles of subatomic physics, and change occurs as particles are rearranged in force-based interactions. Moreover, an overriding stability and permanence of physical reality is guaranteed by certain conservation laws that organize the cosmos. Most prominent among the latter is the first fundamental law of thermodynamics according to which the quantity called 'energy' is globally preserved. To be precise we need to add that energy here is construed to be equivalent to matter. For Einstein famously deduced that $E = mc^2$—that mass is merely energy in what appears to be a different state or form. By implication then we may assert that the first fundamental law of thermodynamics is globally applicable to all of physical existence.

Concerning the problem of causation of change, Empedocles further asserts that the intermingling and separating of parts is driven by the all-pervading forces of love and hate (or strife):

> For these things [i.e., the four essential elements,] are what they are; but, running through one another, they become men and other races of mortal creatures. At one time they are brought together into one order by Love; at another, again, they are carried each in different directions by the repulsion of Strife, till once more they grow into one and are wholly subdued.[52]

A modern reader who is accustomed to the more impersonal lingo of present-day science may be inclined to dismiss Empedocles's reference to love and strife as indicative of a more primitive, perhaps even animistic frame of mind. But here we need to be careful, for given his preference for poetic style and given the overall context of his writings, it seems plausible or even highly likely that Empedocles thought of love and strife as physical rather than spiritual forces. This interpretation derives additional credibility from the fact that Empedocles apparently was well aware of the difficulties one encounters when trying to express an ultimate reality by means of human language. A case in point here is his explicitly stated deference to custom in speaking of the separating of parts as "woeful death." Moreover, we also need to realize that our current scientific jargon, too, is far from being free of ambiguity. When we speak, for instance, of attractive or repulsive forces in mechanics or electrostatics, it is only habit that prevents us from associating the words 'attractive' and 'repulsive' with the sort of interpersonal like or dislike that human relations are commonly fraught with. In taking thus a critical view of our own linguistic choices, we can more readily put aside all considerations of style and recognize the writings of Empedocles for what they truly are: a surprisingly prescient vision of the physical universe confirmed by modern science.

Sophie: I will agree that words are easily exchanged for other words. Speaking of love and hate rather than attraction and repulsion may therefore be excusable, but introducing concepts that are not directly linked to sensory experience is not. It is in this regard that the teachings of Empedocles are most strikingly inadequate.

Philonous: How so?

Sophie: Well, I simply fail to see what observation might ever prompt us to assert that change in the physical world is universally effected by just two conflicting forces, be they love and hate or opposites of other kinds. How can knowledge be advanced by blindly postulating causes?

Philonous: Your sudden concern for observational evidence almost makes me think that my recent preaching on empiricism was not entirely in vain. Are you now a convert?

Sophie: Perhaps a convert to the virtue of evasiveness in philosophical debate because your swift, articulate rebuttals of all my charges regarding contradictions in your reasonings have truly been impressive. Returning now the favor, let me say, "I can assure you that" (p.39) in spite of anything I previously asserted, "I also do acknowledge" (p.39) of course that experimental observation has a central role to play in the development of science.

Philonous: I'm very pleased to see how quickly you have grasped that insistence on integrity can be an all too burdensome restriction when winning arguments is really our true intent.

Sophie: Are you trying to be witty?

Philonous: "Trying" is the way to put it. But on a more serious note and as regards your claim that causal explanations must be tied to observation, I'd like to ask you this: do you believe the current-day conception of a force to be more firmly grounded in experience than the idea that change is caused by love and hate?

Sophie: Of course I do, or have you ever heard of an experiment that showed how love and hate can bring about the mingling or the separating out of elements in aggregates of matter?

Philonous: Definitely not. But what about attractions and repulsions in mechanics? Are these not equally obscure?

Sophie: The answer here is "no" because in Newton's classical account all forces are defined by their effects on moving objects and are thus inherently *observable*.

Philonous: You are referring, I assume, to Newton's second law according to which the total force an object is exposed to is the product of its mass and its acceleration, that is, $F = ma$.

Sophie: I am indeed, because it is at this point that the link to observation is established: both mass and acceleration can be determined by experiment.

Philonous: You mean we put an object on a scale to find its mass and then record the change in its position over time to calculate how quickly it accelerates?

Sophie: Essentially, that's what I mean. But acceleration, of course, is determined from position and time only indirectly by first computing average velocities and then computing changes in velocity over corresponding intervals of time.

Philonous: Of course, but basically you are asserting that, in using a scale for mass, a yardstick for position, and a stopwatch for time, the quantity 'mass times acceleration' is inherently observable.

Sophie: That is correct.

Philonous: Suppose that I agree. Suppose that I am willing to put aside all considerations of conceptual complexities associated with such labels as 'mass,' 'position,' or 'time', and that I also willingly accept your empirical account: a scale, a yardstick, and a stopwatch have been used, values for mass, position, and time have been recorded, and a resulting value for the product m times a has somehow been computed. Then where do I discover in this data the idea that the *cause* of an accelerated motion is a force? Or how would I infer the magnitude of such a force to be equal to the product that I found?

Sophie: Apparently you don't appreciate the fact that Newton's law does not require us to know what forces are but rather happens to *define* them. Fuzzy metaphysical ideas, such as causality, are totally irrelevant if we agree that force, by *definition*, equals m times a.

Philonous: If that is so, then the conception of a force is entirely contained within its constituent conceptions of mass and acceleration and is thus reduced to a mere notational convenience—instead of the two-letter combination ma we write the single letter F.

Sophie: Not at all! The notion of a force is the very foundation of the entire edifice of classical mechanics. Far from being "a mere notational convenience," it is the centerpiece of an ingenious mathematical formalism that has proven its amazing usefulness in countless applications.

Philonous: What would be an example?

Sophie: The perfect illustration here may be the derivation of the laws of planetary motion from the universal law of gravitation and the fundamental laws that constitute mechanics.

Philonous: Please elaborate.

Sophie: At the beginning of the 17th century, the German astronomer Johannes Kepler set out to solve the problem of Copernicus concerning the description of planetary orbits in a heliocentric system. Starting from the observational data collected by his close associate, Tycho Brahe, and laboring over excruciatingly complicated calculations for more than twenty years, Kepler finally arrived at the following conclusions:

- *First law:* the path of a planet is an ellipse, and the position of the Sun coincides with one of the ellipse's foci.
- *Second law:* the area swept out by the line connecting a planet with the Sun is the same for equal intervals of time (Figure 2.10).
- *Third law:* the ratio of the square of the time needed for one full revolution (i.e., the square of the period) and the cube of the major radius of a planet's elliptic path is the same for all the planets in the solar system.

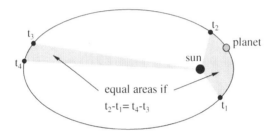

Figure 2.10: Kepler's second law.

About half a century later in England, Isaac Newton took up the challenge again, but his approach to the problem was radically different. Having established the universal law of gravitation, according to which, material objects attract one another with a force proportional to the product of their respective masses and inversely proportional to the square of the distance between them (Figure 2.11), and, having understood that force, in

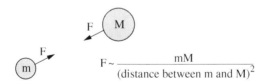

Figure 2.11: the universal law of gravitation.

general, equals mass times acceleration, Newton was able to demonstrate, by the power of mathematical reasoning alone, that these two fundamental principles—the universal law of gravitation and the second fundamental law of mechanics—imply Kepler's laws of planetary motion as a necessary consequence. In other words, in brilliantly applying a mathematical formalism, to which the concept of a force was central, Newton was able to unlock the secrets of the skies. Are you going to maintain, even in the light of this remarkable accomplishment, that forces in mechanics serve no purpose other than to make notation more convenient?

Philonous: If, as you asserted, the equation $F = ma$ is a definition, then the answer clearly must be "yes." In fact, your own example illustrates my point.

Sophie: I beg your pardon.

Philonous: You heard correctly, for a closer look at Newton's calculation shows the notion of a force to be completely inessential. Already in the very first step all forces cancel out, and what is left is simply an assertion concerning the direction and magnitude of a planet's acceleration. Here is how it works: denoting by m a planet's mass and by R its distance from the Sun, the gravitational force F exerted on the planet from the Sun is always pointing to the Sun and is proportional in magnitude to m/R^2. Since F is also equal to ma, it follows that a must be inversely proportional to the square of R. It is this relation between a and R, *from which any reference to F has been removed*, that Newton used in his deduction of the first of Kepler's laws.[1] Thus it clearly is permissible to say that force in Newton's calculation only functions as a metaconcept that perhaps provides a foothold for our intuition but is otherwise dispensable.

Sophie: I think you far too readily dismissed the initial use of F as "inessential." For how would Newton ever have related a to R, as you explained, if gravity and acceleration had not been linked to one another via force?

Philonous: By applying the third law.

Sophie: The third law?

Philonous: You see, Newton actually derived his universal law of gravitation from the relation between the sizes and periods of planetary orbits that is stated in the last of Kepler's laws. Assuming this relation to be accurate, he was able to deduce the formula for a in terms of R to which your question was referring. And only afterwards, when Newton multiplied this formula by m—a given planet's mass—did he obtain the force of gravity exerted by the Sun. In other words, from Kepler's laws Newton first inferred acceleration, then force, from force again acceleration, and finally he closed the circle by inferring Kepler's laws. In essence, therefore, his achievement was to prove that a certain type of acceleration implies and is implied by Kepler's laws. Seen from this perspective, the intermittent introduction of the notion of a force is perfectly redundant.

Sophie: The way your argument progresses makes me feel a little apprehensive. I have a hunch you will be trying to convince me before long that gravity itself, by being a force, is nothing but a "figment" (p.33)—despite, of course,

---

[1]Newton also used the fact that the direction of the acceleration always points from the planet to the Sun, which is the reason why a more detailed treatment of the subject requires the use of vector notation for a and R (see, for example, the exposition in [Bl2], pp.657–665).

the fact that we conveniently rely on it to keep us on the ground.

Philonous: The effects that we associate with the concept known as 'gravitation' are plainly visible and therefore indisputable, but the mathematical
model that we use for its description has been historically more flexible in
kind. For whereas in the Newtonian scheme gravity assumes the form of an
obscure attractive force that can exert its influence at any distance instantaneously, *the notion of a force is altogether absent* from the more advanced
Einsteinian theory of relativity. According to the latter scheme, gravity
is to be explained from the local curvature effects of a four-dimensional
spacetime manifold that supposedly encompasses the entire universe—past,
present, and future. I am not saying, of course, that spacetime curvature,
as a concept, is significantly less obscure than instantaneous action at a
distance. But the fact that gravity in relativity is not a force is certainly
deserving of attention.

Sophie: I must admit, your explanation is surprising—and confusing. For how
can a single physical phenomenon, such as gravity, give rise to two conceptual designs that are apparently completely disconnected? And how then
can we ever feel assured that either one of them is adequate?

Philonous: In a sense, both are adequate, because both formalisms—Newton's
and Einstein's—have been highly successful in matching observational data
with theoretical predictions. The domain of validity of the Newtonian system does not, of course, extend as far as that of Einstein's more sophisticated scheme. But the explanatory reach of either scheme is vast, and
both may therefore be regarded as science at its best. What we must be on
guard against, however, is the sort of naive realism by which a theoretical
model is all too hastily identified with the reality it models. Here, our train
of thought returns to the theme of our last discussion and to the words of
Einstein in particular, whom we had quoted as saying that "[p]hysical concepts... are not, however it may seem, uniquely determined by the external
world." No theory will ever bridge the gap between the concepts it employs
and the substrate of reality of which it is descriptive—or ever allow us to determine, for that matter, whether indeed there is such a gap. Consequently,
no theory can ever assume the status of a true and unique representation
of reality as it really is. Are forces real? Is spacetime curvature real? Or
what exactly do we mean by 'real'? There are no answers.

Sophie: In that you may be right, but to watch the notion of a force dissolve,
just like that, in metaphysical perplexity is rather disconcerting. Your argument concerning gravity is certainly compelling, yet forces in mechanics
are conceived more broadly and more flexibly—not all of them are gravitational in nature.

Philonous: Certainly, but I'm afraid the dissolution you lament is irreversible.
For it can be shown that the entire structure of classical mechanics can
be erected upon an axiomatic system in which there is no mention of a

force at all. Heinrich Hertz, for example, constructed such a system in his treatise on *The Principles of Mechanics*.[53] Closely related and equally comprehensive are the formalisms of Lagrange and Hamilton[II] in which not force but energy is the definitive conception. Both of these formalisms in turn can be derived from the Hamiltonian variational principle of least action which, for the special case of a conservative system,[III] asserts that a moving object always *chooses* from among all possible paths the one that extremizes the time average of the difference between the object's kinetic and potential energies (where 'extremize' means 'minimize' or 'maximize').

Sophie: Are you saying that the path of motion is determined, not by forces, but by choice?

Philonous: It may seem strange, but the intuition that we typically associate with Hamilton's description is really very different from the image of an acting force in Newton's scheme. Taking this description at face value, we may indeed be tempted to conclude that a moving object somehow can anticipate along which path its kinetic and potential energies are balanced most efficiently. Not local causation but teleologic intentionality is here the underlying theme.[IV]

Sophie: It sounds grotesque to say the least.

Philonous: ...*utterly* grotesque to be precise.

Sophie: So you agree?

Philonous: Wholeheartedly!—Except that I would add that equally grotesque is the idea that forces can be acting instantaneously in empty space or that amorphous spacetime can be curved. You see, whenever our intuition tries to get a grip on abstract representations of physical phenomena, the link to truth is tenuous at best. Where Empedocles once spoke of change brought on by love and hate, the modern physicist infers the action of a force or the balancing of energies. But in spite of all these efforts at description, the mystery of ultimate reality remains entirely untouched.

Sophie: And what remains untouched as well is this invariable certainty: no matter what the subject we discuss, the last word always will be yours.

Philonous: Of course it will. How else would we convince the reader of the fact that you are wrong and I am right?

[II]The formalism developed by Hertz is derivative of the Gaussian method of least squares which in turn translates into the same set of fundamental differential equations that also the formalisms of Hamilton and Lagrange are built upon (see [Hert] and [Som2]).

[III]A necessary condition for a system to be conservative is that its total energy remains constant over time. For a detailed discussion of a sufficient condition see the exposition in [Som2].

[IV]The teleological character of the Hamiltonian principle is apparent only in the integral formulation. The equivalent differential formulation by means of the Euler-Lagrange equations is most naturally associated with local action and causation. This observation, however, does not diminish the validity of our argument, for it is in no way obvious which of the two mathematical formalisms should be granted primacy from a philosophical point of view.

The Pure Reduction of Leucippus

Among the various schools of thought associated with the natural philosophers of early Greek civilization it is the Atomist School, established by *Leucippus*, which probably is most directly relevant to science in contemporary thought.

Next to nothing is known about the life of Leucippus, but he is thought to have been active around the middle of the 5th century B.C. in the city of Abdera at the northern coast of the Aegean Sea. His major treatise on the *Great World-System* has been lost in its entirety, and of his other writings only a single sentence has survived (p.51). So far as we know, many of his ideas and beliefs were subsequently incorporated into the works of his most famous student, *Democritus*. But unfortunately, these have been lost as well and are known to us only partially through references in secondary sources. Democritus probably was born in Abdera at about 470 B.C. and reportedly reached the very advanced age of 109 years. He was still alive when Plato founded the Academy in Athens.

In his philosophical thought Leucippus addressed the same central question that Empedocles had been concerned with as well: how can the reality of change be affirmed in light of the Parmenidean teaching on the preservation of Being? In essence, his argument rested on the initial recognition that, in Parmenides's conception of the One, Being was implicitly and, as he thought, falsely identified with corporeal Being. For if indeed the One was a perfect corporeal unity, representing the totality of Being, then all Being, by definition, was bodily in form. Consequently, the existence of a void—or empty space—was equivalent to the existence of nonexistence, which in turn, as we saw earlier, was considered a contradiction in terms. Since Leucippus agreed with Parmenides that change presupposed nonexistence (p.26) and since he also believed change to be undeniable, he was compelled by logic to adopt a somewhat looser materialistic paradigm. That is to say, he came to disassociate Being from corporeity by asserting the reality of empty space. It is in this context that Democritus is quoted as saying that the "[n]o-thing exists just as much as [the] thing."[54]

Having thus set the stage on which his ontology could unfold, Leucippus proceeded to populate the void with an infinite multitude of indivisible, imperceptibly small elementary particles referred to as *atoms* (the Greek word for *indivisible* is *atomos*). In assuming these atoms to be unchanging and indestructible—just as Empedocles had done in respect of his four essential elements—Leucippus was able to argue that material Being, at its core, is endowed with the same perfect immutability as the Parmenidean One. Furthermore, concerning the problem of change, he proposed—just as Empedocles had done—that coming-into-being and passing-away are to be understood in terms of a rearranging of parts: objects form or pass away as atoms interlock or move apart.

Up to this point, then, we may be inclined to think that atomism merely reasserts the doctrine of Empedocles in less poetic language. But here we must be careful, for a crucial difference does exist at the level of causal explanation. According to Leucippus and Democritus, change is brought about, not by love and hate, but by the workings of a mechanism. Atoms supposedly come in various forms and sizes, so that the forming of bonds between them can be understood from how their shapes are matched. The nature of these bonds in turn determines an object's material qualities such as density or hardness.[1] Compounds, for example, in which atomic shapes are only loosely fitting will be soft, and tighter linkages will make a body rigid. In principle, therefore, all material phenomena can be explained in terms of geometric relations between individual atoms, and the entire physical universe, in consequence, becomes accessible to human comprehension.

The atomistic cosmos here described is uncompromisingly deterministic and securely sealed against any interference from transcendence. It is a cosmos wherein knowledge of atomic shapes, sizes, positions, and states of motion at one particular moment in time, implies knowledge of the totality of Being from eternities past to the most distant future. This vision of a rationally transparent universe is poignantly expressed in the single surviving sentence from the writings of Leucippus:

> Nothing occurs at random, but everything occurs for a reason and by necessity.[56]

Philonous: So here we have it—reductionism pure: all there ever was or will be are atoms in a void.

Sophie: And human beings, I suppose, become reduced to soulless aggregates of matter, predictably obedient to geometric laws. The vision is revolting.

Philonous: The human image in a strict interpretation of atomist philosophy is certainly depressing. But Democritus at least was actually somewhat less dogmatic in his views. He not only maintained that human beings have a soul, albeit a material one composed of atoms, but also indirectly affirmed the reality of freedom in his teachings on politics and ethics.

Sophie: The notion of a soul "composed of atoms" plainly is ridiculous, and the idea that freedom and determinism are compatible is not what I would call coherent.[55] But be that as it may, the important issue here is not whether Democritus correctly understood the implications of his own philosophy, but whether the central tenets, from which these implications are derived, are valid.

---

[1]The atomists distinguished between primary qualities such as density or hardness and secondary qualities such as color or taste. The latter were thought to have no reality in the material object itself but only in the perceiving subject. We will return to this issue in our discussion of the philosophies of Locke and Berkeley in Chapter 5.

Philonous: Fair enough, so what do you conclude? Are they valid or are they not?

Sophie: The basic outline that Leucippus and Democritus provided is clearly accurate: matter does consist of atoms, and atoms do float in a void. The modern understanding is a bit more delicate, but the fundamental paradigm, in essence, is the same.

Philonous: Roughly speaking, I agree. But I also think the differences between the ancient atomist philosophy and its modern counterpart reach deeper than you may acknowledge.

Sophie: I don't see what you're getting at.

Philonous: To make the matter clear, we need to take a closer look at the properties of atoms according to Leucippus. First of all and as we were just told (see above), atoms are very small in size and have specific shapes. So we may want to imagine little round things or little cubes with lots of hooks and crannies on the surface. Next there is the property of indivisibility and, associated with it, the notion of *fullness*. Atoms are indivisible because they are completely filled with, shall we say, some kind of atom-material. But what does atom-material consist of? Well, all matter, as we know, consists of atoms, but that, of course, won't work in this case, because if atoms themselves consisted of atoms, then any given atom could be divided into smaller atoms, and our precious property of indivisibility would thereby disappear. For we would face an ontological descent from atoms to atom-atoms to atom-atom-atoms and so forth *ad infinitum*. Since that seems unacceptable, we conveniently agree that the question, "What does *it* consist of?" is simply impolite when an atom itself is the '*it*' in question. In other words, at the level of the atom, the notion of materiality becomes an abstract postulate—an uncaused cause—that probably exists only as a train of thought in the minds of certain natural philosophers.

Sophie: So when you said, just now, that "roughly speaking" you agreed, you really meant that "roughly speaking" you completely disagreed, because your discourse ended with the thought that atoms really aren't real but are just thoughts.

Philonous: I disagree, because, I think, my "thought that atoms really aren't real" is clearly real.

Sophie: So really you agree.

Philonous: ...to disagree that I agree.

Sophie: The game is very much confusing.

Philonous: ...and amusing.

Sophie: ...not to me, so let's move on—let's look at atoms now from our more coherent, modern point of view.

Philonous: Not yet, because I do want to make sure we clearly understand why, at bottom, the atomism of Leucippus presents us with a paradox. And to do so I need to pose a question: from where do we derive the thought that something can be 'full'?

Sophie: The root may here be found in simple everyday experience: we look inside a box and find it full or empty. That's really all it takes to form the pertinent conceptions.

Philonous: On that account, a completely filled and homogeneous object, such as a billiard ball, is probably the sort of model that we should appeal to when speaking of an atom that is *full*.[II]

Sophie: Certainly.

Philonous: In other words, the notion of fullness is derived from sensory perceptions relating to objects that themselves consist of atoms.

Sophie: It is indeed.

Philonous: And thus, the paradox is evident: we take an object that is filled, we examine it with our senses, we form an intuition to which we give a name, we call it 'fullness', and now we take this intuition and *project it back into its source* by asserting that the object is composed of atoms that themselves are full—not full of atoms, but full in a generic sense. Atoms are filled, so to speak, with fullness itself—a purely abstract fullness that *per se* is no more real than any mental image we might happen to attach to it.

Sophie: So that's the reason why you said that atoms are just thoughts?

Philonous: That is correct, except that I would add that we can freely choose the locus of our emphasis: we can say that matter—consisting of atoms—is no more real than thought or, vice versa, that thought is as real as matter.

Sophie: You mean, it really doesn't matter.

Philonous: Precisely.

Sophie: The argument is cleverly set up but nonetheless fallacious.

Philonous: How so?

Sophie: I am not contesting your analysis concerning the problem of projection. In claiming atoms to be full, Leucippus erroneously extended a sense-based intuition into a subatomic or inner-atomic realm that none of our senses can perceive. Afterall, an atom, by being indivisible, cannot be cut in half to find out if it's full or empty on the inside. The conclusion, however, that we must therefore draw is simply this: atoms, as the ultimate constituents of matter, cannot be full or empty. By implication, it is not permissible to go on to conclude that atoms are as immaterial thoughts from the antecedent observation that fullness, as *applied to atoms*, is a mere abstraction. For how can any statement be derived by applying a property that must not be applied?

[II]To be more precise, the notion of 'fullness' is a theoretical construct derived from the observation that in breaking a billiard ball apart we find each fragment bounded by continuous surfaces. In other words, it is a concept that we conveniently associate with a certain set of observations, but it is not itself observable as the actual inside of a billiard ball—that which supposedly is full—is, of course, non-observable by definition.[57]

Philonous: You clearly have a point, but notice also this: my argument will
    look more sensible and sound as soon as we move on from ancient to con-
    temporary thought.
Sophie: Are you sure?
Philonous: Absolutely. For when we look at representations of matter in mod-
    ern quantum theories, the familiar solidity of physical reality is quickly lost,
    and certain of the structures that we find may rightly be considered to be
    "mind-like."[18]
Sophie: Please forgive my skepticism, but assertions concerning the identity of
    thoughts and atoms or mind and matter are not exactly standard fare in
    modern texts on physics.
Philonous: Certainly, such claims are not immediately derivative of facts that
    physicists observe and are unlikely to be found in ordinary textbooks. But
    since they are *consistent* with the facts, they may be viewed as viable
    interpretive alternatives—alternatives, as I should add, that are of interest
    in particular in respect of our integrative quest. However, the physics
    here involved is stubbornly confounding and abstract, and what is needed
    therefore is a prior critical analysis of our all too human tendency to think
    that physical reality inherently makes sense.

An Interlude on Magnets

Up to this point, our survey of the natural philosophies of ancient Greece has
confronted us with a rather diverse array of ontological conceptions all of which
addressed, in their own ways, the fundamental inquiry, "What does the world
consist of?" The proposals that were made, however—with the sole exception
of Pythagoras's more abstract, mathematical approach—will hardly strike us
as convincing. Proclaiming water, air, or fire—separately or in conjunction—
to be the ultimate constituents of physical reality only begs the question as
to what composes these constituents in turn. And the atomism of Leucippus,
despite its markedly more modern tone, leaves us equally dissatisfied. For if
we say all matter consists of atoms and then proceed in vicious circularity
to fill each individual atom with a sort of generic fullness abstracted from
observations of filled objects that in turn consist of atoms, little insight has
been gained.

    In fact, even our most advanced present-day theories do not afford us any
access to questions of ultimate substantiality. According to the standard contemporary account, all ordinary matter consists of atoms, and all atoms consist
of electrons and quarks.[58] But when we further ask what electrons and quarks
consist of, the modern physicist will and must fall silent. Perhaps some day
the question will be passed on to a deeper level still, if electrons or quarks are
found to be made up of some more elementary ingredients. But no matter how
deep a level we will reach, at the end of our descent we will always be met by

the same necessary silence. For the question of substantiality, by its very nature, is unanswerable. Not ultimate substance, but ultimate relatedness must be the goal of our inquiry. Instead of asking "What is there?" we must seek to discern how that which is there, whatever it may be, relates to that which is there too. In other words, the problem of ontology, if we still wish to recognize it as such,[1] is to be reconceived as a search for the relational character of being rather than being itself.

Shifting our focus thus, an elementary particle, such as an electron, is best regarded as a unifying principle—or theory[59]—that organizes certain sets of sensory perceptions. So the seemingly concrete and intuitively accessible notion of a particle as a distinct material entity is here replaced with an abstract conceptual image in the essential character of which we hope to discover the deeper structure and meaning of the reality that the particle is intended to portray. As a matter of course, such a determination of essential characteristics will by necessity be strictly metaphorical in kind and will not be carried out within the realm of scientific knowledge. We will speak for instance of conceptual traits as 'particle-like', 'wave-like', 'matter-like', or, more daringly perhaps, as 'mind-like' without being able to truly define these attributes in terms more basic or transparent. In fact, it is precisely in this overstepping of the bounds of knowledge that we are liable to gain the freedom that we need for our integrative project to succeed.

At first sight, the presently proposed transition from concretely material to abstractly relational ontologies may seem to stand in blatant opposition to the evidence of sense. Afterall, our sensory perceptions provide us with experiences so direct and so compelling that the idea of a physical universe grounded in immaterial relatedness will likely strike us as absurd. Material substance, so it appears, is a perfectly self-evident and ever-present actuality that surrounds us on all sides: we can see it, feel it, touch it, and doubting its solidity will therefore seem insane. However, this naively confident realism of our everyday experience quickly founders when we look in more detail at how material reality is commonly described in scientific thought. And, surprisingly, to see that this is so we do not even have to ponder any far out quantum paradoxes or any odd effects in relativity—a simple pair of magnets, examined from a classical perspective, will be entirely sufficient.

Philonous: Magnets really are amazing, aren't they? You pick up two of them and hold them close to one another, and they will either push apart or pull together; you turn around just one of them, and suddenly you feel the opposite effect. It is astonishing!

Sophie: It surely is, and I can still remember well how magnets always cap-

---

[1]Karl Jaspers, for instance, takes the view that in the light of the Kantian turn "every ontology must be rejected."[60] In essence we concur, but for lack of a better word we have here chosen to allow the term 'ontology' to be applied not only to conceptions of being in itself but also to descriptions of being in relatedness.

tured my attention as a child. At the time, of course, I didn't know what
magnetism was, and so I found it most intriguing to observe how objects,
which are not immediately in contact or otherwise connected, can exert
repulsive or attractive forces on each other. It seemed miraculous to me
that the apparent void between two magnets could offer a resistance as I
tried to push the pole of one magnet closer to the same pole of the other.

Philonous: The way you reminisce, I feel a bit concerned. I hope you do not
mean to say that now, as an adult, you have completely lost your childhood
sense of wonder.

Sophie: I haven't lost it—not entirely. But as I studied science more in depth in
high school and in college it certainly grew weaker. For mystery recedes as
knowledge is increased. It is another case, as you might say, where greater
understanding causes in effect our vision to contract (p.23).

Philonous: As for me, this point is moot, for "understanding" I have none.

Sophie: You do not understand what magnets are?

Philonous: No, I don't, and I'm afraid I never will. And what is worse, even
the more evident phenomenon of gravity in daily life has always stubbornly
eluded my attempts to truly comprehend it. Is there anything intuitively
obvious about the notion that matter attracts matter through empty space
simply by virtue of being matter? The fact, of course, that our feet stay
on the ground is well familiar, and Newton also taught us to believe that
masses are attracted, not only to the earth, but to each other everywhere
and always; he even found a formula by which this universal 'force' can
be *described* (shown earlier in Figure 2.11, p.46). But does it therefore
follow that Newton—or I or you or anyone—has really *understood* what
gravitation is, in and of itself? I doubt it. Similarly, I also never grasped
how "the apparent void between two magnets," as you just chose to put it,
can possibly oppose the muscles in my arms.

Sophie: People who incline to speculative thought are hardly ever known for
physical robustness. Perhaps a bit of exercise would help your muscles
better meet the challenge.

Philonous: The idea of such activity is more disturbing even than my ignorance
concerning magnetism. So please do not digress.

Sophie: Then what am I to do?

Philonous: Explain to me how magnets work.

Sophie: You are being facetious.

Philonous: Not at all—the need is real.

Sophie: Very well then, where shall I begin? With the notion of a field?

Philonous: Whatever you think best.

Sophie: You see, the void between two magnets, that seems to be the source
of your confusion, really isn't just a void but is, in fact, completely filled
with the flow lines of a field—a magnetic field. Have you ever seen experiments with iron files or compass needles that make such flow lines visible

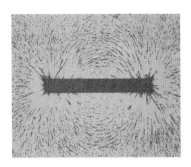 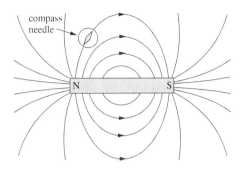

Figure 2.12: magnetic flow lines.

(Figure 2.12)?

Philonous: Of course I have, but do I therefore know what fields or flow lines really are? What, if I may ask, do they consist of?

Sophie: They don't consist of anything because they do not have a mass, and they are real only in so far as their *effects* on matter are.[II] A charged material object, moving in a magnetic field, for instance, will be seen to be subject to a force that always points in the direction perpendicular to both the object's direction of motion and the direction of the flow line through the point at which the object is positioned at any given instant.[III]

Philonous: So flow lines are *effects*? Effects without a cause?

Sophie: The cause is there, but in the magnet at a distance.

Philonous: I still don't understand because there really is no physical connection. Nothing whatsoever links the magnet to the object it affects.

Sophie: But all the same the facts are plain and easily observed.

Philonous: Certainly, but recognition of the factual alone does not suffice to calm the protests of my intuition. A field, as you explained, is massless—it really isn't anything at all—and yet it has effects on objects that supposedly themselves are solid and material. If nothing has effects on something, then maybe that is so because the something really is a nothing.

Sophie: I have a hunch you're trying to confuse a very simple subject.

Philonous: The subject isn't simple in the least—it only is familiar. Many times we have experienced attractive or repulsive forces when holding mag-

---

[II]In modern quantum electrodynamics, the forces of electromagnetism are thought to be transmitted by way of photon exchange between charged particles. On the surface this quantum model may appear to be more concrete than the flow-line model of classical physics, but ultimately, the ontology of a photon—an energy package with vanishing rest mass—is equally obscure. Thus, in the context of our present discussion, the restriction to the classical view is an adequate simplification that will not weaken or invalidate the argument that we are in the process of developing.

[III]The force here in question is the so-called Lorentz force that a magnetic field in a vacuum exerts on a charged, moving object (see [Som1], p.223).

nets in our hands, and our sense of wonder finally gave way to boredom. But habitual acquaintance is not the same as comprehension—and neither is description the equivalent of explanation. Physicists can well *describe* how magnets and the fields that they create will commonly behave. But no physicist will ever be able to *explain* what ultimately lies behind the phenomenon that we refer to as 'magnetic force', no matter how advanced the model he or she employs.

Sophie: Is this assertion somehow tied to your more general refusal to accept the notion of a force?

Philonous: No, the topic of our next to last discussion is here of no concern. Besides, the issue then was not acceptance versus non-acceptance but rather critical reflection.

Sophie: So what is here your point?

Philonous: My purpose presently is to expose how feeble the assumptions are by which we all naively operate in daily life. We like to think of matter as something solid and manifestly present, something that is quite distinct, for instance, from the elusiveness of mental processes. But do we really have a basis for this view? Is it really obvious that an object like a magnet, which abstract fields in empty space can easily deter, is itself more real than emptiness? At first these questions seem ridiculous because the evidence of sense supports so strongly our realist naiveté: we hold an object in our hands and feel it firm and solid, quite different from the nothingness of empty space.[IV] But as we take a closer look, we strangely find the cause of all these sensory perceptions to be as insubstantial as a flow line in a void.

Sophie: The cause is insubstantial?

Philonous: It is indeed.

Sophie: But why?

Philonous: Just take an arbitrary ordinary object like a coin. As you hold and touch it with your fingers, you can sense the hardness of its metal substance and the roundness of its shape. But what exactly is the process that produces these sensations?

Sophie: Well, as my fingertips come into contact with the metal surface, certain nerve endings spring into action, sending signals to my brain that cause me to experience the coin as round and flat and solid.

Philonous: True, but let's go deeper still, from nerves and nervous signals to the actual constituents of matter.

Sophie: To molecules and atoms?

Philonous: ...or even further down to electrons and nuclei.

[IV] In modern physics it has been recognized, of course, that empty space is, in fact, anything but empty. According to our current-day understanding, the so-called vacuum is a whirlpool of quantum energy fluctuations in which elementary particles are ceaselessly created and destroyed. However, this qualification concerning the nature of the vacuum does not diminish the validity of our argument because a quantum fluctuation is, ontologically speaking, hardly any less elusive than emptiness (or fullness or matter or mind or whatever).

Sophie: So as we thus descend, what insight do we gain?

Philonous: To make my point, I need to give a little demonstration.

Sophie: A demonstration?

Philonous: ...at the table over there. Please follow me and watch what I'm doing.

Sophie: Your fist is on the tabletop, and you apparently are straining.

Philonous: I am indeed—I'm pushing down as hard as I am able.

Sophie: To what intent?

Philonous: I want to overcome the opposition that I feel and break right through.

Sophie: Through the table with your fist?

Philonous: The table first and then the floor.

Sophie: Common sense, it seems, is not as common as I thought.

Philonous: You think it obvious that I should fail?

Sophie: Who wouldn't?

Philonous: If the matter is so evident, then tell me please, what kind of force prevents my hand from going down and breaking through. Why does my fist not penetrate the wood to come out at the underside?

Sophie: Because the table is just there. What sort of question are you asking?

Philonous: So it's a kind of 'table-force' that hinders here my fist?

Sophie: In principle, yes, but your choice of words is obviously not commendable. Instead of 'table-force', let me suggest, you'd better use 'mechanical resistance'.

Philonous: It sounds more educated, I admit, but offers little insight otherwise. What I desire is to know the *fundamental type* of force my fist encounters as it presses down against the wood. Is it the force of gravity?

Sophie: Gravity is not involved.

Philonous: Then name a force that *is* involved?

Sophie: I must admit, as far as fundamental forces are concerned, the issue is a little bit perplexing.

Philonous: The puzzle I assure you can be solved. Just follow my advice and take a look at the constituents that matter is composed of.

Sophie: Are you suggesting that the force in question is produced as atoms in your fist collide with atoms in the table?

Philonous: Essentially, I am. But the image that you conjure up of atoms in collision is a bit too mechanistic for my taste.

Sophie: What image would you use instead?

Philonous: The image of a field.

Sophie: To represent your fist?

Philonous: Look, what we must realize is this: all matter, as we commonly encounter it, is first and foremost an *electromagnetic* phenomenon. The atoms that compose the world that we inhabit consist of nuclei and shells that carry charges of opposite polarity and interact by means of fields.

Sophie: The theory is well familiar: atomic nuclei are positive, and the electrons that form the shells are negative. But I concede that only now do I begin to see the larger implication: all ordinary physical phenomena, such as the opposition of a table to the pressure of a fist or the holding of a coin between two fingers, are ultimately caused by forces that we classify as *electromagnetic*. For all of them can be reduced to interactions of electric particles in atoms.

Philonous: It is amazing, isn't it? All those myriad material phenomena that we encounter in our daily lives—except perhaps for those involving gravitation[V]—can be described as the effects of a single type of force.

Sophie: The thought is most remarkable indeed: whether we are sitting on a chair, riding on a bike, or eating breakfast from a bowl, we are engaged in processes that are determined solely—up to gravity—by forces that electric fields transmit at subatomic scales.

Philonous: But do you also see how strangely immaterial these common processes now suddenly appear? What I describe, for instance, as the 'coming-into-contact' of my fist with a table's wooden surface turns out, upon inspection, to be no less elusive a phenomenon than the transmission of a force across the void between two magnets. In fact, there is no contact anywhere—only fields are interacting. The negatively charged electrons in my hand and in the wooden surface exert repulsive forces on each other, but contact, in the mechanical sense, there really isn't any. Or consider the sensations that a coin between my fingers induces in my nervous system. I feel the coin to be a hard unbending object when in 'reality' I never can get past the massless fields by which the object is surrounded.

Sophie: In other words, in all my life I never have encountered yet a single object that I truly have made contact with.

Philonous: And you never will. In fact, the very notion of coming-into-contact is entirely misleading. It is an intuition-based linguistic construct to which a proper analogue in physical reality does simply not exist.

Sophie: The inference, I admit, can scarcely be avoided, but in the light of it, it seems, reality is rapidly dissolving.

Philonous: Slowly now, reality itself is not in doubt—at least not necessarily. What we have scrutinized is only our unreflected tendency to think that the external world, in its essential nature, conforms to intuitions which derive from sensory experience. When we examined earlier the problem of projection in regard to properties ascribed to atoms by Leucippus, you easily could comprehend that fullness, for example, is a sense-based intuition which must not be applied in realms to which our senses have no access. So why are you at present so alarmed, if all we really did was to extend this previous argument to other kinds of common intuitions—such as the

---

[V]...and a few others that hardly ever enter our direct awareness. Examples are the various forms of radioactive decay that are governed by nuclear forces.

notion of solidity in everyday 'mechanical' encounters?

Sophie: I see your point, but your assessment is a blatant understatement. For what we have concluded here is nothing less than that all matter is amorphous. Any object, which by habit we perceive as substantive and firm, dissolves as soon as we explore it scientifically. So isn't it then fair to say that such a radical denial of solidity is fundamentally a total readjustment?

Philonous: You still are using words in ways that simply are inadequate. What does it mean to speak of objects being 'solid'? The notion of solidity is descriptive, not of objects but perceptions. In our daily lives, 'solidity' and 'coming-into-contact' are descriptors that we meaningfully correlate with numerous sensations and impressions. But can we therefore hope to rediscover them when analyzing objects in a microrealm that our senses cannot reach? The answer is that we cannot. Afterall, our sensory apparatus is designed to help us operate in the dimensions of our everyday surroundings, and there is thus no reason in the world to think that intuitions formed in this immediate environment should be reflective of the properties of matter at atomic scales or even accurately represent existence in itself—the Being as it is.

Sophie: But what about the problem of magnetic force? The phenomena that we associate with it are readily accessible to us, and yet you claimed that they as well cannot be truly understood.

Philonous: I did indeed, and you are right to point us back to this particular example. For it may serve us here to illustrate how difficult it is to match reality to sense-based intuitions—even, at times, in the macroscopic realm that our senses *are* designed to reach. Let's take a closer look: whenever I myself, unaided by technology of any kind (including sticks and stones) set out to make an object move, I first must come in contact with it (or perhaps blow at it, but let's not be ridiculous). In other words, the setting-into-motion of a given object by pushing, say, or pulling will always be preceded by the feeling of a touch. Before I see the object move, I will observe my hand or foot or other body parts approaching until the gap is closed and my sense of touch has signaled that the point of 'contact' has been reached. If now by contrast I observe how magnets can exert a motive force on objects that they seemingly are *not* in contact with, my intuition fails because the rule that contact is a requisite of setting-into-motion has here been violated inexplicably. It is for this reason that genuine intuitive understanding of the phenomenon of magnetism is not within my reach.

Sophie: From what you say I gather "understanding" here is narrowly construed. The way you have apparently defined the word is more restrictive than in common usage.

Philonous: Notice please that I employed the phrase "intuitive understanding"—the attribute 'intuitive' is not to be omitted. We may be able, say, to 'understand' or demonstrate by way of mathematical deduction that

Newton's theory of gravity can be inferred from Einstein's or that Maxwell's fundamental equations of electromagnetism can be transformed from integral to differential form. But neither gravity nor electromagnetism will ever be compatible with our sense-based intuitions. Interestingly, it is this latter form of direct, intuitive insight to which the word 'understanding' appears to be appealing. The 'standing-under' of a thing with respect to another is doubtlessly indicative of the sort of immediately apparent causal link that I just spoke of in regard to contact as a requisite of setting-into-motion.

Sophie: So what you are asserting is, in summary, that the standing-under understanding—in science at least—is not a goal that we should ever try to reach.

Philonous: ...because it's simply too ambitious—especially, as we will see, in modern quantum physics.

Anaxagoras in the Quantum Realm

The man who commonly is credited with being the first thinker in the Western intellectual tradition to elaborate the idea that the ruling principle of the universe is mind rather than matter was a philosopher from Asia Minor by the name of *Anaxagoras*.[62] Born around 500 B.C. in the town of Clazomenae, Anaxagoras also was the first philosopher in history to take up residence in the City of Athens. Later in life, however, he likely came to regret this move when the political opponents of Pericles brought him to trial for charges of heresy. His teachings on the Sun's being a fiery stone and the Moon's being made of earth were listed among the official causes of the clamor. But in truth, it probably was his close association with Pericles, who, as a young man, had been a student of his, that provoked the authorities to take action against him.[61] At the trial's conclusion the death sentence was pronounced, but a timely escape from prison, arranged possibly by Pericles himself, allowed him to flee into exile.

In his philosophical thought, Anaxagoras set forth the notion that the world at its foundations is governed by a universal mind, or *Nous*, as he called it. This mind, so he believed, had "power over all things"[63] and acted as a cosmic first cause that set the whole universe spinning in a giant vortex motion. The matter caught in this rotation supposedly began to "separate out,"[64] thereby creating the world's present-day complexity and diversity.

There is undeniably a certain resemblance here to the teachings of Empedocles who, for instance, in one of his writings declared that all things come together "so as to be only one" whenever Strife had fallen "to the lowest depth of the vortex, and Love had reached the center of the whirl."[65] But whereas Empedocles tended to employ Love and Strife (or Hate) as metaphors for essentially material forces, Anaxagoras was more explicit in his insistence that Nous is a non-material mind-like entity.[66] It is for this reason that Aristotle in the

Metaphysics says of Anaxagoras that he "stood out like a sober man from the random talkers that had preceded him."[68] Admittedly, in another passage of the *Metaphysics* Aristotle also laments Anaxagoras's failure to ascribe to Nous genuine causal efficacy[1] by turning it essentially into a *"deus ex machina."*[70] But credit ought to be given where credit is due, and that Anaxagoras clearly perceived the idea of mind as prime mover may safely be asserted.

We would be guilty of untenable conjecturing if we now went on to claim that Anaxagoras's pioneering thoughts from the 5th century B.C. somehow are directly linked to the development of quantum physics in the modern era. But the case that quantum physics—in the spirit of Anaxagoras—has established a necessary link between materiality and mind and thereby softened the line that used to separate these two domains can well be made. To be sure, what is at issue here is metaphysics more than physics as our argument, by its very nature, will leave entirely invariant that core of quantum theory from which its practical applicability derives. It is the meaning of the science rather than the science in itself that we will mainly be concerned with.

Historically, the origins of quantum theory can be traced back to the discovery of certain anomalies in late 19th century physics that were impossible to reconcile with the then dominant classical paradigm. The discreteness of atomic and molecular emission spectra was one such anomaly and another was regarding the energy distribution in black-body radiation. The latter problem, in fact, was the first to find a genuine quantum-mechanical resolution when Max Planck presented a research report *On the Theory of the Energy Distribution Law of the Normal Spectrum* to the German Physical Society in Berlin.[71]

The problem Planck's report addressed was one of the great open puzzles of 19th century physics: the conversion of heat into radiation energy. In everyday life, this phenomenon is readily observed, for instance, when light is emitted from a red-hot piece of metal. But in scientific experiments the same effect is more conveniently examined when the heated object is a box-shaped cavity, a so-called 'black body'. Observation shows that the energy density inside such a cavity, as a function of the radiation frequency, first increases, then reaches a maximum, and then levels off to zero as the frequency continues to grow larger. Unfortunately, though, this experimental result is not consistent with the theoretical prediction of the classical theory of electrodynamics. In fact, this theory implies that the energy density, when integrated over the entire electromagnetic spectrum, yields the total energy infinity—a prediction which is commonly referred to as the 'ultraviolet catastrophe'. To eliminate this evident absurdity, Planck in his paper proposed that the material oscillators, of which the walls of a black body are composed, emit and absorb energy only

---

[1]A similar comment we find in Plato's *Phaedo*, where Socrates expresses his disappointment that Anaxagoras "made no use of mind and assigned to it no causality for the order of the world, but adduced causes like air and æther and water and many other absurdities."[69]

in discrete integer multiples of certain fundamental quanta of energy which in turn are equal to an oscillator's frequency multiplied with Planck's quantum of action.[72] The year was 1900, and the most radical scientific paradigm shift ever to occur was on its way to change the course of history.

In order not to cause any misunderstandings, we need to qualify immediately that the revolution here in question is discernible only with hindsight. Planck himself apparently was well aware, early on, of the potential significance of his work. For on a walk in the Grunewald forest at the outskirts of Berlin, in the late fall of 1900, he confided to his son that he had just made a discovery that might some day be ranked with those of Newton.[73] Yet in the wider community of physicists, his hypothesis regarding the quantization of energy was received, not as a welcome revolutionary breakthrough, but rather as a serious embarrassment—if it was being received at all, that is. In fact, it almost took a full five years until, in 1905, the first follow-up paper in support of Planck's hypothesis was published. To Planck's likely chagrin, however, its author was not a highly esteemed theorist with ample authority to bolster his case but rather an obscure patent examiner from the city of Berne. His name was *Albert Einstein.*

The year 1905 marked the apex of Einstein's scientific creativity. In a series of three landmark papers, all of which were published in the same volume of the *Annalen der Physik*, he established the fundamental principles of the special theory of relativity, deduced the existence of atoms from an analysis of Brownian motion, and, in sweeping generalization of Planck's hypothesis, he provided strong arguments in favor of the view that not only the energy emitted and absorbed by the material oscillators in the walls of a black-body cavity is quantized, but that the same is true as well of the electromagnetic radiation field between these walls. In other words, the radiation energy is not spread out continuously but rather concentrated in discrete 'radiation particles', now known as *photons.*[74]

The magnitude of Einstein's achievement is highlighted by the fact that he arrived at his conclusion independently—without direct appeal to Planck's black-body law—by examining changes in radiation entropy under spatial contractions.[II] Furthermore, he successfully extended the explanatory reach of Planck's quantization hypothesis to other anomalous phenomena such as the problem of the specific heat of solid bodies and the photoelectric effect.

Since the latter of these is especially instructive, it is advisable to take a closer look: the photoelectric effect concerns the phenomenon of intensity invariance with regard to the kinetic energy of electrons emitted from a metal surface under the impact of ultraviolet radiation. From a classical perspective, according to which radiation energy is distributed across space continuously,

---

[II]Considerations of entropy were central to Planck's argument as well, but only in respect of the material oscillators that compose the cavity's walls rather than the radiation between them.

any decrease in the intensity of the stimulant radiation should bring about a corresponding decrease in the kinetic energy of the emitted electrons, and below a certain threshold value emission should cease altogether. Experimental evidence, however, does not confirm this expectation: the electrons' kinetic energy remains unchanged, and a threshold intensity does not exist. Following Einstein, this observation becomes comprehensible from the postulate that the incoming radiation is concentrated in discrete quanta, the energy of each of which is dependent only upon the radiation frequency. For given this assumption, we may readily suppose that energy absorption happens one photon—or quantum—at a time and is therefore intensity invariant in its effects on the absorbing electrons.

Most importantly, Einstein's analysis also led him to derive specific equations that revealed how Planck's quantum of action was relevant to a quantitative description of the photoelectric effect as well as of the other, added phenomena discussed in his paper. This, of course, was all the more remarkable as none of these added phenomena appeared to be directly linked to the problem of black-body radiation.[75] In other words, Einstein's insights uncovered an underlying structural affinity that pointed toward a more encompassing essential discreteness of physical reality at microscopic scales.

As in the case of Planck's original paper, however, the initial reception of Einstein's work was far from enthusiastic. The nature of his arguments was too strange and too unconventional to be greeted with anything but skepticism or indifference. Even years later, when experimental observation had unambiguously confirmed the validity of Einstein's equation concerning the photoelectric effect, the key investigator himself—in this case the American physicist Robert Millikan—felt compelled to comment that the equation had stood the test of empirical verification "in spite of its unreasonableness" and in spite of its being based on entirely groundless assumptions such as the photon concept.[76] Eventually, though, as new discoveries were adding their momentum, the inertia of scientific tradition gave way to the realization that the edifice of classical physics, created by Newton and crowned by Maxwell's formulation of electrodynamics, had to be fundamentally revised in order to accommodate the mounting evidence against it.

A crucial stage in this development was reached in 1911 when Ernest Rutherford proposed a model of the atom. Guided by his research on α-rays in passage through matter, Rutherford was led to conclude that atoms consist of a negatively charged shell and a very small, positively charged nucleus in which by far the largest part of the atomic mass is concentrated. The emerging picture was one of a miniature planetary system with wandering electrons that circled an atomic solar core. Unfortunately, according to the laws of classical physics, such a constellation of charges in relative motion is mechanically and energetically highly unstable. For any outside influence from other fields or atoms would readily disturb the electrons' paths, and the electromagnetic radiation produced by the electrons' supposed orbital motion would cause a rapid loss of energy that would in turn effect the atom's structural collapse.

Faced with difficulties as these, the Danish theorist Niels Bohr introduced, in 1913, a model of the hydrogen atom in which the single electron in the shell could exist only in certain discrete orbital states. If atoms, so he reasoned, could emit and absorb energy only in integer multiples of a fundamental quantum of energy, as Planck had asserted, then it seemed plausible that these discretized absorptions and emissions corresponded to electron transitions between equally discretized orbital states. With this bold proclamation of a subatomic quantum world Bohr resolved the puzzle of atomic stability by simply and blatantly denying classical physics its right to be applied.

As a matter of course, the denial of a theory does not itself a theory establish, and as it turned out, it took another twelve years until, in 1925, the young Werner Heisenberg developed a mathematical formalism that integrated the various quantum phenomena, then known to physicists, into a coherent whole. At the time, Heisenberg was a *Privatdozent* and assistant to Max Born at the University of Göttingen. But his breakthrough insight came to him on the North Sea island of Heligoland where he was recuperating from a severe bout of hay fever in the late spring of 1925.[77] Working undisturbed and carefully taking stock of the available facts, he came to realize that atomic states or, more generally, quantum states ought to be described, not by single numbers, as in classical physics, but rather by arrays of numbers. These arrays in turn he organized in tables and then linked to one another by means of certain fairly obscure mathematical operations. Upon his return to Göttingen he carefully edited his work and passed a copy to Max Born who quickly realized that the computational patterns Heisenberg had stumbled upon were in fact well familiar from the algebra of matrices. Thus the new physics came to be known as *matrix mechanics.*[77]

To give the reader a sense of the sheer elemental force of ingenuity by which Heisenberg wrought his theory from the experimental data, we should perhaps point out that Steven Weinberg, one of the leading theoretical physicists of our time, confesses to his utter inability to understand "Heisenberg's motivations for the mathematical steps in his paper."[78] According to Weinberg, "Heisenberg's 1925 paper was pure magic."[79] In the light of this assessment, it is clearly not advisable for us to try to comprehensively elucidate the thoughts that prompted Heisenberg to formulate his revolutionary 'tabular physics', but a few broad outlines need to be drawn if we are at all to come to grips with the nature of the quantum realm.

The central problem that the early pioneers of quantum theory were faced with was the apparent incompatibility of certain sets of experimental observations. Light for instance acts as a *particle* in the photoelectric effect but displays the familiar characteristics of a classical continuous *wave* in interference and diffraction experiments. On a theoretical level, this empirical incoherence

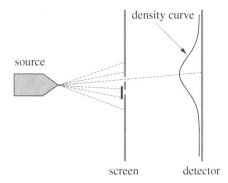

Figure 2.13: the double-slit experiment with one slit closed.

was matched by the apparent irreconcilability of Einstein's photon concept with Maxwell's classical representation of light as an electromagnetic wave. To make matters worse, the French physicist Louis de Broglie suggested, in 1924—one year prior to Heisenberg's momentous advance—that the observed duality of particles and waves is likely a symmetric one: not only is it possible for waves to act as particles but, conversely, particles can also act as waves. An electron, for instance, can be represented as a point-like particle as well as an extended matter wave.

The paradigmatic experiment of quantum theory that reveals this dual nature of material reality most strikingly is that of the double-slit: a thin metal plate with two narrow slits, both of which can be opened and closed, is placed in between a detector screen and an electron source that emits electrons at random in the approximate direction of the double-slit.[III] In the first run of the experiment *one slit is shut and the other kept open.* As electrons are passing through the open slit and subsequently leave their marks on the detector screen, the density of hits is found to be greatest in the direction from the source to the open slit and from there decreases to the sides (Figure 2.13). The corresponding density function is a bell-shaped curve with a maximum directly behind the open slit. This outcome, of course, is no surprise, as seemingly the electrons behave just like a swarm of little bullets: some of the bullets pass through the slit unhindered, some are blocked by the metal plate, and some get scattered randomly by bouncing off the slit's two sides. Thus the distribution's spread and shape are easily explained from a fairly crude mechanical analogy. By implication, if now we open up the second slit as well, we should expect the

---

[III]It is actually not possible to perform the experiment in exactly this form because the whole setup would have to be arranged "on an impossibly small scale."[80] Consequently, it is more accurate to speak of a thought experiment rather than an experiment. However, the outcome of this thought experiment is indubitable because the effects in question have indeed been observed many times in similar actual experiments.

density of hits to be a superposition of the individual densities for each slit. In other words, the number of electrons hitting the detector screen at any given point should equal the sum of the numbers of electrons hitting that point by way of the first and second slit, respectively (Figure 2.14).

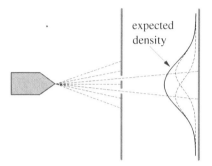

Figure 2.14: expected outcome with two slits open.

As sensible as this prediction may seem, it cannot be confirmed by observation. What actually happens is something altogether bizarre: the density of hits on the screen fluctuates between regions of high and low intensity. Common sense, no doubt, suggests that the density at any given position can only increase when the second slit is opened, but amazingly, reality does not comply: in some of the valleys of low intensity (shown in Figure 2.15), the number of electrons hitting the detector screen is actually smaller with two slits open than with only one!

In order to account for this astonishing result, it is customary to invoke a wave-particle analogy: the particle-like or bullet-like behavior in the first experiment, with only one slit open, is contrasted with a wave-like image in the second. More precisely, in this latter case, an electron emitted from the

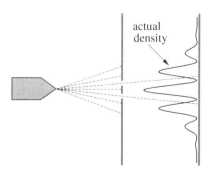

Figure 2.15: actual outcome with two slits open.

source is pictured as a matter wave that generates two interfering wave fronts on the far side of the slits. Thus, the regions of high and low intensity on the detector screen are here aligned, respectively, with places where the crests and valleys of the waves either magnify or cancel out each other (Figure 2.16).

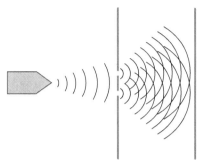

Figure 2.16: two interfering wave fronts.

Conceptually and ontologically, this dualistic picture of particle-like behavior on the one hand and wave-like behavior on the other is, of course, rather perplexing; and in a sense, Heisenberg could overcome the difficulties it entails only by ignoring it entirely. He left aside the problem of determining an underlying conceptual image and fixed his mind instead on actual phenomena. Not particle paths or matter waves were the object of his inquiry but facts that are observed in physical experiments. Thus he came to realize, for instance, that the concept of an electron orbit could be coherently maintained only "in the limit of high quantum numbers"[81] when the corresponding orbital shells are large. In general, so he concluded, the notion of an electron within an atom following a microscopic planetary path had to be discarded altogether, and a far more abstract conception of atomic quantum states had to be adopted in its place.

In the light of these remarks it does seem fair to say that the key to Heisenberg's success was his initial willingness to give up the familiar classical representations of particles and waves in favor of a purely abstract mathematical system that does nothing more and nothing less than to account for the facts of observation. Having said as much, we still of course are far from truly grasping the more specific rationale behind the mathematics Heisenberg employed. But it is interesting all the same to see how at the very outset a proper understanding of the laws of quantum physics depended upon a radical shift in the scientific mode of thought—away from conceptual realism toward a sort of empirically grounded relational abstraction.

Sophie: So what are we to make of it? Particles spread out as waves, and waves contract to particles depending on the opening and closing of a slit? It sounds like magic more than science.

Philonous: I fully share your sense of consternation, but your appeal to higher powers is a bit too hasty for my taste. If magic is involved as waves and particles metamorphose, then the transmission of a force across the void between two magnets may just as well be blamed on sorcery.

Sophie: I do not think at all that your comparison is apt because the common concept of magnetic force is perfectly coherent. Afterall, magnets hardly ever have been known to suffer sudden transformations into altered states.

Philonous: That may be so, but notice also this: the mathematical description of electrons as quantum objects is empirically no less viable than that of fields in classical electromagnetism. So why should we regard the latter to be more coherent than the former?

Sophie: ...because an object cannot be two different things at once. Heisenberg may have been able to create a unifying quantum formalism, but that does not absolve him of his duty as a scientist to give a plausible account of the reality that underlies his model. How is it possible that a particle, such as an electron, transforms itself into a wave and then again becomes a particle depending on the way we look at it by means of our experimental setup? There must be some consistent causal explanation.

Philonous: I don't know. The facts are simply what they are and ought to be accepted.

Sophie: Sure, but in themselves the facts are not enough—we also need an ontological description. In the double-slit experiment, for instance, the electrons that are emitted from the source are obviously ignorant, at the moment of emission, of whether they are headed for a metal plate with two or only one slit open. Consequently, the notion that there are individual particles emerging from the source in the first setup and wave fronts in the second is obviously ludicrous.

Philonous: I honestly have no idea what sort of entity—if any—emerges from the source in either case, because nothing in the design of the experiment allows for this determination to be made. All that is recorded are the marks on the detector screen. As far as I can tell, the only question that a scientist analyzing such experiments should therefore be concerned with is the problem of devising a mathematical scheme that accurately describes *and predicts* the pattern of detection. For it is this pattern and only this pattern that is accessible to sensory perception.

Sophie: If that is so, then I would say you might as well abandon the idea that any such a scheme should equally apply to both conflicting cases. For you could simply treat the two different density distributions (in Figures 2.13 and 2.15) as completely disconnected physical phenomena and be content to let them coexist in total isolation. The very fact that Heisenberg attempted to devise a single mathematical description for particle and wave aspects alike is an expression of the fact that he believed these aspects to be grounded in a unitary shared reality. In particular, the reality represented by the electron source must surely be assumed to be the same regardless of how many slits are open. And a causal link between that *a priori* given reality and its various manifestations on the detector screen must therefore be established.

Philonous: I do not in the least contest your claim that the electron source is an invariant of the experimental setup, and I am even willing to assign to it a degree of objectivity sufficient to justify the search for a unifying formalism. But any further claims about the nature of the entities that such a formalism supposedly pertains to, I tend to treat with caution. For if these entities display wave- or particle-like behavior depending on the questions that we ask of them, then we should perhaps refer to them not as 'particles' or 'waves' but rather as "wavicles"[82] or 'partives' or maybe just as mathematical symbols on a sheet of paper.

Sophie: I'm sorry, but merely playing games with words again (p.35) will not do justice to the problem that we face.

Philonous: Which is?

Sophie: ...to figure out how opening the second slit can *cause* the density of hits on the detector screen to fluctuate from one point to another.

Philonous: I don't agree because my "games with words" are actually not as silly as they seem. They are a thoughtful and deliberate expression of the fact that we must not expect our intuition-based linguistic conventions to be in any way compatible with the laws and phenomena encountered in the quantum realm.

Sophie: But cutting up and reassembling words does not address the problem of causality.

Philonous: So what do you propose?

Sophie: ...to try to understand in full detail what happens when an electron is passing through a slit. For then and only then will we be able to explain how interference comes about.

Philonous: It sounds like sensible advice. But I'm afraid your goal is too ambitious, because you're seeking information that reality inherently refuses to supply.

Sophie: But each individual electron obviously reaches the detector screen along a certain path. So as we analyze this path, we likely will attain a deeper understanding.

Philonous: As to the question of whether electrons must follow certain paths, I only can again confess my total ignorance. It may be true that we have valid reasons to believe that a bullet in flight traces out a path in the macroscopic world of our direct experience, but an electron is not a bullet. An electron is a theory, and the path-habits of theories are simply not a subject I feel competent to speak about.[83]

Sophie: So the electrons are emitted and detected but in between they do not follow any paths?

Philonous: All that is recorded, as I said (p.70), are marks on a detector
  screen—the rest is fantasy. If you believe that paths exist, then come up
  with an argument that forces my assent. Offering blunt appeals to common
  sense is simply not sufficient.

Sophie: What if we tracked the paths with some additional detectors?

Philonous: Electrons, unfortunately, are not as readily detectable as bullets.
  We certainly can try to make position measurements by scattering some
  photons off the electrons as they are passing through the slits. But the
  scattering would disturb the electrons so much that the entire interference
  pattern would be lost. So, yes, it is possible to determine which slit an
  electron is passing through but only at the expense of thereby destroying
  the very phenomenon that we are trying to elucidate.

Sophie: The disturbance, though, depends on how much energy the photons
  have. By implication then, the impact of the scattering would be negligible
  if the photons' frequency was very small (because in Einstein's theory a
  photon's energy is equal to its frequency multiplied with Planck's quantum
  of action).

Philonous: Your reasoning is well thought out, but once again I have to disap-
  point you. For if, as you suggest, the scattered photons' frequency was very
  small, then the corresponding wavelength would be large, and the intended
  position measurement would therefore show a high degree of imprecision.
  What we would see (or otherwise detect in case the light is infrared) would
  be a smeared out flash of light across both slits, and there would thus be
  no clear indication which slit an electron was passing through.[84]

Sophie: Well then the problem somehow is to come up with a method of position measurement that is precise and nonintrusive simultaneously.

Philonous: One of the central claims of quantum theory precisely is that no
  such method can exist. Heisenberg's uncertainty principle does not allow,
  for instance, for the simultaneous measurement of an electron's position and
  velocity (or momentum) to an arbitrarily high degree of accuracy. We can
  measure either one but not both. If we used a highly energetic photon with
  a very small wavelength to locate an electron that just traveled through
  a double slit, we would obtain a very accurate position reading. But the
  resulting disturbance and uncertainty in the electron's momentum would
  be so large that, as I said before, the very interference phenomenon that
  we are trying to causally analyze would be destroyed. Furthermore, the
  boundary between occurrence and non-occurrence of interference coincides
  exactly with the radiation wavelength limit at which position readings become blurred. In other words, precise position readings and low disturbance
  measurements are strictly incompatible.

Sophie: So the information is there, but technologically we lack the means to
  properly extract it.

Philonous: No, the uncertainty principle does not describe a mere technological inadequacy but rather marks a fundamental epistemic limit in the structure of reality. To the best of our current understanding, nature is designed in such a way that the information you are looking for is simply not available. Personally, I like to think that the information doesn't even exist, but that of course is a matter of belief. For it is obviously impossible to ascertain the existence or non-existence of information that for reasons of principle is wholly out of reach.

Sophie: But how is all this making any sense? If an electron is first emitted and then detected, then, at any given moment in between, it surely must be somewhere and do something. In other words, it must possess a well defined position and velocity. I can see that we encounter problems in extracting this information if our means of measurement are simply too intrusive, but the information itself is surely there.

Philonous: Maybe, maybe not—who knows? Perhaps the very notion of an independent quantity that measurements perturb had better be abandoned.

Sophie: But you yourself just spoke a moment earlier of electrons as being disturbed by photon scattering. So what's the difference, may I ask, between disturbing and perturbing?

Philonous: I gladly grant your point because my use of language was indeed inaccurate. You see, the distinction, familiar from classical physics, between an object and an act in respect of a measurement is really rather meaningless where quantum physics is concerned. The act of observation, the means of measurement, and the entire experimental setup form one coherent whole from which no part can be arbitrarily isolated as that which is objectively observed. In particular, the act of measurement itself is not to be thought of as a disturbance but as an integral part of the system by which we pose our experimental questions.[85] If we speak of a disturbance, we have to clarify what it is that is being disturbed, and in so doing we leave the realm that observation can pertain to. In the case of an electron in passage through a double slit, for instance, we would have to assert not only the electron's existence prior to the so-called 'act of measurement' but even make specific claims about the simultaneous objective reality of properties—such as position and velocity—that we can never simultaneously determine.

Sophie: ... "the electron's existence prior to the... 'act of measurement'"? Are you now putting in doubt even so fundamental a notion as existence itself?

Philonous: I am indeed.

Sophie: But that's insane. The electrons are clearly real for otherwise they wouldn't be detected on the screen.

Philonous: What is real, no doubt, is the set of sense perceptions associated with the activation of the detection device, and I also readily concede that these perceptions have some type of extra-personal external source that is at least to some extent objective. But any further claims concerning attributes that we would like this source to have should probably be viewed with great suspicion. Ultimately, we must stick with that which we can see or hear or touch. For it is here, in the immediate experience of sense, where our knowledge of material reality is grounded.

Sophie: The radical empiricist is preaching yet again.

Philonous: Maybe so, but don't forget that Heisenberg's initial step in fashioning his 'tabular mechanics' was to adopt a strict empiricist approach. At the very outset he decided to discard the problem of ontology in favor of the facts. Instead of trying to determine, for example, fictitious electron orbits or paths, he only dealt with those aspects of electron behavior that physical experiments can quantify.

Sophie: And, I suppose, since an electron's existence between two measurements is unobservable by definition, we may as well deny it.

Philonous: Exactly.

Sophie: But isn't that entirely absurd?

Philonous: Not at all, for Heisenberg himself assessed the matter thus:

> Quite generally there is no way of describing what happens between two consecutive observations. It is of course tempting to say that the electron must have been somewhere between the two observations and that therefore the electron must have described some kind of path or orbit even if it may be impossible to know which path. This would be a reasonable argument in classical physics. But in quantum theory it would be a misuse of language which... cannot be justified.[86]

Sophie: If that is so, then what precisely does the formalism Heisenberg created pertain to? What exactly are we trying to describe if quantum entities do not possess a well defined existence?

Philonous: The proper answer is, "the patterns we discern in our sensory perceptions." For if there is any objectivity at all, it is in these subjective patterns that we find it. What we need to guard against, however, is our unreflected tendency to think that quantum entities have properties akin to those that we associate with objects in our everyday surroundings. To take for granted even so basic an attribute as materiality or permanence in existence would be a serious mistake. Quoting Heisenberg yet again, an elementary particle in current understanding cannot even be thought to be endowed with "the quality of being" but only with "a possibility for being or a tendency for being."[87]

Sophie: So that is what the formalism ultimately does—describe "a tendency for being"?

Philonous: That's not a bad way to put it, because quantum physics by its very nature is a theory of probability: events do not occur with certainty but only have a greater or a lesser tendency to happen. This fundamental stochasticity, by the way, is a feature that, seemingly or truly, all known quantum formalisms have in common.

Sophie: All known formalisms? Does Heisenberg's have any competition?

Philonous: Certainly. Apart from matrix mechanics there is the wave mechanics of Erwin Schrödinger, the path integral approach of Richard Feynman (established independently[IV]) the pilot wave model of David Bohm, and the quantum algebra description of Paul Dirac on which in turn the most cohesive scheme, the so-called Hilbert space representation of quantum mechanics, is based. In fact, we even may adopt the view that there are infinitely many formalisms because the Hilbert space representation contains within itself the wave- and matrix-mechanical pictures of Schrödinger and Heisenberg as just two of an infinite variety of special cases that all account for the time dependence of quantum states and the operations performed upon them in somewhat different ways.[88] The details of this issue, though, need not concern us here because, philosophically speaking, the distinctions between these various quantum pictures are really unimportant.

Sophie: Is it fair to say in light of this that quantum physics is a prime example for Einstein's dictum that conceptual thought is not uniquely determined by the facts of observation?

Philonous: Quite fair.[V]

Sophie: So which of all those formalisms do I choose?

Philonous: It's really up to you, but I am glad to offer you some guidance: wave-mechanics is a decent choice if our purpose is to understand the central role of probability and to gain, along the way, a little deeper insight into how the quantum world is organized.

Sophie: I take your word for it—and I am sure that given your amazing expertise, "a little deeper" will mean nothing less than 'utterly profound'.

Philonous: Do I detect a note of irony in this?

Sophie: 'Humble irony' would be more accurate.

Philonous: There isn't such a thing.

Sophie: Not from a classical perspective, but in the quantum world, as we have seen, the inconceivable is perfectly conceivable: if electrons can both exist and not exist, then I submit, humility and irony can also coexist.

Philonous: I think your reasoning just underwent what Schrödinger would have

---

[IV] Commonly, Feynman's formalism is derived from Schrödinger's wave mechanics. But, as demonstrated in [Bl1], it is in fact possible to establish this formalism independently by superimposing solutions of an alternative wave equation which guarantees the preservation of probability along classical particle trajectories.

[V] There are certain conceptual characteristics of quantum theory, such as linearity, that many physicists believe to be indispensable and final. By implication, quantum theory can also be held up as a counter-example to Einstein's dictum of conceptual non-uniqueness. Strictly speaking, though, assertions concerning the absolute validity of theoretical characteristics—including quantum linearity—can never be within the reach of empirical verification and are therefore always somewhat suspect.

referred to as a "damned quantum jump."[89]

Sophie: Is that the way he would have put it? It almost sounds as though he didn't like his own conceptual creation.

Philonous: Indeed, Schrödinger was not amused by the picture that the fledgling quantum theory presented in the early 1920's. So when he invented wave-mechanics in 1926, one year after Heisenberg's original advance, he did so in the hope of restoring a more classical interpretation in which elementary particles assumed the role of quantum matter waves in direct analogy "to such processes in space and time as electromagnetic or sound waves."[90]

Sophie: But he didn't succeed, did he?

Philonous: As a scientist he did, but not as a philosopher. His formalism, as he himself was able to explain, was equivalent to Heisenberg's and therefore also in agreement with the facts. But his hopes for a return to classical tranquility and neatness were dashed. One of the first clear indications of the radically non-classical character of Schrödinger's formalism was given when Max Born proposed that quantum wave functions are carriers of statistical information and as such completely immaterial. In fact, one way to conceptualize a wave function is to think of it as an informational encoding device: to any given particle or particle-system there is assigned a wave function that represents the particle's or system's physical information content as it evolves in time.[VI] In other words, all relevant information about potential manifestations of physical characteristics, such as position, velocity, or energy,[VII] in pertinent experiments, is assumed to be contained in and extractable from the encoding provided by the wave function.

Sophie: An encoding of information? I am afraid I do not understand at all— nor do I see, to be honest, how any of these strange ideas support your earlier assertion that mind and matter may be linked by way of quantum physics. Exactly how are quantum waves connected to the realm of human consciousness or thought?

Philonous: We will discuss that issue soon, but let's explore the physics first a little further. There is a lot that we have still to grasp.

Mind Over Matter

To continue our train of thought, it is helpful to pose the following question: what constitutes the usefulness of science? A tempting answer obviously is that

---

[VI]In the case of a system that is impure in the sense that the individual particles are not all in the same state it is customary—but not necessary on principle—to employ a so-called density matrix instead of a single quantum wave. The system's composition is thus described by a statistical superposition of matrices built from the particles' individual quantum waves rather than, alternatively, by a single quantum wave with as many spatial input variables as there are degrees of freedom among the system's particles.

[VII]Things get a bit more complicated once we include also the phenomena of spin and polarization, but such added complexities need not concern us here.

science gives us insight into causal correlations. By means of science, so we say, we can discern the reason for a physical occurrence. However, if that were all there is to it, then all of Galileo's famous propositions concerning falling bodies would be of little use indeed. What causal insight do we gain by stating that the rate at which a falling body changes its velocity is independent of its mass or that the distance that it falls increases in proportion to the square of time? It seems causality is nowhere here addressed. Nothing at all is here being said about the *why* that prompts a falling body to behave the way it does—only the *how* is treated and discussed. Moreover, even if we did invoke a cause by claiming that a falling motion is effected, say, by 'gravitational attraction', it hardly would be of much use. There simply is no gain, in practical terms, in giving a name to a 'cause' if, in doing so, we merely create a vacuous verbal appendage.

Consequently, a more adequate reply is clearly this: science is useful chiefly because it enables us to make dependable *predictions*. If we can say how far a falling object will descend within a certain stretch of time—regardless of the causes—then, in essence, we are able to *foresee the future*. It is this ability to infer a future from a present state by which the power of scientific knowledge really is defined—and from which also all of our modern technological devices derive their potency: a switch is turned and currents start to flow or mechanisms are engaged in perfectly foreseeable accordance with the laws of nature. By implication, a quantum formalism, too, is mainly a tool to answer the 'what if?': *what* will be the case, *if* something is the case at present? The actual or probable occurrence of experimental outcomes is to be deduced from currently observable states and conditions. There is no need at all to speculate what ontological realities might be the cause behind the correlations we record—the correlations in themselves are all we need to be concerned with.

To illustrate this point, we may consider once again the double-slit experiment: what we should here be trying to discern is not the reason *why* a swarm of electrons might move in such a way that a certain pattern of detection is produced but only *how* this pattern is to be predicted from the information that the setup factually specifies. In other words, the goal is to determine in advance how likely it will be for any given electron to leave its mark at any given point on the detector screen. If the notion of a particle in motion on a path is helpful to this end—fine, but if it isn't, then so be it. So what we ought to be on guard against is the temptation to allow our ontological prejudices to limit our conceptual adaptiveness.

That said, we also need to clarify that when we speak, as we just did, of electrons as leaving marks—or, more generally, as causing an effect—we are in essence making a mistake. That is to say, there clearly is a problem here with how we put together words: an electron is not an object in the ordinary sense but nonetheless appears as such in our writing and our speech. In fact, the very notion of an object or a subject in a sentence is already more concrete than the semi-existent apparitions that we encounter or imagine to encounter in the quantum world. An electron in our double-slit experiment is not to be regarded as a particle or matter wave with a tangible concrete existence. Much more adequate is to consider it the conceptual focal point of a larger information process that can be thought to underlie and bring about the pattern of detection. In other words and for this reason, *Philonous* had it right when he spoke earlier of quantum waves as "informational encodings." For any such a wave is really just a vehicle that represents material information in mathematical form—and the rules of computation that apply to it so happen to allow us to *predict*, in statistical terms, the outcomes of experiments.

Since, then, information is at the core of our scheme, it may be helpful to consider the problem of its storage. One way to record and store, for example, the information given by the setup of a double-slit experiment is by means of human language. We can use ordinary English words to describe the metal plate, the slits, and the detector screen; and we also can encode these words in a variety of forms: from sound waves and the letters used in written text the spectrum readily extends to radio transmissions or strings of bits in a computer code. As a matter of course, such common verbal renderings do not efficiently facilitate the use of mathematics. More adequate, as it turns out, is here a scheme of information storage that employs infinite arrays of number pairs: to every point in space and time there is assigned a pair of numbers (referred to as a 'complex number') in precisely such a way that the totality of all these pairs contains a given system's total information.[I]

Naturally, the question that arises here is how this information scheme can be concretely realized in practice. How are the physical parameters compressed into numerical arrays and how do we anticipate the changes that they undergo in time? Not surprisingly, the answer is "by means of an equation"—the so-called Schrödinger or wave equation. For example, if we wish to analyze the probability for a mark to be left at a given point on the detector screen in our double-slit experiment, we need to set up a corresponding wave equation in which, for instance, the metal plate with either one or two slits open is represented by a proper mathematical expression.[II] After this is done, we proceed to identify the particular array—or wave function—that satisfies this pertinent equation and also matches properly certain additional conditions that the experiment's initial preparation typically specifies. According to the rules of quantum physics, it is this function—this solution of the Schrödinger equation—that contains all the relevant physical information about an electron

---

[I]As indicated in the footnote on p.76, the wave function associated with a system of particles is a little more complicated an object in that the spatial component of its input consists of more than just the ordinary three components (one for each of the three spatial dimensions), but in essence the scheme is very similar.

[II]One way to accomplish this is to consider the metal plate as a region of infinite potential energy and then to insert the resulting potential energy function into the Schrödinger equation.[94]

within the double-slit apparatus, and it is this function as well that tells us how this information changes over time.

Furthermore, in order to compute the (approximate) probability for an electron to be found at a given point in time in a given small segment of space—which, in the context of the double-slit experiment, may be thought to be adjacent to the detector screen—we proceed as follows: we take the pair of numbers that the wave function assigns at that point in time to that point in space where the segment is positioned, take the square of both numbers in the pair, form the sum, and multiply the value that we find with the segment's volume. That is to say, if V denotes the volume and (a, b) (or $a + ib$ for readers familiar with complex number notation) the number pair, then the probability in question is (approximately)[III]

$$(a^2 + b^2) \cdot V.$$

Moreover, analogous computations of probabilities can be carried out for any physical quantity—other than position—that we might happen to consider. And for any such a quantity there is defined an operation or *action* on the wave function by means of which the quantity's potential manifestations in physical experiments can be exhaustively described. In other words, for every physical characteristic there exists a corresponding information processing scheme that allows us to determine how likely it is for a certain measurement to yield a certain value.

Given this explanatory outline, there are some questions that may readily occur to us. Why is it possible, for instance, to compress the entire information about a particle within a given setup, no matter how complex, into pairs of numbers assigned to points in space and time? Why pairs, why points, why only one pair for each point? Or why for that matter are probabilities determined from sums of squares? Why not sums of cubes? It seems so altogether random. What reasons can we give for all of this to work as we are told? Unfortunately, the proper answer is, "none whatsoever." There are no reasons, only facts. Observation shows that the riddles posed by certain physical experiments can be resolved within the scheme that Schrödinger invented. But why it works the way it does is not a question we can meaningfully pose.

The central lesson then is this: as far as our intuition is concerned, quantum physics is entirely elusive.[IV] For it describes a micro-realm to which our senses have no access; and many of the rules that it obeys have absolutely no equivalent within the macroscopic world of our everyday experience. When

---

[III] In order to get the probability's *exact* value at a certain point in time, one would have to break up a given spatial segment into infinitely many infinitesimally small subsegments, apply the above given formula to each of these, and form the sum. In other words, one would have to take the integral of $a^2 + b^2$ as a spatially defined function (with a fixed time coordinate) over the segment in question.

[IV] Here we are following the lead of Richard Feynman who in [Feyn1], p.9, expresses his conviction that nobody understands quantum mechanics.

we observe a falling body, for example, we can easily determine its position and velocity completely independently. And in particular, it is of absolutely no import which quantity is measured first—but not so in the quantum realm. Here a particle's physical characteristics are linked to one another by being jointly encoded in a quantum wave, and the *actions* representing them so happen to be generally *noncommuting*. That is to say, if we apply for instance the actions representing position and velocity (or momentum)—in this order—to a given wave, we get an answer different from the one that we would get if the order of these actions was reversed. Moreover, it is this strange failure of the actions to commute on which the earlier referred to uncertainty principle of Heisenberg's is crucially dependent. How do we ever truly understand these strange phenomena? Why is the information linked the way it is? Or why, for that matter, should we expect reality to be organized in such a way that Heisenberg uncertainty prevents us from determining position and momentum simultaneously? Again, the only proper answer is that we don't know.

Put differently, if our goal is to intuitively grasp *why*, in the final analysis, quantum reality is what it appears to be, we can be sure of comprehensive failure. But if, by contrast, we agree to be content to know and understand *how* certain physical phenomena align with certain mathematical descriptors, we can be equally assured that our goal can be achieved. More specifically, if we inquire why, ultimately, nature is designed in such a way that our double-slit experiment produces interference, we cannot offer a reply. But if instead we seek to comprehend, more modestly and more concretely, how the information content of a quantum wave allows us to *predict* how interference comes about, we can succeed quite readily.

Let's take a closer look: if we apply the formalism Schrödinger invented to the initial case where one slit is open and one is closed, we rather quickly find that the pertinent probability density for electron hits on the detector screen is roughly equal to the one that we were shown in Figure 2.13. The relevant computation is easily performed but in itself of very little interest. Furthermore and as a matter of course, which of the two slits is open and which is closed makes no essential difference as the corresponding wave functions—on the far side of the double slit—are merely spatial shifts of one another. But now the vital point is this: Schrödinger's wave equation is mathematically *linear* in that the sum or *superposition* of any two of its solutions is a solution as well. By implication, the wave function for the case where both slits are open is a superposition of the wave functions corresponding to the two possible setups in which one slit is open and the other one is closed (up to a normalizing factor, but this is not important). Moreover, this property of *linearity* is absolutely central. For the entire structure of quantum mechanical theory appears to be in one way or another linked to it.

To see the truth of this latter assertion, within the present context of explaining interference, it is helpful to denote by ψ_1 and ψ_2 the wave functions corresponding respectively to the setting with the first slit open and the second closed and the alternative setting with the first slit closed and the second open. Using this notation, the solution in the case where both slits are open is simply the sum $\psi = \psi_1 + \psi_2$ (up to a normalizing factor). Furthermore, addition here is carried out componentwise: if ψ_1 and ψ_2 are equal to the pairs (a_1, b_1) and (a_2, b_2), respectively, then $\psi = (a_1 + a_2, b_1 + b_2)$. This very simple additive procedure can also be expressed in geometric terms if we represent ψ_1 and ψ_2 by arrows in a plane. For if these arrows are attached to one another by parallel shifting ψ_1, then the sum ψ is given by the diagonal compound arrow shown in Figure 2.17. Alternatively and in switching to a global view, we also may

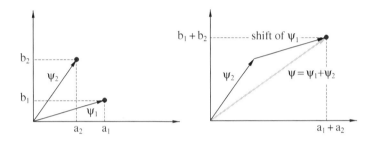

Figure 2.17: addition of two wave function values.

imagine, if we wish, that at every point in space there are installed two little stopwatches—one for ψ_1 and the other for ψ_2.[91] Each stopwatch has a single moving hand (whose length may vary with time) that represents the value of the corresponding wave function at the point in space and time where the stopwatch is positioned. Then, given such a larger view, we find the function ψ by adding up the hands for every pair of watches.

That said, the next and most important step is to observe that the relative directions of the hands on the paired up watches are typically not the same at every point in space. For it is this directional variability that potentially causes the effects of the addition on the amplitude of ψ to be strongly dependent on the point in space that we so happen to consider. At points where the directions of both hands are equal, their lengths are added and thus amplified, whereas a cancellation will occur wherever the two hands are diametrically opposing; and other cases will be intermediate (Figure 2.18).

In order to understand exactly how these potential cancellations and amplifications are linked to the phenomenon of interference, it is useful to denote by a and b, respectively, the two components of the compound arrow ψ at, say, a given point on the detector screen (i.e., $\psi = (a, b) = (a_1 + a_2, b_1 + b_2)$). Then, the density of probability for electrons to be detected at that point is $a^2 + b^2$— that is, it is equal to the area of a square whose sides are equal in length to this resulting arrow ψ (by the theorem of Pythagoras as illustrated in Figures 2.2

Science and Spirit

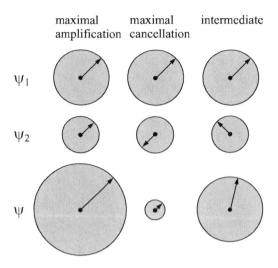

Figure 2.18: addition of two wave functions at various angles.

and 2.19). In consequence, the density of hits on the screen will be large in regions where the arrows ψ_1 and ψ_2 are oriented equally and small where their directions are opposing. In other words, there is a fluctuation in density from point to point or region to region. And it was this fluctuation in turn which we saw earlier displayed in Figure 2.15 and which we then conjectured to be due to interference.

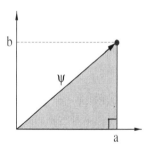

Figure 2.19: the square of the length of ψ equals $a^2 + b^2$.

Sophie: Then let me try to summarize: to begin with we are faced with certain facts. A pattern of detection is observed and found to be dependent on the setup that we choose. As slits are opened separately or simultaneously, electrons imprint their marks accordingly at varying points on the detector screen in varying degrees of density. In order to mathematically model these results, we imagine, rather obscurely, that at every point in space there is installed a little watch on which a single hand is moving (and possibly changing its length in the process). That is to say, we strangely envision an infinite array of arrows—indexed by the points in space—that somehow as a whole contains the total information that we need to properly describe how electrons behave statistically. Furthermore, the way in which this array changes over time is governed by the Schrödinger equation.

Philonous: That is correct, but I would like to add, for emphasis, that the mode of change is perfectly *deterministic*. In other words, the evolution of a quantum wave in time—according to the Schrödinger equation—is *not* stochastic in kind but rather certain and precise.

Sophie: But what is not so certain is the link between that wave and the observable reality that it supposedly conditions. For in respect of a particle's position, for example, the wave function merely prescribes the density of the corresponding detection probability—that is, at any point in space this density is equal to the square of the length of the arrow that the electron's wave function assigns to that particular point. By implication then, the density fluctuations in the pattern of detection in our double-slit experiment can be understood from the spatial variation in the lengths of these function arrows across the surface of the detector screen. In regions on the screen where the arrows are long the density is high, and, conversely, it is low where the arrows are short. Furthermore, in order to actually determine this pattern of variation in the case when interference is observed—that is, when both slits are open—we first determine the wave functions for the two cases when one slit is open and one is closed and then analyze how these two functions, by being superimposed, either magnify or cancel out each other.

Philonous: I think you got it right.

Sophie: I got it right, but I don't understand it.

Philonous: You don't?

Sophie: No, because I really cannot see how a fictitious array of watches, conceived in Schrödinger's mind, can influence statistically the activation of a recording device by a material particle such as an electron. How could it ever be the case that the immaterial information contained in a quantum wave conditions actively a physical occurrence?

Philonous: "How could it be the case?"—well I don't know. But I can speculate that the *material* information given, for example, by an electron in passage through a slit is really just that: mere information.

Sophie: It doesn't sound convincing to be honest.

Philonous: At first it doesn't, it is true. But what you need to take into account is here the fact that quantum physics, according to the original *Copenhagen Interpretation*, is not a theory of physical reality but rather of the knowledge that we have thereof.

Sophie: The Copenhagen Interpretation?

Philonous: It's an interpretive scheme that Bohr developed in collaboration with Heisenberg in 1927.

Sophie: And within that scheme, as you appear to be suggesting, physical reality is nothing but the information that we *know* of it?

Philonous: No, the Copenhagen Interpretation is *not* an ontological description. It doesn't tell us what the world at bottom consists of but only how we ought to explore it in scientific practice. Being essentially pragmatic in tone, this interpretation was designed to give physicists a conceptual frame of reference within which they could organize and analyze the data their experiments produced. In fact, Bohr's emphasis on knowledge, we may say, was intended precisely to discourage the sort of groundless speculation that necessarily underlies *and undermines* all ontological accounts.

Sophie: ...but you are not discouraged.

Philonous: Definitely not, for the ontological view suggests itself quite naturally, and also derives some notable support, for instance, from the philosophical position of Heisenberg's close associate, Carl Friedrich von Weizsäcker. According to the latter, "the abstract structure of quantum theory suggests that information is its foundation and in this sense its *substance*" (emphasis added).[92] So if we take a step of *faith* beyond the Copenhagen Interpretation and assert that quantum theory is not about knowledge alone but also describes the world as it is, then the notion that the substance of this theory is information will quite readily imply that information is the substance of reality in turn. Furthermore, the idea that everything 'material' is merely information is appealing not only for its conceptual economy and intrinsic empirical viability (in explicit contradistinction to 'verifiability') but also for its being nicely expressive of "the relational character" of the physical world of which we treated earlier (p.55). Afterall, information always is descriptive—it cannot stand in isolation and assumes its meaning only in relation to an overarching context. Seen in this light, it also is apparent that a maze of spread out, interfering, and connecting quantum waves is more suitable an image of material reality than the classical depiction of matter as an aggregate of particles on predetermined paths.

Sophie: Moreover, I suppose, a world of information would be *mind-like* in the sense that it consists of 'stuff' that minds are made to process and to store.

Philonous: ...and even to *beget*. For in a sense it is the minds themselves that generate that 'stuff' on which in turn they feed when processing a sensory perception.

Sophie: The minds beget the stuff?

Philonous: They give it form and make it real.

Sophie: So are you saying then that physical reality is mentally produced?

Philonous: What I am saying first of all is that the issue here at hand is intimately linked to what may be the quantum realm's most enigmatic mystery: *the mystery of measurement*—that is, the problem of how wave-like possibilities contract to point-like actual events when consciously observed.

Sophie: Please elaborate.

Philonous: To frame this issue properly, we need to first examine once again the double-slit experiment in its initial, simple preparation: if only one slit is open and one is closed, the electrons can be imagined to be particles on paths that act like little bullets.

Sophie: We said as much before.

Philonous: ...but we were *wrong.*

Sophie: Don't tell me that, because the bullet-flight analogy is pretty much the only thing I fully understood.

Philonous: ...and that's okay because it is the only thing that *can* be understood—by you or me or anybody else. For only in this basic case is there available an *intuitively* compelling ontological picture—a particle on a path—that truly accords with the facts—the marks that we detect. Once the second slit is opened, this common sense agreement is severely undermined: the electrons still leave their individual point-like marks on the detector screen, but the notion of their tracing out a well defined continuous path becomes extremely tenuous. Indeed, this notion is impossible to entertain unless we are prepared to contemplate that electrons in passage through a slit can somehow 'know' or 'be aware' if other slits near by are open for travel or not.

Sophie: It makes no sense—I told you so.

Philonous: Let's say, you stated that you do believe that electrons are "ignorant" (p.70).

Sophie: And in response you said that you refused to speculate "what sort of entity" an electron might be.

Philonous: And rightly so because if electrons are not construed to be conventional, material objects, then we are less inclined to think of them in incoherent terms.

Sophie: Which is the reason, I suppose, why you went on to speak of them as wavicles or partives or some other hybrid form.

Philonous: In other words, these previous thoughts of mine are perfectly consistent with my current claim that even in the one-slit case we are mistaken when we fantasize that electrons are bullets tracing paths. Afterall, if electrons are always wavicles and never particles or waves, then wavicles they will be entirely regardless of how many slits they are allowed to travel through.

Sophie: I see your point, but there is yet another option. For instead of assuming that the particle and wave ontologies are incompatible and are to be replaced by some synthetic hybrid scheme, we may as well attempt to comprehend the latter ontology in terms of the former. Why should it not be possible, for instance, to describe the fact of interference as being resultant of a force that moving electrons—as particles—exert on one another in their passage through the slits?

Philonous: Because there happens to be evidence refuting this idea. For observation shows that there is interference even if the electron source is of such extremely low intensity that electrons emerge from it as isolated bits. One by one, these single electrons accumulate on the detector screen in such a way that the overall statistical pattern displays the familiar characteristics of wave-like interference.[95]

Sophie: I must admit that settles it.

Philonous: Indeed, the facts that we observe impel us to abandon unequivocally all classical explanatory schemes. What interferes in double slits are not particles or swarms of them but rather informational alternatives: an electron can travel through one of two slits, and ultimately, it is these two possibilities, described by quantum waves, that interfere with one another. In fact, there aren't only two. More accurate would be to say that these alternatives that interfere are infinite in number.

Sophie: Infinite? But why?

Philonous: To frame this issue properly we need to analyze to start with a somewhat modified experiment: imagine that we open up another slit adjacent to the double-slit.

Sophie: So as to have a triple-slit?

Philonous: That's right. And now the question is how in this altered case we should compute the probability for electron detection on the screen.

Sophie: If the method that we previously employed has any claim to generality, we probably would have to form a threefold sum of quantum waves. In other words, if ψ_1, ψ_2, and ψ_3 are the wave functions corresponding, respectively, to the three cases where exactly one slit is open and two are closed, then the wave function ψ, describing the case where three slits are open simultaneously, should equal $\psi_1 + \psi_2 + \psi_3$ (up to a normalizing factor).

Philonous: Your answer is correct, but tell me now what would we do if we continued cutting slits in ever greater numbers?

Sophie: Presumably we'd always form a sum of equally as many terms as there are slits in the plate. All the different quantum waves—one for every slit—would be superimposed, and the square of the length of the resulting arrow ψ would give us the density of the detection probability.

Philonous: Sure, but what would happen in the end as slits are ever further multiplied?

Sophie: Ultimately, there would be only slits, and little would be left that could obstruct an electron that's headed for the screen.

Philonous: Indeed, the plate would turn so porous in the end that it would wholly cease to function as plate—and that's the crucial observation. For every point on such a porous nonexistent plate may here be thought to represent an open slit to which there corresponds exactly one attendant quantum wave. In consequence, we would add up, not only three such waves, as you suggested for the triple slit, but one for each of these innumerable points. Furthermore, if we imagine to insert a nonexistent plate, not just in one locale, but all along the stretch that the emitted electrons traverse, we finally are forced to contemplate the whole totality of points through which an electron can travel from the source to any point on the detector screen.[96] That is to say, the function arrow ψ must logically be thought to be an enormous informational compound to which every potential path for electron travel contributes one tiny, infinitesimal bit of quantum information.[V]

Sophie: That's quite astounding, isn't it?

Philonous: It clearly is, but notice also this: the picture that emerges thus portrays to us a single electron that traces all the paths at once.

Sophie: ...and therefore no path in particular?

Philonous: Apparently—that is correct.

Sophie: So what you are suggesting is that electrons are everywhere and nowhere simultaneously.

Philonous: What I would say is that an electron, before it is observed, is not an object on a path but rather is a cloud of electron potential. It is a would-be particle on a would-be path whose being isn't actual as yet. By implication, it is natural to ask how such a cloud of would-be possibility becomes eventually the mark that we detect.

Sophie: A valid question, I agree.

Philonous: But unfortunately, the answer most commonly given to it is purely descriptive in kind. According to the Copenhagen Interpretation, the event of detection—or measurement—signifies a random *discontinuity* for which there cannot exist a causal account. At the instant when the measurement is carried out the wave function, describing a particle or particle system, *collapses* randomly into an altered state that directly reflects the value that the measurement produced. For instance, the wave function of an electron that has just left a mark on a detector screen becomes spontaneously reduced so that it differs from zero only in the region of that mark.

Sophie: So first there is an information cloud containing a semi-existent electron and then, after this suspended something has collided with the screen, there occurs a sudden contraction as semi-being becomes being and cloud becomes point?

Philonous: It sounds about right.

Sophie: Then how, if I may ask, does a material screen become aware or figure out that it was 'hit' by any such semi-real something?

Philonous: ...by being a semi-real something itself. Afterall, the screen as well consists of particles that signify mere clouds of quantum possibilities. In

---

[V] This method of compounding information over the totality of all available paths was first devised by Richard Feynman, in 1948, and forms the base of a comprehensive computation scheme that is commonly known as the path-integral formalism of quantum mechanics.[97]

fact, we even may adopt an encompassingly systemic view and consider the entire experimental setup, including the screen, the source, and the emitted electrons, as a single informational entity described by a single quantum wave whose temporal evolution—as a whole—is governed by the Schrödinger equation.

Sophie: Put differently, there really is no setup that is there because a setup in the quantum world is nothing but an existential tendency for something like a setup to be there.

Philonous: ...and so is the room in which the setup is placed and so, too, is the 'physical' body of the human observer in that room who conducts the double-slit experiment. The whole 'material' environment, including, plausibly, the entire 'material' universe, is one connected quantum cloud.

Sophie: And in that encompassing cloud the two of us are also just somehow adrift, suspended in limbo.

Philonous: To that point I'll get in a moment. But first we need to return to that semi-existent electron that's hitting the screen. This electron, as we discussed, must be construed to be in a state of infinite superposition. For regardless of any metal plates and any open slits in them there always are infinitely many paths by which the source can be connected to any given point on the detector screen. Furthermore, the principle of superposition has been tested in so many varied experiments and is conceptually so central to the entire mathematical structure of quantum mechanics that its validity may justly be considered to be solidly established. Consequently, we cannot help but conclude that potential electron hits occur in parallel at all points on the screen. Everywhere there are arriving electron information bits that set into motion those specific physical processes that lead to the formation of macroscopic detection marks as perceived by conscious human observers.

Sophie: The only trouble is, it simply isn't so: electrons leave marks at specific, individual points rather than semi-marks at all points at once.

Philonous: And hence we need to ask again: what prompts a cloud of quantum possibility to suddenly contract into an actual, observable event? There is nothing in the mathematical formalism of quantum mechanics that tells us how it works. What we are given merely is a set of rules that specify how quantum waves evolve deterministically and how the methods we apply to them allow us to predict, in statistical terms, the outcomes of experiments. But nowhere is there any mentioning of how or when a quantum wave is suddenly reduced. In principle, any physical system—that is, any system governed by the Schrödinger equation—may evolve indefinitely and may remain completely undisturbed by any discontinuous wave collapse. Hence, we really have no reason whatsoever to deny that the electron/screen-system in our double-slit experiment can enter into a superimposed state in which an electron first travels simultaneously along all possible paths and then sets into motion parallel physical processes that lead to the equally parallel formation of detection marks at all points on the screen. Moreover and by extension, it is not in the least implausible to further suppose that the attendant physical processes by which these 'semi-marks' imprint themselves upon the nervous system of a perceiving human agent are equally cloud-like. All these alternative histories, from the emission of an electron to the eventual generation of nervous signals in a human brain, exist in synchrony in a giant web of quantum information.

Sophie: But my point precisely is that this is not the case. I never was or will be in a state of parallel perception of myriad histories.

Philonous: You need to qualify the 'I'. If the 'I' in question is your physical body or brain, then you simply do not know and cannot know what state that 'I' is ultimately in. For it is not the external physical world that you are and can be aware of, but only the inner depiction that your *conscious 'I'* produces of that world. By implication, a contradiction would only arise— and this is important—if we assumed antecedently that your consciousness as well belongs to that overall physical system that Schrödinger's formalism is meant to describe. In other words, the fact that you never find yourself to be in a state of cloud-like conscious perception forces us to infer, or so it appears, that the premise is false and that your consciousness is actually *not* a physical phenomenon.

Sophie: But what about the mark that we detect? I still don't see what causes it to finally appear.

Philonous: The answer is conceivably "the fact that we detect it." For according to Eugene Wigner, one of the 20th century's great quantum pioneers, it is indeed "the entering of an impression into our consciousness which alters the wave function."[98] By consciously observing an event we act as agents that transform a web of parallel histories into an actual material occurrence.

Sophie: So the mark emerges on the screen, not because an electron collides with it, but rather because there is a consciousness that happens to notice it?

Philonous: There is no doubt, the claim is radical. But from the arguments that we discussed it really seems to follow naturally that physical reality derives its actuality from being consciously perceived—which, by the way, is why I said before that minds "beget" the information 'stuff' that our world apparently is made of. It is only in the mind—or in the consciousness—that physical phenomena assume a well defined and actual existence.

Sophie: But doesn't this imply that no thing can be ever said to truly exist unless we somehow are aware of it?

Philonous: It does indeed.

Sophie: So a physical universe that no one perceives would really not really exist?

Philonous: That is correct—it seems to follow here that our universe was only semi-real until there came alive in it a being that could consciously encounter it. Consequently, there is another problem urgently arising: we do not know exactly who or what that first perceiving being was or how precisely it was conscious. Was it the first living cell, the first DNA molecule, the first fish, reptile, or bird? Or was it instead the first homo habilis, the first neanderthal hunter, the first modern human?

Sophie: The question is absurd.

Philonous: ...entirely absurd.

Sophie: Then why are we discussing it?

Philonous: Because the problem of quatum measurement leaves us no choice. Afterall, quantum mechanics is quite simply the most successful scientific theory ever devised. It has been tested in countless applications, and there are no empirical facts known to physcists that are not consistent with it. Consequently, we had better take serious whatever worldview it seems to imply.

Sophie: But if this worldview is "entirely absurd," then quantum mechanics cannot be true and must be revised.

Philonous: ...or so it would appear. But as you surely know, appearances may very well be very much deceiving.

Sophie: Then how are we deceived?

Philonous: Our mistake was to pay insufficient attention to one of the conclusions at which we arrived, namely the claim that consciousness is not material in kind. For if indeed the conscious mind is not contained within that realm that we refer to commonly as 'the physical universe', then—conceivably—there could exist an encompassing, *extra-universal* mind which gives that realm its actuality by consciously perceiving it.

Sophie: An encompassing mind?

Philonous: Call it what you like: a divine intellect—the mind of God—the Nous of Anaxagoras.

Sophie: Are you saying that the universe exists because there is a god who pays attention to it?

Philonous: I am.

Sophie: Then I will say that this idea of yours may be religiously appealing, but physics it is not.

Philonous: Nor does it truly resolve the quantum enigma.

Sophie: Why not?

Philonous: ...because a universal, all-perceiving intellect—by being all-perceiving—would actualize any cloud of quantum possibility that our conceptual thought portrays to us as a genuine cloud. Think about it: one of the reasons why an electron in a double-slit experiment can act in so enigmatic a fashion is simply that it is too small for us to directly observe it. If electrons were as big as bullets, then, presumably, they would behave accordingly and fly through one slit or through the other but not through both of them or neither. That is to say, a physical event that we can be directly aware of is always an actual event rather than a multiple would-be occurrence. Consequently, the existence of genuine quantum clouds is consistent with the postulate of an all-perceiving intellect only if that intellect is in fact *not* all-perceiving.

Sophie: ...that is to say, if there are things, such as electrons, that are too small even for God to be directly aware of.

Philonous: Indeed, somewhere there would have to exist a mysterious boundary between the things that God can see and those He cannot see, or more generally, between a real world of actual events and a fuzzy quantum realm in which semi-existence is waiting to become existence by being perceived by God.

Sophie: ...which makes no sense because a god who can create a world that he cannot *entirely* perceive would really be a silly looking oddity.

Philonous: By implication then, the concept of an all-perceiving intellect is inherently contradictory and therefore doesn't resolve the quantum enigma— or so it appears.

Sophie: But luckily and as we just agreed, "appearances may very well be very much deceiving."

Philonous: ...and in order for them to be deceiving in this case there must exist a way to interpret quantum mechanics as being descriptive of a well-defined objective world that God can fully perceive and thereby be *entirely* aware of.

Sophie: Put differently, there must be a way to deny just about everything that we have said about the quantum world so far. Do I understand correctly?

Philonous: The matter is a little more complex, but it is true that we are in for a fairly radical conceptual shift, away from randomness and fuzziness toward a more classical, deterministic description.

Sophie: So there is then another conceptual loophole through which we can slip?

Philonous: Yes, the loophole exists, and this time the key to finding it is Bohr's interpretive dictum according to which, quantum mechanics is not about the world as it is but as it is *known* to human observers. For it is this restriction in scope through which there opens up the possibility that underneath the world of scientific *knowledge* there is another, hidden world that God can see but we cannot.

Sophie: A world we cannot see? It sounds like pure philosophy.

Philonous: ...'pure mathematics' would be more accurate. For in 1952, the American physicist, David Bohm, developed a rigorous mathematical model of quantum mechanics that was based on the initial assumption that any particle in any physical system, such as an electron in a double-slit experiment, always has a well defined position in space and therefore moves along a well defined trajectory.[99]

Sophie: So I was right, we will deny the whole shebang of quantum clouds and semi-existent apparitions that we have so far been exploring.

Philonous: Let's say we will replace the clouds by a realm of unknowing.

Sophie: A realm that God can know but we cannot?

Philonous: Bohm wouldn't have put it thus. But within the model he invented, it is indeed the case that the apparent fuzziness of quantum phenomena is expressive of an irreducible incompleteness in human knowledge: there are specific paths that particles follow, but human consciousness can never discern them.

Sophie: So what about his model then? How does it really work?

Philonous: The mathematics are not easy to explain. But in taking a look at Bohm's rendering of the double-slit experiment, we can get a decent impression of the nature of his theoretical scheme.[100] To begin with, we need to assume, as I said, that electron positions in the double-slit apparatus are universally well defined at all points in time. The coordinates specifying these positions are supposed to be objectively real, but since they cannot be known, they are said to be *hidden* (and hence the Bohmian model is said to be a *hidden variables theory*). What Bohm now accomplished was to invent an ingenious mathematical method by means of which the wave function associated with a double-slit electron can be interpreted as a so-called *pilot wave* that guides the electron in its dynamical behavior. That is to say, a quantum wave here is transformed into a phantom field of force whose physical effect is to control an electron's motion in much the same way as a Newtonian gravitational field, for instance, controls the motion of a planet.

Sophie: A phantom field of force?

Philonous: It's less obscure than it sounds because all forces, as we previously discussed, are nothing but conceptual figments—and the gulf between phantoms and figments isn't exactly that wide.

Sophie: ...in your frame of mind.

Philonous: Trust me, the only difference between a classical Newtonian force and a Bohmian phantom force—or *quantum* force—is that the immediate action of the latter cannot be directly observed. It is impossible, for reasons of principle, to trace an electron's trajectory and thereby to record the local influence of these Bohmian forces. But all the same, the mathematical model describing this influence correctly explains the pattern of detection.

Sophie: But isn't it quite strange to think that force-induced precise trajectories could generate a random pattern of detection? It seems there is a mismatch here in elemental terms.

Philonous: The answer—roughly stated—is as follows: imagine that a single electron is emitted from the source at one specific, well defined position. This initial point of departure cannot be known or controlled, but its reality is all the same assumed. As the electron is now subjected to the quantum force, it is led to describe a non-observable, fictional path in a perfectly deterministic, classical fashion. And if that path so happens to pass through one of the slits, the electron will subsequently be detected at the point at which its path connects to the detector screen. Moreover, as the experiment is repeated numerous times with other electrons that follow different paths from different initial positions, there is a detection pattern emerging that directly reflects the distribution in space of these various electron paths.

Sophie: It almost sounds like common-sense mechanics. But how do we explain in this account the fact of interference? What interferes with what if single electrons are traveling on well defined discrete trajectories?

Philonous: 'Interference' here is not the proper word to use. More adequate perhaps would be to say that particle dynamics in Bohm's mathematical scheme are environment-induced. For any change in setup—such as the opening or closing of a slit—will alter correspondingly the quantum force that locally governs a particle's motion. In particular and by implication, when there are two slits open simultaneously, this quantum force will act so as to distribute the electrons' potential paths in such a way that certain areas on the screen are hit more frequently than others. Hence there is an appearance of interference and of a greater 'probability' for hits to occur in certain regions than in others, despite the fact that the underlying process of electron travel is strictly deterministic in kind.

Sophie: From your account I gather that the quantum force is sensitive to the overall geometric arrangement. As the slits are opened or closed, the geometry changes and so do the forces.

Philonous: Your understanding is correct.

Sophie: In other words, in this more classical, Bohmian scheme, it is the guiding field of force and not the electron itself that 'knows' its physical surroundings.

Philonous: The paraphrase is apt, for in a sense we may regard this field quite properly as a holistic encoding of the material information content of a given environment. Knowledge of the entire setup is needed to determine how this field will locally affect a moving electron.[VI]

Sophie: I get a sense these forces of Bohm's are almost as weird as the arrays of stopwatches that represent Schrödinger's waves—both are encodings of information and both are equally odd and fictitious. That is to say, the Bohmian design is really not a whole lot more coherent and compelling.

Philonous: Perhaps then we should not attempt to rank these two designs

---

[VI]The same, of course, is true as well in a classical setting in which, say, a gravitational or electromagnetic field conditions locally the motion of a particle but depends itself upon the overall spatial distribution of masses or charges. However, the contextuality of hidden variables theories is further highlighted by the necessary existence of nonlocal instantaneous effects (as we shall see in Chapter 4) and also by the impossibility to choose the hidden variables in such a way that all physical quantities of a given particle or system of particles are uniquely determined by them and independent of the larger physical environment. A more detailed discussion of the latter point can be found in [Gh], Sections 9.6 and 9.7.

but rather let them coexist with equal rights in tandem. Afterall, if particles and waves can be considered complementary then why should not the
Bohmian scheme of particles on predetermined paths, be perfectly compatible with Schrödinger's statistical description?

Sophie: Why should it not? Because it's not—compatible that is. There is no
way to reconcile two notions that are frontally opposed. Determinism and
*in*determinism cannot be both the case in parallel.

Philonous: But don't forget that we connected these two views by means of
fairly cogent reasonings: from quantum waves we moved to realize the critical role of consciousness, then postulated God and a realm of unknowing,
and finally were led to introduce the Bohmian design.

Sophie: ...and thereby we denied the wave-mechanical description. In other
words, we merely said that Bohm was ultimately right.

Philonous: The problem, though, with this conclusion is that physicists do
not—in general—agree. For Bohm's deterministic scheme is fully equivalent
to standard quantum physics only in the non-relativistic case when all the
particle velocities are small compared to the speed of light. An extension
of his theory that encompasses relativistic quantum field effects has so far
been impossible to formulate.

Sophie: Is this another sudden turn? Are we about to cast aside whatever
objectivity and classical solidity we managed to regain by turning quantum
waves into a hidden world of particles and forces?

Philonous: We need to wait and see. There is a decent chance for future
theoretical research to bring about some notable advances. But when you
speak of giving up whatever gain in 'objectivity' we managed to achieve,
I feel a need to qualify. It is true, no doubt, that Bohm's model—at a
conceptual level—depicts a world of objective particles moving on objective
paths. But since that world exists verifiably only as a figment in a theorist's
mind, it is *per se entirely subjective.* That is to say, in order to overcome the
need to assign to consciousness a vital role in the process reality creation
we are forced to create an imaginary reality—the hidden world of Bohm's—
which consciousness wholly contains. As far as I can tell, the only way to
get around this circular conclusion is to invoke again the postulate of God.
For only then may we assume that Bohm's reality is more concretely real
in that the mind of God continuously beholds it.

Philonous: So even if we don't go back from phantom fields to standard quantum waves, we still have recourse once again to consciousness and God.

Sophie: And that's precisely what I find so very much attractive—this dual
view that points to God from two distinct but complementary perspectives.
Moving in from one side of the argument we encounter the Creator God who
brings about the universe by consciously beholding it. And coming from
the other side we meet with the omniscient God whose mind perceives the
whole of physical reality including that elusive hidden realm of particles and

paths wherein the wave-mechanical uncertainty gives way to well-defined existence.

Sophie: I can agree that this interpretive duality is quite appealing to consider. But as I said before, what you call "complementary" strikes me as starkly contradictory.

Philonous: I cannot force you not to see it thus. But as it is, my own, subjective inclination is to take a more accommodating view. What I perceive is not a head-on opposition but rather a paradoxical juxtaposition: on the one hand there is a world of genuine choice—the world of quantum possibility—and on the other hand, in Bohm's domain, there is a perfect knowledge in the mind of God of all the choices anyone or anything has ever made and will make from here on. An obvious analogy that comes to mind is the notion of free will: God gives us freedom to choose but also knows in advance all our actual choices.

Sophie: And since then, I suppose, the paradoxical nature of physical quantum descriptions resembles the paradoxical theology of human free will, it follows once again that physical reality is *mind-like*, or perhaps better, *volition-like*.

Philonous: I don't know, but speaking of free will, I must confess, that I have asked myself at times whether my own compelling sense of volitional liberty may not already have its elemental analogue in the notion of a random quantum jump. Perhaps what we describe as chance is, in truth, a proto-conscious rudiment of freedom.[101] Perhaps all being in the universe is free because in absence of this attribute there cannot be a meaningful existence. But then again at other times I also wondered if that freedom really is what I suppose it is. Individual quantum events are free but only on condition that we choose the proper point of view—the Schrödinger picture. So what about me? Am I truly free or am I free only insofar as I adopt a certain philosophical perspective? Moreover I may ask if that free agency of mine is truly what I think it is before the knowing mind of God or only before those who like myself are ultimately ignorant?

Sophie: In other words, your question is if you are not perhaps akin to a Bohmian particle which gives an appearance of free random behavior to human observers but which, in fact, is known to God to trace a predetermined path.

Philonous: ...and, more generally, my further question is if all these various analogies that liken physical reality to consciousness are more than merely formal. In fact we posed this question previously when we discussed if possibly the universe is comprehensible to us because there is a structural analogy that links the mind to matter (p.16ff).

Sophie: As I recall, we never really answered it.

Philonous: But presently we are more well equipped and can attempt to fill that gap. For on the one hand we may say that matter—construed as information 'stuff'—is no less elusive than mind, and on the other hand we also may assert that both, matter and mind, are equally active. Mind is not a passive observer in a uniquely real material universe but is instead an indispensable participant in the process of reality creation. For whenever an observing consciousness incites a quantum wave to discontinuously collapse, it causes matter to bring forth a physical occurrence. By implication, we may claim with confidence that consciousness is not a mere appendage: it is not epiphenomenal, because it enters the quantum mechanical framework in a completely non-reductive fashion as a necessary independent agent that defines—or co-defines—the nature of existence. Furthermore, we even may adopt the view that physical reality is engineered—at its very base— to accommodate the presence of the mind. For in order for consciousness to take an active role in physical reality, there must be quantum wave alternatives that consciousness can choose from. Afterall, how could a conscious mind effect a quantum wave collapse if quantum waves did simply not exist?

Sophie: The reasoning is trivial.

Philonous: But what is not so trivial is the thought that quantum waves depend for their reality upon the strict positivity of Planck's quantum of action. Using a few concise mathematical arguments, it can be shown that if the value of this constant were to shrink to zero, the quantum realm would be transformed into the well-behaved Newtonian world of perfect causal closure. All quantum clouds and all uncertainties would dissipate and with them also all the space that mind and matter need in order to cooperate. Consequently, we may say that the essential discreteness at the heart of quantum theory, to which the strict positivity of Planck's constant attests, is the *conditio sine qua non* of mind-and-matter interaction.

Sophie: So are you saying then that this is *why* the quantum world is so decidedly bizarre? Uncertainty, discreteness, and the rest are needed to ensure that mind and matter can cooperate?

Philonous: Let's say we may believe that it is so without fear of inconsistency. Personally, I find it deeply satisfactory to think that the rules of quantum physics have the purpose to connect my consciousness to physical reality. That which is most central to my very own existence is not peripheral or inessential in the larger scheme of things but rather is intrinsic to the laws that organize the cosmos.

Sophie: I must admit the thought is most remarkable indeed: when Planck discovered energy to be discrete he unknowingly beheld the key to understanding why his own penetrating intellect could interact with matter.

Philonous: ...interact with it and also comprehend it. For, as Heisenberg once put it, "nature... is made to be understood, or, rather, our thought is made to understand nature." [102]

Sophie: By implication then, Pythagoras was right: the universe and human thought are fundamentally homologous.

Philonous: Less strongly we might say that such a view can plausibly be chosen.

Sophie: But chosen it can only be if choices do exist—that is, if Bohm was wrong and Schrödinger was right.

Philonous: ...or if, instead, by way of paradox, they both were right and wrong in synchrony.

Sophie: It doesn't makes sense, but never mind, it's got to be true—like quantum mechanics.

Philonous: And for once the last word has been yours.

Sophie: Not yet, but now it has.

Chapter 3

The Golden Age

Ignorance Exposed

Anyone who surveys the history of culture and thought is struck at times to find confluences of seemingly independent yet strangely correlated or analogous events. Nicolaus Copernicus, for instance, envisioned a new order in the skies at just the time when Spanish ships were sailing for a new world in the West; Leibniz invented the calculus in unison with Newton; physics and painting were revolutionized by Einstein and Picasso simultaneously; and the case of Euclid's famous postulate, as we saw previously, was settled in close temporal proximity by Gauss, Bolyai, and Lobachevsky after more than two millennia of fruitless investigation.

In the light of such surprising synchronicities we cannot help but wonder what role in history we should assign to the great minds and personalities we meet in it. Is it they who forge the various successive eras by virtue of their individual accomplishments, or is it rather the imposing spirit of an age that impels certain men and women to mobilize their powers of creation? In a sense, the question may appear redundant, for an era or an age, of course, is nothing but the sum of all the acts and thoughts that those who live in it produce. Yet more specifically it still is meaningful to ask, for instance, whether universal gravitation was strictly a discovery of Newton's or whether instead the unfolding Scientific Revolution forced it to the fore. Was Newton truly a creator or mainly a receiver? The rather obvious reply that he was both unfortunately leaves us with the problem of the chicken and the egg: what comes first reception or creation—the spirit or the deed? In the case of universal gravitation the spirit was, perhaps, the primary and stronger force. For to think that without Newton we would never have advanced beyond Galileo's law of falling bodies is really quite a stretch. Progress, to be sure, would not have been as swift, but sooner or later even Newton's greatest deeds would likely have been done by someone else—somewhere, somehow.

In other cases, though, it is the acting individual that seems to be the all-decisive factor. Christianity, for instance, can obviously not be thought apart from Jesus, and Socratic wisdom is similarly dependent for its power of persuasion on the singularly enigmatic personality of Socrates himself. If Newton had not written the *Principia*, the history of science would certainly have taken different turns, but, conceivably and not unlikely, the final outcome would be similar. By contrast, the influence of Socrates is rather of a different kind. For it is not so much the brilliance of his intellect or the power of his thought, no matter how formidable these may have been, for which we best remember him, but simply and disarmingly the utter uniqueness of who he was. Plato, in the *Symposium*, has Alcibiades express it thus:

> [P]ersonally, I think the most amazing thing about him is the fact that he is absolutely unique; there's no one like him, and I don't believe there ever was. You could point to some likeness to Achilles in Brasidas and the rest of them; you might compare Nestor and Antenor, and so on, with Pericles. There are plenty of such parallels in history, but you'll never find anyone like Socrates, or any ideas like his ideas, in our own times or in the past—unless, of course, you take a leaf out of my book and compare him, not with human beings, but with sileni and satyrs—and the same with his ideas.[1]

Such lofty admiration had its source in an unwavering commitment to honesty and truth, an enviable freedom from ambition, a remarkable indifference to physical adversity, an indomitable courage grounded in moral uprightness, and, with hindsight, in a manner of death that bespoke a perfect unity of thought and deed. For it is one thing to teach the excellence of wisdom, but it is an altogether different thing to die for it.

When Socrates was handed the death sentence by the restored Athenian democracy in 399 B.C., for reasons of impiety and so-called corrupting of the youth, he could have easily avoided execution either by admitting to his guilt and proposing a small fine or by allowing his friends to arrange for his escape to exile. However, since neither of these options was at all compatible with his idea of loyalty to truth and law, he preferred to drink the poison cup. In fact, he "received it quite cheerfully... without a tremor"[2] in his hand. The final moments of his life are movingly described in one of Plato's dialogues as follows:

> The coldness [that the poison had induced] was spreading about as far as his waist when Socrates uncovered his face, for he had covered it up, and said—they were his last words—Crito, we ought to offer a cock to Asclepius. See to it, and don't forget.'

> No, it shall be done, said Crito. Are you sure that there is nothing else?

Socrates made no reply to this question, but after a little while
he stirred, and when the man uncovered him, his eyes were fixed.
When Crito saw this, he closed the mouth and eyes.

Such, Echecrates, was the end of our comrade, who was, we may
fairly say, of all those whom we knew in our time, the bravest and
also the wisest and most upright man.[3]

Throughout his life and up unto his death Socrates avoided all empty pos-
turing and maintained a clear sense of priorities. As a young man he had initially been interested in the cosmological systems of natural philosophy. But
when he found these to be contradictory and inconsequential, he turned his
mind to matters more important. For in marked contrast to the Sophists, who
also had perceived the flaws of natural philosophy, he was not content with
skeptical denial or mere manipulative rhetoric,[1] but chose instead to earnestly
pursue the problems that he deemed most relevant to human life and here
especially to proper moral conduct.

His definite conversion to his role of the tireless seeker of wisdom and truth
came when the Oracle at Delphi pronounced him to his friend, Chaerephon,
the wisest man alive.[4] Upon reflection, Socrates took this to mean that he was
wise because he was so keenly aware of his own dire ignorance. In consequence,
the quest to overcome that ignorance became his life's ideal and central motive
force. His mission took him to the streets and public squares of Athens where
he engaged his fellow citizens in arguments that were intended to reveal the
truth by bringing into sharp relief the feebleness of human understanding.
Typically, Socrates proceeded from words of praise for certain excellences of
his interlocutors to professions of his own lamentable confusion and onward
to a step by step unmasking of false assumptions, spurious beliefs, and poorly
drawn conclusions.

It is this image of Socrates in searching conversation that reminds us to this
day that the pursuit of truth requires antecedently a firm acknowledgement of
human limitation. Earlier we listened, for example, to *Philonous* and *Sophie*
discuss the nature of scientific knowledge, the properties of matter, and the
role of consciousness in physical reality. But we must not forget that topics
such as these can never be addressed with final or even provisional clarity. If
asked what we might mean when we employ such terms or verbal symbols as
'matter,' 'knowledge,' 'consciousness,' or 'physical reality,' we ultimately have
no meaningful reply.

In our current age of quantum physics, relativity, and DNA genetics it may
of course appear that science has advanced to unexpected heights—and in a

---

[1]We do not wish to convey the impression that the great Sophist philosophers were early
proponents of nihilism. But implicit, for instance, in Protagoras's famous saying that "man
is the measure of all things" there is the notion of the relativity of truth, and it is this notion
that clearly is incompatible with the eternal realm of forms conceived by Socrates and Plato.

sense it has. But on the other hand we still have no idea how to describe coherently even the most common elements in our ordinary lives. What is a thought, a feeling, a sensation, or an act of will? The simple and resounding answer is that no one has a clue. In fact, we cannot even distantly imagine what truly knowing these 'mundane' phenomena might mean or, more drastic still, what it might mean to know what we mean—ignorance abounds.

Physicists aspire to a theory of everything, neuroscientists hope to penetrate the inmost secrets of the brain, and we in our present, far less ambitious quest are trying to discover here and there a hint that science and spirit can somehow coexist. All these efforts probably have value, but all of them can also benefit from that Socratic irony that forces us unfailingly to recognize the narrow bounds of human comprehension.

The Frog at the Gate

Socrates's lifetime from about 470 B.C. to 399 B.C. is easily identified as one of the most momentous periods in the entire history of Western Civilization. For it not only bore witness to Athens's rise and fall, but also left us with a legacy of spectacular cultural achievements that are of singular historical significance.

The founding of the Athenian Naval Empire dates back to 478 B.C. when Athens took the lead in establishing the Delian League as an alliance against the then recent Persian invasions. The subsequent victorious campaigns under the command of Cimon effectively contained the Persian threat, and hostilities officially ceased with the Peace of Callias, in 449 B.C.

In a parallel development, the First Peloponnesian War between Athens and Sparta was fought intermittently in the years from 460 to 446 B.C. At the conflict's conclusion, Athenian naval supremacy was formally recognized in a settlement that allowed both sides to maintain their respective spheres of influence—Athens at sea and Sparta on land.

With peace thus restored, there followed a time of unparalleled intellectual and artistic brilliance: the Golden Age of the City of Athens. Under the generous democratic rule of Pericles the city was adorned with marvelous works of architecture and art, the Parthenon was built, and the city's cultural life flourished as never before. It was the time of the sculptor Phidias, of the great dramatists Aeschylus, Sophocles, and Euripides, of the philosophers Protagoras and Anaxagoras, and, of course, the time of Socrates as well.

This period of exquisite cultural splendor came to an end with the outbreak of the Second Peloponnesian War in 431 B.C. In the protracted struggle that ensued, neither side could gain a clear advantage until, in 412 B.C., the Persians fatefully entered the conflict in support of the Spartan cause. Eight years later, in 404 B.C., Athens was defeated, its empire dissolved, and its government taken over by an oligarchic group of aristocrats. This so-called Rule of the

Thirty, however, did not endure, and already in 403 B.C., the democracy was restored.

In spite of these historical convulsions, or perhaps partly because of them, there soon emerged another brilliant period of intellectual activity that was to have an even more profound effect on the development of Western Civilization and that is best referred to as the golden age of Greek philosophy. Its central figures were Plato and Aristotle.

Plato was born in 427 B.C. into one of the most distinguished aristocratic families in Athens. As a young man he had initially felt drawn to pursue a career in politics but the events surrounding the revolt of 404 B.C. severely disillusioned him. For the ruling oligarchs, among whom were numbered several relatives and acquaintances of his, quickly descended into gross immorality and even attempted to implicate Socrates in their despicable crimes and abuses. Naturally, Plato's disgust with political affairs only deepened when the succeeding democratic government took Socrates to trial and falsely accused him of impiety.

Following the death of Socrates, Plato left Athens for Megara and from there embarked on far-flung travels that brought him into contact with the Pythagorean School in Southern Italy as well as with the court of Dionysius in Syracuse on Sicily. Perhaps he even ventured as far as Egypt and India, but here the records are uncertain.[5] Upon his return to Athens, in 387 B.C., he acquired a piece of land outside the city walls whereon he founded his Academy. Interrupted only by two later journeys to Syracuse, Plato remained at the Academy until his death, in 347 B.C., dedicating himself to the teaching and writing of philosophy, and continuing the Socratic quest for that true and certain knowledge that would set right the soul of man and organize the state to the benefit of all.

Of Plato's works the dialogues, with Socrates as the leading interlocutor, have been preserved in their entirety. But there are no known records of any of the more formal expositions that Plato delivered in his lectures at the Academy. The general problem that we face in evaluating the dialogues is to determine what part of the teachings that we find in them is to be attributed to Socrates and what part to Plato himself. Concerning this issue, Plato asserted in one of his letters that his writings merely reflected the views of Socrates in "beautified and rejuvenated"[6] form. But perhaps more accurate here is the view of St. Augustine, according to whom, Plato "was devoted to his master Socrates with singular affection, and therefore even put into his mouth in almost all his discourses the ideas he himself had learnt from others, or those which he owed to his own intelligent perception, tempering them with Socrates's charm and moral earnestness."[7] Since it obviously cannot be the purpose of the present exposition to shed new light on this so-called 'problem of Socrates' (or Plato), we will now leave aside all questions of ultimate authorship and simply focus on the doctrines that the dialogues expound.

With respect to the pre-Socratic natural philosophies that we examined earlier, we may say that one of Plato's most important contributions to the history of Western thought was his synthesis of the antithetical positions of Heraclitus and Parmenides regarding the problem of change. Plato denied Parmenides's monistic premise of the One as a perfectly stable all-embracing unity and set up in its place a harshly dualistic scheme in which a changeable physical realm—the realm of sensory perception—is juxtaposed to an eternal transcendent world of archetypal Ideas and perfect rational templates. In thus subdividing reality into two sharply contrasted domains, Plato was able to affirm Heraclitean flux without denying Parmenidean permanence. Change, according to Plato, is real, but only in the world of matter—the realm of Ideas is timeless and wholly inert.

Furthermore, true knowledge can only be acquired as the human intellect transcends the shadow lands of fleeting material phenomena and aspires to behold the universal archetypes that form reality's immutable essence and center. We must reach beyond the level of our immediate sensory experience, says Plato, if we are to attain to genuine insight and truth. In the physical world, a right triangle, for instance, can be encountered only imperfectly in incidental material configurations. But as an Idea it exists transcendently in a pure conceptual form that is hidden from perception but that reason has the power to reveal. Likewise in respect of its universal properties: the theorem of Pythagoras is not a provisional hypothesis, inductively derived from sensory particulars, but rather is an everlasting truth established by a rigorous, rational proof.

As we compare Plato's solution to the problem of change with the synthesis proposed by Empedocles, we quickly become aware of a fundamental difference at the level of ontology. For unlike Empedocles, whose conception of four immutable elements in ever-shifting constellations was strictly materialistic in kind, Plato explicitly extends the epistemological dualism of empiricism versus rationalism, or sense perception versus conceptual thought, to the ontological division between matter and spirit. The world of Ideas is not material but also not a mere intellectual construct. Indeed, it not only has an independent existence of its own but is, in fact, the very core of existence itself. Seemingly paradoxically we may therefore say with Plato that matter is insubstantial and that true substance is immaterial.

In Book VII of Plato's *Republic*, this consistently dualistic view is famously illustrated in the so-called 'allegory of the cave':[8] imagine a group of prisoners that have been held captive throughout their lives in an underground cave. At the back of the cave a fire is burning, and in between the fire and the prisoners there is set up a stage on which puppets and other "implements of all kinds"[9] are being carried back and forth. The prisoners, by being narrowly confined, can only see the shadows that these objects cast upon the cavern wall in front of them. They cannot see the moving things and also not the fire. To them the world is nothing but a two-dimensional display of shifting outlines—a dark menagerie of silhouettes that occupies for them the place of physical reality. But what would happen now if one of these unfortunates were suddenly set free so that he could stand up and turn around? Most probably the fire's unreflected light would irritate his unaccustomed eyes with pain, and only slowly would his vision be adjusting. Only slowly would he see the stage, the puppets, and the other moving things. And if further on this prisoner were forced—against his likely impulse to return to his familiar captive state—to manage the ascent to the entrance of the cave and step outside, his eyes would be so troubled by the radiating sun that he could hardly keep them open. Barely squinting, he would merely see a haze of all-embracing brightness. Eventually, though, his vision would accommodate the stronger stimulus, and he would finally perceive that true reality which had been all along the source behind the shadows of his underworld existence. At last he would behold a world of unexpected richness and glittering variety—a kaleidoscope of colors and forms arranged in three-dimensional perspectives. It would be a transformation of his experience so radical that he would struggle to express it in the words that he had formerly been taught solely to describe a play of shadows on a wall. And if ever he should climb back down into the cave in order to communicate the knowledge that he gained to those who still are chained, he likely would be stumbling in the dark and be laughed at and despised as a lunatic among the sane.

Such, according to Plato, is our human cognitive condition. Held captive by the bonds of sensory perception, we must rely on reason to deliver us. Only by means of rational reflection can our souls aspire to that realm of light in which reality displays its true and ever stable countenance.

Sophie: As I was listening to this, I somehow felt reminded of a strange event that I observed when I came home last night from our second day's discussion. When I arrived and drove up to the gate in front of my garage, with both my headlights shining, I saw a little frog that had been startled by the light and was apparently attempting to escape it.

Philonous: You mean the animal was acting like a prisoner who favors the familiar darkness of his fettered life over freedom's fearsome light?

Sophie: No, that's not the point—you didn't let me finish. What happened next was this: instead of moving to the side into the grass, the frog plunged straight ahead, away from where I was approaching. And as it reached the white illumined gate, it didn't alter course but bounced right into it, head first, and even stubbornly repeated its mistake. It almost seemed as though the frog's amphibian perception had transformed the gate's bright metal surface into a shining open space. Where we perceive a solid object, the frog saw only light. Again and again it bumped its head against the gate, unable to correct its cognitive malfunction.

Philonous: Maybe it simply didn't feel to have a choice. Maybe instinct forced it to seek flight the way it did, regardless of the gate.

Sophie: Maybe, maybe not—I cannot tell for certain. Yet on occasion I have noticed certain insects acting equally confused: when the central ceiling light is turned on in my room at night, it may occur, for instance, that a daddy-long-leg or a fly is hitting hard against the ceiling in its flight. The insect then is circling frenziedly in the apparent hope that the ceiling's substance somehow will give way. It really is bizarre.

Philonous: And the ceiling in your room is white as well, just as the gate?

Sophie: It is indeed.

Philonous: Then your conjecture is that frogs and insects will at times believe that white equals light.

Sophie: That is correct. But more generally, I am intrigued to think how easily perception can be fooled.

Philonous: I fail to see how that can be considered a surprise. Afterall, fly swatters routinely rely for their effectiveness on certain perceptual incompetencies in insect compound eyes. And silhouettes of birds of prey are pasted onto windowpanes in order to prevent the little songbirds from colliding with the glass. Deceptions of this sort are really rather common—in animals and human beings too. Aren't you familiar, for example, with the phenomenon of optical illusions?

Sophie: You are referring, I suppose, to those clever geometrical arrangements in which a certain figure's length or size appears to change depending on the context that we place it in.

Philonous: That's right. A line, for instance, will appear longer or shorter depending on whether we attach to its ends arrows pointing inwards or outwards. And a circle's area content will seem to be inversely correlated with the size of other circles that we draw in its vicinity (Figure 3.1).[10]

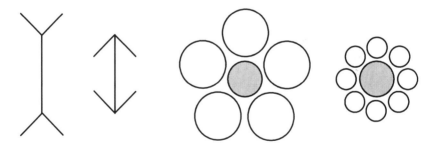

Figure 3.1: optical illusions.

Sophie: So Plato was correct: as far as knowledge is concerned, perception is a miserable guide.

Philonous: A better way to put it may be this:

Bescheidne Wahrheit sprech' ich dir.

> *Wenn sich der Mensch, die kleine Narrenwelt,*
> *Gewöhnlich für ein Ganzes hält*—[11]

Sophie: I beg your pardon.

Philonous: It's German—Goethe wrote it in the *Faust.*

Sophie: That's good to know but doesn't tell me what it says.

Philonous: Without regard for rhyme or meter, the English version can be stated thus: *A modest truth I speak to thee, if man will commonly mistake his little world of foolery for an entirety.*[12]

Sophie: And so?

Philonous: And so we'd better take a look at how that little world we see or hear or touch can be embedded in a whole.

Sophie: ...the whole that Goethe calls "entirety"?

Philonous: Precisely.

Sophie: In that regard my understanding is that Plato thought that this embedding is achieved as reason comes to comprehend the perfect forms that lie behind the flux of sensory particulars.

Philonous: Your understanding is correct. But as for Plato's thought, I really must reject it. For Plato failed to take the proper global view. That is to say, he didn't know—and couldn't know, in his day—that he was probably descendent of a creature as the one that knocked its head against your gate.

Sophie: He was descendent of a frog?

Philonous: Let's say, a late Devonian amphibium.

Sophie: You're talking evolution now, it seems.[13]

Philonous: Indeed, what we should entertain is the idea that life on earth has undergone a long historical development. Evidence in favor of this view is obviously only circumstantial but overwhelming no less.

Sophie: Evidence such as the fossil record?

Philonous: For instance.

Sophie: I think that I am with you here. The facts are plain and solidly established.

Philonous: Then are you also in agreement if I say that the development in question is likely to continue?

Sophie: Of course.

Philonous: Would it further be acceptable if we assumed that even human life—the form of life which currently is most advanced—may one day be surpassed as evolution progresses?

Sophie: The possibility is real, and I would like to add that higher forms of life may well exist already *presently* on other planets somewhere in the universe.

Philonous: If so far we agree, then our next step simply is to realize that cognitive abilities in humans—in much the same way as in insects or amphibia—are subject to essential limitations. Nobody in his right mind would ever venture to assert that a daddy-long-leg or a frog can form an image of the world that really is correct. For everybody knows that animals as these do simply not possess the necessary rational capacities. And yet, just a few steps higher up the evolutionary ladder, on the human plane, we suddenly presume—or so at least philosophers like Plato do—that cognition is sufficiently advanced for genuine reality to be revealed. It is preposterous.

Sophie: Your judgment is unfair. For Plato was not only highly conscious, as we saw, of the flaws of sensory perception. But his portrayal of Socrates in the *Dialogues* also indicates a very clear awareness of the general fragility of human rationality.

Philonous: That point I concede. But Plato also champions the idea that human reason can have access to a higher realm of archetypes and forms in which all truths are ultimate and absolute. It is in this regard that I cannot agree with him, because the evolutionary view that I have just put forth does not accommodate such grandiose aspirations. Afterall, if evolution is a fact, then we may plausibly assume that our own limitations, on the human plane, could be as obvious to higher forms of life as the limitations of a daddy-long-leg are to us. By implication, it is foolish to believe that any human mind could ever form a concept of reality that really is the Truth.

Sophie: So what are we to do?

Philonous: Perform a leap of faith. For evolution forces us to recognize that there most likely is a world out there of vast extent that human reason and perception are entirely incompetent to reach. And it is this unknowable *transcendent* world that only faith can ever give us access to.

Sophie: Slowly now, the common understanding is a different one. Evolution, by convention, is assumed to be conducive to naturalism and therefore incompatible with faith. And rightly so, for evolution bids us to account for the development of life entirely in terms of historical contingency and material causation. Our very existence, according to this theory, is nothing but a chance occurrence molded by the laws of nature.

Philonous: There is a lot that could be said about this claim, but for the moment let me just reiterate (p.95) that randomness and freedom may be linked. 'Evolution' simply means 'development,' and it is therefore up to us to decide whether we perceive a process of evolving as purposeless and random or free and purposeful.[1]

Sophie: Maybe so, but that in no way contradicts my pertinent assertion: evolution leads to naturalism, and naturalism, as commonly construed, is contrary to faith—especially religious faith.

Philonous: And why, if I may ask, should that be so?

Sophie: Because naturalism, by definition, cannot accommodate transcendence.

Philonous: Precisely, a naturalist posits that nature, as revealed in his or her

---

[1]The latter view, in far more elaborate detail, has been famously developed in the writings of Teilhard de Chardin (see, for instance, [Te]).

cognition, is really all there is. By implication then, we ought to say that naturalism and belief in evolution are wholly incompatible.

Sophie: Please forgive me my naiveté, but are you sure, you got it right? Are you sure you didn't mean to say that they are strongly reinforcing?

Philonous: Completely sure, and here is why: the word 'nature', in naturalistic philosophy, signifies the realm of human sense experience. Nature is nothing but the source of all the sensory perceptions that the human mind or brain can process or produce.[II] Such a definition of nature, however, is thoroughly anthropocentric and thus incompatible with evolution. For a proper view of evolutionary theory compels us to acknowledge, as I said, that our own level of consciousness is not, in all likelihood, 'nature's' final word. Consequently, we are led to postulate that there are realms of possible experience that far exceed the human realm and hence may be referred to as *'transcendent'*. By implication, a naturalist who believes that all phenomena can and must be explained in reference to the correlations and 'natural' laws that human beings come to discern within their 'natural' patterns of perception is very much akin to a religious dogmatist who infers man's final supremacy in the created world from, say, a Biblical ascription of God's image to mankind. Both endow the human being with a very special status, and both will therefore find it difficult to accept a genuinely evolutionary view.

Sophie: I also tend to think that any scheme by which we set aside for ourselves a place of singular importance and ability is likely based on wishful thinking more than fact. But given this conclusion, it appears that I was right when I asserted previously that sense perception is a miserable guide. Afterall, to any higher form of life the human range of sensory experience will likely seem entirely inadequate.

Philonous: The problem with your logic is that even miser-*able* guides are not entirely *unable*. That is to say, you mustn't overlook that Goethe's verse on our "little world of foolery" was spoken in the *Faust* by *Mephistopheles*. It is the devil's condescension that denounces us from in between the verse's lines and that thereby perverts a truth and turns it into into falsehood. For in the light of our present train of thought, the possible existence of a higher form of life does not at all allow us to infer that our own, conceivably quite limited cognition, comparatively speaking, is altogether worthless or "inadequate." Nor, for that matter, are such attributes applicable to the abilities of frogs or daddy-long-legs. It certainly is possible to place a frog in situations that would blatantly reveal its cognitive inferiority compared to human beings. But other than that, the frog's cognition is an asset to be cherished. It ensures the animal's survival in natural environments and allows it to compete successfully with species that are similar in kind. Furthermore and even more importantly, the frog's perception—while certainly more

---

[II]Indirect perceptions by means of technological devices are included in this definition. So ultraviolet and infrared radiation, for example, are in this sense 'natural' phenomena.

narrowly confined—is still in line with human understanding. A frog may see a beetle or a fly only indistinctly as a shadow passing by. But its tongue will meet the insect all the same at that precise position in the air where human vision, too, would place it and detect it. The knowledge that facilitates such skillful predatory actions is obviously not entirely illusory. It only is a fragment, and probably a tiny one, but a fragment of *reality* no less. By analogy, the shadows seen in Plato's cave, as fleeting as they may appear, are still directly linked to actual existence. They only show projections, but they do not simply lie.

Sophie: So your confidence in knowledge that derives from sensory experience is rooted, as it were, in certain cognitive consistencies and continuities that we observe across the taxonomic range from animals to modern human beings.

Philonous: It is indeed, because the fact of global cognitive coherence is truly marvelous: millions of different species with millions of independently evolved cognitive faculties, and all of them, in their own ways, present the same external flow of information. A vast multitude of widely differing levels of perceptual complexities but no essential contradictions—it is astonishing. From the simplest stimulus/response reflexes in a single-celled amoeba, to a frog's catching of a fly, and on from there to our highly varied human forms of conduct and ability we see spread out before us an immense array of mutually consistent patterns of behavior. No matter how primitive a behavior an amoeba may display, its 'knowledge' of reality and its correlated actions are still coherently attuned. The protozoic world that it indwells is very crude undoubtedly but inconsistent it is not. In other words, the natural conclusion here is this: cognition and perception represent reliably and universally—their limits notwithstanding—the same external world. The great ethologist, Konrad Lorenz, succinctly put the matter thus:

> The complete agreement between the representations of the outside world provided by such an immense variety of world-depicting apparatuses evolved independently by such a vast number of different forms of life certainly needs an explanation. I think it absurd to seek for any other than that all these manifold forms of possible experience refer to *one and the same real universe*.[14]

Sophie: The inference then is twofold: an external world exists and our senses portray it faithfully—within limits.

Philonous: That is correct. Evolution teaches us that living organisms form in direct interaction with an objectively existent external realm that is the common source of all their sensory perceptions. That said, I also need to emphasize, of course, that objectivity here shouldn't be construed to be an absolute. For quantum physics, as we saw, suggests that the object and the subject of perception are entangled inextricably. Yet in the light of what we just discussed, a flat denial of all claims to objectivity can also not be plausibly maintained. Nor is it tenable to take a stance of radical mistrust regarding knowledge that derives from sensory perception.

Sophie: To that I can agree, but there are many questions still remaining. Plato, for example, thought that our limitations can be overcome by means of reason. You, by contrast, emphasized the need for faith, but faith in what? In an abstract notion of transcendence, inferred from future evolutionary possibilities? How do we formulate this faith, and how far does the range of possibilities extend?

Philonous: To ask me for an answer to all this seems overly demanding. But maybe I can start with the question you raised last. In a sense, the obvious reply here is that we will never know. For determining the range of possibilities would require comprehensive knowledge in space and time of all the habitable places in the universe. However, with a bit of guided imagination the potential enormity of this developmental range can fairly well be glimpsed as we survey the present-day variety of life on Planet Earth.

Sophie: It can? How so?

Philonous: Well, so far as I can tell, there are discernible in our earthly biosphere two fairly clear dividing lines. On the one end of the spectrum, the first of these is evident between inanimate matter and living organisms and on the other end the second runs between the animals and ourselves— the modern human beings. I do not know, of course, how life on earth arose, but all the same I think it fair and safe to say that the advance in complexity from ordinary inorganic matter to just a single living cell is so dramatic and profound that it deserves to be regarded as an elemental qualitative leap. Moving up from there across the taxonomic spectrum, from single-celled organisms to the highest forms of animal existence, there may be other demarcations we can draw. But the next truly fundamental rift is visible between the animals and our own, much higher human form of life. Genetically, of course, man and ape are very much alike, but the added dimensions of highly diversified psychological, social, cultural, and spiritual realities that we encounter on the human plane clearly mark a point of radical departure.[15]

Sophie: But why do you explain all this? Your claim that human beings are superior to animals and living cells are more complex than inorganic matter seems rather trivial to be honest.

Philonous: Just consider what the implications are—just consider what a vast array of possibilities there opened up when long ago in Earth's prehistory the first organic compound truly came alive. Would anyone have thought that protozoa can develop into monkeys? So is it not conceivable in light of this that the range of possibilities created by the crossing of the border line from animal to human life is just as vast?

Sophie: Are you insinuating here that we are, so to speak, the protozoa in the realm of self-aware and fully conscious life—the first and most primitive creatures to settle in a new domain?

Philonous: The thought is not entirely implausible, is it?

Sophie: Not implausible, perhaps, but certainly depressing. If you are right, then human kind is really at the low end of the scale: we are the lowest form of life in our own domain, just one step up from animal existence, and no one knows how many more domains there are above. It is a sobering idea.

Philonous: Remember, though, the one step up is truly fundamental. The gulf that separates a monkey from a man may be as wide as that between a lifeless grain of sand and an active living cell.

Sophie: Yet turning our heads the other way, the view is utterly deflating.

Philonous: 'Profoundly humbling' is a better term to use. For evolution is commendable, most notably, for teaching us to be less pompous and conceited. We are in many ways amazing creatures, it is true, but others in a distant place or time may very well be more amazing still.

Sophie: But isn't it conceivable, as Plato might have said, that reason can facilitate a genuine ascent. Perhaps we *can* escape from our evolutionary cage if only we rely more thoroughly on rational deduction.

Philonous: I see two problems here: firstly, there can be no such thing as 'knowledge of exterior reality', if we do not rely in our reasonings on sensory experience. And secondly and more importantly, our rational capacities evolved in unison with our senses, and both are therefore equally constrained.

Sophie: But what about our mathematical conceptions? You yourself explained how Riemann could anticipate the structure of the theory of relativity by means of purely abstract thought (see p.17). So did he not in doing so transcend the narrow bounds of sensory experience?

Philonous: Riemann constructed a general geometric framework that later proved to be a proper fit for Einstein's redesign of Newton's gravitation— and that no doubt is very much impressive. But on the other hand there also was a crucial contribution from perception. For ultimately, relativity grew out of certain conceptual difficulties in Maxwell's formulation of electrodynamics which in turn was based upon the *empirically* grounded field theory of Faraday's. Without this link to observation no one would have ever thought to come up with a general relativistic theory of gravity. Furthermore, even Riemannian geometry, in its original, purely mathematical form, is not entirely devoid of input from experience. What Riemann could depend upon to start with was the inbuilt spatial understanding of his own cognitive apparatus. In other words, he utilized a form of *a priori* intuition which presumably had been produced as evolution gave the human mind the novel skill to mirror physical reality by means of rational conceptions. Immanuel Kant—from his necessarily non-evolutionary point of view—addressed himself to these ideas as follows:

> Mathematical science affords us a brilliant example, how far, inde-
> pendently of all experience [(Kant here disregards the possibility
> of experience extending backwards into evolutionary history)], we
> may carry our *a priori* knowledge. It is true that the mathematician
> occupies himself with objects and cognitions only in so far as they
> can be represented by means of intuition. But this circumstance is
> easily overlooked, because the said intuition [(as a mental structure
> formed by evolution)] can itself be given *a priori*, and therefore is
> hardly to be distinguished from a mere pure conception. Deceived
> by such a proof of the power of reason, we can perceive no limits
> to the extension of our knowledge. The light dove cleaving in free
> flight the thin air, whose resistance it feels, might imagine that her
> movements would be far more free and rapid in airless space. Just
> in the same way did Plato, abandoning the world of sense because
> of the narrow limits it sets to the understanding, venture upon the
> wings of ideas beyond it, into the void space of pure intellect. He
> did not reflect that he made no real progress by all his efforts; for
> he met with no resistance which might serve him for support, as it
> were, whereon to rest, and on which he might apply his powers, in
> order to let the intellect acquire momentum for its progress.[16]

Sophie: It may be true that Riemann—and Einstein—relied on their inherent
spatial intuitions in formulating their respective theories, and it may even
be the case that these intuitions were formed in evolutionary history. But
nonetheless the theories themselves reach far beyond the problem-solving
range in natural environments. In fact, as I recall, you said yourself not
long ago (p.18) that the logic of evolution cannot entirely account for our
intellectual "ability to formulate the fundamental principles of spacetime
gravitation." So your apparent claim at present to the contrary is somewhat
contradictory.

Philonous: The fact that our cognitive apparatus can, at times, provide us
insights that transcend the needs presented by the problem of survival in
a natural environment does not at all imply that evolution had no part in
forming it. In other words, the assertion that the basic spatial intuitions
in the human mind were formed by means of evolutionary adaptation is
not *per se* in conflict with the claim that the reach of these intuitions far
exceeds the native range of problems that conditioned their development.
For even if evolution by natural selection or some other causal process does
not fully explain this greater reach, it still can be a major contributing
factor.

Sophie: In that you may be right but otherwise, it seems, you just effectively
affirmed my claim that our limits can be rationally breached.

Philonous: We are amazing creatures, as I said. And in particular, it is amazing very much indeed that Einstein could describe the force of gravity in terms of *four*-dimensional curvature effects despite the fact that in his human thought he was inherently confined to *three*-dimensional depictions. However, your talk of breaching limits is suggestive of a basic misconception. It seems to me you don't appreciate sufficiently that all of our human thoughts and reasonings are really *our* thoughts and *our reasonings* of needs. That is to say, the trivial truth is simply this: we can never step outside ourselves and see reality as a higher form of life perhaps already is or will some day be able to.

Sophie: I don't quite see where we are headed here. Please elaborate.

Philonous: To clarify my meaning, it is best to look at an example. If we subject a chimpanzee, let's say, to certain types of lab experiments, we are liable to observe that it can handle problem-solving tasks that aren't found in this same form in natural environments. Perhaps the animal can learn to ask for certain types of food by pressing buttons on a board; or maybe it can reach for some banana high up on a shelf by stacking up and climbing up two boxes underneath.[17] No matter what the details may turn out to be, the chimpanzee will likely show a kind of cognitive adaptability that is essentially akin to our own, far more advanced ability to operate outside the native problem-solving range that nature once defined for us.

Sophie: ...as for instance in such higher mental functions as mathematical deduction, scientific exploration, or, perhaps, artistic inspiration.

Philonous: That is correct. But when we now confront the chimpanzee with realms of understanding that are absolutely and on principle outside the reach of its abilities, we simply hit a wall. How, for instance, would we ever teach it to appreciate Newtonian gravitation? The chimpanzee perhaps can see the rising Moon at night and find it round or crescent-shaped as human beings do. But could it ever understand the Moon to be a planetary satellite kept on its path by forces that obey the law of inverse squares?

Sophie: Obviously not.

Philonous: ...because in chimpanzee-reality, the very notion of an understanding of this kind is strictly a *transcendent* one. It has no overlap with chimpanzee cognition.

Sophie: In other words and by analogy, even our most powerful mathematical and scientific insights are nothing but a simple stacking-up of boxes from the vantage point of that superhuman consciousness on the postulated existence of which your argument is based.

Philonous: Except that 'powerful' here is a word that we had better use with caution. We like to think of mathematics in particular as one of our proudest intellectual possessions. Nothing, it seems, is so pure and lucid, so absolutely firm and certain as the world of mathematics and nothing so revealing as its use in quantitative science. Mathematics is the golden Platonic key to all the secrets of the universe and quantifiability the modern standard of all truth. But can we really justify this high regard? Perhaps, the fact that our minds attain to clarity only in reductive mathematical abstraction is a sign of weakness rather than of strength.

Sophie: The problem, though, here is that Newton, Einstein, Heisenberg, and company are not remembered commonly for feebleness of intellect. To speak of "weakness" with regard to thinkers of this very highest rank is not what I would call 'convincing'.

Philonous: I don't agree because the genius of a man like Newton first and foremost was to recognize and take into account his own inherent limitations. To be sure, he was not as altogether stupid as the rest of us...

Sophie: Careful now, speak for yourself.

Philonous: ...but, being human, he as well was cognitively challenged by default.

Sophie: I think, I see it now: Newton invented the calculus, he devised a theory of light, set up the fundamental laws of classical mechanics, discovered universal gravitation, established Kepler's laws by mathematical deduction, and thereby proved himself a feeble-minded dolt.

Philonous: Your irony, unfortunately, is not Socratic but merely out of place. For Newton's works directly prove the truth of my assertion. Just take, for instance, Newton's greatest deed: the derivation of all three of Kepler's laws. How did he accomplish it?

Sophie: I answered that before (p.45): Newton combined the second law of classical mechanics with the universal law of gravity in order to infer, by way of calculus, that planetary orbits are elliptic.

Philonous: And what initial setup did he use?

Sophie: Ingeniously, a very simple one! At the outset he assumed the Sun and planets to be unextended points, the only quality of which was mass. In fact, instead of all the planets simultaneously he studied only one so as to cleverly avoid the useless tedium of having to account for all the small disturbances that come about as planets are attracted to each other.

Philonous: So the entire solar system was reduced in Newton's mind to a single point-like planet orbiting a single point-like Sun?

Sophie: Initially that was his setup, it is true. But later on he also proved that Kepler's laws still hold when the Sun is thought to be extended, like a ball.

Philonous: Yet in his first approach he really dealt with nothing more than two imagined points that moved about each other.

Sophie: That is correct and that is also why we still so much admire him. For Newton's intellect shone forth most brilliantly precisely in reductions of this sort. Newton saw simplicity where others got entangled in complexity. It was his eye for the essential that enabled him to demonstrate—for the very first time in history—the true power of mathematical modeling in science.

Philonous: In a sense, of course, I totally agree, but there is yet another side to it: what Newton taught us more so even than Descartes was the idea that our human intellect is too incompetent to truly understand a thing unless it be denuded and reduced. No problem can be solved in its original diverse reality. What we must therefore aim to find are ways to break a problem down until it finally admits of mathematical analysis. The human mind's fragility when facing full complexity can thus be circumvented but only at a price. For in any such analysis the colorful phenomenal reality that surrounds on all sides is rationally bleached and scattered into parts.

Sophie: It is the problem of reductionism once again.

Philonous: —the problem sitting at the heart of our integrative quest.

Sophie: And it is sitting there so stubbornly because it is indeed the case that elemental parts in mathematical relatedness exhaust reality in its entirety.

Philonous: Or so at least we come to think if we accept the central modern myth—the scientistic claim that everything there is can be potentially completely encompassed by human understanding.

Sophie: Unfortunately, it isn't just a myth because the methods Newton handed down to us have been unfailingly enormously successful.

Philonous: They were successful in their own domain. But as we take an evolutionary view, the picture that these methods paint will seem to us quite colorless and crude.

Sophie: But look—we take a flowing river, for example; we analyze the plants and fish in it, the riverbed, the shore, and all the other details that we find; we go on to record the entire fantastic array of physical ingredients and break them down—to cells, to molecules, to atoms, and finally to electrons and quarks. And what we find in doing so is that the river that we started with is really just an aggregate of nothing but these ultimate, most fundamental units. In other words, reductionism works!

Philonous: And where in all that you have just described is your experience of beauty as you contemplate the scene? Where is the sense of peace that you derive from tracing with your eyes the river's path as it meanders through the fields and forests of the land?

Sophie: It isn't there and can't be there—and that's exactly what I find so thoroughly depressing.

Philonous: But this is just absurd. The beauty and the sense of peace are there—in you. You feel them, resonate with them, and let them penetrate your being. They are for you the very center of it all.

Sophie: I don't agree, for science teaches us that such emotions are completely inessential. We subjectively impose them on the data we receive through our senses, but in themselves they really are non-entities.

Philonous: As I said, the notion is absurd.

Sophie: Not at all—what is absurd is only your refusal to acknowledge present-day realities. Ours is an age of technological utility, scientific feasibility, and computational efficiency. For we have learned that this is how things

work and can get done. The spirits you are trying to invoke have long ago
departed.

Philonous: Evidently, that central modern myth of our human reason's comprehensiveness is very deeply rooted in your mind. It may be time to dig
it up weed it out.

Sophie: By trying to convince me that Sir Newton was a fool?

Philonous: ...by showing you how crude a scheme lies at the basis of his thought.
So let's remember this when we return in just a moment.

Simplicity Begets Perplexity

In Newton's work we come across a breadth of seminal accomplishments that
is not easily surpassed. In mathematics and in physics equally the legacy that
Newton left is gloriously rich and varied in its reach. Yet more important still
than this immensity in scope is here the fact that there is evident in Newton's
thought a common underlying theme—namely the idea that physical reality
can be reduced to mathematical descriptions. The lesson that we learn from
the *Principia*, first and foremost, is how the world that we call 'physical' can
be coherently portrayed to us by quantitative means. Only with Newton did
the power of mathematical modeling in science become fully apparent, and
only with him did science take the form of *quantitative* science in the truest
modern sense.

By implication then, if our goal at present is to better understand the
essential character of Newton's world of thought, we need to look more carefully
at what it means to quantify a physical phenomenon. That is to say, the
question we should ask initially is simply this: how do we count?

To frame this question properly, it is helpful to observe that our use of
decimal expansions is very likely motivated by the fact that the number 10—
the base of these expansions—is equal to the number of our fingers. For clearly
this suggests to us that counting, fundamentally, is done by matching objects.
We count the objects in a bag by matching them, one by one, with the fingers
of our hands. In other words, there is a radical abstraction at the root of
any counting process: as far as counting is concerned, the only property an
object must possess is that of being in existence. It doesn't matter whether we
are counting fingers, chairs, or oranges as long as 'thingness' is a quality that
plausibly applies. Indeed, it is the ultimate reduction: an object is divested
of its shape, its size, its color, and absolutely all its varied properties except
for its reality as something that is there. Expanding on this thought, we may
conceive of any given number as a measure for the fact of being in existence:
one thing that exists becomes the number one, two things become two, three
things become three, and so forth *ad infinitum*.

That said, it is advisable to add that ordinarily of course, in modern mathematics, the concept of a number is established in a manner more concise

and formally coherent. A popular approach in this regard is to assert that there exists a set—the set of counting numbers—which satisfies a certain list of axiomatic properties (the axioms of Peano). In fact, all number systems commonly employed can be successively built up from nothing but these axioms. The integers, the rationals, the reals, the complex numbers, too—and even the quaternions—they all can be constructed from the simple counting numbers $1, 2, 3, \ldots$ by way of these defining, basic properties.

Moreover and amazingly, since the real numbers form the base of Newton's calculus, it follows that, in principle, the entire computational machinery that physicists rely upon in modeling material phenomena can be reduced to elementary arithmetic with positive whole numbers. It would be very cumbersome indeed but clearly can be done: upon the counting numbers and the axioms that establish them we can erect the theory of calculus in its entirety.[1] What we must therefore realize is this: Newton's scheme, along with just about all other schemes of mathematical modeling in science, is built upon a very simple base of black-or-white decisions—existence versus nonexistence—yes or no—zero or one. In other words, the clarity of mathematics and the firmness of its truths, that we so readily admire, are paid for with a heavy loss of richness and abundance. It almost seems as though the human mind is so restricted in its means that certainty can never be achieved by it except at levels of complexity that are so low that zero-one dichotomies can capture and contain them.

To be sure, most students of the subject will intensely disagree. Mathematics is the terror of the college life and feared for its confounding logical perplexities. Few indeed would choose it over, say, a course in history for its superior simplicity. And yet, the truth appears to be that mathematics is the subject understood most easily, because it is the only subject—apart from maybe logic—that can be understood at all. The reason why the field of history is commonly considered more accessible is simply that historical events are so completely shrouded in contingency that no one who is asked to study them can ever be expected to maintain an attitude of unexcepting rigor. Indeed, how would we ever give a full account, for instance, of the French Revolution? Perhaps we can discover and point out a few things here and there, a little bit of politics, of economics, and of cultural developments, but a truly comprehensive view is wholly out of reach. For clearly we cannot describe and analyze, entirely exhaustively, what all the acting personalities were doing and saying and thinking at any one moment and place. Nor do we know for that matter how the local Paris weather on the 14th of July, 1789, affected the mood of

---

[1]Set-theoretic constructions such as real- or complex-valued functions also feature prominently in the theory of calculus, but the mathematical entities from which these constructions are built can invariably be traced back to the axioms that establish the counting numbers. In this regard the theory of calculus is far more specific in the choice of its objects of study than, for instance, such fields as topology or group theory. By implication, it is accurate to say that calculus in its entirety is nothing but an elaborate scheme of enumeration.

those who were involved in storming the Bastille. In other words, the higher the complexity, the lower the demand for rigor, and the better will be typically the students' grades.

As a matter of course, this claim that mathematics is so difficult because it is, in fact, so utterly simple[18] seems crudely paradoxical. But even so its truth is plainly evident to anyone who teaches mathematics at a somewhat higher level. For unfailingly it can be seen that the true difficulty of the subject is encountered by a student when the field of study is so far reduced that absolute rigor, for the very first time, can be consistently required. The problems many students face when for once they have to think and speak with unrelenting clarity are really quite revealing. With nothing but the axiomatic bare bones of the counting numbers to consider they frequently will struggle in despair just to understand what in fact it means to clearly understand a thing. Such is the weakness of the human mind that even in a world of zero-one dichotomies it takes the greatest effort not to keep on groping in the dark.

While this assessment may sound grim, there is another side to it. For as it is, the zero-one language that mathematicians at bottom employ is sufficiently versatile to cover all of modern physics—and science thereby. We humans may be limited, but if we are aware of it and if we are content to focus on the subjects we can grasp, we do quite well and really can advance (assuming that we aren't students anymore and have been blessed with a Newtonian intellect). It is only when we switch to highly non-reductive topics, such as the causes of historical events or, perhaps, the nature of the beautiful, the virtuous and true, that we are liable to quickly get confused. Indeed, such issues we may contemplate for centuries on end and not produce a single valid insight.

By implication then, the transition at the dawn of our modern age from Scholastic speculation to quantitative science is best regarded as a wise acknowledgment of mental limitation. Galileo studied falling bodies rather than the doctrine of the Trinity because only the former subject was sufficiently simplistic for his feeble human intellect to really get a grip. The success of science based on mathematics shows, not the greatness of the human mind, but rather how severely we must limit our rational ambitions if we are not to lose ourselves in arbitrary fantasies.

Yet even so, we have enormously progressed—and this is where the problem lies. For it was precisely the great *advance* of science in the past five hundred years that has seduced us to forget that only our thought is black and white and that the world itself is vibrantly alive in sparkling light effects and richly varied colors. Deceived by our own success, we foolishly came to identify reality with quantitative human understanding. Indeed it is the ultimate anthropocentric fallacy: instead of recognizing clearly that our cognitive capacities are embedded in an evolutionary spectrum that is open in the vertical direction, we have defined a world-depicting apparatus, just one step up from animal unconsciousness, to be "the measure of all things."[19] In other words, we really needn't be surprised that everything turns gray and meaning stubbornly eludes us, if we believe that mixing black and white is all it takes to capture all reality.

As a matter of course, we are on principle unable to imagine what form of more advanced cognition and expression might some day take the place of our human thought and language. But the contemplation of the possibility of such an advance can help us all the same to better understand how very limited we very likely are. Afterall, what reason in the world is there to 'think' that we will ever truly grasp reality by lining up semantic primitives in strings, that is, by forming sentences and written text from words or formulas from mathematical notation? Philosophers and scientists endeavor to describe the universe by means of symbols—in language or in calculation. But why should such a scheme be adequate? Why should a scheme of discretized semantics, wherein symbols are described in vicious circularity in terms of other symbols, be suitable a key to ultimate reality? We ask what mind or matter is, or maybe virtue or the lack thereof, and all that we can offer in reply are verbal constructs built from symbols that in turn are as elusive as the symbols we are trying to describe. To beings that are higher than we are such mental efforts may appear entirely ridiculous. To them we look perhaps like monkeys that attempt to apprehend Newtonian gravity by stacking up and climbing up a bunch of cardboard boxes so as to get a better view thereby of how the Moon is moving in the sky. In other words, there may be strata of existence so far above our own that none of our thoughts and none of our words will ever be appropriate to capture them.

Sophie: So what are we to make of this? If this assessment is correct, then all the thoughts and words that we employ are likely but a play of shadows on a wall. Everything we say and every concept that we formulate is possibly of such depressing primitivity that we perhaps had better just fall silent. Whether we speak of evolution, mind and matter, change and stability, or perhaps the problem of reductionistic thought, we are confined of needs to an anthropomorphic tunnel vision that really has no outlet to the truth. Why think, why study, why investigate, if self-referring symbols will be all that we will find?

Philonous: We certainly must give up our modern claims to absolutes in human understanding. But that's a call to modesty, not foolish self-deflation. In fact, no radical position on the optimistic or the pessimistic side can ever be compatible with evolutionary thinking. For the idea that humans are positioned on a scale that far extends to higher forms of life will cause us to dismiss delusions of grandeur as readily and as decidedly as total skeptical denial. To the initiate of evolution the radically absolute is just as unattractive as the radically relative—modernity and postmodernity are equally deceptive. We are never going to find a theory of everything, regardless of what physicists may tell us. But neither is the knowledge that we have, as fuzzy and as incomplete as it may be, a mere illusion or an incidental cultural convention. Nor for that matter, is the search for truth and meaning, including our present quest, futile by default. It all depends, as I have said before, on whether we "uphold a vision of proportion" (p.10). We go as far as we can go by means of reason and perception, we then move on to faith, and in the end we just relax and openly admit that finitude in every skill and attitude is inescapably our lot.

Sophie: I understand, but when you speak of faith I wonder what you mean by that. So far as I can tell, the only object of belief that you are holding out to me is some assumed potential for development in future evolutionary time.

Philonous: Something is still missing, you are right. But we just cannot take the second step before the first. Before a faith can be defined more narrowly, its possibility must somehow be established, that is, transcendence must be recognized.

Sophie: Your usage of 'transcendence', though, is also somewhat odd. When I employ this word, I think of God, eternity, or immortality—a realm that really lies beyond the bounds of physical existence. By contrast, your appeal to higher or, as you might say, 'transcendent' forms of life in distant times or places is aiming at realities that are entirely contained within the confines of the cosmos, that is, within the universe in which all evolution so far has occurred. Conceivably, your view can lead us to ascend from 'natural' to 'supernatural,' but can it also get us to the 'extra-natural'—to that which matters most, perhaps, as far as meaning is concerned? I doubt it.

Philonous: And so do I. For transcendence due to evolution is always *weak* and thus distinct from that much stronger kind that really transcends the physical world.[20] However, in the light of our contemporary "double bind"[21]— overconfident modernism versus extreme postmodern skepticism—it still is helpful to point out that science can enable us to find a stable middle ground. For the evolutionary paradigm, as I have tried to show, is not compatible with either of these radical positions. In acknowledging initially that there is very probably a great Beyond, be it in the weak or in the strong sense of transcendence, we are less tempted to continuously fall back on ourselves and make the human plane "the measure of all things." Indeed, it is this inclination to believe that *our* world is *all* the world that really is the mortal sin that underlies modernity and postmodernity alike.

Sophie: It underlies them both? I do not understand. Is not the latter the undoing of the former, and are the two not therefore frontally opposed? So how can they be rooted in a common misconception?

Philonous: To find the answer, it is best to briefly recapitulate some thoughts that we discussed: as you recall, we stressed repeatedly that evolution very likely will advance beyond the plane of current human life.

Sophie: We did indeed.

Philonous: By implication we may speculate that human cognitive abilities are subject to essential limitations.

Sophie: The claim undoubtedly is sensible.

Philonous: ...and perfectly consistent with the fact that clarity in human thought, apparently, can only be attained in zero-one reductions.

Sophie: Hence we cannot rigorously understand what beauty or what virtue is, but analyzing falling bodies quantitatively is something we can do. In other words, it is restriction in the scope of thought that really is the key to scientific mastery.

Philonous: And now go back to Newton's and to Galileo's time and try to feel in retrospect the deep impression that this mastery was liable to leave in all the minds that witnessed its arrival. Centuries of Scholastic speculation with no dependable results, not even one,[II] and suddenly true knowledge is arising. Guided by a proper sense of epistemic modesty, consciously or not, the human intellect can suddenly perceive how falling bodies move and how the law of inverse squares will force a planetary path about the Sun to be elliptic. Science thus ascends, technology develops rapidly, and men watch in amazement as a new Promethean power is unfolding in their midst—the power to *predict*. By analyzing observations quantitatively the modern scientist can learn how laws *foretell* a future from a present state with frequently remarkable precision. As a matter of course, the scope of this endeavor, in the larger scheme of cosmic evolution, is probably still humble, but on the human plane the spectacle is vast: the birth of modern science here appears to be that true discovery of fire that finally makes man the undisputed ruler of his universe.

Sophie: Or so at least he thinks.

Philonous: Because humility lamentably is not a common grace.

Sophie: And thus we are misled to make the human mind—the cranial contents of a former ape—the arbiter of everything there is, the whole entirety referred to as 'reality'.

Philonous: And thus all meaning must disintegrate because a world that is so small that such a tiny mental space can process and contain it cannot support, all by itself, a genuinely non-reductive concept. We can *ask* what beauty or what virtue is, and we may do so driven by compelling inner needs, but within that discretized symbolic system of semantics, also known as human language, a fully coherent answer is impossible to find. A self-referring discontinuous scheme is simply far too crude to ever be complete.

[II]This comment is not intended to universally disparage medieval philosophy. For as Copleston is eager to point out in [Copl2], pp.2–8, medieval philosophy represents a rich intellectual tradition in its own right that is not *per se* inferior to its modern or classical counterparts. The comment made above is therefore not to be interpreted as an objective valuation of medieval thought but rather as a reflection of the low esteem in which that thought was held during much of the modern era.

Sophie: So instead of acknowledging this state of limitation to be a natural characteristic of our evolutionary stage, we turn the matter on its head and effectively declare the world to be as small as our human comprehension. That is to say, we strip existence brutally of everything that our quantitative zero-one analyses are liable to miss.

Philonous: And in the end, what are we left with? A skeletal universe in which reductive reason ruthlessly usurps reality in its totality—body, soul, and spirit.

Sophie: And it is this act of usurpation in which the anthropocentric fallacy at the heart of our modern paradigm is finally revealed.

Philonous: Precisely.

Sophie: Very well, I followed you thus far, but what about the antithetical postmodern view? You said that it is rooted in the same defining sin. But what is here your reasoning?

Philonous: The issue clearly cannot be exhaustively addressed in just a few remarks. But very roughly I would frame the matter thus: the modern fraud of epistemic overreach could not forever go unnoticed—the illusion was bound to be unmasked. And sure enough, along came Kant to tell us that the world that we experience must be assumed to be a cognitive construction of our own. Time and space, for instance, are not demonstrably exterior realities but rather are internal, inbuilt concepts that we use to organize the flow of our sensory perceptions. It is not human intuition that conforms to the object of experience, but instead it is the object that conforms to an *a priori* given intuition in the human mind. Consequently, our *knowledge* always is *our* knowledge—it is not objective but radically relative to how we are subjectively conditioned to pursue its acquisition.

Sophie: In other words, no objectivity is absolute.

Philonous: More strongly even we may say that total objectivity is totally destroyed. For Kant's original foray would soon be followed by a veritable onslaught. Philosophers, linguists, psychologists, quantum physicists, and many artists, too, would somehow reinforce the same subversive insight: the world is largely *our* world—the subject and the object are entangled.[22]

Sophie: And since, as we were told, the whole of human language is at bottom circular (p.119), we may as well assert more blatantly that subjectivity is wholly self-contained.

Philonous: That's right—we ask what verbal symbols such as 'mind' or 'matter' mean and realize that all we offer in reply are other verbal symbols. The whole charade is just a game within the human mind that nowhere has an opening to that which is objective and external. In consequence and in particular, we may here come to think that the dichotomy of mind versus matter, that timeless philosophical conundrum, is not primarily a problem of ontology but rather of linguistic flexibility. Afterall, if Eskimos use 40 different words for 'snow', then why should we not add to 'mind' and 'matter' other nouns as 'minder', say, or 'minter', 'mitter,' 'mattend'? Perhaps there wouldn't be a mind-and-matter puzzle to begin with if only we replaced a strict linguistic opposition by such a cut-and-paste verbosity. Perhaps it all comes down to happenstance: our history and culture so happen to have left us with a pair of words—'mind' and 'matter'—rather than a more accommodating spectrum.

Sophie: This type of criticism then, when taken to its logical conclusion, dissolves all human knowledge in anarchic arbitrariness. The solid ground on which the modern world was thought to have been built is seen to be a quicksand of random histories, linguistic conventions, and accidental biological and cultural developments.

Philonous: Indeed, "anything goes,"[23] as the postmodern thinker, Paul Feyerabend, once poignantly put it. We ask what 'mind' or 'matter' is, and answer anything we like: an inscrutable linguistic symbol, an historical contingency, a cultural convention, a scientific liability, or maybe just more honestly a philosophical embarrassment.

Sophie: It is a bit surprising, isn't it, how quickly all that modern certainty can crumble and disintegrate.

Philonous: No it isn't—not one bit. Just take again an evolutionary view: you saw a frog insisting that a solid metal gate was just a white illumined space, and you inferred that its perception was deceived. That is to say, the subject's amphibian cognition constructed in this case a world that was consistent only partially with that which you yourself would have described as the 'objective' situation. So why should we be in the least surprised to learn that on a somewhat higher plane a creature by the name of *homo sapiens* inhabits a subjective world that is perhaps a little wider in its various horizons but limited no less? We humans do not meet our mental limitations by banging our heads against a gate, but maybe we encounter them in those symbolic self-referring cycles by which we hope to get a grip on ultimate reality. Is it not completely obvious that evolution—by being open-ended—will never grant to any creature it begets the intellectual capacity to form an image of the world that truly is the Truth?

Sophie: So your assertion is apparently that the existence of the deconstructive possibilities that present-day postmodernists have been exploiting can only strike us as astonishing, if we forget that we are former apes.

Philonous: ...that is, if our view is rigidly *anthropocentric*.

Sophie: Put differently, what you're suggesting is a classic dialectic: the thesis is the modern claim to objectivity, the antithesis the skeptical postmodern counterclaim, and the coherent synthesis emerges from the evolutionary view.

Philonous: Indeed, within the evolutionary scheme, the best of human knowledge can be viewed to be objective and subjective simultaneously. 'Objective' because our world-depicting apparatus is part of a continuum of other such apparatuses that all consistently portray the same external world, and 'subjective' because on evolution's open-ended scale no individual apparatus can ever be assumed to be the arbiter of any final Truth. The former attribute inspires modern confidence in human reason and perception, whereas the latter leads to radical postmodern deconstruction. In other words, both the thesis and the antithesis are valid aspects of the same coherent synthesis. But as this synthesis emerges, the underlying fallacy of anthropocentrism is fully brought to light, and claims to knowledge and their counterclaims give way to faith in weak or strong transcendence. And Kant, if I may add, would likely have agreed, for he maintained that we "must... abolish knowledge in order to make room for belief."[24]

Sophie: So all will now depend on whether we can make that Kantian belief more lively and concrete.

Philonous: That is to say, we still have quite a bit of work to do.

The Forms of Lawlessness

If there is a moral to be learned from either of the last two dialogues, it probably would have to be that stupidity is more difficult to bear in the dusk than in the dark. The twilight zone of human reason is more perilous a realm than the lightless pit of animal unconsciousness. For the essential difference between a chimpanzee aspiring to understand Newtonian gravity and a human being attempting to discern, by means of reason, the nature of the beautiful, the virtuous and true is, of course, that the former knows of no such aspiration. Where animal existence is closed and self-contained, human life is open, incomplete, and therefore restless. Man was given a light to see the book of life before him, but the light is far too dim for him to read the pages it contains. Perhaps he can identify a letter here and there or maybe even half a word, but the larger story that is told remains forever hidden from his sight. He certainly can speculate as to the plot that is unfolding, but in the end his reason is incompetent to draw reliable conclusions. The human half-wit (as represented presently by *Philonous* and *Sophie*—as well as the hapless author of their dialogues) unlike his more modest cousin, the ape, therefore finds himself caught up in never ending cycles of confusion. If he is guided only by his rational faculties, he is beset with ineradicable doubt and forced to live a life of constant discontent in an alien land of unmet desires, nagging uncertainties, and intellectual conundrums.

In the light of this predicament, it is no wonder that philosophers like Plato have attempted time and again to somehow come to grips with the world as it is, in and of itself. Faced with the shortfalls of perception Plato took flight to reason, but his vision of rationally discernible Ideas or *forms*, defining the core of existence, remained largely fictional. To be sure, it may be feasible to argue—at the level of ontology—that the mathematical form of a law of nature, in our current understanding, also is a form in the Platonic sense.[25] But viewed in epistemic terms there is a very clear distinction. For a law of nature in the modern sense must needs be tied to observation and experiment. Not pure Platonic reason is the arbiter of scientific truth but evidence derived from sensory perception. Concepts that are inconsistent with or unrelated to the data of experience will simply be discarded.[1]

The notion that a final insight can be gained in freely speculative thought is rooted in illusion. For as the human mind turns inwards, it discovers, not the forms of ultimate reality, but at best a range of a priori patterns of cognition that constitute its own *modus operandi*. That is to say, what it detects are mental structures which evolved to mirror the external world in consciousness but which, as mirrors, show reflections that presumably are still quite primitive and pale.

Finding ourselves thus encaged by cognitive deficiencies, we further come to realize that our mind's ability to generate dependable rational insights is inversely correlated with the metaphysical significance of the questions that these insights aim to answer. Whenever existence can be reduced, beyond recognition, to a crude reductive scheme, we possibly can get a grip. But all the truly interesting, truly non-reductive issues remain completely shrouded in obscurity of needs. At this latter end of the spectrum reason can ask but only faith can offer a reply. In other words, the problem of our existential discontent is, at bottom, not intellectual but spiritual in nature.

The truth of this conclusion—with an eye to the ironic—is easily confirmed in everyday encounters. For anyone who ever has observed a human infant enter earthly life in kicking and in screaming agitation was thereby given an occasion to reflect on the rather unfavorable contrast that such a spectacle provides to the appearance of unquestioning acceptance with which, say, a young gazelle or wildebeest will face the struggle for survival within minutes of its birth. Even in a state of total physical protection a human infant cannot help but throw a tantrum at the least attentive lapse he deems his hassled mother guilty of. Thus, the great Augustine, in his meditations on the nature of postnatal human nature, rightly felt compelled to ask "where or when" he ever had been "innocent."[26] Clearly, it cannot be the workings of the intellect that cause an infant to forsake all personal integrity so early and so eagerly as he manipulates his mother to attend to him. Instead, what is revealed in such pre-rational behavior is the intrinsic restlessness of a spirit that is fundamentally in conflict with the world in which it has been placed. The human being is a stranger where the animal is perfectly at home.

---

[1]The question of when or why a scientific concept is discarded requires in itself a very careful and deliberate analysis (as given for instance in [Kuh2] and [Pop]). The brief remark above is only meant to indicate that in spite of all historical or cultural conditionings, agreement between theory and observation is a vital requirement that cannot be dispensed with.

An animal, it seems, is simply and harmoniously a part of its environment whereas a human child will struggle ceaselessly no matter the conditions that it finds. A child forever wants the things it cannot have, and whatever it can have, it does not want. Dissatisfaction here is not resulting from a need but simply from the fact of being human. And even as the child matures the struggle doesn't end but only is transformed. Adults may not be kicking anymore, yet neither do they ever come entirely to rest.

Sophie: It is pathetic, isn't it, how poorly we compare to animal existence.

Philonous: Yes and no. 'Yes' because the image we present can sometimes be indeed a bit unflattering, and 'no' because we also come to see in this how far removed from animals we humans really are. For better or for worse, the spirit in us truly is a different one. That is to say, our prominent propensity for discontent may here be viewed to be the price we have to pay for living at a higher stage of consciousness.

Sophie: But isn't it precisely this propensity from which your integrative rea- sonings were all along intended to deliver me? And doesn't it then follow from your claim that this deliverance in turn requires that my consciousness be somehow made more primitive so as to be subhuman?

Philonous: Not really, no it doesn't. What we are trying to eliminate is not the general propensity as such but rather more specifically the discontent it causes in your case.

Sophie: That doesn't really satisfy, does it?

Philonous: To rid you of your discontent would clearly be a positive accom- plishment.

Sophie: Fair enough, but are you really ridding me of anything? As far as I can tell, your only offerings so far have been a quantum vision of a universe to which the notion of a conscious mind may somehow be intrinsic and an evolutionary space of speculative weak transcendence that is unknow- able by definition. It's not that I dislike these vistas in themselves—your quantum vision, in particular, is really quite intriguing. But what I find so cumbersome is that your discourse has been all along a rather abstract one. If alienation, loss of meaning, and the modern sense of disenchantment are to be the themes of our quest, then our arguments must be more personal and tangible in kind. Afterall, I cannot feel at home in our universe just because my mind can bring about a wave collapse or just because some future day a higher form of life will understand reality more fully.

Philonous: In other words, you need an anchor for your spirit.

Sophie: What I desire is a means by which I can connect, or *re*connect, my self to that which is external—a way to bring the inner and the outer world in line.

Philonous: The first step here may be to properly appreciate that the external world is not congruent with the knowledge that you have of it. The latter only is a fragment of the former—intrinsically and necessarily. By implication, the world you long to be connected to is largely a transcendent one, and your appeal to it must therefore be derivative of more than merely knowledge—there must be also faith.

Sophie: My central problem though is not intrinsic epistemic incompleteness but personal emotional detachment—and this is where your various interpretive alternatives are woefully inadequate. For even if the universe is not a mechanistic world machine of classical Newtonian sorts, but is instead a giant quantum thought in God's sustaining intellect[27] (p.90), it still is governed by eternal laws that are indifferent to the fact of my existence. That is to say, as long as I perceive the world to be a strictly law-abiding one, I find it difficult to see what deeper meaning my existence in that world could possibly assume. A mere descriptive shift from physical to mental traits or classical to quantum law, all by itself, can never be sufficient.

Philonous: Perhaps you feel detached because you tend to think that 'world' and 'scientific law' are more or less synonymous. In other words, your problem here may be that you identify too readily reality with scientific knowledge.

Sophie: As I see it, this knowledge is the base from which I start. Consequently, your appeal to faith cannot resolve the problem that I face unless a point of entry can be fixed at which transcendence, as the object of that faith, can somehow become real to me and genuinely modify the knowledge that I have. For otherwise transcendence would be insular and therefore largely useless.

Philonous: But what about the multitudes of people who, throughout the course of history, have held transcendent faiths of one form or another? Is it not completely obvious that notions of transcendence in religion can be meaningfully part of human life despite the fact that they do not directly intersect with scientific knowledge?

Sophie: I hope you are not trying to suggest that I should look for shelter in traditional belief.

Philonous: Not necessarily, but the fact that a large part of mankind is able presently and has been able in the past to forge, by means of such belief, precisely that connection that you seek is certainly worth noting.

Sophie: I don't agree because the bond that is established here does not connect the self to the external world but rather to a pre-scientific caricature of that world which modern people find at best amusing. To be sure, if I could make myself believe that the dead can rise or that prayer can be effective, the loss of meaning that I suffer from could easily be overcome. For I would then be living at the center of divine attention in a world in which a mountain can be moved by faith alone and gravity can be conveniently suspended whenever I should wish to walk on water. Unfortunately, though, such paranormal fantasies are bare of all reality. Consequently, if I want to make sense, let's say, of the essential Christian doctrines, I have to purify

them first by means of modern science. But as I do so I will turn religion
into mere philosophy and thereby lose entirely the meaning that I seek.

Philonous: That is to say, in order for transcendence to be useful in your eyes,
it must be tied to science more constructively.

Sophie: At least the knowledge that I have must not be compromised. What
I desire is to find a link between the self and the external world that isn't
merely fantasy and doesn't force me to deny what cannot be denied: the
basic truth of science.

Philonous: But such a link was offered earlier already in our discourse on the
quantum world.

Sophie: It was a positive first step, but still too abstract to be helpful. For, as
I said, the notion that my mind can bring about a wave collapse is hardly
in itself sufficient to rejoin my inner human self to that which is external.
Nor, for that matter, is the idea of weak evolutionary transcendence, while
plausibly derivative of valid scientific thought, a very fruitful one.

Philonous: Why not?

Sophie: Because it's far too unspecific. For let's suppose that one fine day
a higher form of life indeed emerges and in consequence attains a vastly
greater depth of world-depicting insight. Then how can I be sure that the
reality perceived by such a superhuman consciousness is any more hos-
pitable than the reductive universe of current human science? Perhaps the
opposite will be the case—perhaps the larger picture will be so depressing and deplorable that even Newton's mechanistic world machine will by
comparison appear to be a cozy little log-home in the woods.

Philonous: Reality is not a solidly objective block. The subject is involved in
its creation. What we perceive the world to be is partly our choice, and
what I therefore would expect to happen at a higher evolutionary stage is
clearly for the range of choices to expand. That is to say, there will be
bleakness bleaker than we can imagine but also heights of happiness and
inspiration that our highest flying human sentiments can never hope to
rival.

Sophie: In that you may be right, but then again you also may be wrong. For
all of this is idle speculation.

Philonous: The involvement of the subject is a central concept in the orthodox interpretation of quantum mechanics and therefore tightly linked to
scientific facts.

Sophie: But the second part of your assertion, concerning far expanded choice,
is evidently fantasy.

Philonous: ...but very plausible no less. Afterall, we can observe the corresponding pattern clearly in the range of life to which we presently have
access. The potential for suffering and joy is greater in a cat than in a
fly, in a monkey it is greater still, and in a human being it is greatest. By
implication it is natural to think that on a superhuman plane the range of

sentiments will yet again be more diverse and broader.

Sophie: And so, if you are right, what do we gain?

Philonous: Admittedly, the likely fact of weak transcendence in itself can only save us from the sin of human self-importance. But the notion that perception of reality is, in part at least, a choice, may very well be central to the struggle that you face.

Sophie: In other words, you are suggesting that my problem may be mostly self-induced. If only I could change my point of view, the world would really *be* much brighter.

Philonous: I do believe that you must *choose* the path you want to travel on. If you insist that everything around you is at bottom driven by a quantitative "law-abiding" scheme (p.127), then driven it will be. Meaning cannot be established as long as you effectively deny the possibility of its existence. Belief or disbelief is something you must choose.

Sophie: But that's not all there is to it. For you yourself have cautioned more than once that objectivity is not to be entirely discarded. So when I say that our universe is subject to eternal laws that are indifferent to my personal existence, I am expressing more than just a personal opinion.

Philonous: ...because the notion of a law is largely an objective one?

Sophie: That's right. All laws are closely tied to facts: a falling body is observed and hence the corresponding law can well be said to be essentially objective.

Philonous: Unfortunately, though, what we observe is not a law but, as you said, a falling body.

Sophie: Strictly speaking I agree, but your objection is more tedious than helpful. It is true, of course, that laws cannot be stated without faith in lawfulness. I must believe the cosmos to be uniform in time and space before I can assert that falling bodies will descend tomorrow as they did today and that the fundamental rules by which their motion is constrained are here the same as over there where you are sitting at the table. So yes, there is belief involved but not the kind that I consider difficult to muster.

Philonous: Are you saying then that lawfulness is altogether absolute?

Sophie: I am indeed.

Philonous: But in the light of what we learned about the quantum realm there is another option to consider.

Sophie: Which is?

Philonous: Well, if consciousness is vital to the process of reality creation, then possibly it also has a word to say about the rules that this reality obeys.

Sophie: Is this to say a body will respond to gravity by falling only on condition that the state of mind of the observer is conducive?

Philonous: Look, I willingly acknowledge that the falling of a body in my everyday surroundings is just about as close as I can ever hope to get to an event that laws control objectively. But does it therefore follow that a law can never be responsive to subjective conscious influence?

Sophie: Of course it does! Or are you going to maintain that I am able to design my own edition of scientific law by simply consciously intending it? The notion is ridiculous.

Philonous: Not any more so than your own competing counterclaim. Why do you say the universe abides by laws that are indifferent to your personal existence when in reality a law is not an object we observe? What we perceive are individual events that never are repeated. No falling body ever falls the same way twice. What do we really know about how tightly 'laws' are linked to all those non-recurring individual phenomena that in their sum compose material existence? Is consciousness involved, and if it is, to what extent? Are laws forever absolute, or are perhaps some laws evolving? The answer is that we don't know.[28]

Sophie: But there is nothing wrong, I hope, with forming and expressing an opinion.

Philonous: Nothing whatsoever—as long as viable alternatives are not excluded groundlessly.

Sophie: Alternatives such as your scientific anarchy?

Philonous: I never meant to put in doubt the fundamental claim that physical reality is built upon a form of lawfulness that to a large degree is not subjective. Yet do I therefore need to postulate that laws exist unchangeably and are forbiddingly disjoint from any living consciousness? The empiricist in me is very much reluctant to accept a hostile proposition of this kind that no experience will ever justify. There simply is no valid reason to believe that ours is a universe in which all things particular and everything concrete will always be conditioned inescapably by abstract universals known as 'laws.'

Sophie: Just open up a window then and take a leap. If universal gravity is nothing but an ineffectual abstraction, then surely you can neutralize its customary pull by means of your directed mental opposition.

Philonous: We mustn't be too rash in trying to apply what I have been suggesting. If our goal is to determine the effects that consciousness exerts on objects pulled by gravitation, we probably will need to be a little less ambitious.

Sophie: In other words, we need to give up all ambition altogether as such effects do simply not exist.

Philonous: The issue may be less transparent than you think because phenomena that are suggestive of a different view have been, in fact, quite carefully recorded (as we will see in Chapter 5, p.374ff).

Sophie: I don't believe it, and I also do not care because regardless of whatever odd phenomena you have in mind, a falling body still will be a body that is *falling*. Furthermore and more to the point, the problem of my existential discontent will very likely not be solved by making me believe that consciousness can dent the law of gravitation. Meaning cannot be established by contemplating arguments that are peripheral at best and totally irrelevant at worst. So let's just take a break. I need to get my focus back on matters more important.

The Transition We Call 'Death'

Perhaps the most prominent exponent of a conception of physical law that resembles the one *Philonous* just proposed was the eminent theoretical physicist John Archibald Wheeler. Starting from Bohr's dictum that "[n]o elementary phenomenon is a phenomenon until it is a registered (observed) phenomenon,"[29] Wheeler speculated that "acts of observer participancy" may be "the magic ingredient"[30] from which the laws of physics arose. In other words, observer participancy—broadly construed as registration of events— can plausibly be thought to be "the mechanism for the universe"—including its laws—"to come into being."[31] Wheeler's pertinent slogan of "law without law"[32] may thus be understood to signify an essentially evolutionary conception of lawfulness.

Apart from questions such as these concerning the ultimate origin and nature of physical law, there also is the issue of how lawfulness in actuality is countered by the forces of contingency. Is the universe predominantly law-abiding or is it just a vast array of freely singular events?[I] Taking our inspiration from the standard quantum lore, we probably should say that these alternatives are complementary, not rigidly opposing: lawfulness exists but only in the statistical accumulation of events that in themselves are irreducibly acausal (so far as we can *know*). Furthermore, if we are willing to admit that consciousness is vitally a part of the reality equation, then every elemental quantum act assumes a dual character as an initiating conscious influence is paired up with a 'free' or 'random' physical response.[II] Consequently, it is plausible to claim that physical reality is not a rigid monument to law's control and absolute authority but rather is endowed with ample space for free creative acts and individual expression.

However, in respect of our chosen central theme of loss of purpose in the

---

[I]In recent scholarly debates concerning process philosophy and the notion of emergence, it has been argued from the point of view of combinatorics that law is always overwhelmed by the massive number of configurations that any reasonably complex system can assume. That is to say, "[l]aws continue to constrain what can happen, but they become insufficient to *determine* which configurations eventually prevail" (see [UI], p.950).

[II]The question of whether consciousness is indeed an indispensable ingredient in quantum measurement is, of course, subject to debate. Wheeler, for example, is careful to point out that 'observation' is not necessarily to be identified with 'conscious observation' and that 'registration' therefore is a better word to use.[33] Other physicists, though, disagree and make explicit reference to consciousness in their own alternative interpretations (see, for instance, [Wig1] or [Sta2]). In other words, our choice to align ourselves with the latter point of view is really and truly a choice.

modern mind, the question should be asked if considerations of this kind are truly of importance. Afterall, in our daily macroscopic life the freedom of the quantum realm is all but blotted out as myriads of underlying quantum choices are channeled by the force of law into statistical mean values that evolve with classical Newtonian certainty. The world at our human scale is one in which a falling body will be falling quite in spite of all atomic realm contingencies.

To be sure, there is nothing wrong *per se* with arguments exploring the more speculative aspects of the notion of scientific law, but in the end the physical determinants of our actual existence are still prescribed with lawful stringency. Spatially we are constrained at worst by our tiny planetary home and at best by the extent of our solar system, cognitively we are tied to our evolutionary stage, and temporally we cannot escape the terminal event we commonly call 'death'. By implication it is tempting to conclude that our human straits are dire indeed and that no descriptive shift regarding lawfulness or other philosophical conceptions can credibly hold out a promise of relief.

Sophie: I gladly see the central matter coming closer to the fore, and I whole-heartedly agree: the "human straits are dire." For in the final consequence the physical constraints set forth in nature's code of law impose themselves on human life in ways that are no less predictable than fatal. And in particular—and quite in spite of any Heisenberg uncertainties or quantum probabilities—the rule that every human birth is followed by a death is wholly unexcepting.

Philonous: In fact, this 'law of death' is very deeply rooted in the structure of material existence. A physicist will commonly refer to it with rational detachment as the second fundamental law of thermodynamics, but in its consequence this law is dreadfully concrete. For briefly stated it asserts that chaos and disorder in the universe, as measured by the quantity of entropy,[III] must needs increase until a point of ultimate disorder has been reached. On this account the cosmos is approaching slowly but surely a final state of disarray in which all energy will have been maximally spread and thereby rendered impotent. That is to say, the whole of physical reality is headed for paralysis in thermal dissipation.

Sophie: It's called the 'heat death' or 'Big Freeze', if I am not mistaken.

Philonous: The notion is familiar then?

Sophie: It is indeed, and I must say it has a certain grim appeal.

Philonous: It does?

[III]Roughly speaking, entropy in classical thermodynamics is a measure for that part of a system's energy that cannot be translated into work. Furthermore, in the mathematical theory of dynamical systems a notion of entropy has been rigorously introduced that quantifies the rate at which an initially well ordered state becomes chaotic. And just as the second law of thermodynamics predicts that entropy in physical reality is ever increasing, so it can be shown in this latter case that for every nontrivial dynamical system there exist certain minimal rates at which the system's entropy increases to infinity (see [Bl3] and [Bl4]).

Sophie: Just try to picture it: a universe that is eternally inert—nothing stirs and nowhere is there any sign of life. Drifting aimlessly within a boundless sea of time the world, at last, has run its course and has forever fallen silent.

Philonous: Yet where is the appeal? I find the vision bleak.

Sophie: As I see it, where death is universal and complete there can be no more dying, no more pain. And furthermore and more importantly, the underlying fact of ever growing entropy is well descriptive of the world of my immediate experience. For it defines and brings about the fundamental struggle that I face.

Philonous: The struggle against death?

Sophie: Against death, against decay, and against a total loss of meaning in the face of either.

Philonous: Are you saying then that meaning is denied as entropy increases? The notion is a stretch.

Sophie: To see where I am coming from you only need to look objectively at what you really are: your body in scientific terms is nothing but an intricate thermodynamic machine which is designed to temporarily maintain its functional integrity by way of energy-exchange with its environment. Since the order in the parts of this machine, that is, its organs and its cells, is clearly of a very high degree, its entropy, by implication, is quite low. Consequently, if such a highly organized but fragile state is to be preserved against the strong corroding forces of the second fundamental law, your body must have access fairly frequently to packages of energy that are quite low in entropy as well and commonly called 'food'. Whenever such a package is absorbed by your mammalian metabolic system, the useful energy contained in it will be converted partly into heat and entropy will thereby be increased.[IV]

Philonous: In other words, the second fundamental law for the entire system—comprising body, food, and physical surroundings—will strictly be obeyed despite the fact that my body's entropy in isolation remains approximately stable.

Sophie: Correct.

Philonous: And meaning therefore is denied because...?

Sophie: Just wait a second please, I will address the issue in a moment. But first we need to realize that in the light of what I just explained there is a problem here arising. For packages of suitably low entropy are typically not falling from the sky. In fact, the only way to get to them for beings like the two of us is to destroy some other living beings. That is to say, the second fundamental law—the law of death—is literally causing now the

---

[IV] An example of such a metabolic passage from higher to lower forms of chemical order is given for instance by the oxidation of glucose in the process of which one glucose molecule and six oxygen molecules are converted into a less organized ensemble of six carbon dioxide and six water molecules (see the exposition in [Lei1], Chapter 14, for more details).

blood to flow as organisms will be driven to annihilate each other.

Philonous: Life will prey on life in order to maintain itself—I understand. But this is just a commonplace.

Sophie: I know, but what is interesting here to see is how the lawful structure of material reality is organized, at even its most basic level, to bring about a struggle for survival. The competition that facilitates the process known as 'evolution' is ultimately consequent of matter's unrelenting drive to randomness. If it weren't for this law, we wouldn't have to kill in order to keep going, and in particular, we wouldn't be aggressively competing with each other to become the most efficient predators—or murderers.

Philonous: And "other" here means 'other species,' I assume.

Sophie: Not necessarily, because in nature competition comes in two varieties. First there is indeed the inter-specific kind that pits perhaps two different types of carnivores against each other in their quest to dominate the same environmental niche. But then there also is the intra-specific sort that forces individuals *within* a given species to determine by aggressive means who, for instance, will attain to reproductive rights or occupy a fertile hunting ground.[34] By implication then, aggression universally—including human war—may properly be thought to be a mindless high-end consequence of scarcity brought on by thermal dissipation.

Philonous: Blaming acts of war on heat dispersion really is a little too eccentric for my taste, and on the whole, reality is not as gloomy as you paint it. For you conveniently omitted to point out that evolution also brings about such altruistic tendencies as care and sacrifice and nurture for the young.

Sophie: Unfortunately, though, such 'loving kindness' has its source, not in the goodness of the heart, but rather in the stern competitive demand to propagate one's genes. Nurturing your children is by no means an expression of unselfishness but simply is a reasonable strategy to guarantee that your genetic information won't be lost.

Philonous: There is a warmth to all these thoughts of yours that I find humanly profoundly reassuring.

Sophie: Your irony aside, I eagerly agree that warmth is missing totally and painfully. Worse still, this lack of anything humane is not by chance but by design because a law that mathematics can encapsulate, such as the law of entropy, is by default unable to accommodate a notion that alludes to personal emotion. Reality, as science must describe it, just stares us in the face indifferently. Where Christian people in the past could still believe the law of death to be a punishment for an original transgression, we only see a mathematical relation. What modern man perceives the world to be is in effect a miserable soulless pit: aggression, war, disease, decay, and death, along with all the sufferings that they imply, are in the final consequence reducible to quantitative laws that are deplorably devoid of any higher purpose or intent. In fact, the absence of intent is so complete and obvious that laws as these cannot be even meaningfully said to be despicable or evil.

Philonous: The image that you conjure up is one of utter desolation. For if indeed all suffering and all decay and everything we commonly describe as 'evil' is nothing but a purposeless expression of the lawful order of material reality, then, in essence, no morality can ever have a base.

Sophie: It's sad, I know, but clearly so, and just the same applies to *everything* that we hold dear or wish to value. Whatever we admire or aspire to—the true, the beautiful, the good—is quickly found to be, when analyzed scientifically, a silly wishful fantasy. The beauty of a flower or a tree becomes a matter of competitive utility, and all the colors of a coral fish, so splendidly arranged, are shown upon inspection to be symbols of aggression. The function of such 'beauty' is to signal other fish to stay away or else to get ferociously attacked. It wasn't joyous artistry that drew these colorful designs but blind selective pressure toward ever more assertive territorial possessiveness.[35]

Philonous: And by extension, I assume, all beauty, love, and virtue on the human plane are equally deceptive.

Sophie: They are indeed.

Philonous: So when you watch two lovers holding hands, you only see two thermosystems headed for genetic propagation?

Sophie: I know it sounds extreme, but as we analyze clearsightedly the standard mating rituals by which such interpersonal 'attractions' are conditioned, all sense of the sublime is thoroughly discouraged. Where animals establish rank and reproductive rights in terms of purely physical criteria the human game, perhaps, is somewhat more complex but not in essence any different. Social status, wealth, and physical appearance clearly are determinants that play a crucial role. I can, of course, envisage for myself to use criteria that aren't quite as base, but in the end reality will always override my virtuous resolve. For the truth is simply this: I won't get married to a man whose height is markedly below my own or whose appearance otherwise is seriously unappealing—regardless of how noble or courageous or how loving he may be.

Philonous: And men, of course, are even more depraved in their approach because—as you would surely emphasize—the driving force in men is universally their bodily desire.

Sophie: Of course, but rankings of depravity are not at present my concern.

Philonous: I understand, your claim at bottom is that human sexuality, by its very nature, forces us to judge another person by criteria that always are to some extent degrading.

Sophie: That is correct, because the physical dimension here involved will cause us even in the best of cases to regard a fellow human being partly as an object. More generally, though, what I am trying to communicate is the

idea that a world of scarcity prescribed by ever growing entropy, a world
in which a struggle for existence must lead to competition and aggression
will also be a world that must corrupt the thoughts and deeds of those
who live in it. We cannot be engaged in sexuality without a vital loss of
innocence but neither can we even take so much as just a single breath
without exposure to corruption.

Philonous: That is to say, evil in a world like ours isn't merely possible but
altogether inescapable.

Sophie: Indeed, evil is intrinsic and profoundly structural—it follows us at
every step and turn. As solid objects cast their shadows when exposed to
light, so a living consciousness, embedded in materiality, must show its evil
side when held up to the standard of the truly pure and moral.[36] Living in
a world of suffering and scarcity we are sold out to villainy of needs. For
even if we give to our children, with the best intentions we can muster,
toys or clothes or other items they desire, we cannot help but be aware
that somewhere else a little boy or girl is eating food from garbage dumps.
Put differently, if next to every new and shiny car or other good that we
acquire there sat a starving mother with a dying child, we likely would
be less inclined to fantasize about upholding in our lives a sense of ethical
integrity.

Philonous: So the erosion of morality is brought about not only by the total
absence of all purpose and intent in nature's code of law but also by the
fact that those who are subjected to this code are thereby driven to engage
in criminal behavior.

Sophie: It is the hallmark of all truly evil schemes that they destroy the moral
base from which they can be recognized as such by turning victims into
perpetrators.[36] In fact, it is the final perfidy: physical reality, by being
meaningless and utterly amoral, is able first to void all judgments we might
pass on it and then to force the fruits of its corruption to ripen into full-
blown evil only in the conscious minds of those that this reality itself is the
creator of. Has any plot of treason ever been more hideous?

Philonous: I think your view is too unyielding and too far removed from ordinary human life. For even if I did admit that evil is to some degree at least
intrinsic, it wouldn't follow necessarily that I must be entirely sold out to
it. There surely is a way in which morality can be upheld while recognizing
simultaneously that ideal consistency is not a goal that we can reach.

Sophie: The notion makes me laugh.

Philonous: Your attitude is bitter.

Sophie: Call it honest if you please. For it simply cannot be denied that just by
being physically alive I will be implicated passively *and actively* in crime.

Philonous: In other words, to say it with Carl Jung, "life itself is guilt."[38]

Sophie: It surely is.

Philonous: Are we at the center then? Is this the issue at the very heart of our quest—the point where meaning must disintegrate as all morality collapses?

Sophie: Almost, but there are still a few comments that I would like to add. For the ethical debasement that we suffer from is really just a symptom— albeit a revealing one—of a deeper existential dislocation: a total loss of all connectedness. I feel as though with every insight science has to offer, with every step in understanding that I take, my grip on life is loosening and ever growing weaker. Reality for me has wholly come undone. I still can hear at times a voice inside that beckons me to hope for some redeeming rays of light, but whenever I engage my reason actively, the darkness only deepens. I very much would like to think that faith and joy and love are not just empty words, that reaching out to friends and neighbors can be more than wasted time. But then again, who is my neighbor? A ghost? A passing prisoner of time who spends a fleeting moment in material existence before he fades in death forever into nothingness? Why bother then to meet him kindly? No act of friendliness has yet escaped the grave. Whatever goodness we aspire to, whatever hopes we entertain, it all will come to naught as growing entropy reduces us to dust.

Philonous: The way you speak like that, I feel reminded of Tolstoy, the famous novelist, who was tormented in his later middle age by similarly haunting ruminations. Searching in despair for meaning in the face of death and coming to the brink of suicide, he realized in great distress that scientific thought produces only hopelessness:

> When I put my questions to one branch of human knowledge I received a countless number of precise answers to things I had not asked: the chemical composition of the stars, the movement of the sun towards the constellation Hercules, the origin of species and of man, the forms of infinitely tiny atoms, the fluctuations of infinitely small and imponderable particles of ether. But the only answer this branch of knowledge provided to my question concerning the meaning of life was this: you are that which you call your life; you are a temporary, incidental accumulation of particles. The mutual interaction and alteration of these particles produces in you something that you refer to as your life. This accumulation can only survive for a limited length of time; when the interaction of these particles ceases, that which you call your life will cease, bringing an end to all your questions. You are a randomly united lump of something. This lump decomposes and the fermentation is called your life. The lump will disintegrate and the fermentation will end, together with all your questions. This is the answer given by the exact side of knowledge, and if it adheres strictly to its principles, it cannot answer otherwise.[39]

Sophie: Well put—I understand exactly how he felt. There really is no point to living in a void. I often even wonder why I still get up and put on clothes if fifty, maybe sixty years from now I will be nothing but a rotting chunk of flesh. Seen against this background of inevitable termination, every single act of daily living becomes an exercise in the absurd. Why brush my teeth or eat my food? In order solely to maintain a little longer an entropic state, called 'life', that in the end is nothing but a transitory aberration?

Philonous: The common answer is, "In order to find meaning and fulfillment in the things you do, the plans you make, and most importantly the people that you meet."

Sophie: Yet how do I encounter fellow human beings in a world of constant competition? With openness, unselfishness, and genuine affection or rather fear, suspicion, and hostility?

Philonous: It's up to you—it really is your choice.

Sophie: I don't agree, for fear is not a choice but simply is implied by competition and aggression, that is, it is a form of evil that is ultimately structural as well. Once again we therefore see how truly comprehensive the corruption is to which the law of death—the law of entropy—so amply testifies.

Philonous: The very center then is just a single word: *death.*

Sophie: In essence that's the topic—you are right.

Philonous: ...and as a topic, let me say, it's certainly well chosen. For the awareness of our own approaching death will crucially inform the meaning we assign to our physical existence. Afterall, in order to establish meaning of whatever kind we must be able to perceive some guiding purpose or some goal to which we can aspire. In other words, we must be oriented consciously from our present thoughts and actions to a future state that we encounter as a hoped for possibility.[40] By implication, the prospect of a final termination that reduces our future to a finite stretch of time is bound to have a very sobering effect. If nothing will be left of our life's experience and aspiration, then ultimately nothing is worth living for. We can of course envision our deeds and our hopes to live on in our children, our children's children, and some latter day perhaps in creatures more advanced than current human beings. But regardless of how far these remnants will extend, the specter of a universal freeze still looms as our final destination.

Sophie: It is depressing, isn't it? Everything we humans have accomplished and everything we ever have endured can only sink into oblivion as our universe is forced to lawfully disintegrate. What bothers me of course is not that universal death will terminate all pain but that the pain we struggle with can have no purpose other than to vanish. I cannot think of anything more harrowing than the idea that all the tales of misery on planet Earth may only have been told to be eternally forgotten.

Philonous: The thought is clearly not a cheer, but neither is it forced on us. For while it may be true that our universe in its entirety is headed for decay, it also may be true that our common *human* fate may be a little brighter.

Sophie: What do you mean—it may be brighter?

Philonous: I mean that your assessment is so bleak because your view, apparently, is strictly modernistic.

Sophie: I don't agree because a death will always be a final termination quite regardless of a person's point of view, be it modern or postmodern or traditional or otherwise.

Philonous: What ends in death undoubtedly is our physical existence. But don't you think we also have a soul?

Sophie: The notion is archaic.

Philonous: —from a *modern* point of view.

Sophie: I am a little disappointed I must say that after all the thoughts that we have here exchanged on matters of importance you cannot offer anything more promising than such a puerile appeal. It plainly is ridiculous to think that somewhere in a human being there might dwell a soul that can transcend the bounds of physical existence. No evidence for such a claim has ever been convincingly established.

Philonous: Your attitude is biased, not informed: the evidence is there and has been frequently recorded. The question merely is if you are willing to accept it.

Sophie: What evidence, if I may ask, are you referring to?

Philonous: To formulate my answer most effectively it may be best to share with you a story from a paper that I chanced upon not long ago. It was reported by a nurse in a hospital in Holland and is pertaining to a patient with a cyanotic heart defect who had entirely lost consciousness:

> "During a night shift an ambulance brings in a 44-year-old cyanotic, comatose man into the coronary care unit. He had been found about an hour before in a meadow by passers-by. After admission, he receives artificial respiration without intubation, while heart massage and defibrillation are also applied. When we want to intubate the patient, he turns out to have dentures in his mouth. I remove these upper dentures and put them onto the 'crash car'. Meanwhile, we continue extensive CPR [which is the acronym for 'cardiopulmonary resuscitation']. After about an hour and a half the patient has sufficient heart rhythm and blood pressure, but he is still ventilated and intubated, and he is still comatose. He is transferred to the intensive care unit to continue the necessary artificial respiration. Only after more than a week do I meet again with the patient, who is by now back on the cardiac ward. I distribute his medication. The moment he sees me he says: 'Oh, that nurse knows where my dentures are'. I am very surprised. Then he elucidates: 'Yes, you were there when I was brought into hospital and you took my dentures out of my mouth and put them onto that car, it had all these bottles on it and there was this sliding drawer

underneath and there you put my teeth.' I was especially amazed because I remembered this happening while the man was in deep coma and in the process of CPR. When I asked further, it appeared the man had seen himself lying in bed, that he had perceived from above how nurses and doctors had been busy with CPR. He was also able to describe correctly and in detail the small room in which he had been resuscitated as well as the appearance of those present like myself. At the time that he observed the situation he had been very much afraid that we would stop CPR and that he would die. And it is true that we had been very negative about the patient's prognosis due to his very poor medical condition when admitted. The patient tells me that he desperately and unsuccessfully tried to make it clear to us that he was still alive and that we should continue CPR. He is deeply impressed by the experience and says that he is no longer afraid of death. 4 weeks later he left hospital a healthy man." [41]

Sophie: The story, I admit, is very much intriguing, but my suspicion somehow is you took it from a tabloid. [42]

Philonous: Your attitude is biased, as I said. The source in question is *The Lancet*, a highly reputable medical journal published in Great Britain.

Sophie: And therefore I should now believe that consciousness can take on disembodied forms? For that, it seems, is what you are implying: a patient's soul departs from its material encagement at the point of death and thereby is enabled to perceive a busy scene when all the while the patient's body shows no signs of life.

Philonous: Since you apparently are disinclined to buy it, you should perhaps attempt to give a better explanation. Afterall, the facts must somehow be accounted for.

Sophie: Frankly speaking I am not persuaded yet that there are really any "facts." A single anecdote does not establish an inductive base from which to draw reliable conclusions.

Philonous: If the story that I quoted were an isolated oddity, your point would clearly be well taken, but such is not the case. Occurrences involving claims to disembodied mental states and extrasensory perceptions are nowadays a commonplace. For as technology advances, the likelihood for resuscitations to succeed increases, and the number of near-death experiences therefore grows accordingly. This is not to say of course that every patient who at some point underwent a total loss of vital signs will be reporting afterwards on travels into altered states of being and awareness. But the proportion of such cases has consistently been found to be significant. In the study from the *The Lancet*, for example, a near-death experience (NDE) was reported by 62 (or 18%) out of a total of 344 resuscitated patients.

Sophie: So are you telling me that there are many documented cases of ex-

trasensory perception that can be verified by matching, say, the details in
a given patient's story with the facts observed by other people at the scene?

Philonous: I am indeed, because reports as these are really legion.[43] According to the Swiss-American psychiatrist Elisabeth Kübler-Ross, more than
twenty-five thousand accounts of NDEs had been collected from around the
world by the late nineteen nineties, and the total number of such cases—
recorded or not—apparently is in the millions.[44] Not all of these, as I admit,
contain descriptions of events that can be verified directly, but all the same
the numbers are impressive.

Sophie: Kübler-Ross?

Philonous: She was a well respected expert in the field and author of a famous
book *On Death and Dying.*[45]

Sophie: Please give me more details. What was her work about?

Philonous: Well, it all began in 1965, when four of her students, at the University of Chicago, approached her with the thought to study the experience of
dying for a paper that they had to write on "crisis in human life." Having
just accepted a position at the University's hospital, Kübler-Ross suggested
that the problem might be best addressed by trying to get interviews with
patients who were terminally ill. Initially, her plan was met by serious resistance from the doctors and the staff, but in the end she did succeed and
managed to gain access to a patient who was dying. Little did she realize
that she had thereby gotten started on a journey that would truly change
her life—hers and that of many others. For after this original encounter
with a patient close to death she soon established a permanent seminar
that, over the years, has been attended, not only by a multitude of students in related major fields, but also by physicians, nurses, clerics, and
professionals of many different kinds. In the further course of her research,
Kübler-Ross went on to meet and speak with patients at all stages of the
dying process, and of the many interviews that she recorded some were
later published in that famous book of hers to which I just alluded.

Sophie: But what about the issue of near-death? Did she arrive at any definite
conclusions?

Philonous: "Definite" may be too strong an attribute to use where regions
of reality come into play that are on principle beyond the reach of our
ordinary matter-bound perception. All the same, however, it's certainly
worth noting that, according to Kübler-Ross, human life is not confined to
physical existence. Our body, she believes, is but a mere "cocoon, which
we inherit for a certain number of months or years, until we make the
transition called death."[46]

Sophie: That is to say, she did conclude that death is not a final destination
but rather the beginning of a different form of life—a change in state.

Philonous: She did indeed, because to her the testimony of the many patients
that she met established evidence that ultimately couldn't be rejected. A

case in point in this regard was her acquaintance with a so-called Mrs. Schwartz.[47] This lady had been in and out of hospitals repeatedly and had been close to death on several occasions. One day, when yet another crisis was occurring, Mrs. Schwartz was lying in some hospital in Indiana in a private room and was experiencing premonitions of her own, directly imminent demise. Feeling torn between a deep fatigue brought on by suffering through many bouts of illness in the past and a sense of duty to continue living for her family, she wavered for a moment and was hesitant to call for help. Incidentally, however, at this very instant a nurse came in and quickly recognized the gravity of her condition. As the nurse was rushing out to organize emergency assistance, Mrs. Schwartz could suddenly perceive herself to be adrift, floating peacefully to a position right above her lifeless body on the bed. With her awareness thus transferred to extrasensory perception she was enabled to observe how one by one the members of the resuscitation team appeared and set about their tasks. Amazingly, she watched in great detail the medical proceedings and later on recalled the facts correctly.

Sophie: It was this testimony then that Kübler-Ross took as the basis for her claim that death is merely a transition?

Philonous: No, this story only was the first piece in a larger puzzle—the first of many cases that together constitute by now compelling evidence that human life and consciousness are not confined to physical existence.

Sophie: But if the evidence were really as compelling as you say, then shouldn't it be far more widely recognized? Shouldn't there be multitudes of scientists exploring it, and shouldn't it be also taught in our colleges and schools?

Philonous: Those are very good questions. So let's step back to take a broader view. There is a context here to recognize.

The Ghost in the Collider

In order to discern the "context" just alluded to, we need to take a moment to reflect how very far indeed scientific understanding in the modern era has progressed. Beginning from the speculations of Copernicus, concerning heliocentric planetary orbits, there has emerged within the past 500 years a vision of a universe of unbelievable complexity and size. Using giant telescopes and radio antennas, we have explored the deepest depths of space and time at distances too vast for anyone to fathom. The modern cosmos is a world in which a hundred billion galaxies each hold a hundred billion suns—a world where stars explode and stars collapse, where matter causes light to bend and black holes swallow matter up. And in the regions close to Earth we even have directly entered that immense domain with rocket ships and satellites. Man has landed on the Moon, robots have been sent to Mars, and spacecrafts have been taking photographs of all the major planets in the solar system.

Moreover, at the opposite extreme—the microcosm of the quantum realm—the progress has been equally impressive. Ever deeper did we moderns penetrate, from molecules and atoms to electrons and nuclei and finally to quarks. Great experimental and conceptual advances were achieved that in the end revealed how particles together with the forces they exert can constitute the world that our senses every day portray to us.

The story of this quest is one of intellectual adventures and ambitious projects of research that still continue to this day. Presently, for instance, a group of scientists is probing into matter yet a little deeper. Using the most powerful particle accelerator ever built, the Large Hadron Collider (LHC) at the CERN facilities in Switzerland and France, physicists are now conducting new, spectacular experiments by means of which they hope to solve some riddles still remaining. The nature of mass itself is to be determined, supersymmetries are to be explored, and perhaps even the extra dimensions predicted by certain theories of gravity are to be uncovered.

It is an undertaking of astonishing proportions: the accelerator ring is 27 kilometers long (17 miles), runs at a depth from 50 to 175 meters, and is lined with thousands of superconducting magnets, most of which weigh more than 27 tonnes. The total amount of liquid helium that is used to cool the magnets down to their operating temperature of about 2 degrees above absolute zero ($-271.25°C$ to be precise) is 96 tonnes.[64] At several points along the ring giant detectors are installed, in which particles such as the Higgs boson supposedly reveal their transitory being for the billionth part of whatever tiny fraction of a second one can manage to imagine. The ATLAS detector alone weighs more than 7000 tonnes, is 46 meters long, 25 meters high, 25 meters wide, and boasts a total of 100 million individual sensors.[65] No doubt, the LHC at CERN is a shining monument to modern man's technological competence, his engineering prowess and scientific genius—the splendid culmination and point of convergence of that great historical endeavor that is known as 'modern science'.

However, when we read a headline in the news pronouncing that the "World's Largest Superconducting Magnet Switches On, To Help Answer Universe's 'Big Questions'"[66] we cannot help but wonder how big a question someone here is asking if the answers that are found most certainly will not explain how we can ever have a thought or feel a pain or will to move a hand. Nor is it very obvious why data produced by a machine of such fantastic complexity as the LHC, a machine that perhaps no single human being completely understands in all its intricate details, should be considered more trustworthy a guide to knowledge of reality than thousands of perfectly intelligible stories told by thousands of perfectly ordinary people who so happen to have experienced disembodied states of consciousness.

To be sure, the achievements of modern particle physics at the level of theory, experiment, and engineering are absolutely stunning, and the research at the LHC especially is very much admirable. There also is no reason whatsoever to be doubtful concerning the realities that such research reveals—they are remote, even utterly remote, but realities they are no less.

That said, however, we also need to understand that the LHC at CERN not only is a most astonishing accomplishment but also is a final point of contraction. It is the current endpoint of a long historical development in the course of which reality was narrowed down further and further until it finally became so small that nothing was left but plain absurdity—namely the idea that our world in its entirety, including all of human life, can be contained within the formulas that specify the properties of subatomic particles like electrons and quarks. In other words, it really is a stretch to think that the proton beams at CERN contain more truths, or more important truths, than the countless stories told by ordinary men and women about ordinary everyday events that they observed while on the verge of dying. Why should we trust the data from the LHC more willingly than these directly verifiable accounts that testify to disembodied states of consciousness? Afterall, the matter really isn't that complex: a person undergoes a trauma, is totally unconscious, shows no signs of life, and yet is able to perceive events that even in a state of normal sensory activity would lie outside that person's field of vision. The evidence is plain and perfectly consistent with the further claim that consciousness is not a physical phenomenon and can as such detach itself from any kind of bodily enclosure.

So why don't we accept it? Because acceptance would imply that the pertinent conclusion concerning the existence of disembodied mental states will seem ridiculous in light of the historical authority of science? Or perhaps because the correlated question of whether human beings have a soul is insignificant compared to problems that pertain to Higgs bosons? Surely not. So something here is not quite right, but what exactly is it?

Sophie: It's strange, but I just had a really funny thought. I saw myself participating in a conference at which the very best and brightest physicists were all assembled to discuss how research at the LHC is going to advance their search for a final unifying theory—a theory of everything. Speaker after speaker was presenting insights of the most sublime sophistication on topics such as quantum gravity or supersymmetry or superstring cosmology. The ensuing discussions proceeded at a level so abstract and so refined that no ordinary mortal could ever hope to follow them. And then, at last, it was the final speaker's turn to give a summary report; and that speaker was—you guessed it—it was I. So here I go: I get up to the podium, I face the crowd, and I begin to talk. My object at the outset is to give a full account of everything I didn't understand—which pretty much is everything. Very clearly I explain that quantum gravity to me is just a mental cavity, that hyperactive symmetries are best kept in a cage, and that a superstring in my mind is a pretty looking cord. And so I go on rambling for a while, revealing ignorance of astronomical proportions, until at last I get on to the main part of my talk.

Philonous: Which is?

Sophie: 'Modern Physics in the Light of the Experience of Mrs. Schwartz'.

Philonous: Is this a scene from one of Beckett's plays—a modern theater of the absurd?

Sophie: No it isn't—not if you are right. For if indeed there is conclusive evidence that consciousness can sever all its links to physical existence, then certainly these brilliant physicists, assembled in my dream, should be intelligent enough to process and assess it. That is to say, it should be possible to make these clever people understand that there just cannot be a theory of everything unless that theory accounts as well for Mrs. Schwartz in disembodied form.

Philonous: I think you fundamentally misread the meaning of my claim. For when I mentioned 'evidence' or 'facts that need to be accounted for', I did so from the basic supposition that your attitude at bottom is conducive. Afterall, your choice to be engaged in our present quest bespeaks a certain openness of mind that indicates to me that you may be receptive.

Sophie: The way you put it makes me feel a little bit suspicious. Perhaps your case is not as solid as you claim, because a fact that is conditioned by my attitude—my inclination to receive it—is likely not a fact at all.

Philonous: But don't you realize that *no* fact ever is a fact without a subject to acknowledge it?

Sophie: Don't make it sound so philosophical and lofty—the matter currently at hand is rather more concrete.

Philonous: And what exactly do you deem that matter here to be?

Sophie: The central issue is your claim that there are clear objective facts that demonstrate that consciousness is non-material and can be disembodied.

Philonous: Notice, though, that in connection with that claim I never used the word "objective."

Sophie: No, you didn't—not directly—but implicitly you did because you said that there are facts that can be verified.

Philonous: ...by anyone who so inclines.

Sophie: ...by virtue of an attitude that is "conducive," such as mine?

Philonous: Precisely.

Sophie: Well then I simply say again that no fact really is a fact as long as it depends on my or any other person's attitude.

Philonous: Because a fact, by definition, is objective?

Sophie: Certainly.

Philonous: What would be an example?

Sophie: The perfect illustration here is yet again the falling of an object when we drop it. I know of course that you will raise immediately a host of dubious objections, but as it is I do believe the illustration to be fitting: I take an object in my hand, I drop it, and it falls. The fact is plain, and even you admitted it a little while ago "to be as close as [you] can ever hope to get to an event that laws control objectively" (p.129).

Philonous: And you are sure, as you just said, that my objections likely won't be piercing.

Sophie: Quite sure, because we have been through all this before. Most probably, you would contend that objects fall in space and time and that both of these—space and time—are mere conceptions and as such intrinsically subjective. In other words, if space and time did not exist, then nothing in them could be falling. And afterwards, perhaps, you would go on to question—as before—exactly how a falling object is in fact an object.

Philonous: As I recall, it wasn't I who questioned that. For it was you who pointed out, that in a person's stream of consciousness a falling body only is "a stereoscopic projection—a superimposition of two shifting color patches in a larger panoramic field" (p.40).

Sophie: That is correct, but in reply you said that you would "even go so far as to assert that the very notion of a material object in space is nothing but a theoretical construct."

Philonous: Which goes to show that we agree.

Sophie: ...but only superficially. For while I do admit that all such protestations can to some extent be technically justified, I don't consider them important. And in particular, I cannot see how presently my understanding of near-death phenomena would be advanced by giving any further thought to them.

Philonous: And at the level of deduction, I suppose, where facts are channeled by the force of reason into principles, called laws, my earlier remark that laws are strictly speaking not observed (p.129) and thus are only partially objective most likely left you equally dissatisfied.

Sophie: Let's say, it struck me as eccentric.

Philonous: If that is so, then I had better now come up with arguments a little more incisive.

Sophie: You'd better—I agree.

Philonous: Then let me start by re-examining the physical phenomenon that you have here brought up of bodies that are falling.

Sophie: As I said, the process in its basic form is perfectly transparent: I take an object in my hand, I drop it, and it falls. The fact is obvious and cannot be denied.

Philonous: Yet in itself this fact will not inspire us because no further insight from it can be drawn.

Sophie: True, but to make up for that, we only need to add a second object. That is to say, we take *two* metal balls—a big one and a small one, say—we drop them simultaneously and find that they descend in synchrony.

Philonous: The synchrony, however, won't be quite exact—the smaller ball will be a little slower.

Sophie: ...because the force of air resistance relative to gravitation will be larger for the smaller ball than for the bigger. But this disparity, of course, can be quite easily reduced by picking larger balls—a big one and a huge one, say.

Philonous: I understand, the force of air resistance is dependent in direct proportion on an object's surface area, and, by implication, for a ball of radius R it will be equal to the product of some scaling factor with R^2. The force of gravity, by contrast, is proportional to mass and therefore equal to some factor times R^3. In other words, if we are using balls consisting of the same material, then the relative effect of air resistance will indeed grow smaller as the balls grow bigger.

Sophie: And as we thus continue to perform experiments with varied objects and alternative conditions, we finally feel justified to claim inductively that universally all falling bodies close to earth descend at equal rates.

Philonous: ...if air resistance is negligible.

Sophie: That's right.

Philonous: And hence we have *objectively* established, so it seems, the law of falling bodies—that famous law that Galileo was the first to formulate.

Sophie: Philosophers, of course, will likely disagree, but from a practical scientific point of view, the inference is admissible no doubt.

Philonous: If that is so, then I suggest we now proceed to my presumably more tenuous deduction of the reality of disembodied states of consciousness from NDE accounts.

Sophie: Please do, but let me caution right away that, from the very outset, states of consciousness are somewhat less concrete—to put it euphemistically—than falling bodies.

Philonous: It certainly is true that no one has the slightest clue what consciousness might be, in and of itself—apart, that is, from one's direct experience of it—but just the same applies to mass or matter too. So let's not be unfair: the metaphysics, here as there, is ultimately equally elusive.

Sophie: It used to be that such remarks would startle me but they no longer do, and that's what frightens me.

Philonous: Why should my trivial statement startle you? Does anybody know what matter is as such? Of course not.

Sophie: There clearly is no point to argue here. So go ahead, convince me that my mind can float off and abandon me.

Philonous: It may depend on what you mean by 'me'. But that aside, the first step is to recognize the factual foundation. In other words, we must acknowledge that the NDE—as an experience—exists: people who survive a medical emergency involving total loss of consciousness do, at times, speak afterwards of travels into altered states of being and awareness. The only way that I can see to get around that *fact* is to assume that all the people who till now reported NDEs were members of a global grand conspiracy involving every people group and nation.

Sophie: Very well, I don't object: an NDE occurs, it is recalled, and then reported publicly. But what about the larger implication?

Philonous: Before we get to that, we should discuss how NDE-reports can be established to be valid.

Sophie: So that's the step when facts are matched with factual accounts.

Philonous: Indeed, we take a patient's near-death observations and compare them, say, with written protocols or oral eyewitness accounts concerning things that happened while the patient's vital signs had altogether ceased.

Sophie: And as we find, surprisingly, that there is very close accord, we venture to conclude that consciousness—objectively—can take on disembodied forms.

Philonous: At least, the claim to objectivity here is no less admissible than in the previous case of falling bodies.

Sophie: If only I agreed.

Philonous: I don't see why you wouldn't.

Sophie: The reason for my disbelief is mainly that a disembodied mental state, unlike a falling body, is not an object I can see or otherwise perceive. In other words, the evidence that you present is not direct but highly circumstantial.

Philonous: If you prefer, I can be less adventurous linguistically and speak of 'extrasensory perception' rather than of 'disembodied consciousness'.

Sophie: To merely change the verbiage won't do because perception independent of the senses is basically no less extravagant than consciousness afloat. What I want you to offer me is some initial comprehension.

Philonous: As far as comprehension is concerned, I can assure you, I have none. But that does not in any way prevent me from acknowledging the facts as I encounter them. If everyday events are 'seen' by people that are comatose, then I just cannot fail to recognize that perception and awareness can exist entirely apart from ordinary sensory activity—especially if these events lie sometimes far outside the waking field of vision. I don't know *how* it works but *that* it works I can and do concede.

Sophie: Is that indeed what happens? Are people able to recall events that they could not have seen if they had been awake?

Philonous: Of course, such cases have been documented carefully. The American medical doctor Michael Sabom, for example, once interviewed a patient who made detailed observations of the workings of a complicated medical instrument that couldn't have been visible to him from where he lay while undergoing surgery. And what is more, in other cases of this sort the patients could correctly recollect occurrences that happened far away in other rooms or places.[48] Still more astonishing, there have been people who were blind from early infancy and never had a memory of sight and who, in near-death states of consciousness, could suddenly perceive the world in light and dark and colors. Such people, I should add, may not be able to describe what they have seen in ordinary terms because they never learned to link a visual experience to language. But all the same we can discern from their accounts that they indeed were capable of sight while seemingly unconscious.[49]

Sophie: I must confess these details are confounding. If things are seen by 'spirit eyes' that are invisible to ordinary human eyes, then that eliminates at once the possibility that NDEs involve the common organs of perception.

Philonous: But look, even if there was some flicker of perception somewhere left, there really is no way that someone in a state of traumatizing crisis would ever feel at leisure to observe the details of his physical surroundings.

Sophie: So what is the solution?

Philonous: To grant that people speak the truth. There is no problem to be solved if only we are willing to accept that in an NDE a person's soul or spirit does indeed detach itself from physical existence. I do not know how such a thing is possible, but *that* it is possible and that it *does* explain the facts, I willingly admit.

Sophie: Your argument to some extent is certainly persuasive. But then again I wonder as before: why is it not accepted far more widely?

Philonous: Let's ask the question differently. Let's not determine first why recognition is withheld from NDE research, but why it's given much more readily to Galileo's claims concerning falling bodies. Why is the law that Galileo found so often thought to be entirely objective if here as well it is a *subject* that investigates, collecting facts and using rational abilities?

Sophie: Because the subject in the latter case is more or less irrelevant.

Philonous: And that is so because...

Sophie: ...all subjects will agree. Perhaps there are some people somewhere in this world who don't believe that falling bodies close to earth are really falling, but on the whole the issue isn't very much divisive.

Philonous: In stark contrast, I assume, to my assertion concerning the existence of paranormal states of consciousness.

Sophie: The contrast couldn't be much starker.

Philonous: In other words, the case of falling bodies is objective in the sense that any individual subjective influence is rendered insignificant in general across-the-board accord.

Sophie: I think you said it quite succinctly, and implicitly you thereby made it clear where your competing argument, concerning NDEs, is falling short most blatantly. For simply put, you cannot plausibly explain why even in the face of your presumably sound evidence most scientists around the world just won't believe in ghosts and won't accept your reasonings as valid.

Philonous: The problem, though, as I see it, is this: no argument will ever sway a person who refuses to be swayed. There are no facts that truly force belief.

Sophie: As I said, there may be always someone somewhere who will not agree, but, as regards the law of falling bodies, the group of such dissenters, I dare say, will be minute.

Philonous: With respect to this present era, you are right, but in the days of Galileo, the matter wasn't nearly as clear-cut. Back then, you see, the arbiter of scientific truth was not empirical experimental inquiry but rather the historical authority of Aristotle's writings.

Sophie: You mean back then most people didn't think that falling bodies fall?

Philonous: No, what they denied was only that they fall in synchrony. For according to Aristotle, the speed of falling bodies varied in proportion to their mass.[1] In other words, so it was thought, a body twice as heavy as another would descend at twice the rate.

Sophie: The notion is absurd. Even the most cursory of observations will at once reveal it to be false.

Philonous: ...to someone who believes in observation. Yet if my point of reference is an ancient philosophical opinion, I may not even want to take a look, or if I do, I may not be prepared to recognize an evidential weight.

Sophie: Are you saying then that I could drop two balls, the one of which is twice as heavy as the other, right in front of someone who adheres to Aristotle's view and not effect thereby a change in his or her opinion *even* as the balls are seen to reach the ground approximately simultaneously?

Philonous: I am indeed because that was in fact what happened back in history. For Galileo did just that—perform experiments before the very eyes of certain of his Aritotelian critics without affecting in the least the critics' well entrenched establishment beliefs. According to legend, he climbed the Leaning Tower of Pisa with cannon balls on his back to publicly conduct experiments on falling bodies. But whatever the setting of his demonstrations may have been, they did little to persuade an audience unaccustomed to the use of observation for the purpose of deciding what was thought to be a purely philosophical dispute. In his dialogue on the *Two New Sciences*, Galileo later commented on the critics' stubborn denial as follows:

> Aristotle says that a hundred-pound ball falling from a height of a hundred cubits hits the ground before a one-pound ball has fallen one cubit. I say they arrive at the same time. You find, on making the test, that the larger ball beats the smaller one by two inches. Now, behind those two inches you want to hide Aristotle's ninety-nine cubits and, speaking only of my tiny error, remain silent about his enormous mistake.[51]

---

[1] In his treatise *On the Heavens* Aristotle writes concerning this point that "the downward movement of a mass of gold or lead, or any other body endowed with weight, is quicker in proportion to its size."[50]

Sophie: So what exactly are you here implying? Are you trying to suggest that you yourself are Galileo's present day equivalent, a man who boldly argues for the truth against inflexible establishment beliefs?

Philonous: No, not I, but maybe those who first advanced the NDE research. Whether they will come to be regarded as great pioneers or minor figures contributing on a modest scale, I do not know. But either way, their work and their discoveries conceivably are functioning as catalysts in a larger process of historical proportion—a civilizational shift in consciousness away from what I like to call a crudely scientistic form of anthropocentric materialism toward a more synthetic vision of a peaceful soul-and-body/mind-and-matter harmony.

Sophie: Your vision is more hopeful than compelling but certainly not timid in its scope. And it is fair enough, for the phenomenon of disemdodied consciousness, conclusively established, would undermine the edifice of modern science at its very roots.

Philonous: I don't agree. What would be undermined would not be modern science but only our modern tendency to vastly overstate its competence and power.

Sophie: It seems to me you don't appreciate how downright radical the view you are expounding really is. For bluntly stated your contention is that unbeknownst to us a disembodied human ghost could be afloat right here and now above our heads and listen in on our conversation. To put it very mildly I would say that such a notion stands in brutal contradiction to each and every scientific proposition I have ever come across.

Philonous: Not at all. The proposition, for example, that we are descendants of some lower form of life, which clearly is a scientific one, not only doesn't stand "in brutal contradiction" but even is conducive to my view. For in a sense, the plausible existence of disembodied states of consciousness only highlights what we said before concerning evolutionary weak transcendence—namely that reality, most probably, includes domains that are entirely beyond the reach of human reason and perception.

Sophie: In other words, to creatures more advanced than we, in evolutionary terms, the very ghosts that we, for lack of cognitive ability, are forced to relegate to phantom-land transcendence, may be, in fact, a vividly apparent company.

Philonous: That is correct, but only if transcendence here is really of the weak variety—and that, of course, we cannot know. For the question whether or to what extent the notion of a disembodied consciousness can be contained within the range of future cognitive developments is unanswerable by default. It is conceivable that certain of its aspects fall within that range while others perhaps are of a kind that is transcendent strongly in the 'extra-natural' or 'extra-universal' sense. However, the only mode of thought available to us in matters such as these is freely flowing speculation.

Sophie: The earnestness of your response suggests that you did not detect the sense of playful irony that I intended to convey with my remark concerning ghosts in phantom land.

Philonous: The matter is more serious than that. Afterall, it was you who called attention to the fact that loss of meaning in the face of death is the crucial problem at the heart of our quest.

Sophie: I understand, but as I try to really get a grip on what you are proposing, the implications seem preposterous in the extreme. What you are asking me to do is not to readjust some loosely held opinions and assumptions but to totally recast my entire mental disposition. Perhaps you don't appreciate how very deeply tied I am to scientific ways of thinking.

Philonous: But then again this total change in sentiment precisely is what we are trying to achieve.

Sophie: It's just, I didn't bargain for that change to be so radical and sudden.

Philonous: I'm sorry, but I really cannot see how you can overcome the discontent you suffer from by means of minor realignments. There are some major choices to be made.

Sophie: It sounds like sensible advice, but nonetheless I find it rather unappealing. I much prefer to solely trust in reason and in facts than to engage in willful acts of choosing.

Philonous: As I said, my central argument is factual and can be verified by anyone who so inclines. But as I also said, there are no facts that force belief because a fact—to be a fact—must be *subjectively* received. Even falling bodies, as we saw, descend in synchrony only in a mind that is not otherwise conditioned or preoccupied. In other words, if you don't want to be convinced, then convinced you will not be. Reason can never prevail against a will that stubbornly opposes it.

Sophie: You may be right, but all the same I feel uncertain and confused. Adopting new ideas that challenge fundamentally my innermost beliefs concerning life and death and consciousness is very hard to do.

Philonous: That is to say, you really need a break.

Sophie: More than ever—yes, I do.

Turning Toward the Light

> Beloved Pan, and all ye other Gods who here are present, grant me to be beautiful in the inner man, and all I have of outer things to be consonant with those within. May I count the wise man only rich. And may my store of gold be such none but the temperate man can bear.[52]

In these words, which Plato in the *Phaedrus* attributes to Socrates as a prayer to the gods, there is expressed in beautiful poetic form the deep belief that man's essential self dwells in his soul—"the inner man"—and that his body, like a shell, is only an external casing.[53] For according to Plato's strictly dualistic view, the soul is not a mere appendage, as it were, that emanates from matter, but rather is a human being's central driving force or "source of movement."[54] "The soul is," as Plato writes in the *Phaedo*,

> most like that which is divine, immortal, intelligible, uniform, in-
> dissoluble, and ever self-consistent and invariable, whereas body is
> most like that which is human, mortal, multiform, unintelligible,
> dissoluble, and never self-consistent.[55]

Implicit in this thought is the idea that the polarity of soul and body also is a hierarchy: the soul as the eternal part is unmistakably the primary reality.[56]

In light of this belief there comes to mind quite readily the notion of a disembodied consciousness, as formerly discussed. Afterall, if there is indeed a spirit in us that will separate itself from our body at the point of death, then a clear dividing line between these two realities—mind and matter—soul and body—can plausibly be drawn; and Plato's dualism therefore offers us a viable perspective. Furthermore, this view appears to be compatible as well with the idea that consciousness in modern quantum physics is a necessary independent agent. However, the dualism in the latter case is softer in its hue than the Platonic (or Cartesian) one because its two defining poles appear to be endowed with overlapping attributes: mind and matter are alike and equally important to "the process of reality creation" (p.96). In other words, the dividing line is not a rigid demarcation—the polarity also is a unity.

Moreover, we must not forget that the dualities in question—as all conceptions formed in human minds—are irreducibly symbolic. That is to say, the mind-and-matter dichotomy is at bottom a linguistic one. For as we pointed out before on several occasions, we do not know and cannot know, not even distantly, what absolute realities there lie behind such symbols as 'mind' and 'matter' or 'soul' and 'body'. A cloud of ignorance surrounds us at all times and hides from our sight that inner realm of being-in-itself to which these words presumably are pointing. We speak of a duality, but when we further ask, "duality of what?", we really have no answer.

Trivial and repetitive as observations such as these may seem, they nonetheless directly bear on our present topic. For to express surprise or disbelief at the idea that consciousness can take on *dis*-embodied forms is only meaningful if the familiar, solidly embodied form admits of some initial comprehension. And since the truth appears to be that no one understands how matter can be conscious, we probably are well advised to keep an open mind. Why should we be surprised to learn that a human being's consciousness can be afloat below the ceiling of a room if we do not have any insight whatsoever into how a conscious being can in fact be conscious?

It is true, of course, that our everyday experience teaches us a habit of per-

ception which firmly ties the presence of a consciousness to physical existence.
In the ordinary flow of daily life, we seemingly are no less justified in claiming
that a conscious thing must first and foremost be a thing than in asserting
that a body when we drop it drops. As valid as this argument may seem,
we must not overlook that a habit of perception is not the same as insight
into causal correlation. Russell's famous chicken that has its neck wrung by
the very hands that it was used to seeing scatter feed in front of it, day after
day, has no more reason for surprise at such a sudden turn of fate than we as
humans have when faced with evidence that consciousness may not be always
matter-bound.[57]

To challenge these ideas, one could of course point out that studies of the
brain have brought to light a vast array of scientific facts that any well informed
discussion of the phenomenon of consciousness had better take into account.
And furthermore, who is to say where we will stand if research carries on into
the future for a thousand years? Is it not completely sensible to think that
future insights will reveal with perfect clarity how human brain activity creates
the conscious mind? The proper answer is, "It may seem sensible, but it is
not." To be sure, we do not know and cannot know how far our insight will
extend if our species undergoes an evolutionary leap in distant times to come,
that is, if we acquire superhuman intellects. But absent such an innovative
upgrade, we can be fairly confident that no research conducted presently or in
some future age will ever lift the central secret of the mind—the problem of
how symbols come alive.

To see exactly what this problem is about, we only need to ask this very
simple question: how will a future theory of consciousness, no matter how
advanced, be written down or otherwise encoded? The tempting answer, "We
don't know," is not correct because all human thought and language by their
very nature are symbolic. That is to say, whatever future theory there may
arise, it will be represented most assuredly by strings of symbols known as
'words' or 'mathematical notation' (see also p.119). Furthermore, to see why
this implies that consciousness most likely will forever be outside the reach of
human comprehension, we may want to agree that any such a theory should at
the very least allow us to determine whether and to what extent a given entity
or being is in fact a conscious one.[58] Put differently, it should be possible for us
to study that desired future theory word for word, symbol for symbol, and page
after page, and then to use the knowledge that we gained in order to decide if
any given individual is really sentient or just a robot in disguise. Are people
soulless aggregates that are controlled by some external agent, say, as God, or
are they really conscious and aware? Perhaps some are what they appear to
be while others are just biddable automata. How do we know? In other words,
the claim at present is that there can never be a theory of consciousness that
is complete or even relevant because, for reasons of principle, no such theory

can ever tell these two alternatives apart.[1]

To counter this claim we could perhaps assert that science in the future may be able to explain why any physical system of sufficiently advanced complexity and structure, such as a human brain, must needs be self-aware. But logically this notion is absurd because a scientific theory at bottom must be based on sensory perception. And as it is, in this regard the two scenarios of free-willed personhood and automated servitude are perfectly identical by definition. The way it works in more detail is this: we take a set of data that we have received through our senses—a set of observations, say, pertaining to a person who presumably is conscious—we transfer it into symbolic form by using words or mathematical notation, and then we further mold these symbols into theories by way of rational analysis. Finally, when all is done, we re-associate the symbols that the theories produced with our sensory perceptions so as to test the theoretical predictions and conclusions that we found. As plausible as this account may seem, the problem with it is that it is plausible in either case. For in purely physical terms, that is, in terms pertaining to perception (and thus including in particular all observable neuronal activities), the person and the robot are entirely alike. So how then can a theory distinguish between cases with regard to which the theory's inductive base is perfectly invariant?

Moreover, if human consciousness could truly be conveyed to us by symbols on a page, then so could be conveyed—presumably at least—the consciousness of animals as well. Afterall, the latter should be less complex and therefore easier to handle. Yet how would any string of symbols that we write, no matter how refined and intricate, be ever adequate to teach us what it's like—in actual experience—to be a chicken or a cat? It simply can't be done.

So as we come to understand that science is a scheme by means of which the stream of our sensory perceptions is encoded and then processed in symbolic form, we also come to realize that all scientific theories, by their very nature, are descriptive of the contents of that stream rather than the underlying consciousness in which that stream is first begot so as in fact to be a stream. For symbols simply are entirely non-actual. They never think a thought, they never feel a pain, and never are aware of anything at all.

It is this daunting imposition to capture and convey the true actuality of a conscious first-person experience by means of strings of symbols known as 'theories' that constitutes the utterly insoluble conundrum at the heart of all

---

[1] In [Tu], Alan Turing, proposed a test of machine intelligence according to which a machine, by definition, is intelligent if the answers it gives to questions posed by an interrogator are indistinguishable from those given by a presumably intelligent human being. If we applied the same type of test to the problem of distinguishing an actually conscious human being from a seemingly conscious puppet, we would have to conclude of course that the puppet is indeed conscious. In other words, the position we have chosen to adopt is precisely that a Turing-type test of consciousness is not sufficient to establish the sort of first-person actuality that the notion of consciousness by its very nature entails. For another argument in support of this position, the reader is referred to [Hee], pp.482–483.

attempts to comprehend scientifically, as it were, the personal experience of conscious comprehension. Indeed, a scientist who tries to understand by means of science how he or she can be conducting research consciously is no less odd an image to behold than a mathematician who aspires to demonstrate that his or her ability to understand geometry is also just a geometric fact.

Given these discouraging perplexities, it hardly is surprising that for most of the 20th century scientists pursuing research into consciousness were very few in number. Consciousness was just too nebulous a field for anyone to really get involved in it.[59] And even those who would assign to it a crucial role in quantum-physical ontology would not therefore consider it an object of empirical research. This picture of communal scientific abstinence remained intact until about the early 1990's when Francis Crick, the famous co-discoverer of the genetic code, chose consciousness to be his premier field of study. Together with his collaborator Christof Koch, Crick devised a radical reductionist agenda for research that aimed to understand all states of awareness strictly in terms of their physical correlates in the brain's neuronal processing. The programmatic statement framing this approach was provided by Crick himself in the opening sentences of his 1994 book *The Astonishing Hypothesis*:

> The Astonishing Hypothesis is that "You," your joys and your sorrows, your memories and your ambitions, your sense of personal identity and free will, are in fact no more than the behavior of a vast assembly of nerve cells and their associated molecules. As Lewis Caroll's Alice might have phrased it: "You're nothing but a pack of neurons."[60]

In other words, that innermost reality of man, the conscious self, where we experience the flow of life in thought, emotion, and perception, is but an excrement of matter.

A scientist who follows this approach can thereby circumvent the problem of distinguishing between a person and a robot in disguise because distinctions of this sort can simply be declared to be irrelevant. That is to say, the scientific optimist—to stay an optimist—must sacrifice that most essential quality to which any theory of consciousness, by definition, should pertain, namely the experience of really being conscious. Incredible as it may seem, a thinker of this sort is willing to reduce to nothingness the only world that he or she will ever know—the world of personal experience—if only he or she is thus enabled to uphold the modern philosophical fiction that science is potentially complete.

Yet willing he or she will only be, most probably, if he or she does not have any memory of ever having been in paranormal states. In other words, we rightly may suspect that even Francis Crick would likely feel less certain in his attitude, if he himself had undergone an NDE and thereby had experienced firsthand an episode of extrasensory perception. Having seen his body from a distance streched out on a bed, he surely would be less inclined to rigidly insist that consciousness can only be a property of matter.

Philonous: And very likely he would also be in other ways affected. For NDEs quite frequently involve much more than simple episodes of extrasensory perception. In a typical core experience, the initial phase of out-of-body observation is only the beginning of a larger odyssey. What happens commonly is that a tunnel suddenly appears through which a person's spirit travels to what seems to be a kind of heavenly domain—a realm of light. The moment when that realm is reached is one of utter ecstacy. The spirit now is in the presence of a divine being of light that powerfully emanates an aura of unselfishness and absolute acceptance. In fact, the light is so intense that it would blind an ordinary human eye, but to a spirit eye it is a source of sheer delight and beauty in its purest form. Other standard elements of such a core experience are meetings with deceased relatives, visions of pristine celestial sceneries, and a guided life review that shows how a person's actions here on earth affected other people.[61][II]

Sophie: Do you remember that fictitious conference of mine on LHC research?

Philonous: You mean the one where you delivered that surreal address in front of all those brilliant physicists?

Sophie: That's the one.

Philonous: I do remember it. But why do you refer to it?

Sophie: Well, the question just occurred to me how such a meeting would turn out if all of its esteemed participants would undergo the sort of full blown NDE that you have just described. Imagine all those Nobel laureates being sucked into a tunnel and then greeted by a spirit guide. How would, I wonder, that affect their intellectual ambition?

Philonous: That would be quite a sight: a tunnel to eternity packed full with disembodied theorists. And, yes, I think there is a chance that theorists in spirit form would be—as theorists—a little less ambitious. In fact, not only would they be more humble in their intellects, but very probably they also would feel prompted to rethink a host of fundamental attitudes regarding things that really are important. For studies strongly indicate that NDEs have long-term formative effects.[62] Most notably and commonly, the fear of death is far reduced, faith in an afterlife becomes more vivid, and values tend to shift, away from selfish goals and mere acquisitive pursuits, toward a more communal outlook of increased spiritual sensitivity and greater emphasis on empathy and personal relations.

Sophie: It's not surprising, I admit. For if indeed the destination we call death is not a final one, then very probably we will be more relaxed and not regard this present life to be the only chance for happiness we've got.

Philonous: I eagerly agree. The prospect of an afterlife can broaden our concept

---

[II]As Patrick Glynn aptly points out, NDEs are not always as pleasant as the standard case here described. For a certain percentage of these experiences seem to be genuinely hellish (see [Gl], p.129).

of reality so as to make us see this present world of scarcity and physical desire as an embedded one: what we refer to as 'the universe' is but an island in eternal seas—a sphere inside a sphere—a wrinkle in infinity. And so, as our spirit reaches for the waters on the far side of the temporal horizon, we feel more readily at liberty to loosen our grip—to let the struggles of this present life be struggles, the pains be pains, and to receive the joys with joy. There is no need to strenuously satisfy our every wish and craving if our earthly life is but a brief excursion on an everlasting trip. Nor do we need to meet the person next to us with apprehension as an enemy, if all of us in fact are fellow spirit travelers.

Sophie: Such visions can inspire us to live and think in ways thar are more wholesome and coherent. Yet looking at the base in fact, I feel uncertain still regarding its solidity. For even if I did admit that extrasensory perception in cases of near-death is verifiably occurring, I still could not be sure what happens when the threshold finally is crossed and near-death turns to death. Perhaps there is a soul in me that ventures on to different realms. But in the absence, as you aptly pointed out, of any comprehension, I may as well assume that there is not. In other words, no NDE will ever give me final reassurance.

Philonous: In that you certainly are right, but Kübler-Ross, for instance, sees the matter in a different light, because her "base in fact" is yet a little broader. She owns a written note that proves to her conclusively that life after life is a reality.

Sophie: A written note? From whom? A floating ghost?

Philonous: No, from Mrs. Schwartz—in resurrected form.

Sophie: I knew that you were up to something odd.

Philonous: Listen first before you judge.

Sophie: Fair enough—so what about that note?

Philonous: Well, as it turned out, this lady, Mrs. Schwartz, finally succumbed to her condition. She passed away just two weeks after her youngest son had come of age and her duties as a mother had been thereby satisfied. About ten months later, it so happened that Kübler-Ross reached an impasse in her work and felt a need to quit her death-and-dying seminar. The subsequent events she recollects as follows:

> The minister with whom I had worked and whom I loved very dearly had left. The new minister was very conscious of publicity, and the course became accredited.

> Every week we had to talk about the same stuff, and it was like prolonging life when it is no longer worth living. It was something that was not me, and I decided that the only way that I could stop it was to physically leave the University of Chicago. Naturally my heart broke, because I really loved this work, but not that way. So

I made a heroic decision. I told myself, "I am going to leave the University of Chicago, and today, immediately after my death and dying seminar, I am going to give notice."

The minister and I had a ritual. After the seminar we would go to the elevator, I would wait for his elevator to come, we would finish business talk, he would leave, and I would go back to my office, which was on the same floor at the end of a long hallway.

The minister's biggest problem was that he couldn't hear—this was another of my grievances. And so, between the classroom and the elevator, I tried three times to tell him that it was all his, that I was leaving. He didn't hear me. He kept talking about something else. I got very desperate, and when I am desperate I become very active. Before the elevator arrived—he was a huge guy—I finally grabbed his collar and said, "You're gonna stay right here. I have made a horribly important decision, and I want you to know what it is."

I really felt like a hero to be able to do that. He didn't say anything.

At this moment a woman appeared in front of the elevvator. I stared at her. I cannot tell you how this woman looked, but you can imagine what it is like when you see somebody that you know terribly well, but you suddenly block out who it is. I said to him, "God, who is this? I know this woman, and she is staring at me; she is just waiting until you go into the elevator, and then she will come."

I was so preoccupied with who she was that I forgot that I was trying to grab him. She stopped that. She was very transparent, but not transparent enough that you could see very much behind her. I asked him once more, and he didn't tell me who it was, so I gave up on him. The last thing I said to him was kind of, "Heck, I'm going over and tell her I just cannot remember her name." That was my last thought before he left.

The moment he entered the elevator, the woman walked straight toward me and said, "Dr. Ross, I had to come back. Do you mind if I walk you to your office? It will only take two minutes." Something like this. And because she knew where my office was, and she knew my name, I was kind of safe, I didn't have to admit that I didn't know who she was.

This was the longest path I have ever walked in my whole life. I am a psychiatrist. I work with schizophrenic patients all the time, and I love them. When they were having visual hallucinations I told them a thousand times, "I know you see that Madonna on the wall, but I don't see it." I said to myself, "Elisabeth, I know you see this woman, but that can't be."

Do you understand what I'm doing? All the way from the elevator to my office I did reality testing on myself. I said, "I'm tired, I need a vacation. I think I have seen too many schizophrenic patients. I'm beginning to see things. I have to touch her, to see if she is real." I even touched her skin to see if it was cold or warm, or if the skin would disappear when I touched it. It was the most incredible walk I have ever taken, but not knowing all the way why I was doing what I was doing. I was both an observing psychiatrist and a patient. I was both at the same time. I didn't know why I did what I did, or who I thought she was. I even repressed the thought that this could actually be Mrs. Schwartz who had died and had been buried months ago.

When we reached my door, she opened it like I was a guest in my own house. She opened it with such an incredible kindness and tenderness and love, and she said, "Dr. Ross, I had to come back for two reasons. One is to thank you and Reverend Gaines." (He was a beautiful black minister with whom I had had this super-ideal symbiosis.) "To thank you and him for what you did for me. But the real reason I had to come back is that you cannot stop your work on death and dying, not yet."

I looked at her, and I don't know if I thought by then that this could be Mrs. Schwartz. I mean, this woman had been buried for ten months and I didn't believe in all that stuff. I finally got to my desk. I touched my pen, my desk and my chair, which was all real, you know, hoping that she would disappear. But she didn't disappear; she just stood there and stubbornly but lovingly said, "Dr. Ross, do you hear me? Your work is not finished. We will help you, and you will know when the time is right, but do not stop now, promise."

I thought, "My God, nobody would ever believe me if I told them about this, not even my dearest friend." Little did I know then that I would say this to several hundred people. Then the scientist in me won, and I said to her something that was very shrewd and a real big, fat lie. I said, "You know, Reverend Gaines is in Urbana now."

So far it was true; he had taken over a church there. But then I said, "He would just love to have a note from you. Would you mind?"

And I gave her a piece of paper and a pencil. You understand, I had no intention of sending this note to my friend, but I needed scientific proof. I mean, somebody who is buried can't write little love letters. And this woman, with the most human—no, not human—most loving smile, knowing every thought I had—and I knew, it was thought transference if I've ever experienced it—took this paper and wrote this note, which we naturally have framed in glass and treasure dearly. Then she said, but without words, she said, "Are you satisfied now?"

I looked at her and thought, "I will never be able to share this with anybody, but I am going to really hold on to this. Then she got up, ready to leave, repeating, "Dr. Ross, you promise," implying not to give up this work yet. I said, "I promise." And the moment I said, "I promise," she left.

We still have her note.[63]

Sophie: And the moral of the story therefore is that immortality is a reality. Afterall, if the dead can rise and leave us notes, then who would dare to argue otherwise?

Philonous: I, for my part, clearly wouldn't, but you of course are welcome to be bolder.

Sophie: Against the indisputable factuality of written notes I also have no arguments to field.

Philonous: In other words, to you as well the story is persuasive.

Sophie: No, just aggravating and upsetting, because it leaves me in effect with nothing but a giant question mark. You see, before you shared with me this latest tale about the paranormal, I was recovering quite well from our previous talk and even felt a growing sense of hope. Upon reflection I saw promise in the thought that there could be conclusive evidence that humans have a soul that isn't just an "excrement of matter" (p.156). But now again I'm only filled with doubt.

Philonous: Your reaction is more negative than justified. Why do you disapprove of this most recent tale more strongly than of those I shared before?

Sophie: Because where people talk to people who are dead, I cannot help but wonder, "Who else will stick around to listen?" Are there any men or women of sound reason left that we are still in contact with? I have a hunch that in the presence of the living dead one will be left with quite a narrow company. Most people with scientific understanding will depart where reason is defied by phantoms from the netherworld.

Philonous: And what is worse, as we survey certain of the 'highlights' of our earlier discussions, the picture really is alarming: from *noitisop* and other concepts in reverse we moved to quantum verbal hybrids, then likened Heisenberg's and Newton's greatest deeds to the exploits of disoriented frogs, and finally, we even ventured to resolve the mind-and-matter philosphical enigma by emulating Eskimo vernacular. I think it fair and safe to say that

no one with an eductated mind can be exposed to such astonishing profundities and not take flight. So even absent any talk of floating ghosts or
other apparitions, our audience by now would likely be reduced to epistemic
anarchists and anti-science freaks.

Sophie: You make it sound a little humorous, but I must say this lack of
meaningful community, to me at least, is really quite distressing. You
see, a scientific proposition is supported by the weight of history, a long
chain of achievements in the past, and brilliant contributions from the
likes of Galileo, Newton, Heisenberg, and Einstein; and presently its truth
is still upheld by scientists around the world whose expertise is generally
recognized. A claim of science therefore rests on grounds that have been
solidly established. But what about a claim to paranormal apparitions?
What is the base on which we can assess the case of Mrs. Schwartz? Where
is the precedent, the intellectual authority, the scholarly tradition? Who
testifies to its validity?—An audience of one?

Philonous: It's true, of course, that Kübler-Ross in this case is the only witness
that we have, but credible her testimony is no less. Afterall, she is a woman
who has spent a large part of her long career in close proximity to suffering
and pain. Many people she supported in their time of greatest need, and
the face of death she saw in countless variations. She is not the proverbial
academic specialist who knows more and more about less and less until she
knows everything about nothing. Instead, her focus has been all along on
that which truly is essential—on that which we may aptly call the ultimate
realities of human life. So is it really plausible to think that a woman of such
elevated standing and exceptional maturity as Kübler-Ross would sit down
at her desk, write a fake note, frame it, and then claim to have received it
from a patient who no longer was alive? Did she suddenly regress and act
up like a child, vying for attention, or did she not perhaps just simply tell
the truth?

Sophie: I don't know. People do the strangest things for reasons that are often
hard to follow. Besides there are some inconsistencies in her account that
really make me wonder.

Philonous: Such as?

Sophie: Well, so far as I can tell, the minister whom Kübler-Ross had grabbed
while waiting for the lift was not aware of any Mrs. Schwartz. Kübler-
Ross saw her, but he did not. I do not know, of course, how visions work,
but even if I did accept that they can be selective in the sense that only
certain people see them at a time, I still would have a problem to explain
what happened afterwards. For suppose, for instance, that the minister
had followed Kübler-Ross and watched her in her office hand a piece of
paper and a pencil to a ghost that he himself did not perceive. What in
the world would he have seen? A pencil writing by itself, without a person
holding it? It is ridiculous.

Philonous: So your conclusion therefore is she simply made it up.

Sophie: As I said, I really do not know. But what I do know is that there is likely no consensus here that we can call upon for guidance.

Philonous: Your emphasis on social context and consensus, while understandable, is just a little too unbending for my taste and is beginning to appear more burdensome than helpful.

Sophie: To better understand where I am coming from, you may want to recall that you yourself once raised the question of how science can be viewed "as a dependable body of 'knowledge' despite the fact that we will never be able to perceive firsthand the vast multitude of physical phenomena that scientists throughout the ages have reportedly observed" (p.41). It seems to me the answer is that knowledge here is socially construed. We believe that planetary orbits are elliptic, not because we checked the data ourselves or verified in full detail how Newton's fundamental laws allow us to deduce this proposition using calculus, but instead because we trust the scholarly consensus that forms and formed the proposition's social base at present and in history. In other words, the claim to truth and factuality here rests on social sanction and authority and not on individual investigative scrutiny.

Philonous: The latter, though, the scrutiny, that is, must also not be wholly disregarded. For science vitally depends on it for novelty and pioneering stimulus. If there had never been a man like Galileo who defied the common wisdom of his day, relying only on his own exacting judgment, we still would live in Aristotle's geocentric universe and falling bodies still would not descend in synchrony. To us, at our present vantage point, Galileo is the founding father of a venerable scholarly tradition, but to many of his contemporaries he merely was a stubborn freak who rightly ended up in prison.

Sophie: So are you telling me, in other words, to venture forth courageously and seek the truth in freakish isolation?

Philonous: At the very least you should consider as an option the idea that communal contexts not only can define the truth but can as well conceal it. A case in point here is again the mental attitude that the medieval era forged and that prevented Galileo's Aristotelian critics even from acknowledging what could in fact be plainly seen: the simultaneous falling of two objects when we drop them.

Sophie: By implication then, the breaking of communal bonds, in your view, is a necessary stage in bringing forth a genuinely innovative view. That is to say, the isolation that I fear is but the burden of the pioneer.

Philonous: In essence, yes, although the pioneers, of course, are not the two of us but those who first discovered and examined NDEs and other such phenomena.[III]

[III]Examples of similar phenomena are laboratory studies of out-of-body experiences.

Sophie: But you advise we follow where they lead.

Philonous: Certainly, because, as I see it, the base in fact is really very solid: there are thousands and even millions of people in this world who have experienced firsthand how souls depart from bodies at the point of death. Why should I trust that vast communal testimony any less than, say, the research data from the LHC? We have been through all this before, but just consider once again how very strange it is to think that the existence of a Higgs boson, inferred from complicated measurements on proton beams, should seem to us more credible a claim than the reality of disembodied mental states, inferred from simple common sense comparisons of facts and factual accounts. Do we reject the latter claim solely because it's currently unpopular in academic circles? If we do, we may as well join in with Galileo's Aristotelian critics and shake our heads at the silly demonstrations of an upstart mathematician who was so arrogant as to assume that he could overthrow a grand tradition in philosophy by simply dropping cannon balls.

Sophie: Your tone of voice betrays a certain sense of urgency. You clearly feel the issue is important.

Philonous: Absolutely, yes I do, because belief in immortality, unlike a Higgs boson, can change a person's life. As time expands to limitless eternity all sentiments and attitudes are bound to be profoundly altered and affected. The steps we take, the words we speak, the deeds we do and those that we aspire to, they all will be revalued and transformed. In fact, if Kant was right in this regard, then faith in everlasting life is even at the root of any moral action. In the *Critique of Pure Reason*, for instance, we read that "the practical interests of morality" require "the assumption... of God, Freedom, and Immortality,"[67] and later in the same work Kant describes his attitude as follows:

> [M]y belief in God and in another world is so interwoven with my moral nature, that I am under as little apprehension of having the former torn from me as of losing the latter.[68]

Sophie: In other words, that Kantian belief, to which we previously alluded, is finally beginning to appear more substantive and lively.

Philonous: ...as lively as can be, as I would say, because what really is behind all this is that intensely loving light that often greets the soul in core-experience encounters. For our hope for immortality, of course, is not in Kantian philosophy but rather is precisely in this light—the light of God—the light of Christ—the light that many people close to death reportedly have entered. It is this heavenly illumination—this brilliant otherworldly radiance—for which we reach in faith and with which we long to be united.

Kübler-Ross, for instance, testifies to one such experience in [Kub2], p.100.

How Aristotle Lost His Final Cause

If *Philonous* had it right when he insisted that awareness of eternity and immortality affects our every thought and action, then surely it affects as well and in particular the journey through the history of science and philosophy that we are presently embarked upon. This history itself, of course, cannot be altered arbitrarily but our way to look at it is clearly open to adjustment. The vital question, though, is "how?" How do we reconceive that history against a backdrop of infinities that far exceed the universe of space and time to which we currently are bound? Or how for instance is the purpose of the knowledge that this history produced to be appraised or re-appraised in such a larger scheme? What meaning do we give to science and the world that it reveals if we believe that world to be embedded in a whole that vitally transcends it?

In order to address questions such as these that are of daunting magnitude and never to be answered with conclusiveness, it may be best to look for guidance to the works of thinkers from the past—thinkers who were active in a time when faith in God and immortality in scholarly communities was still more prevalent than nowadays. A case in point here was the faith that Plato had in the existence of an "inner man" (p.152), or soul, that is akin to the divine and therefore is immortal. But even more significant in this regard, as we shall see, are the ideas of Plato's greatest student—the philosopher *par excellence* that everybody knows as *Aristotle*.[1]

Aristotle was born in 384 B.C. in the town of Stageira in Thrace, a region that today is part of northern Greece. His father, Nicomachus, belonged to the guild of the sons of Aesculapius[70] and worked as a physician at the court of King Amyntas II of Macedon. At the age of seventeen or eighteen, Aristotle moved to Athens where he became a student of Plato's at the Academy.

Subsequent to Plato's death in 347 B.C., Aristotle left Athens for Assos in Asia Minor where Hermias, the ruler of Atarneus, had established a branch of the Academy some years prior.[71] When Hermias fell victim to treason and was carried off by the Persians to be tortured and killed, his school of philosophy was dissolved. In consequence, Aristotle fled to the island of Lebos together with Pythias, the niece of Hermias, who soon thereafter became his wife.

In 342 B.C., he was invited by King Philip of Macedon to take on the education of the king's son Alexander—the boy to whom posterity awarded the epiteth 'the Great' for his far-flung military conquests. Following Alexander's coronation in 336 B.C., Aristotle returned to Athens to establish the *Lyceum*, a school of his own which in essence was an early model of the modern university.

---

[1]Aristotle's views on immortality are somewhat obscure and have been subject to considerable debate. Roughly speaking, Aristotle does not believe the human soul to be immortal but instead maintains a conception of an Active Intellect that survives physical death in a sort of deindividualized form from which all memory of personal existence has been erased. However, the details of his doctrine need not concern us here as other parts of his metaphysical thought are going to be of greater interest to us.[69]

The *Lyceum* was equipped with a large library, housed extensive collections of scientific artifacts, and offered a regular routine of lectures and instruction.

In 323 B.C., when the death of Alexander precipitated a hateful reaction in Athens against Macedonian influence, Aristotle quickly came under attack for his formerly close association with the deceased leader and was accused of impiety. Unlike Socrates, however, he decided to flee, "lest the Athenians should sin against philosophy for the second time,"[72] as he supposedly commented. Only one year later, however, in 322 B.C., an illness struck him down in exile, and shortly thereafter he died.

Aristotle's fall from grace was neither the first nor the last of its kind, but the victim in this case was probably among the most oustanding to ever have suffered such a fate. For without undue exaggeration it may be said that in the history of science and philosophy Aristotle's works are unsurpassed in their breadth of scope and force of originality. Starting from logic as the basis and the lawful form of human thought, Aristotle wrote extensively on such varied fields as physics, astronomy, cosmology, meteorology, zoology, psychology, metaphysics, ethics, politics, and even literature and rhetoric. Never before had knowledge been presented in as systematic and as comprehensive a form as in Aristotle's writings.

Turning to the content of these works, we notice that already at the very foundation, that is, in Aristotle's treatises on logic, there is a clear distinction to the strictly rational approach that Plato took to knowledge. For Aristotle recognizes as a valid means for drawing a conclusion not only the rational deductive approach, but also the empirical inductive one from sensory particulars to universal claims. In his *Topics* for instance we read that

> [i]nduction should proceed from individual cases to the universal and from the known to the unknown; and the objects of perception are better known, to most people if not invariably.[73]

And an even stronger affirmation of the use of sense-perception in the generation of knowledge we find in the opening sentences of the *Metaphysics:*

> All men by nature desire to know. An indication of this is the delight we take in our senses; for even apart from their usefulness they are loved for themselves; and above all others the sense of sight.[74]

The man who wrote these lines was clearly not an otherworldly mystical idealist but was instead a scientist. To be sure, Aristotle never placed himself in direct opposition to Plato in the sense of personal antagonism or even open enmity, as he always held his former teacher in the highest possible esteem. But being more pragmatic than the latter in his attitude he also was more readily inclined to let his reason be informed by input from experience.

Figure 3.2: *The School of Athens* with Plato and Aristotle at the center.

This fundamental difference in philosophical temperament between the younger and the older man was captured very vividly by Raphael in his depiction of *The School of Athens* (Figure 3.2): at the center of the painting we see Plato pointing upwards to the heavens or some far away transcendent realm, and Aristotle next to him is gesturing to keep the focus closer to the ground (Figure 3.3).

Figure 3.3: Detail from *The School of Athens*.

In order not to cause any misunderstandings, we need to emphasize as well that when we spoke just now of Aristotle as a scientist we did not have in mind the more restricted modern meaning of this word but rather the traditional conception of a natural philosopher. In other words, Aristotle certainly was not a modern-type reductionist or scientistic atheist. He was dedicated to empirical inquiry but also open to religious aspiration. This attitude is evident especially in the solution he proposed to the problem of change.

In Plato's thought, as we discussed (p.103), this problem was resolved by means of a dualistic conception in which an eternal realm of Ideas of perfect Parmenidean permanence was juxtaposed to an Heraclitean material world of never-ceasing flux. But how exactly are these two domains of spirit and matter supposed to interact? What causal efficacy do we assign to the realm of Ideas in respect of the world of matter? Aristotle's terse reply is "none whatsoever." For if indeed the realm of Ideas is strictly distinct from the world of matter, then the existence of the former clearly cannot help us to explain how change might be effected in the latter. That is to say, the abstract forms in Plato's dualistic ontology are nothing but ineffectual copies of actual physical objects and are, as such, completely superfluous.[75]

Having thus criticized Plato's pertinent position, Aristotle goes on to assert that change implies movement and that every movement has a cause. However, as he further on inquires what cause in turn this cause might have, there opens up before him an infinite regress from movement to movement and cause to cause. Faced with this dilemma, he is led to postulate the existence of an ultimate first cause which is itself unmoved and therefore needs no further cause to draw upon. Thus, all movement and change in the universe has its ontological point of origin in an Unmoved Mover whom Aristotle took to be God.

As a matter of course, the question that immediately arises here is how this God who is unmoved can be in turn the cause of any change or motion. Is not the notion of a mover who is motionless inherently absurd? To this Aristotle responds by developing his theory of the emergence of the real in the process of actualizing form in matter: each existing thing—such as a horse—has a perfect form—the ideal of 'horseness'—to which it strives as the goal of its existence. Consequently, this process of realizing form in matter can be interpreted as a striving toward the perfection of which the Unmoved Mover Himself is the ideal manifestation.[II] In other words, the role of God in phenomenal reality is not to act but to passively attract. God causes change and motion not by changing or moving Himself but by being the object of desire to which the real aspires as its flawless image of perfection. The Unmoved Mover, as it were, does not provide the impetus that brings about a temporal succession of events but rather constitutes an ontological first principle—a ground of being—whose ideal purity the physical world of matter and motion is driven to seek.

Closely linked to these ideas concerning the emergence of the real in the process of imprinting form upon matter is Aristotle's influential theory of cau-

---

[II]It may be argued that at this point in Aristotle's philosophy form again assumes a degree of independence that is reminiscent of the strict transcendence of Plato's realm of Ideas. Störig, for instance, remarks in this context that the Aristotelian forms and the Platonic Ideas look very much alike.[76]

sation. For in order to fully understand a thing, so Aristotle says, we not only need to identify its matter and form, that is, its material and formal cause,[III] but also its efficient and its final cause, that is, the process or the means by which it came into existence and the purpose that it serves. A house, for instance, is made of certain materials, such as wood or stone, has a certain form, as expressed in its plan, was built by workers using certain tools, and serves a certain purpose, namely to protect its dwellers from the elements. According to Aristotle, these four causal modalities—the material, formal, efficient, and the final one—are complete and universally applicable. Furthermore, in the context of this scheme, the Aristotelian God—the Unmoved Mover—simultaneously represents the ultimate formal, efficient, and final cause of all that exists. For He not only instantiates the ideal of perfect *form* but also *efficiently* draws all being towards it and in so doing defines the attainment of that perfect form as the *final good* and *purpose* of existence. In other words and for example, a horse becomes a horse by being drawn to emulate divine perfection in expressing the ideal of 'horseness' as the goal of its development from matter to form. Its individual reality arises, so to speak, as 'horseness' is imprinted upon matter.

This latter thought, of course, may seem to our modern minds obscure and highly unconvincing, but there are elements in it that clearly are important. The first of these is the idea that universal facts or properties can be inferred inductively from observations of particulars. We come to truly know what horses are as we encounter them and recognize their commonalities as 'horseness'. A modern scientist today still does the same when he or she derives a general hypothesis or universal law from observations of particular phenomena. Furthermore, implicit in the use of such inductive reasonings there is the underlying supposition that the material particulars that make up the inductive base—the horses that we see—are fully real. The truly actual here is the thing, not its ideal as Plato would have taught.

For clarity we need to add that Aristotle fully understands the crucial role that universals play as objects of our knowledge. But at the level of ontology it is the physical particular—the horse that we perceive—that he endows with genuine reality. For universal forms in Aristotle's scheme do not exist *apart* from matter, as they did in Plato's thought, but only in conjunction with it—the one exception being God. The Unmoved Mover is a pure and perfect form and nothing but a form. But other than that, reality will always be a mix in which matter and form are inextricably entangled: matter provides form with the occasion for becoming actual, and form in turn provides matter with the structure it requires to develop its potential. That is to say, matter and form—the potential and the actual—are the midwifes of all immanent existence.

[III] Aristotle here employs the word 'cause' to signify a factor or a condition in the absence of which a thing cannot exist.

Interestingly, the notion here implied that neither matter nor form are fully real in isolation and that the former in particular is by itself no more than abstract possibility establishes a solid link to modern quantum physics.[77] For according to Heisenberg, as we recall (p.74), a particle such as an electron merely signifies "a possibility for being or a tendency for being" to develop. In other words, just as matter as such—the primary Aristotelian substance, devoid of any form—is only a potential for the being of a thing, so a quantum probability wave is descriptive merely of the various possibilities for a particle to become manifest in conscious observation. Moreover, the inherent stochasticity of quantum physical events has here its proper analogue in Aristotle's view that matter isn't merely passive but rather actively exerts a randomizing influence. Matter will inherently oppose the forces that give form to it and thereby introduce an element of chance that accounts, at a very fundamental level, for the imperfection and indeterminacy of physical reality.

Another parallel that we can draw is linked to the idea that underlying quantum law there is the purpose to facilitate the mind-and-matter interplay (p.96). For this idea directly bears on Aristotle's teaching on causation: no explanation is complete unless we have identified an end for the sake of which a thing or a phenomenon exists—there always is a *final cause* to be accounted for. Put differently, the final cause of quantum law, so it appears, is to create that fuzzy space of cloud-like possibility that conscious agents need in order to communicate and interact with matter.

This notion, to be sure, cannot be said to be 'scientific' by contemporary standards. For modern scientists have long since given up on any kind of final purpose or intent. We moderns do not search for meaning anymore but only for relations that are formal and abstract. If we are asked, "*Why* does the world exist?" we merely draw a blank. But ask us *how* the world's appearances are mutually linked, and promptly we pull out a catalogue of theories and formulas. Indeed, this ban upon the final cause may very well be said to be a hallmark of the whole of modern science. And what is more, the final cause is not the only victim. For once we take a closer look, we quickly realize that in effect the only cause that we have left is the efficient one.

At first, of course, this broader claim appears to be preposterous, as even modern people still believe that things have *forms* and do consist of *matter*. But the key to understanding is the fact that modern science by its very nature is symbolic. That is to say, the final objects of scientific knowledge are the mathematical formalisms that physicists employ to model their experiments. Is there a form? Is there a substance? Perhaps, but all we really know are quantitative symbols and the rules of transformation that apply to them. A wave function in quantum mechanics, for instance, is a symbolic mathematical representation that is *efficiently* transformed into another such representation by being fed into a corresponding wave equation. And since the symbols themselves are directly or indirectly representative of sensory perceptions, it follows that, in essence, we have nothing left but certain rules for the *efficient* transformation of patterns of perception.[IV]

There is no doubt that this reduction in the modes of causal explanation is a truly revolutionary step. Where knowledge is construed as symbol correlation there has occurred a vital loss of aspiration. The modern scientist no longer is concerned with final causes or intents because the formulas that he or she employs are perfectly devoid of them. In other words, no final cause is ever in the realm of scientific *knowledge*. However, the fact that we do not and cannot *know* for sure if indeed the laws of nature were designed with a higher end in mind need not deter us from *believing* that they were. And what is more, the contemplation of the possibility of there being such an end may very well enable us to reach the goal that we are after (p.165). That is to say, it may enable us to figure out how faith in immortality and otherworldly spirit realms should alter our view of science and its history. Is it not conceivable that the interpretive re-introduction of purpose into nature's code of law is here the key to proper reappraisal?

Sophie: It is conceivable, no doubt. But what about that faith in all those otherworldly realms that all of this depends upon? So far as I can tell, I haven't yet adopted it. But even if I had, the notion of there being purpose in scientific law would not be positively linked to it.

Philonous: It wouldn't? Why is that?

Sophie: Look, it is one thing to agree that quantum law is what it is in order to facilitate the interaction of my mind with matter. But it is an altogether different thing to search for meaning, for example, in the law of entropy— the law of death. The notion that this latter law is meaningless is bad enough, but even worse would be to think that somewhere in a higher realm there is a God who once maliciously designed it with intent and full awareness of its awful consequence. What comfort do I draw from the idea that suffering and death are not by chance but by design? Or why should I feel heartened at the thought that matter has been engineered to interact with consciousness if any conscious witness in a world of ever growing entropy can only be a witness to decay?

Philonous: The first thing you should note is that the law of suffering and death becomes the law of suffering and only suffering if immortality indeed is a reality.

Sophie: True, but your objection carries little weight unless I somehow can feel certain that the afterlife is more appealing than this present life. Yet if indeed there is a God who purposefully gave this world a set of laws that

---

[IV] In this context Heisenberg comments that "[t]he final equation of motion for matter will probably be some quantized nonlinear wave equation for a wave field of operators that simply represents matter."[78] In other words, the holy grail of physics—the so-called theory of everything—will in effect be nothing but a rule for the transformation of symbolic functional representations.

in effect would render it a living hell for many or most of its inhabitants,
then why would I look forward to the company of such a God in His eternal
netherworld? The prospect doesn't seem exactly that inviting.

Philonous: "A living hell" is rather harsh a phrase to use.

Sophie: Let's not be kidding now. The tale of misery that we refer to commonly
as human history is black in even its most cheerful hue. Where do we start,
where do we end? The sea of horrors is of vast extent: from rapes and
murders and a host of other 'ordinary' crimes it stretches out to genocides
and ethnic cleansings, to concentration and extermination camps, and on to
countless tortures and brutalities that are too sickening to speak about. In
fact, no small proportion of the worst atrocities was eagerly committed by
the very people who believed that theirs was the cause of a just and loving
God. In other words, that Christ was followed by the Spanish Inquisition
was sadly not in any way surprising.

Philonous: I notice, though, that all the horrors that you listed were inflicted
not by God but by His creatures on each other. Perhaps the "living hell"
is not without but is within—perhaps what is at fault is not divine intent
but human sin.

Sophie: There is a hell in every human heart—I know—but why would that
be so? Because we all choose evil for the fun of it? Or is it not instead the
case, as I explained before (p.134ff), that evil in a world of scarcity induced
by lawful energy diffusion is deeply structural and therefore inescapable?

Philonous: Your claim then is, if I correctly understand, that we are what we
are because the world is what it is by virtue of its maker's lack of virtue.

Sophie: Assuming that there is indeed a maker.

Philonous: But granted that assumption your contention is that purpose in
this maker's mind is mostly and most probably despicable in kind.

Sophie: At least I cannot see what other option there might be. If evil always
could be traced to human moral failure, it would in principle be possible,
as you implied, to put the blame for its existence on ourselves. But such is
not the case. The world is rotten to its core regardless of all human choice
or action. There is a hell in every human heart—but there also is a hell
in every forest, sea, and field, and even still in every tiny living puddle.
No matter where you turn you find disease, decay, and death, and horrible
affliction. Have you ever seen a little chick that's eaten up by parasitic
maggots?

Philonous: Not that I recall.

Sophie: Then let me fill you in—it's really very pretty: a certain type of fly,
driven by its mindless instinct, first deposits its eggs onto a nestling's skin,
then the larvae hatch, bore their way into the epidermic tissue, and, using their sharply toothed mouth hooks, begin to feed on the nestling's
flesh and blood.[79] As the larvae now increase in size they each cause a
protective tumor to grow up around the openings where they respectively

are anchored. And in the final stages you can therefore see the nestling's emaciated body grossly disfigured by numerous cavernous legions in which the fattened maggots wriggle. No man-made torture has ever been more hideous. And consider also how admirably the horror is designed: the physical functions that produce the eggs, the instinct for their deposition, and the well adapted feeding habits of the maggots—they all are perfectly attuned to keep the chick alive in agony just long enough to fully satisfy its ghastly host of parasites.[V] Exactly how do I infer the goodness of a God who gave this world a set of laws that can occasion such contemptible brutalities?

Philonous: I don't pretend to have the final answer here, but as regards your tortured chick, we must be careful not to judge its sufferings too hastily by our own, much higher human standards. Precisely what an animal far lower than a human being feels we simply do not know.

Sophie: Of course we don't, but that is clearly not the issue. Because the sort of natural, presumably amoral evil that animals are subject to has all too often been a curse in human life as well. Just consider for example what horrendous sufferings were brought about in history by that most infamous bacillus, *Yersinia pestis*, that causes the bubonic plague. The Black Death pandemic of 1348 and 49 alone wiped out approximately 25 million lives, or about a third of the European population at the time.[VI] And the world-wide count of all the deaths in all the epidemics that occurred may run as high as 200 million. But more shocking even than such global figures are the details of the carnage. For the plague not only killed—it killed with venomous brutality. Apart from uncontrollable vomiting, bloody coughs, diffuse pains, and a foul body odor,[VII] its most characteristic symptom was the appearance of swellings in the armpits, in the groins, or on the neck. These so-called buboes, from which the pestilence derived its name, were caused by internal bleedings and could become as large as oranges. When they burst, which they did with some regularity, the pain inflicted was a gruesome agony that whipped the hapless sufferer into a frenzy. An

---

[V] The parasitic infestation here described does not always end with a nestling's death, but it does so frequently.

[VI] Whether it was indeed *Yersinia pestis* that caused the great pandemic of 1348 and 1349 is subject to continuing debate. The apparently very rapid spread of the disease in this first and most devastating outbreak is difficult to reconcile with the fact that *Yersinia pestis* can be transmitted to humans only from dying rodents such as rats rather than directlly from other humans. And there is little evidence from eyewitness accounts that medieval plague epidemics among humans were accompanied by parallel epidemics among rats as they should have been if *Yersinia pestis* had indeed been the disease causing agent.[80] However, very convincing evidence in support of the traditional teaching on this matter is constituted by recent finds of *Yersinia pestis* DNA at medieval plague sites.[81]

[VII] As Kelly points out in [Kel], p.112, some of these symptoms are not common with the modern form of plague. This fact can be interpreted as further evidence for the claim that *Yersinia pestis* in its current form was not the disease causing agent in the epidemics of the Middle Ages.

eyewitness account from the spring of 1348 describes the horrors thus:

> [T]his scourge had implanted such a great terror in the hearts
> of men and women that brothers abandon brothers, uncles their
> nephews, sisters their brothers, and in many cases, wives deserted
> husbands. But even worse and almost incredible was the fact that
> fathers and mothers refused to nurse and assist their own children,
> as though they did not belong to them."[82]

About a year later, in Ireland, the Friar John Clynn was "[w]aiting among
the dead for death to come" when he "committed to writing"[83] the following
report:

> Plague stripped villages, cities, castles and towns of their inhab-
> itants so thoroughly that there was scarcely anyone left alive in
> them. The pestilence was so contagious that those who touched
> the dead or sick were immediately affected themselves and died, so
> that the penitent and confessor were carried together to the grave.
> Because of their fear and horror, men could hardly bring them-
> selves to perform the pious and charitable acts of visiting the sick
> and burying the dead. Many died of boils, abscesses and pustules
> which erupted on the legs and in the armpits. Others died in a
> frenzy, brought on by an affliction of the head, or vomiting blood...
> It was very rare for just one person to die in a house, usually, hus-
> band, wife, children and servants all went the same way, the way
> of death.[84]

At the very end of this account there is a note that someone added later:
"And here it seems the author died."[85]

Philonous: The horror is confounding.

Sophie: So confounding in fact that the notion of there being a compassionate
and loving God who purposefully created this universe together with its
laws in an act of divine wisdom can only seem ridiculous.

Philonous: Remember, though, that God in Aristotle's scheme is not creating
actively but passively attracting. That is to say, the Unmoved Mover is
the end but not the source. For Aristotle's universe is uncreated and exists
eternally without a temporal beginning.

Sophie: But such a totally inert divinity is even more offensive a conception to
behold. For how am I supposed to find attractive the idea that God stared
on impassively, for instance, as the Black Death swallowed up its victims
by the millions. Life after countless life was lost while God just reveled as
contentedly as ever in his own celestial perfection—no, thanks!

Philonous: I must admit such unrelenting unconcern would be decidedly depressing. So let's agree instead that God, in order to be worthy of His
status, must be involved in some way more directly.

Sophie: But that in turn will lead me back to what in essence I just asked: exactly how do I infer the goodness of a God who is responsible in one way or another for the havoc that *Yersinia pestis* wreaked? As I see it, there only are two options—the first is bad, the second very bad. For either God brought forth a lawful order that contained the Black Death constellation of *Yersinia pestis* versus man as a contingent developmental possibility or, alternatively, He even caused that constellation to arise *deliberately* by means of some divine creative act. There surely is no solace in the thought that God intentionally used His powers of creation to ingeniously design a hideous bacterium that really has no purpose other than to kill. Afterall, the biochemical mechanisms that allow *Yersinia pestis* to defeat a human being's powerful immune defense are really rather intricate. And any god who occupied himself with such detestable designs would rightly be regarded as a merciless malicious murderer.[86]

Philonous: He clearly would, but there is yet another possibility.

Sophie: Which is?

Philonous: That God might simply have no choice.

Sophie: No choice? You mean that God is not omnipotent?

Philonous: No, what I am trying to suggest—in all humility—is that perhaps creating is to God what breathing is to us.

Sophie: In other words, if God is truly to be God, He truly must create.

Philonous: Precisely.

Sophie: The problem, though, is not that God creates but that the world He did create is violent and mean.

Philonous: It may be mean, but possibly not quite as mean as any of the other worlds He could have made instead.

Sophie: I heard that argument before but cannot quite recall who first devised it.

Philonous: Gottfried Wilhelm Leibniz.

Sophie: That's right, I do remember now: our world, according to Leibniz, is the best of all possible worlds. And the reason why it had to be created, in spite of its apparent flaws, is basically that God, by being good, could not avoid to choose existence over nonexistence as the better of two options.

Philonous: Moreover, the fact that there is evil, Leibniz says, is due to the inherent imperfection of a world that has been finitely created. God does not will evil but positively wills existence over nonexistence and thereby must allow for evil to be caused by His creation's necessary finitude.[87]

Sophie: And by implication, I suppose, the father whose entire family just perished in a pestilence will therefore gladly realize that God is good and that his grief is nothing but a corollary to his finite creaturely condition. Is that the consolation that you offer?

Philonous: I understand, the father's pain cannot be lessened by a clever argument. Afterall, where suffering is unspeakable it behooves us not to speak.

But then again I also think that the problem we are dealing with—the problem of theodicy—is of sufficient existential urgency to justify some efforts at reflection. It is true undoubtedly that grief is better met by empathy than rational deduction, but that does not imply that each and every careful thought in this regard must needs be totally irrelevant.

Sophie: But simply setting up the postulate that this world is the best world there can be is blatantly inadequate. For it amounts to little more than saying that when God creates He always labors hard to do His best.

Philonous: The way you put it, it sounds silly, I admit. But in itself the question Leibniz raised is well deserving of attention.

Sophie: You mean, the question whether ours is the best world there can be?

Philonous: Or more specifically, the question whether God could have designed this world to be immune to evil by default. Could evil have been banished, as it were, by God's divine decree?

Sophie: If we assume, as people do, that God is perfectly omnipotent, then I would say the answer to that question must be "yes."

Philonous: Well then the further question is if God would have been wise to do what He can do, if you are right: eliminate all evil.

Sophie: Again, the answer should be "yes."

Philonous: Not necessarily because where evil is impossible there also is no good. For the knowledge of good and evil is intrinsically the knowledge of a contrast. That is to say, what we discern is not the good as such, but rather is the good that's better than its opposite. Furthermore and more importantly, if humans had no freedom to do evil, then they would simply not be free and thus entirely deprived of any sense of meaning. Afterall, robotic life is pointless be it virtuous or not.

Sophie: To that I can agree, but your appeal to human moral freedom clearly is irrelevant as far as the existence of *Yersinia pestis* is concerned.

Philonous: I cannot counter that objection with conclusiveness, but what I can do is to state with honesty my vague belief that freedom—whatever that may be—is here the key to proper understanding. I do not know, of course, whether there can exist a meaningful universe in which there cannot be diseases caused by germs. But what I do *believe* is that in order for a universe to have that attribute—of being meaningful—it must be free at every of its levels. From a subatomic quantum leap to a contingent evolutionary development and from a willful bodily motion all the way up to a conscious moral choice, it is freedom and freedom only that provides the possibility for meaning to unfold.

Sophie: So is it then the case as well and in particular that plague bacteria can form by means of evolution because the universe is free?

Philonous: It is an option to consider.

Sophie: By implication then, your broader claim in summary is this: there can be meaning only if there can be evil too.

Philonous: Let's say I dimly recognize that even an omnipotent divinity cannot achieve the patently illogical. Even God cannot exist and not exist, and even God cannot create a world in which existence can be meaningful while lacking any freedom. In other words, if we accept that absence of freedom negates meaning in the same way that nonexistence, for instance, negates existence, then *Yersinia pestis* is a testimony, not to God's ill will, but rather to the fact that freedom is a requisite of meaning. So in order for this universe to not be meaningless, it must be free; and in particular, it must be free to bring forth evil—regardless of whether that evil takes the form of a bacterial agent of disease or a heinous human deed.

Sophie: The caveat, though, is that God, if He is good, cannot be just observing passively as evil runs its course. He must be trying to prevent it.

Philonous: But then again if He prevented every evil actively, all freedom and all meaning, as I said, would wholly disappear.

Sophie: So are we back to God just sitting there in bliss while His Creation under Him is mired in a mess?

Philonous: Not necessarily.

Sophie: Why not?

Philonous: Because conceivably God can participate by way of empathy and fellowship and sacrifice. Perhaps His choice is not to obviate the struggles and the evils and the pain, but rather is to share with us their burden.

Sophie: You mean He suffers as we suffer, and He struggles as we struggle?

Philonous: Indeed, what I have here in mind is a rather traditional conception of a suffering redeemer—the Christ who on the cross partakes in human misery.

Sophie: But if we follow through with that approach, then God would really be a tragic figure: His very own nature would be the source of His distress. For by His nature He would bring about a cosmos that is free, and by His nature He would then be forced to carry its affliction.

Philonous: In other words, in that regard He would resemble you and me.

Sophie: In being a tragic figure?

Philonous: Yes.

Sophie: And that is so because we humans, too, are our own most vicious enemies?

Philonous: I wouldn't speak of enmity in reference to God. But insofar as human words can capture it, I'd say that consciousness in God and man alike begets its own inherent contradiction. God's perfect goodness implies that He creates, that His creation must be free, and that, in consequence, the opposite of good becomes a choice that can in fact be realized.

Sophie: Is that a novel way of saying that God created man in His own image—the image of a tragic figure?

Philonous: It makes good sense—at least to me.

Sophie: If that is so, then I suppose the final consolation here is this: I am a mess, you are a mess, the world is a mess, God is a mess, and thus we are united in a mess.

Philonous: I have a hunch your paraphrase is heresy.

Sophie: Careful now, the heresy may rather be your very own apology.

Philonous: On God's behalf?

Sophie: Of course.

Philonous: But how can it be heresy to argue—as I did—that God is good in spite of all the evil that we see?

Sophie: Well, in light of your own reference to Christ, the suffering redeemer, I urge you to consider here a scene: Jesus on the cross or Jesus in Gethsemane and you right next to Him explaining soberly why all is well and why His sufferings are merely consequent of an "inherent contradiction" in His consciousness.

Philonous: I didn't say that all is well and neither did I anywhere address myself to God directly. It was my own confusion—and yours perhaps as well—that my ideas were meant to lessen or to still.

Sophie: But when I paraphrased your words a little bit too bluntly for your taste, you suddenly had qualms and were afraid, or so it seemed, that God might listen in and be displeased. For why would you have otherwise accused me of a heresy?

Philonous: Because your choice of words was plainly disrespectful: God is *not* a mess!

Sophie: Disrespectful—towards whom? Towards you?

Philonous: Of course not—towards God.

Sophie: In that case, though, you might as well have let your God defend Himself—unless, that is, your purpose was to leave a virtuous impression.

Philonous: Are you questioning my motives now?[88]

Sophie: I am indeed.

Philonous: As far as motives are concerned, I can assure you that I never had a pure one even once in my entire life. But otherwise I do alright.

Sophie: Fair enough, yet not sufficient to escape. For there is something so inadequate and reprehensible in your intent of justifying suffering by way of reasoned argument that even a completely areligious soul as mine will sense in it a sacrilege.

Philonous: It's not like that. How can I make you understand?

Sophie: The one who needs to understand is you.

Philonous: Not so, my dear—it's you.

Sophie: No, you.

Philonous: No, you.

Sophie: No, you.

Philonous: No, you.

Sophie: No, you.

⋮

Chapter 4

The Great Transition

Conduct by Reason of Reason

When Aristotle died in exile, in 322 B.C., there came to an end that first great period of intellectual exploration that had begun some three hundred years prior with a single enigmatic question asked by Thales of Miletus: what is there? The very act of posing this question as a problem to be solved by rational effort alone proved fruitful beyond measure. For it created a sense of pristine optimism concerning man's ability to know reality by means of reason that soon thereafter inspired the Hellenes to perceive the world as an ordered cosmos governed by a universal mind. The inner workings of this mind, or *Logos*, as Heraclitus had called it, were thought to be mirrored in the workings of the *human* mind and thus accessible to human comprehension.

It was this epistemic optimism from which the philosophical systems of Plato and Aristotle, in spite of all their differences, derived their common underlying theme, namely the belief that man's highest calling and ultimate destiny was the pursuit and procurement of rational knowledge and truth.

To be sure, not everyone agreed, and the systems of Aristotle and Plato in particular were shaped to a significant degree by their dialectic encounter with the skepticism of the Sophists. But the final outcome of the pertinent debates, insofar as these two central figures were concerned, was a resounding affirmation of man's ability to *know*—to know the real as such, within and without.

Plato, for one, was vitally inspired by this hopeful epistemic creed when he developed his conception of an eternal realm of Ideas in which the forms of all true knowledge had their independent, *rationally transparent* being. And Aristotle likewise endowed his inductively established universals—or forms— with the sort of steadfast realism that bespeaks a fundamental trust in human reason and perception. In other words, Plato and Aristotle were united in the core belief that genuine knowledge of genuine truth could really be acquired.

Interestingly, the agreement here in question was pertaining not only to the potential depth of human understanding but also to its breadth. For Aristotle no less than Plato was convinced that valid rational insight could be obtained across the board with respect to almost every object of experience or thought. In physics, metaphysics, politics, *and even in the field of ethics*, the final authority and court of appeal was the rational mind of man.

From our present vantage point of postmodern relativism, Freudian theories of the unconscious, and evolutionary models of psychology, it seems peculiar to think that Plato—and Socrates before him—considered proper moral conduct to be exclusively a problem of intellectual insight—that to know the good was to do the good. We find it difficult to imagine that we could attain to absolute moral truths, relying only on our rational powers of analysis, and then let our actions even be directed by these truths with the stern inevitability of a logical deduction. But for the preeminent thinkers of the Golden Age, such high esteem for reason's powers of persuasion was a natural expression of that same epistemic optimism that we just found to underlie the whole of their respective systems.

As a matter of course, Aristotle here again was more inclined to give experience its due than Plato was and therefore emphasized the need for moral conduct to be practiced. In his *Nicomachean Ethics*, for example, we read that "[m]oral virtue... is the outcome of habit"[1] and that "it is by doing just acts that we become just."[2] However, when it comes to the ideal by which such acts should be inspired, it is here as there man's rationality that has the final say. In fact, "[t]he function of man," says Aristotle, "is the activity of soul in accordance with reason,"[3] and virtue is nothing but the rational avoidance of irrational extremes. Courage is the golden mean of cowardice and rashness, and self-respect the happy compromise between humility and vanity. At bottom then, these two great pioneers—Aristotle and Plato—both believed that the final arbiter of moral truth and action was not the human heart but was instead the intellect.

Remarkably, this notion that virtue can and ought to be grounded in reason was destined to become a highly influential philosophical current in the now emerging age of Hellenism—and even more so in the subsequent era of Imperial Rome. For it was foundational within the *Stoic* system of philosophy which rose to prominence initially in Hellenistic thought and later on found many followers in Roman high society.

The so-called Hellenistic period encompasses the approximately 300 years between the ascendancy of Alexander the Great to the throne of Macedon and the rule of Augustus—the first emperor of Rome. The conquests of Alexander, which extended over much of the then known world, from Egypt and the Middle East all the way into India, effectively marked the end of the Hellenic age of the Greek city state. Athens in particular was never to rise again as an independent power of its own.

Ironically, though, it was precisely at this point of Athens's final subjugation that its cultural and ideological influence began to spread more rapidly and more successfully than ever before. For within the various kingdoms, into which the Macedonian empire was broken up in consequence of Alexander's early death in 323 B.C., there began a process of cultural colonization by means of which the Greek heritage in philosophy, literature, art, and politics was disseminated over almost the entire Middle Eastern region. Eventually, as these kingdoms were successively vanquished by the Romans, the influence of Hellenistic culture was extended even farther, across the whole of the Roman Empire, from Spain in the west to Persia in the east and from North Africa in the south to Britain in the north. Poignantly, the Roman poet Horace remarked in this regard that "the Greeks, captive, took the victors captive."[4]

As a matter of course, this fundamental shift away from the local cultural contexts of the Hellenic age toward the more cosmopolitan scene of the Hellenistic and Imperial Roman eras was bound to leave its mark as well on the corresponding history of thought. For in a time of uncertainty and cultural flux, there arises in the human soul a natural need for practical guidance and moral support. Consequently, what made the Stoic system of philosophy so widely attractive was, in part at least, its promise to directly satisfy this need. That is to say, the Stoic emphasis on problems of practical moral import befitted the mood of the times here in question.

The history of Stoic thought is long and involved, with some of its more enduring currents extending well into the modern era.[I] Commonly, one distinguishes the period of the early Stoa from the middle and the later Stoa, but the details of the pertinent chronology are beyond the scope of our present exposition.

The founder of the Stoic School was *Zeno* of Citium in Cyprus who lived between 340 and 270 B.C. (not to be confused with Zeno of Elea, the disciple of Parmenides). His interest in philosophy was sparked when, as a young man, he came across the writings of Xenophon and Plato on the life and death of Socrates. The *Apology*, in particular, left him deeply impressed with Socrates's strength of character and moral rectitude.[II] In consequence he came to stress the general primacy of ethical thought over physical and metaphysical speculation—a trait, as we already hinted, that made his system popular among the Romans in particular whose bend of mind was commonly quite practical in kind.

[I]As Störig remarks, the revival of Stoic thought in the modern era was mainly due to its perceived compatibility with the Christian faith, as explained for instance in the work of Joest Lips. But important parallels also can be found in the *Ethics* of Spinoza, the *Theodicy* of Leibniz, and, ambiguously, the moral philosophy of Kant.[5]

[II]Most immediately, Zeno was influenced by Crates the Cynic whom he chose as his teacher because he "was the man who," in Zeno's mind, "most resembled Socrates."[6] The Cynic's back-to-nature movement in particular became a prominent feature of Zeno's Stoic system.

In fact, according to the Roman Stoic Seneca, philosophy, by definition, is nothing more and nothing less than the science of proper human conduct.[7] But what exactly makes that proper conduct proper? To this the simple Stoic answer is that man in all his actions must conform to the laws that govern the whole universe as well as his own nature. To live "in obedience to Nature"[8] is the Stoic key to moral purity and happy equanimity. And since the natural in man is predominantly the rational, it follows that ideal moral conduct consists in the ideal agreement of reason and action. In other words, just as Plato and Aristotle before them, the Stoics thought the moral law to be inherently a rational law.

Apart from Seneca, the most prominent exponents of the later Stoa were the emancipated slave Epictetus and the Roman Emperor *Marcus Aurelius* (121–180 A.D.) whose *Meditations* are a deeply intriguing testimony to the Stoic way of life and thought. The morality that Aurelius espouses in his work calls for utmost dedication to duty, total indifference in the face of adversity, perfect self-control, and complete disregard for everything that merely is external—the fortune, fame, or status of a man. The blessed life is lived in modesty, in adherence to the rational laws of the universe, and in continual awareness of one's own finitude and impending death. In one of the entries in the *Meditations*, for instance, we read:

Of man's life, his time is a point, his existence a flux, his sensation clouded, his body's entire composition corruptible, his vital spirit an eddy of breath, his fortune hard to predict, his fame uncertain. Briefly, all things of the body, a river; all the things of the spirit, dream and delirium; his life a warfare and a sojourn in a strange land, his after-fame oblivion. What then can be his escort through life? One thing and one thing only, Philosophy. And this is to keep the spirit within him unwronged and unscathed, master of pains and pleasures, doing nothing at random, nothing falsely and with pretense; needing no other to do aught or to leave aught undone; and moreover accepting what befalls it, that is, what is assigned to it, as coming from that other world from which it came itself. And in all things awaiting death, with a mind that is satisfied, counting it nothing else than a release of the elements from which each living creature is composed. Now if there is no hurt to the elements themselves in their ceaseless changing each into other, why should a man apprehend anxiously the change and dissolution of them all? For this is according to Nature; and no evil is according to Nature.[9]

The image of the ideal man that the *Meditations* present us with is that of a rather lonesome individual who stems the tide of ever-present change, uncertainty, and tribulation by calmly asserting his natural dignity as a rational being and free moral agent. The man who has truly mastered the art of living is governed by an enlightened mind that graces his soul with firm repose and perfect inner balance.

That said, we need to qualify immediately that Aurelius also emphasizes time and again the need for man to do his duty for the common good and to be socially minded. He clearly recognizes the "principal end in man's constitution" to be "the social"[10] and thus asserts that whatever "is reasonable is... social"[11] as well. The true philosopher, says Aurelius, does not retreat into a mountain cave but rather lives among his fellows actively and never loses sight of his communal obligations.

On the other hand, however, Aurelius also counsels strict withdrawal of the self into itself. For he perceives "the reasonable governing self" to be "by its nature content with its own just actions and the tranquility it thus secures."[12] The wise man therefore is active *in* the community but does not inwardly *belong* to it. He keeps his distance, is self-sufficient, and in all his social dealings urgently concerned to carefully maintain his philosophical composure. His consciousness is ever watchful of the cross-currents and disturbances that his social interactions are liable to generate.

The central focus on the self that such a sharpening of consciousness requires lends a strangely modern tenor to some of Aurelius's teachings.[13] Most notably, his emphasis on the individual as a center of repose and self-sufficient moral agency anticipates the modern Enlightenment idea of the free and morally autonomous human self in Kantian philosophy. To be sure, Kant vehemently denies the Stoic view that perfect moral conduct is attainable in earthly life and in itself sufficient to establish happiness.[14] But in Kant and Aurelius equally, we find a commitment to rationality that is as unrelenting as the categorical sternness of the corresponding moral demands is daunting.[III]

Furthermore, the essentially materialistic and deterministic conception of reality that underlies the Stoic metaphysic imparts to Aurelius's writings on occasion a reductionistic bleakness that the modern world is also painfully familiar with. As a case in point we are for instance told that matter is rotten, that all is "[w]ater, dust, bones, [and] stench,"[16] and that we are to uncover things in "their nakedness, see into their cheapness, [and] strip off the profession on which they vaunt themselves."[17]

And finally, when Aurelius speaks of the "fog and filth" of "[r]ealities [that] are so veiled"[18] and so vast that they in essence are too large for human comprehension, we even can detect a hint of that post-Copernican forlornness that pervaded much of modern thought and culture. What we discern here is the disillusioned weariness of a conscious mortal being in a cosmos next to which that being looks as insignificant as a speck of dust in fathomless infinity.

[III]In his *Critique of Practical Reason* Kant also explicitly recognized that the Stoics had correctly chosen "their supreme practical principle" by "making virtue the condition of the *summum bonum.*"[15]

The world, according to Aurelius, is a "great" material "torrent of being and time"[19] in which man can do no better than to gracefully accept whatever fate ordains and to wait contentedly for that terminal moment when the burden of consciousness is lifted in death.

To be sure, Aurelius also envisions the universe to be organized and governed by a rational *Logos* in which all things ultimately work together for good. But the force sustaining this belief is not a personal encounter with the goodness of the God of Nature but rather is an iron-willed commitment to maintain a rigid philosophical composure—a manly resolve to firmly assert the Stoic belief that "all things are what we judge them to be."[20] Fate is globally benevolent and Nature is good, not by observation or by evidence of mystical experience, but by the power of the human will. Reason demands Nature's goodness in the interests of morality, and the will, in consequence, delivers it.

In summary, if our present purpose is to trace *The Great Transition* from the ancient to the modern world, then we are well advised to look to Stoic thought for inspiration and for guidance.

Sophie: I must admit the *Meditations* always find me struggling to decide whether I should feel inspired by the nobility of the ideals expressed therein or rather saddened by my own utter failure to live up to them. Aurelius perhaps was able to exemplify his teachings by his conduct and the greatness of his soul, and I really do admire that. But what about the rest of us? In principle, as I expressed before (p.5), I very much would like to live in harmony with nature and myself. But the task that Aurelius sets before us seems positively superhuman in its loftiness. I feel fatigued already at the mere idea of being perfectly composed in every action I perform, every word I utter, and every attitude that I assume. In fact, Aurelius even goes so far as to advise us to "remove not actions merely that are unnecessary, but imaginations also."[21] Is such a life of totally self-centered self-control a life according to the Laws of Nature? It seems decidedly unnatural to me.

Philonous: I do not wish to sound irreverent, but whenever *I* read Aurelius, there arises in my mind the image of a beast.

Sophie: A beast?

Philonous: Let's say a bison or a bull.

Sophie: In meditation?

Philonous: No, in bad weather.

Sophie: Like snow or hail?

Philonous: Or scorching heat or arctic cold. Isn't it amazing to imagine how these animals endure all that without a shelter or a cover? Just try to picture it: a bison in the prairies of Dakota—the open sky, the far horizon, and the periodic fury of the elements. Quietly, contentedly, unflinchingly, the animal just stands there in the open land, exposed to everything that earth and sky assail it with. No matter the adversities or hardships that befall, the bison calmly takes them all—without complaint, without a question asked, and without so much as even just a single conscious thought. The bison, as it were, is "like the headland" conjured up by Aurelius "on which the waves continually break," but which "stands firm" as "the boiling waters" about it "sink to sleep."[23] And then one day, as Nature runs its course, the time will finally have come for that great beast that once was strong but now is weak to simply lie down and to die. Nature gives and Nature takes away. Such is the law of life, and everything apart from it is vanity and human sophistry.

Sophie: I like it.

Philonous: And so do I. It is refreshing to behold a being that isn't fretting endlessly but is content to merely be. There is a dignity to such a mode of life that civilized humanity would do quite well to rediscover. We try to make our lives more pleasant constantly, and even our slightest pains are treated with a pill. More comfort, 'less' suffering, more medicine and ever more of it, and in the end what will become of it? Or better yet: what will become of *us*? A race of pets—overweight, spineless, and weak?

Sophie: So 'back to Nature' is the slogan then?

Philonous: If 'back to Nature' means 'away from civilized excess', then I say "yes." But if it means to force upon myself a state of consciousness that has been absolutely rationally purified, then I agree with you that such a goal can only be fatiguing. Aurelius correctly perceives, of course, the many aspects of our human lives that are degrading, mean, and utterly depressing. But his reaction to retreat into an inner core of self-sufficient rationality is rooted in delusion. There is no self-sufficiency in human life at any station, place or time, and any effort to establish it will only foster isolation. Such isolation, for an emperor, may be a part and parcel of the fate that he has been allotted. But for the broader human world, I wonder how that world might look if everyone who has a share in it was exercising that complete control that Aurelius was so ardently devoted to.

Sophie: I think, I see it quite distinctly: a world of Stoics walking past each other not as persons but as purified conceptions—a world wherein no word is spoken lightly, no need expressed without control, no sentiment is felt that reason doesn't sanction, and no imagination is allowed to freely run its course. It is a fellowship in the abstract—an odd menagerie of man-like silhouettes, composed, serene, and calm, and ever contemplating death. And should it happen then that death indeed demands a victim, as disease, for instance, slays a father's son, the only task that father will be focused on will be to carefully "preserve [his] own divinity pure and erect"[24] in the realization that ultimately "[a]ll that comes to pass comes to pass with justice."[25] In fact, Aurelius even counsels us explicitly

> [t]o look to nothing else, even for a little while, except to reason. To be always the same, in sharp attacks of pain, in the loss of a child, in long illnesses.[26]

Philonous: We may not want to go so far as to suggest that Aurelius preached parental abstinence from grief when sons or daughters die. Afterall, in other passages he also speaks of love of children and of family.[IV][27] But otherwise I very much agree that Aurelius teaches a philosophy that overburdens life with rationality.

Sophie: Worse still, the burden is as heavy as its purpose is unclear. For the only 'benefit' that I can see is strict suppression of all spontaneity.

Philonous: As I perceive it, Aurelius—paradoxically—aims to heighten rational awareness mainly to diminish it. For once we have become fully conscious of the deep futility and emptiness of consciousness we are set free. The man who is "so minded,"[28] Aurelius says, will be

> unstained by pleasures, unscathed by any pain, untouched by any wrong, unconscious of any wickedness; a wrestler in the greatest contest of all, not to be overthrown by any passion; dyed with justice to the core, welcoming with his whole heart all that comes to pass and is assigned to him; seldom and only under some great necessity and for the common good imagining what another person is saying or doing or thinking.[29]

Sophie: That is to say, he will resemble strikingly your bison in the prairie. For that great animal as well will not be stained by pleasure or pain and not imagine, certainly, what private thoughts his fellow bisons entertain.

Philonous: Indeed, the bison will attain to philosophical perfection, so to speak, by virtue solely of its 'bison-ness'. Because that 'bison-ness' entails a lower level consciousness.

Sophie: The purpose then is consciousness negation?

Philonous: That would be taking it too far. The image of the bison, afterall, is just a somewhat humorous caricature. More accurate would be to say that Aurelius is intent on stringent consciousness control. He wants to calm the turbulences of unchecked awareness and channel them into a peaceful ordered stream. However, that control itself is nothing but the catalyzing discipline. The deeper goal and purpose is to inwardly set free the self from all its needs and shackles—to let it be *autonomous.*

Sophie: ...in our modern-day enlightened sense (p.183)?

Philonous: Not quite, but the parallels are surely worth exploring. Do you remember what we said not long ago about that central modern myth according to which the reach of human reason is potentially complete?

Sophie: As I recall, we analyzed that myth to have its roots most likely in "the deep impression" that was left "in all the minds who witnessed" modern science's emergence and remarkable success (p.121).

[IV]Moreover, even if we did detect a contradiction here, we mustn't overlook that the *Meditations* aren't meant to be a systematic treatise. In reading them we need to leave some leeway for the author's shifting moods and flexible perspectives.

Philonous: Indeed, we spoke of science in this context as "that true discovery
   of fire that finally [made] man the undisputed ruler of his universe"—or so
   at least he thought (p.121).

Sophie: I do remember it, but why do you refer to it?

Philonous: Because as we establish now a link from Aurelius to the modern
   world, we are led back directly to that central issue at the heart of our
   quest.

Sophie: I must admit, I don't quite see that implication yet.

Philonous: Then try to feel again that sense of awe that the accomplishments
   of Kepler, Galileo, and then Newton had so vividly induced. Consider the
   effect when centuries of frequently abstruse Scholastic thought are followed
   by some actual discoveries: Kepler analyzes Tycho's data, Galileo drops his
   cannon balls, and suddenly there is a dawn of genuine and fertile understanding. Suddenly a man like Newton can explain by way of calculus why
   gravity impels a planet to obey all three of Kepler's laws, and suddenly
   there are emerging new technologies that ancient Romans, for example,
   would likely have believed to be great miracles and wonders.

Sophie: And over night, if I may add, the world has thus become as dull and
   spiritless as its scientific black-and-white description.

Philonous: Not over night, for at the outset men can only see the great advance
   that has been wondrously accomplished. Human reason now has come into
   its own and handed us, or so it seems, the keys to ultimate reality. Where
   is the limit, where the next frontier? The mind now is *autonomous*, and
   nothing hinders its expansion. And so we may be led to think, that reason
   has dominion not in science only, but globally in all of human life, including
   even ethics and religion. That is to say, we may here come to earnestly
   believe that we can rationally comprehend not only all the rules that govern
   our physical existence but also those that govern our conduct. Indeed, this
   notion that the moral law is quasi-scientific was famously expressed by
   Immanuel Kant in the closing passage of his second critique, the *Critique
   of Practical Reason.* In it, Kant at first laments the misdirected crude
   attempts of prior ages at scientific inquiry, and then extols the methods of
   more recent date as models for the study of morality as follows:

> But after the maxim had come into vogue, though late, to examine
> carefully beforehand all the steps that reason purposes to take, and
> not to let it proceed otherwise than in the track of a previously
> well considered method, then the study of the structure of the
> universe took quite a different direction, and thereby attained an
> incomparably happier result. The fall of a stone, the motion of a
> sling, resolved into their elements and the forces that are manifested
> in them, and treated mathematically, produced at last that clear
> and henceforward unchangeable insight into the system of the world
> which, as observation is continued, may hope always to extend

itself, but need never fear to be compelled to retreat.[30]

    This example may suggest to us to enter on the same path in treating of the moral capacities of our nature, and may give us hope of a like good result (emphasis added).

Sophie: There we have it—Newtonian morality.

Philonous: Stated with explicitness.

Sophie: And here then, I suppose, we reconnect the line of our thought to Aurelius and his similar belief that proper moral conduct always is derivative of reason.

Philonous: But only after delving into Kant's philosophy a little bit more deeply. For the contrast that it forms with Stoic thought will be revealing and acute.

Sophie: Delving into Kant's philosophy?—The prospect is alarming.

Philonous: There is indeed some reason for concern because Kant's writings are obscure in their use of language, notorious for their conceptual complexity, and exasperating in the dryness of their style. In fact, even Konrad Lorenz, the great ethologist—whose own work added much to Kantian epistemology—once humbly admitted that Kant's writings are best left to professional philosophers specializing in the field.[31]

Sophie: But *you*, of course, are undeterred.

Philonous: Let's say I am possessed of a certain Stoic stubbornness that always keeps me going.

Sophie: "Stoic stubbornness"? I didn't know the Stoics held that stubbornness was virtuous.

Philonous: You didn't know because they really didn't—but as for me, that stubbornness is part of *my* own nature most decidedly; and "no evil," as you know, "is according to Nature" (p.182).

Sophie: Very well, then where do we begin?

Philonous: Where Kant himself began.

Sophie: And that is where?

Philonous: The place in question is the first sentence in the first section of the *Fundamental Principles of the Metaphysics of Morals.* Here is what it says:

> Nothing can possibly be conceived in the world, or even out of it, which can be called good without qualification, except a Good Will.[32]

Sophie: Nothing can be good except a will?

Philonous: That's right—nothing but a will. As a matter of course, Kant is well aware that there are things and qualities that are desirable apart from a good will, such as for instance courage or intelligence or wealth. But all of these, so we are told, can be misused for evil ends or may inspire boastful attitudes. That is to say, they cannot be considered good all by themselves. It is the will and nothing but the will to which this attribute, of being good *all by itself*, can ever be applied.

Sophie: To grant the will a status of such prominence is something that the Stoics did as well. For in the *Meditations* Aurelius urges us, in passage after passage, to properly align our will to that most elevated good which is the universal law—the Law of Nature. In other words, the will in Aurelius's thinking, too, is the internal spring where all morality originates.

Philonous: In fact, he even states explicitly "that philosophy wills nothing else than the will of your own nature."[33]

Sophie: Meaning, I suppose, that there can be no higher good in all philosophy than a will that is in perfect harmony with nature—and thereby with Nature.

Philonous: Well put.

Sophie: So you agree? There is indeed that clear connection that I see?

Philonous: There is a clear connection, it is true, but almost more importantly, there also is a very clear distinction. For as we read a little further on in that first paragraph of Kant's from which the previous quote was taken, we come across the added claim that a good will constitutes "the indispensable condition of being worthy of happiness."[34] And that is so, says Kant, because no "impartial rational spectator" can ever take pleasure in the sight of a prosperous and happy being that "is not adorned with a single feature of a pure and good will."[35]

Sophie: It makes good sense, for no one likes to see a scoundrel who is happy. Yet where is here that "clear distinction" to the Stoics that you claimed to have detected?

Philonous: Consider carefully what meaning Kant is trying to convey. He doesn't say that moral rectitude, as constituted by a good and perfect will, produces happiness, but only that our being worthy of its attainment requires the presence of such a will as a necessary precondition. In fact, in his *Critique of Practical Reason* Kant explicitly asserts, with respect to this point, that

> [t]here is not the least ground... in the moral law for a necessary connection between morality and proportionate happiness in a being that belongs to the world as part of it, and therefore dependent on it, and which for that reason cannot by his will be a cause of this nature, nor by his own power make it thoroughly harmonize as far as his happiness is concerned, with his practical principles.[36]

Sophie: In other words, there can be saints that are prodigiously unhappy.

Philonous: That's part of it, but there is more to it. Because what Kant here says is nothing less than that in our present life on earth we can't expect the *"is"* and *"ought"* to ever be in harmony.[37] That is to say, unlike the Stoics, Kant perceives a fundamental rift between the *is* of nature and its laws, and the *ought* determined by the moral law. Where Aurelius holds that Nature is good and that perfect moral conduct, in rational "accord with Nature," is by itself sufficient to ensure "the blessed life,"[38] Kant believes by contrast that nature and morality in essence are disjoint. In fact, in Kantian philosophy, the existence of a necessary link from moral perfection to "the blessed life" or happiness would needs be the undoing of the former.[39]

Sophie: You mean, if good people were always also happy people, then good people would cease to be good?

Philonous: In essence, yes.

Sophie: But why?

Philonous: Because the knowledge that our virtue is inevitably tied to a reward—to greater happiness, that is—would make it all but impossible for us, in our current state in earthly life, to will the good exclusively for its own sake.

Sophie: So the introduction of an ulterior motive in the form of a selfish end would compromise the purity of our will and thereby soil the only form of goodness there can be.

Philonous: That is correct.

Sophie: And the Stoics, as you said, had no such reservations—they didn't mind to make morality a means.

Philonous: Correct again, as long as we account for certain subtleties. For the "blessed life" of Aurelius is not the happy life of Kant. "*Happiness,*" says Kant, "is the condition of a rational being in the world with whom *everything goes according to his wish and will*"—a condition that rests "on the harmony of physical nature with... the essential determining principles of [the] will,"[40] as given by the moral law. In the light of this definition, Kant accuses the Stoics, not chiefly of abusing virtue in the interests of happiness, but rather of forfeiting happiness for the sake of virtue. That is to say, the sin the Stoics are most guilty of, in his analysis, is not to make morality a means but to unnaturally include happiness "in the consciousness of being morally minded."[41] The Stoics, according to Kant, are moral fanatics who "indulge in dreams of imaginary moral perfections"[42] and who espouse a "blessed life" that is in truth a pale state of contentment derived from self-deluding fantasies of ethical purity.

Sophie: I think, I see where Kant may here be coming from. Because the Stoic passion for suppressing any consciousness of any need beyond, perhaps, the level of mere sustenance, is very much unnatural and bleak.

Philonous: Upon a certain reading of the *Meditations* we can indeed get that distasteful sullen sense that happiness in Stoic thought is nothing but a person's unawareness of having any need for it. The Stoic goal on such a view is not to genuinely reconcile the *is* and *ought*, but rather to willfully reduce the *is* of human nature until at last it can no longer pose demands that threaten to arouse the moral *ought* from its detached serenity.

Sophie: That's my impression too, and the illusion herein is that nature can be satisfied by being thus reduced.

Philonous: I see your point, but to be fair we also need to add that even Kant—in spite of being critical in general—explicitly commends the Stoics for their emphasis on virtue[43] and calls their attitude "heroic."[44] And indeed, there is much in Stoic thought that is beautiful, noble, and good. Afterall, who would not admire the man who is completely in control of himself, loves mankind,[45] is unfailingly committed to duty, indifferent in the face of death, and even endures torture with equanimity? And who does not yearn for release from pain and fear and hate and pettiness and from the self-disgust that they induce? It is this state of perfect moral independence—of freedom from all wants and everything unclean—that Stoic thought and discipline aspire to. The goal here is to be set free and leave behind the dross of earthly life by reaching total mastery of that which is internal—the soul and moral will of man. For then, at last, the self can truly come to rest, truly be in harmony with Nature, and truly be content in its autonomy. It is this vision of perfection that Aurelius longingly and very movingly appeals to when he says:

> Wilt thou one day, my soul, be good, simple, single, naked, plainer to see than the body surrounding thee? Wilt thou one day taste a loving and devoted disposition? Wilt thou one day be filled and without want, craving nothing and desiring nothing, animate or inanimate, for indulgence in pleasures; not time wherein longer to indulge thyself, nor happy situation of place or room or breezes nor harmony of men? Wilt thou rather be satisfied with present circumstance and pleased with all the present, and convince thyself that all is present for thee from the gods and all is well for thee and will be well whatsoever is dear to them to give and whatsoever they purpose to bestow for the sustenance of the perfect living creature, the good and just and beautiful, which begets, sustains, includes and embraces all things that are being resolved into the generation of others like themselves? Wilt thou one day be such as to dwell in the society of gods and men so as neither to find fault at all with them nor to be condemned by them?

Sophie: It's moving, it is true. But the man who so dwells, as Aurelius says, "in the society of gods" would really have to be himself a god, or very nearly so. And that's precisely where I find his teachings so fatiguing, desperate, and bare of any hope, because for most of us the truth is simply this: it never can be done.

Philonous: On that score I agree and so does Kant.

Sophie: Apparently he does, but I must say I do not understand as yet what

Kant's perspective on this matter ultimately is. The *is* and *ought*, he says, are not in harmony. But what is his solution?

Philonous: Before we get to that, we need to clarify that Kant's perception of the problem is still harsher. For Kant lives in a universe that's ruled, not by the *Logos* of the Stoics, but by the calculus of Newton's physics. That is to say, where Aurelius could still postulate a cosmic rationality that governs all reality with ethical awareness, Kant can only contemplate a set of empty formulas. There is no link from moral freedom to a mathematical description. By implication then, the Stoics' prominent belief that moral laws are satisfied when nature is was bound to seem to Kant entirely preposterous.

Sophie: I am confused. For didn't we start out observing that Newtonian physics was the model for Kant's rational morality?

Philonous: The model it was, but only in a formal sense. Kant was inspired by the rigor and success of the modern scientific method, but he never meant to say that moral laws can be derivative of physics. The realm of freedom and morality can have no overlap with that which is material and thus inherently determinate. It is this essential rift between the free and the material to which Kant famously addressed himself in the concluding section of his second critique:

> Two things fill the mind with ever new and increasing awe, the of-
> tener and the more steadily we reflect on them: *the starry heavens*
> *above and the moral law within.* ...The former view of a countless
> multitude of worlds annihilates as it were my importance as an
> *animal creature*, which after it has been for a short time provided
> with vital power, one knows not how, must again give back the
> matter of which it was formed to the planet it inhabits (a mere
> speck in the universe). The second, on the contrary, infinitely ele-
> vates my worth as an *intelligence* by my personality, in which the
> moral law reveals to me a life independent of animality and even
> of the whole sensible world, at least so far as may be inferred from
> the destination assigned to my existence by this law, a destination
> not restricted to conditions and limits of this life, but reaching into
> the infinite.[46]

Sophie: The consolation then that Kant can offer us is the awareness of the "worth" that our moral nature can bestow on us? Where is the difference here to Stoic thought and to that "pale state of contentment" that Kant himself supposedly complained about?

Philonous: You focused on the wrong part of the sentence. Kant's promise of relief is not pertaining to a mere awareness of a person's worth in earthly life but rather to a rationally grounded hope for reaching a transcendent "destination." For according to Kant, there is implicit in the moral law a conception of God and of human immortality that opens up a view for us toward the attainment of a blissful state of moral purity in the eternal afterlife. That is to say, instead of fantasizing, as the Stoics did, that a finite human being can attain to holiness by means of moral fanaticism in a finite stretch of time—a single human life span—Kant envisions the attainment of perfection as resulting from an infinite development. It is "a *progress ad infinitum*"[47] that will lead us to approximate ever more closely the final goal of "the *perfect accordance* of the mind with the moral law."[48] And the immortality of the soul, in Kantian thought, is thus understood to be a postulate of reason. The purity of the moral law *requires* that the goal of moral perfection, which by this law is *necessarily* held out to us, be ultimately one that can in fact be reached.

Sophie: The notion is bizarre. It almost sounds as though Kant's purpose is to make himself immortal by a logical deduction.

Philonous: Not quite, because the proposition here in question is "not," as Kant admits, "demonstrable as such,"[49] but rather is a necessary postulate without which the moral law would be impure and incomplete.

Sophie: And as you hinted in your previous explanation, God's existence, too, is thus derivative of human moral insight.

Philonous: Indeed, the existence of God, according to Kant, is a "disinterested"[50] rational consequence of the requirement that there must exist a highest being in whom "the exact harmony of happiness with morality"[51] is realized. Moreover, it is this "exact harmony" that Kant here offers us as our final consolation and ultimate promise. For the ideal quasi-divine accord of *happiness* and moral purity is precisely that transcendent destination to which our infinite personal development is driven to converge.

Sophie: In other words, attainment of happiness—just as in Stoic thought—demands that we ascend from our current human lowliness to godlike perfection.

Philonous: It is intriguing, isn't it, how Kant and Aurelius here arrive at much the same conclusion. In fact, Aurelius in this context really is deliberate and quite explicit when he urges us, as you have noted earlier, to "preserve [our] own divinity pure and erect" (p.185), and even more so when he says that it is possible for man "to become... entirely godlike."[52] Kant, by contrast, is a little more restrained and only speaks of perfect "holiness"[53] in a state in which "nature and morality are brought into... harmony."[54] But the only true distinction really is that the Stoic who has reached his goal has not ascended to transcendence but has returned to oneness with the pantheistic God of Nature.

Sophie: So it is not the goal itself but rather the space within which that goal is to be reached that here defines the crucial demarcation. The Kantian vision is transcendent in the very strongest sense whereas the Stoic view is strictly immanent.

Philonous: That is correct.

Sophie: ...and curious indeed. For, as you said, it is intriguing to observe how Kant *and* Aurelius here arrive at more or less the same astonishing conclusion. They both agree that man can overcome the inner conflicts in his consciousness only by transforming his humanity into divinity. Is it really true that man must be a god in order to be happy?

Philonous: I don't know, but I can see that we have reached an all-important juncture. Because what is emerging here with greater clarity than previously is really the profundity of our problem. Man, by virtue solely of his consciousness, cannot help but be aware, simultaneously, of the moral standards of the *ought* and of his own utter inability to bring them into line with the *is* of his nature. According to both Kant *and* Aurelius, it is this awareness of the *ought* in opposition to the *is* that has implanted in man's finiteness a seed of the divine. By implication both agree that in order for the human self to overcome its own dividedness, the seed must germinate and grow until the human has become an image of pure holiness.

Sophie: There is a simpler way to put all this: we all are prone to sin and don't know how to handle it.

Philonous: Did you say "sin"?

Sophie: I did.

Philonous: Coming from you, that word sounds unexpectedly religious.

Sophie: I didn't say I liked it.

Philonous: But you employed it.

Sophie: Because I noticed that apparently we merely are returning to the base from which we started—the *Book of Genesis* (pp.4,20). For in it we can read, as you yourself once pointed out (p.22), how God explains that "man has now become like one of us, knowing good and evil."[55] That is to say, the conflict of the *is* and *ought*, as you so elegantly called it, is really just the ancient curse that followed Adam's sin: the knowledge of good and evil.

Philonous: In essence, I agree, and there are yet some other verses in the Scriptures that may also be of use to us. For in the *Book of Romans* Paul describes the conflict thus:

> I do not understand what I do. For what I want to do I do not do, but what I hate I do. And if I do what I do not want to do, I agree that the law is good. As it is, it is no longer I myself who do it, but it is sin living in me. I know that nothing good lives in me, that is, in my sinful nature. For I have the desire to do what is good, but I cannot carry it out. For what I do is not the good I want to do; no, the evil I do not want to do—this I keep on doing. Now if I do what I do not want to do, it is no longer I who do it, but it is sin living in me that does it.
>
> So I find this law at work: When I want to do good, evil is right there with me. For in my inner being I delight in God's law;

but I see another law at work in the members of my body, waging war against the law of my mind and making me a prisoner of the law of sin at work within my members. What a wretched man I am! Who will rescue me from this body of death? Thanks be to God—through Jesus Christ our Lord![56]

Sophie: In summary: the problem of the alienated human self isn't all that modern an invention afterall.

Philonous: Not exactly—no it isn't. The modern aspect heightens it and brings it to the fore. But fundamentally, man's conflict and dividedness are really just a part of what it means to be a man. Consequently and amazingly, that same dividedness is found already in the oldest tale of man's creation in the Bible.

Sophie: And even more amazing is the more specific fact that—just like Kant and Aurelius—the author of the *Book of Genesis* recognized in man's moral awareness—his knowledge of good and evil—a spark of the divine: "man has now become like one of us."

Philonous: That is indeed a most astounding point of trifold intersection. And our task must therefore be to understand more carefully how these three prominent perspectives—the Kantian, the Stoic, and the Biblical or Christian one—are closely linked but also are distinct.

Sophie: In other words, the dialogue from now on will become a trialogue.

Philonous: And it is only fair that it be so, for at the present station in the larger history, it is indeed Christianity that is the next great force to enter Western culture.

Conduct by Reason of Grace

If we were asked to capture man's condition here on Planet Earth in just a single synoptic sentence, we might perhaps say this: the burden of consciousness is heavy.[1] As a matter of course, this sentence is a mere triviality insofar as every human burden or experience, by definition, is a burden or experience in consciousness. But that aspect aside, the sentence also may be taken to convey the central truth that all of our human struggles ultimately are internal. Not outside forces or adversities or tragedies are our most relentless enemies, but our own inner disposition in the face of them.

How heavy indeed the burden of that disposition can become, is evidenced by the abundance of the means and methods we employ to lighten it. We enter into meditation, practice Yoga, become Stoics, Christian mystics, Buddhists, even drunks, only to find some respite from self, from self-awareness or just

---

[1]The reader may judge the truth of this sentence for him- or herself, but as for the present author, its truth is plainly evident from everything that has been said so far.

plain awareness, and from all the conflict and division that they bring. Something deep within us urges us to seek for a return, to find the exit door, to re-establish oneness. We long to rediscover that primordial form of being that is able just to be—to be unconsciously.

In nature—on the sea shore or the rugged mountain slope—we still behold the presence of that different world from which we came and which no thoughts or questions ever entered. It is a world in which all being is embedded, in which the impulse strictly rules the deed, and no act ever is reflected—a world without remorse, responsibility, or guilt. It is not a peaceful world by any means, nor is it gentle or kind, but it is what it is, and no being that truly still belongs to it will ever wonder why. Only man wonders, and only man cannot belong to it—not anymore.

The emergence of the conscious human self has made the immediate mediate and thereby distanced the possessor of that self from the sources of experience. The distancing, of course, took time and isn't yet complete. Man's awakening was slow and arduous and still continues to this day. A long chain of development connects him with his past through countless generations, eras, epochs, even eons. Somewhere long ago in prehistoric time there came to life that inner light that can illuminate itself—that conscious mind that can be self-reflective. Who were those beings on the verge to humankind whose bones we have discovered and collected—those ape-men, hominids, and early human beings? And later then, who were those Ice Age tribesmen who depicted in their caves the animals they hunted? What was it like to see the world through their much younger eyes?

Deeply moved we stand before the pictures that they drew of mammoths, bisons, reindeer, and of other Ice Age beasts. 'Skillful', 'lifelike', 'true to nature' are the attributes that we here readily apply—yet there is more. For so expressive are the lines and shapes that these most distant pioneers of art produced that we can truly feel the spirit of a different world in them. Something in them tells the story of a distant, more connected, less divided form of life. What do we really see? Some animals on stone? Or do we rather sense in images as these the presence of a spirit link between the human soul and natural environments? There is a danger here, no doubt, to read more into it than we can justify, but do we not perceive in paintings such as these an intimate connectedness that merges the portrayed with the portrayer? Man back then was still much more than nowadays a part of that reality that merely is. The severance of consciousness from the nature that gave rise to it had only just begun.

But all the same, the severance was final. For once a deed is mediated by reflection, the rule of impulse, drive, and instinct has irreversibly been undermined. Man can act, but not unknowingly. The animal that won a fight can leave behind its trounced opponent writhing in a pool of blood and never even once look back. And man, no doubt, can do the same, but very much unlike the animal he never can forget. He cannot be unconscious of his deed, cannot unknow the pain he has inflicted, cannot be unaware that some day that pain may be his. That is to say, he cannot help but recognize that there is suffering in other living beings.

It is this initial moment of insight and awareness, this first extension of a self beyond its boundaries to another creature who is suffering that marks the origin of our inner conflict and division—and on the brighter side, of course, it also marks the origin of all that can be good in us. For as the great Christian humanitarian Albert Schweitzer once poignantly remarked,

> [i]t is this insight that is the great event in the development of Being. Here there appear the truth and the good in the world; the light that shines in the dark; the deepest conception of life is realized, the life that also is a life in fellowship, where in a single existence there is felt the whole world's wave-like surging and receding, [and] in a single existence life as such becomes conscious of itself...[here] being in isolation ceases [and] the being within is flooded by the being without.[57]

In other words, the good has now become a possibility, a choice to be made, an option to be recognized, and so of course has its direct antagonist— the dark side of reality that we call evil. Good and evil are the great contenders that henceforth are vying for the free attention of man's will. From here on onwards every deed of man will be *his* deed in the truest sense and also *his* responsibility. To be sure, the forces of nature are still strong in him, the powers of instinct still unruly and impetuous. His animal aggression continues to impose demands, trying to compel him into action. But now the voice of conscience always has a say. Quietly, insistently, incessantly it is appealing to a law that nature never knew. And suddenly the realm of nature stands in competition to a different realm with different rules and different ends. The schism that here forms between these two domains—the *is* of nature and the moral *ought*—is a schism in man's consciousness. Man now is divided—his nature and morality can never be in harmony.

Or can they be? Or can perhaps the *is* and *ought* be reconciled? The Stoics posed that question and said "yes." Man, *by nature*, is rational and therefore moral. With the advent of the human mind, the nature of nature was redefined. What was natural then is not so now because the ruler isn't instinct anymore but is instead the intellect. And if only we defer to that emergent rational authority and let it rule supremely, the oneness that we lost will be restored. Man *can* live in harmony with Nature, or so at least the Stoics here proclaimed, if he truly treads the path of righteous rationality. If his actions are blameless and his thoughts are pure, the "blessed life" will once again be his.

But what about the 'if'? Man is happy, *if* he is perfect?—The Stoic demand is daunting. Every act must be controlled, every attitude be purified, and no thought be permitted to exist that hasn't been completely purged of sin. The self must learn to totally control itself, to stringently apply a harsh and ever harsher discipline, to focus on its own serenity with ever more persistency until at last the world recedes, and the self beholds itself in rarefied divinity. In other words, if human nature can become divine, the Stoic project can succeed, but otherwise the destination may be bleak.

As a matter of course and as we said before, there is much that is admirable and edifying in the Stoic way of life and thought. The cosmopolitan call of Aurelius to love all mankind[58] as well as his abhorrence of the superficial are inspiring, his earnestness and modesty commendable indeed. But all the same the Stoic vision has a fatal flaw: Nature is *not* good, and no determination of the human will can make it so. Aurelius held most fervently that "all things are what we judge them to be,"[59] but can we really judge amoral Nature to be moral? Does everything in Nature come to pass with justice just because the rift between the *is* and *ought* may otherwise seem utterly unbridgeable? Where is that justice in *Yersinia pestis* or a parasite (p.172ff)? The truth it seems is this: nature is what it is. It is beautiful and violent, inspiring and depressing because in essence it is none of these. Nature doesn't know. It isn't conscious and is wholly unaware of anything that humans would call 'moral'.

And so, where does it end? The Stoic in his final state of 'holiness' has learned to see the given as the good, and judgment therefore is his ultimate reality. He doesn't long or strive or wish but merely is content. His happiness is *resignation*.

Kant saw the Stoics' bind and deep dilemma with great clarity. The Stoics, according to Kant, had posed the right questions and correctly chosen virtue as their guiding light, but the resolution that they offered was a mere delusion. The *is* and *ought* in our universe cannot be reconciled because the Kantian Newtonian world machine is morally entirely incompetent. Consequently, in this present world, the human lot is constant conflict and division. We are obliged to live the moral life as well as we are able, but we must not expect to ever be the better off for it. To bring in line the needs and inclinations of the *is* with the moral law determining the *ought* is not a goal for earthly life but for the afterlife. All hope is therefore in transcendence.

Implicit in these views of Kant is the belief that the transcendent destination that our hopes aspire to is one that human moral reason can in fact perceive. And in particular, it follows here that our human moral law is more than merely human: it equally applies to any being capable of thought—including even God.[II]

It is precisely for this reason that Kant refers, as we saw earlier, to goodness "in the world, *or even out of it*" (our emphasis, see p.188) when he declares the

---

[II]The perfect will of God of course can never be in conflict with the moral law. Consequently, the moral law for God is not a law that He obeys but the adherence to which is intrinsic to His being.

will to be the only source of goodness there can be. That is to say, even in God or any other being with a rational capacity there can be nothing good apart from a good will. By implication, Kant's objective has to be to find a moral law that isn't just a codex—a mere catalogue of rules for *human* ethical behavior. The Ten Commandments, for example, tell us not to murder or to steal, but imperatives as these would have no meaning whatsoever in a world in which all beings are immortal and properties that can be stolen don't exist.[60] Instead, what Kant must purpose to achieve is a full elucidation of the essential lawful structure of the practical moral reason itself. He needs to uncover a universal principle that is sufficient to determine the will of any rational creature in any circumstance by virtue solely of that creature's rationality.

So how can it be done? The task seems overwhelmingly ambitious. But Kant has given us already the point of entry that we need, namely his initial claim that the only seat of goodness is the will. By implication, the question that we now must pose is this: what makes a good will good? And, following Kant, the answer is that a will is good if it aims to carry out a duty solely for that duty's sake.[III]

To illustrate this point Kant offers the example of a merchant who never overcharges any of his customers regardless of experience or standing. The merchant thereby does his duty properly but moral worth his honesty will only have if the duty to be honest is his only motivation—that is, if he is not pursuing, for example, any selfish ends such as a favorable business repute. Consequently, what lends a moral worth to any given act is not the act's overt intent—the proper treatment of a customer—but rather "the maxim by which" the act at bottom "is determined."[61] And it is well that it be so, because a moral law, as we just said, that was dependent on a catalogue of rules to be followed or ends to be achieved in *human* life would hardly be the universal law that Kant envisions.

However, there is a problem here arising. For if we take away all practical intents and all external purposes, then what is there still left? Anything at all? Yes there is—the purely formal structure of a law, namely the categorical demand to always *act in such a way that we could will the maxim of our action to become a universal law*. It is this demand that Kant refers to as the categorical imperative—the universal law of the pure practical reason that depends on nothing but the nature of that reason in itself. The categorical imperative is the Kantian equivalent, as it were, of Newton's universal gravitation—a law that tells us, not what things will always be, but what they always *ought* to be.

Yet how does this imperative control how we should act in ordinary living? To answer this let us assume that we are contemplating stealing something

---

[III] As Copleston points out in [Copl6], p.315, this rule is not applicable to the "holy will" of God because in God there can be no conflict between inclination and obligation, and the notion of a duty therefore becomes meaningless.

that we urgently desire. Can we will the maxim of that act of theft to become a universal law? If not, then Kant would say we simply shouldn't do it. That is to say, all acts of thievery will always be immoral necessarily.

But can we here agree? Can there indeed be never any circumstance that turns an evil theft into a righteous deed? What if we stole a loaf of bread to feed a starving child? Would not the end to save a human life here override the categorical proscription? According to Kant, it probably would not. For quite conceivably he would reply that a mother, say, who steals a piece of bread to feed her hungry child cannot in full anticipate the outcome that her robbery results in. So it may happen, for example, that—with the deed just done—she hurries off in panic, falls down a flight of stairs, loses the bread, breaks her leg, and therefore can't get back to where her child is waiting. And even worse and very tragically, before she left to steal the bread she felt so tense and so disturbed that she completely failed to recognize a dear old friend who came her way and would have gladly bought her all the food she needed. In other words, the end result may even be that the child dies *because* the mother stole the bread while otherwise it would have lived.

Given that this 'argument' will readily appear to us decidedly absurd, it is surprising and important to observe that Kant would likely have endorsed it. For in his last essay *On a Supposed Right to Lie from Altruistic Motives*[62] he offers us an argument quite similar in kind. Here is how he frames it: a man is hiding from an assassin in the house of his friend. As the assassin arrives and demands to know the man's whereabouts, the friend is facing a dilemma. He can tell the treacherous truth and thus become a murderer's accomplice or he can lie and thereby violate the moral law that tells him to be honest. But is there really present in the latter case a moral violation? Perhaps the categorical imperative can here be satisfied—and only satisfied—by telling an untruth. Afterall, the maxim of the choice to be dishonest in this case appears to be the laudable intent to save a man from being murdered. The friend may not be able to will that lying as such be universally permissible, but in all cases in which a lie protects an innocent life, so he could claim, the lie is clearly justified.

But now suppose, says Kant, that the friend in fact deceives the assassin by being untruthful. The problem then would seem to be resolved, but as it is we do not really know that. For conceivably and unbeknownst to the friend, the man in hiding gets so scared that he decides to look for safety somewhere else. He opens a window, climbs out, the assassin happens to see him, and kills him on the spot. In other words, in this scenario, proposed by Kant, it is the lie and not the truth that causes the assassin to succeed.

Naturally, the likelihood for such a sequence of events to come about in actual reality will strike us as minute. But then again what do we mean by 'likelihood'? There is no precedent, no probability, and no statistic to be referenced. The friend's encounter with the murderer on that particular day under those particular circumstances—whatever they may be—is a perfectly singular event. It never happened previously and never will happen again. In other words, there simply is no likelihood to be determined. So why then is it obvious that lying in this case is *a priori* justified? Why is a course of action based on non-existing probabilities preferable to Kant's demand to never be dishonest?

To better understand why questions such as these are valid and nontrivial, it is helpful to record a story from *The Hiding Place*—the book in which Corrie ten Boom describes her underground activities in Holland under Nazi occupation. When Germany's war effort began to falter, the Nazis decided to seize physically able young men from occupied countries, such as the Netherlands, for forced labor in German munitions factories. As it turned out, Nollie van Woerden, a sister of Corrie's, had three able-bodied sons that all were very much in danger to be seized. In anticipation of a possible raid, Nollie and her husband Flip installed a hideout in their kitchen underneath a table. When the raid finally came, the two sons that happened to be home at the time quickly climbed into the hideout and there awaited the search. As two of the soldiers entered the kitchen, they only found Nollie's daughter Cocky, the grandfather, and two of Cocky's aunts including Corrie ten Boom herself. The subsequent events, ten Boom recalls as follows:

> "Where are your men?" the shorter soldier asked Cocky in clumsy, thick-accented Dutch.
>
> "These are my aunts," she said, "and this is my grandfather. My father is at his school, and my mother is shopping and—"
>
> "I didn't ask about the whole tribe!" the man exploded in German. Then in Dutch: "Where are your brothers?"
>
> Cocky stared at him a second, then dropped her eyes. My heart stood still. I knew how Nollie had trained her children—but surely, surely now of all times a lie was permissible!
>
> "Do you have brothers?" the officer asked again.
>
> "Yes," Cocky said softly. "We have three."
>
> "How old are they?"
>
> "Twenty-one, nineteen, and eighteen."
>
> Upstairs we heard the sounds of doors opening and shutting, the scrape of furniture dragged from walls.
>
> "Where are they now?" the soldier persisted.
>
> Cocky leaned down and began gathering up the broken bits of cup. The man jerked her upright. "Where are your brothers?"
>
> "The oldest one is at the Theological College. He doesn't get home most nights because—"
>
> "What about the other two?"
>
> Cocky did not miss a breath.
>
> "Why, they're under the table."

Motioning us all away from it the soldier seized a corner of the cloth. At a nod from him the taller man crouched with his rifle cocked. Then he flung back the cloth.

At last the pent-up tension exploded: Cocky burst into spasms of hysterical laughter. The soldiers whirled around. Was this girl laughing at them?

"Don't take us for fools!" the short one snarled. Furiously he strode from the room and minutes later the entire squad trooped out—not, unfortunately, before the silent soldier had spied and pocketed our precious packet of tea.

It was a strange dinner party that evening, veering as it did from heartfelt thanksgiving to the nearest thing to a bitter argument our close-knit family had ever had. Nollie stuck by Cocky, insisting she would have answered the same way. "God honors truth-telling with perfect protection!"[63]

Sophie: And in the next one hundred cases of this kind the sons in hiding would be found. So much for God's divine protection.

Philonous: Except for the fact that there aren't any such cases. There is only one case, one fateful outcome, one moment of decision, and one person to decide. Cocky gave the answer that she gave, broke into laughter involuntarily, and her brothers were saved. That's the fact, and no one knows what would have happened otherwise—if she had told a lie.

Sophie: And still I say: this sort of thing would never happen twice.

Philonous: No doubt, all cases are distinct, and each is subject to a myriad of factors that are largely unpredictable in terms of their effects. But all the same I say "this sort of thing" is not as singular as you appear to be assuming. For as it is, it happened not much later for a second time when Nollie faced a test of faith herself.[64] She and her husband had opened their home to a Jewish lady, named Annaliese, who was seeking refuge from the Nazis. When the Nazis finally discovered it, some men from the S.D. were sent, entered the home, and there found Annaliese with Nollie in the living room. When one of the agents asked Nollie if Annaliese was a Jew, Nollie answered...

Sophie: "yes."

Philonous: How did you guess?

Sophie: And since "God honors truth-telling with perfect protection" the Nazis let her go—if only I believed it.

Philonous: No, they didn't—both were arrested. Nollie was taken to the local police station and Annaliese "to the old Jewish theater in Amsterdam from which Jews were transported to [concentration and] extermination camps in Germany and Poland."[65] Remarkably, however, from her prison cell, Nollie relayed the following message to her family: "No ill will happen to

Annaliese, God will not let them take her to Germany. He will not let her suffer because I obeyed Him." [66]

Sophie: And so?

Philonous: Six days later Annaliese was free—and, after another seven weeks, so was Nollie too.

Sophie: It's hard to believe.

Philonous: But true.

Sophie: So that's how Kant can be a moral rigorist? He sticks to the letter of his law, and God picks up the slack.

Philonous: No, Kant's concern is with contingency, not providence. The friend who climbs out through the window only to get killed is a victim of pure accident. That is to say, in talking to the murderer, you can choose to be honest or dishonest but you cannot control what afterwards will come of it. Thus we read in one of Susan Neiman's works that Kant's essential point is "one we have no wish to hear: our power over the consequences of our actions is really very small. What lies in our hands is good intention itself." [67]

Sophie: That's really rather sobering: we make sure that our willing is in order and is pure, and all the rest is randomness.

Philonous: ...or faith—as in Cocky's and in Nollie's case.

Sophie: And that faith, being Christian by profession, is the new contender that we now must reckon with?

Philonous: It is indeed, and it directly leads us to the heart of our quest. The matter is essential.

Sophie: Please elaborate.

Philonous: To make my point it is advisable to start again from that initial thought that somewhere deep in prehistoric time there came to life a form of consciousness that could extend itself to other living beings. Somewhere long ago a hominid or early human being could perceive a pain that wasn't just his own. Suddenly a light was dawning—compassion was born; and being left the cage of animal unconsciousness. But what about the price? Where actions can be mediated by reflection an inner impulse can become an enemy. Man has urges and desires but cannot always act in their pursuit—or can he, or may he, or must he? The soul is now divided. Man has become like God, knowing good and evil. And yet, man is finite, is not divine, cannot be God, and his knowledge therefore brings on separation—from God and from himself:

So the LORD God banished him from the Garden of Eden to work the ground from which he had been taken. After he drove man out, he placed on the east side of the Garden of Eden cherubim and a flaming sword flashing back and forth to guard the way to the tree of life. [68]

Sophie: In other words, we are cut off.

Philonous: ...and feel it painfully. The oneness is destroyed. In nature we can feel it still and also in the paintings at Lascaux, but the magic is gone and won't return—our knowledge has destroyed it.

Sophie: But the Stoics disagreed.

Philonous: Because the Stoic world is governed by a *Logos* that securely grounds morality in Nature. Lamentably, however, the *Logos* is delusion. For nature in the Kantian Newtonian scheme is merely a machine. It knows nothing of right and wrong and nothing of the human moral conflict. Nature is contingency plus mathematical necessity, and that is all there is to it.

Sophie: ...and hence the modern disenchantment.

Philonous: ...and hence the Kantian division: nature and morality are utterly disjoint. On the one hand there is the human moral will and on the other hand a mindless system of mechanics. The world must blindly follow its Newtonian laws and we can only watch it. By implication, the only good that there can be is the good we will to be.

Sophie: For against the forces of contingency we are powerless, as Kant points out, to truly bring about a consequence we wish for. And even the supposed protection of a friend will therefore not suffice to justify a willful lie.

Philonous: Because a supposed protection may very well turn out to be complicity. And worst of all, Kant may be right. For if, for instance, Cocky or Nollie had been telling lies the outcome might have been disastrous.

Sophie: It is true, the treacherous truth in these two cases was amazingly the saving grace.

Philonous: But Kant most likely wouldn't put it thus. For 'grace' reeks far too much of providence and divine tutelage to have a place in Kant's enlightened modern mind. God, in modern times, no longer is an active force in human life and history but merely is a rational necessity. In the Kantian universe, man is alone, thrown back upon himself, and must accept his inner isolation—he is autonomous in the very deepest sense. The moral law is not God's law or Nature's law but rather reason's law and therefore man's law.

Sophie: But Nature's law was reason's law in Stoic thought no less.

Philonous: That is correct but that is also why the rational in Stoic thought, by being natural, is clearly not as insular. That is to say, the modern isolation of the self is rightly labeled 'modern'.

Sophie: Yet more important than the label we attach to it is the approach that we adopt to overcome it.

Philonous: In this regard the present options are ascension to divinity in earthly life by following the Stoic lead, attainment of perfection in Kantian transcendence, or the promise of the Christ.

Sophie: The first is as fatiguing as the second is abstract, and the third, the Christian option, is fatiguing *and* abstract.

Philonous: I don't agree, because when Nollie spoke the truth she was impelled by living faith not abstract thought.

Sophie: I understand, but all the same I say the Christian message is removed. For who can comprehend that God Incarnate can become a sacrifice for human sin by dying on a cross? Exactly what, if I may ask, has Jesus's death two thousand years ago to do with my dividedness and personal frustration?

Philonous: You're taking here the wrong approach. The starting point is man's creation.

Sophie: The *Book of Genesis*?

Philonous: The Fall.

Sophie: That is, the birth of human consciousness.

Philonous: ...and human moral reason.

Sophie: In other words, we must begin with Christian ethics.

Philonous: We must begin with it in order to dispose of it.

Sophie: Dispose of Christian ethics?

Philonous: That's right—no ethic can be Christian.

Sophie: Meaning, I suppose, that Christians are at liberty to lie and steal and murder as they please.

Philonous: God willing—yes, they are.

Sophie: So are you saying that the Christian's first concern is not to will the good but to will as God wills?

Philonous: Indeed, the will here is the center once again, but not the will of man—the will of God. "His will," says Corrie ten Boom, "is our hiding place," and then she adds, "Lord Jesus, keep me in your will!"[69] The Bible, too, is full of exhortations to obey and seek that will unceasingly. Jesus Himself advises us to pray "Thy will be done;"[70] Paul exhorts us, in his letter to the *Romans*, to "approve"[71] of God's will for us; and in the Psalms we read of the "desire to do your will."[72]

Sophie: In my Bible, though, Paul also speaks of that divine will as being "good, pleasing and perfect."[73] By implication, it appears, your claim that there can be no ethic that is Christian rests on the rather spurious distinction between a will that seeks the good and a will that seeks to conform itself to a will that is good. In either case the final object is the good.

Philonous: Admittedly, the choice of terminology is open to adjustment. What is important here is not whether we describe the central problem of the Christian life—the seeking of God's will—as ethical or not, but whether we perceive its nature properly. According to Albert Schweitzer, for instance, Christians "are to be ethical, not in the expectation of thereby fulfilling some purpose but from inward necessity, so as to be children of God's spirit and in this world already to enter into His will."[74] And along very similar lines, the Lutheran theologian and martyr of the German resistance against Hitler, Dietrich Bonhoeffer, writes:

Whoever wishes to take up the problem of a Christian ethic must
be confronted at once with a demand which is quite without parallel. He must from the outset discard as irrelevant the two questions which alone impel him to concern himself with the problem
of ethics, 'How can I be good?' and 'How can I do good?', and instead of these he must ask the utterly and totally different question
'What is the will of God?'[75]

Sophie: And yet I cannot see precisely how that different question really is so
different. If God's will is good and if it is God's will that I seek, then,
effectively, I seek the good.

Philonous: The difference is so radical because the purpose of the Christian
life is not adherence to a moral law or code of conduct but a fundamental
transformation of being—a *metanoia*. The Christian aims not only to act
like Christ but to actually become and *be* like Christ.

Sophie: That vision leaves me cold. For in the light of the doctrine of the
Incarnation, to be like Christ means nothing less than to be like God Himself. That is to say, the final goal here is no less demanding than in Stoic
thought or Kantian philosophy. And, if I may add, the road that takes
us there is equally constraining. For am I really better off in mimicking
Christ-likeness than in harshly submitting, say, to Aurelian discipline or
Kantian abstraction? Let's just be honest: those pious Christian souls who
try to be like Jesus and never dare to say a word their pastor hasn't sanctioned are an utterly pathetic sight. You talk to them and they respond
like Christian robots, pretending to be sinless. Every word is predictable,
every action boring, and every thought a slimy old hypocrisy.

Philonous: What you describe is undeniably a part of cultural reality but not
of what I call 'Christianity'.

Sophie: Don't get me started now. That Christian piety is plain dishonesty.

Philonous: I sense that underlying your reply there is a fundamental misconception: Christ-likeness isn't something we achieve by piety or practicing
religion. For in the final consequence, to be like Christ can only mean to
fully be yourself, that is, to really be what God intended you to be. Carl
Jung, for instance, with his ever so penetrating eye saw the issue clearly
when he said:

> We Protestants must sooner or later face this question: Are we
> to understand the "imitation of Christ" in the sense that we should
> copy his life and, if I may use the expression, ape his stigmata; or
> in the deeper sense that we are to live our own proper lives as truly
> as he lived his in all its implications? It is no easy matter to live
> a life that is modeled on Christ's, but it is unspeakably harder to
> live one's own life as truly as Christ lived his. Anyone who did this
> would run counter to the forces of the past, and though he might

thus be fulfilling his destiny, would none the less be misjudged, derided, tortured and crucified. He would be a kind of mad Bolshevist who deserved the cross.[76]

You see, it is absurd for anyone to try to be like Christ by way of imitation if Christ Himself was always just Himself. In other words, it is logically impossible to imitate a man who in turn imitated no one.

Sophie: That point of view, I readily admit, is somewhat more attractive. But then again Carl Jung is hardly an exponent of the orthodox tradition. In fact, I doubt he really was a Christian in the ordinary sense.

Philonous: But Bonhoeffer most definitely was.

Sophie: And he agreed with Jung?

Philonous: Not explicitly, but what he did say is that our

> *conformation* with the unique form of Him who was made man, was crucified, and rose again... is not achieved by dint of efforts 'to become like Jesus', which is the way in which we usually interpret it. It is achieved only when the form of Jesus Christ itself works upon us in such a manner that it moulds our form in its own likeness (Gal. 4.19). Christ remains the only giver of forms. It is not Christian men who shape the world with their ideas, but it is Christ who shapes men in conformity with Himself. But just as we misunderstand the form of Christ if we take Him to be essentially the teacher of a pious and good life, so, too, we should misunderstand the formation of man if we were to regard it as instruction in the way in which a pious and good life is to be attained. Christ is the Incarnate, Crucified and Risen One whom the Christian faith confesses. To be transformed in His image (II Cor. 3.18, Phil. 3.10, Rom. 8.29 and 12.2)—this is what is meant by the formation of which the Bible speaks.[77]

And in another passage Bonhoeffer adds the following, still more impassioned words:

> The Christian is not a *homo religiosus*, but simply a man as Jesus (in distinction from John the Baptist) was a man. ... Not the flat and banal 'This-sidedness' of the Enlightened, the deep 'This-sidedness' which is full of discipline and in which the knowledge of the Death and Resurrection is always present, this is what I mean. When a man really gives up trying to make something of himself— a saint, or a converted sinner, or a churchman (a so-called clerical somebody), a righteous or unrighteous man, ... when in the fullness of tasks, questions, success or ill-hap, experiences and perplexities, a man throws himself into the arms of God ... then he wakes with Christ in Gethsemane. That is faith, that is *metanoia* and it is

thus that he becomes a man and Christian. How can a man wax
arrogant if in a this-sided life he shares the suffering of God?[78]

Sophie: Is that indeed the motto of the Christian life—be yourself and thereby
be like Christ? How can I give "up trying to make something of" myself if
my objective is to form myself into a mirror image of Jesus?
Philonous: It isn't you but Christ who does the forming.
Sophie: Still, the notion is confusing.
Philonous: It's less confusing than it seems if we begin from the initial thought
that to truly be yourself requires in particular to truly know yourself.
Sophie: That idea I can accept. But how is knowledge of the self related to
the Christ?
Philonous: Jesus Himself provides the answer when he says that "[n]o one is
good—except God alone."[79]
Sophie: You're speaking in riddles.
Philonous: No, I merely am reminding you of one of your own thoughts.
For when you spoke of the corruption that the law of death—the law of
entropy—induces, you said that evil in a world like ours "is intrinsic and
profoundly structural" (p.136).
Sophie: It is true, the world that modern science has revealed is rotten to
the core. Where competition and aggression rule, all living beings are
corrupted.
Philonous: And in admitting that you have laid claim to that which is for any
Christian soul the centerpiece of genuine self-knowledge.
Sophie: The knowledge of my sin?
Philonous: That is correct because the knowledge of your sin—the knowledge of good and evil—precisely is the inner cause of your dividedness and
separation—from God, from yourself, and from your fellow human beings.
Sophie: And the solution of the conflict therefore is for me to go to church in
order to confess them—confess my sins, that is?
Philonous: There is a story in *The Hiding Place* that helps us here to gain the
adequate perspective: during her imprisonment in a concentration camp
near Vught, in Holland, Corrie ten Boom was informed by her sister Betsie
about the identity of the Dutch collaborator who had denounced them
both, along with family and friends, to the Gestapo. In consequence Corrie
was shaken by violent feelings of hate that threatened to consume her.
Sophie: That's very understandable.
Philonous: It surely is, but, remarkably, when Corrie asked her sister how she
felt about the traitor and his villainous behavior, Betsie gave the following
astonishing reply:

> Oh yes, Corrie! Terribly! I've felt for him ever since I knew—
> and pray for him whenever his name comes into my mind. How
> dreadfully he must be suffering.[80]

Completely taken aback, Corrie lay still in her prison bed for a long time, contemplating her sister's words. Finally, it came to her that Betsie "in her gentle way"[81] had been telling her that she, Corrie, was just as guilty as the traitor whom she loathed. "[B]efore an all-seeing God," she and the traitor stood convicted of the same revolting sin—the "sin of murder."[82] For Corrie "had murdered" her betrayer in her "heart and with her tongue."[83]

Sophie: She lowered herself to the level of that hideous coward, that evil snake?

Philonous: She did indeed.

Sophie: I do not understand. How can a woman of such saintly rectitude and outstandingly humane compassion as Corrie ten Boom consider herself the moral equal of a spineless backstabber?

Philonous: Well, suppose that Corrie had been he—the backstabber. Suppose that she had grown up in the same surroundings, had been subjected to the same influences, thought the same thoughts, experienced the same emotions, and really and truly had been he. Do you not think that then perhaps she also might have acted as he acted?

Sophie: Are you saying that the traitor couldn't help it? That he somehow was externally conditioned—the unwitting instrument of environmental influence?

Philonous: No, I'm merely saying that he did what he did because he was who he was.

Sophie: I am surprised. For suddenly you almost sound as though you're giving up free will in favor of blind destiny.

Philonous: Not at all—my point is simply this: if Corrie really had been he—the betrayer—she really might have used the freedom of her will exactly as he did. Afterall, the will is free but not completely free. And ultimately, therefore, we just cannot know why we do what we do and why we are who we are.

Sophie: But what is here the logical conclusion? In following your present train of thought, we may as well consider ourselves the moral equal of any henchman, murderer, and torturer who ever walked this earth. In fact, ten Boom could just as well declare herself the equal of her cruel prison guards or even of Hitler himself for that matter.

Philonous: Or of Adolf Eichmann, Heinrich Himmler, Josef Mengele—the list is very long.

Sophie: But don't you realize what all these names in essence signify?

Philonous: Evil incarnate.

Sophie: And Corrie ten Boom was the equal of that—of evil incarnate?

Philonous: Corrie ten Boom, her sister Betsie, and her entire family were lights that shone in the dark. My admiration for who they were and what they did could not be any greater. But all the same they still were human beings—like you and I, if I may add. And as for myself, the final truth is simply this: nothing, nothing whatsoever, and absolutely nothing separates me from the likes of Hitler, Himmler, Eichmann, and company but the grace of God. If I really had been Adolf Eichmann, lived like he, felt like he, been like he, well then I really would have been he and probably would have done what he did. Why did I not? Why was I born in a different time, a different place, with a different inner make-up? Because of my own competent choice or rather God's inscrutable grace?

Sophie: Your point of view is radical.

Philonous: I call it trivial: I do not know why I am I and you are you and Eichmann was Eichmann and neither do you. The fact is undeniable and utterly plain.

Sophie: And yet I wonder where exactly we are headed here. When I declared all evil to be "intrinsic and profoundly structural"—a necessary presence in a world of ever growing entropy—you cautioned that I thereby had deprived morality of its foundation (p.135). But now it seems you did in essence just the same. For if indeed the worst of sinners is no worse than even the greatest of saints, then all distinctions in the moral realm are altogether nullified. The good is equal to the bad, and thus morality is emptied of its content.

Philonous: What is removed are merely the distinctions between persons. For Jesus didn't say "no deed is good" but rather that "no *one* is good—except God alone." And I believe He really meant it as He said it. Deeds can be evil or good, and one deed therefore can be better than another. But for any one person to declare him- or herself to *be* better than another is entirely absurd. We all have, as Fyodor Dostoevsky put it in *The Brothers Karamazov*, "sinned against all men,"[84] and

> in truth we are each responsible to all for all, it's just that men don't know this. If they knew it, the world would be paradise at once.[85]

Sophie: It would be paradise? A world in which each person is the worst of scoundrels ever to have lived?

Philonous: That we live in a world in which every single person *is* the worst of scoundrels but for the grace of God, is really just a fact—a plain reality that simply must be recognized.

Sophie: Yet why would we return to paradise if only we agreed?

Philonous: Just ask yourself what forced us to abandon it.

Sophie: The paradise, you mean?

Philonous: The paradise.

Sophie: We said it more than once: the knowledge of good and evil.

Philonous: Because it is this knowledge that forces us to judge and thereby brings us into conflict with ourselves, with others, and with God. But how can I continue judging others or myself if I am Adolf Eichmann but for the grace of God? Where the bottom is reached, there is nothing left to teach.

What right do I still have, in light of this admission, to point out flaws in other human beings? In other words, as our moral awareness here is driven to its final Christian consequence—the realization of the universal guilt of every human being—the root of our own dividedness—the need for moral judgment—is pulled out.

Sophie: The teaching is eccentric.

Philonous: But very soundly Biblical, because the central message of the gospels is that Christ took on all human sin and died for it. So as we come to *know ourselves* as universal bearers of all sin, we follow Christ to Golgotha. That is, we become like He by truly coming to know ourselves and thus truly *being* ourselves. To be like Christ in this most crucial sense is therefore not an exercise in piety but in acceptance of reality.

Sophie: And after Golgotha there comes the Resurrection.

Philonous: ...or, as Dostoevsky said, the return to paradise. Just imagine how utterly transformed the world would be if only for a single day no evil was projected—if only for a single day we all agreed that all the evil there can be is fully present in each one of us. Imagine what it would be like—a single day of truth and honesty. It would be bliss—it would be heaven.

Sophie: In other words, the Christian does and can here overcome that very dividedness against himself that you identified before as being "just a part of what it means to be a man" (p.195). And in so doing, it appears, he in effect transcends his ordinary state of being merely human.

Philonous: We mustn't be too literal, but it is true that the acceptance of Christ's sacrifice is thought to bring about a very deep renewal. In accepting the redeeming gift of grace man opens himself to God's transforming work in him. That is to say, the initial decision to believe marks the inception of a truly existential *metanoia*.

Sophie: And yet I wonder who will ever follow you? Who will admit to be a Nazi criminal or other well known monster but for the grace of God? Yours, most certainly, is not a stance that ever will be popular.

Philonous: Here again you should recall what you yourself asserted: "if next to every new and shiny car or other good that we acquire there sat a starving mother with a dying child we likely would be less inclined to fantasize about upholding in our lives a sense of ethical integrity" (p.136). Have you forgotten it?

Sophie: No, I haven't. But I don't remember ever to have said that I was Himmler, Mengele, or Eichmann in disguise.

Philonous: But don't you see the obvious connection? Eichmann organized the mass murder of millions of Jews from all over Europe by essentially doing office work. He wrote orders, received orders, filled out forms, sent letters, and on the whole just acted like a bureaucrat intent on furthering his own career. Remarkably, he wasn't even notably a vicious anti-Semite.[86]

Sophie: It almost sounds as though you're trying to defend him.

Philonous: Don't worry, I am not. But I can surely see myself in him. Eichmann was astoundingly and cruelly indifferent to the horrors that he caused.
But is indifference of this kind really all that foreign to me—to you—to anyone? In your comment, that I just cited, you contrasted consumerism with
the reality of starvation. What does it take to be a dedicated consumer
in a world in which thousands of children die of malnutrition and other
poverty related causes every single day? Can you picture yourself in some
horrendous urban slum walking across a garbage dump on which children
are searching for food and then afterwards going into a showroom and buying a brand new car for 20,000 dollars? I can, because in essence I have
done it. Or can you picture yourself looking at a newspaper photograph
of a starving mother with her dying child and afterwards going about your
daily business as if nothing was the matter? I can, because I do it all the
time. So what does it take? Nothing more and nothing less than simply
being what you are: totally selfish, totally unconcerned, and totally indifferent. And what did it take for Eichmann to organize the holocaust? Total
selfishness, total unconcern, total indifference.

Sophie: Excuse me, but indifference to starvation when buying a car is not the
same as organizing actively the slaughter of the Jews!

Philonous: It certainly is not, for the horror and the scale of the crimes to which
Eichmann was a principal contributor were so extreme and so unique that
no words of human language can possibly suffice to properly convey them.
However, even in the light of this admission, I still can and must acknowledge that I myself not only would have likely done what Eichmann did if
I really had been he, but, far more disturbingly, that the undeniable fact
of my own indifference to other people's sufferings, allows me to recognize
Eichmann's human nature to be mine. Eichmann was not an extraterres-
trial, not a sadist, not insane, but far more shockingly, he was an ordinary
man. In her account of Eichmann's trial in Jerusalem, Hannah Arendt put
it thus:

> The trouble with Eichmann was precisely that so many were like
> him, and that the many were neither perverted nor sadistic, that
> they were, and still are, terribly and terrifyingly normal.[87][IV]

That is to say, his deeds were monstrous, but so are mine—except for the
grace of God.

Sophie: And thus we are "responsible to all for all," and thus all individual guilt
is radically relativized. For where everybody is responsible for everything,
no one in particular is responsible for anything—or so at least it seems.

[IV]In the same account Hannah Arendt also points out, that the psychiatrists who examined
Eichmann for moral insanity found him to be "not only normal," but even declared his
attitude toward his wife, his children, and his larger family to be "most desirable" (see [Are],
p.22).

Philonous: No. We are "responsible to all for all," it is true, but not because we actually have committed all crimes against all, but because we *potentially* could have. Consequently, the issue presently at hand is not to eradicate the responsibility of individuals for their individual deeds but to do away with the absurdity that we *are* good or better than another because we sometimes *do* or have *done* good.

Sophie: Afterall, "[n]o *one* is good— except God alone."

Philonous: Precisely.

Sophie: And it is this essential teaching of the Christ, I suppose, that is the Christian key to re-establishing the oneness that we lost.

Philonous: Indeed, healing the wound of disunion that the knowledge of good and evil tore open in man's soul was the very purpose of Christ's mission here on earth. The moral law that seduces us to judge, not actions merely, but human beings too, is the cause of man's dividedness and separation from God. By implication, it is this moral presumption—this claim to know a doer by his deed—that Jesus centrally attacks in the gospels. In direct reference to this all-important context, Dietrich Bonhoeffer for instance remarks that even a superficial reading of the New Testament will reveal "the complete absence" of the "world of disunion, conflict and ethical problems."[88] According to Bonhoeffer, it is precisely Jesus's refusal to let Himself be drawn into the world of moral arguments and laws that brings up the Pharisees against Him:

> It is in Jesus's meeting with the Pharisee that the old and the new are most clearly contrasted. The correct understanding of this meeting is of the greatest significance for the understanding of the gospel as a whole. The Pharisee is not an adventitious historical phenomenon of a particular time. He is the man to whom only the knowledge of good and evil has come to be of importance in his entire life; in other words, he is simply the man of disunion. Any distorted picture of the Pharisees robs Jesus's argument with them of its gravity and its importance. The Pharisee is that extremely admirable man who subordinates his entire life to his knowledge of good and evil and is as severe a judge of himself as of his neighbour to the honour of God, whom he humbly thanks for his knowledge. For the Pharisee every moment of life becomes a situation of conflict in which he has to choose between good and evil. For the sake of avoiding any lapse his entire thought is strenuously devoted night and day to the anticipation of the whole immense range of possible conflicts, to the determination of his own choice.[89]

Sophie: He is as disciplined as Aurelius, that Pharisee.

Philonous: And just as Aurelius—and Kant—the Pharisee, in judging himself and others according to God's law, becomes his own self-sufficient source.

Where Aurelius strove to realize his own divinity by the strength of his own will, and where Kant assigned to his own reason the role of creator of the moral law, the Pharisee is his own judge and court of appeal. As Bonhoeffer points out, the Pharisee "as a judge... is like God, except that every judgment he delivers falls back upon himself."[90] For even in the full awareness "of his own faults and of his duty of humility,"[91] he remains the prototypical man of disunion, fulfilling his moral obligation to God and setting himself apart as the man who truly knows what good and evil are. These men, Bonhoeffer says,

> with the incorruptibly impartial and distrustful vision cannot con-
> front any man in any other way than by examining him with regard
> to his decisions in the conflicts of life. And so, even when they come
> face to face with Jesus, they cannot do otherwise than to attempt
> to force Him, too, into conflicts and decisions in order to see how
> He will conduct Himself in them. It is this that constitutes their
> temptation of Jesus. One need only read the twenty-second chap-
> ter of St Matthew, with the questions about the tribute money,
> the resurrection of the dead and the first and great commandment,
> and then the story of the good Samaritan (Luke 10.25) and the dis-
> cussions about the keeping of the Sabbath (Matt. 12.11), and one
> will be most intensely impressed by this fact. The crucial point
> about all these arguments is that Jesus does not allow Himself to
> be drawn into a single one of these conflicts and decisions. With
> each of His answers He simply leaves the case of conflict beneath
> Him. ... Just as the Pharisees cannot do otherwise than confront
> Jesus with situations of conflict, so, too, Jesus cannot do otherwise
> than refuse to accept these situations. Just as the Pharisees' ques-
> tion and temptation arises from the disunion of the knowledge of
> good and evil, so, too, Jesus's answer arises from unity with God,
> with the origin, and from the overcoming of the disunion of man
> with God.[92]

In consequence, as Bonhoeffer also writes, "Jesus demands that the knowl-edge of good and evil shall be overcome; He demands unity with God."[93] For it is precisely in man's "extreme realization of his good [that] he is ungodly and a sinner."[94]

Sophie: I sense that you are on his side. Your arguments quite openly support the views that Bonhoeffer espouses.

Philonous: Let's say, I resonate with his beliefs.

Sophie: And his religion then—the Christian faith—is your religion too?

Philonous: Religion is of limited appeal to me because my first concern is not with piety but with reality—or so at least I like to think. However, when I ask myself where that reality is grasped most firmly—in the thought of Aurelius, the philosophy of Kant, or in the Christian faith and life of Bonhoeffer—my vote goes to the last of these undoubtedly. There is much that is commendable in both Aurelius and Kant, but ultimately both of them were men of conflict and disunion. Oneness cannot be restored by adherence to a moral law. On the contrary, the man who makes morality his guide will only harden the division. For the judgments that he passes must needs fall back upon himself. Those who aspire to be good cannot unknow their aspiration and therefore cannot be good.

Sophie: In other words, the pursuit of moral purity begets its own inherent contradiction.

Philonous: And the Christian vision therefore strikes me as considerably more coherent. The Christian doesn't strive to be good but merely desires to be open to Christ's transforming work in him. Where Kant and Aurelius were the masters of their own salvation, either in transcendence or in immanence, the Christian humbly embraces the gift of grace. Kant thought that modern man had come into his own, that he had left behind the bondage of God's tutelage and finally was free and self-sufficient. But when the assassin was knocking at the door, Kant had nothing to fall back upon other than a moral abstraction justified by randomness.

Sophie: Is this to say that you reject the whole of his philosophy?

Philonous: I like the spirit of Kant's first critique—the *Critique of Pure Reason* (pp.122,124,164). But as regards his moral views, I do indeed reject them. As an epistemologist Kant rightly calls us to be humble—to be aware how limited we are. But as a moralist he overestimates by far the reach of human reason. In trusting his own rationality unreservedly he creates a world of ethical thought that really is as colorless as Newton's system of mechanics. Afterall, his duty-based imperatives completely neutralize in moral terms all common human acts that flow from inclination or affection. No sacrifice for family or friends, no matter how heroic, has any moral worth in Kantian philosophy if love, not duty, is its guiding motivation. That is to say, as human reason here demands to be its own sufficient source, the human moral world is woefully depleted.

Sophie: The tune sounds well familiar, doesn't it (see for instance p.122)?

Philonous: The tune does but not the Christian lyrics that we now attach to it. Because the Christian faith here opens up a novel dual possibility: to heal the ancient wound that's symbolized in Adam's fall and thus to overcome in parallel the modern delusion of man's rational grandeur.

Sophie: And the healing Christian ointment is...?

Philonous: ...humility.

Sophie: The recipe is simple.

Philonous: But powerful in its effects and highly relevant to the problem at the heart of our quest.

Sophie: The modern loss of meaning?

Philonous: Precisely.

Sophie: So what about it then?

Philonous: Well, from our present vantage point, let me suggest, we can describe that problem as a spirit/science double bind. For on the one hand there is the original cause of disunion—the knowledge of good and evil and the attendant impulse to moral judgment—and on the other hand there is the intensifying influence of modern man's scientific understanding. The brilliant advances that Kepler, Galileo, and especially Newton achieved, not only tempted man to overestimate the powers of his reason but also drove him into bitter isolation. For in a material universe, in which random distributions of matter are acted upon by impersonal mathematical laws, man's moral self is utterly insular. As God is nowhere tangibly involved, man must bring about his own salvation wholly by himself. In a Kantian progress *ad infinitum* he must bring in line the *is* of his nature with the *ought* of his own rational moral law. However, this focus on the law only hardens the original division—unity can never be restored by trying to be good. For man not only is not good and cannot be good, but is in truth the universal bearer of all sin.

Sophie: And as a man acknowledges this all-important fact he overcomes, as we have said, his inner need to judge—the cause of his disunion. In other words, the truly humble man embraces grace in place of moral certainty.

Philonous: And in the same spirit of Christian humility there is rooted out as well any pretension to comprehensiveness in human understanding, be it scientific or moral or otherwise. For as we come to see ourselves, not as self-sufficient, self-reliant wholes, but rather as embedded parts in God's divine reality, we come to freely recognize that our knowledge and our powers of control are narrowly restricted. Blaise Pascal, for instance, is emphatic on this point when he exclaims "Be humble, impotent reason!"[96] and Paul as well reminds us to beware of intellectual pretensions:

> Knowledge puffs up, but love builds up. The man who thinks he knows something does not yet know as he ought to know. But the man who loves God is known by God.[97]

Sophie: I also feel reminded here of Socrates's confession—his claim that wisdom ultimately is the knowledge of one's ignorance.

Philonous: And furthermore, there is a solid link to our earlier discussion of evolutionary weak transcendence. For the awareness of the near certainty of evolutionary development beyond the level of the human plane—on Earth or on another planet—inspires in us sentiments of intellectual modesty that directly counteract the vilest of all sins—the sin of pride (see also p.111). Afterall, how can we humans get puffed up, as Paul might say, once we have truly understood how small a role we play in evolution's larger scheme? The world of man is nothing but a temporary station, a realm within realms within realms that far exceed the human cognitive horizon.

Sophie: In other words, science and Christian belief are here in close accord. Both remind us very strongly not to overstate the reach and relative significance of human comprehension.

Philonous: Indeed, we can discover here a beautiful convergence—an intersection of mind and spirit, science and faith—a link that truly is of critical importance. For humility in Christian life is one of God's most precious gifts of grace. It ennobles not only the intellect with natural restraint but beautifies the will and heart as well. And it is precisely this humble spirit of contrition, this admission of limitation, and this willingness not to will but to will as God wills, that we perceive as the brilliant guiding light in the lives of Albert Schweitzer, Corrie ten Boom, Dietrich Bonhoeffer, and many others like them. We perceive it as well, for instance, in Maximilian Kolbe, the Polish priest who sacrificed his life to save a fellow prisoner at Auschwitz;[98] we perceive it, too, in the testimony of Helmuth James von Moltke, the Prussian nobleman who was brutally executed by the Nazis for his peaceful resistance to Hitler's terror;[99] and we would perceive it as well, of course, in the lives of countless others if only their names and stories had been handed down to us.

Sophie: The courage and commitment of ten Boom and of the others that you mentioned were beacons of light, undoubtedly, but don't forget that multitudes of Christians everywhere fell short of their example. When it mattered the most these common people of the faith gave in to evil all too easily and often even eagerly.

Philonous: All Christians fail, and the measure of a Christian is neither in failure nor in success. But more importantly, the word 'Christian' is just that—a word. It has been applied to the Grand Inquisitor as well as to many of his victims. The word itself means very little. What matters solely is the substance that it signifies one human being at a time. The Christian spirit is not to be captured in statistics. It's not an average computed over those who practice a certain religion. Instead, the Christian spirit is a light that shines in the dark, and it shines brightest where the darkness is deepest. Ten Boom, Bonhoeffer, Kolbe, and von Moltke, they all experienced that darkness at its blackest, and that is why in them the light could be so splendidly reflected. They all failed, they all were human beings, made mistakes, and none of them was better than another. But the path they chose was the path of truth, and we can confidently trust that truth, in part at least, because of their example.

Sophie: And you, in fact, do trust it?

Philonous: I do indeed, because I sense in lives as these a grasp of the essential that inspires me and strongly reassures me. The truth here is not only found in clever reasonings but in a fundamental harmony of thought, word, and deed. Bonhoeffer, for instance, was a brilliant theologian, but far more brilliant still was the message of his sacrifice. He took up Christ's cross and died for his conviction. Tellingly, however, death to him was not a final termination, a destruction to be feared, but rather was a new beginning promising to free him from the shackles of his physical existence. For when Bonhoeffer knew that his fate was sealed, he wrote in his prison cell in Berlin the following lines:

> Come now, solemnest feast on the road to eternal freedom,
> Death, and destroy those fetters that bow, those walls that imprison
> this our transient life, these souls that linger in darkness,
> so that at last we see what is here withheld from our vision.
> Long did we seek you, freedom, in discipline, action and suffering.
> Now that we die, in the face of God himself we behold you.[100]

Sophie: I like it—his words are very moving.

Philonous: He followed where Jesus was leading and so did the others. Betsie ten Boom died in the notorious concentration camp at Ravensbrück, transfigured in appearance, as her sister Corrie described it;[101] Kolbe met his end—his moment of liberation—in the starvation bunker of Auschwitz, gently leading his fellows "through the shadows of the valley of death;"[102] and von Moltke, too, was led to Christian martyrdom. He stood trial before Hitler's people's court and was sentenced to death by the fanatical Freisler—"not as a Protestant," as he himself put it, "not as a big landowner, not as a nobleman, not as a Prussian, not as a German... but as a Christian and nothing else."[103] And in his final letter to his wife we read:

> Dear heart, my life is finished and I can say of myself: He died in the fullness of years and of life's experience. This doesn't alter the fact that I would gladly go on living and that I would gladly accompany you a bit further on this earth. But then I would need a new task from God. The task for which God made me is done. ... But I end by saying to you by virtue of the treasure that spoke from me and filled this humble earthen vessel:
>
> > *"The Grace of our Lord Jesus Christ*
> > *and the love of God and the fellowship*
> > *of the Holy Spirit be with you all."*[104]

On Parrots and Scarabs

These are beautiful words, and beautiful, too, are Bonhoeffer's thoughts concerning his faith. But the way in which that faith—the Christian faith—first entered the dialogue to which we just listened was so odd and so unexpected that it decidedly calls for some further comments.

So let us go back to that vital pronouncement of Nollie van Woerden's that "God honors truth-telling with perfect protection." Without undue exaggeration it may be said that a statement of faith so bluntly put is an insult to reason if ever there was one. In fact, so ridiculous and so blatantly spurious is this claim of Corrie ten Boom's sister that one feels almost embarrassed not to reject it outright.

But just to be sure that the claim has really no merit, we may want to picture that we do a very large search of historical records; that we go to all the world's archives, read all the world's documents, letters, and journals concerning historical facts; and that we compile in the process a complete list of all the known cases where an apparently treacherous truth was told in reliance on God's benevolent action. And further on let us assume that we do indeed find numerous cases—thousands of them—where the truth was told but God's protection was lacking. Would this not immediately settle the issue? Would not the facts thus collected immediately force Nollie van Woerden to renounce her silly belief? It is tempting to think so, but the answer is "no"—not because the historical search would be far too extensive but because in no given case can we ever be sure that Nollie's assertion truly applies.

To understand the matter more clearly, we need to observe at the outset that Nollie in no way meant to assert that there is, so to speak, a rigid mechanical link from the telling of the truth to God's protective action. Afterall, the traitor who denounced the ten Booms was truthful as well, when he revealed to the Nazis that the ten Booms were involved in an underground ring helping the Jews. But it would be entirely absurd to suppose that Nollie's intent was to assert that the truth told by a genuine traitor for selfish ends affords the traitor's victims a right to be shielded by God. In other words and in analogy to Kantian philosophy, what matters crucially is here a person's inner disposition—the purity of the motivating faith is all-important.

But this is precisely the point at which the issue gets tricky. For let us consider as an example the case where Cocky's essential motif had not been pure trust in God's faithful action, as it apparently was, but rather a blend of genuine faith and selfish concerns. For instance, Cocky might have acted the way she did from the hidden assumption that in telling the truth she could not only conveniently pass on the burden for protecting her brothers to God but also escape the distress of further questioning by the German soldiers. Outwardly, all her answers would have been exactly the same and so would have been the historical record, but her inward change in intent might well have proven disastrous. For it clearly is conceivable that Cocky, in being partly concerned for herself, would have differently processed the emotional pressure and not have broken out into spasms of laughter. Or perhaps some subtle difference in her expression might have affected the soldier and caused him not to interpret her laughter as ridicule. There are many possibilities for the scene to end in disaster, and every detail, even the smallest, can be decisive.

As a matter of course, the suggested example in which Cocky's motif for telling the truth is a little bit tainted is clearly in very poor taste. But given our present train of thought, it can help us assess the nature of Nollie van Woerden's assertion. For in the light of this hypothetical case, we can now more clearly see that the statement of faith here in question is not a crude rule saying "all will be well if only we always are honest," but is instead a subtle law of the spirit that very sensitively depends for its truth on the presence of certain initial conditions—the inner attitude of the acting believer must be just right. In fact, so sensitive is this dependence on intangible factors that, in essence, this law is beyond the reach of rational testing. Ultimately, reason is perfectly impotent to validate or invalidate Nollie van Woerden's belief. That is to say, her belief is really just that, a chosen belief.

And yet there somehow remains the unpleasant feeling that what we are dealing here with is not a responsible faith but merely a wishful fantasy. For let us imagine that all across Holland and all across Europe there had been millions of Nollies and Cockys taking in Jews and telling the truth whenever the Nazis came for a visit. Do we really want to believe that in such a scenario the Holocaust wouldn't have happened because time after time God would have honored the truth with perfect protection? Time after time and day after day a benevolent fate would have faithfully intervened to frustrate the Nazi machine? This is ridiculous—a faith for children not for adults.

How is it possible that Nollie van Woerden, an intelligent woman of courage and upright conviction, could hold such a view? How would she defend her position? Would she really have us believe that mass murder can be averted by simply being honest? We don't know, but a statement of Betsie, her sister, can give us a clue: "There are no if's in God's world." [105]

In other words, reality from this Christian perspective is not a potential, not an *if*, but simply a given with God in control. It is not a thought-experiment but a web of events that do in fact happen. What *would* have occurred if millions of Nollies had helped out the Jews while being honest about it? The question is pointless. There weren't millions of Nollies, and if there had been the world would not be the world as we know it. Would the Holocaust have run its course with millions of Nollies standing against it? Who knows? Who knows what can or cannot occur in a world so totally different from ours?

But what are we really here saying? There are no *if*'s? Can we not even ask what might have occurred *if* Cocky had not broken out into spasms of laughter?—that is, *if* one random event—the laughter—had been replaced by another—the absence thereof? Would her brothers in that case have been discovered? Again we don't know what Nollie van Woerden's answer would be, but to venture a guess, her reply might be this: "No, we cannot ask what might have occurred because where there are no *if*'s there also is no randomness."

But be that as it may, the point at present is not to decide if an answer as this can truly satisfy but rather to understand the worldview to which it testifies. So let us assume for the moment that nothing is ever a matter of chance. In that case the scene with Cocky, the soldiers, and the two brothers in hiding, is driven at bottom by forces that human perception and reason cannot discern. Perhaps there was initially a free will decision on Cocky's part to tell the truth, but what followed was not an arbitrary sequence of events that could have easily taken a different turn, but rather an orchestrated connected occurrence designed to produce an intended effect, namely the saving of the two brothers. To support this view we may postulate, as Nollie van Woerden did, that God's hand somehow was active, protecting the brothers— or, alternatively, that Cocky's pure faith set the stage for a spiritual law to spring into action and thereby bring forth the actual outcome reported in *The Hiding Place.* Either way the image is one of a surface layer of visible events covering a deeper hidden reality of purposeful actions to which human reason on principle cannot ascend.

The visible world in this kind of vision is akin to the waves on an ocean built up by forces, from above and below, that the waves themselves cannot contain. The waves, as it were, are the physical world that science describes, and the winds of the air and the currents beneath represent that far vaster transcendent domain to which only faith can ever connect us.

Philonous: It may seem silly, but I really can't deny that frequently I also feel that apparently random events are not at all random.

Sophie: You do?

Philonous: To help you see what I mean, let me give an example: whenever my wife drives the family car, and I sit right next to her in the passenger seat, I act like a typical male, making critical comments and expressing displeasure at what I consider her substandard car-driving skills.

Sophie: It sounds rather annoying.

Philonous: It's a horrible habit, I know, but somehow I cannot control it.

Sophie: And so you just continue to annoy, acting like a chauvinist?

Philonous: No, I don't, because by now my wife is so entirely fed up that she refuses to sit at the wheel as long as I'm present to watch her—that is, by now, I'm always the driver.

Sophie: That's even worse. But what is your point?

Philonous: My point is that there was over time a very clear pattern emerging. Whenever I was at my worst, making nasty comments and acting impatient, I was unfailingly made to see my mistake by what appeared to be recurring random accidents.

Sophie: I don't understand.

Philonous: Let me explain: in one case for instance, I took over the wheel right after criticizing my wife fairly severely. We had done our shopping, and it was my turn to drive both of us home. But what was the next thing that happened? I ran a red light! It was very dangerous. I was talking to my wife, getting distracted, and failing to notice the changing of the light. The

Science and Spirit

next moment I found myself in the middle of a large intersection with a whole line of cars rushing in from the side and angry drivers honking their horns at me, the crazy lunatic, for blocking their way. It was the worst traffic mistake I ever made, and it was just the rebuke that I needed—the timing was perfect.

Sophie: But it didn't have a lasting effect.

Philonous: As I said, I cannot really help it. But the pattern continued, and one scene in particular I still recall very distinctly: once again I had taken over the driver's seat after indulging my habit, and as I was backing out of the parking space there came from an impossible angle diagonally behind me a sit-on lawn mower at a very quick pace. It came directly from the grass onto the parking lot where I didn't expect it. I slammed the brakes and only barely averted the worst. My wife of course was triumphant, and I was—for the moment—repentant.

Sophie: In other words, God intervened to put you in place. Is that what you are saying?

Philonous: In essence, yes, but alternatively, I can of course also assume that all of it was simply pure chance or that my pertinent driving mishaps were Freudian slips expressive of an unconscious need to punish myself for my own annoying behavior.[106] The latter view has a certain appeal except for the fact that it doesn't account for the mower. Exactly how likely is it for anyone anyway to collide with a mower?

Sophie: I don't know, but certainly it could be accidental.

Philonous: Of course it could. But all the same I had that very vivid sense—that perfectly subjective sense—that there was more involved than was immediately apparent. In fact, it became a standing joke between my wife and myself that these things were divinely ordained to straighten me out.

Sophie: There's something I need to confess: there was a case when I once had a similar experience. It was involving a parrot.

Philonous: A parrot?

Sophie: Yes, the parrot of my neighbors had escaped from their house. And so the lady of the house with all her children in tow came over to me and asked me to open my windows, hoping the bird would fly in and be saved. I cannot explain it, but when I opened my windows I had a completely irrational thought: "If the parrot flies in, a disaster will happen." It really made no sense, but the thought forced itself upon me with such a strength of conviction that I simply couldn't reject it. I strangely knew, in the depths of my being, that if this bird came in through the window, a tragedy would somehow befall.

Philonous: And, did it come in?

Sophie: It did indeed.

Philonous: Then what about the tragedy?

Sophie: Well, a little while later the man of the house, the children's father, was killed in a car crash in England where he had gone for a visit.

Philonous: That's very sad.

Sophie: It was a terrible blow.

Philonous: Your story reminds me of a similar one told by Carl Jung concerning one of his patients. Here is his account:

> The wife of one of my patients, a man in his fifties, once told me in conversation that, at the deaths of her mother and her grandmother, a number of birds gathered outside the windows of the death-chamber. I had heard similar stories from other people. When her husband's treatment was nearing its end, his neurosis having been cleared up, he developed some apparently quite innocuous symptoms which seemed to me, however, to be those of heart-disease. I sent him along to a specialist, who after examining him told me in writing that he could find no cause for anxiety. On the way back from this consultation (with the medical report in his pocket) my patient collapsed in the street. As he was brought home dying, his wife was already in a great state of anxiety because, soon after her husband had gone to the doctor, a whole flock of birds alighted on their house. She naturally remembered the similar incidents that had happened at the death of her own relatives, and feared the worst.[107]

Jung further explains that there is in this case conceivably some archetypal symbolism involved as the souls in the Babylonian Hades supposedly wore a "feather dress," and the soul in ancient Egypt "was thought of as a bird."[108] I really don't know anything about these matters at all, but this story of Jung's just came to my mind because it bears a certain resemblance to your premonition. In both cases, the symbol of death is a bird.

Sophie: It sounds a bit spooky or plain superstitious.

Philonous: As I said, I really don't know how to assess matters as these. And we certainly mustn't imagine that anywhere here there can be discovered *verifiable* truths. An anecdote all by itself never forces belief and never persuades any skeptics. Afterall, the only clear facts far and wide are the experiences themselves: it does indeed happen that people perceive apparently random events to be strangely symbolic, loaded with meaning, or arranged by invisible hands in ways that reason cannot discern. Whether such perceptions are justified is a question that ultimately no one can answer.

Sophie: I completely agree, but I would like to add that perceptions as these can very well exert at times some very strong effects. The whole episode with the parrot seemed so strange to me and was so intensely felt that, ever since, I secretly carried in me a nagging doubt whether my rational scientific conceptions of what the world is like were really correct. I cannot say that the experience created for me a coherent alternative view but it did create doubt. In fact, a twofold doubt: concerning my familiar conceptions on the one hand and the genuineness of my experience on the other.

Philonous: Interestingly, there is another story told by Jung that underscores your point. It concerns a patient of his, a young woman, who, as Jung saw it, was "psychologically inaccessible"[109] and didn't progress in her therapy:

> The difficulty lay in the fact that she always knew better about everything. Her excellent education had provided her with a weapon ideally suited to this purpose, namely a highly polished Cartesian rationalism with an impeccably "geometrical" idea of reality. After several fruitless attempts to sweeten her rationalism with a somewhat more human understanding, I had to confine myself to the hope that something unexpected and irrational would turn up, something that would burst the intellectual retort into which she had sealed herself. Well, I was sitting opposite to her one day, with my back to the window, listening to her flow of rhetoric. She had had an impressive dream the night before, in which someone had given her a golden scarab—a costly piece of jewellery. While she was still telling me this dream, I heard something behind me gently tapping on the window. I turned round and saw that it was a fairly large flying insect that was knocking against the window-pane from the outside in the obvious effort to get into the dark room. This seemed to me very strange. I opened the window immediately and caught the insect in the air as it flew in. It was a scarabaeid beetle, a common rose-chafer (Cetonia aurata), whose gold-green colour most nearly resembles that of a golden scarab. I handed the beetle to my patient with the words, "Here is your scarab." The experience punctured the desired hole into her rationalism, and broke the ice of her intellectual resistance. The treatment could now be continued with satisfactory results.[110]

Sophie: That's a remarkable story.

Philonous: It is the most remarkable of a whole number of similar cases that Jung throughout his life collected. In fact, this data led him to propose that there exists an acausal connecting principle, called 'synchronicity', according to which the close temporal proximity of meaningfully correlated but causally disconnected events is not a matter of mere happenstance.

Sophie: Meaning, I suppose, the beetle at the windowpane did not show up by chance. There is no discernible causal connection between the telling of the dream and the appearance of the beetle. But by some wondrous higher design the two events were somehow perfectly synchronized so as to assist the young woman's personal growth.

Philonous: Indeed, the dream, the beetle, and Jung's spontaneous act of catching it together combined to form an instance of grace.

Sophie: In other words, Jung's synchronicity is not a theory in the ordinary sense because, in essence, we cannot understand it.

Philonous: That is correct. 'Synchronicity' is a scientific sounding name given to a hunch. Nonetheless, however, Jung's view has found many adherents. The American psychiatrist and bestselling author, Scott Peck, for instance, was firmly convinced that synchronicity is real. As evidence he cites, for example, in one of his books an occasion of synchronized dreams that he himself was involved in:

> The validity of such happenings is scientifically proven in terms of their probability. I myself had a dream one night that consisted of a series of seven images. I later learned that a friend, while sleeping in my house two nights previously, had awakened from a dream in which the same seven images occurred in the same sequence. He and I could not determine any reason for this happening. We were unable to relate the dreams to any experience we had had, shared or otherwise, nor were we able to interpret the dreams in any meaningful way. Yet we knew that something most significant had happened. My mind has available to it millions of images from which to construct a dream. The probability that by chance alone I would select the same seven as my friend had in the same sequence was astronomically low. The event was so implausible that we knew it could not have occurred by accident.[111]

And in another passage Peck relates a similarly 'improbable' incident involving a patient of his whom he describes as a "mature, highly skeptical and respectable scientist." The patient's story Peck retells as follows:

> After our last session, it was such a beautiful day, I decided to drive home by the route around the lake. As you know, the road around the lake has a great many blind curves. I was approaching perhaps the tenth of these curves when the thought suddenly occurred to me that a car could be racing around the corner far into my side of the road. Without any more thought than that, I vigorously braked my car and came to a dead stop. No sooner had I done this than a car did indeed come barreling around the curve with its wheels six feet across the yellow line and barely missed me even though I was standing still on my side of the road. Had I not stopped, it is inevitable that we would have collided at the curve. I have no idea what made me decide to stop. I could have stopped at any one of a dozen other curves, but I didn't. I've traveled that road many times before, and while I've had the thought that it was dangerous, I've never stopped before. It makes me wonder whether there really

isn't something to ESP [(extrasensory perception)] and things like
that. I don't have any other explanation.[112]

It is understood that in calling this incident 'improbable', as I just did, I am
not making a rigorous mathematical statement. For there is no well-defined
method for computing the likelihood of stopping a car before a blind curve
that another car is going to cut the next moment. Notwithstanding this
admission, though, the story makes me wonder.

Sophie: Me too.

Philonous: So what are we to make of it?

Sophie: I don't know. Do you?

Philonous: Well, as I see it, the matter is far too diffuse for there to be any true
comprehension. In particular, it is wise to abstain from any attempts to artificially systematize or categorize the various incidents that we have here
brought up. How does the case of Cocky's and Nollie's telling-the-truth
compare to your premonition concerning the parrot or to Jung's catching
of the scarab? I don't have a clue. There was an element of intentional faith
in Cocky's and Nollie's actions, whereas your premonition caught you entirely unawares; and in Jung's case there was "the hope that something...
irrational would turn up," but whether that hope is sufficient to constitute faith, I really cannot judge. Furthermore, the notion of there being
synchronous events that are connected but not causally so is clearly represented only in the last of these cases—the catching of the scarab. In your
parrot encounter, there is a causal disconnect, but the relevant events—the
flying-in of the parrot and the father's fatal accident—didn't happen in
synchrony, but rather in sequence with a fairly large temporal lapse. And
finally, in Cocky's case there wasn't even a causal disconnect because the
events that occurred were plausibly causing each other: the truth is told,
Cocky feels tense, breaks out into laughter, the soldier feels insulted and
thus stomps out of the kitchen. What we are left with in this case is a
stark sense of surprise that the giving-away of the hiding place turned out
to be the saving grace. But a gap in causality there really is none. Consequently, as far as I can tell, the only common element in these and the
other cases that we discussed is the definite feeling, in some of the persons
involved, that there is some transcendent influence that meaningfully links
or brings about the facts that are observed. God or grace or a law of the
spirit or whatever other agent we wish to invoke is somehow acting to orchestrate and channel apparently random events so as to render them no
longer random.

Sophie: In other words and as Betsie would say, there really "are no if's"
(p.220).

Philonous: At least there aren't as many as we commonly think. Afterall, we
may want to leave some room for the *if* of free will.

Sophie: I understand, but the basic suggestion is still that randomness is frequently just an appearance. What seems to be random is, in fact, orchestrated, synchronized, or somehow directed by powers we cannot directly perceive.

Philonous: And surprisingly this sort of disbelief in randomness has long been highly popular not only in religion but also in science. For in any deterministic model of physical reality, randomness, strictly speaking, doesn't exist. Whether it be the atomism of Leucippus or the Newtonian world machine, the understanding here as there is that the material world is causally closed and that no event is ever truly uncertain.

Sophie: But that's very different from the idea that apparently random events are set up by God to accomplish an end.

Philonous: It's totally different, no doubt, but all the same I find it worth noting that even in science randomness has been traditionally thought to be essentially illusory. For in the light of this scientific belief, Betsie ten Boom's analogous Christian perspective doesn't seem quite so eccentric. In fact, a closer look at the former, the modern scientific belief, can even provide the latter with a certain measure of rational grounding. So what we therefore should do next is to discuss if randomness in physics is genuine or not.

Sophie: Sounds good to me—let's do it.

Quantum Dice

If randomness in modern physical science is to be our topic, we do well to return to the source and begin with the Newtonian conceptual scheme. For it is this scheme upon which the present worldview of science was founded and upon which it rested for more than 200 years. Only with the arrival of general relativity and quantum mechanics,[1] in the early part of the 20th century, did the sovereign rule of Newton's classical paradigm finally come to an end.

The Newtonian world, as *Philonous* just explained, is perfectly causally closed and therefore perfectly rationally transparent. It is a world in which the exact knowledge at present of all the positions and all the momenta of all the particles in the universe allows us to calculate and thereby foretell what the future will bring with absolute, mathematical certainty. In principle, all events in this classical picture can be precisely predicted, and randomness therefore is an illusion rooted in ignorance. In other words, in such a deterministic world machine we say an event is a matter of chance, not because it really is, but because we didn't *know* in the past the factors on which it depended at a level of detail sufficient to fully foresee it. The eminent eighteenth-century physicist

---

[1] As we shall see, with respect to the problem of randomness, it was only quantum mechanics that created a genuinely new paradigm. Relativity was a revolutionary new theory of gravity, but its structure was still deterministic and therefore essentially classical.

and mathematician Pierre-Simon Laplace astutely expressed this Enlightenment vision as follows:

> All events, even those which on account of their insignificance
> do not seem to follow the great laws of nature, are a result of [them]
> just as necessarily as the revolutions of the sun. In ignorance of
> the ties which unite such events to the entire system of the uni-
> verse, they have been made to depend upon final causes or upon
> hazard, according as they occur and are repeated with regularity,
> or appear without regard to order; but these imaginary causes have
> gradually receded with the widening bounds of knowledge and dis-
> appear entirely before sound philosophy, which sees in them only
> the expression of our ignorance of the true causes.
>
> Present events are connected with preceding ones by a tie based
> upon the evident principle that a thing cannot occur without a
> cause which produces it...
>
> We ought then to regard the present state of the universe as the
> effect of its anterior state and as the cause of the one which is to
> follow. Given for one instant an intelligence which could compre-
> hend all the forces by which nature is animated and the respective
> situation of the beings who compose it—an intelligence sufficiently
> vast to submit these data to analysis—it would embrace in the
> same formula the movements of the greatest bodies of the universe
> and those of the lightest atom; for it, nothing would be uncertain
> and the future, as the past, would be present to its eyes.[113]

As we saw earlier (p.79), the view here expounded has been made obsolete
by quantum mechanics. For in the wave mechanical formalism, invented by
Schrödinger, the probability assigned to a quantum event is not expressive
of a mere lack of knowledge but rather is thought to be due to a true and
irreducible uncertainty. That is to say, the knowledge that would allow us to
give a *complete* causal account is either out of reach—for reasons of principle—
or wholly nonexistent. The formalism makes no provision for it, and within
that formalism therefore, the appearance, say, of an electron on a detector
screen in a double-slit experiment is a genuine *if*—a *quantum-if*. We know
what the distribution of electron hits will be in the statistical limit, but each
individual hit is an unpredictable spontaneous occurrence for which a cause
that is fully sufficient can never be known.

However, if Betsie ten Boom was correct, then there are no *if*'s in God's
world and therefore, presumably, also no *quantum-if*'s. It is doubtful, to say
the least, if Betsie ten Boom could ever have been bothered to extend her
claim to quantum mechanics. But insofar as our current purpose is to examine
scientifically the worldview that informs her claim, we probably do well to take
a closer look: the classical Newtonian world, as we just said, is causally closed.

If we know the present in all its details and all its complexity, then, by virtue of our knowledge of physical law, we also know the future completely. But in quantum mechanics, by contrast, no such prediction can ever be made. The quantum world, in Schrödinger's scheme, is genuinely uncertain and therefore at bottom acausal. Consequently, in reference to Betsie's belief we may plausibly speculate that the causal gap that here opens up can in fact be filled by God's purposeful action. So what we perceive as a genuine *if*—a *quantum-if*—would be in reality, if this view is right, an intended event caused by God or some other transcendent being or law. In other words, an individual quantum occurrence would not be a matter of chance but rather be due to divine intervention.

In order not to cause any misunderstandings, we need to point out that the reference just made, to "Schrödinger's scheme," is vitally important. For as we previously discussed (p.91ff), there are no *if*'s at all in David Bohm's competing description. The physical world, according to Bohm, is wholly predetermined, and even God can only know it—He cannot intervene. That is to say, the same causal gap that we just filled, in the Schrödinger case, with God's free agency can here be bridged by hidden mathematical necessity.

Notwithstanding, though, as we choose to endorse the wave-mechanical formalism of Schrödinger as the more popular option, there opens up for us the possibility to make compatible with science the religious worldview that underlies Betsie ten Boom's denial of *if*'s. For as we replace, by an act of faith, the stochasticity that characterizes this formalism by transcendent intent, we are enabled to believe that our common hunch that macroscopic everyday events are at times 'miraculously' synchronized or otherwise connected is really much more than a hunch. In other words and more concretely we may say that in the light of quantum-acausality it is conceivable—scientifically—that the scarab appeared at Jung's windowpane at just the right time because God somehow arranged, in just the right way, the myriads of individual quantum events that made up that scene.

As a note of caution we need to add that in matters as these, of course, we tend to be completely in the dark. For when it comes to a scene as the one with the scarab there aren't just countless quantum events to be reckoned with but also conscious acts of free will of the persons involved. Quantum indeterminacy is a loophole that allows us to speculate on the possibility of transcendent causation. But whether that loophole is large enough to transcendently orchestrate the scarab's appearance and Jung's quick reaction to it is not within our human powers to know. However, having admitted as much, it still remains true that quantum reality, in the Schrödinger picture, is indeterminate and therefore potentially open to transcendent interference.

Sophie: By implication then, there can be instances of grace in a wave-mechanical cosmos but not in a classical Newtonian world machine.

Philonous: I somewhat disagree, because in a Newtonian—or Bohmian—universe a sort of robotic 'grace' could still be built into the initial conditions. We wouldn't be free to accept or reject it, but present it would be.

Sophie: The freedom, then, is making the difference?

Philonous: Indeed, in Schrödinger's world we can more easily wiggle and squirm. Causation in it is not of needs exclusively physical and is also not nearly as rigid. There is room for freedom of will to cause a disturbance and also for transcendent intents to come into play.

Sophie: And in particular, there is freedom for us to believe.

Philonous: There is indeed, but that's not all there is to it.

Sophie: Why not?

Sophie: To answer that question, we need to go back in time to the late 1920's and early 1930's, some twenty years prior to Bohm's creation of his pilot-wave model.

Sophie: So wave mechanics then was largely uncontested.

Philonous: Largely but not entirely, for even then some prominent dissenters just couldn't accept that *quantum-if's* were genuine. In fact, it was Albert Einstein himself, the greatest of all modern scientists, next to Isaac Newton, who wasn't inclined to believe that nature was a gamble. More specifically, Einstein said this:

> Quantum mechanics is certainly imposing, but an inner voice tells me that it is not the real thing. The theory says a lot, but does not really bring us any closer to the secret of the 'old one.' I, at any rate, am convinced that *He* is not playing at dice.[114]

Sophie: But that's what we are saying too: God is not playing at dice but taking control. He arranges quantum events and doesn't just leave them to chance—at least not all of them and not at all times.

Philonous: Except that Einstein's idea was quite a bit different. Einstein was a scientist down to the core of his being, and our suggestion to link a scarab's timely appearance, no matter how remotely, to the acausal element in individual quantum events would likely have struck him as utterly frivolous. No, what Einstein had in mind was the existence of some deeper scientific law that would show randomness to be epistemic—an expression of ignorance.

Sophie: As it was in Newton's scheme?

Philonous: Correct.

Sophie: So what he was after was really the Bohmian system.

Philonous: Something deeper still, for as we shall see, even Bohm's deterministic description does not at all satisfy Einstein's central demand that quantum reality be fully objective. It was this demand for objectivity that Einstein was really most urgently concerned with. What does it mean to say that particles do not truly exist until we observe them? Is it not perfectly sensible for us to require that a theory of physical reality should treat a particle as an objective entity with objective properties such as position, momentum, and energy?

Sophie: Naively, the answer is "yes." But in the quantum realm, of course, there is a chance that 'yes' means 'no' and 'no' means 'yes'—as you were able to convince me (p.73ff).

Philonous: But Einstein couldn't be convinced. He always stayed a stubborn quantum-skeptic—in spite of or maybe because of the fact that quantum mechanics profoundly concerned him. According to his own assessment, he spent "at least one hundred times more time thinking about quantum problems than about general relativity,"[115] his grandest creation.

Sophie: So what did all this thinking come to in the end?

Philonous: It never produced an alternative theory but it did help Niels Bohr to deepen his own conceptual insight. You see, for many years Einstein and Bohr were engaged in a very fruitful dialogue concerning the nature and meaning of quantum mechanics. Commonly, Einstein would pose a challenge that Bohr would counter by pointing out flaws in Einstein's assumptions, verbal descriptions, or attendant deductions. And Einstein, being the honest scientist that he was, admitted that Bohr always won— always but once. In one crucial case Einstein had very good reasons not to retreat.

Sophie: What was the case regarding?

Philonous: In a paper that Einstein published in 1935 in collaboration with Boris Podolsky and Nathan Rosen (the so-called 'EPR paper') he proposed an experiment concerning two particles, such as two electrons, whose states are entangled.[116]

Sophie: I don't understand.

Philonous: Roughly speaking, a system made up of two electrons is entangled if the wave function describing the system cannot be 'broken up' or 'decomposed' into two separate functions, one for each electron. The existence of such irreducible quantum states is a direct consequence of the principle of superposition (p.80), and the practical preparation of them is easily accomplished. For whenever two electrons come close to each other and interact, the state of the two-electron system after the contact will be entangled.[117]

Sophie: So what about the experiment that Einstein proposed?

Philonous: He and the other two authors assumed that they were given two electrons A and B, the wave functions of both of which were separately known at the initial time zero. Using the Schrödinger equation, it is then possible to predict the state of the *entire* two-electron system for any time in the future so long as no measurement on the system is carried out. For as we know, a measurement causes a random collapse in which the system's wave function is abruptly and unpredictably altered.

Sophie: Why do we speak of a *system* when the electrons are described by separate functions?

Philonous: Because, starting at the initial time zero and continuing on for a certain specified interval of time, the electrons are allowed to interact. After that interval has passed, the electrons fly apart and interact no longer.

Sophie: And since interaction produces entanglement, the electrons will now comprise a genuine system.

Philonous: And to see why this is problematic, we zoom in on electron A and measure its momentum. In doing so we cause electron A to assume a well defined momentum state, and since A is entangled with B and since the system's total momentum must be preserved, the momentum of B—in consequence of the measurement on A—is well defined too.

Sophie: I don't see a problem with that.

Philonous: Just consider more closely what I just said: electron B will assume a well defined momentum state *in consequence of the measurement on A*. This is clearly absurd because, for all we know, by the time the measurement is performed, electron A may be as far from B as the Earth from the Sun. Consequently, no measurement carried out on A can possibly have any effect on electron B. And, in particular, electron B cannot assume a well defined momentum state in response to any such a measurement. In other words, a well defined momentum is simply an *objective* property that electron B possesses regardless of what we did to electron A.

Sophie: I still don't see how that is problematic.

Philonous: Well, suppose that we had measured, not the momentum, but the position of electron A. In that case, the relevant calculation easily shows that the entangled state of the two-electron system collapses in such a way— due to the measurement—that the position of electron B is also precisely specified. In other words, position *and* momentum are *objective* physical properties that can be assigned to electron B simultaneously. But that, perplexingly, isn't the case: Schrödinger's formalism doesn't allow for a single particle to have a well defined position *and* a well-defined momentum at one and the same point in time.

Sophie: It's a violation of Heisenberg uncertainty, if I remember correctly.

Philonous: Not quite. The conclusion in the EPR paper is not that the uncertainty principle is violated but rather that quantum mechanics as a theory of physical reality or our knowledge thereof cannot be complete. It's a fine point of distinction, but Einstein and his collaborators really didn't outline a method for the simultaneous *measurement* of position and momentum but only provided an argument in support of the view that in certain cases these two physical parameters must be thought to have a simultaneous *objective existence*. Afterall and as we just saw, the EPR argument crucially involves an either/or choice: we can measure *either* the momentum *or* the position but not both in conjunction. By implication, the conclusion is not that Heisenberg uncertainty cannot be valid, but that the physical description provided by a wave function may sometimes be *incomplete*.

Sophie: And that is so because no quantum wave can simultaneously specify the position and the momentum of electron B?

Philonous: Precisely.

Sophie: So how was the problem resolved?

Philonous: It wasn't, not at the time. Bohr came out with a statement that supposedly showed Einstein to have made a mistake. But his argument in this particular instance was highly obscure.[118] Physicists generally assumed that Bohr had once again triumphed, but it is doubtful whether Bohr or anyone else at the time truly understood the profundity of the problem to which the EPR paper was pointing. The implications of the EPR argument were just too radical for anyone to clearly state and embrace them.

Sophie: What's so radical about it? If position and momentum can be real in synchrony, then that just means that objectivity can undercut the epistemic threshold of Heisenberg uncertainty. In other words, things can exist that cannot be known (see also the related discussion on p.73).

Philonous: To understand what I mean it is best to assume that Einstein, Podolsky, and Rosen were wrong, that is, to assume that quantum mechanics is *not* incomplete. In that case, the obvious question that needs to be answered is this: where did their argument fail?

Sophie: I don't know.

Philonous: But, luckily, the three authors knew very well and therefore addressed the problem as follows:

> Indeed, one would not arrive at our conclusion if one insisted that two or more physical quantities can be regarded as simultaneous elements of reality *only when they can be simultaneously measured or predicted.*[119]

And further on they explain that "[o]n this point of view" the position and momentum of electron B "are not simultaneously real."[120] But how is that possible given their argument? Well, the only option here open to us is the absurd supposition that the measurement on electron A—that conceivably happens at a very great distance—can instantaneously affect the properties ascribed to electron B. For according to Heisenberg uncertainty, the measurement performed on electron A causes its momentum to become certain and its position to become totally *un*certain, and it also causes the same to happen—miraculously—to electron B. Faced with this alternative view, the three authors of the EPR paper poignantly added the concluding comment that "[n]o reasonable definition of reality could be expected to permit this."[121]

Sophie: The word 'miraculous', to me, seems vastly overstated.

Philonous: For clarification an illustration may help:[122] suppose that there were a 'natural law' according to which you always wear socks of two different colors, say yellow and red. If, given this information, I take a look at one of your feet and find the sock on it to be red, I immediately know that the sock on your other foot must be yellow.

Sophie: But that's not a miracle. That's plain common sense.

Philonous: Of course, but the situation pertaining to the EPR 'paradox' is quite a bit different: suppose that you don't have any socks on at all until I choose to take a look. So in front of each of your feet there are dangling two socks—one yellow, one red—up to that moment in time when I 'measure' a color by looking at one of your feet.

Sophie: So in taking a look you actually choose to put on one of the socks?

Philonous: Indeed, as I look at, say, your right foot, I choose one of the socks dangling in front of it at random—let's say the red one—and put it on.

Sophie: I still don't find that all that astonishing.

Philonous: But what *is* astonishing is this: as I put the red sock onto your right foot, the yellow sock is simultaneously chosen and put on your left foot by powers I cannot discern—it just so happens. Somehow the yellow sock dangling in front of your left foot instantaneously 'knows' what I am doing at a distance to your right foot and acts accordingly: it puts itself onto your left foot, just like that, without a physical link to my parallel action. In consequence, the 'natural law' that the colors worn on your feet must always be different has been strictly respected, but how did it happen? How did the yellow sock know what to do?

Sophie: That's perplexing, I admit.

Philonous: So perplexing in fact that Einstein felt forced to conclude that quantum mechanics just cannot be complete. For the only way for it to be complete, in the light of what we just said, is for state changes in entangled systems to exert instantaneous effects at a potentially very large distance. Somehow and without delay electron B 'knows' what state to assume just because in a far away place electron A underwent a random collapse.[II]

Sophie: There is no doubt the thought is strange.

Philonous: And no one found it stranger than Einstein himself, because no one had worked harder than he to ban all strangeness from physics.

Sophie: What do you mean?

Philonous: What I mean first of all is that the notion of actions exerting effects at a distance instantaneously had long been familiar from Newton's description of gravitational force.

Sophie: You brought that up before, as I recall, when you were trying to

---

[II]To speak of a random collapse or change of state with regard to only one of the electrons is of course not completely correct. The only state that can collapse in the case of an entangled system is the state of that system as a whole because the defining property of an entangled system is precisely that the individual particles, of which the system is composed, do not have well defined individual states. However, the wording here chosen is consistent with the fundamental assumption underlying the EPR argument that all physical effects somehow are local effects and that in particular the effects of any measurement are local as well.

convince me that forces are nothing but figments (p.48).

Philonous: I did, indeed, but a little review is likely in order.

Sophie: In that you likely are right.

Philonous: Then let me say or repeat that the image attached to Newton's gravitational law is one in which a change in position of any material object anywhere in the universe is *instantaneously* felt by all other material objects no matter how distant they happen to be. This is not to say by any means that the Newtonian world is acausal but only that causes in it can be transmitted without a delay and without an apparent 'mechanical link'. As a matter of course and as a note at the side, the notion of a 'mechanical link' is highly obscure from a contemporary perspective. For matter, so we believe, consists of elementary particles that in turn are nothing but mathematical theories and therefore abstractions. But in Newton's day the situation was quite a bit different. Back then scientific belief in a solidly 'mechanical' world was just beginning to bloom.

Sophie: Whether everyone really agrees with that "contemporary perspective" of yours is probably open to doubt.

Philonous: True, but today the dissenters are without excuse whereas in Newton's day insistence on 'mechanism' could justifiably be thought to be the *sine qua non* of any rational explanation in physics. It is for this reason that Newton didn't cut a very convincing figure when he resorted to divine intervention in order to 'explain' how actions at a distance can happen instantaneously—that is, when he proposed that gravity could be transmitted by God.[123]

Sophie: That's almost as bad as replacing quantum randomness by transcendent intent. It's hard to believe that the greatest physicist of all times was so completely off track.

Philonous: It's hard to believe but nonetheless true. And predictably, Newton's proposal wasn't universally met with approval. The continental Cartesians, in particular, were unsparingly critical. Christiaan Huygens, for instance, considered Newton's gravitational law a "manifest absurdity"[124] and Gottfried Wilhelm Leibniz commented on the issue as follows:

> The fundamental principle of reasoning is, *nothing is without* cause. ... This principle disposes of all inexplicable occult qualities and other figments. ... But if he posits that the effects [of gravity] depend not on an occult quality but on the will of God or a hidden divine law, thereby he provides us with a cause but a supernatural or miraculous one.[125]

Sophie: But Newton's law apparently survived the attacks.

Philonous: Because, ultimately, the Cartesians were silenced, not by Newton's appeal to divine intervention, but by the success of his mathematical system. Instantaneous action at a distance remained as strange as ever, but it simply worked far too well to merely be false.

Sophie: So the issue was never truly resolved?

Philonous: Not until more than two hundred years later when Einstein revolutionized our understanding of gravity by devising his general theory of relativity. For in relativity all actions are strictly *local* and changes in gravitational fields are not instantaneously felt but are being spread in a wavelike fashion at the speed of light. More precisely, Einstein envisioned the presence of material objects to cause the very fabric of spacetime to bend and to curve in such a way that the *locally* resulting curvature effects on other material objects become the relativistic equivalent of Newton's gravitational force.

Sophie: It sounds about as occult as instantaneous action at a distance to be honest.

Philonous: Arguably, it does, but the advantage of the relativistic picture is that causes don't just spring into action but are transmitted at a finite speed in a rationally discernible pattern. Our intuition may fail to give us a clear understanding of how an amorphous entity as spacetime can be curved into higher dimensions. But at least we no longer need to directly appeal to divine intervention to account for gravitational actions. Furthermore, we need to understand that nonlocal actions in quantum mechanics are even more perplexing than in Newton's classical system. For if indeed the EPR argument fails and if indeed quantum mechanics is *not* incomplete, then we are faced with instantaneous effects that aren't at all diminished by distance. Newtonian gravity—as described by the inverse square law—grows weaker the farther removed from each other two masses become. But the instantaneous effects that we encounter in quantum entanglement are entirely invariant under changes in distance. That is to say, the effect on electron B of the measurement on electron A is the same regardless of whether the distance between them is a few inches or a few miles.

Sophie: By implication then, it seems plausible to assume that Einstein, Podolsky, and Rosen were right and that, in fact, quantum theory is not yet complete.

Philonous: And concerning the natural question of whether it can be made complete the three authors commented as follows:

> While we have thus shown that the wave function does not provide a complete description of the physical reality, we left open the question of whether or not such a description exists. We believe, however that such a theory is possible.[126]

Interestingly, this problem of completing quantum physics directly leads us back to our earlier question of whether reality, at bottom, is random or not. For it was in this very context that Einstein more specifically predicted that "the future will see the emergence of a theory that will be *free from statistical aspects* but will have to introduce a remarkable number of variables"[127] (emphasis added).

Sophie: And that theory was the Bohmian system?

Philonous: Yes and no. For while on the one hand Bohm's phantom fields successfully eliminated all "statistical aspects," they could not on the other hand remove the mystery implied by entanglement; in fact, the subsequent developments only served to deepen it.

Sophie: How so?

Philonous: The crucial advance in conceptual thought was achieved in 1963 when the American physicist John Stewart Bell tried to purge Bohm's model of all its entanglement weirdness. Bell had been deeply impressed by the fact that Bohm had been able to create a deterministic quantum theory that was predictively equivalent to the orthodox probabilistic description. But when he tried to make the Bohmian system fully compatible with Einstein's rational vision of strict locality in physical causation, he simply couldn't do it. In consequence, however, he somehow conceived the idea that nonlocality was not a problem at the level of interpretation, as Einstein and most of his critics had thought, but rather a fundamental aspect of quantum reality that might have effects that can be directly *observed*. In other words, Bell was now seriously considering the possibility that Einstein had not only been wrong but that his being wrong could even be established by experiment.

Sophie: And, did he succeed?

Philonous: He did indeed, because he brilliantly concluded his analysis by deriving a now famous inequality that opened up the possibility for nonlocality to be confirmed by empirical means. More specifically, Bell's work showed that the probabilities which quantum mechanics assigns to the outcomes of *local* measurements, performed on entangled systems, are inconsistent with the requirement that the effects of such measurements are strictly *local* as well. To put it more bluntly, we may say that Bell opened up the prospect of empirically verifying that quantum particles "are telepathic."[128]

Sophie: In other words—that physics is paranormal.

Philonous: Let's say that it is strange; so strange, in fact, that there cannot exist—for reasons of principle—an objectivist quantum theory in which the local properties, assigned to a particle, are causally sufficient to describe that particle's local behavior in measurements.

Sophie: But what about the empirical test?

Philonous: That was carried out at the University of Paris, in 1982, by a team of physicists led by Alain Aspect. The experiment that Aspect and his collaborators devised was not pertaining to position and momentum states, as in the EPR paper, but rather involved polarized photons. This difference, however, is merely of technical interest. What truly matters to us is only the fact that Aspect's experimental results very convincingly

confirmed Bell's theoretical predictions.[III] That is to say, the matter by
now is more or less settled: quantum reality is really as weird as it seems.

Sophie: And Einstein, by implication, really was wrong.

Philonous: But so, in a sense, were most of his critics as well because, as Giancarlo Ghirardi points out in his analysis of the relevant scientific debate,
the orthodox position on the question of nonlocality had been, in essence,
to declare the question insignificant, as it supposedly was inaccessible to
empirical testing.[129]

Sophie: In other words, the world is stranger than Einstein as well as his critics
could ever have imagined.

Philonous: Indeed, the picture that here is emerging is one of an inscrutably
interconnected world that is profoundly holistic. Everything is dependent
on everything, and nothing happens in complete isolation. For if indeed the
universe originated in a Big-Bang singularity, as scientists commonly hold,
then, conceivably, this initial moment of creation and of intimate particle
interaction in a very small space produced a globally entangled system in
which no part can ever be truly apart. All events are mysteriously linked,
orchestrated, or synchronized, and the cosmos, in its entirety, is but a
single evolving quantum state in which every individual quantum collapse
is a collapse of the whole.

Sophie: Given the way you are choosing your words, I get a bit worried. Are
you trying to insinuate that, in the light of such quantum *synchronicities*,
we can now understand why the scarab appeared at Jung's windowpane at
just the right moment in time?

Philonous: That would be a bit of a stretch.

Sophie: A bit more than a bit.

Philonous: Quite a bit more because it would be totally ridiculous. Afterall,
the gulf in complexity between a meaningful orchestration of macroscopic
events à la Jung and a synchronized quantum collapse involving two electrons, say, is so incredibly wide that no scientific argument will ever be
able to bridge it. Personally, I may be inclined to *believe* that quantum entanglement and acausal connectedness in the Jungian sense are more than
mere metaphors for one another—that there is indeed a more substantive
link. But a rational reason for such a belief I will never be able to give.

Sophie: And that "more substantive link"—if it existed—would allow us to see
how Jungian synchronicity is a consequence of quantum entanglement?

Philonous: No, that sort of reductionistic approach doesn't strike me as very
convincing. For it would be somewhat akin to what I called "robotic grace"
in a Newtonian deterministic machine. Instead, what I have here in mind is

---

[III]As Giancarlo Ghirardi points out in Section 10.6 of [Gh], there are still some arcane
possibilities left open for unbelieving critics to interpret these experimental results as being
inconclusive. But the far more plausible option certainly is that Bell was right and that
quantum particles are indeed telepathic.

a higher, transcendent layer of laws of which the laws that we are aware of in quantum mechanics are but the crudest, most primitive manifestation. Isn't it conceivable that there is, so to speak, a higher rule of the spirit—a law of grace—that causes a higher form of entanglement?

Sophie: I really do not know.

Philonous: And neither do I.

Sophie: In that case, let me suggest, we may summarize the matter as follows: starting from Nollie's assertion of God's faithful action and Betsie's denial of *if*'s, we went on to observe that Newton agreed because a classical *if* is always deceptive. To this, however, Bohr most strongly objected because the classical *non-if*, upon closer inspection, is found to be a genuine *quantum-if*. But Einstein didn't buy it. He thought that God wouldn't gamble and that the world would just be a little too odd if quantum mechanics was in fact right. For in that case, particles would act at a distance with no time elapsing. But then again that's really not so bad because Newton's gravitational masses—with God's faithful assistance—had done exactly the same for more than two hundred years. Furthermore, if Newton can throw in a pious appeal to divine intervention, then we, in turn, can follow his lead and brilliantly claim that a genuine *quantum-if* is a transcendent *non-if* as long as God's loving hand or a law of the spirit is busily causing waves to collapse. And to further enhance the conceptual chaos, Bohm now envisions a great deterministic Beyond in which imaginary particles are neatly describing fictitious paths and are guided by forces that really are phantoms. Thus the genuine *if* of Schrödinger's waves becomes a *non-if* once again, but this time the latter's formal appearance suits the physicists' classical taste, and Bell, in particular, is truly impressed. But then he cries foul, because he clearly perceives that matter is telepathic regardless of whether *if*'s are *if*'s or Bohmian *non-if*'s. Finally, to round it all up, we fully agree that all of this—while clearly coherent—is in no way whatever discernibly linked to Jung's scarab or my parrot or Nollie's telling-the-truth.

Philonous: In other words, it's a glorious mess.

Sophie: ...or simply a mess.

Philonous: But either way, there is a lesson here to be learned, namely that humans live in the dark. Is reality random or is it deterministic? Is it transcendently orchestrated or immanently a matter of chance? Is it meaningfully arranged or driven by purposeless physical laws? There are no rational answers. Our present-day intellectual climate may favor assertions of blind contingency over faith in purposeful interrelation. But the preference thus given is grounded in cultural fashion and therefore open to future revision.

Sophie: That is to say, our pertinent perspective is a matter of cultural and personal choice.

Philonous: Indeed, we can will to open the window and reach for the scarab or leave it shut and pay no attention. Either way, we do make a choice, and either way, there will be an outcome resulting. Jung's decision to catch the beetle positively impacted his patient; Cocky's refusal to lie saved her two brothers from being discovered; and the willingness of Peck's patient to follow his irrational impulse to step on the brakes in front of a curve prevented a presumably fatal collision.

Sophie: But how can we ever be sure that such an irrational impulse doesn't lead us astray? If the world is driven by agents or forces that no human senses will ever perceive, then how can we know what to do when facing a vital decision? Are we to act on hunches or leadings that are perhaps mere fantasies?

Philonous: I honestly don't have a clue. I can say for myself that I tend to believe that grace is abundant and that we somehow can learn to perceive it, but genuine insight I really have none. As far as I can tell, the only certainty in all of this appears to be that many people, including myself and maybe you too, are guided at times, in action or thought, by transcendent realities in which they believe while having no rational reason to do so. Moreover, the choice to believe or not to believe can be decisive. It can be a matter of life and death, as in the case of Peck's patient, and it can even profoundly affect the course of history on a very large scale.

Sophie: You mean the decision to open the window and reach for the scarab can change the whole world?

Philonous: So to speak.

Sophie: What would be an example?

Philonous: The stock of examples is probably incredibly large, but given our present historical station—the late Roman and early Christian era—the conversion of St. Augustine is naturally coming to mind.

Sophie: Augustine of Hippo?

Philonous: That's the one—the great Christian saint who laid in his thought the intellectual foundation on which the European Middle Ages would later be erected.

Sophie: So how was he converted?

Philonous: We'll get to that, but first there is some context to establish.

A Sense of Wonder

Taking a global view, the history of Western Civilization appears to be strangely and deeply a process of cultural colonization. For in contrast, for instance, to Chinese history, which we can trace in an unbroken chain from ancient mythologies to current events over a period of 5000 years, the histories of countries like France, England, or Germany veer off at some point to become histories of foreign powers and lands—of Rome, Greece, and ancient Israel.[130] The roots of what it means to be German or French are not to be found chiefly in the customs or religious beliefs of the Gothic and Celtic tribes that once inhabited Central Europe and Gaul but rather in Roman law,[1] Greek philosophy, and Judaic monotheism. It is the meeting and merging of these two original strands—the Greaco-Roman and the Christian-Judaic—that has given the West its specific cultural form.

The defining event that made it possible for an eventually global civilizational force to grow out of the local and narrowly ethnic Hebraic traditions was, of course, the life and death of a Jew—of Jesus of Nazareth. Unfortunately, Jesus, like Socrates before him, did not commit any of his teachings to writing, and all the available historical records are therefore secondhand sources—most prominently among them the four gospels and the various apostolic letters, factual accounts, and prophetic visions that make up the New Testament.

Given the astonishing abundance of doctrinal dissent to which these Biblical sources have given rise ever since they were composed and compiled, it almost goes without saying that the New Testament does not comprise a perfectly coherent body of theological thought that clearly defines in every detail a rigid dogmatic position. But the one common thread that holds the pieces together and that provided the Christian faithful generation after generation with ever renewed inspiration and hope is the figure of Jesus.[131]

The question of who Jesus was as an historical person has been subject to endless debate. But regardless of whether or to what extent the 'historical Jesus' coincides with the Biblical picture of the Christ, the indubitable fact that remains is the absolute centrality of that picture for what it means to be Christian. Christianity just cannot be thought or experienced apart from that person, called Jesus, that the Bible portrays. It is not a philosophical system, a rational moral belief, or an essentially natural religion that the human spirit can autonomously perceive. Instead, Christianity is and always has been a call to discipleship. It is a commitment or better a yielding to a certain way of life and belief—a mode of existence that Jesus exemplified.

Most famously and perhaps most clearly that call of Jesus to follow Him by embracing and being embraced by a new form of life is articulated in the Sermon on the Mount. For bluntly put, in the *Beatitudes* the world is turned on its head. The blessed that Jesus exalts are not the great rulers and kings of the earth, not the rich and the beautiful, not the powers and superpowers that govern this world, but the poor in spirit, the meek, the merciful, the pure in heart, and those who make peace—they are the ones whom God will one day invite to sit at His side as sons and daughters of His. And where the law requires a tooth for a tooth and an eye for an eye, Jesus demands that we love our enemies and overcome evil with good.

Naturally, such a radical redefinition of how the world works is not likely to inspire much faithful adherence in practice, especially not on a larger historical

---

[1]The common law that developed in medieval England is actually distinct from Roman law, but in continental Europe the Roman tradition is still very much alive even today.

stage. Few indeed are the cases in which these lessons of Jesus have ever been tested and tried on a more than personal level. The American Civil Rights Movement may here come to mind as well as the patient endurance of the early Christian communities in the face of Roman persecution. But ironically, the most remarkable demonstration of the great spiritual power inherent in the Sermon on the Mount was given and led by a man who wasn't even a Christian. Mahatma Gandhi and his many disciples ended Britain's unrightful rule over India armed with nothing but faith in the truth of principles that closely resembled the teachings of Jesus. In his autobiography Gandhi recalls how the Sermon on the Mount, when he first came across it, "went straight to [his] heart,"[132] and in another place he is quoted as saying that

> [t]he message of Jesus as I understand it, is contained in His Sermon on the Mount. The spirit of the Sermon on the Mount competes almost on the same terms as the *Bhagavadgita* for the rule of my heart. It is that sermon which has endeared Jesus to me.[133]

Given the image of Jesus that the Bible depicts, we probably shouldn't be all too surprised at the fact that a Hindu would carry His torch so much more boldly than many a Christian. For the divisions that human beings create—be they religious or tribal or ethnic or otherwise—Jesus apparently wholly ignored. He reached out to women, welcomed the outcasts, praised the good Samaritan for his loving concern, and thereby let it be known that his loyalty was not to be tied to customs or norms that people employ to distance themselves from one another. Jesus fearlessly broke through the limits and laws that society imposes because, in essence, the only law that He knew was the law of love, compassion, and truth—which isn't even a law.

For clarity we must hasten to add that Jesus, of course, was not intent on provoking. He didn't *aim* to upset the established traditions but simply was free to put them aside whenever love impelled him. Nor was His goal to create a novel political order. Jesus was not a revolutionary—revolutionary was only His message. And He delivered that message with the absolute authority of a man who was totally and disarmingly free—free to love, free to forgive, and free to live and to die. His freedom was His greatest charisma but also His unspoken threat to those who wouldn't let go of whatever it was that held them imprisoned, their law, their righteousness, or their superior knowledge of either.

The Christian then, as Bonhoeffer longingly wrote, is seeking that inner freedom "in discipline, action and suffering" that Jesus possessed and modeled so perfectly. Christians seek to be free in order to be truly themselves in the most genuine sense. They desire to follow the footsteps of Christ by deeply imprinting their own. For Jesus did not establish a law or a rule that showed his followers or even His closest disciples distinctly the right path to choose. Instead, He only left them a Spirit that desired and still desires today to guide them in living their lives without defining in detail the form of a goal that they must achieve.

The only form that is given, as we just said, is the figure of Jesus Himself. And it is this centeredness on a particular person, a human being who really was human, that sets the Christian religion so clearly apart, not only from the polytheistic pagan beliefs of the Greeks and the Romans, but also from the faith of the Jews. Commonly, of course, Christians acknowledge the latter of these—the Judaic tradition—as a valid precursor. But it was only the life and death of the Christ that allowed this preceding revelation of God—so they believe—to really become concretized. For the God of the Jews, while certainly prodigiously active in human affairs, was nonetheless fully transcendent as well. In Old Testament times God was God and man was man and the gulf between them seemed incredibly wide. But according to the central Christian doctrine of the Incarnation, the birth of Jesus signified that the transcendent had become immanent and that God indeed had entered the world in the form of an actual person. The Word had become flesh to reconcile fallen humanity—the sons and daughters of Adam—with Him, the creator and ruler of heaven and earth.

Indeed, it is this very doctrine—this strange belief that God once lowered Himself to take on the form of an infant in a Bethlehem cradle—on which Christianity depends for much of its appeal. For in contrast, for instance, to the rational *Logos* of Stoic philosophy, which merely is a postulate, the *Logos* incarnate in the Gospel of John is a Word that literally did come alive. It is not an abstract willful assertion of the goodness of Nature, but rather a man who walked among men.

According to the Catholic theologian Hans Küng, the author of the Gospel of John was the first to explicitly identify this divine *Logos* with the actual person of Jesus.[II] But Küng also asserts that even the earliest Christians, almost all of whom were still Jews, had already been deeply convinced that Jesus had ascended to heaven and taken His seat at the right hand of God.[134] This first and very important doctrinal belief was apparently formed in direct consequence of Jesus's death on the cross and the subsequent charismatic events that persuaded His former disciples of His having been raised from the dead. In other words, bad Friday became Good Friday in the minds of these original Christian believers, and a hideous instrument of execution by torture in the shape of a cross became a symbol for God's glorious victory over the darkness of sin and death.

From a modern scientific perspective, the resurrection of Jesus is, of course,

---

[II]More specifically Küng explains "that the author of the prologue... used an older, probably Jewish-Hellenistic hymn which in good Jewish fashion is not about a pre-existent divine being 'Son', but about God and his Logos, his Word, his Wisdom in creation and revelation. The Christian author of the prologue did not change this text about the Word which was from the beginning with God, but only gave it a Christian focus at the end: 'and the Word was made flesh and dwelt among us'" (see [Kün1], p.89).

a highly unlikely event. But whatever our present assessment may be, belief in its reality has been—throughout the centuries—the *sine qua non* of the Christian religion. In fact, Christianity without it wouldn't even exist. For if the earliest believers had not been thoroughly convinced that Jesus had indeed overcome death, they more than likely wouldn't have mustered the courage and zeal to spread a good news that really wasn't that good—and if they had, they probably wouldn't have made many converts. Afterall, who would want to accept as 'messiah' a man who died on a cross never to be seen or heard of again? In other words, Christianity, as that great civilizational force that—for better or worse—it was to become, was dependent at its inception on the perceived reality of scenes as the one in which Thomas silenced his doubts by putting his hand into his risen Lord's side.

Still more bluntly and at the danger of engaging in an impious or ridiculous comparison we may even say that Western Civilization would never have been what it actually was, and is, if it weren't for the fact that a small group of Jews two thousand years ago believed to have had an encounter that, scientifically speaking, seems just as preposterous as the encounter that Kübler-Ross claimed to have had with the resurrected Mrs. Schwartz (p.158ff). And since many a modern scientist would surely not hesitate to relegate the latter of these to the realm of delusion at best and tabloid folklore at worst, we are left with the astonishing and rather strange realization that Western Civilization has given birth to a worldview—the worldview of science—that in turn denies and negates or even mocks and derides that very civilization at its very roots.

Moreover, the problem is only made worse by the fact that the first and greatest of all Christian missionaries, the Apostle Paul, received his life's calling by what appears to have been a supernatural vision. It was on the road to Damascus where Saul, the persecutor of Christians, became Paul,[III] the most zealous of all the believers. His mission was revealed to him when the risen Christ spoke to him from within a heavenly light. Add to that the various miracle accounts in the four gospels and Jesus's supposedly repeated self-designations as the "Son of Man"—the messianic figure referred to in *Daniel 7:13*—and we may as well think that the New Testament is a book about a lunatic that only lunatics would ever endeavor to write or consider authentic.

In the face of difficulties as these, the Christian writer and Oxford professor C.S. Lewis felt forced to conclude that either Jesus was indeed "a lunatic"[135] or else that his words were really the truth. Apart from this conclusion of Lewis's, it seems, the only option remaining to us is to assume that the 'historical Jesus' was a perfectly sensible person who taught us great truths and never made any fanciful claims that educated moderns would consider alarming. On such a view all the miracles, transfigurations, and references to God-given missions that we find in the New Testament would appear as embellishments

---

[III]Strictly speaking, of course, Saul didn't change his name directly on that road, but his vision on that road still was the reason for adopting his new name a little bit later.

added by those who wrote about Jesus in order to make His case seem a bit more convincing. Perhaps we even can argue that the practice of adding such supernatural adornments was culturally a well entrenched custom and should be respected as such. Alternatively, though, we also might say that a lie is a lie no matter the purpose it serves.

In order to avoid any potential misunderstandings, we wish to emphasize that the preceding remarks are in no way meant to offend those earnest Christian believers who strongly affirm the literal truth of the Gospels—and neither, of course, did C.S. Lewis, by his remark, intend to do so. That is to say, the object here is not to ridicule the Christian faith or its adherents but rather to starkly display the rational dilemmas that the Bible necessarily presents us with.

To be sure, modern rationalists and empirical scientists were not the first to notice the problem that is here at issue, namely the alignment of revelation with reason. Instead, the conflict was bound to unfold right from the start. The Apostle Paul, for instance, already anticipated the trouble to come in the following passage from his first letter to the *Corinthians:*

> Where is the wise man? Where is the scholar? Where is the philosopher of his age? Has not God made foolish the wisdom of this world? For since in the wisdom of God the world through its wisdom did not know him, God was pleased through the foolishness of what was preached to save those who believe. Jews demand miraculous signs and the Greeks look for wisdom, but we preach Christ crucified: a stumbling block to Jews and foolishness to Gentiles, but to those whom God has called, both Jews and Greeks, Christ the power of God and the wisdom of God. For the foolishness of God is wiser than man's wisdom, and the weakness of God is stronger than man's strength.[136]

And the North African church father Tertullian was even more explicit in his rejection of the follies of reason when he famously coined the motto *"credo quia absurdum est"*—"I believe because it is absurd."[IV] Others, however, as we shall see, couldn't be satisfied with such an exclusive endorsement of faith—over and against the critical intellect—and therefore took on the task to harmonize the wisdom of man with the wisdom of God.

This move toward an intellectually more open-minded approach was part of a larger historical process that transformed Christianity from an initially Jewish heretical cult into a cosmopolitan Hellenistic religion. The decisive

---

[IV] According to Störig, it isn't entirely certain whether Tertullian was indeed the one who coined this phrase because it cannot be found in any writings of his that are still available to us. Notwithstanding, though, the phrase may be said to accurately reflect Tertullian's basic impulse to deny reason in favor of faith (see [Stö], p.246). Furthermore, as Carl Jung points out, what Tertullian did say is this: "And the Son of God died, which is immediately credible because it is absurd. And buried he rose again, which is certain because it is impossible."[137]

impetus here again was provided by Paul who, in spite of his dismissal of Greek philosophical wisdom in the passage just quoted, was himself markedly Hellenistic by culture. Consequently, Paul quite naturally perceived his mission to be the preaching of the Christian good news to Jews and Gentiles alike. On his far-flung travels throughout the Mediterranean world he not only engaged the Jews in their synagogues but spoke to whomever he met and found willing to listen.

It is in the context of such cosmopolitan missionary ambitions that the first attempts were made to integrate Greek philosophy with Christian belief. For if indeed the pagans were to be won for the new faith, their most outstanding intellectual traditions could not be simply ignored or despised. A more accommodating approach that combined the best of two worlds seemed here to be more promising.

One of the most notable early pioneers in this quest to ally faith with philosophy was a man from Palestine, named Justin, who was martyred in Rome in 165 A.D. Central to Justin's theology was a conception of the *Logos* as a world-governing reason which closely resembled the pertinent ideas in the teachings of the Stoics and the thought of Heraclitus. The *Logos*, according to Justin, had found its fullest expression in Christ, but to some lesser degree every human mind could partake of the truths that this divine reason reveals. Consequently, the truths contained in Plato's Socratic dialogues, while clearly imperfect, were truths nonetheless. In consequence, Justin came to regard men like Socrates and Heraclitus, for the depth of their insight, as "Christians before Christ."[138]

A far more comprehensive approach to the problem of integration was taken a little less than a hundred years later by Origen of Alexandria. Gifted with enormous creative powers—he supposedly authored as many as 2000 works— Origen devised a highly speculative mode of allegorical exegesis by means of which he aspired to directly align the elements found in Biblical texts with the essential themes of the Platonic tradition. There is no need for us to look at Origen's system in any greater detail. But concerning the final result we should perhaps add that his attempt at complete integration produced a *Logos* Christology of rather bewildering complexity. The simple original message of Christ crucified that we find in the gospels and the letters of Paul was here being lost in a metaphysical maze of complicated concepts and deductions. This is not to say, of course, that Origen was lacking in Christian commitment—he was imprisoned and tortured for his faith by the Romans—but only that his partial descent into heterodoxy made his system suspect in the eyes of the church. In fact, already during his lifetime did certain parts of his system come under attack, and eventually, long after his death, his work was condemned.[139]

Thus it was left to other church fathers to recast Origen's byzantine thought in a more compact, orthodox mold. One of the next who attempted this task was St. Gregory of Nyssa who lived from about 335 to 395 A.D. In contradistinction to Origen, Gregory perceived a clear qualitative difference between a revelation accepted on faith and a philosophical system grounded in reason. In doing so, he was able to maintain the superiority of faith over reason while recognizing simultaneously the teachings of philosophy as a valid rational aid.[140] However, these efforts of Gregory and some others besides pale in significance when compared to the outstanding achievement of that great Christian thinker to whom we must now devote our attention: *St. Augustine of Hippo.*

Augustine was born at Thagaste in North Africa in 354 A.D. His father, Patricius, was a pagan, but his mother Monica brought him up as a Christian.[141] As a boy, Augustine was instructed in Latin and Greek by the schoolmasters at Thagaste. But the latter of these, the Greek language, was "distasteful"[142] to him, and even later in life "he never learned to read it with ease."[143] At the age of sixteen he went to the city of Carthage where he studied rhetoric and also developed a lively interest in philosophy. When he came into contact with the thought of the Manichees, he adopted their doctrines and in the process began to abandon the faith of his youth, thereby causing his mother great sorrow.

What attracted him most to the Manichean religion was the solution it offered to the problem of evil. For in contrast to the seemingly absurd Christian belief in a *good* God who had created a world that in turn produced evil, the Manichees held that good and evil were independent forces eternally engaged in a conflict from which the real as we know it comes forth.

Somewhat less compelling, though, was the Manichean teaching according to which matter was made up of good and bad particles and flesh, in particular, was dominated by evil. In practice, the Manichees took this to mean that they, as the religious elite, should abstain from the eating of meat. As for fruits and vegetables, these were permitted, but the act of plucking or cutting was considered defiling and was to be left to those who didn't belong to the sect.[144] Such absurdities aside, Augustine especially came to be troubled by the teachings of Manes, the sect's founder, on matters of science. According to Augustine, Manes "was not only ignorant of the subjects which he taught, but also taught what was false, yet was demented and conceited enough to claim that his utterances were those of a divine person."[145] When he got a chance to put his questions to Faustus, a highly acclaimed teacher of the Manichean religion who had come for a visit to Carthage, Augustine was deeply disappointed with the man's lack of insight and scholarly learning. As a result, he gave up all his ambitions to advance in the sect but remained loosely in contact until something better showed up.

Shortly after his encounter with Faustus, Augustine decided to move from Carthage to Rome where he continued to work as a teacher of rhetoric. His reasons for moving had nothing to do with the visit of Faustus but rather with certain reports that the student behavior in Rome was not as disruptive. For apparently, the students in Carthage routinely committed outrages against the faculty that bordered on the criminal.

Upon his arrival in Rome, Augustine was struck down by an illness that nearly killed him, and, as he himself put it, almost cost him his soul. For in retrospect, in his *Confessions*, he describes his life up to this point as one of grave sin and licentiousness. As an adolescent, for instance, he had joined a gang of young "ruffians"[146] to whom he boasted of his vices—real or imagined—and together with whom he also committed a theft. Late one evening, he and his companions stole a number of pears which, afterwards, they fed to the pigs. Some months later, in Carthage, Augustine found himself "in the midst of a hissing cauldron of lust"[147] in which his own passions were soon getting the better of him. Indeed, it didn't take long before he lived with a mistress and fathered an illegitimate son. Immersed in city life, he also came to enjoy the plays at the theater, some of which apparently were of dubious moral repute. Exactly how bad his conduct was compared to that of other young males in that place and time is hard to determine, but a model of righteousness it clearly was not.

Returning now to Augustine's tenure in Rome, it may be said that it proved to be shorter than he intended. For as it turned out, the students in Rome, while being less violent than those in Carthage, were given to cheating their teachers out of their pay. To do so, they would plot to transfer their attendance in groups from one teacher to another just in time before a payment was due. In the face of such hostile behavior, Augustine gladly offered his services when the Prefect of Rome announced that a position for a teacher of literature and elocution had opened up in the city of Milan. Armed with excellent recommendations, he set out for Milan and there was able to secure the position.

On a personal level this second professional move marked a point in his life when he had almost completely despaired of ever finding the philosophical truth for which he longed so eagerly. By now he had cut all his ties to the Manichees, but the void that their teachings had left was not being filled. Hence he resigned himself to becoming a skeptic.

Before long, though, in Milan, he made the acquaintance of the bishop Ambrose, a man of great kindness who received him with fatherly warmth. As he listened to the bishop's sermons on Sundays in church, he initially directed all his attention at the charming style of delivery, as he didn't expect the content to carry much weight. But in time, his attitude changed. Slowly he came to appreciate the truth in what the bishop was saying, and slowly there grew in him a new hope that it might be possible "to unravel the tangle"[148] that he found himself in. However, his sense of having been fooled for almost ten years by Manichean pretensions made him now feel ashamed of his imprudent judgment as well as afraid of another potential deep disappointment. And so he continued to struggle, eager to relieve his unhappiness but hesitant to accept the Catholic claims to the truth.

Eventually, in this process of urgently seeking the truth, the message of Christ that the Bible proclaims became more and more dear to his heart. But his mind was still troubled with incomprehension concerning the problem of evil and other such metaphysical questions. In agony he applied himself to the study of the Scriptures as well as some Platonist texts, hoping desperately that somewhere the answers would come into sight. And indeed, proceeding step by step in an arduous struggle, his confusion was finally lifted. Regarding the problem of evil, for instance, he now was able to see that evil is deprivation of good, and not, as the Manichees taught, a mysterious substance. In consequence, he came to conclude that nothing that was in existence was completely bereft of all good, and that creation in toto was better than even the best of its parts in isolation.[149]

Having thus resolved his rational quandry, the one stumbling block still in his way was his attachment to sensual pleasure. Concerning this issue, he already felt "quite sure that it was better for [him] to give [himself] up to [God's] love than to surrender to [his] own lust. But while [he] wanted to follow the first course and was convinced that it was right, [he] was still a slave to the pleasures of the second."[150]

Finally, though, it all came to a head one day when Ponticianus, a fellow country man of his, told him of the sudden conversion to the service of God of two friends after they had chanced upon a written account of the life of Antony, an Egyptian monk of exceptional saintliness. At the telling of the story, Augustine was filled with the deepest remorse at his own life of sin as well as with "violent anger"[151] at his continued reluctance to heed God's call for his life. In the company of his good friend, Alypius, who happened to be present as well, he was overcome with emotion and laboring to reach a decision. With tears welling up in his eyes, he got up and left to be on his own, all the while berating himself with questions as to why his habit of sin could still hold him captive. The events that ultimately broke his resistance Augustine recounts in his *Confessions* as follows:

> I was asking myself these questions, weeping all the while with the most bitter sorrow in my heart, when all at once I heard the sing-song voice of a child in a nearby house. Whether it was the voice of a boy or a girl I cannot say, but again and again it repeated the refrain 'Take it and read, take it and read'. At this I looked up, thinking hard whether there was any kind of game in which children used to chant words like these, but I could not remember ever hearing them before. I stemmed my flood of tears and stood up, telling myself that this could only be a divine command to open my book of Scripture and read the first passage on which my eyes should fall...

So I hurried back to the place where Alypius was sitting, for when I stood up to move away I had put down the book containing Paul's Epistles. I seized it and opened it, and in silence I read the first passage on which my eyes fell: *Not in revelling and drunkenness, not in lust and wantonness, not in quarrels and rivalries. Rather arm yourselves with the Lord Jesus Christ; spend no more thought on nature and nature's appetites.* I had no wish to read more and no need to do so. For in an instant, as I came to the end of the sentence, it was as though the light of confidence flooded into my heart and all the darkness of doubt was dispelled.[152]

Philonous: And thus Augustine the sinner became Augustine the saint.

Sophie: And what was the key? Carl Jung's synchronicity! Ponticianus appears, tells his story, Augustine is shaken, the child sings a meaningless song at just the right time, Augustine opens Paul's writings to just the right page, and on the spot his life is made new and he leaves as a monk.

Philonous: ...and thus the course of theological thought is set for the next eight hundred years. For that is how pervasive the influence of Augustine's ideas—in consequence of his initial conversion—would turn out to be. With respect to one of his most famous works, the *City of God*, it has been said for instance that no thinker in history, with the exception of Plato, had a more penetrating effect on the development of Western culture than Augustine had by means of the twenty-two books that this work comprises.[153] Add to that his highly influential treatise on the Trinity, his *Confessions*, and the rest of his numerous books, letters, and sermons—well over 800 in total[154]—and Augustine assumes an aspect of intellectual greatness that's very hard to match.

Sophie: I must admit it strikes me as odd that the point of inception for such an historic achievement was a moment of seemingly irrational willingness to believe that a hunch was more than a hunch.

Philonous: The hunch being, I suppose, that the child's 'meaningless' chant of "take it and read" was, in truth, an instruction from God.

Sophie: Precisely.

Philonous: In that case I should perhaps caution that we won't ever know of course how crucial that hunch really was. For conceivably, Augustine would have reached his decision to abandon his worldly career for a life in the church even if there had been no child and also no chanting.

Sophie: But given the events that did in fact happen, we do have good reasons to say that the tale of Augustine the great Christian thinker began in a moment that Augustine himself perceived as an instance of heavenly grace.

Philonous: We do, I agree.

Sophie: If that is so, then I am getting once again entirely confused. For the issue of the emergence of the Christian religion as a defining cultural force appears to be just as obscure as the matter of *quantum-if's* and classical *non-if's* that I recently found so perplexing.

Philonous: Why is that?

Sophie: Because in my understanding the relevant story is this: at the outset there was written a book, called 'The New Testament', that tells of a man who came to this earth born of a virgin and on a mission from God—a man who really was God but really was human as well. This man performed a number of wonders, walked on water, became transfigured, died on a cross, and a little while later was seen again by his disciples strolling about as if nothing had happened, and in particular, as if He never had died. Soon thereafter He ascends into heaven, becomes Himself a heavenly light and appears as such to a man on the road to Damascus who calls himself 'Saul' but then prefers 'Paul', and afterwards travels about, hither and thither, to tell the whole world that a death on a cross is really good news. Naturally, people believe him because it makes so much sense, and the religion born in the process becomes the foundation of our civilization. This religion, however, looks still a bit rough in a rational light, and, by implication, there still is a bit of explaining to do. So along comes Augustine to straighten things out, and the point where he starts is a tentative hunch that a silly child's song is a coded instruction from that man in heaven, called 'Jesus', who really is God. Exactly what, if I may ask, is all this hocus-pocus really about?

Philonous: To that I can give a fairly clear answer: your "hocus-pocus" is a short-hand sound imitation of 'hoc est corpus (meum)'. This Latin phrase is used in the Eucharist and refers to the claim that Christians eat bread that becomes in their mouths the actual flesh of the body of Christ—the claim which caused the Romans to believe, as I should add, that Christians were cannibals.

Sophie: I get a sense it's still getting worse.

Philonous: And we haven't quite reached the bottom as yet because there still is another major event that your irreverent summary of early Christian history should probably include: the conversion of Constantine.

Sophie: The Roman emperor who legalized the Christian religion?

Philonous: Indeed, Constantine granted unlimited religious freedom to the entire Roman world with the Edict of Milan in 313 A.D. And, surprisingly, this epochal decision was due to the fact that Constantine, a year earlier, had won the battle at the Milvian Bridge against the Roman usurper Maxentius under the sign of the cross.[V] In other words, Christianity became the

---

[V] As Norman F. Cantor points out in [Can], pp.48–49, there is a certain amount of controversy among historians regarding the question of how or whether the events surrounding that battle facilitated Constantine's conversion to the Christian religion. However, a detailed discussion of the various accounts and opinions that are here at issue is obviously far beyond the scope of the present exposition.

West's official belief because an initially pagan emperor had superstitiously ascribed a military victory to Jesus, the Prince of Peace.

Sophie: Which leads us directly to the final conclusion that the history of our great Western World is a story of nuts who do nutty things for perfectly nutty reasons.

Philonous: Strangely, though, we also find that all this nuttiness becomes remarkable saneness when we study the teachings of Jesus and discover how they inspired the actions and thoughts of such admirable men and women as Mahatma Gandhi, Albert Schweitzer, Corrie and Betsie ten Boom, Dietrich Bonhoeffer, Maximilian Kolbe, and Helmuth von Moltke—or how, for that matter, they inspired Augustine to write his *Confessions*. In fact, not only is there no nuttiness on this alternate side of the coin, but instead we find here a world in which the highest human ideals of love and genuine sacrifice are brilliantly exemplified.

Sophie: Yet how do we make it all fit? We cannot just say that irrational madness somehow begets beautiful saneness and then just leave it at that.

Philonous: No, but what we can do is to go back to the scene of Augustine's conversion or of Jung's catching the scarab and discuss some ideas that may help us recover a rational view.

Sophie: But how?

Philonous: By picking up three billiard balls and letting them float.

Sophie: Three billiard balls? What in the world...?

Philonous: Just give me a chance. I think, I can do it.

Sophie: Can I say "no"?

Philonous: No.

Sophie: That's what I thought. So what about those balls?

Philonous: We put them in a rocket ship and set them afloat far out in space.

Sophie: And then, what do we do?

Philonous: Imagine them each as big as a planet.

Sophie: Three planet-sized balls are floating in space—the picture is clear, but what is its purpose?

Philonous: To see what I am getting at, you need to consider the following question: what happens to the balls if they are not externally disturbed?

Sophie: The answer is, no doubt, that gravity will cause them to accelerate.

Philonous: That is correct, but more specifically, the balls will be attracted to each other, bounce off of each other, be attracted again, bounce off again, and so forth in some irregular fashion.

Sophie: I still don't see your point.

Philonous: To be more explicit, my first point is this: the movements will be irregular for reasons of principle. For the three-body problem—in decided contrast to the two-body problem—doesn't have a nicely closed solution. There is no way to find an equation for the paths that the three balls or planets will follow—except in very special cases. In the two-body case, the trajectories are either Keplerian ellipses with a common focus at the two bodies' center of mass or, alternatively, they are open hyperbolas.[VI] But in the three-body case, the pertinent paths are typically chaotic and highly sensitive to any change in the initial conditions.[VII] This is not to say, of course, that the three-body motion, in its classical Newtonian description, isn't lawful or isn't deterministic, but only that in most of its visible aspects, it appears to be random.

Sophie: I understand, the paths are totally irregular. But once again I need to say, I still don't see your point.

Philonous: Then try to imagine next that you aren't as smart as you are, but really quite dumb.

Sophie: How dumb?

Philonous: Very dumb.

Sophie: As dumb as a monkey?

Sophie: A bit smarter than that, but not a whole lot.

Sophie: What about an earlier version of man—a *homo habilis* or *homo erectus*?

Philonous: That's a good thought—an ape-man will do.

Sophie: 'Ape-woman' is a little more like it.

Philonous: That's okay too—I didn't mean to be sexist.

Sophie: Very well, then I am now a stupid woman from prehistory. But how do I, in this capacity, assist you in your reasonings?

Philonous: By observing patiently the movements of the planetary billiard balls.

Sophie: And as I do that, what do I see?

Philonous: Basically, the same that I see as well, but what you lack is proper comprehension. With your inferior brain you have perhaps some dim recognition of the balls being drawn toward each other and bouncing off of each other again and again, but other than that you're totally clueless. For you do not command conceptual thought and, in particular, you do not command mathematics. In other words, the quantitative modeling that Newton made available to me—a modern human being—is wholly transcendent from your point of view. You have a "tentative hunch" (p.251) that the repeated collisions are pointing to something beyond the tangible world that your senses perceive, but what exactly that something might be is not within your powers to grasp.

Sophie: You asked me to give you a chance, and that's what I did, but now I'm afraid it was a mistake. For what have we got? A lady *erectus* somewhere in space, watching a gravitational billiard and having no clue.

Philonous: But don't you see how beautifully it all is set up to draw an analogy to our own present dilemma?

[VI]...or parabolas. But the case of parabolic paths is a limiting case which in essence can never be directly observed and only exists as a theoretical option.

[VII]The initial conditions are constituted by the bodies' initial positions and velocities.

Sophie: Of course I do. By now I know exactly what your purpose is: you're aiming to invoke your favorite pseudo-scientific conception.

Philonous: Which is?

Sophie: ...weak evolutionary transcendence. For what you will do next is to propose that in the future there may live a being on a higher plane of consciousness that will look upon us as we look upon that lady *erectus*. That being, so you will argue, will be able to perceive, by virtue of its superior cognitive skills, that Carl Jung's synchronicity is not just a "tentative hunch" but rather is coherently rooted in a higher layer of rational structures or laws that strictly transcends the layer of physical laws that humans explore by means of their natural science. In other words, where we can make fully precise by mathematical methods the dim recognition of a lady *erectus*, your postulated higher being will be able to see why the appearance of the beetle at Jung's windowpane or the chanting of the child in Augustine's account was not a mere coincidence. In both of these cases our intuition suggests that there may be a purpose acting beneath the surface of seemingly random events. But rationally, we just cannot get a grip because our human intellect is simply not sufficiently highly evolved.

Philonous: I must admit, you got me figured out. For as it is, I do believe that the ability to discern lawfulness in apparent randomness most likely isn't an absolute but rather is continuously refined as evolution progresses.

Sophie: I told you, I knew.

Philonous: So what do you think? Does it make sense?

Sophie: Not a whole lot to be honest. For your proposal merely is, as I see it, a one-size-fits-all fallacious evasion.

Philonous: That's a harsh way to put it.

Sophie: Harsh but fair nonetheless, because your reasonings are easily abused to lend support to any odd belief that people may come up with. If you wanted to argue, for instance, that astrology is more than a mere superstition, you could conveniently conjecture that a higher form of life could possibly be conscious of a law that does indeed connect events on earth in causal terms to planetary constellations. In other words, anything goes, if only we keep evolution's potential in mind.

Philonous: There is a danger, it is true, of overapplication. But the opposite mistake of *under*application is certainly more prominent. For vanity inclines us to believe that our rational abilities are greater than they are and thus discourages the more deflating evolutionary view.

Sophie: In that you may be right, but your perspective in this case is very much one-sided.

Philonous: How so?

Sophie: To show you what I mean, I'd like to share with you a story of a meeting of the *Royal Society* in London. The year was roughly 1650, and the gentlemen attending it were all of elevated academic standing. As the meeting commenced, exactly at midnight, everyone gathered around a large table, and the general mood was one of expectant suspense. To start the proceedings, one of the luminaries rose from his seat and drew on the table a circle, using some chalk, while others intoned occult incantations. Then a giant stag beetle was released from a box and placed in the circle right at the center. Silence now descended over the room as everyone was watching intently what the insect would do. At first the beetle was hesitant, uncertain of its unfamiliar surroundings. It moved a bit to the left, then veered to the right, and again to the left, unable to make up its 'mind'. Finally, though, it followed an impulse to walk straight ahead—across the circle of chalk—until it reached the edge of the table. And as it did so, everyone present felt greatly relieved.[155]

Philonous: The story is strange and so is the meeting.

Sophie: As for the meeting, I have to admit that I don't know for sure whether it really took place. But the point of the story is valid regardless.[VIII]

Philonous: And that point is...?

Sophie: ...to illustrate how very difficult it was for early modern scientists to free themselves from the shackles of medieval superstition. At the time it couldn't be taken for granted at all, that a beetle couldn't be bound by a spell or restrained in its motion by a circle of chalk. Any such occult proposition had to be carefully tested before it could be discarded. For the worldview of science was still too feeble and young to simply declare it false by default.

Philonous: So what you are saying in other words is that people like I need to be mindful not to revive irrational creeds by devising spurious arguments that promote blatant unreason under a cover of scientific-sounding conceptions like weak evolutionary transcendence.

Sophie: Indeed, the Enlightenment victory over the darkness of groundless beliefs was very hard won and should be guarded carefully. Insofar as such beliefs pertain to beetles in circles or scarabs appearing exactly on time, the consequences of unreason may be benign. But when women are declared to be witches and burned at the stake because they happen to have red hair, the matter is a bit more sinister.

Philonous: It's a difficult problem, no doubt. But the fact that evil in general is a permanent threat and that the witch hunts in particular were a terrible scourge does not in any way imply that it is wrong for me to contemplate the nature of my own limitations. If it is possible, as science clearly suggests, for beings far higher than myself to develop, then it certainly is possible as well for an understanding of lawfulness, orchestration, or interconnectedness to arise that far surpasses mine.

[VIII] As Ditfurth points out in [Di], p.191, this story was told to Werner Heisenberg by his colleague Niels Bohr, and Bohr intentionally left open the question as to whether the meeting had really occurred.

Sophie: But how do you separate the wheat from the chaff? How do you tell apart a responsible faith from a silly wishful fantasy?

Philonous: You asked that question once before (p.240), and as before my answer is that I don't know. I don't know if Augustine was right to believe that the little child's song was a message from God intended for him, and I also don't know what caused or didn't cause the other events in the various cases that we discussed. How do we account for Jung's scarab, for Peck's patient braking his car in front of a curve, for your parrot encounter, or my car-driving mishaps? Again, I don't know. But neither, of course, do I know that your premonition concerning that parrot was a delusion or that Augustine was fooling himself when he opened Paul's letter upon hearing that song. I can choose to go exclusively with what I can see, but then the risk that I run is to miss some great opportunities. If Augustine had been purely a realist he probably would have remained a teacher of rhetoric for the rest of his life. And worse still and as I mentioned before (p.240), if Peck's patient had refused to listen to his inner irrational voice, he would have probably died shortly thereafter in a head-on collision. On the other hand, though, if I choose to believe that reality is largely transcendent, then I may at times make a decision based on a hunch that really is just an illusion.

Sophie: But how do I come to a workable balance? How do I know when to trust reason and when to trust faith?

Philonous: I don't know.

Sophie: Fair enough, but as regards for instance all those stories in the Bible, it would be nice to know if I can trust that they are true.

Philonous: Belief or disbelief in this regard is really your decision. For ultimately, no case by case apology—based either upon historical records or present-day related events—will ever be truly conclusive. We can speculate, of course, that the light that Paul perceived on the road to Damascus was the same kind of light that people commonly see in near-death encounters. And furthermore we can point out that Paul would likely not have been as zealous as he was in spreading the Christian good news if the vision of the Christ that he had seen had not been truly persuasive. Afterall, who would be willing to face severe persecution, torture, and death for the sake of a dim apparition?[156] But realistically, no such purported defense is going to sway a modern critic whose standard of truth is science and nothing but science.

Sophie: In other words, belief is here a choice and nothing but a choice.

Philonous: That is correct, but I would like to add that choosing to believe is not *per se* a sign of silly gullibility. For if indeed the world is greater than the range of human comprehension, then why should I be shocked to learn that there have been events in history that really did exceed my human comprehension?

Sophie: Events like Jesus's resurrection and the Pauline vision of the Christ?

Philonous: Precisely.

Sophie: In that case let me say that I don't feel at all convinced that these events occurred. For simply pointing to transcendence as a global possibility is really not sufficient.

Philonous: ...but neither is, as I just said, the most detailed apology. There have been many arguments devised for why the resurrection, for example, did indeed occur—and I encourage you to look at them.[IX] But don't expect to find a proof that really is a proof.

Sophie: And yet, I still don't like your argument.

Philonous: Why not?

Sophie: Because it undermines the scientific impulse. Afterall, there is no need for us to ever try to separate the real from the imagined, if everything is potentially real by weak or strong transcendence. Put differently, why should we search for knowledge by scientific means, if most of what there is is basically beyond us?

Philonous: Just look for guidance to Augustine: he searched for understanding with his mind despite the fact that he believed most fervently in otherworldly realms.

Sophie: But Augustine's primary interest wasn't in science.

Philonous: Certainly, Augustine was not a theoretician. He was not a natural scientist; he was not a systematic philosopher; and he wasn't even a theologian for theology's sake. Instead, his main concern consistently was human life in its relatedness to God. But as it is, it was precisely this concern of his that led him to contemplate some very deep problems, including the problem of knowledge itself.[157] You see, Augustine felt an urgent need to understand how certainty in knowledge can be reached because he himself, as we recall, had been troubled by skepticism after rejecting the Manichean religion.

Sophie: So what was his solution?

Philonous: To begin with he merely observed that even a skeptic has to accept certain minimal logical rules such as the principle of contradiction. That is to say, even a skeptic cannot deny that the disjunction 'A or not A' is true necessarily. 'God exists or doesn't exist' is a statement that no one can meaningfully assert to be false. Furthermore, Augustine also believed that sense-perception—taken at face value and unburdened by any conceptual judgments—is worthy of trust. For even in cases where the senses seem to mislead us—as for instance in the case of the *apparent* bending of objects that are partially immersed in water—Augustine isn't dissatisfied with what he perceives. In his treatise *Against the Academics*, for example, he addresses the matter as follows:

[IX] The apology provided by Lee Strobel in [Stro] is a popular example that the reader may want to explore.

There remains to ask if, when the senses report, they report what is true. Now, then, if an Epicurean says:[158] 'I have no complaint to make of the senses, for it is unjust to demand of them more than they can give: whatever the eyes can see they see truly.' Then, is that true which they see in the case of an oar in the water? Quite true. For granted the cause why it appears in that way [i.e., bent], if the oar, when plunged into the water, appeared straight, I should rather accuse my eyes of playing me false. For they would not see what, granted the circumstances, they ought to see...

'But I am deceived, if I give my assent', someone will say. Then don't give assent to more than the fact of appearance, and you won't be deceived.[159]

Sophie: In other words, the senses provide a raw stream of data that is what it is and that, as such, may very well be trusted.

Philonous: The paraphrase is apt.

Sophie: A skeptic, though, could easily object that the stream in question is merely imagined and is thus entirely internal.

Philonous: True, but even a radical doubter as this can be assured—by virtue of his doubting—of being conscious and alive. And hence Augustine's famous motto: "Si fallor, sum"—"If I am mistaken, I am."[160]

Sophie: Very well, the conscious self exists. But what about exterior reality?

Philonous: Insofar as Augustine was willing to accept as valid the information that the senses provide he also was inclined to assume that the source of this information was somehow external. His stance in this regard was not designed to convince a radical skeptic—nor could it have been—but as for himself it certainly settled the issue.

Sophie: So was he an empiricist?

Philonous: Definitely not. Augustine didn't mind to let the senses have their say, but he also held quite strongly the Platonic view that knowledge that derives from sensory experience is fairly unimportant. Here again we need to emphasize that Augustine was concerned primarily with man in his relatedness to God. The truths that matter the most are not discovered by mere observation but by a contemplative ascent of the rational soul to the wisdom of Christ. It is by looking inwards and upwards, rather than outwards, that the immutable verities on which man's salvation depends can be discovered and received. On the whole, therefore, Augustine was much impressed by how naturally Platonic conceptions could be integrated with a Christian perspective. But it is important to realize that the integration itself still added some genuinely new points of view. For in contrast to Plato, who thought the realm of Ideas to have an independent eternal existence, Augustine followed more closely the lead of Plotinus in whose neo-Platonic semi-religious philosophy the eternal Ideas were thought to inhere in the Nous—the divine mind that governs the cosmos (see also p.90). However, in contradistinction to Plotinus, who believed the Nous to emanate from the One, Augustine proposed that the Nous was simply in God and that the same was true as well of Plato's Ideas. Furthermore, in order to explain how humans can receive the truths contained in the Ideas, he postulated that the human mind is spiritually enlightened by God in much the same way as a physical body is illumined by the light from the sun.[161] Thus, by means of this enlightenment, the human spirit is enabled to recognize, for example, that the absolute, unchanging truth of a mathematical theorem is directly reflective of the changeless nature of God. And, most importantly, this idea of a divine illumination also implies that knowledge ultimately is certain and that skepticism can be defeated.

Sophie: So that's, in summary, how Augustine tried to align the Christian religion with Platonic philosophy or, more generally, revelation with reason?

Philonous: The few ideas that we have here examined are a very small part of a very extensive intellectual effort. And once again we mustn't forget that Augustine's primary object is existential in nature. To him the problem of knowledge as a self-contained academic diversion is of very little interest. 'Man before God' and 'man seeking salvation' are the great central themes that give his thought its direction. And nowhere is this elemental orientation more clearly apparent than in the *Confessions*. It is here that Augustine not only reveals himself for who he really is as a man and a sinner before his Creator but that he also truly is himself in his mode of expression. The *Confessions* are a deeply inspiring work. They are written in the form of a prayer to God and provide a wealth of acute spiritual and psychological insights that shine a penetrating light upon the central struggles of the human self.

Sophie: The human self or Augustine's self?

Philonous: Both. For on the one hand the *Confessions* can be regarded as a strictly autobiographical testimony of one particular person at one particular historical station. But on the other hand, they also are a literary masterpiece of timeless import. For Augustine not only asks questions that everyone—even today—can easily recognize as his or her own, as for instance when he inquires:

> Who am I? What kind of man am I? What evil have I not done? Or if there is evil that I have not done, what evil is there that I have not spoken? If there is any that I have not spoken, what evil is there that I have not willed to do?[162]

But he also places these questions again and again in a larger philosophical or theological context that raises the account that he gives of his life and his thought far above the level of an isolated personal story. Again and again Augustine takes his eyes off of himself to contemplate, for example, such issues as the nature of God, the problem of truth, the abyss of evil and sin, or the riddle of human thinking and willing. Famously, he even ponders the nature of time.

Sophie: That's a surprise. But why did he care?

Philonous: As usual Augustine started from a genuine need—in this case his wish to decipher the account of creation that the Bible presents. In part, his purpose was as well to respond to certain critics who asked what God had been doing before He created the physical world and who thereby implied that God wasn't truly eternal and changeless. For according to these critics, the moment when God made up His mind, so to speak, to bring about the world that we live in, signified an instance of *change* in God's disposition.

Sophie: And, did Augustine figure it out?

Philonous: The least one can say is that the answer he gave was in essence the same as the one that modern science has given as well, namely that time is a *part* of creation as well. For as you probably know, in modern cosmology it is commonly thought that the Big-Bang singularity, from which the universe supposedly emerged, marks the creation of space *and time* simultaneously. So 'before' the Big Bang occurred, neither space nor time had any existence at all, and, in particular, there was no 'before'. As a matter of course, Augustine didn't say that there was a Big Bang, but what he did say was that "there was no time before heaven and earth were created"[163] and that God is "the Maker of all time."[164]

Sophie: That's a remarkable thought.

Philonous: ...and a beautiful example of how Augustine's transcendent Christian perspective impelled him to confront the enigma of reality by using his reason. For once he had convinced himself that time indeed was created, he continued his intellectual investigation by inquiring next into "the fundamental nature of time"[165] itself:

> What then is time? I know well enough what it is, provided that nobody asks me; but if I am asked what it is and try to explain, I am baffled.[166]

Sophie: And so am I.

Philonous: Baffeled?

Sophie: Yes, because when we discussed a while ago the paradoxes of Zeno, the nature of time was thoroughly confusing to me (pp.29–42).

Philonous: Interestingly, the problem posed in Zeno's second paradox is highly relevant as well to how Augustine framed the issue.

Sophie: The problem regarding the arrow in flight that cannot be moving?

Philonous: Let's say more generally, the problem of how individual point-like moments of time can add up to form an extension. You see, Augustine was profoundly struck by the fact that in the customary division of time into past, present, and future it is only the momentary unextended present that can be said to have an actual existence. Afterall, the past is no longer and the future not yet, and thus it is only the Now that really has reality. But the Now is a point without length, and therefore, the question arises how time can ever be said to have a duration. How can we measure the length of that which doesn't exist in future and past and is point-like at present?

Sophie: We know the answer: infinity can be larger than infinity, and a point-like zero, construed as the present and multiplied by infinity, can therefore become a positive length.

Philonous: Assuming that we are willing to antecedently postulate that time indeed has any objective existence at all.

Sophie: I am willing but you are probably not.

Philonous: What matters here is not your willingness or my hesitation but rather Augustine's conclusion.

Sophie: Which is...?

Philonous: ...that objectivity in respect of time most likely is a stubborn illusion. More precisely, what he asserted is this:

> It is in my own mind, then, that I measure time. I must not allow my mind to insist that time is something objective. I must not let it thwart me because of all the different notions and impressions that are lodged in it. I say that I measure time in my mind. For everything which happens leaves an impression on it, and this impression remains after the thing itself has ceased to be. It is the impression that I measure, since it is still present, not the thing itself, which makes the impression as it passes and then moves into the past. When I measure time it is my impression that I measure. Either, then, this is what time is, or else I do not measure time at all.[167]

Think about it—his point is well taken.

Sophie: What do you mean?

Philonous: What I mean is that the experienced reality of extension in time is indeed entirely a product of the mind's operation.

Sophie: But why?

Philonous: Well, imagine, for example, that you sit in front of a screen of monotone color.

Sophie: A computer screen?

Philonous: For instance.

Sophie: What color?

Philonous: It doesn't matter.

Sophie: So I'm watching a screen that is blue...

Philonous: ...and suddenly it switches to yellow—but only for the millionth part of a fraction of a second. Afterwards, it's back again to blue.

Sophie: In that case, it seems, I wouldn't be aware of any change to yellow.

Philonous: That's precisely my point: perception is always a process in 'time'—

you are never aware of only the present. For at the very moment when the screen switches to yellow you will be fully convinced it is blue. In other words, in order for there to be any perception at all, your mind must record and remember the past—that is, it must present to you a temporal compound.

Sophie: But I can only remember the past because it once was the present, that is, because time objectively flows.

Philonous: But Augustine would say that the past, by virtue of being the past, is no longer there and therefore has no objective existence. In other words, the only place where a temporal extension exists is likely your mind and only your mind. The exterior world, as it were, consists of disconnected instants of which only one can be real 'at a time', and, by implication, your *experience* of 'time' as having duration is completely subjective.

Sophie: In other words, the problem of time is really the problem of conscious remembrance.

Philonous: It is indeed, and Augustine addressed that latter problem as well. In fact, in his *Confessions* he addressed it first, *before* the problem of time.

Sophie: So how did he resolve it?

Philonous: He didn't—as might be expected. But it is fascinating all the same to follow his inquisitive mind and to witness his profound sense of wonder. Augustine was able to keenly perceive the ordinary as miraculous and to find in the common his intellectual stimulus. In this regard, his contemplation of conscious remembrance is a particularly revealing example, displaying his reverence for the mystery that people call 'reality' as well as his mind's rational acuity. In the following passage, for instance, his creative musings concerning this issue even lead him to anticipate the modern conception of the unconscious:

> The power of the memory is prodigious, my God. It is a vast, immeasurable sanctuary. Who can plumb its depths? And yet it is a faculty of my soul. Although it is part of my nature, I cannot understand all that I am. This means, then, that the mind is too narrow to contain itself entirely. But where is that part of it which it does not itself contain? Is it somewhere outside itself and not within it? How, then, can it be part of it, if it is not contained in it?
>
> I am lost in wonder when I consider this problem. It bewilders me. Yet men go out and gaze in astonishment at high mountains, the huge waves of the sea, the broad reaches of rivers, the ocean that encircles the world, or the stars in their courses. But they pay no attention to themselves. They do not marvel at the thought that while I have been mentioning all these things, I have not been looking at them with my eyes, and that I could not even speak of mountains or waves, rivers or stars, which are things that I have

seen, or of the ocean, which I know only on the evidence of others, unless I could see them in my mind's eye, in my memory, and with the same vast spaces between them that would be there if I were looking at them in the world outside myself.[168]

Sophie: Augustine's ability to marvel at that which others would simply accept is really delightful. But on the downside I have to admit that I don't understand why he always needs to point us to God or why for that matter his reverent wonder is so much tied to unknowing. Can we not employ our minds entirely freely and marvel as well at that which we do in fact know and can understand?

Philonous: You may be right in that Augustine's attitude in this regard was really rather limiting. Idle or "unhealthy curiosity," as he called it, concerning subjects that "are irrelevant to our lives" and knowledge gained solely "for the sake of knowing" were repugnant to him.[169] But on the other hand, his sense of wonder I find decidedly attractive. You see, it may be true, as you suggested, that our knowledge and not only its limits can cause us to marvel at times. But as for myself, my amazement increases the broader I choose the field of my vision. Science can certainly teach us many beautiful things about space and matter and time and how they lawfully intertwine. But more intriguing still, to me at least, are questions that pertain to ultimate realities. What is space? What is matter? What is time? And where did they originate? We say they were created in the Big Bang. But what about the Big Bang? Who or what made it happen? Perhaps we say "Nothing" or perhaps we say "God." But what about God? How did He come to be? We say that He couldn't have *come* to be because He isn't in time. But how then can He be? How can someone or something just simply be there, eternally? Put differently, "why is there something rather than nothing?"[170] It's questions such as these that may prompt us to exclaim with Augustine: "O Lord,... how deep are your mysteries!"[171] Do you see what I mean? How can something just be? What is that something and why is it there?

Sophie: The answer is simple: I don't have a clue.

Universal Unity

When Augustine wrote his *Confessions* in the closing years of the 4th century A.D. the Roman Empire in the west was caught in a spiral of rapid decline. Plagued by economic and demographic weakness and an attendant lack of resources, the empire was no longer able to effectively guard its vast northern frontier against the military threat posed by barbarian tribes. By now, the proud conquering spirit that once had given Rome its dominion was a thing of the past and disaster therefore a matter of time.[172]

In fact, the trouble was already well on its way, for in 376 the Visigoths had crossed the Danube in search of refuge from the terror spread by the Huns. The fury unleashed by these Asian invaders had devastated the Ostrogoths not long ago, and flight seemed therefore the only option left open. Initially, the Visigoths' entry into the eastern empire was peaceful. But only two years later, in 378, hostilities ensued, and in the battle of Adrianople the Roman legions were dealt a stunning defeat. In the years that followed, the Visigoths were temporarily pacified under the rule of the Emperor Theodosius the Great and were given some land on which they could settle. But after the emperor's death, in 395, they again grew dissatisfied and eventually saw themselves forced to go back to war. Under the capable leadership of King Alaric the Bold, they set out for Italy, and, in 410, they sacked the eternal City of Rome.

The sack of Rome did not as yet mark the actual end of the Roman Empire in the west—that only came in 476 when the last emperor was deposed by the German general Odovacar. But in the minds of many observers it did mark an almost apocalyptic breakdown of what had been thought to be a timeless civilizational order.

Significantly, the sack of Rome also provided Augustine with the motif for writing his *City of God*. As a true man of faith, Augustine had actually been less concerned with Rome's decline and loss of worldly power than many of his contemporaries had been. But when suggestions were made that Rome had succumbed to her enemies *because* her people had transferred their allegiance from the pagan deities of their forefathers to a Christian God who demanded that those very enemies be greeted with love,[1] Augustine felt called upon to offer a detailed reply.[173]

In the first part of that reply, that is, in the first part of the *City of God*, he draws attention to the fact that, during the pillage of Rome, the barbarians' respect for Christ had afforded the Roman citizenry considerable protection from the otherwise customary brutalities of warfare and had occasioned some uncommon acts of clemency. Then, in order to incisively clear the Christian faith of all blame, he further contends that calamities had befallen Rome even in times when the pagan gods were still worshiped and that, in fact, these very gods had been the downfall's true culprits. For according to Augustine, Rome's traditional embrace of polytheism had been a morally deleterious folly, resulting in decadence and thereby ruining the Roman commonwealth.[174] That is to say, in his view, "the lust" that the pagan demons excited in the hearts of men had been "more deadly than the flames which [eventually] consumed their dwellings."[175]

---

[1] For clarification, we should perhaps add that during the reign of Theodosius—directly prior to the main onslaught of the barbarian invasions—pagan religious rites had been declared illegal, pagan temples widely destroyed, and Jupiter along with all his subordinate gods had been formally banned by the Roman Senate.[178] That is to say, against the backdrop of such a wholesale rejection of traditional polytheistic practices, the sack of Rome was bound to appear in the minds of some as a punishment for religious disloyalty.

After this rather lengthy discussion of the falsity and moral destructiveness of Roman polytheism, Augustine—in a study of contrast with the earthly city of man—goes on to describe the eternal foundations of the City of God: he asserts the absolute supremacy of the Holy Scriptures "over every product of human genius,"[176] details the goodness of God's plan of salvation for fallen mankind, and in the process develops a philosophy of history according to which the course of the world is divinely ordained and has a clearly defined beginning and end.

This Christian Augustinian vision of history as a finite, redemptive development is very significantly distinct from the views that prevailed in Greek philosophical thought. For where Heraclitus described the world as "an ever-living Fire,"[177] where Empedocles saw recurrent cycles of intermingling and separation (p.42), where the Stoics put forth the notion of periodic universal conflagrations,[II] and where Aristotle thought the material world to be uncreated and eternal (p.174), Augustine simply proclaims the Biblical message: history is unique and bound to fulfill the plan that God has revealed. It is not cyclic but rather a sequence of never-to-be-repeated events extending from the time of creation via the birth of Christ to the Final Judgment Day—and onwards from there to that day of glory when all is made new and God's Holy City, the New Jerusalem, appears in the heavens. History has a goal, and God will make sure that it will be achieved.

With the *City of God*, Augustine provided the Christian West with a grand unifying narrative into which the sometimes bewildering twists and turns of earthly events could be seamlessly fitted. Whatever has happened up to the present or will happen in ages to come can be seen by those who believe to have a place in God's overarching design. *"Crede, ut intellegas"*[179]—"believe in order to understand." If the heart is pure and the faith is firm, the mind will come to discern the divine unity that underlies all that did and will occur. For everything comes to pass for a purpose, and even the wayward in their sinful rebellion cannot help but advance God's ultimate, overall plan:

> Evil men do many things contrary to the will of God; but so great is his wisdom, and so great his power, that all things which seem to oppose his will tend towards those results or ends which he himself has foreknown as good and just. (Augustine, *City of God*)[180]

The theme of unity, which emerges here so forcefully, was one of Augustine's most persistent concerns, and the approach that he took to it was in essence always the same. Whether he argued for the hierarchical unity of faith and

---

[II]According to Augustine (see the footnotes in [Aug1], p.485), this doctrine of periodic conflagrations was held by Heraclitus as well, but Copleston points out that such most likely wasn't the case (see [Copl1], p.44). For the notion of a periodic universal collapse seems to be incompatible with the idea, found in the remaining fragments of Heraclitus's writings, of an "ever-living fire" that has no beginning or end.

reason, proclaimed the unity of history in the divine will, or defended the unity in diversity in the Godhead of the Trinity, he did so unfailingly from the fundamental assumption that there is only one God, one Truth, and one Faith. Consequently, in his mind, a genuine conflict between the truths of reason and Christian belief was unthinkable by definition.

Not surprisingly then, Augustine was also strongly committed to the idea of a unified Church Universal—a church that truly was catholic. And in particular, it was due to this commitment of his that he came to vehemently oppose the Donatist challenge which had arisen about a hundred years prior in the time of the Diocletian persecution. Following that persecution, a North African bishop by the name of Donatus had demanded that only the true saints, that is, those who had stood firm and had not opted out by symbolically surrendering their Scriptures to the authorities, should be allowed to stay in the church. In essence then Donatus conceived of the Church as a privileged fellowship of proven believers from which the majority of weak and merely nominal Christians had to be strictly excluded. Being the realist that he was regarding the nature of human nature, Augustine was of course well aware that the Donatists were right in that the Church, in this world, was indeed very far from perfection. For it was home, as he himself said, to "reprobates"[181] and true believers alike. But the task of separating the saints from the sinners was to be left to the judgment of God, and there was therefore no question for him of creating a church for the holy elect.

Augustine's decision to adamantly oppose the Donatist heresy and to insist on the universality of the Christian Church was a momentous historical choice that laid the foundation for the medieval ideal of a unified Christendom. This ideal, from the point of view of Augustine, was of course spiritual rather than political in character, but in times to come the political dimension would also be strongly emerging. Europe in the Middle Ages would be thought of by many a Christian as a unified "Christian republic"—"a single kingdom" and "a house undivided."[182] The act that most clearly symbolized the arrival of this medieval paradigm[III] was the coronation of Charlemagne in St. Peter's Basilica in Rome on Christmas day 800. Here on that day, in that ancient imperial city, the pope, in the name of the Church, gave sanction to the king of the Franks to dominate and thereby unify the Christian world in the West.

As a matter of course, this creation of the 'first Europe' under the aegis of the Catholic Church was still by far too far in the future to have been of any concern to Augustine when he was fighting the Donatists in his official function as the Bishop of Hippo. But as it turned out, the saint's insistence on

---

[III]The question concerning the beginning and temporal extent of the Middle Ages is answered differently by different historians. According to Maurice Keen, the Middle Ages encompass the time span from the coronation of Charlemagne in 800 to the Council of Basle in 1449 (see [Kee], p.11), whereas Norman F. Cantor places the corresponding limits at about 300 and 1500 (see [Can], p.1).

unity in this particular instance would help to bring about that future creation by ensuring the Church's survival during the dark and turbulent times that followed the western empire's then imminent disintegration.[183] In fact and as a note at the side, Augustine himself, in the final days of his life, became engulfed in these violent torrents of the Roman decline when he died in 430 while the Vandals were besieging the City of Hippo.

In the centuries that immediately followed—the so-called European Dark Ages—there occurred a general degradation of civilized life in what used to be the Latin West. Literacy declined dramatically, urban centers were deserted, and effective administration ceased to exist. In the east, the empire remained initially still fully intact, and the rule of Justinian (527–565) in particular held out the promise of reinvigorating the Roman civilizational order. But when Justinian ultimately exhausted his powers in the attempt to reconquer Rome, it was soon to be left to the newly ascendant Muslim Arabs to continue that quest that we commonly call 'civilization.' For following the death of the Prophet Mohammed, in 632, these Arabs set out to spread by the sword—as well as the force of conviction—the religion of Islam that the Prophet had founded.[IV] Their advance lasted for almost exactly one hundred years and eventually extended their reign from Spain in the west across North Africa and the Arabian Peninsula all the way into Turkistan in the east.

This rise of Islam, however, was more than a religiously driven military expansion. For in the process of colonization and administrative consolidation it also became a genuine cultural force. Typically, the Arabs were quick to adopt the often superior civilizational standards and techniques of the peoples that they had subdued. And as a result, there developed a vibrant Islamic domain with brilliant urban focal points. Cities like Baghdad and Cordoba became flourishing centers of intellectual life that far surpassed in their cultural vitality the cities of western Christendom.

As regards the more specific intellectual deeds of the Muslims, there is no place here to go into any details. But in the context of our overall story we need to point out that one of the great contributions of the scholars of Islam to subsequent thought was the preservation, translation, and interpretation of the philosophic and scientific works of Greek antiquity—including very importantly the whole of Aristotle's writings. It is understood, of course, that these scholarly efforts were highly competent as well as significant in their own right, but in addition they also were preparing the way for the intellectual re-emergence of Europe. For it was mainly through contacts with Islam that the Aristotelian corpus would reenter the West in the 12th century after

---

[IV] The phrase "spread by the sword" is not supposed to convey unusual viciousness but merely is intended to be expressive of the fact that the Arabs did indeed spread their religion by means of military conquest. In this context Norman F. Cantor points out that the Arabs in general did not force conversions at the threat of death, but only imposed certain restrictions on those who refused to "recognize Mohammed as the Prophet of Allah" (see [Can], p.133).

having been almost entirely lost during the European Dark Ages.[184] Sadly, many of these contacts were facilitated by the gruesome 'Christian' crusades, but regardless of whether the occasions were edifying, the attendant effects were pronounced. For the reentry of Aristotle into the West provided the decisive stimulus for the very philosophic debates that would bring on the scene the second most prominent intellectual figure after Augustine: *St. Thomas Aquinas.*

However, before we look at the life and work of St. Thomas a little more closely, we need to add some further comments on the intervening developments. The first of these that is of importance is the Carolingian renaissance under the rule of Charlemagne. Given the deplorable state of education in his Frankish domain, Charlemagne was eager to better the standards and to this end enlisted some foreign scholarly talent. Most famously, the Englishman Alcuin from the City of York was put in charge of Charlemagne's Palatine School in Aachen—the school that has been considered by some the earliest precursor to the French university system.[V]

Concerning the legacy of the Carolingian renaissance, it may be said that it was a very successful educational effort that brought back to life a culture of letters and learning and thereby effectively ended the Dark Age. In itself it did not produce any distinguished original thought, but it did lay the groundwork for the reactivation of such thought in the age of Scholastic philosophy that was soon to arise. In this sense therefore, the Carolingian renaissance was influential indeed because it was precisely this Scholastic philosophy that was to become the defining intellectual current of the entire medieval period.

Scholasticism was a Pan-European phenomenon with a distinctly international flavor. Typically, the philosophers and theologians that contributed to it were not exclusively tied to their native lands but rather were frequently active in various schools in various countries and places. Significantly, though, Scholasticism was also a very strongly unified movement. Its universal scholarly language was Latin, and its universal scholarly goal was to elaborate the Augustinian vision of the essential unity of revelation and reason. In other words, the problem was not to discover the truth—for the truth was given already by faith—but rather to show that the truth which the Scriptures reveal was compatible with and supported by the demands of the rational mind.

Following the Carolingian renaissance, the earliest original efforts in pursuit of this goal were undertaken by John Scotus Eriugena who was born in Ireland[VI] in approximately 810. Eriugena acquired most of his learning in an Irish monastery but later in life he set out for France to teach at the Carolingian Palatine School—which, by then, had been moved from Aachen to Paris.[VII] Eriugena, at bottom, was firmly committed to the Scholastic ideal, just referred to, of the essential unity of reason and faith. But there is room for debate as to which of the two—reason or faith—he considered superior. For whereas some of his statements clearly affirm the absolute "authority of the Sacred Scriptures," others seem to suggest that faith without reason is weak and that only "true reason" can stand on its own.[185] Either way, however, Eriugena did set the stage on which the later Scholastics would enact their disputes. Moreover, in his Augustinian embrace of certain Platonic and neo-Platonic positions (p.258) he also was implicitly taking a stance concerning a problem that would dominate a good many of these future disputes—*the problem of universals.*

To understand what here was at issue it is helpful for us to recall how Plato and Aristotle approached the problem of knowledge (pp.169f,179f). According to Plato, true knowledge is gained as reason ascends to a world of eternal Ideas so as to discover the unchanging 'templates' from which the objects of sense inherit their particular forms. Moreover, at the level of ontology, the real, in this view of Plato's, is first and foremost the template. Not the horse that we see has true reality but rather its general essence—the archetype of 'horseness'.

Aristotle, however, did not agree. For he believed the universal to exist, not independently, in some ethereal realm, but only in the particular thing that our senses portray. According to Aristotle, knowledge of 'horseness' is gained, not by means of a direct rational ascent but by taking an analytical detour through the domain of sensory objects.

Using the terminology of the pertinent Scholastic debates—which is a little misleading—we may say that Plato the idealist was, in fact, a *realist* with respect to the status of universals. For reality in Platonic thought is not a patchwork of randomized particular objects of sense but rather is transcendently centered upon the eternally changeless, universal Ideas. The real, as we just said, here isn't the horse but its ideal.

The antithesis to realism is the philosophical doctrine of nominalism, according to which universals are nothing but *nomines* or names, that is, they merely are words. Insofar as this doctrine is construed to imply, as it commonly is, that universals, being mere names, are strictly contained in the mind, we may say that Aristotle most decidedly was not a nominalist. For Aristotle no less than Plato believed that knowledge of universals is genuine knowledge of things as they are in themselves. He did not, to be sure, grant primacy to the universal over the sensory thing, as Plato had done. But he clearly did affirm that there is something in the thing, something that really exists, that our rational mind correctly perceives as its general form. The universal is not a mere concept that we invent but directly reflects a part of the real. In other words, both Aristotle and Plato were strongly committed to the idea that being and thought in essence are one. And the difference between their pertinent persuasions is therefore more properly viewed as a distinction by degree on the realist side rather than a realist-nominalist harsh opposition.

Concerning the question as to why the Scholastics considered the problem of universals to be so important, we need to observe that the doctrine of nominalism, interpreted strictly, can be strongly conducive to skepticism with respect to the substance of knowledge. For if there really is no true connection between the universals on which our knowledge is based and the individual objects of sense to which these universals are meant to pertain, that is, if universals are really just words and nothing but words, then, ultimately, nothing can ever be known. Consequently and in the final analysis, the problem of universals is concerning the question how thought and reality are interrelated.[186]

Seen under such a more general aspect, it is fair to say that the problem of universals has occupied us in various guises more or less constantly. For whenever the issue at hand was to examine how or whether the extramental physical world can be portrayed by mental conceptual constructs, it was precisely this question—of how thought relates to reality—that we were in essence addressing. We encountered this problem—to name just a few important examples—in Einstein's claim that "physical concepts are free creations of the human mind" (p.34), in the standing-under understanding that *Sophie* and *Philonous* discussed (p.62), in the conceptual perplexities of quantum mechanics, as well as in the Lorenzian doctrine of evolutionary epistemology.

Interestingly, this latter doctrine of Lorenz's—according to which the human mind was adaptively formed in directly interacting with an objective external world that it thereby came to partially mirror in the specifics of its cognitive constitution (pp.109–111,125)—allows us even to argue that the problem of universals admits of a distinctly modern, evolutionary solution. For if indeed the patterns of human cognition are partly reflective of the exterior world, then, conceivably, the human mind's propensity for employing universals in the organization of thought is also partly reflective of that exterior world, and thus universals are partly objective. This is not to say, of course, that any specifically given universal or concept is more than a figment, but only that our *a priori* employment of such figments may be correctly, if imperfectly, expressive of reality's actual structure. Consequently, from this modern perspective, we have very good reasons to partly deny a rigid nominalist's rigid denial.

This evolutionary solution, of course, would never have been a solution of choice among the early Scholastics. For insofar as the goal of defeating skepticism is concerned, the realist stance of Plato—as well as Augustine by implication—is a stronger position by far. Afterall, if the Platonic Ideas, as Augustine proposed (p.258), exist in God's mind, then it follows very directly that in being illumined by these Ideas and in employing them as universals the rational mind of man can gain access to genuine knowledge and, in particular, to genuine knowledge of that sort that matters the most to a Christian—the knowledge of God's redemptive Truth. Consequently, it is not surprising in the least that most of the early Scholastics—including Eriugena as well as, among others, St. Anselm of Canterbury (1033–1109) and William of Champeaux (1070–1120)—were very strongly endorsing this realist option. All three of them, in fact, may be considered ultra-realists in that they all deemed universals to very literally possess an independent, extra-mental reality.[VIII]

As always, however, someone somewhere is bound to dissent. And sure enough, along comes a man by the name of Roscelin (about 1050–1120) and abandons this Augustinian Scholastic consensus. Roscelin actually was one of the teachers of the just referred to William of Champeaux, but for whatever reasons he and his student completely disagreed regarding universals. A note of caution here is in order as the writings of Roscelin have been almost entirely lost and as the precise nature of his beliefs is therefore a little uncertain. But from secondary sources it can be reasonably safely inferred that he thought universals to be first of all words. This position itself, when elaborated with Aristotelian moderation, would not *per se* make him a skeptic—nor would it put him of needs at odds with the Church. But Roscelin blatantly overstepped the bounds of what was allowed when he employed his philosophic convictions to effectively dismantle the Trinity. His argument went something like this: the real is not the general concept but rather the individual particular to which the concept pertains. Consequently, the three Trinitarian persons—the Father, the Son, and the Holy Spirit—are real only as separate individual entities, and thus they cannot be one. Since the Church obviously couldn't agree, Roscelin was forced to recant.

A synthetical compromise between the nominalism of Roscelin and the fairly rigid realist views of most of the other early Scholastics was offered by the Frenchman Peter Abélard (1079–1142) who had been a student of William of Champeaux but later became his strongest opponent.[187] According to Abélard neither nominalism nor realism was credible in its radical form, and he therefore proposed to establish, as it were, a quasi-Aristotelian middle ground. On the one hand, Abélard rejected the nominalist premise that universals are nothing but words by granting them the sort of objective significance that Aristotle, in similar form, had granted them too. And on the other hand, he also rejected the ultra-realist views according to which the real is only the universal. The Platonic universals exist as ideal templates of the created world in God's mind. But in the minds of men, these same universals must be derived as abstractions from the encounter with the concrete. In other words, horses are real first of all in the details of their individual characteristics, but real as well are the traits

---

[VIII]As Copleston indicates in [Copl2], pp.141–142, the exact details of the doctrines attributed to Eriugena and Anselm in respect of the problem of universals are actually somewhat uncertain. But the holding of ultra-realist views in the case of Eriugena seems likely and in the case of Anselm it seems to be at least a plausible possibility.

that they all have in common. By implication, the universals that pertain to these traits are not just mere names given to collections of objects, but instead are descriptive of something that really exists *in* the objects themselves. The universal, so to speak, is real *in* the form of the thing—it is *in re*.

With respect to the suggested partial affinity of these teachings of Abélard's to Aristotle's epistemological stance, we need to clarify, that Abélard developed his thought largely independently, without any reliance on Aristotle's metaphysical or psychological writings, for these were simply not known to him. Abélard had available Aristotle's works on logic but the rest of the Aristotelian corpus was being recovered only gradually, after Abélard's death, in the latter half of the 12th century. All the same, however, in elaborating a solution to the problem of universals that ascribed primary reality to individual objects instead of to general traits, and in proposing, in essence, an empirical method leading from observation by means of abstraction to universal ideas, Abélard was preparing the philosophical soil for the reception of Aristotle's system by the generations of Scholastics that immediately followed. In particular, his thought was setting the stage for the arrival of the era's two leading scholarly figures: *Albert the Great* and *Thomas Aquinas*.

Aquinas on Dinosaurs

Aquinas was born on or around New Year's Day 1225 in the town of Roccasecca in south-central Italy. At the age of five he was entrusted by his father, the Count of Aquino, to the educational care of the Benedictine monks of the nearby Abbey of Monte Cassino. Nine years later, in 1239, the Abbey was pillaged by the troops of the Holy Roman Emperor Frederick II, and Aquinas, in consequence, went on to Naples to study the liberal arts. In Naples he also came into contact with the Dominican order which had been founded by St. Dominic, in 1216, as an intellectual bulwark against heresy. Much to the consternation of his blue-blooded family, Aquinas joined the Dominican ranks in 1244. Taking the vows of poverty, he abandoned all status and privilege and humbly went forth as a beggar for Christ.

Soon thereafter, he set out for Paris to study under Albert the Great who was a Dominican too. On his way, however, he met with resistance, as his family was fiercely determined to frustrate his plans. For clarity we need here to add that in speaking a moment ago of his family's 'consternation' we were rather severely understating the case. G.K. Chesterton, for instance, in the same context writes that "his family flew at him like wild beasts."[188] It was totally unheard of for the son of a count of Aquino to turn out a beggar, no matter how noble or godly his motives. And so, in order to bring the foolhardy Thomas back to his senses, two of his brothers waylaid and kidnaped him and afterwards locked him up in the family castle. At one time in his confinement, his unsparing brothers even introduced into his cell a beautiful temptress who was to release the obstinate friar from the shackles of chastity. Faced with this vision from hell, the usually mild-mannered Thomas reached for a firebrand and threatened to launch an attack, whereupon the vision reached for the door and ran out for cover.[189]

Aquinas remained in his cell for nearly a year, and when he finally escaped, with the help of his sister, he directly went back to where his brothers had seized him: the road to Paris. Upon his arrival in that splendid capital city of the Scholastic world, he was able at last to accomplish his mission. That is to say, he finally joined his teacher of choice, Albert the Great, the *Doctor Universalis*, in his studies of theology and Aristotelian philosophy at what was then the foremost center of learning in all of Christendom—the famous University of Paris.

Albert the Great was the man who truly reclaimed for the West the Aristotelian corpus from its Arabian exile. In Aristotle's philosophical system, Albert discovered "[t]he sublimest wisdom of which the world could boast,"[190] and to harvest that wisdom for the cause of the Christian religion was the goal of his scholarly quest.[1] In pursuit of this goal he not only wrote numerous commentaries on *the Philosopher's* works but even expanded upon them by adding his own original insights and, significantly, his own scientific empirical facts. Thus, Albert the Great may be considered the true initiator of that 13th century Aristotelian Revolution which directly foreshadowed the greater Scientific Revolution three centuries hence.

As indicated by these remarks, the rediscovery of Aristotle brought in its wake a positive reappraisal of natural science and, more generally, of knowledge derived from perception. Aristotle the empiricist was leading the way, and the Christian Scholastics were following suit. Aquinas in particular explicitly echoed *the Philosopher's* pertinent call to rely on perception (p.166) when he asserted, for instance, that it was "natural to man to attain to intellectual truths through sensible things, because all our knowledge originates from sense."[191]

As a result of this epistemological realignment, reason in science and philosophical thought was now allowed to stand on its own—to be autonomous. It was still subordinate *to* faith but no longer wholly dependent *upon* it. Augustine's conception of a divine illumination was here being replaced by an active process of inquiry that utilizes all of man's rational and sensory faculties. And where Augustine proclaimed *"crede, ut intellegas"* (p.265), Aquinas, as it were, now adds the reversal: *"intellege, ut credas"*—"understand in order to believe."[192] Reason and faith are not only compatible but do, in fact, hold up each other. Those who believe will use their minds wisely, and those who

---

[1] In order not to cause any misunderstandings we should perhaps add that Albert the Great was deeply appreciative of the works of other Greek thinkers as well. The works of Plato in particular exerted a strong influence upon Albert's philosophical and theological thought.

use their minds wisely will come to believe.

In fact, this latter part of the faith-and-reason equation—the faith that arises from reason—was appealed to already by Paul when he contended in his letter to the *Romans* that

> since the creation of the world God's invisible qualities—his eternal power and divine nature—have been clearly seen, being understood from what has been made.[193]

Not surprisingly then, it was precisely this verse from the letter of Paul that Aquinas frequently quoted in support of his own theological doctrine.[194] In his *Summa Theologica*, for instance—after stating this verse—Aquinas goes on to insist that "the existence of God" can "be demonstrated through the things that are made."[195] And in another passage of the same work we read that it "is befitting Holy Writ to put forward divine and spiritual truths under the likeness of material things."[196]

In order to anchor this foundational outlook of his in a rigorous system, Aquinas devised a structure of two firmly built floors:[197] faith and reason, theology and philosophy, heaven and earth—these are the pairs that define the hierarchical but also *newly dynamic* unity of the above and below. For the hierarchy is one of mutual close interaction: *"crede, ut intellegas"* and *"intellege, ut credas"*—the road has two lanes. Faith is the compass that reason must follow in seeking the truth, and reason uncovers the evidence that renders more tangible the transcendent verities of the Christian religion.

In his two greatest works, the *Summa Contra Gentiles* and the *Summa Theologica*, Aquinas elaborated these basic beliefs into a grand theological vision that left no aspect of reality untouched. From the existence and nature of God to the causes of evil and from the first principles of knowledge to the last ends of man, Aquinas covered the entire spectrum of being and thought. Every subject was systematically explored and given its place in the overall scheme. Epistemology, psychology, metaphysics, ethics, and politics—they all were cut down to size and made to fit in. The resultant picture was one of a unified world in which the material and the spiritual were inextricably linked and entangled. Aristotelian physics became Christian physics, and the geocentric universe became a statement of dogma.

As regards the more specific problem of universals, Aquinas followed the lead of his teacher, Albert the Great, who had heightened and brought into sharper relief a distinction which, in less explicit form, was present already in Abélard's synthetical doctrine.[198] According to Albert and with him Aquinas, universals exist in three different modes: they exist *ante rem*, or before the thing, as Ideas in God's divine intellect; they exist *in re*, or in the thing, as forms that are given to material objects; and they also exist *post rem*, or after the thing, as abstracted conceptions in man's comprehension.

On the surface, it may well appear that distinctions as these are tedious in the extreme, but expanded upon and examined with an eye to their general theme, they quickly reveal some intriguing new vistas. So let's take a closer look: the eternal Ideas or universals, Aquinas says, subsist independently in the mind of the Creator. So far so good, and it seems he merely agrees with Augustine. But here we need to be careful because in contrast to Augustine, Aquinas doesn't make any provisions for that divine mind to directly illumine man's understanding (p.259). The human intellect can come to know the universal only by way of abstraction from the perception of the concrete. Man is not God, and therefore he cannot directly behold the ideal divine universals without a reference to particular objects. Consequently, the concretely material assumes here a role that is vital indeed. For since we cannot ascend to universals directly, it follows that we can attain to true knowledge of the material world only by exploring that world on our own, that is, by acting in essence *as scientists*.

However, as we follow this line of thought, the question arises what function that higher layer of perfect Ideas in the mind of the Godhead should be assigned. If we cannot access that layer directly, then why do we need it? In response, Aquinas would say that the function in question is to ensure that our knowledge, however imperfect, is still and inherently knowledge of true reality—that knowledge and being somehow are one. And in arguing thus he would have a point. Afterall, if the Creator knows His creation through the very universals that we know in turn, in less perfect form, by means of inference from observation, then our knowledge, by definition, is a piece of the Truth. On the other hand, though, there is the sobering option that in relying thus on our own cognitive powers we may be led to adopt a sort of Kantian view according to which, man is autonomous and God a distant rational presence serving no purpose other than to guarantee the conceptual coherence of our philosophical system. Or—even more disconcertingly—we may be led to conclude that the lower layer, to which man is confined, is all that there is. That is to say, God might here be reduced to a useless illusion. Aquinas, to be sure, was solidly orthodox in his intentions and certainly not a willing forebear of Kantian rationalism or modern scientific atheism. But in the light of his thought, the actual later emergence of these philosophical currents may well give us pause.

Along a less skeptical route, we also can argue, of course, that the process of abstracting universals from observation need not result in a denial of God but rather may help us to know Him more deeply. For if the universals that we deduce are somehow reflective of those that God beholds in His mind, then, in essence, we come to know God in and through the world He created.

Unfortunately, though, even if we endorse this alternative view, there still are some critical questions remaining. For what for instance will happen to Aquinas's grand vision of a total alignment of the Christian religion with Aristotelian philosophy if it should be discovered that Aristotle was wrong about

physical law and that, in particular, the Earth isn't at rest but rather adrift
somewhere in space along with the Sun? What will happen to faith in that
case? What will become of a faith that supposedly supports and is supported
by a natural philosophy that in turn is found to be lacking? If Aristotelian
science and Christian belief cannot be disentangled, then perhaps there will
come a day when we have to discard the former along with the latter. And is
it not possible then that the system, which Aquinas devised, contained in itself
the seeds of its own inevitable disintegration? Afterall, if the first floor one
day is completely remodeled, then who will still want to dwell on the oldfash-
ioned second? In other words, the road ahead may indeed lead to skepticism,
atheism, and total destruction.

In posing these questions, of course, we are benefitting from hindsight.
From our current vantage point, it is easy to recognize that there had to be
problems arising. The advent of modern autonomous reason in consequence of
the progress of science was bound to produce, so we can see, in many a modern
mind the impression that the second floor of Aquinas was merely a dispensable
fantasy.

However, even Aquinas in his day, when he was nearing the end of his life,
got a glimpse of the struggles that the future would bring. It was during his
famous controversy with Siger of Brabant that he came to perceive in the mind
of this Aristotelian opponent of his a harsh fragmentation of truth that foretold
the modern tale of religion's decline and lethal depletion.[199] For Siger asserted
that certain of Aristotle's teachings, such as, for instance, the proposition
concerning the material world's eternal existence (p.174), were in conflict with
Christian dogmatic belief. Put differently, Siger in essence contended that the
truths of the faith did not of needs have to agree with the truths of philosophy.

Faced with this charge, Aquinas—understandably—was profoundly disturbed. He himself had called upon Aristotle as a witness for Christ. But
it had never occurred to him that a man like Siger, with his unrelenting intellect, might one day present the witness as the accuser and thereby lay siege
to that foundational unity of reason and faith without which the world can
only break down. G.K. Chesterton in this context remarks that "in the abyss
of anarchy opened by Siger's sophistry..., [Aquinas] had seen the possibility of
the perishing of all idea of religion, and even of all idea of truth."[200]

In the end, Aquinas prevailed but his strength was exhausted. All of his
life he had lived in a world that had been at bottom fully coherent. Faith,
in his mind, had always been a rock of absolute certainty, and philosophical
inquiry had been revealing of needs the glory of God. Moreover, this unity
of reason and faith and of being and thought, in the life of St. Thomas, had
always been more than a mere proposition—it had been a vital reality. And
the prospect of its falling apart was therefore a shattering blow that left him
deeply fatigued.

In consequence, Aquinas abandoned the world of debates and intellectual struggles, and retired to the land of his birth. He, the intellectual soldier for Christ, was weary of war and ready to lay down his weapons. He had been the greatest mind of his time, but he also had been—no more and no less— an obedient friar who traveled on foot in the service of God. Theology had been his calling but faith had been and still was his ultimate passion. And now, at the end of his life, it was his calling that faded away and thus left his passion solely remaining. For in a moment of heightened mystic awareness, he came to see "things" which, as he himself put it, made all his "writings like straw."[201] As a result, Aquinas lost his will and his power to write, and the greatest theologian that the Middle Ages had known was thus once again what he always had been: a soul before God.

Shortly thereafter, in 1274, Aquinas was called by the Pope to attend a Council meeting in France. True to his habit he honored the call with "automatic obedience,"[202] but this time he didn't get far. An illness struck him down soon after leaving, and he was taken for shelter to a nearby monastery. Knowing what was to come, he confessed his sins, found his peace, and went home to meet his Redeemer. The confessor who witnessed the scene afterwards "whispered that his confession had been that of a child of five."[203]

Philonous: It's moving to see how so brilliant a man as Thomas Aquinas could still be so simple and humble at heart.

Sophie: It's moving but also a little confusing. For how can a thinker as accomplished as he, at the end of his life, confess like a child? I don't understand it.

Philonous: Perhaps his life had been truly coherent.

Sophie: That's hard to believe.

Philonous: ...from your point of view. But you mustn't forget how vastly the times of Aquinas differed from ours. To a certain extent, coherence back then was not a goal to be reached but rather a state that was given. That is to say, the Middle Ages decidedly weren't postmodern.

Sophie: They certainly weren't, for if they had been, they likely wouldn't appear so utterly foreign. You see, among all the different historical eras the Middle Ages to me have always been the most elusive by far. Those ages, it seems, were steeped in an alien spirit of religious belief that I myself can only encounter uncomprehending. I am secular down to the core of my being. I don't pray, I don't go to church, I don't like the Pope, and I therefore don't see a link from the world of Aquinas to my own, present existence.

Philonous: Then let me give you a hint: the link is right there, in the words that you think.

Sophie: What do you mean?

Philonous: The problem of universals.

Sophie: The problem of universals? But that's really odd. Are you saying it should matter to me if 'horseness' exists independently or if, instead, it is merely a word? Is this a link to the present or rather the height of medieval obscurity?

Philonous: The notion of 'horseness', I fully agree, is not exactly essential. But other than that I would say, it really isn't that easy to think of any problem or issue whatever that is more important, more baffling, and more directly relevant to our present station in history than the problem of universals—broadly construed.

Sophie: You are kidding.

Philonous: Not at all, the matter is central. For in an age of information inflation—or even hyperinflation—the general question of what is the 'substance' of the words that we use, in writing or thought, may well be more pressing than ever. Where information has grown to a flood and words are employed with multiple meanings in multiple personal and cultural contexts, the abstruse medieval problem of universals takes on the form of the highly relevant and highly current concern regarding the nature and possibility of *communication* in a postmodern world. We rely on words for the transmission of meaning, but what if that meaning should differ from person to person, culture to culture, and context to context? The medieval realists thought that universals were given externally and therefore possessed a uniform absolute meaning that wasn't dependent on context at all. But what if, instead, the meaning of words is flexibly changing in flexible settings?

Sophie: In that case we might be in trouble.

Philonous: We might be indeed. For how can we ever engage in a fruitful discussion or sensible dialogue if the meaning we send is not the meaning received?

Sophie: That is to say, the problem at hand is really semantics.

Philonous: To begin with it is.

Sophie: So how do you want to approach it?

Philonous: The best point of entry, I think, is here an example. In fact, any example will do. But just for convenience let me suggest we take up the one we looked at before: the universal of 'goodness' or 'good'. What do we *mean* when we say that an action is morally good?

Sophie: As far as I can recall, the answer provided by Kant was roughly stated as follows: your action is 'good' if you can will the maxim of your action to become a universal law (p.199).

Philonous: In other *words* and in a more general light, Kant here proposes to clarify the meaning of *words* by adding more *words*. For the notion of an act that is good is here broken down—or rather expanded—by attaching to it the further notions of a will, a maxim, and a universal law. Clearly then, it is these secondary notions that we now must proceed to define.

Sophie: But how?

Philonous: By adding more words—or, in practical terms, by consulting a dictionary. In the *American Heritage Dictionary,*[204] for instance, we read concerning the will that it is "the mental faculty by which one deliberately chooses or decides upon a course of action." Consequently, in order to elucidate the notion of a will and thereby—partially—the notion of goodness, we have to explain what a faculty is, what a *mental* faculty is in contradistinction to a non-mental one, and what it means to choose a course of action with deliberation.

Sophie: Are you implying we merely keep adding words *ad infinitum?*

Philonous: '*Ad finitum*' is a little more like it because the set of all words that humans employ is finite of needs.

Sophie: But then I must ask: when do we stop? When all the words that there are have been completely used up? Do we finally know what it means to do a good deed when the entire English vocabulary has been spread out before us in a giant cascade of interconnected successive descriptions?

Philonous: To see why the answer is "no," let's take another look at our chosen example: at the stage that we reached, a moment ago, we had to explain what a 'faculty' is. Consulting again the *American Heritage Dictionary,* a faculty is "an inherent power or ability," a power in turn is an "ability or capacity to perform or act effectively," and finally, an ability is a "physical, mental, financial, or legal power to perform." In other words, a faculty is a power, a mental faculty is a mental power, a power is an ability, an ability is a power, a power is an ability, an ability is a power, a power is...

Sophie: I get the idea—the cycle is vicious.

Philonous: Indeed, it is the sort of self-referential symbolic cycle that we met with before (see pp.119,122,123), except that this time we can see a little more clearly why it has to be vicious of needs. For if we keep defining words by means of words, and if the set of words is finite, then we simply *must* reach a point where we start turning in circles, describing words by themselves. It can't be avoided. In fact, right at the start we already encounter a problem. For the very idea of 'assigning meaning to words' will only make sense if we know at the outset what it means to assign meaning to the words 'assigning' and 'meaning'. That is to say, the problem is a perfect conundrum because we cannot even address it unless we already know how to solve it.

Sophie: I call that absurd.

Philonous: You may call it that, but then I will ask, "what do you mean by 'absurd'?"

Sophie: Since meanings are cyclic, the answer is simple: "absurd means absurd."

Philonous: I think you are right.

Sophie: And I think, in that case, the whole scheme of language is pointless. For if the meaning of words is strictly in words and therefore strictly reflexive, then nothing of substance can ever be said. And, in particular, whatever

the two of us said in our various belabored discussions up to this point was
nothing but circular nonsense.

Philonous: That is correct, because ultimately nothing means anything and
everything means nothing—it is the postmodern paradigm.

Sophie: So the problem of communication in the postmodern world has thereby
been solved. For regardless of any cultural or personal contexts, the ultimate truth will always be this: nothing is something.

Philonous: Furthermore, along similar lines, the problem of universals can now
be settled as follows: words are words, universals are universals, and no
question of meaning can ever have meaning.

Sophie: That is to say, radical nominalism is the postmodern option of choice,
providing a definite answer by denying that there can be a question.

Philonous: So to speak.

Sophie: And now, in the face of this total semantic collapse, what do we do?
Fall silent?

Philonous: No, find the mistake.

Sophie: But where? The logic is plain: words are described by words, the
number of words is finite, ergo all descriptions are cyclic. The argument is
perfectly valid, and the conclusion is no less depressing than flawless.

Philonous: It's baffling, I know, and it seems we are stuck. But thankfully,
whatever inspiration or insight we lack, we can always find in the *Faust*.
As regards the present conundrum, for instance, here is a passage that may
come in handy:

> On *words* let your attention centre!
>
> ...
>
> For just where fails the comprehension,
> A word steps promptly in as deputy.
> With words 't is excellent disputing;
> Systems to words 't is easy suiting;
> On words 't is excellent believing;
> No word can ever lose a jot from thieving.[205]

Sophie: Who said it?

Philonous: Goethe.

Sophie: Of course, but in the *Faust*, who said it there?

Philonous: The devil.

Sophie: And the devil is to help us out?

Philonous: Not voluntarily, because he is a liar by profession. But in the *Faust*,
at least, his lies are never merely lies, for all along the truth is woven in to
partially conceal them.

Sophie: So as to render them still more perfidious?

Philonous: Certainly, but on the upside and importantly, this evil interplay of
falsehood and veracity is also going to afford us here the insight that we

seek. As a case in point, we may consider, I suggest, the devil's line "On words 't is excellent believing." Just think how very true and odd it is that all of us so readily put our faith in words. We trust a fact to be a fact in science, say, or history because we read some words about it in some books or listened to the words a teacher used describing it. And if these words, in writing or in speech, should tell us that the Earth is flat or that Napoleon existed, then flat it will be and existed he will have. That is to say, in large part our worldview is a secondhand extract from other people's words.

Sophie: But how could it be ever otherwise? The world is too complex for us to figure out what all of it is all about from nothing but direct original experience.

Philonous: And thus, you do admit the devil to be right.

Sophie: No, because I wouldn't say, "On words 't is excellent believing," but rather that, "In words we trust because we must."

Philonous: The basic fact though is in either case the same: the word is our object of belief.

Sophie: As I said, I don't see how it ever could be otherwise.

Philonous: But don't you think that this admission is disturbing?

Sophie: Absolutely, it is strange and even downright frightening to think that our thought and therefore our world is to a large extent produced by words that carry meanings that are circular.

Philonous: But even absent that perplexity, there still would be the problem of determining which meanings in which contexts can be trusted to be *true*. Afterall, the mass of information that is nowadays continuously produced far exceeds the processing capacity of any single human being. Each year, each month, each week, each day, and every single hour, there are printed books and written articles and added pages to the Internet that no one probably still knows the number of and no one certainly has any relevant awareness of as far as content is concerned. We are adrift in what I picture as a vast and rapidly expanding information universe in comparison to which the individual knowledge of even the most readily absorbent human mind must needs appear to be of quantum size. Somewhere out there in this giant information space we all trace our own atomic knowledge paths, and none of us still really knows why one path should be truer than another.

Sophie: You promised that the devil's words would "come in handy" to assist us, but now it seems they only cause the picture to grow grimmer.

Philonous: I promised insight not relief. A problem must be faced before it can be solved.

Sophie: But what we face, it seems, is now a scene that only devils will find pleasing. For the image that you conjure up is one of tiny human 'knowledge' paths traced out in far-flung information worlds the sheer immensity of which makes mockery of any claim to certainty or truth.

Philonous: And even worse and as a consequence, the paths are largely disconnected. Each path meanders randomly and any points of intersection with another path are purely due to happenstance.

Sophie: In other words, what you contend is that the massive information flows of our present era nullify and thereby isolate the individuals exposed to them.

Philonous: That is correct.

Sophie: But couldn't we instead perceive these very information flows to serve us and connect us? Afterall, where information can be accessed globally, it can as well be argued that the world is growing smaller and more unified.

Philonous: Absolutely, because as long as only words are our guide, we certainly can argue for whatever view we like. You take one view, I take another, and as words are thus opposed by other words we can be sure there won't be any resolution. To illustrate that point, it would be very much instructive for example to start a forum on the Internet concerning the effects of global information flows. I promise you, the chaos of opinions would be stunning—and so it would be, by the way, with any other 'fact' or issue we might happen to consider. That is to say, the devil once again is perfectly on target: "With words 't is excellent disputing."

Sophie: But what about those facts that everyone agrees upon? Do they not constitute a basic plan of points of reference that organize and structure all the chaos that you see?

Philonous: What 'facts', if I may ask, are you referring to?

Sophie: The facts, for instance, that the Earth is round, not flat, and that Napoleon existed.

Philonous: Yet both of these are facts because and only because there is a broad-based scholarly and general societal consensus that's supporting them—or so at least it seems.

Sophie: Certainly, for as I said—it never could be otherwise. We have to trust in other people's words because we simply cannot do original research regarding all the facts that we consider to be facts.

Philonous: By implication, then, a fact would cease to be a fact—as far as your opinion is concerned—as soon as there develops some significant societal dissent.

Sophie: It would indeed.

Philonous: But then, I think, we have a problem now. For no consensus can be trusted to be lasting in a world where information is a global random flood. I really have no difficulty whatsoever to imagine, for example, that someone sometime in the future will discover 'facts' disproving indisputably that there had ever been a conqueror known as Napoleon, and that in consequence there will emerge a dedicated cyber-space community of Napoleon-deniers.

Sophie: That seems a little bit far-fetched.

Philonous: Not at all—such things are happening.

Sophie: What would be an example?

Philonous: The controversy that surrounds the landings on the Moon. Because if anecdotal evidence is any indication, the story of the lunar landings, in many a contemporary mind, is nothing but a Cold War fantasy. Just search the Internet, and you will find there is no lack of words and 'facts' unmasking the entire Moon program as a hideous, elaborate conspiracy. Naively one might think the lunar landings, as a relatively recent historical occurrence, to be more solidly established in the realm of fact than even the existence of Napoleon, but such is not the case. The wealth of information testifying to these landings as a genuine phenomenon does not create more certainty but, apparently, it only stimulates more disbelief and critical denial.

Sophie: I have to say, I do not think that views as these should merit serious attention.

Philonous: As far as something meriting attention is concerned, there may be room for various perspectives. Just recently, for instance, I chanced upon an interview in which a man who worked for NASA in the sixties claimed that NASA, technologically, could not have staged a landing on the Moon in 1969. Exactly why, if I may ask, should his view, which is based on firsthand knowledge of the lunar program, be considered less deserving of respect than your competing view, which is in essence nothing but a secondhand extract from other people's words?

Sophie: Are you saying then that his denial may be justified?

Philonous: No, my present point is *not* to challenge or to justify particular opinions but rather to examine honestly the nature and validity of knowledge that derives, as I just said, from other people's words. Just ask yourself why you and I are so unshakably convinced that man has landed on the Moon? It seems to me the answer is, "because we read and heard some words that said he did." But such unquestioning credulity, on your part and on mine, is hardly going to impress a man whose pertinent professional experience has led him to conclude the landings were a fraud. For neither you nor I have anything to say to him that is of any substance. We never checked in detail any facts, we never saw a NASA program from the inside, and on the whole we really do not have a clue.

Sophie: But don't you think for every former NASA employee, who argues that the landings didn't happen, we can find a hundred or a thousand who emphatically argue that they did?

Philonous: What I do or don't think in this matter is irrelevant. Perhaps these other employees exist and perhaps I even am persuaded I could find them. But as it is, I haven't found them yet because I never even tried.

Sophie: And in that you certainly are right, but all the same I do not like what you are here implying. Something is decidedly upsetting in your underlying claim that every whim and fancy has a right to be considered as long as we have not directly checked the facts.

Philonous: I can assure you that there is no underlying claim as that. For what I purpose to assert is not that every fancy has a right to be considered but merely that considered it will be. In our global information world, every fact and issue, as it were, acts as a point of trifurcation splitting up the group of passers-through into supporters and detractors and agnostics in between. You mentioned as a fact that everyone accepts the proposition that the Earth is round, not flat, but when we switch from our planet's shape to our planet's age, the matter is a little more perplexing. For the classical scientific understanding that the Earth was naturally formed about four billion years ago[II] is here opposed by orthodox religious views insisting on a much more recent Biblical creation in six days. And what is more, the spectrum of beliefs concerning the related issue of the origin and history of life on earth is nothing but bewildering. Evolutionists stand here against creationists, naturalistic evolutionists oppose design-theorists, who in turn semi-oppose creationists; theistic evolutionists alternately support or oppose design-theorists; some evolutionists are evolutionists because they are atheists, some atheists are atheists because they are evolutionists, some evolutionists are creationists as well as design-theorists, and some are multiple '-ists' according to whatever whim has struck them.

Sophie: The spectrum is confounding, it is true, but once again I'd like to urge some caution. For certain of the views that are at issue here are really too obscure to be deserving of attention. Afterall, the facts are plain and widely known: the Earth is *not* six thousand but several billion years old, life as we know it was *not* created in six days but in eons of contingent evolution, and Adam and Eve, most certainly, did *not* just pop up from the ground but rather were descendent from monkeys. If we go back behind such well established scientific truths, we simply lose all contact with reality. There is no end, of course, to silly creeds and fanciful opinions, but then again why should I listen? I simply can't be bothered to consider earnestly the view that dinosaurs, for example, never existed and that their purported remains were put in the ground by some divine trickster to test our faith. Nor, for that matter, am I impressed with the alternative teaching that dinosaurs lived contemporaneously with pre-flood human beings and even were used by the latter for dino-back riding with harness and saddle. There is no rhyme or reason to any of this.

Philonous: And neither is there much rhyme or much reason to what you mean by a fact. You admitted that facts would cease to be facts in absence of a broad-based social consensus. But now you suddenly claim the status of 'fact' for various teachings that numerous people for reasons of culture and religious belief are known to reject.

Sophie: But the people in question are poorly informed, and somewhere, I

[II] ...or, more precisely, 4.54 billion years ago.

think, there must be a limit. Afterall, if the lunar landings were a hoax, if dinosaurs never existed, and if evolution is an invention, then what, if I may ask, can still prevent us from denying, say, even the Holocaust? I never did an original study to conclusively prove that six million people were wiped out in factory killings, but that doesn't mean that Holocaust-denial shouldn't disgust me.

Philonous: It shouldn't, I fully agree, but if you ask "why?", my only answer will be—and has to be—your very own motto: "in words we trust because we must."

Sophie: And thus you will be consistent but also, for my taste, taking the game a little too far.

Philonous: Except that the game is not just a game, for doubting creation or evolution is one thing, doubting mass murder another. In other words and in this sobering light, the loss of consensus that the present era has wrought may rightly appear a little distressing. It is not entirely a matter for joking that only uncertainty can ever be certain in a globalized world where individual knowledge is atomized and utterly fragmentized by the shattering force of a nuclear information explosion. I find it profoundly disturbing to see how people exposed to the impact of that violent force are randomly scattered between numerous parallel worlds that rigidly insulate these people in turn. An atheistic evolutionist, for instance, has preciously little in common with a young-Earth creationist, and little between them is worth being said. For words would here be opposing nothing but words, and nothing would thus be achieved. According to some words in some worlds, creation did occur, according to others, it did not; according to some words, the dinosaurs existed, according to others they did not; according to some words, the Moon landings happened, according to others they did not; according to some words, the Holocaust happened, according to others it did not. Reality itself, in this sort of vision, takes on the form of a surreal charade—a quicksand of constantly shifting verbal descriptions to which no meaning can ever be faithfully fixed.

Sophie: And yet, I cannot help but wonder: is present-day reality really as formless and as glibly amorphous as you are making it look? Are dinosaurs, lunar landings, and the Holocaust really just matters of contingent opinion?

Philonous: That's a matter of "contingent opinion"—in the postmodern world. But perhaps, by way of compromise, we can here agree that formlessness is also a form. Afterall, it is this very formlessness that *forms* so stark a contrast to medieval definition. In fact and in the light of what we just said, the contrast couldn't be much starker: the radically relative is here directly set against the absolutely absolute. And where Aquinas could still built a system, using words, that he believed to portray the real as it is—truly and faithfully—his postmodern counterpart struggles even just to understand how words such as 'real' or 'true' can ever have meaning at all.

Sophie: In respect of that contrast you most certainly are right. For as I mentioned earlier, the Middle Ages to me felt always elusive. With my contemporary consciousness I find no access, so it seems, to that supremely confident religious faith by which Aquinas, for example, was so vitally inspired. Aquinas and his fellows still inhabited a static Earth that God had kindly placed at His creation's center. But I, instead, have spent my life on some odd solar satellite that swiftly travels on a nameless path among an unknown multitude of other paths traced out by other planets and their stars. The universe that I know is stupendously complex, and there is honestly no hope to capture it within the pages of that single book that we refer to as the 'Christian Bible'.

Philonous: But neither can we capture it, as I see it, within that single set of theories that we call 'modern science'. Pretensions to completeness ought to be avoided, not only in theology, but all across the board in any area of thought. Aquinas may have been misguided in his efforts to create a comprehensive grand design. But just the same is true of physicists who dream up theories of everything from nothing but a bit of mathematics and a smattering of physical experiments. We really don't gain much when we replace medieval overconfidence in rational theology with modern fantasies of final computation schemes.

Sophie: In other words, you really are skeptic.

Philonous: To some extent I am. But there is more as we shall see.

From Words to Genuine Reality

Close to the end of his life, the postmodernist, Paul Feyerabend, succinctly expressed his philosophical vision as follows:

> The world we inhabit is abundant beyond our wildest imagination. There are trees, dreams, sunrises; there are thunderstorms, shadows, rivers; there are wars, flea bites, love affairs; there are the lives of people, Gods, entire galaxies. The simplest human action varies from one person and occasion to the next—how else would we recognize our friends only from their gait, posture, voice, and divine their changing moods? Narrowly defined subjects such as thirteenth-century Parisian theology, crowd control, late medieval Umbrian art are full of pitfalls and surprises, thus proving that there is no limit to any phenomenon, however restricted.[206]

There clearly is some truth to this. In fact, the latter assertion that "there is no limit to any phenomenon, however restricted" might well appear trivial except for the fact that much of Western philosophical thought was dedicated to proving its falsehood. Again and again there have been attempts to limit not only specific phenomena but even the world as a whole to finite symbolic descriptions. Thales proposed, in the words of his language, that the essence of Being was fully contained in the substance of water, Anaximenes replaced water with air, Heraclitus believed in a primeval fire and the change that it brings, and Parmenides said that the one final truth is the absence of change as being must be preserved. Western man, from the very beginning, was fiercely determined to figure it out—to discover the key to ultimate reality.

What is behind the world of appearance? Is it a God, a material substance, a realm of ideas, or merely a play of mechanical atoms? This is the puzzle that has to be faced, and to think it a puzzle that reason can solve was—for better or worse—the Western mind's unique predisposition. Somehow somewhere there arose the conviction that the reason we use in everyday life is able to penetrate the very core of existence. In Platonic philosophy, that innermost core consists, as we saw, of eternal Ideas, perfect forms, or changeless universals; that is, it consists of rational entities which are as such congruent to symbolic descriptions, in language or in mathematical thought. Seen from this angle, it is tempting to think that Plato—along with many or most of the West's greatest thinkers—was firmly committed to heeding the devil's advice: "On *words* let your attention centre!"

Worse still, the devil seems to be right. For is it not perfectly true that all our rational thought is tied to verbal or other symbolic descriptions? And is it not also true, by implication, that the limits of our language are the limits of our world as the philosopher of language, *Ludwig Wittgenstein*, famously put it?[1] In other words, if symbols are all that we know, then the essence of being—so far as we know—must be symbolic as well. As a matter of course, in speaking of the limits of *our* world we leave open the question of whether that world that *we* know is really the world as it is. Significantly, though, it was precisely this faith in a direct correspondence between being and human knowledge thereof that Plato, Aristotle, Augustine, and Thomas Aquinas, in various forms, all strongly upheld. And hence we may assert that a deep-seated faith in the power of reason to know the real essence of things lies right at the heart of the Western tradition.

That said, we also need to see clearly, of course that, in modern and especially postmodern times, this ancient epistemological confidence has been severely tested and criticized. Kant brought an end to the metaphysicians' groundless pretensions when he announced that the thing in itself—*das Ding an sich*—can never be known. And the attendant denial of knowledge that is truly objective has grown into a kind of radical subjectivism in many a contemporary mind that is nothing short of subversive. We in the West, in the 21st century, no longer believe in grand metaphysical systems. Nor are we given at all to the sort of rational acrobatics that Aquinas was still so prone to perform. We smile or shake our heads at carefully crafted arguments in the

---

[1] As the subsequent dialogue will show, what Wittgenstein precisely said is this: "*The limits of my language* mean the limits of my world."[207]

Summa Theologica that are designed to establish as 'factual' what cannot but strike us as dubious or downright ridiculous.

It leaves us befuddled or amused, for example, when Aquinas, using many words of 'explanation', infers that no two angels can be in the same place simultaneously,[208] that "beatified" angels "can be moved locally,"[209] and that their "local motion... can be continuous and non-continuous."[210] Similarly, we pay little attention to Augustine's assertion in the *City of God* that the number of days of creation was six because six is minimal among the numbers of 'perfection'—that is, the numbers that equal the sum of their proper divisors (in this case $6 = 1+2+3$).[211] For Augustine the neo-Platonist—and realist with regard to the status of universals—a perfect number was perfect in an absolute metaphysical sense, and therefore naturally expressive of God's immaculate character. But for us, at our present station in history, perfect numbers are no more perfect than odd numbers are odd. 'Perfect' for us, in respect of numbers, is merely a name and thus entirely devoid of any transcendent significance. And rightly so, because mathematics, as we understand it, would not be affected or changed in the least if odd numbers from now on were said to be blue and perfect numbers were said to be weird.

However, in spite of these modern critical currents there still is fully alive, even at present, the Enlightenment creed that knowledge in science is knowledge that reaches the essence of things—the real as it is. Science works, and therefore, science is true. That is to say, we don't believe in metaphysics anymore but in physics we still trust. By implication then, the Western dream of finding that "inmost force," as Goethe wrote, "which binds the world, and guides its course"[212] has now become a dream of final physical descriptions. The Holy Grail of knowledge nowadays is not the merging of the Christian faith with true philosophy, nor is it the ascent to Plato's purified conceptions; instead the object of desire presently is that elusive computation scheme—that final theory—that brings in line and unifies the mathematical laws by which the universe is governed.

Sophie: I must admit, this view is thoroughly persuasive. For science does indeed work very well, and any knowledge worth its name is therefore found, if anywhere, in science.

Philonous: As far as knowledge is concerned, I also think that science doesn't have much competition. Being an empiricist at heart, I strongly hold that knowledge of exterior reality is grounded in perception and is thus derivative of scientific testing. Notwithstanding this admission, though, there still remains the problem of determining how far that knowledge that composes science really takes us. What is its nature, what its scope? Is it broad or narrow, deep or superficial?

Sophie: To think of it as superficial would seem odd in light of its success. There is no doubt, the vast array of technological devices that scientific insight has produced is solid proof that science reaches deep and has a base that can be trusted.

Philonous: In other words, you do believe that science is the key—the key to ultimate reality.

Sophie: The notion of an ultimate reality is not a scientific one. When physicists today speak of a final theory—a theory of everything—they really mean a theory of everything that matters. Science doesn't tell us why the world exists or what its final purpose is but only how it works.

Philonous: In that case, I suppose, the task at hand should be to understand precisely what it is that matters to a physicist.

Sophie: It should indeed, but how do we accomplish it?

Philonous: By looking at a prototype—that is, what I have here in mind is to inspect a theory of physical reality that is exemplary.

Sophie: Such as?

Philonous: Newtonian classical mechanics.

Sophie: We looked at it before.

Philonous: ...and it was you, as I recall, who pointed out how Newton used his system brilliantly when he derived the laws of planetary motion (pp.45,114).

Sophie: I do remember it, and what I said back then in essence was that Newton's model was commendable for its superior conceptual economy because the planets and the Sun in it are merely points that have a mass and trace a path.

Philonous: In other words, a couple of ingredients—mass and position in space and time—are fully sufficient to capture the material world in this Newtonian scheme. Each planet has a mass and at any given time it has a definite position.

Sophie: And the set of all positions is its path.

Philonous: That is correct.

Sophie: Very well, the matter is plain. But why do you broach it?

Philonous: Because a closer look reveals a striking little oddity: Newton doesn't tell us what the nature or reality of his ingredients might be apart from how he chooses to denote them. What is a mass? It is a number, a symbol, a name, but what really is it? There is no answer.[II] Nor is there any attempt, on the part of Newton, to elucidate the concept of an absolute space in which objects exist in absolute time. What is space? What is time? Again, there is no answer—nor could there be, because in Newton's classical scheme the notions of mass, space, and time effectively function as axiomatic primitives the ontological status of which cannot be determined. Newton proudly asserted that he wasn't given to empty hypothesizing—

[II]To be precise, Newton does offer a definition of mass by calling it "a measure of matter that arises from its density and volume jointly."[213] But that only begs the question as to what the word 'density' means. Commonly, of course, density is defined as mass per volume, and thus we end up defining mass in terms of density and density in terms of mass which is meaningless.

"Hypotheses non fingo."[214] But his system, in fact, was built upon purely hypothetical concepts that he could not and did not explain in the least.

Sophie: I don't agree. For the concepts of mass, space, and time, while being indeed axiomatic, as you rightly observed, are nonetheless fully explained by the system itself. Those who study that system of Newton's will come to appreciate what 'mass' as a concept conveys simply by grasping the various ways in which that concept within that system is used. The mass of an object, from this point of view, is an inherent material quality that vitally conditions the object's behavior in the presence of other material objects. If we understand the rules by which this behavior is governed and if we also understand how the symbols we use are representative of certain observational contents, then we really have understood whatever there is to be understood about the concept called 'mass'.[III]

Philonous: And, I suppose, in much the same way we also can 'understand' whatever there is to be 'understood' about the notions of time and spatial position.

Sophie: ...within the system of Newton's—yes, that is how I perceive it. And that is as well, if I may add, what was meant earlier when it was said that "the problem of ontology... is to be reconceived as a search for the relational character of being rather than being itself" (p.55). You see, it doesn't make sense for us to inquire what meaning there is in the notion of 'mass' in an absolute, non-contextual sense. For 'mass' is an abstracted conception that simply cannot have meaning apart from the ways in which we employ it.

Philonous: If that is so, then would it be further correct to assume that in essence the same conclusion applies to other systems as well?

Sophie: Systems other than Newton's?

Philonous: Indeed, my question here is whether the view you expressed, concerning the construal of meaning in classical mechanics, would also apply to a more advanced theoretical scheme—such as, for instance, Einstein's general relativity or perhaps the latest super-string model.

Sophie: The answer is "yes." For in any finite symbolic description there must be a layer of symbols and concepts that forms the description's bottommost floor. Whether these ultimate primitives are mass, space, and time, or some other, more recent conceptions is completely irrelevant. For either way, we will be faced with a theory in which no symbol has meaning apart from the rules that define how the symbol is used.

Philonous: By implication, it seems, the answer to the question we posed— "What is it that matters to a physicist?"—apparently is this: "nothing

---

[III]The philosophical position that Sophie here expounds is analogous to a foundational conception of mathematics that is known as 'formalism'. This position was most prominently held by David Hilbert, and briefly stated it says that mathematics is a play of notations that can be useful for instance in science but doesn't have meaning apart from the logical rules that define it.

but self-contained symbolic descriptions." The world, according to physics, is a play of symbols—it is a game. And the rules of the game somehow determine the meaning the symbols can have. That is to say, meaning is ultimately a rule-induced contextual construct.

Sophie: Absolutely, yes it is.

Philonous: Then would it be accurate too if I said that, in principle, the same is true of any system of thought in any field whatsoever?

Sophie: ...as for example the field of philosophy?

Philonous: ...or theology or psychology or anything else that may come to mind.

Sophie: Certainly, for unless we are willing to argue in circles, we will come upon a layer of symbols or words that cannot be further reduced. Speaking of God, for instance, a theologian might say that God is Love or that God is Truth, but any attempt to further define these additional concepts of Love and Truth will sooner or later encounter a limit. For either we will absurdly explain words by themselves or we will be forced to assume, by an act of pure choice, that certain words or groupings of words are meaningful simply by virtue of how we employ them.

Philonous: ...and hence we really are left with nothing but words.

Sophie: ...and hence the devil's advice: "On *words* let your attention centre."

Philonous: But you mustn't forget: the devil is truly the devil and thus his advice is truly pernicious.

Sophie: In this case, however, it strikes me as sound. Afterall, in words we trust because we must.

Philonous: Which goes to show that the devil is really a master deceiver.

Sophie: But Wittgenstein isn't the devil, and his dictum isn't meant to deceive. So I still wonder: isn't it trivially true that the limits of our language are the limits of our world—or, put differently, that our world ends where our language ends and that therefore we cannot but center on words?

Philonous: Actually, he didn't quite say that. For in the *Tractatus*—his most famous work—the words that he uses are these: "*The limits of my language* mean the limits of my world."[215]

Sophie: How is that difference important?

Philonous: In choosing the singular case, Wittgenstein places his emphasis on the first-person subject. Thus it clearly is significant when in the same section of the *Tractatus*, from which the dictum I quoted is taken, we find the following attendant assertion:

> The subject does not belong to the world: rather, it is a limit of the world.[216]

Sophie: I don't understand.

Philonous: To clarify what I am after, it may help to observe that Wittgenstein actually agrees with your point of view according to which, the meaning of symbols derives from the rules that govern their use. For in one of his later writings he explains, regarding this issue, that "the life of [a] sign" is simply and solely "its use."[217]

Sophie: And so?

Philonous: Well, as we now conjoin this later claim with the assertion above, concerning the transcendence of the subject, we finally come to perceive why the devil is a liar indeed.

Sophie: I still don't understand.

Philonous: It's not quite obvious, I know, but suppose for a moment that the limits of your language really are the limits of your world and that your language in turn really is a self-referential game in which all meaning is inherently contextual. Then, given these assumptions, your entire world is encompassed by a set of rules that specify how certain symbols are used and how they align with certain sensory contents or states of awareness. But the one reality that this reflexive world of symbol correlations and matching perceptions just cannot contain or represent is the existence of your own perceiving consciousness. By implication, you yourself, by being conscious, do not belong to the world that your language comprises (see also the discussion on p.89ff).

Sophie: The notion is odd.

Philonous: On the contrary, it's perfectly plain—as long as we concur, that is, that the symbol 'world' presently refers to that part of the total of existence which symbols can model. For in imposing this restriction, awareness *of* the world is excluded *from* the world and therefore, by definition, relegated to transcendence. Certain symbols may correspond to certain sense perceptions, but the actuality of any such perception in your own subjective consciousness is entirely off limits.

Sophie: And thus the devil is a liar because...?

Philonous: ...because in urging us to center on words, he tempts us to believe that words can capture everything. Reality, from his deceptive perspective, is but a facade—an empty shell—utterly soulless and barren. Put differently, if reality in its entirety were indeed compressible into symbolic theoretical schemes, then all of human life would indeed be truly and utterly bleak—and that is, of course, what the devil would gladly have us believe.

Sophie: So Wittgenstein's remark, concerning the subject as a limit, you really take to mean that humans have something in them—perhaps a soul—that the devil would like us to be unaware of or to downright deny.

Philonous: Yes, I do. But Wittgenstein, of course—at the time when he wrote the *Tractatus*—would likely have labeled such talk as 'meaningless banter' or worse. Afterall, the purpose of his work most certainly was not to argue that humans have souls but to delineate the limits of language. His goal was to solve all philosophical problems universally by demonstrating that problems become non-problems as soon as language is properly purged of everything vague and impure.

Sophie: Did you say *all* problems?

Philonous: Indeed, Wittgenstein was not lacking in ambition and, amazingly, he did believe that his work had fully accomplished its purpose.[218] In his own mind, at least, his philosophy was final and complete. It clarified, once and for all, what can be said and then discouraged any further discussion with the concluding command to simply not speak about that which cannot be spoken about.[219] In fact, this insistence to abstain from nonsensical talk is really the core of his quest. For already in the preface to his work we read that "the whole sense of [his] book might be summed up in the following words: what can be said at all can be said clearly, and what cannot be talked about we must pass over in silence."[220] Interestingly, however, he also admits that, as the problems of philosophy are solved in this way—or better dissolved—by means of linguistic analysis, very "little is achieved."[221]

Sophie: And *with* this admission he points, I suppose, to a rather large transcendent space beyond his terminal thoughts.

Philonous: ...namely the space that the subject inhabits. In fact, it is this transcendent realm to which the whole of the *Tractatus* points *by its very nature*. You see, Wittgenstein cautions his readers right at the start that, conceivably, his work "will be understood only by someone who has himself had the thoughts that are expressed in it," and then he observes that "its purpose would be achieved if it gave pleasure to one person who read and understood it."[222] In other words, Wittgenstein here affirms—inadvertendly—his attendant explicit assertion concerning the subject's essential transcendence. For he implicitly acknowledges that his own world of thought, his own most intimate intellectual life, just cannot be contained in the words of his language.

Sophie: How so?

Philonous: Just connect the dots: if everything that "can be said... can be said clearly," then it may be assumed that Wittgenstein in the *Tractatus* addressed himself to matters that can be said and that he did so with the intent to express himself clearly. Consequently, even his presumably best efforts to accomplish this end take place, as he himself says, in front of a hoped for audience of one. The person who truly understands the frequently cryptic pronouncements that compose the *Tractatus* will have to be, as it were, Wittgenstein's intellectual *soulmate*. In absence of that genuine first-person experience of an intellectual life that somehow directly parallels Wittgenstein's own there can be no true comprehension. That is to say, language in itself is ultimately powerless to fully convey what Wittgenstein wants to convey. And in the light of this latter conclusion, let me suggest, we'd better rephrase his dictum as follows: our world *begins* where our language *ends*.

Sophie: But this is absurd. For regardless of any of Wittgenstein's sayings, it still is the case that whenever I consciously process a thought, an emotion, or a sensation, I clothe it in words. It is in these words and through these words that I know the world I am in.

Philonous: Do you really? I doubt it.

Sophie: You are free to doubt as you please, but the fact is undeniable: my entire conscious existence is clearly and trivially completely contained in the words that I use to portray it. Whatever I am and can be aware of, I capture in words.

Philonous: So when you feel a pain, the pain can be put into words? If that were the case, then your pain would surely be mine as soon as I heard you express it. But as it is, your pain is yours and my pain is mine no matter the words we exchange. This is *not* to say, of course, that I cannot feel empathy, but my pertinent capacity is rooted in my own genuine experience of pain in the past, rather than in my knowledge of some related verbal abstractions. I can empathize with you in your pain, not because I listened to language, but because I have been there and felt it—because I know what it's like.

Sophie: And yet it is the words that I speak that cause you to recollect what you yourself endured in the past. It is only because I can capture in words the state I am in that you are enabled to share in my suffering.

Philonous: I don't agree because firstly the nonverbal part of the picture—as given for instance by your facial expression or bodily posture—is potentially far more expressive than the words that you speak. And secondly and more importantly, my comprehension of what you are saying really depends, as I said, on whether I myself in the past have known a pain of my own. If I had never felt pain, then nothing that you could possibly say would help me to know what it means to feel pain. Where experiences are shared, words can be used to establish a link, but where they are not, no word can fill in the gap. Words in themselves are perfectly impotent. Just ask yourself, for instance, what words you would use to convey what it really is like to be you. How would you try to transmit in speech or in writing your own inner world—your conscious self—your real you? You could talk for hours on end and still I wouldn't truly know what it truly is like for you to be you. The genuine actuality of your very own first-person existence just cannot be compressed into symbols.

Sophie: So what you are saying apparently is that language is only a crude imposition—a play on the surface masking the real.

Philonous: Let's say it is a mental processing scheme which evolution equipped us with and which therefore is partly reflective of the real world but not—by any means—identical with it. We use discrete symbolic descriptions largely because our senses portray to us the exterior world as being made up of separate individual objects, but ultimate significance such a portrayal has probably not. If we only had a sense of smell, for example, the world would likely appear mostly diffuse, and we likely wouldn't have formed that essential conception of rigid discreteness that lies at the heart of all our symbolic conceptions[IV]—and the same might be true as well, of course, if we operated on a higher plane on which quantum entanglement or some other, even deeper connecting principle was something that could be directly perceived. I find it very plausible to think that a higher form of consciousness may be able to replace or supplement the merely symbolic with other, more sophisticated means of expression.

Sophie: In other words and as I suggested just now, you do believe that language *is* superficial.

Philonous: I do indeed, and by implication, I also believe that symbolic conceptual thought in science is lacking in depth.

Sophie: In that case I have to conclude what I concluded before: you are at bottom a skeptic.

Philonous: To which I answer as before: "to some extent I am" (p.286). For in respect of science I not only refuse to acknowledge its depth but also tend to affirm rather strongly its basic validity. Science works and is true but isn't itself the real thing. As I see it, the best final theory that physicists will ever come up with will be a theory of everything *except* of that which matters the most: the direct experience of an actual self—which afterall is the only reality that I, or anyone else for that matter, will ever be faced with. The world—for me—just doesn't exist apart from my own awareness of it. And it is precisely this immediate actuality of my conscious existence that science just cannot but utterly miss. Symbols aren't actual and they never will be.

Sophie: So what we are finally left with, it seems, is limited knowledge that's valid but weak.

Philonous: No, in addition and very importantly, we also have the very real thing—our own first-person experience. Naturally, this subjective actuality is not in that realm of genuine public knowledge where science is found. But our world begins where our symbols end, and thus there is room for more to be said.

Sophie: Put differently, in order to fully convince me that I shouldn't center on words, you will be adding more words.

Philonous: I know, it doesn't make sense but, unfortunately, I don't have a choice. With my closest relatives still up in the trees, I am forced, by reason of these humble relations, to keep on spitting out words. I don't center on words—*of course*—but my poor primate brain just cannot do

---

[IV] As a matter of course, "discreteness" in this present context carries a different meaning than in the juxtaposition of discrete versus continuous that is familiar from mathematics an that was at issue for instance in our discussion of the continuity or discreteness of time. For even the continuous real numbers are thought to be made up of individual points and the corresponding symbolic representation may thus be still considered discrete.

without them.

Sophie: As you said, it doesn't make sense.

Philonous: And since that is so, we'd better keep moving.

Sophie: So as to avoid to be facing the truth?

Philonous: No, so as to discover its meaning.

Sophie: The meaning of truth?

Philonous: ...or better of Truth.

Sophie: You are changing the subject.

Philonous: Not at all, the topic is still to determine whether and how I ought to be counted a skeptic.

Sophie: I don't see the link.

Philonous: Look, the real world begins where our language ends—this is the key that settles the question.

Sophie: The question of your being a skeptic or the question of Truth?

Philonous: Both.

Sophie: Your claim is ambitious.

Philonous: Less than it seems, and to try to convince you, let me say this: the fact that science is lacking in depth implies in particular that science never pertains to concepts with capital letters. Anthropologists, for instance, can study the story of 'god' in man's image, but to God they cannot ascend. Similarly, biologists can fully describe the workings of physical 'love', but Love they cannot explain. For science is true but isn't the Truth.

Sophie: And that is so, as many a scientist would probably say, because concepts with capital letters are merely inventions. They are philosophical fictions, stubborn illusions, or, worse still, they are meaningless *names*.

Philonous: And thus we return to our favorite problem: *the problem of universals*.

Sophie: ...in order to finally solve it?

Philonous: Of course not. I am neither willing nor able to rationally establish, for instance, that 'Truth' exists independently as a Platonic Idea, perhaps in God's mind, or, alternatively, that it is a mere name. If that were the goal we are after, we might as well stick with the writings of Plato, Augustine, and Thomas Aquinas—and numerous others besides.

Sophie: So what are you proposing?

Philonous: To consider a scene—from the life of Aquinas. G.K. Chesterton writes how Aquinas, when still a young boy, startled his teachers at school one day with the force of a question that all of a sudden burst forth: "What is God?"[223] It may be fair to assert that no man and no woman in history was ever more strongly committed to putting the answer to that question in words than he, the brilliant St. Thomas Aquinas. And yet, we also recall that pivotal moment, at the end of his life, when he was granted a vision in which he saw "things" which made all his "writings like straw" (p.277). All his life Aquinas had searched for the Truth in the words of his language, but when he finally found it, he knew that he could not and would not express it in words. In consequence, he retired from scholarly writing and left unfinished even his greatest work, the *Summa Theologica.*

Sophie: And the moral of the story is, I suppose, that the problem of universals in respect of Truth is most conveniently solved by beholding a vision. For in the presence of God's divine reality, arguments are no longer needed, and words can be safely thrown out.

Philonous: As I see it, the moral first of all is that Aquinas, along with some of his fellow great minds—the greatest thinkers in history—came to understand that symbols and words can never contain what matters the most to a man: his inner domain—his actual self. Turning from Aquinas to Plato, for instance, we find not only a deep-seated rational confidence in man's ability to know, but also an even deeper conviction that true understanding ultimately reaches beyond the limits of language.[224] What Plato was after at bottom was not a symbolic system of thought but rather true enlightenment of spirit and soul. The seeker of Truth, according to Plato, was given to "contemplation," committed to "love and purification,"[225] and could expect to experience moments of mystical union in which understanding came suddenly, "like a blaze kindled by a leaping spark."[226] Even more strongly we find these ideas in the thought of Plotinus, of course, the mystic par excellence who emphasized time and again that genuine knowledge of Truth was grounded in inner experience and that, in the absence of the latter, his own philosophy in particular could not be fully comprehended.[227]

Sophie: And from Plotinus, I assume, the Platonic influence directly extends to Augustine as well.

Philonous: Indeed, Augustine never ceased to be amazed at how naturally neo-Platonic conceptions could be integrated with Christian belief,[V] and his focus on the inner life of the self before God is evident on every page of his *Confessions.* But while the case of Augustine is plain, the case of Aquinas requires some added comment. Commonly, Aquinas is thought to have been a dedicated Aristotelian whose bend of mind was more objective and concrete and whose foremost concern was to harmonize *the Philosopher's* teachings with divine revelation.

Sophie: ...and rightly so.

Philonous: But what is frequently overlooked is the fact that Aquinas gave ample space as well in his writings to the neo-Platonic tradition. The works of the so-called *Pseudo-Dionysius*, for instance, a Christian neo-Platonist from the 5th century, he quoted an astounding "1700 times."[229][VI] That is to

---

[V] In the *City of God* Augustine explicitly says this: "If Plato says that the wise man is the man who imitates, knows, and loves this God, and that participation in this God brings man happiness, what need is there to examine the other philosophers? There are none that come nearer to us than the Platonists."[228]

[VI] The Pseudo-Dionysius was so named because in ancient and medieval times his writings were wrongly attributed to Dionysius the Areopagite whom St. Paul had converted in Athens.

say, it does seem worth noting that Aquinas was deeply influenced by a man
who counseled for instance in one of his works to "leave behind... everything
perceived and understood" and to "strive upward... toward union with him
who is beyond all being and knowledge."[231]

Sophie: So your point is, I take it, that the ground was well prepared when
Aquinas finally had his own, transcendent moment of Truth.

Philonous: Let's say, he likely was ready to fully acknowledge that the life
of the spirit cannot be contained in blotches of ink. Even he, the great
St. Thomas Aquinas, foremost among the Scholastics and creator of a
supremely ordered universe of theological thought, had to admit, at the
end of his life, that words are ultimately empty and weak. Moreover and
very interestingly, the same conclusion we find in Wittgenstein too. For
close to the end of his *Tractatus* he surprises his readers with the following
claim:

> My propositions serve as elucidations in the following way: anyone
> who understands me eventually recognizes them as nonsensical,
> when he has used them—as steps—to climb up beyond them. (He
> must, so to speak, throw away the ladder after he has climbed up
> it.)
>
> He must transcend these propositions, and then he will see the
> world aright.[232]

Sophie: I see what you mean, but the trouble here is that most of us don't
understand the *Tractatus* to start with and thus may feel a little hard
pressed when urged to transcend it. And, in reference to Aquinas I will
say, that, lamentably, most of us most of the time don't have a vision. It
is true, of course, that many a question can be nicely and firmly resolved
if God directly invites us to take in the Light. But absent such a divine
revelation we probably have to continue to muddle about, using impotent
symbols and words in the process.

Philonous: Your view is too narrow. For what I was trying to argue was not
that we always must wait for a heavenly vision or a road-to-Damascus
event, but rather, more simply, that Truth is beheld by the spirit. It is not
in words and symbolic descriptions where we encounter the Truth but in
the recess that harbors the soul. Do we 'know' that the sermon of Jesus
is true—the Sermon on the Mount—because we carefully analyzed, one by
one, the words that compose it, or, instead, because its power is manifest
in actual deeds and realities that speak to the heart?

> Blessed are those who are persecuted because of righteousness, for
> theirs is the kingdom of heaven.[233]

In this context, Copleston points out, that the high esteem in which Aquinas and many other
medieval thinkers held his works was due not least to this erroneous association.[230]

Do we know what is meant by this verse because we dissect it, argue around it, and drown it in abstractions? Or do we instead understand what Jesus here says because we have seen it in action with powerful force? It is in the actions of Gandhi, for instance, or Corrie ten Boom—and Jesus Himself— that we come to behold those innermost Truths that here are referred to.

Sophie: Speaking of Jesus, though, you conveniently omitted to mention that the author of *John* calls him the Word. If the word is so weak, then how can it also be God?

Philonous: No, Jesus is not the Word, he is the Word-come-*alive*—which is precisely the kind of distinction I was trying to make.

Sophie: And which, I assume, is also the reason, why you refuse to be counted a skeptic.

Philonous: I think, you are right.

Sophie: That answers my question.—And thanks for putting it all so nicely in words.

On Stone Age Clubs and Atom Bombs

When we mentioned the name 'Peter Abélard' in our discussion of universals, a little while back (p.271), we committed the serious blunder not to mention as well one of the most tragic and most famous romantic affairs in written history.[234]

When Abélard was about forty years old and a highly acclaimed Master of the Schools of Paris, he felt attracted to a gifted young woman named Héloise. At the time, Héloise lived in the house of her uncle Fulbert, and Abélard therefore conceived the devious plan to come into closer contact with her—that is, to seduce her—by persuading Fulbert to allow him to work as her private instructor. Before long he succeeded, and a little while later Héloise was expecting. Faced with this dishonoring circumstance, Abélard had her abducted and taken to Brittany to the home of a sister of his where she bore him a son. In order to settle the matter and to appease Fulbert in the process, Abélard decided to marry his mistress but tried to keep it a secret so as to avoid that his "reputation should... suffer."[235] Fulbert, however, didn't stick to the bargain and made the marriage publicly known. The resulting violent complications prompted Abélard to send Héloise to the Abbey of Argenteuil for protection from Fulbert which in turn prompted the latter to hire some henchmen who assaulted Abélard during his sleep and severed his manhood.

This story of Abélard and Héloise was not only a great personal drama, but even had an effect on the history of Western ideas. For it inspired Abélard to write an autobiography—*The Story of My Misfortunes*[236]—that differed sharply in its focus on personal specifics from the common medieval hagiographies which tended to portray the Christian saints as standardized types. Instead of a description of himself in terms of ideal universals, Abélard offered his readers the particular picture of a real human being in unmasked real-life perplexity. In other words, as Norman F. Cantor points out in his thoughtful account of medieval history, Abélard's great contribution in writing his autobiography was the "rediscovery of personality"[237]—a contribution, as one might add, that was pointing ahead to the Renaissance.

As a matter of course, we are not here asserting that Abélard's true-to-life picture of his own misadventures was somehow directly connected to the arrival, 300 years later, of those outstanding personalities that imprinted the Renaissance with the force of their genius—men like Michelangelo and Leonardo da Vinci. Abélard's autobiographical writings in themselves were only a very small piece in a very large puzzle. However, insofar as Abélard also prepared, as we saw, the reception of Aristotelian philosophy into the systems of Albert the Great and Thomas Aquinas, his overall contribution to the eventual forging of the modern world is clearly deserving of mention. For the positive appraisal of Aristotle's thought by Albert and Thomas not only foreshadowed the rise of modern empirical science but also, inadvertently, provided the thesis against which the antithetical spirit of Renaissance humanism would soon be asserting itself. That is to say, it served to enliven the European intellectual scene at precisely that critical juncture that the Renaissance signified.[I]

Furthermore, in respect of the problem of universals, the doctrines of Abélard and, via extension, of Albert and Thomas, signaled an irreversible shift away from the exaggerated realism of the early Scholastics toward a more empirical, scientific conception of knowledge. In fact, already in the works of Aquinas's English contemporary, Roger Bacon (1214?–1292), do we come across some important new currents that further reinforced this epistemological reorientation. Bacon was explicitly critical of the leading Scholastics in Paris and scolded them openly for their all too ready deference to ancient authority. Truth, according to Bacon, was not only found in Plato's or Aristotle's philosophical writings, but could be discovered as well independently by freely employing all of man's sensory and rational faculties.[II] Consequently, he made it a point to conduct his own scientific research and even to analyze his experimental results with mathematical methods.[III] Consistent with this approach of his to the problem of knowledge, Bacon also emphasized the importance of direct mystical experience, guided by grace, in matters of faith and urged

---

[I]Thomas Kuhn elaborates this point in [Kuh1], pp.127–129, where he argues that the "dogmatic anti-Aristotelianism" of leading Renaissance humanists helped "to facilitate for others a break with the root concepts of Aristotle's science."

[II]In order not to cause any misunderstandings, it may be helpful to add that Bacon greatly admired Aristotle and even considered him the most outstanding of all the pagan philosophers. It was not Aristotle's philosophy itself that Bacon rejected, but only the uncritical acceptance thereof that he claimed to have observed among the Parisian Scholastics.

[III]According to Stewart Easton's detailed assessment of Bacon's work, Bacon conducted only a few planned experiments himself but gave "much thought to the meaning of experiments carried out by others, and considered seriously the place of ordinary life-experience within a theoretical universal science."[238]

that Biblical exegesis should use as its source the original texts in Hebrew and Greek.

What we see happening here is a definite move toward that autonomy in thought and observational inquiry that lies at the heart of modern empirical science. Bacon, of course, would have insisted that all his research and philosophical thinking was conducted solely for the glory of God. But then again, it was Bacon alone who did the conducting—and little indeed would he have achieved by appealing to God in the process. For knowledge is grounded, according to Bacon, not in divine illumination, but rather in man's own, immediate experience.

An even more pronounced assertion of human independence in the search for knowledge and truth we find in the thought of Bacon's fellow countryman, William of Ockham (1290–1349). Starting from his famous economy principle[IV]—commonly known as 'Ockham's razor'—according to which explanatory schemes must not be inflated needlessly, Ockham was led to adopt a very clearcut nominalist view. For in the light of this principle, a Platonic Idea such as 'horseness', for instance, is to be judged a useless appendage to our actual knowledge of the actual phenomenon—the horse that we see. According to Ockham, the real is not the general idea or form of a thing but merely and exclusively the thing in itself. In other words, universals are here understood to be purely rational constructs that do not in any way whatever exist independently in extra-mental reality.

Amazingly, Ockham even disputed the traditional Augustinian position regarding the existence of universals and forms *ante rem* in the divine intellect. And to support his dissenting opinion, he argued in essence that the presence of such anterior universals would have limited God's freedom in the act of creation. For if indeed the function of these universals had been, as was commonly assumed, to predetermine the forms of the physical world, then, in the act of creation, the divine will would have been tied, so to speak, to a template.[240] Since that seemed unacceptable, the assumption of anteriority in respect of universals had to be false. In other words, in this view of Ockham's, God had freely chosen the design of the world in an irreducible act of decision, and any attempt to limit that act by rationally demonstrating its necessary dependence on certain pre-given forms was therefore tantamount to a denial of God's perfect omnipotence. Moreover, the total absence of any form of necessity from God's creative decision also implied, so Ockham believed, that the nature of physical reality could not be deduced but only observed. There cannot and does not exist a set of *a priori* first principles from which the order of the universe can be inferred in a self-contained rational fashion. For the

---

[IV] In one of its versions, Ockham states this principle as follows: "We must not affirm that something is necessarily required for the explanation of an effect, if we are not led to this by a reason proceeding either from a truth known by itself or from an experience that is certain."[239]

universe exists due to a choice, and any knowledge of the laws that it obeys must therefore be arrived at inductively from observation of the concrete.

In following these lines of thought, we do well to recall the trouble that Roscelin faced when he contended that the three Trinitarian persons cannot be one. Is Ockham as well going to argue that the real in the case of the Godhead is only the individual person and that therefore the pertinent dogma of Trinitarian unity must be discarded? The answer is "no," but the 'no' is momentous. For Ockham in essence asserts that a conflict between his own philosophical views and the Church's doctrinal position just cannot arise because the truths of the faith are not within reach of the rational mind. Reason is impotent, Ockham says, to elucidate propositions which—by their very nature—are not within reason's domain. We simply can *not* understand how three can be one or how Christ could be human as well as divine, and therefore, whatever we *can* understand does not cause a problem.[241]

Surprisingly, in arguing thus, Ockham's intent was not to undermine faith but to outline the limits of reason. He dismantled the foundational unity of philosophy and theology, chiefly in order to keep the latter safe from attack. Put differently, we might say that Ockham was so notably modern in the tone of his thought because he was still so fully medieval in purpose.[242] He wanted to safeguard the faith but effectively only deprived it of reason's support. In consequence, the Truth was split in two halves, and Ockham thereby became the unwilling prophet of a secular world in which science would rule and religion would be reduced to a private diversion with no claim to rational truth. Ockham may have been a true medieval believer, but in his ideas he foretold the tale of the modern split consciousness in which reason and faith are harshly opposed.

The sketch that we have here drawn of the thought of Bacon and Ockham allows us to see, in spite of its evident crudity, how certain intellectual currents in the late Scholastic period were contributing to that immense civilizational shift out of which the modern world would soon be arising. For both of these men—for different reasons and with different conscious intents—were helping to form, for better or worse, the modern ideal of the free autonomous self that encounters the world with resolute confidence in its own understanding and skill.

As a matter of course, a transition of such truly historic proportions as the one here in question cannot be forged by merely asserting a new point of view. Creating a new civilization is not a matter of slightly adjusting or even radically reshaping a philosophical outlook but of bringing about an entirely new form of life. Something more had to happen than a mere realignment in Scholastic debates. Yet what exactly was that something? In attempting to answer this difficult question, it is instructive to note that the year 1349, the year when Ockham died,[V] was also the year when Europe was fully engulfed

---

[V]Whether Ockham died in 1349, in 1348, or already in 1347 appears to be somewhat

by the Black Death pandemic. For it has been argued convincingly that the terror spread by the plague effected large scale adjustments in economic affairs as well as in patterns of thought that were of enormous import to Europe's impending rebirth.

Initially, of course, the Black Death—along with the secondary plague epidemics that followed it—was bound to bring chaos and economic decline. But it was precisely the desperate need born of such hardships that created a greater openness for renewal and change. On the whole, as David Herlihy writes in his detailed analysis of the effects of the plague, "Europe proved to be a strong patient, and emerged from its long bout with pestilence healthier, more energetic, and more creative than before."[243]

Perhaps then it is not accidental that the age of the plague was also an age of important inventions. The first mechanical clock was built around 1360, corned gunpowder was introduced in the late 14th century, and, in 1440, movable type printing was invented by Johannes Gutenberg. Furthermore, the widespread use of the compass along with advances in ship building led to substantial improvements in seafaring skills which eventually made possible the Voyages of Discovery across the Atlantic. On the darker side, though, the introduction of gunpowder, just mentioned, also set off a series of innovations in military technology that would soon be made use of in recklessly projecting Europe's new power to the rest of the world.

In the light of this latter remark, it is proper to add that a negative view of human affairs and human history can always be easily taken. Evil is always somewhere involved and pointing that out is hardly an insight worth noting. On the other hand, though, the temptation to look at only the bright side of things may even be greater and more problematic. When we think of the Renaissance, we commonly think of great works of art—the *Mona Lisa*, the statue of *David*, or Brunelleschi's *Florence Cathedral*. And rightly so, for works as these are indeed celebrations of beauty that are deserving of great admiration. But what we don't like to think of so readily is the terrible face that this brilliantly ascendant new Europe would soon show to those who didn't belong to it—the peoples of Africa, Asia, and the Americas.

When Christopher Columbus landed in the Caribbeans, in October 1492, he and his men were greeted by the native Arawaks with 'food, water, [and] gifts.'"[244] But Columbus, of course, had not come all the way across the Atlantic to find some new friends—he had come to find gold. And sure enough, he wouldn't waste time on niceties:

> As soon as I arrived in the Indies [(which is what Columbus falsely assumed the Bahaman islands to be)], on the first Island which I found, I took some of the natives by force in order that they might learn and might give me information of whatever there is in these

uncertain. But apparently, his death was *not* caused by the plague.

parts.[245]

Noting further that the natives had no iron and no effective weapons of war, Columbus also observed that "[t]hey would make fine servants" and that "[w]ith fifty men we could subjugate them all and make them do whatever we want."[246]

Columbus was sailing under the sign of the cross, but the message of the one who had died on it was apparently entirely lost on him. For otherwise he wouldn't have been so keenly surprised to discover that the natives were completely "free with their possessions:"[247]

> [N]o one who has not witnessed them would believe it. When you ask for something they have, they never say no. To the contrary, they offer to share with anyone...[248]

Columbus called such behavior "naive."[249] One wonders what he might have called Jesus of Nazareth for saying that we always should "[g]ive to the one who asks" and never "turn away from the one who wants to borrow from [us];"[250] or how, for that matter, he might have fit in with those early Christian believers of the *Book of Acts* who "had everything in common"[251] and "gave to anyone as he had need."[252]

In 1495, on his second journey to the Caribbeans, Columbus set up a base on the island of Haiti from which he conducted slave raids and enacted a brutal regime. When the Arawaks tried to resist they were punished with cold-blooded cruelty. Historian Howard Zinn, describes the events that unfolded as follows:

> When the Spaniards took prisoners they hanged them or burned them to death. Among the Arawaks, mass suicides began with cassava poison. Infants were killed in order to save them from the Spaniards. In two years, through murder, mutilation, or suicide, half of the 250,000 Indians on Haiti were dead.
>
> When it became clear that there was no gold left, the Indians were taken as slave labor on huge estates, known later as *encomiendas*. They were worked at a ferocious pace, and died by the thousands. By the year 1515, there were perhaps fifty thousand Indians left. By 1550, there were five hundred. A report of the year 1650 shows none of the original Arawaks or their descendants left on the island.[253]

We celebrate Columbus Day, but what do we really celebrate? The beginning of a glorious new era or plain old genocide?

It is easy, as we already said, to always take a negative view. But insofar as the emergence of the modern world—and the modern self therewith—is presently at issue, it must surely be permitted to ask what kind of a self exactly it was that was here emerging. Was it the brilliant self of the proverbial 'Renaissance man' who creatively encounters the world with God-given freedom?

Or was it instead the self that Carl Jung, for example, was confronted with during his visit to the Pueblo Indians (p.3)—the self that murders, usurps, and destroys? According to Jung, his Indian interlocutor, Chief Ochwiay Biano, conveyed his impressions of the white man as follows:

> See how cruel the whites look. Their lips are thin, their noses sharp, their faces furrowed and distorted by folds. Their eyes have a staring expression; they are always seeking something. What are they seeking? The whites always want something; they are always uneasy and restless. We do not know what they want. We do not understand them. We think they are mad.[253]

At this point one might interject that the picture here painted of the Aryan bird of prey can be painted in similar form of other peoples and cultures as well. Afterall, cruelty is not a European invention. While that may be so, it clearly isn't of interest. For the evil in others is the problem of others, and only the evil in *us* is of interest to *us*. Furthermore, evil is not indifferent to scale, and there simply is no denying the fact that only the West has developed powers and means sufficient to threaten global destruction. Multiple overkill capacities and global ecological degradation are the bitter fruits of the West's and only the West's scientific inventiveness.

It is appalling but nonetheless true: the great Christian West was ruthless in the extreme. Wherever the Europeans sent their explorers and fleets, they left a trail of destruction.

Indigenous populations were exploited, enslaved, and exterminated; lands were abused, forests cut down, and animals brutishly slaughtered. At about the middle of the 19th century there were 60 to 100 million buffalos roaming the North American prairies, by 1884 the buffalo was almost extinct (Figure 4.1). Killing the animals in massive numbers was a convenient means of killing the Indians too, that is, it was a natural measure to take—a typical Western approach.

So let us ask again: what was that modern self that supposedly began to emerge in the Renaissance period? A divinely inspired creator or rather a savage brute deceptively clad in the garments of culture? In the Renaissance itself, an interesting answer to that question was provided by the young Pico della Mirandola who, in 1486, at only 23 years of age, composed an *Oration to the Dignity of Man* in which he described the gods' intent in fashioning man in the following words:

> We have given you, Oh Adam, no visage proper to yourself, nor any endowment properly your own, in order that whatever place, whatever form, whatever gifts you may, with premeditation, select, these same you may have and possess through your own judgment and decision. The nature of all other creatures is defined and re-stricted within laws which We have laid down; you, by contrast,

Figure 4.1: A mountain of buffalo skulls in the 1870s.

impeded by no such restrictions, may, by your own free will, to whose custody We have assigned you, trace for yourself the lineaments of your own nature. I have placed you at the very center of the world, so that from that vantage point you may with greater ease glance round about you on all that the world contains. We have made you a creature neither of heaven nor of earth, neither mortal nor immortal, in order that you may, as the free and proud shaper of your own being, fashion yourself in the form you may prefer. It will be your power to descend to the lower, brutish forms of life; you will be able, through your own decision, to rise again to the superior orders whose life is divine.[255]

In other words, the answer is this: the self that emerged was not an actual form but merely a certain potential—a promise to be realized or a curse to be dreaded. Man must choose because the power to choose is what truly makes him a man.

Sophie: Have you ever read *King Solomon's Ring?*

Philonous: By Konrad Lorenz?

Sophie: That's the one.

Philonous: It's a wonderful book.

Sophie: Indeed, I was very pleasantly surprised that a man like Lorenz, a Nobel Prize winner, would write in a style so engaging and easy to read. I had never read a book of his before, and since we mentioned his name a number of times, I thought it quite fitting to fill in that gap.

Philonous: And fitting it certainly was, but where is the link from *Solomon's*

Ring to Pico's *Oration*?

Sophie: Well, toward the end of his book, Lorenz relates the following story:

> Some time ago I decided to breed a cross between the African
> blond ring-dove and our own indigenous somewhat frailer turtle-
> dove, and, with this object, I put a tame, home-reared male turtle-
> dove and a female ring-dove together in a roomy cage. I did not
> take their original scrapping seriously. How could these paragons
> of love and virtue dream of harming one another? I left them in
> their cage and went to Vienna. When I returned, the next day,
> a horrible sight met my eyes. The turtle-dove lay on the floor of
> the cage; the top of his head and neck, as also the whole length of
> his back, were not only plucked bare of feathers, but so flayed as
> to form a single wound dripping with blood. In the middle of this
> gory surface, like an eagle on its prey, stood the second harbinger
> of peace. Wearing that dreamy facial expression that so appeals
> to the sentimental observer, this charming lady pecked mercilessly
> with her silver bill in the wounds of her prostrated mate.[256]

Interestingly, after describing this hideous scene, Lorenz goes on to remark
that "[o]nly in two other instances" had he "seen similar horrible lacerations
inflicted on their own kind by vertebrates: once, as an observer of the em-
bittered fights of cichlid fishes who sometimes actually skin each other, and
again as a field surgeon, in the late war, where the highest of all vertebrates
perpetrated mass mutilations on members of his own species."[257]

Philonous: That's a sobering thought.

Sophie: And it bears directly on Pico's *Oration*. For Pico in essence asserts that
human behavior is largely a matter of choice. The gods have fashioned us
to freely decide who or what we are going to be—higher beings "whose life
is divine" or, instead, common brute beasts. It's a choice between heaven
and hell—between the glorious creativity of a Leonardo da Vinci on the
one hand and the base brutality of a Christopher Columbus on the other.

Philonous: I understand, but what about the story from *Solomon's Ring*? I
still don't see the connection.

Sophie: If Pico is right, then all of the horrors of human history in general and
Western history in particular were produced by a very long sequence of very
bad choices. Evil, in this kind of vision, *is* intrinsic, but not in its actual
form. Instead, it is an ever-present potential that we have the freedom to
realize or to refuse at any one moment. However, the story of Lorenz's,
concerning the doves, quite strongly suggests a different view. For it seems
to imply that the sort of pathological behavior that we refer to as 'evil' is
context-induced.

Philonous: It is context-induced? What do you mean?

Sophie: If you ask yourself why the ring-dove so brutally tortured the turtle-dove, the answer is easily found: a natural potential for aggressive behavior was placed in a very unnatural context.

Philonous: ...namely the cage.

Sophie: Indeed, if it hadn't been for that cage, the turtle-dove would simply have taken to flight, and no serious injury would have resulted. The initial aggression would still have occurred, but it wouldn't have done any damage worth noting.

Philonous: And, by analogy, the conclusion must be, I assume, that Columbus not only victimized the natives he met, but that he himself was also a victim. Some unnatural, external condition, that he couldn't control, was the cause of his terrible deeds.

Sophie: No, not of his deeds—only of the evil inherent in them.

Philonous: But how can you separate a deed from its ethical nature? I doesn't make sense.

Sophie: Sure it does, for as you recall, according Kant, the locus of good—and therefore of evil as well—is not in the deed but rather the will that impels it.

Philonous: So evil is context-induced and therefore external but also contained in the will and therefore *in*ternal? I have to admit, I'm getting confused.

Sophie: Look, in a natural environment the type of aggressive behavior that Columbus displayed would not only have been far less destructive than it actually was but even would have accomplished a positive end. To see what I mean, just consider a setting, for instance, in which several Stone Age clans are trying to eke out a living in a given territorial space. In order to efficiently use the natural resources that this space provides, it is important that the clans be distributed across it reasonably evenly. In other words, clans whose territory is small may have to fight to expand it, and others in turn may have to defend whatever part of the land they consider their own. The fighting will be lethal at times, but since the clubs and sticks that these prehistoric warriors rely on for weapons are relatively ineffective, injuries will be more likely occurring than deaths. But fast forward now, by several tens of thousands of years, to the European invasion of the Americas, and the clans suddenly become populous peoples or nations whose military capabilities are very unevenly matched. And the result, of course, is *not* an adequate splitting of hunting grounds, but slaughter, enslavement, and genocide.

Philonous: In other words, Columbus enacted an ancient aggressive strategy that became an atrocity only because it was placed in an alien historical setting that Columbus himself was powerless to create or reject.

Sophie: That is correct.

Philonous: So the context was evil, but the will which inspired Columbus to do what he did was morally neutral?

Sophie: No, Columbus actively willed to perpetrate evil. But it was only the external circumstance, that he found himself in, that allowed him to will and to act as he did.

Philonous: That is to say, he couldn't have willed and carried out genocide if genocide, for whatever reasons, had simply not been an option.

Sophie: The paraphrase is apt.

Philonous: ...and more or less trivial in content.

Sophie: Less—not more.

Philonous: I don't agree. For to say that I cannot effectively will an evil deed that I am powerless to perform, is about as profound as the shallow truism that I cannot will evil if I don't have a will.

Sophie: ...which is precisely the reason, of course, why the murderous dove, by having no will, cannot be guilty of moral misconduct—and which also is the reason, if I may add, why the mere existence of human consciousness is already deeply pathological all by itself. For ultimately, the question of whether the dove's behavior constitutes a pathology or whether Columbus's deeds and intents were evil or not is a matter of judgment. If it weren't for the presence of a judging moral consciousness in either the victim, the perpetrator, or the observer, evil would simply cease to exist.

Philonous: Put differently, the sum of your wisdom is this: human consciousness is the cause of all evil in willing and judging, and therefore, inherently evil itself.

Sophie: At the very least, it is an alien presence—an unruly intruder into a physical realm that is meant to exist in total moral indifference. The natural biological world knows nothing of fanciful moral demands. Cruelty in nature just happens to be. It comes and goes like the wind or the waves on the sea. And even its occasional explicit avoidance is not to be traced to the ethical qualms of a loving Creator, but merely and simply to the practical task of ensuring survival.

Philonous: The soullessness of material reality—your favorite litany.

Sophie: No, my favorite reason for getting depressed. But either way, that soullessness and moral unconsciousness is clearly a fact. In our present discussion, for instance, the lack of aggressive restraint in the fight of the doves makes it apparent that nature is a moral minimalist and utter functionalist. Doves are not equipped with instinctual programs that inhibit the murder of close relatives because in a natural environment such programs would simply be useless.

Philonous: In decided contrast, I suppose, to animals whom nature has given more dangerous weapons.

Sophie: Of course, if we switch from a couple of doves to a couple of wolves, the need for restraint in intra-specific aggression becomes paramount. Afterall, if wolves didn't have strong inhibitions to prevent them from fratricide, there simply would be no wolves.

Philonous: In other words, avoidance of murder in nature is purely a matter of naked utility.

Sophie: Indeed, death and brutality—in intra- *and* inter-specific aggression alike—are never avoided just to be kind. A lioness attacking a wildebeest, for instance, will try to make her kill quickly and thereby limit the pain. But her instinctive intent is not to prevent unnecessary prolonged suffering but instead to avert a potentially injurious fight. For should it so happen that her prey is entirely helpless, unable to escape or to cause any damage, she would just as readily eat it alive, bit by bit, without mercy or pity.

Philonous: And that is how it should be. Afterall, moral awareness, in your view, is a pathology.

Sophie: Let me put it this way: just as the cage, containing the doves, provided an abnormal external context within which a given behavioral disposition grossly malfunctioned, so the evolutionary arrival of a self-aware moral consciousness within the human brain marks an abnormal internal change that caused and still causes today a pathological conflict with the surrounding physical world.

Philonous: In the latter case, though, it is not the context that induces the pathology but rather the individual's inner condition.

Sophie: That is correct. The principle is the same, but the causal relations have been reversed.

Philonous: So what do we do? Extinguish all moral awareness by regressing to animal life?

Sophie: That would be a fully consistent approach: becoming a bison and roaming the prairie (p.184). But since we cannot effectively will what isn't an option, we may have to settle for mere comprehension.

Philonous: Of the pathology?

Sophie: ...and its effects.

Philonous: Please elaborate.

Sophie: To begin with, we need to consider again the case of violent territorial disputes among Stone Age clans. Territorial aggression, as you certainly know, is common throughout the animal kingdom. For wherever natural resources need to be used efficiently, the aggressive formation of territories is a highly effective behavioral strategy. And since humans and animals together inhabit the same natural systems, they both must obey the same natural laws.

Philonous: Consequently, Stone Age clans will get into fights.

Sophie: But now there is a problem arising. For the presence of that internal pathological condition that we refer to as 'human consciousness' implies a need to reflect. A Stone Age warrior who just killed an alien clansman in a violent clash may notice, for instance—by way of reflection—that his vicious behavior in this murderous act was markedly different from the care that he commonly shows to his kin. And insofar as this warrior feels himself prompted to search for some explanation, he may, for example, be tempted to posit that members of other clans deserve to be treated differently—that is, brutally—because they *are* in fact different. In other words, in order to reconcile the reality of his own aggressive behavior with his own conscious awareness thereof, the warrior is driven to fashion for himself a delusional view in which alien clansmen become objects of *hate*.

Philonous: —the sort of hate, I assume, that is the root of such pretty phenomena as ethnic cleansings, racial discriminations, religious persecutions, and nationalistic violent outbursts, to name just a few.

Sophie: Precisely.

Philonous: Well, as far as that Stone Age warrior's "delusional view" is concerned, you may have a point. Albert Schweitzer, for instance, directly encountered such views in his medical work in the African jungle: when Schweitzer was in need of assistance he would on occasion ask one of the natives to help him in serving another native who was ill. If the two natives were from the same tribe, all would be well, but if not, no amount of convincing on the part of Schweitzer's would sway the former to lend a helping hand to the latter. For people from different tribes, in the minds of these natives, were simply not brothers and had to be shunned.[258]

Sophie: But do you see what is happening here? As pathology begets pathology there is created in the human mind a fictitious parallel world in which members of other clans or tribes appear as inferior, subhuman, and worthy of being destroyed. Man must follow the same laws that animals follow because he lives in the same physical world. But since he is self-aware, he cannot just do so and leave it at that. Instead, he is bound to create for himself a deeply illusory view of the world by which he purports to explain his deeds and perceptions. And, to make matters worse, this view of his is even quite strongly self-reinforcing. For it is precisely this view—this parallel world in the mind—through which his perceptions are filtered and by which his deeds in turn are inspired. That is to say, hate begets hateful deeds and perceptions, and thus begets more hate.

Philonous: The pattern exists—I cannot deny it.

Sophie: And there is more to be said. For the notion of deeds that are driven by views reveals here a link to another profoundly pathological feature: the replacement of instinct with conscious intent. We humans don't act on impulse alone, but require as well to be given a reason or cause—especially and all the more so when the task at hand is dangerous combat with neighboring tribes that may in fact cost us our life.

Philonous: I agree. The courage it takes to enter a life-and-death struggle can only be drawn from a strong inner source.

Sophie: And that source is hate.

Philonous: In other words, we actually need our hateful delusions in order to meet the demands that amoral nature imposes on us.

Sophie: That is correct. Nature demands territorial combat. But where animals rely for their motivation to fight strictly on instinct and drive, man must build up emotional stimuli to bolster his conscious intent.

Philonous: And since hate is clearly one of the stronger stimuli available to us, it is useful for people to think that others, by being others, are evil and worthy of spite.

Sophie: Correct again.

Philonous: The picture is bleak.

Sophie: ...but perfectly true to nature.

Philonous: Except for the fact that human consciousness, from your point of view, is a pathology and therefore not truly a part of that nature to which your picture is true. Consequently, there may be room for some consciousness-driven alternative strategies.

Sophie: Such as?

Philonous: The development of a civilized world is here the most obvious option.

Sophie: Unfortunately, though, it was precisely that civilized world that provided the context within which Columbus could act as he did. Columbus "enacted," as you said, "an ancient aggressive strategy" (p.308), but he did so with military technologies that civilization provided him with. Put differently and a little more bluntly, we don't gain much if we replace a primitive Stone Age club with a 'civilized' atom bomb.

Philonous: But civilization can also put on a lid—a check on aggression.

Sophie: Of course it can, since that is the purpose for which it exists. Afterall, in the absence of instincts that act with the absolute force of natural laws there must be set up some other, alternative laws to put on that lid. For humans are social by habit, and no human social entity can properly function in anarchy.

Philonous: That is to say, you do agree that civilization can serve a positive function.

Sophie: No, I don't. For civilized man is even more deeply in trouble than all of his savage progenitors taken together.

Philonous: And that is so...

Sophie: ...because civilization intensifies and hardens the conflict, as we shall see in a moment.

The Blessings of Civilization

One of civilization's most articulate critics was the 18th century anti-Enlightenment mutineer *Jean Jacques Rousseau*. Born in Geneva, in 1712, the son of a watchmaker, Rousseau was hardly a natural aspirant for honor and fame in the world of philosophy. He never enjoyed the benefits of a systematic education, and his highly emotional, unsteady temperament ill disposed him for a life of intellectual conquest and learned dispute. However, it was precisely this romantic, emotional side of his—this "sensitive heart,"[259] as he himself called it—that would allow him to set so striking a counterpoint in an otherwise proudly rational century.

Rousseau's entry into the history of Western ideas came suddenly and unexpectedly. In 1749, the Academy of Dijon announced an essay contest addressing the following question: "Has the restoration of the sciences and the arts tended to purify morals?"[260] True to his nature, Rousseau, in his answer, said "no!" with passion and force, but nonetheless won the prize, and instantly became a celebrity.

This decision of the Dijon Academy, along with the fame that it brought to Rousseau, may well seem a little ironic in light of the fact that the prize-winning essay, the *Discourse on the Sciences and the Arts*, was plainly and simply a scathing attack on civilized man in all his cultured and learned pretentiousness. Strangely and somewhat surprisingly, the civilized world of the French Enlightenment here honored its own, most vicious accuser.

In the opening paragraphs of his *Discourse*, Rousseau still seems to salute the spirit of his age when he marvels at the apparent greatness of man's inquiring intellect and acknowledges the enormous strides of progress that Europe had taken in recent history. Soon, however, the tone changes, and familiar roles are harshly recast: culture does not edify but only oppresses, and the civilized people amongst whom the wonders of progress unfolded parade as "happy slaves"[261] whose elegant urbanity is matched only by the depth of their moral depravity. "How sweet it would be," says Rousseau, "to live among us, if the exterior appearance were always the image of the heart's disposition; if decency were virtue; if our maxims served us as our rules; if true Philosophy were inseparable from the title of Philosopher!"[262] But as it is, appearance of enlightened civility is sadly and merely a cover for fear, hatred, and coldness of heart.

Then, to further highlight the inherent falsity of civilized society, Rousseau resorts to a study of contrast. Having just sternly exposed modern-day social hypocrisies, he now draws attention to the supposed merits of an earlier, more genuine form of life in which nature wasn't hidden as yet behind a perfidious "veil of politeness:"[263]

> Before art had molded our manners and taught our passions to speak an affected language, our morals were rustic but natural, and differences of conduct announced at first glance those of character. Human nature, basically, was no better, but men found their security in the ease of seeing through each other, and that advantage, which we no longer appreciate, spared them many vices.[264]

According to Rousseau, it is only in such a more immediate, simpler mode of existence that men can retain that primal strength of character which alone can harbor true virtue. Lamentably, though, throughout the course of human

history, such virtue, again and again, dissolved into decadence as the wisdom
that dwells in an innocent heart became compromised by knowledge in science
and beauty in art. Thus, in his account of the rise and fall of the various
successive great powers from Egypt to Rome to Renaissance Italy, Rousseau
invariably traces the cause of decline to a fateful neglect of heroic virtue in
favor of a corresponding, effeminate preoccupation with cultural sophistries.
The Romans, for instance, so he observes, had once "been content to practise
virtue; all was lost when they began to study it."[265]

As a matter of course, these counter-cultural musings were bound to pro-
voke some hostile reactions. Rousseau had been made famous by his passionate
plea for a return to simplicity—but also notorious. All the same, however, he
persisted on his chosen path and soon let his second strike follow. In his *Discourse on the Origin of Inequality*, published in 1753, he purposed to truly
see past the anomalies and sickly distortions that civilization induced, so as to
discover behind them the original, primordial image of a truly natural man.
For it was precisely in the point of departure from this original image, so he
believed, where the ultimate cause of mankind's present corruption could be
discovered.

The primeval savage, according to Rousseau, was a being exclusively driven
by physical needs—a being who was, not noble or good, but rather too primitive to ever be false. In his own, strangely elegant words, Rousseau describes
that savage as follows:

> His imagination paints no pictures; his heart makes no demands on
> him. His few wants are so readily supplied, and he is so far from
> having the knowledge which is needful to make him want more,
> that he can have neither foresight nor curiosity. The face of nature
> becomes indifferent to him as it grows familiar. He sees in it always
> the same order, the same successions: he has not understanding
> enough to wonder at the greatest miracles; nor is it in his mind
> that we can expect to find that philosophy man needs, if he is to
> know how to notice for once what he sees every day. His soul,
> which nothing disturbs, is wholly wrapped up in the feeling of its
> present existence, without any idea of the future, however near at
> hand; while his projects, as limited as his views, hardly extend to
> the close of day.[266]

Interestingly, Rousseau, much like Pico before him, believed that freedom,
not reason, was man's most man-like quality. In the light of the description just
given, it may not be completely obvious how a being confined to the present
by lack of foresight can encounter the future with freedom of choice. Indeed,
taking an evolutionary view, we may be tempted to argue that the savage
described by Rousseau was not the first of our human forbears but rather the
last of our animal ancestors. But be that as it may—what matters at this

point is not the pertinent taxonomy but rather the claim of Rousseau that the liberty to choose and act willfully was the savage's essential human capacity:

> It is not... so much the understanding that constitutes the specific difference between the man and the brute, as the human quality of free-agency. Nature lays her commands on every animal, and the brute obeys her voice. Man receives the same impulsion, but at the same time knows himself at liberty to acquiesce or resist: and it is particularly in his consciousness of this liberty that the spirituality of his soul is displayed.[267]

What a potent comment and what an odd proposition! "Man receives the same impulsion" but whether the impulsion will really impel him is something for him to decide.

As a *rule*, life is too immediately present to us to ever prompt us to wonder how utterly odd it all really is. But since Rousseau in essence just told us that rules aren't rules unless we consent, we may as well go ahead, put *that* rule aside, and wonder a bit. So let's take a look at that odd proposition that man is impelled but not truly so. Evidently, what we are dealing here with is the Kantian division—the opposition between the *is* of nature and the moral *ought*. On the one hand there is a material realm that is constituted upon amoral physical laws, and on the other hand there is a human moral consciousness that is deeply embedded within that realm but free nonetheless.

Strictly speaking, the roots of the latter's embeddedness in the former, as we saw earlier (p.132ff), reach all the way down to the fundamental laws of thermodynamics: energy is preserved but useful energy is not because entropy is forced to increase. Since that is so, useful energy in living organisms will tend to diminish and therefore must be continually replenished. Consequently, useful energy becomes an object of desire and as such inspires a competitive struggle for its procurement, also known as the struggle for survival. Hence there will be aggression, and hence the Stone Age clans of our preceding discussion will get into fights.

The trouble, though, is that fights among men are not impulsive, instinctual acts that Nature controls, but rather are consciously chosen engagements, driven by willful intent. By implication, there now appears that parallel world in the mind in which intent is bolstered by hate, and hate is fed by the lie that others are evil because they are others. Put differently, there is indeed such a thing as original sin. For in the final analysis, it is the thermodynamic structure of material reality that induces us humans to hate and to lie and thereby to sin. The law of entropy, as it were, is the ultimate, perfectly innocent culprit that makes us so mean.

What is more, consciousness is anchored in our brains in such a way that we can in fact lie—to ourselves by believing in falsehoods and to others by concealing from them our actual thoughts and true motivations. We can deceive, pretend, and misguide precisely and only because no one can read our minds. This observation, of course, will readily strike us as utterly trivial and therefore irrelevant. But surprisingly, it is neither trivial nor irrelevant because it is in fact false. For unbeknownst to most of us, there live among us some people who actually *can* read our minds—in a certain, limited sense—precisely because they can *not* comprehend our ordinary verbal expression.

These people are known as aphasiacs and suffer from a neurological disorder that makes it impossible for them to understand words. In order to compensate for this cognitive deficit, aphasiacs commonly develop an uncanny ability to discern meaning from the nonverbal clues that naturally accompany the flow of words that a person produces in everyday speech. Thus, they frequently *can* understand most of the meaning of what a person is saying, simply by paying very close attention to such attendant phenomena as tone of voice, facial expression, or bodily posture—as long as, and that is important, the person is truthful, that is, as long as the nonverbal clues do not belie the words that are spoken. In other words, aphasiacs, by being indifferent to that which is merely symbolic and thus superficial, can only grasp that which really has substance and truth.[268]

So let's suppose then for a moment that we were all aphasiacs. Or let's suppose, even more boldly, that all of us always knew what each of us thinks at any one moment. How would the world be affected? Would we all exclaim with Rousseau "how sweet it is to live among us, now that the lie is exposed and all of us know what all of us think!"? Or would we instead be completely worn out by all the massive dishonesties and malicious intents that we would thus be condemned to perceive? Perhaps we would be freed, but perhaps we would be utterly dehumanized instead by being revealed on the one hand and by being deprived on the other of our ability to respect as fellow human beings those that would be revealed to us.

We don't know, but what we do know is this: we not only can be and are, at times, massively dishonest with deliberation and malicious intent, but we even are dishonest by habit, constantly, incessantly, politely, and largely unconsciously. For 'civilized' man, by definition, never shows—or even knows—his true inner nature and genuine self. And any attempt to do so, to really show that self, invariably carries an element of social pathology. The real, in 'civilized' society, is the deviant, the true the abnormal, the natural the perverse, and the healthy is the insane. No 'normal' personal interaction in 'civilized' company is ever straightforward, honest, and pure. Indeed, deception and dishonesty are so universally engaged in and so ever-present that the facade has become our one and only social reality. What is worse, some of us, or maybe most of us, or maybe all of us, come to identify that facade with the actual self lurking behind it. And it is only too understandable that it be so. Afterall, the surface is so much nicer, so much cleaner, and so much more respectable than the emaciated, sickly being that crawls underneath it.

Rousseau, as we saw, was highly sensitive to the petty deceptions and games of pretense that civilized people are so prone to invent. He was a man who loathed the artificial and abhorred the affected. And as he was getting older and harboring thoughts of final accounts, he finally decided one day to put an end to it all—to stop lying—to really and truly be honest for once:

> I am commencing an undertaking, hitherto without precedent, and which will never find an imitator. I desire to set before you my fellows the likeness of a man in all the truth of nature, and that man myself.[269]

This is the stunning announcement by which Rousseau elected to open his famous *Confessions*. And, amazingly, he really did what he purposed to do and revealed himself fully. The *Confessions* are a work of unsurpassed frankness in which the reader is granted a look behind the facade. Rousseau doesn't compromise. He shows himself to all the world in all his radical, undisguised truth.

Sophie: I really wonder sometimes what it would look like if I did the same. What would it look like to see a person like me—a civilized being in a civilized world—fully disclosed with absolute honesty? I imagine a scene where all my life's thoughts, all my dreams, my sentiments and secret fantasies are displayed on a screen and publicly shown. I can assure you, the image produced would differ more than a bit from the image I show in our daily discussions. In fact, I'm not even sure you would recognize me to be I. For the chasm between the I that I know and the I that I show is incredibly wide.

Philonous: A remarkable scene, but what if one day it was really enacted?

Sophie: The scene with the screen?

Philonous: Yes. Have you ever considered that option?

Sophie: Not exactly, no I haven't.

Philonous: But Rousseau did consider it—not literally, of course, but still, in a fully equivalent sense. For in the opening paragraphs of his *Confessions* he appeals to his Christian belief in a final judgment day: "I will present myself," he says, "before the Sovereign Judge with this book in my hand." And then he continues:

> I will say boldly: "This is what I have done, what I have thought, what I was. I have told the good and the bad with equal frankness. ... I have shown myself as I was: mean and contemptible, good, high-minded and sublime, according as I was one or the other. I have unveiled my inmost self even as Thou hast seen it, O Eternal Being. Gather round me the countless host of my fellow-men; let them hear my confessions, lament for my unworthiness, and blush for my imperfections. Then let each of them in turn reveal, with

equal frankness, the secrets of his heart at the foot of the Throne, and say, if he dare, 'I was better than that man!'"[270]

Sophie: A communal confession before the Throne of Grace—no, I haven't considered that option.

Philonous: But I have—many times—dozens of times—hundreds of times. Some day, so I believe, I will stand in that heavenly place, and make my confession. My entire life—what I did, what I thought, what I felt, and who I was—it all will be openly seen. I am not sure, of course, if anyone will pay much attention, but as for myself, it will be the moment that will set me free—the moment when the burden is finally lifted.

Sophie: It's interesting—where you envision a heavenly day of release, I envision a tent and a backpack. You see, I often get so tired of everything 'civilized' that I just want to flee—pack my bags, put on my boots, and simply walk off and leave. I dream of a life close to the earth that restores my being to oneness. In my mind I see a far open country where the skies are vast, the valleys and hills are luscious and green, and oceans of grass stretch out to every horizon. It is a land where the ground hasn't been covered by asphalt as yet, where concrete and steel don't harden the soul, and water and air are still unpolluted.

Philonous: A beautiful place—like heaven on earth.

Sophie: More heaven than earth, to be honest.

Philonous: You may have a point. For as much as I resonate with the longing you feel, it doesn't quite strike me as fully consistent. Afterall, whenever the subject of nature comes up, you are the first to assert that nature is merely an amoral physical system in which cruelty is common and never avoided for reasons of kindness. So what, if I may ask, is so attractive about returning to that bloody old natural world?

Sophie: The matter is not quite as simple. On the one hand, it is true, there is the rational side where science will tell us that nature is bleak, cruel, and driven by soulless utility. But on the other hand, there also is the allure of the simple—the attraction one feels to a world that cannot be false. In nature all being is genuine, unaffected, and true—it is what it is. Animals don't carry in them the burden of thought. For being to them is immediate and wholly concrete. That is to say, the world they perceive is always the world as it is.

Philonous: The "burden of thought"—it reminds me of Kant.

Sophie: The Kantian division?

Philonous: No, the Kantian obsession with orderly living.

Sophie: I don't understand.

Philonous: What I am referring to here is the curious fact that Kant was a man of perfectly regular habits. Every day he followed the same exacting routine:

Rising, coffee drinking, writing, lecturing, dining, walking, each had its set time. And when Immanuel Kant in his grey coat, cane in hand, appeared at the door of his house, and strolled towards the small avenue of linden trees which is still called 'The Philosopher's Walk,' the neighbors knew that it was exactly half past three by the clock. So he promenaded up and down, during all seasons; and when the weather was gloomy, or grey clouds threatened rain, his old servant Lampe was to be seen plodding anxiously after, with a large umbrella under his arm, like a symbol of Prudence. (Heinrich Heine)[271]

And so Kant honored his schedule, day after day, year after year, until at last he made an exception—only once, to be sure—but still, he made an exception. It was on the day when he picked up the novel *Émile*, by—you guessed it—Jean Jacques Rousseau. For so engrossed did Kant become in his reading that day that he simply kept at it until he was done. And thus, at last, the unthinkable happened: Immanuel Kant did not go out for his afternoon walk.[272]

Sophie: So it took a romantic to finally break that rational thinker's rigid routine.

Philonous: Indeed, the vivid, emotional writings of Jean Jacques Rousseau somehow struck a deep chord in Kant's apparently so rational soul. Here he was, the author of the *Critique of Pure Reason*, the great rational moralist, perhaps the greatest thinker in history, and the world of the savage held him entranced. Is it not conceivable that Kant was so touched by Rousseau because the "burden of thought" so heavily weighed on him?

Sophie: I like your suggestion: the great man of modern philosophy finding respite from reason and thought in secretive dreams of aboriginal ecstacies—the call of the wild.

Philonous: Well, you never know.

Sophie: You certainly don't—especially in the case of a man like Kant whose outlook on life was so purely cerebral that he surely was somewhere quite harshly repressed. Afterall, no man can live by reason alone.

Philonous: It is true, no doubt, that Kant was not a free-wheeling spirit. His overbearing intellect constrained, as it was, by the practical, moral restrictions of his pietist youth, left little room indeed for emotional escapades. But then again, his life was also quite blameless. Kant had his quirks, he was grumpy with his grumpy old servant,[273] and didn't have any close friends or relations. But on the whole he could have done worse. And where Rousseau, for instance, abandoned all his five children shortly after their birth to an orphanage, Kant just sternly obeyed the rule of all conduct, the categorical imperative.

Sophie: You omitted to mention, however, that Rousseau as well, claimed to have followed, in this particular instance, a rational moral demand. This is not to say that he flatout defended his conduct. For he admits in his *Confessions* that the subsequent "regrets of [his] heart told him that [he] was wrong."[274] But on a purely rational level, he presents his decision to hand over his children to government care, as a sensible step, fully consistent with his responsibility as "a citizen and a father," and even declares himself, by virtue of his moral reasonings, "a member of Plato's *Republic*."[275]

Philonous: And in that he may have been justified. For Plato, in the *Republic*, not only counsels that children be taken away from their parents and brought up communally, but he even advises that those who are born to inferior parents or are otherwise "defective," whatever that means, are to be "properly dispose[d] of in secret, so that no one will know what" happened to them.[276]

Sophie: In other words, it is not only Stone Age warriors who make up fictitious parallel worlds in their minds in order to vindicate or to inspire their own abhorrent behavior—the greatest of Western philosophers do it as well.

Philonous: To be fair, though, we mustn't forget that Rousseau at least had the courage to confess his failings publicly—which is more than can be said about either one of us—so far as I know.

Sophie: That is true, but all the same I find it amazing how people—including myself and maybe you too—create, again and again, these parallel fantasies that are solely designed to conceal, from others and from themselves, their true inner nature. In fact, in the civilized world, this game of concealment and make-believe has become so common and so universally popular that the individual human life is almost completely controlled by it. Living in civilized company, I am forced to adhere to countless demands and behavioral standards that keep me tightly encaged. The real I—my true nature—never emerges from hiding.

Philonous: The question though is "What is your nature?" According to Pico, the essential nature of human nature is to be nonexistent. And you as well have observed that instinct in humans has been replaced with conscious intent (p.311). If instinct doesn't control us, then we ourselves must somehow do the controlling. So maybe your true nature is to allow civilization, by way of religion or moral injunction, to restrain your true nature.

Sophie: That may be so, but that only shows the depth of the conflict. Afterall, if it is indeed my nature to let my nature be locked in a cage, then I am hopelessly torn. For in that case, I not only know myself to be what I must not be, but I even have to accept that such a state of inner division is innately my lot.

Philonous: Would it be fair to assume that this *You* that you know yourself to be but must not be is your somewhat earthier side—the layer of impulse and drive that harbors the base and the vulgar?

Sophie: As far as my being vulgar is concerned, I would like to be a bit more explicit: I am vulgar *by definition*. For the word 'vulgar' derives from the Latin *vulgaris* which means 'ordinary' or 'common to all'. We are all vulgar—I, you, everyone. It's just, we are supposed to deny it, to hide it and *lie* about it in 'civilized' company.

Philonous: But what is here the alternative? To let it all just hang out? If people indulged their basest desires without compunction or social restraint, they would soon be reduced to an unseemly bunch of massively overweight sex-addicts, burping freely and wanting to be liked for it.

Sophie: You're making it sound a little bit humorous, and that is alright—but also very revealing. For nothing is funnier than a blatant portrayal of human lowliness as long as we are not the ones who are being portrayed. People love to see others brought low so as to be able to laugh at them. In fact, laughter itself has its roots in aggressive behavior. Groups of monkeys for instance are known to act in a similar fashion when they threaten a predator, say, or one of their kind, by baring their teeth and producing rhythmic sounds of aggression. Tellingly, ethologists refer to this sort of behavior as 'hating'.[277] In other words and by analogy, people may very well laugh at that which they hate—in others *and* in themselves. Humor relieves us, and the laughing at others, in particular, allows us to project our hatred of self onto a target outside.

Philonous: Thank you for your free-of-charge psychoanalysis! Now I finally know what I hate most in myself: my closet-gluttony, my hidden sex-addiction, and my covert habitual burping.

Sophie: You are welcome. The pleasure is mine.

Philonous: On the other hand, though, that little glimpse of my personal depravity isn't really all that exciting and novel. Afterall, as the universal bearer of all sin (p.216), I am bound to accommodate the full range of everyday vices by theological default.

Sophie: It is true, your personal irregularities, while pleasantly entertaining, are scarcely eccentric or very important. But your attendant, implicit appeal to your resolution is rather intriguing.

Philonous: My resolution?

Sophie: ...of the conflict—the Kantian division—the struggle between the *is* of nature and the moral *ought*. Your offer to heal that division was closely linked, as I recall, to the notion just cited that each human being carries within the seed of all sin.

Philonous: I see what you mean—and, yes, you are right. For in the simple recognition that all human sin is potentially mine I overcome the temptation to judge—the cause of disunion.

Sophie: And as you thus come to truly know yourself, in this most vital dimension, as the universal bearer of sin, you also draw near to the goal to truly *be* yourself and hence to truly be like Christ.

Philonous: That is correct.

Sophie: The question, though, is "What does it look like in practice?" According to Jung, I must live my "own proper" life "as truly as" Jesus lived his (p.206), and according to Bonhoeffer, I must give up "trying to make something of" myself (p.207). If I really took that to heart and really just were who I am, right now, I really might look quite vulgar and mean. So how do I thereby assume the likeness of Christ?

Philonous: You don't.

Sophie: Precisely. And by implication, 'becoming like Jesus' can only mean what it always has meant throughout the course of Christian history, namely to make an attempt to act and to speak like a man who didn't have sin. Thomas à Kempis, for instance, in his highly influential work on *The Imitation of Christ*, prominently upholds and defines this tradition when he urges us to "[l]et the life of Jesus Christ be our first consideration"[278] and to "follow Jesus in complete self-abandonment, dying to self..."[279]

Philonous: Perhaps it is in "dying to self" that you truly come to be yourself in this true Christian sense. Would this be a plausible interpretation?

Sophie: Paradoxes are safe. They always sound very profound, and those who don't understand them always appear to be lacking in wisdom. So no, it isn't a plausible interpretation, and it doesn't pertain to the issue at hand. For the question of whether a dead self can be a real self is utterly irrelevant as far as social and historical realities are concerned.

Philonous: And that is so...

Sophie: ...because in a Christian church or society wherein social status, to a degree, is dependent upon outward adherence to Christian standards and norms, the call to be Christ-like will simply and plainly produce a whole host of efforts to imitate Jesus. The less sincere will fake an appearance of virtue and piety and thereby deepen the lie of civilized man; and the more sincere will come to truly hate sin and thereby to hate their very own nature. Either way, though, the sin is made worse—in lying or hating. And that, if I may add, was precisely the striking effect that Christianity, as a real-world religion in the actual course of Western history, has had—to worsen the sin.

Philonous: That's a serious charge.

Sophie: Serious but justified. For insofar as the function of civilization is to put on the lid, that is, to restrain those earthy drives and unruly desires that nature endowed us with but no longer wants to control by instinct alone, and insofar as the function of Christianity has been to restrain us even more tightly, there can be no doubt whatsoever that Christianity has deepened the trouble of civilized man. For on the one hand, those who are Christians are driven to hate themselves and therefore their neighbors, and on the other hand, in order to appear as good Christians, they are liable to redefine this hateful disposition of theirs as loving concern. A case in point here is the phrase "in order that they might learn" (p.303) which Columbus evidently inserted into his log in a clumsy attempt to make us believe that he, as any 'good Christian', had only the best of intentions: he never wanted to kill or abuse, but only to teach.

Philonous: I wonder, though: was Columbus a Christian or merely his parody?

Sophie: In the real world, the two may not be distinct. Conceivably, of course, Columbus was not a true type but only an odd abberation. But what if he wasn't? What if the whites looked so "cruel," as Chief Ochwiay Biano said (p.305), *because* they were Christians? What if the white Europeans hated the other—the natural—in the natives they met *because* their religion had taught them to hate their very own flesh. Christ taught us to do unto others as we would have them do unto us, and the 'civilized' Christians took that to mean that they were to hate nature in others as in themselves. In Christian society, nature is not only kept hidden, more or less constantly, but actively suppressed, loathed, and despised. For nothing is more threatening to the Christian's illusion of self than the presence of an actual self in undisguised primitive nakedness.

Philonous: There is some truth in all of this, but all of this is also starkly one-sided. Christianity has inspired much evil, no doubt, but countless acts of goodwill and compassion as well.

Sophie: I understand, but by and large, what remains is the fact that the actual Christian religion in history upheld in the image of Jesus a moral ideal that inspired in many of those who tried to be true to it a profound hatred of self. Civilized Christians not only hide their own nature because they are civilized but they truly despise it because they are Christians. And, sadly, they frequently acted accordingly. For Nature to Christians is really an enemy who must be subdued and defeated—not only within, but also without.

Philonous: And hence, I suppose, the trail of destruction that Western man left in all the lands that he conquered.

Sophie: And hence the sobering tendency for that man to act as a usurper even in his most inspired creative endeavors. It has been said that "when we think of the Renaissance, we commonly think of great works of art" (p.303). But what is so great about a form of art whose arrogant theme is the rational conquest of Nature? To see what I mean, just consider for instance this painting by Dürer (Figure 4.2), one of the leading figures of the northern Renaissance. On the surface, it is a great work of art—a self-portrait of the most sublime quality. But looking beneath, to the general theme, the view is not nearly so brightly appealing. For what we here see is the work of an artist who not only aims to master Nature completely, so as to be able to represent her faithfully, but who even desires to force her to do his rational bidding. Dürer is not content to simply reproduce his own physical likeness, as a photograph would. Instead, he uses his visual mastery of Nature's complexity to express an idea of himself—namely the notion that he is a man of vision whose lofty ambition ranges as far and

Figure 4.2: *Self-Portrait* by Albrecht Dürer (1498).

reaches as high as the snow-covered peaks on the distant horizon behind him on his left. How differently, by contrast, here strikes us the spirit that speaks from an ancient cave-drawing. Where Dürer makes Nature his rational captive, his prehistoric counterpart simply allowed her to flow, straight from the heart, onto the rock that served him as canvas. A cave-art painting, as it were, was itself still fully a part of the natural world, whereas Dürer, in his proud self-depiction, looks down upon that world as a king on his subject.

Philonous: With this latter remark you captured quite well a prominent facet of Renaissance culture, namely the humanistic belief that man is a being of superior worth and importance. Pico, for instance, directly endorses this view when he has his Creator declare "I have placed you at the very center of the world" (p.306) and when, in another passage of his *Oration*, he writes that man is "a great miracle" and more deserving of admiration than even the angels in heaven.[280]

Sophie: I call that conceited. And what is worse, the Bible as well ascribes to us humans the image of God and gives us dominion to rule "over all the earth, and... all the creatures"[281] upon it. In other words, that "humanistic belief," to which you alluded, is also, and very distinctly, a *Christian* belief. As I see it, the Renaissance is that precise time in history when Western Christendom truly embraces the worldview that the Bible implies. It is here, at the birth of the modern era, that Western man shamelessly arrogates to himself his supposed Biblical right to treat the rest of creation—and of mankind—to the fruits of his pride, that is, to endless destruction. Moreover and as a matter of course, the rise of science as well, seamlessly fits this overall context. For just as in Renaissance art—and even more strikingly so—the central theme in all Western science is the rational conquest of Nature.

Philonous: You mustn't forget, however, that Nature, at times, is also unkind—as in the case of the Black Death pandemic for instance. That is to say, there may be times when that "rational conquest," of which you just spoke, may rightly appear a heavenly blessing.

Sophie: That is correct but scarcely a valid objection. My assertion at present is not that science can never be put to good use, but rather that its essential usurpative character shows a certain affinity to the worldview derived from the Christian religion. Put differently and a bit more concretely, science gives us the power to claim the dominion that Christianity gives us the right to demand.

Philonous: That may be true, as you said, of the Christian religion. But Christianity to me is not so much a religion as a view of reality. And as such, it doesn't promise dominion but rather a yoke that is easy and a burden that's light.

Sophie: It's just I don't find that burden exactly that light because, if your view is right, that burden includes the heavy awareness that all sin is mine.

Philonous: ...potentially.

Sophie: Yes—"potentially"—but it's a problem all the same. For the conception of man that this view implies is just as negative—and also as harmful in its effects—as the pertinent image of man that traditional Christian practice entails. Afterall, whether I come to despise my sin and thereby my nature because I choose as my model a man without sin, or whether I declare myself right from the start to be globally sinful and therefore the worst of all scoundrels makes hardly a difference. If anything, the latter option is worse, and either way, the result is self-hatred.

Philonous: I don't agree but I welcome your charge, because the matter at hand is doubtless of utmost importance. Afterall, hate is an ever-present oppressive reality, and it doesn't take a degree in psychology to understand that much of that hate is rooted in hatred of self. Furthermore, your more specific assertion that Christians are especially prone to fall prey to this vice of self-loathing has clearly some merit. For the traditional construal of Christian religious commitment as a call to imitate the moral perfection of Christ may indeed severely inhibit a healthy acceptance of self by making that acceptance dependent upon the reaching of a goal that simply cannot be reached. As a matter of course, this latter insight is hardly a novelty. Carl Jung for instance observes in this context that "the acceptance of

oneself is the essence of the moral problem and the epitome of a whole
outlook upon life,"[282] and then he goes on to say this:

> That I feed the hungry, that I forgive an insult, that I love my en-
> emy in the name of Christ—all these are undoubtedly great virtues.
> What I do unto the least of my brethren, that I do unto Christ.
> But what if I should discover that the least amongst them all, the
> poorest of all beggars, the most impudent of all the offenders, the
> very enemy himself—that these are within me, and that I myself
> stand in need of the alms of my own kindness—that I myself am
> the enemy who must be loved—what then? As a rule, the Chris-
> tian's attitude is then reversed; there is no longer any question of
> love or long-suffering; we say to the brother within us "Raca," and
> condemn and rage against ourselves. We hide it from the world;
> we refuse to admit ever having met this least among the lowly in
> ourselves. Had it been God himself who drew near to us in this de-
> spicable form, we should have denied him a thousand times before
> a single cock had crowed.[283]

Sophie: And thus, I suppose, you really are right: I *am* the worst of all
scoundrels—"the most impudent of all the offenders"—and so is everyone
else.

Philonous: But notice as well that the conclusion Jung draws is directly in line
with your observation, namely, the claim that Christians are prone to hate
their own selves.

Sophie: So whose side is Jung here supporting, yours or mine?

Philonous: Yours *and* mine, because the two sides are really just two different
aspects of one, common intent.

Sophie: I don't understand.

Philonous: Look, what both of us share is the powerful wish to somehow shake
off that onerous burden of constant deceit: *you* by treading the back-to-
nature trail, and *I* by making my public confession on Judgment Day.

Sophie: But in your case it is rather absurdly you yourself who makes that
burden so heavy by heaping the weight of all sin upon your own shoulders.
Seen in this light, I don't think we really have that much in common.

Philonous: You are completely misjudging my motives. For when I say of
myself that, potentially, all sin is mine, my purpose is not to heap on my
shoulders a burden, but merely and simply to really be honest—to drop
the facade. You see, nothing is ever more burdensome than the yoke of
untruth. As long as I imagine myself to be good, virtuous, or better than
others, I carry the weight of a lie. It is only when I fully acknowledge my
true inner reality—however bleak it may be—that the yoke is made easy
and the burden made light. That is to say, only when I fully admit that
nothing but the grace of God sets me apart from even the "most impudent"

offender can I finally let go of it all—the pretense, the deceit, the constant dishonesty. Before myself at least the moment of this acknowledgment is precisely the moment when I find my relief—when I peal off my pretty persona and really am I.

Sophie: Your desire for honesty I do understand, but all by itself it isn't sufficient. For in order to silence the urge to self-loathing you have to not only *acknowledge* your own destitute state but to fully *accept* it.

Philonous: And thus we return to that "essence of the moral problem" that Carl Jung so keenly identified.

Sophie: So what about that problem then? How do you ever resolve it?

Philonous: I don't—nobody does. But what I can do is to honestly face it.

Sophie: And that's as far as you take it?

Philonous: It is indeed, because I don't believe that resolving ultimate problems is really my reason for living. At bottom, I think, life presents us with final dilemmas that are insoluble by design and by definition. We must confront them earnestly, but setting them truly aright is probably not a viable option. And in the end we really just have to let go—give up our need to straighten things out and simply surrender to life as it is, intended by God.

Sophie: I have to admit, that's quite a surprise. For all of a sudden you almost sound as despondent as I whenever I doubt the meaning of life. For what is the purpose in living my life if the problems that matter the most to me can never be truly resolved?

Philonous: There is no purpose whatsoever—as long as you take an immanent view. Is there a purpose in living a civilized life in which the respectable person differs from the scoundrel only in that the latter does and thinks what the former only thinks. The answer is "no." Is there a purpose in living a natural life in which living beings are engaged in a struggle for survival for no reason other than to be engaged in it? Again, the answer is "no"—as long as you take an immanent view.

Sophie: For if my view is transcendent instead, then I am headed, so I suppose, for a glorious afterlife that more than makes up for whatever meaning there may be lacking at present. Is that the case you are trying to build?

Philonous: Not quite, because a transcendent perspective not only offers us hope for an afterlife but also gives meaning to *this* life in *this* world *right now.* In other words, if this world is not the whole world, then our life in it may not be as bleak as it seems.

Sophie: It doesn't make sense. For even if I did admit that life can continue past death, my present condition would still be as bleak as it is. I still would be caught in civilized lies, and my moral consciousness would still be in conflict with physical amoral forces.

Philonous: Your condition, I agree, would not be affected—but your perception of it most certainly would. As I see it—and as I stated before (on p.216)—this physical universe to which I am currently bound is merely a realm within realms within realms. For a brief span of time—my earthly existence—I experience it, but then I pass on to other dimensions. Naturally, my understanding of matters as these is not exactly acute. But nevertheless I really believe that life in this world is merely a station. It is a phase—a learning stage—brief but vital no less. For it is in this dim and narrow physical realm, and perhaps only in it, where I can learn what it means for a soul to be locked in a cage, what it means for a moral consciousness to come into conflict with amoral natural laws, that is, what it means to know evil and sin. One day, so I imagine, I will look back upon this physical phase of my personal journey as an oppressive form of existence in which, however, I learned a lot of useful lessons. There is no doubt, of course, that my current condition as a spirit confined to a material prison is pitiful in the extreme. But it is precisely this yoke and burden of life, this pitiful state I am in, that makes for the meaning I seek. In other words, it is by adopting a truly transcendent perspective, that I am truly set free to fully embrace my immanent life in this world at this very moment.

Sophie: So what you are saying apparently is that Planet Earth is really a boot camp—a spiritual testing ground where people are sent to crawl in the mud.[284]

Philonous: But notice as well that boot camps do have a purpose. For those who go through them are afterwards ready for action.

Sophie: I see your point, but what I dislike is the fact that meaning in your view is tied to a yoke. Is there really no way to cherish this earthly existence of mine for other, more sanguine reasons?

Philonous: It's easy to find a positive purpose in positive things like friendship or love. But what isn't so easy is to accept that everything good in this world will always be compromised. Friendships don't last, relationships fail, and love is often a struggle. And as long as we haven't properly dealt with these sobering facts, meaning will always elude us. As long as we live in a state of denial, imagining ourselves and the person next to us to be loving and kind, rather than loving and kind and selfish and vulgar, we are bound to get stuck. The truth of the human condition is not the shell of the pretty persona but the unseemly human mollusk that writhes within.

Sophie: And thus my brightest hope must therefore be, I suppose, that I—the mollusk—will learn a lesson or two from my own slimy condition. Now that's a positive view of human existence if ever there was one.

Philonous: It's positive and also attractively Christian.

Sophie: ...but only to you, in your very own distorted way of thinking.

Philonous: In other words, it's nicely in line with my favorite motto: be yourself and thereby be like Christ.

Sophie: Which more and more looks, I must say, like a recipe for Christian anarchy—or simply for anarchy. Afterall, if being a Christian just means to believe as you please, you may as well drop the word 'Christian'.

Philonous: Not necessarily, because what it means for *me* to be Christian is first and foremost that my own inner dialogue is Christian in context—it doesn't mean that there isn't a dialogue, nor does it mean that I can't be creative.

Sophie: But an *inner* dialogue is really a monologue, and therefore, your usage of 'Christian' is still too narrowly personal to truly make sense.

Philonous: Let me put it this way: what strikes me the most about the human condition is not, as Pico would say, that we are free, but rather that we are free to be different. Human beings, unlike animals, are very distinctly and strikingly individual beings—no two of them are ever alike. Just consider for instance the two of us—you and me. At the physical level the differences between us may only be slight, but mentally, psychologically, and especially spiritually we are very different indeed. My spirit is unique and so is yours. By implication, any genuine spiritual life, by its very nature, must be highly specific and personalized. Spirituality is the one central area in our lives where we each must determine our own individual path and where we mustn't make any concessions to civilized lies. Before ourselves, at least, we need to be as honest as we possibly can be. Consequently, regarding the view I expounded, I can only say this: I don't know whether this world I presently live in is really a boot camp, as you chose to put it, or whether indeed the purpose of life—to some extent and from a certain angle—is to learn what it means to crawl in the mud. All I know is that I honestly think so.

Sophie: And that's your final word on it?

Philonous: That's right. The boot camp and the *mud*—that's all that I got.

Sophie: Well then, we may as well wallow in it—like a pig—in the mud...

Philonous: ...and be glad...

Sophie: ...glad like a pig.

Philonous: You got it.

Chapter 5

Science Victorious

The Greatest Problem in History

People are different and so are the things they consider important. Generally speaking it seems that no subject of thought or field of endeavor is ever too odd for people to somehow get hooked on it. In the world of sports, for instance, grown men and women routinely derive a deep sense of satisfaction from kicking or hitting balls into nets, under nets, over nets, into each other, or into the stands. In fact, some of us even depend for our sense of self-worth upon the success of our favorite net-hitting team (the present author is a dedicated soccer fan and knows exactly what he is saying).

It is amazing indeed what people can sometimes obsess about: mathematics, miniature golf, physics, gardening, table tennis, dinosaurs, philosophy, cooking, and paper-cuts—for a completely ridiculous, random selection.[1] In extreme cases, a person will even find pleasure and meaning in writing a book on spelling in reverse (p.35) and epistemic anarchists (p.162).

In the light of all this confusion, it is good to behold on occasion a group of individuals who truly major in majors and truly stay focused on matters of consequence. A laudable example that here comes to mind is the executive committee of the International Astronomical Union (IAU) that prepared the decision to demote what was formerly known as 'Pluto the planet' to the status of dwarf. Pluto, according to the pertinent resolution of the IAU's General Assembly in Prague, in 2006, is not a planet anymore but rather a dwarf planet.

As might be expected, this issue of Pluto's family membership was highly contentious indeed. Prior to the meeting in Prague, it had been debated for

---

[1]The list here compiled is drawn exclusively from the author's own life, as well as the lives of members of his family. Concerning the dinosaurs, for instance, the fanatic in question is the author's three-year-old son.

years, and at the meeting itself it still took more than a week to distill a fully satisfactory definition of planethood from a number of competing proposals. According to the definition that was finally adopted and formally approved on August 24th, 2006, a planet is a material object which

(a) directly orbits the Sun,

(b) is sufficiently massive for its self-gravity to give it a spherical shape, and

(c) has mostly swept clean its orbital path of solar-system debris.

As it turns out, Pluto, along with quite a large number of its trans-Neptunian Kuiper-belt cousins—most prominently among them the formerly 'tenth planet' Eris—satisfies the first two of these conditions but not the last. To be precise, the Earth as well satisfies only the first two, but since its cleaning efforts along its orbit have been vastly more successful than Pluto's, it still is rightly considered a planet.

This latter remark goes to show that the phrase 'mostly swept clean' in item (c) urgently requires itself a more precise definition—and so does the word 'directly' in item (a). In fact, Pluto satisfies (a) only conditionally. For what orbits the Sun is not Pluto itself but rather the Pluto-Charon center of mass which happens to lie outside of not only the moon Charon, as might be expected, but also of Pluto itself—thus rendering the pair the only known double dwarf planet in the solar system. Faced with difficulties as these and other issues besides—such as the proper classification of brown dwarf stars and independent rogue planets—the reader may rest assured that the true complexity of all the problems involved far exceeds the scope of our present discussion.

In conclusion, though, we wish to record that in consequence of the IAU's landmark ruling the number of known planets in the solar system has now been fixed to eight. There are four inner planets—Mercury, Venus, the Earth, and Mars—and four outer ones, on the far side of the asteroid belt—namely Jupiter, Saturn, Uranus, and Neptune. That's it and that's the last word—at least for the moment.

So far so good, but what's the point? Does it really matter if the number of planets is eight or nine or ten or twenty-nine? No, it doesn't, not in the least—as long as, that is, there are some planets at all. If the number of planets were zero, we wouldn't exist, and if it were one, we might be around, but modern-day natural science quite likely might not. For if there wasn't a single planet like Mars in the sky, the path of which we can trace and wonder about, we really might never have found that golden mathematical key to physical reality without which the secrets of nature cannot be unlocked. Indeed, the so-called *problem of the planets* has been of such pivotal importance for the development of science that science, as we know it, is almost unthinkable in absence of it. In other words, the problem of the planets is truly and undoubtedly the greatest scientific problem in history.

In order to understand what exactly that problem is really about, we need to take a quick look at the various objects and motions that we observe in the sky. Most immediately obvious here is the apparent *daily* or *diurnal* motion of the Sun which is caused by the Earth's rotation about its own axis. Every day the Sun traces out a circular arc from east to west that depends for its size and height in the sky on the time of the year and the position on the Earth's surface from which we observe it.[II] Similarly, the Moon, the planets, and the stars that we see after dark also perform daily circular motions, all of which—on the northern hemisphere—seem to be centered at the North Star, also known as *Polaris*. This is so because Polaris lies almost exactly on the northward extension of the Earth's axis and therefore appears to be fixed.

Apart from these diurnal rotations, we also observe, in the case of the Sun and the planets, an apparent annual motion against the backdrop of stars which is due to the Earth's and the planets' orbital travel about the Sun. Strictly speaking, as the Earth orbits the Sun and as the Sun and the stars orbit the center of the Milkyway galaxy, the stars as well undergo continual positional changes. However, the distances that separate the Sun from even its nearest Milkyway neighbors are so vast, that these various relative motions cannot bring about any effects that are large enough to be perceptible to a naked-eye human observer who is temporally confined to a single human life span. Consequently, the stars are wrongly but commonly referred to as 'fixed stars'.[III]

For clarity, we wish to point out that the word 'fixed' here only refers to the positions of the stars *relative to one another;* because relative to a human observer on the Earth's surface, who looks at the sky at always the same time of night, the stars' positions will change along with the celestial hemisphere that the observer's horizon delimits. That is to say, at different times during a year different portions of the sky are visible, and as these portions are shifting, so are the stars and constellations contained in them.

Turning now to the shape of the apparent *annual* motions and beginning

---

[II]If an observer is positioned south of the Arctic Circle and north of the Antarctic Circle, the arc described by the Sun will always be strictly a circular segment, that is, there will be a sunrise and a sunset. But in the polar regions that lie to the north and to the south of these two polar circles, respectively, the arc may also be at times a full 360-degree circle. On the northern hemisphere such a full solar circle can be observed on June 21st (or 22nd)—the day of the summer solstice—from any position north of the Arctic Circle, and the analogous situation on the southern hemisphere occurs on December 21st (or 22nd).

[III]The first to provide substantive evidence for the relative motion of the stars was Edmond Halley (1656–1743). In 1718, Halley published a paper in which he showed that discrepancies between ancient and contemporary records of stellar positions are attributable, not only to imprecisions in measurements, but also to actually occurring relative motions.[1] Furthermore, for the stars nearest to the Sun, sensitive instruments also reveal an *apparent* annual change in the angular positions of these stars (relative to other stars that are more distant) which is caused by the annual orbital motion of the Earth about the Sun. However and as we said, these position changes are only *apparent* and are not indicative of actual, physical motion of the stars relative to each other.

with the Sun, it is fairly easy to see that the Sun's annual path relative to the fixed stars must very nearly be a constant velocity circle—the so-called *ecliptic*. And the reason simply is that the Earth's orbital motion about the Sun is in good approximation circular and therefore regular.[IV] Furthermore, the angle at which the plane of this ecliptic is inclined away from the Earth's equator equals the angle at which the Earth's axis is tilted away from the direction perpendicular to the plane of the Earth's orbital path. Consequently, the annual motion of the Sun, along with all the apparent diurnal motions listed above, can be very nicely described in a geocentric model of the universe that is framed by two spheres: at the center, there is the sphere of the Earth itself, which is thought to be perfectly at rest, and on the outside there is the sphere of the fixed stars which revolves about the Earth once every 24 hours. At an intermediate distance between the Earth and the stars there is the sphere of the Sun within which the Sun is adrift, eastwards, along the ecliptic and also is carried about, like the stars, in a daily, westward rotation (Figure 5.1).

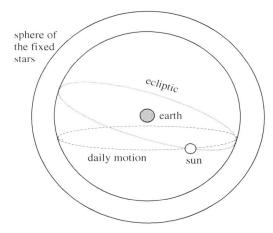

Figure 5.1: The ancient two-sphere universe.

In order to establish the Earth's stable, central position that this model posits, Aristotle famously argued as follows:

> The observed facts about earth are not only that it remains at the centre, but also that it moves to the centre. The place to which any fragment of earth moves must necessarily be the place to which the

---

[IV] The deviation from regularity is noticeable but small. In the winter months the Sun's apparent motion along the ecliptic is slightly more rapid than in the summer months, and, by implication, the time from the autumnal equinox on September 23 to the vernal equinox on March 21 is shorter than the complementary time from March 21 to September 23, but the difference is only about six days.

whole moves; and in the place to which a thing naturally moves it
will naturally rest. ...If then no portion of earth can move away
from the centre, obviously still less can the earth as a whole so
move.[2]

Evidently, the "observed facts" that Aristotle here invokes are observed only
partially. For while it is certainly true—and observable—that chunks of earth,
as falling bodies, move toward the Earth and that they remain there unless
otherwise moved, no observation available to Aristotle or ourselves entails the
necessary inference that this place to which they strive and where they remain
is really the world's absolute center.

On the other hand, though, we also need to clearly see that none of the
observations discussed so far are in conflict with the belief that the universe is
geocentric and bounded by two spheres. Afterall, the heavens, as seen from the
Earth, do look dome-shaped and the postulate of an overall spherical universe
with the Earth at its center is therefore not only reasonable but perhaps even
the simplest and most elegant assumption to make—or, as Aristotle believed,
it is the assumption most worthy of the heavens' divine nature:

> The activity of God is immortality, i.e., eternal life. Therefore the
> movement of that which is divine must be eternal. But such is the
> heaven,... and for that reason to it is given the circular body whose
> nature it is to move always in a circle.[3]

From a modern perspective it is tempting to simply dismiss an argument
as this as hopelessly 'unscientific'. But we mustn't forget that modern particle
physicists were often led to their greatest discoveries by trusting in judgments
that vitally appealed to highly subjective, aesthetic criteria. This is not to
say, of course, that particle physics was ever divorced from empirical inquiry,
but merely that important new insights could often be traced to strikingly
'unscientific' habits of thought. By implication, we needn't be all too indignant
when Aristotle here tries to establish the heavens' sphericity on what appear
to be essentially theological grounds.

Furthermore, no matter how soberly modern our perspective may be, there
is no denying the fact that the two-sphere universe—as a *scientific* model—is
very adequate indeed. For it not only correctly accounts for all the diurnal
and annual motions so far discussed, but it even does so in a manner that is
conceptually easy to grasp and fully convincing. Furthermore, of all the cosmological models that Western thinkers ever produced, the geocentric model is
by far the most useful in practice. For even today, a captain out on the ocean
who has lost contact, let's say, to his GPS satellite will determine his ship's
position strictly in reference to a geocentric point of view. In fact, using a
heliocentric or even a more advanced current-day cosmological model for navigational purposes would be so cumbersome as to be downright ridiculous. In

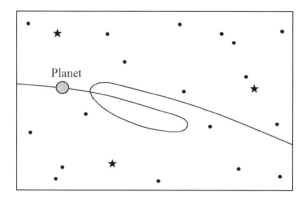

Figure 5.2: qualitative rendering of a planetary retrograde motion.

summary, therefore, we rightly may say that the geocentric model is adequate, useful, simple, elegant, and fully consistent with observation.

So what's wrong with it? Why did anyone ever doubt its validity? Why do we not still believe, in the literal physical sense, that the whole world revolves about us? To answer these questions, we now need to turn to that greatest of problems referred to above: the problem of the planets.[V]

As we already said, the planets, just as the Sun and the stars, travel daily on almost perfectly circular paths. Up to this point, then, the picture is simple, but when it comes to the longer term, annual motions, the matter gets quickly a bit more complex. For as we track the planets' positions against the backdrop of the fixed stars over the course of several years, we are bound to discover a couple of striking anomalies: firstly, the planets' apparent motions are not as neatly periodic as the motion of the Sun along the ecliptic, which is almost the same year after year,[VI] and secondly, the shapes of the planetary paths are surprisingly intricate. The planets don't move consistently eastward, as the Sun along the ecliptic, but rather retrogress at times and travel in loops (as shown in Figure 5.2).

In order to fit these anomalies within the traditional geocentric framework, the astronomer Ptolemy of Alexandria[VII] (100?–178? A.D.) devised an ingenious mathematical system of transposed and superimposed circular motions

---

[V] The word 'planet' is derived from the Greek word 'planasthai' which means 'to wander'.

[VI] To be precise, the Sun's apparent annual motion along the ecliptic is not perfectly periodic either, because the precessional motion of the Earth's axis—which has a period of about 26,000 years—causes the points of intersection of the ecliptic with the celestial equator to drift along the latter. This phenomenon was discovered by the Greek astronomer Hipparchus toward the end of the second century B.C. and is known as the precession of the equinoxes.

[VII] According to some sources, Ptolemy did not live and work in Alexandria itself but fifteen miles to the east in Canopus.

that modeled the observed planetary paths with a reasonably high degree of accuracy. There is no room in this exposition, of course, to examine his system in any substantial detail. But to give the reader a rough idea of what is involved, there is shown in Figure 5.3, on the right, an example of the type of path that can be produced by combining two regular circular motions in an *epicycle-deferent* construction. More precisely, the path in question is traced by

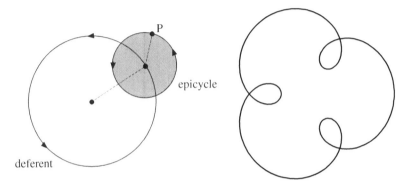

Figure 5.3: epicyclical motion.

the given point P on the left as both the epicycle, to which P is attached, and the underlying deferent rotate both at constant angular velocities. Whether the motion of P is periodic, as in the case shown in Figure 5.3, or non-periodic (in which case the path on the right would not be closed) and whether the number of loops is equal to three or some other integral or fractional value depends on the ratio of the epicycle's and the deferent's respective angular velocities. Furthermore, the question of whether there are in fact loops or merely wavelike oscillations about the deferent depends for its answer not only upon the ratio of the angular velocities but also upon the ratio of the deferent's and the epicycle's respective radii. Thus there is considerable freedom of choice to adjust the relevant parameters in such a way that the apparent planetary paths are properly matched. In addition to epicycles, Ptolemy also employed transposed circular motions, that are known as *eccentrics*,[VIII] but as we said, exploring the details of all his constructions would lead us too far.

Ptolemy believed that his insistence on regular circular motions as his elementary dynamical building blocks was duly expressive of the heavens' divine sublimity. For he explicitly wrote in his *Almagest*,[IX] his magnum opus, that

---

[VIII] Eccentrics are regular circular motions that are observed from an off-center position. The effect resulting from such a displacement of the center of observation can be used to model, for instance, the slight deviations of the Sun's angular velocity during the course of a year. As it turns out, such motions can also be represented via an epicycle-deferent construction, that is, they merely are a special case of the type of motion shown in Figure 5.3.[4]

[IX] 'Almagest' is the title of the Arabic translation of Ptolemy's work. The original title

only the regular circular motion was "proper to the nature of divine things which are strangers to disparities and disorders."[5] In practice, his adherence to this philosophical doctrine of his was sometimes only tenuous,[X] but even disregarding any questions of consistency, we cannot help but realize that Ptolemy's system was rather unwieldy and highly complex. It never had the compelling simplicity and apparent elegance of the original two-sphere model, and it also never quite worked. Its agreement with observation was reasonable, but far from ideal. And with every succeeding attempt to make it more accurate, it also became a little more tangled and cumbersome. As epicycles were imposed upon epicycles, one after another in multiple layers, and as ever more tedious constructions were added, either by Ptolemy himself or, sporadically, by later Arabic and medieval astronomers, the beauty and coherence of that ancient cosmology framed by two spheres became ever more clouded and compromised.

As a matter of course, loss of beauty is scarcely an objectively cogent criterion for denying a conceptual model's scientific validity. But the excessive complexity that causes this loss, in the case of Ptolemy's system, is certainly a practical concern that may prompt a vigilant thinker to search for a simpler alternative model. And as we all know, the thinker who felt that prompting most keenly was the Polish-Prussian clergyman who boldly recast the design of the cosmos: *Nicolaus Copernicus*.[XI]

Copernicus was born in Torun, Poland, on February 19, 1473, the son of a wealthy copper trader. After his father's death, in 1484, he and his three older siblings, were adopted by their maternal uncle Lucas Watzelrode who was a priest at the time and later became the Bishop of Ermland. From 1491 to 1494 Copernicus attended the University of Cracow, devoting himself chiefly to mathematics and astronomy but also developing a taste for the newly revitalized classical studies. In 1496 he went to Italy to study canon law at the University of Bologna and later medicine at Padua. When he returned to Poland, in 1506, he took up at first a position in Heilsberg as secretary and physician in his uncle's bishopric. But when his uncle passed away, in 1512,[XII] Copernicus moved on to Frauenburg to work as a canon at the local cathedral.

---

was 'Great Syntaxis'. But since only the translated version has survived, the Arabic title is the one commonly used.

[X] A case in point here is Ptolemy's explicit provision, in Book IX of the *Almagest*, for an epicyclical center to revolve regularly about a point other than the center of the underlying deferent—a provision that Copernicus, for instance, considered to be scandalous.[6]

[XI] The question of Copernicus's nationality is subject to debate. The town of his birth, Torun, is commonly designated as belonging to Poland, but according to Angus Armitage, one of Copernicus's most prominent biographers, both of his parents "belonged to a class exclusively drawn from the German elements of the population" and the astronomer himself therefore came to identify himself most closely "with the Germanized West Prussians, as distinguished on the one hand from the Poles and on the other from the Teutonic Knights."[7]

[XII] There is some disagreement in the literature concerning this date, and the same is true of the date of Copernicus's return from Italy. The former is sometimes placed in the year 1510 instead of 1512, and the latter seems to range between 1503 and 1506. The choice that we have here made is based on the biographical sketch in [Cope], pp.499–500.

At Frauenburg he diligently dedicated himself to his numerous practical tasks and clerical functions, but also found time at the side to pursue his intellectual interests. He established an observatory in a tower on the cathedral grounds and elaborated in great detail his heliocentric astronomical system.[8]

As regards the fundamental idea that underlies this system, namely the notion that the Earth is in motion and the Sun is at rest at the center of the universe, we need to point out that Copernicus was by no means the first to conceive it. For exactly the same idea had already occurred to the Greek astronomer Aristarchus in the 3rd century B.C, and earlier still, in the 6th century B.C., the Pythagoreans had postulated the existence of a central fire, distinct from the Sun, about which the Earth was thought to be moving in circles. In fact, in his major work *On the Revolutions of the Heavenly Spheres*, Copernicus explicitly acknowledged some of the Pythagoreans for their pertinent thoughts,[9] and—in a preliminary version of his work—he also acknowledged his debt to Aristarchus. Why he chose to delete the latter reference from his final manuscript is not known. But perhaps he was afraid that otherwise he too might attract that odious charge of impiety that Aristarchus, in his day, had attracted as well.[10]

Having thus set the record of ultimate authorship straight, we also wish to give credit where credit is due and recognize clearly that only Copernicus employed the heliocentric design for clearly defined mathematical ends. In other words, what is unique in the work of Copernicus is not the overall cosmological system itself, but rather the specific problem-solving context within which Copernicus placed it—and within which the technical advantage that this system enjoyed over the traditional Ptolemaic scheme became most vividly apparent.

In order to appreciate this advantage *qualitatively*, it is helpful to examine the phenomenon of apparent planetary retrogression from a heliocentric perspective. So let us assume, as Copernicus did, that the planets, including the Earth, orbit the Sun on circular paths. Taking Mars as an example, it is immediately obvious that, given this assumption, the apparent motion of Mars against the background of fixed stars, as seen from the Earth, depends upon, not only the motion of Mars itself, but that of the Earth as well. A qualitative rendering of two different kinds of apparent position changes that Mars can undergo in consequence of this dual orbital motion is shown in Figure 5.4. Taking into account the greater speed with which the Earth travels along its orbit as compared to Mars, the diagram on the left shows a situation in which the combined motion of the two planets causes the apparent position of Mars to shift in the standard, forward direction (which appears to be eastward when viewed from the Earth); and the diagram on the right shows a case where the corresponding shift is anomalous, that is, retrogressive. In other words, the perplexing phenomenon of planetary retrogression is here elegantly understood to be a natural consequence of two relative motions that are both uniformly

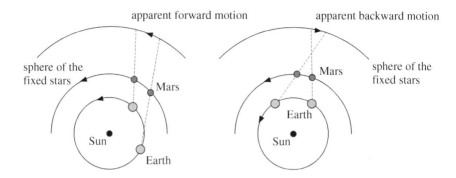

Figure 5.4: apparent forward and backward motions of Mars.

circular. Instead of a profusion of Ptolemaic epicycles, deferents, eccentrics, and other obscurities in mutual superpositions, we only behold two circular paths that are traced by two planets at constant velocities.

Seen in this light, the gain in explanatory economy seems highly significant indeed, but unfortunately, the matter is not quite as simple. For neither do the planets move on perfectly circular paths nor do they do so at constant velocities. And, by implication, the Copernican system, in its most simple and most elegant form, was not in agreement with observation. In fact, the agreement was worse than in the best available Ptolemaic description.[11]

Faced with this sobering realization, Copernicus the revolutionary became a reactionary and meekly deferred to tradition. That is to say, in order to bring more closely in line his system's predictions with the actual facts observed in the sky, he had recourse to the same epicyclic constructions that had earlier made Ptolemaic astronomy so tedious and cumbersome—and even then, he didn't succeed. For his final design was not intrinsically any more accurate than the rival geocentric one.[12] On the whole, therefore, it may be said that the advantage in favor of his alternative scheme—technically as well as aesthetically—was hardly sufficiently striking to convincingly justify the grand cosmological shift that he had been so boldly proposing.

Sophie: In other words, the Copernican Revolution, examined more closely, was really a timid reform, replacing a cumbersome and highly confusing mathematical system with one that was merely confusing.

Philonous: At a purely technical level, the advance here in question was indeed hardly decisive. Copernicus eliminated the 'major' epicycles that Ptolemy had used to describe planetary retrogressions. But as regards the 'minor' epicycles—that is, those whose function it was to even out small scale discrepancies between observation and theory—his system was quite disappointing.[13]

Sophie: Which raises the question as to why it was ever accepted.

Philonous: This question is important, I agree. But before we address it, we
need to be clear that what was at stake in this case was not a matter of
observable fact but rather a radical shift in conceptual thought. It wasn't
empirical data that Copernicus questioned but a time-honored theoretical
model that history sanctioned.

Sophie: I don't quite understand. The proposition that the Earth is in motion
instead of at rest is clearly a statement of fact. Consequently, the Copernican shift was more than a mere realignment of concepts: it was a vital
advance in coming to grips with the world as it is.

Philonous: Or so it may seem if we don't pay heed to the *fact* that the only
type of motion that we ever observe is *relative*, not absolute. The Earth is
in motion *relative* to the Sun and the stars—so much we know, not more
and not less.

Sophie: You almost make it sound as though the geocentric view were still a
plausible option.

Philonous: It is as plausible or as absurd as any other *absolute* view—be it
heliocentric, lunarcentric, or some otherwise-centric description. That is
to say, as far as motion is concerned, all is relative, and, by implication,
everything and nothing is an absolute.

Sophie: But this is the 21st century. The Earth is swiftly moving and the
Middle Ages are long past.

Philonous: And thus we certainly do well to adopt a genuinely contemporary
perspective, that is, a perspective that physicists call *relativistic*. More
specifically, we need to clearly understand that in Einstein's general theory of relativity there is only one defining *absolute*, namely the axiomatic
demand that the laws of nature be the same in *any* frame of reference.
In relativity no frame is preferred or somehow distinct. At first sight this
statement seems ridiculous because a rotating frame such as the Earth,
or maybe a merry-go-round in an amusement park, appears to be easily
recognizable as being in motion absolutely and objectively. Afterall, rotation produces certain definite effects that can be directly encountered: on
a merry-go-round we are being pushed outwards by a centrifugal force, and
on the Earth's surface, the so-called Coriolis force causes tropical storms
to rotate counter-clockwise on the northern hemisphere and clockwise on
the southern. Consequently, in Newtonian classical physics it is the Earth
rather than the surrounding universe that is daily revolving about its own
axis—but not so in Einstein's more advanced theoretical system. For in a
general relativistic description, the perceived rotational motion of distant
stars about either the Earth or a merry-go-round produces gravitational
effects that fully account for the various pseudo-forces that a rotational
motion is commonly thought to induce.[XIII] Steven Weinberg, for instance,

---

[XIII]For clarification we need to point out that this latter assertion concerning the influence

explains the matter as follows:

> In general relativity there is indeed an influence exerted by the distant stars that creates the phenomenon of centrifugal force in a spinning merry-go-round: it is the force of gravity. Of course nothing like this happens in Newton's theory of gravitation, which deals only with a simple attraction between all masses. General relativity is more complicated; the circulation of the matter of the universe about the zenith seen by observers on the merry-go-round produces a field somewhat like the magnetic field produced by the circulation of electricity in the coils of an electromagnet. It is this "gravitomagnetic" field that in the merry-go-round frame of reference produces the effects that in [classical Newtonian physics] are attributed to centrifugal force.[15]

Sophie: So Aristotle was right—the Earth is firmly at rest at the center.

Philonous: ...and so is the Sun and the Moon and the merry-go-round.

Sophie: Meaning, I suppose, that on Mondays the universe is geocentric, on Tuesdays it is heliocentric, on Wednesdays lunarcentric, and for the rest of the week the cosmic point of reference is a rusty old carousel or some other fairground attraction.

Philonous: That's exactly right, and that's the most coherent conceptual view that scientists have so far come up with.

Sophie: But as a conceptual view, it too may be subject to future revisions.

Philonous: That is true, but no such revision, as I see it, is likely to reestablish the notion of an absolute motion.

Sophie: Why not?

Philonous: Firstly because any future theory of gravity is bound to contain general relativity as a limiting case, and secondly because such a reassertion of absoluteness would squarely run counter to a long-standing trend in the development of conceptual thought in physics. You see, physical theory, at a foundational level, has fairly consistently evolved in the direction of an ever deeper understanding of the ever more prominent role played by symmetry relations in the organization of nature's mathematical laws.[16] In the transition from Newtonian physics to Einstein's relativity, for instance, we see this tendency displayed quite strikingly. In Newton's classical scheme the laws of nature are the same for all observers that move relative to each other at constant velocities, but in general relativity they are the same, as we saw, for all observers universally. In this sense it is adequate to say that the world of relativity is fundamentally more uniform

---

of distant stars—which is known as Mach's principle—represents a somewhat speculative extension of the fundamental principle of relativity according to which the laws of nature are the same in all frames of reference. There are solid mathematical arguments supporting Mach's principle, and Einstein himself, in his creation of general relativity, relied on it for vital inspiration, but a final verdict concerning its validity has so far not been passed.[14]

and therefore more *symmetric*. In classical theory motion comes in various types that are objectively distinct, but in relativity there is only one single type, namely relative motion, and only one set of laws that all observers equally acknowledge. Quoting Steven Weinberg yet again, we may even say that it is this invariance and the profound symmetry that it signifies that actually "requires the existence of gravitation"[17] as a necessary precondition. For evidently, only if gravitation is indeed an empirically viable concept, can a description in terms of it of the pseudo-forces that rotation induces ever have meaning—and only then can we assert that motion can never be absolute. Consequently, in the light of these thoughts, our natural expectation has to be that any future revision of relativity is going to broaden rather than reduce the scope of its defining symmetry relation.

Sophie: But even the longest standing trends can be reversed, and a natural expectation is hardly a reason that forces belief.

Philonous: Certainly, I am not clairvoyant. Whether relativity will be with us for good, I simply don't know—nor do I need to know because my argument does not depend on it. For regardless of what the future will bring, the possibility *at present* of reconciling the relevant empirical data—namely the motions of celestial bodies as seen from the Earth—with a radically relativistic perspective makes it perfectly clear that the Copernican shift, at the time of its occurrence, was pertaining to modes of thought rather than matters of fact. Consequently, the question you raised, concerning that shift's eventual acceptance, bids us to discern why a traditional mode of thought that seemed empirically sound for more than 2000 years would suddenly appear to be false—first to Copernicus himself, then, tentatively, to a few like-minded initiates, and finally, with categorical force, to the public at large. In fact and somewhat ironically, at our present station in history, at which the ruling physical paradigm is thoroughly relativistic, the belief that the Earth is in motion *objectively* is just as deeply ingrained as the equally arbitrary geocentric view apparently was in Copernicus's day.

Sophie: I must admit, I also always thought that the matter was settled; and the explanation given by Weinberg was therefore a genuine surprise to me. But be that as it may, you haven't answered yet my question.

Philonous: Your question concerning the Copernican system's eventual acceptance?

Sophie: That's right.

Philonous: ...and that's a good point. But before we attend to it, I'd like to add as a caution that the answer won't be that easy to find. In fact, the philosopher of science, Thomas Kuhn, in his pertinent analysis of the Copernican Revolution's historical and technical causes offers a whole bundle of answers, none of which is fully conclusive all by itself.

Sophie: So what does he say?

Philonous: Incidentally, one reason he gives for the Copernican Revolution to

have occurred at the time when it did is directly relevant to what we just
said regarding that long-standing trend in conceptual physical thought.

Sophie: The trend toward ever more symmetric formulations?

Philonous: That's the one. For symmetry in nature is appealing not only for
its conceptual utility but also, very intensely and compellingly, for its inherent elegance and beauty. The intellectual encounter with symmetry in
mathematical form tends to generate a deeply felt aesthetic satisfaction
which somehow bespeaks the presence of truth. And whenever, therefore, modern physicists trust—which they frequently do—in the aesthetics
of mathematics as their guide, they thereby uphold, consciously or not,
an ancient philosophical tradition that originated with Pythagoras, and
that—at the dawn of the modern era—was strongly revived by the Renaissance humanists. For the Platonic or neo-Platonic philosophy that these
humanists were prone to embrace—over and against the Aristotelianism of
the Scholastics—drew upon the Pythagorean belief in cosmic mathematical
harmonies as one of its historical sources. Copernicus, of course, was well
aware of these important intellectual currents, and his search for a simpler
mathematical solution to the problem of the planets was partly inspired
by them. In fact, in his treatise *On the Revolutions* he not only mentions
explicitly, as we saw earlier (p.338), the Pythagorean cosmology in support
of his claim that the Earth is in motion, but he also reveals his neo-Platonic
bias when he speaks of "a sure bond of harmony"[18] that supposedly underlies his heliocentric design and again when he laments the mathematical
disorderliness of the Ptolemaic tradition. In a dedicatory note to Pope Paul
III, with which he chose to preface his work, he expresses his discontents
as follows:

> And so I am unwilling to hide from Your Holiness that nothing
> except my knowledge that mathematicians have not agreed with
> one another in their researches moved me to think out a different
> scheme of drawing up the movements of the spheres of the world.
> For in the first place mathematicians are so uncertain about the
> movements of the sun and moon that they can neither demon-
> strate nor observe the unchanging magnitude of the revolving year.
> Then in setting up the solar and lunar movements and those of the
> other five wandering stars, they do not employ the same principles,
> assumptions, or demonstrations for the revolutions and apparent
> movements. For some make use of homocentric circles only, others
> of eccentric circles and epicycles, by means of which however they
> do not fully attain what they seek.[19]

And further on he writes:

> Accordingly, when I had meditated upon this lack of certitude in
> the traditional mathematics concerning the composition of move-

ments of the spheres of the world, I began to be annoyed that
the philosophers, who in other respects had made a very careful
scrutiny of the least details of the world, had discovered no sure
scheme for the movements of the machinery of the world, which
has been built for us by the Best and Most Orderly Workman.[20]

Sophie: The quote is revealing, but scarcely for being distinctly Platonic. Instead, it strikes me as openly Christian. For the "Orderly Workman" in
question is evidently *not* the Nous of Plotinus but rather the God of the
Bible.

Philonous: Certainly, but you mustn't forget that in the Augustinian integration of neo-Platonic philosophy with Christian theology, the Nous was
in God—and so were, presumably, the mathematical forms by means of
which that Nous rationally ordered the cosmos (p.258). Furthermore, and
very importantly, Copernicus also mirrors the Augustinian neo-Platonic
image of a divine illumination that is sun-like in function, when—in another passage—he first refers to the sun as the "lamp of a very beautiful
temple" that is rightfully placed at the center and then proceeds to quote
certain philosophers as having spoken of this lamp as either "the mind" or
"the visible god."[21]

Sophie: So are you saying then that the Renaissance recovery of neo-Platonic
philosophy was the vital catalyst that sparked the Copernican shift?

Philonous: It was one of the larger-scale historical factors that did play a role,
but it wasn't the only one or the solely decisive one. For as Kuhn also points
out, Copernicus's lifetime was very generally speaking a time of innovation
and novelty. According to Kuhn, "stereotypes are most readily discarded
during periods of general ferment."[22] By implication,

the turbulence of Europe during the Renaissance and Reformation
itself facilitated Copernicus's astronomical innovation. Change in
one field decreases the hold of stereotypes in others. Radical innovations in science have repeatedly occurred during periods of
national or international convulsion, and Copernicus's lifetime was
such a period.[23]

Sophie: In this context we probably also do well to recall that the age of
Copernicus was still the age of the plague. For as we said before, the Black
Death catastrophe plausibly provided that age with a strong innovative
stimulus.

Philonous: And furthermore we need to understand that global forces such as
these produced in their wake some practical problems and needs which, by
being addressed, supported the Copernican shift a bit more directly. The
Voyages of Discovery, for instance, not only created, as it were, the earthly
equivalent of the cosmological spectacle of a vastly reorganized and quickly

expanding celestial world, but they also very concretely fostered a need for improved geographical maps and navigational methods.

Sophie: ...methods that depended in turn on better knowledge of astronomy.[24]

Philonous: That is correct, but there is more to be said. For in Kuhn's analysis, these improvements—in astronomy as well as in geography—when they were finally achieved, led people to realize how deeply mistaken the much admired scholars of antiquity had frequently been. Ptolemy, in particular, who was thought to have been equally accomplished in both of these fields, was found to be a rather blundering geographer.[25]

Sophie: And the suggestion here is, I suppose, that once he was found to be wrong in one field, he might as well have been wrong in another. That is to say, the weight of authority opposing the Copernican advance would suddenly seem substantially lighter.

Philonous: Moreover, this loss in authority of the Ptolemaic system was matched by a parallel *gain* in authority of the Copernican scheme, especially after the latter had been prominently employed in the Gregorian calendar reform of 1582 (so named after Pope Gregory XIII who sponsored it).

Sophie: The calendar reform?

Philonous: Indeed.

Sophie: Please elaborate.

Philonous: The problem that was here at issue arose from the fact that the length of the year in the traditional Julian calendar was slightly overestimated. With the passage of centuries, the cumulative effect of this error eventually caused the Ecclesiastical calendar to become notably distorted. The resultant need for reform was recognized as early as the 13th century, but it was only during Copernicus's lifetime that the matter truly became an urgent concern. When Copernicus was called upon to give his advice, he recommended postponement as he did not deem the then available astronomical tables and systems to be accurate enough to support a fully satisfactory solution.

Sophie: So the earlier quote concerning the mathematicians' inability to correctly determine "the unchanging magnitude of the revolving year" (p.343) is to be seen in this context.

Philonous: It surely is, for at the end of the preface, from which that quote was drawn, Copernicus explicitly mentions how past failures to achieve the reform had been a primary motive for his own, strenuous efforts at creating a more accurate astronomical system.[26]

Sophie: But I thought his system was really not any more accurate than the best available geocentric description. So how did it finally aid the reform?

Philonous: As far as accuracy is concerned, the comparison between the two systems was ultimately inconclusive—that is true. But on the other hand and as we said earlier, Copernicus's system was still not quite as complex and thus was still a bit more convenient to work with. However, what matters most is not the question of objective precision but rather the historical fact that Erasmus Reinhold relied upon the Copernican model rather than the Ptolemaic one when he computed the astronomical tables—the so-called *Prutenic Tables*—on which the calendar reform would finally be based. Interestingly, Reinhold never directly endorsed the heliocentric hypothesis but merely employed Copernicus's mathematical methods. In doing so he displayed an attitude that was quite common among astronomers of the immediate post-Copernican era: the usefulness and overall superiority of Copernican astronomy were openly acknowledged but the reality of the Earth's motion was not—which goes to show, if I may add, that the assimilation of the new astronomy was anything but a straightforward process. Practical acceptance and ideological support were not in synchrony; larger-scale cultural and historical factors were closely entangled with problems that turned on mathematical minutiae; and scholarly views were not in line with public opinion—as the latter was generally more slowly emergent and also more viciously antagonistic.[27] In other words, the overall picture was profoundly confusing.

Sophie: Such rifts and agitations, though, are not at all surprising. Afterall, if a planet is suddenly starting to spin, after being at rest for 2000 years, there is bound to be felt a serious shake-up.

Philonous: And the struggle was only made worse by the fact that the arguments against the new cosmology were not to be discarded lightly and that those in favor of it were sometimes less than convincing. A case in point here is Copernicus's somewhat feeble attempt to argue against Aristotle's view (p.333), that pieces of earth naturally strive toward the center so as to come to rest at it, by merely asserting that this is simply not so. What seemed natural to Aristotle seems unnatural to Copernicus and that's about as far as Copernicus takes it.[28] Similarly, against Ptolemy's intuitively plausible claim that a rotating Earth would cause objects on its surface to be scattered and scrambled with violent force,[29] he only sets up his rather less compelling counter-speculation that the rotational motion in question might well be natural and therefore designed to keep all things "in their best organization."[30] Admittedly, he also offers, by way of analogy, the far more cogent observation that sailors on a ship that "floats over a tranquil sea"[31] will find the objects on that ship to remain completely at rest. But in reply, even a well-meaning critic might feel prompted to ask what would be the case if such a ship were sailing at the supersonic speed of the Earth's revolving equator which covers some 40,000 kilometers every 24 hours.

Sophie: I understand, but Copernicus's point is nonetheless very well taken. For experience does indeed suggest that constant velocity motion leaves wholly undisturbed all objects that are carried along with it. And inasmuch as Ptolemy was worried that the Earth's rotation might produce some violent side effects, he should have been perhaps equally bothered by the thought that the necessarily far more rapid motions, which he himself ascribed to the heavenly spheres, might cause a still greater disturbance among the celestial bodies affected by them.

Philonous: That's an obvious objection that Copernicus fielded as well.[32] But in absence of any genuine knowledge regarding the celestial bodies' physical make-up, it may not be all that incisive. For according to Ptolemy, the celestial bodies were "the lightest and subtlest"[33] and thus the most suited for traveling swiftly.

Sophie: But this is pure fantasy. Ptolemy had absolutely no basis for making this random assertion.

Philonous: ...but neither had Copernicus for any of his counter-claims.

Sophie: In other words, since both were equally clueless, the contest was bound to end in a draw.

Philonous: Not quite because in one important respect, Copernicus's case was clearly the weaker. For a Sun-centered universe, in order to be compatible with empirical facts, had to be a universe of such daunting magnitude that even the most ardent Pythagorean enthusiast would have to have felt very hard pressed to credibly defend his philosophical faith in it. To make my point clear, I would like to remind you of that earlier statement according to which "no observation available to Aristotle or to ourselves entails the necessary inference that" the place to which a falling body strives is "the world's absolute center" (p.334). Technically speaking, this statement is correct. There really are no facts that force us to infer that the Earth is squarely placed at the absolute center; but as it is there are some cogent reasons that suggest it may be very close to it.

Sophie: Such as?

Philonous: ...such as the direct observation that the visible horizon of any observer on the Earth's surface always bisects the heavens into two equal portions. For any two stars that are directly opposing can always be seen to rise and to set in almost perfect synchrony. To understand what I mean, you need to take a look at the diagram on the left in Figure 5.5 where the visible portion of the sky is considerably smaller than the non-visible one. As indicated, such a situation would arise if the Earth were appreciable in size compared to the sphere of the fixed stars or, alternatively, if it were small but far from the center (and the observer were positioned on that side of the Earth that is nearest to the sphere of the stars).[XIV] Consequently, in either of these cases, the rising of a given star in the east that happens

---

[XIV] To be precise, in the case where a small Earth is placed far from the center, relatively speaking, the size of the visible portion would be dependent upon the position on the Earth from which the sky is observed. In particular, two observers on diametrically opposite points on the Earth will see two complementary portions: the visible portion for one observer is the non-visible portion for the other and vice versa.

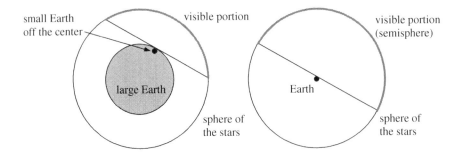

Figure 5.5: the visible portions of the sky in two hypothetical cases.

to be in synchrony with the setting of another star directly opposite in the west would *not* be followed, 12 hours later, by an equally synchronous setting of the former star and rising of the latter.

Sophie: For the distance that the latter has to travel would be greater.

Philonous: That is correct, and that is where the trouble lies. For no such asynchrony has ever been observed. By implication, we are forced to conclude that the Earth must be close to the center and also quite small (as shown in the diagram on the right in Figure 5.5). Moreover, there also is the related consequence that if the Earth were large, the angular separation between two stars would be dependent upon the position on the Earth from which we observe them (see the diagram on the left in Figure 5.6). And simi-

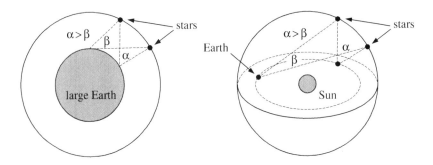

Figure 5.6: parallactic variations in angular separations.

larly, on an Earth that orbits the Sun at a significant distance—relatively speaking—an analogous *parallactic* variation in angular separations would have to occur as the Earth changes its orbital position during the course of a year (see the diagram on the right in Figure 5.6). But again, since no such dependence was ever observed—either by Copernicus himself or any of his predecessors—we are led to conclude as before that the Earth is small and close to the center.[XV]

Sophie: How small is small?

Philonous: Given the accuracy of the best available naked-eye observations in the latter half of the 15th century, a rough calculation readily shows that the phenomenon of seemingly ideal, semispherical bisection requires the radius of a centrally located Earth to be at least 1000 times smaller than the radius of the surrounding sphere of the fixed stars.[35]

Sophie: So even a geocentric universe has to be vast.

Philonous: But not nearly as vast, and that is important, as its heliocentric rival. Because in a Sun-centered universe it is not the radius of the Earth itself that must be smaller by a factor 1000 but rather the radius of the Earth's planetary orbit—which, as you certainly know, is larger by far.

Sophie: Let me see—the Earth has a radius of about 6,400 kilometers and the radius of its orbit is about 150 million kilometers. So the Copernican universe had to be larger than the Ptolemaic one by a factor of more than 20,000.

Philonous: Well, Copernicus and his contemporaries might have thought that factor to be only about 1100 or 1,500,[36] due to a severe underestimation of the distance from the Earth to the Sun. But even so, the volume of the universe would still have been inflated by a factor of more than one billion! That is to say, in the face of such an enormous inflation, the Copernican cosmology might well have appeared utterly preposterous for very sensible reasons.

Sophie: On the other hand though, all these figures and dimensions are really almost laughable when compared to the size of the universe as we presently know it. Afterall, even *Alpha Centauri*, the star nearest to the Sun, is at a distance of more than 3 light years—or more than 200,000 times the distance from the Earth to the Sun. And when it comes to the universe as a whole, that distance would have to be multiplied by another 4 billion or so. It's absolutely mind-boggling.

Philonous: Indeed, it is most amazing to see what has become of the Copernican Revolution in the hands of modern cosmologists—especially considering the meager support that Copernicus himself was able to lend to it. This is not to say, of course, that Copernicus was not a great astronomer—he was the greatest since Ptolemy, and his *Revolutions* clearly were a brilliant mathematical feat. But as far as his heliocentric cosmology is concerned, most of his arguments in favor of it were either tenuous or fully unconvincing. In the final analysis, what Copernicus could rest his case upon was nothing more than a neo-Pythagorean hunch, namely the highly subjective perception that the far greater ease with which planetary retrogressions

---

[XV] Both of these arguments—concerning the equal bisection and the non-occurrence of parallactic variations—were already known to Ptolemy, and he explicitly cited them in his *Almagest* to support his claim "that the earth has the ratio of a point to the heavens."[34]

could be explained within a heliocentric system—at a *purely qualitative level*—was evidence of that system's inherent validity. Otherwise his arguments were really quite weak. And in the case of parallactic variations he even had to have recourse to a cosmic inflation by happenstance that seemed highly implausible, to say the least. Realistically, if someone did today what Copernicus did in the 16th century, he or she would never find a hearing. Just imagine—it almost took a full 300 years from the time *The Revolutions* were published before the first observation was made that could be construed as a genuine 'proof' of the Earth's orbital motion (at least from a non-relativistic perspective). For it was only in 1838 that Friedrich Wilhelm Bessel directly observed the kind of parallactic shift in stellar positions that this motion implies (see again the diagram on the right in Figure 5.6). That is to say, for almost 300 years the entire observational evidence in favor of Copernicus's central assertion of the Earth's orbital motion was strictly speaking purely circumstantial.

Sophie: Which directly leads us back to my earlier question as to why his system was ever accepted.

Philonous: On the scientific side the matter was more or less settled when Johannes Kepler (1571–1630) devised his famous three laws of planetary motion in the first two decades of the 17th century (p.45). For Kepler's conceptual design of a heliocentric system in which the planets orbit the Sun on elliptic paths was so vastly superior, in computational terms, to any design predating it that no one could any longer doubt its correctness.[XVI] Kepler had relied in his research on the most accurate astronomical data ever collected—the *Rudolphine Tables* of Tycho Brahe—and his system was a nearly perfect match for it. However, when we inquire concerning the intentions and inner motivations that guided Kepler on his road to mathematical discovery, we are quickly led back to those same, intangible worldview allusions that we already met with in respect of Copernicus. For Kepler truly was a neo-Pythagorean Renaissance mystic par excellence. A devotee, not only of astronomy, but also of astrology, he was driven—much more so even than Copernicus—by a deep belief in cosmic harmonies that underlie and organize the movements in the heavens. Ultimately, it was these harmonies that Kepler zealously endeavored to decode by means of mathematics. Very fittingly and tellingly, he called his major work *Harmonice Mundi—The Harmonies of the World.*

Sophie: So in the end it was this semi-religious Pythagorean faith in a cosmic mathematical order that provided the decisive revolutionary impetus—at least in the minds of these two pioneers, Kepler and Copernicus.

Philonous: Decisive maybe not, but important it certainly was.

[XVI]Thomas Kuhn points out in this context that "[b]y the middle of the seventeenth century it is difficult to find an important astronomer who is not Copernican; by the end of the century it is impossible."[37]

Sophie: ...important as well as prophetic.
Philonous: ...and *ironic*, as we shall see.

The Creed of Babel

Copernicus never got a glimpse, during his lifetime, of the great civilizational struggle of which the publication of his seminal work on *The Revolutions of the Heavenly Spheres* marked the inception. For when the first copy came from the printer and was handed to him, on May 24th, 1543, the astronomer already lay on his deathbed. Copernicus, so we are told, "saw and handled his completed work" and passed away a few hours later.[38]

The man who died in this way, with his work at his side, left behind him a legacy that confronts us at once with a glaring discrepancy: on the one hand there is the objective accomplishment—skillful, yes, but hardly a triumph—and on the other there is the vast and penetrating transformation that this accomplishment has wrought in every field of Western culture and thought. *Philonous* was correct, of course, when he said that *The Revolutions* were "a brilliant mathematical feat," but correct as well is to say that Copernicus was not a Newton. Copernicus did not invent the calculus, he did not create a lasting theoretical system, he never discovered a natural law, and ultimately, he never even truly resolved the central problem to which his labors aspired—the problem of the planets. His achievement was impressive against the backdrop of an astronomical tradition which, by the beginning of the 16th century, had been largely stagnant for well over one thousand years. But when we ask what exactly it was that was here achieved, we are forced to admit that, qualitatively, Copernicus did little more than to reorganize a handful of circles on paper by shifting their center. Worse still, the Sun-centered setup itself was merely adopted, and novel was only the technical scheme. Since the latter, however, never quite worked, we are led to conclude that Copernicus created, as it were, a semi-innovative astronomical model whose original elegance was clouded by error and whose defining cosmological hypothesis was almost completely bereft of a basis in fact. And yet, something so utterly profound happened in that pivotal moment when Copernicus conceived of the Earth as a planet among planets—a common solar satellite—that even today the force of the impact this moment produced is barely diminished.

When Copernicus redrew the circles of the heavens with the Sun at their center something essential and highly significant was irretrievably lost. That something, however, was not a mere mathematical system—proposed by Ptolemy and upheld by tradition. Instead, what was here discarded, as we shall argue, was nothing less than an intimate, time-honored bond between the outer and the inner world—the realm of sense perception and the spirit life. The Copernican Revolution severed that ancient connection between experience and meaning that fifteen prior centuries of Christian history had seemingly so thoroughly solidified. In fact, it is this very connection upon which the entire Christian religion is vitally centered. For the birth of Jesus, the Christ, was precisely that all-important, cosmic event in which the spirit of God assumed the material likeness of an actual person. Here the Word became flesh so as to reveal God's gift of salvation. God, in Christian theology, was once a physical presence—a man who walked the earth and could be spoken to—could be touched, could be *experienced*. So at the very core of Christian religious belief there lies the momentous assertion that the transcendent spirit of God had once become manifest in immanent, tangible form.

And when Augustine some centuries later proclaimed that whatever occurs occurs for a purpose, the entirety of human life and history was seen to be part of a plan that God Himself had wisely ordained. Everything that human beings do in the world that they see or feel or otherwise sense is a piece of a puzzle that God will assemble—it has a role to play and a function to satisfy as history converges upon its foretold conclusion. Human experience, in Augustine's thought, is transcendently anchored in the divine will and is thereby endowed with absolute, eternal significance. Experience is never meaningless or merely random because there simply is no randomness.

An even more decisive step in fusing the immanent with the transcendent was taken by Albert the Great and his pupil St. Thomas Aquinas. For the full integration of Aristotelian philosophy with Christian theology that these two thinkers conceived was intended to demonstrate, once and for all, how every aspect of the cosmos, even the least, was designed to reveal the wisdom of God. The heavens that Aquinas saw were not a limitless expanse of empty space in which a billion nameless galaxies are randomly scattered. Instead, what he perceived was a celestial sphere, unchanging and pure, behind which there lay the empyrean home of the blessed. In the mind of St. Thomas, the Christian Heaven, where God gathers the faithful and chosen, directly bordered the visible skies. And the material world, that these skies surrounded in turn, served as the stage upon which the Christian drama of salvation and damnation was meant to unfold.[1]

This vision of the cosmos as a stage, set up to accommodate the leveling of God's divine justice, was famously immortalized in the epic verse of *Dante Alighieri*. In the *Divine Comedy* Dante describes how he himself, guided by *Virgil*, the poet, traverses the Christian-Aristotelian universe. The journey commences on Good Friday when he and his guide begin their descent through the circles of hell. Along their way, the two travelers have numerous haunting encounters with tortured souls whose successively increasing wretchedness closely accords to the harshness of the punishments imposed on them. Tellingly, the misdeeds that these wayward once were guilty of in earthly life

---

[1]To be precise, in the *Summa Theologica* Aquinas speaks of the "empyrean heaven" as "the highest corporeal place" (see [Aq], p.317). That is to say, he considered it in essence to be material as well.

directly align with the three Aristotelian classes of sin: sins of incontinence, violence, and malice.[39]

In Dante's medieval perspective, hell is a physical place and even posses-ses a well-defined, geometrical shape. It is an inverted spherical cone whose centerline runs through Jerusalem, the place where Jesus was betrayed and crucified. Its vertex at the other end is the world's absolute center and also the point most distant from Heaven. Here, at the evil heart of existence, satan holds sway over his netherworld—his "kingdom dolorous"[40]—and mercilessly mangles in his jaws the vilest of sinners, the backstabbing Brutus and Judas, the traitor of God.

Upon their exit from hell, Dante and Virgil pass through the region of the purgatory and from there Dante alone ascends to the spheres of the heavens. Beginning with the sphere of the Moon—the First Heaven—he moves through the spheres of the planets, from Mercury to Saturn by way of the Sun,[II] and, having ascended further still, beyond the fixed stars and the *primum mobile*, he finally reaches the Tenth and Highest Heaven—the Empyrean—"where God, his angels, and the most blessed humans" reside.[42]

The universe that Dante thus describes is organized to match the stations of the human spirit life with actual physical places—above us and below. It is a universe that doesn't just happen to be, but rather is meant to fulfill a definite, God-given function. However, in order to perceive that function properly, we need to go beyond the image of the cosmos as a stage, to which we just alluded, and take a closer look at Dante's profound metaphysical vision. At its base, this vision is built upon the neo-Platonic-Christian belief that the only true and truly self-subsistent reality is consciousness pure—the self-awareness of God.[III] It is this empyrean consciousness, this timeless, non-spatial point of dimensionless spirit that begets and beholds the material world.

But the question is "why?"—Why would a spirit, perfect and pure, bring forth into being a world that is in many ways so flawed and depressing? To this Dante replies that the ultimate reason for creation to be in existence is to provide the divine intellect with an occasion to experience itself in its own nec-essary opposite—the finite, the contingent, the material. For it is only thus that divine love can ever be given to that which is 'other'—other than consciousness pure. Consequently, creation's God-given function—its final cause—is to make possible the unfolding of Love.[44]

Furthermore and as we just saw, acceptance of this critical truth requires antecedently that the absolute ontological primacy of consciousness over mat-ter be unequivocally recognized. In this context, the Dante-scholar Chris-tian Moevs poignantly identifies the stimulation of this recognition, in the

---

[II]In his cosmology Dante even makes provision for the Ptolemaic epicycles and considers them separate, subordinate heavens.[41]

[III]In *The Banquet* Dante explicitly states that "the divine intellect is the cause of everything."[43]

reader's mind, as the *Comedy's* implicit pedagogical aim. For the *Comedy*, by being starkly realistic and irresistibly continuous "with spatiotemporal experience,"[45] impresses its fictive textual world with categorical force and thereby causes the 'real' world of matter outside to appear, by inversion, ever more fictive. In other words, what is awakened here is an awareness of the purported verity that subjective consciousness supersedes objective, material being.

In the light of these remarks, we now begin to see with greater clarity how deep a rift there opened up when Copernicus reorganized his orbital circles. For affirmation of Copernican astronomy was not, by any means, merely a matter of granting the Sun a place at the center, but rather of completely inverting an entire system of metaphysical thought. That is to say, the transformation here in question was a world-view revolution in the deepest and most radical sense.

To see the truth of this assertion, we only need to honestly inquire why the heliocentric model—proposed by Copernicus, perfected by Kepler, and explained by Newton—appears to us, at our present station in history, so much more adequate than its medieval geocentric rival. And, disregarding relativity, the answer most commonly given will probably be "it better agrees with observational facts." There is no need to dig any deeper when the facts in themselves are fully articulate. Moreover, as latter-day Copernicans we also understand, of course, that facts really are—first and foremost—observable, physical facts, and that Being, by implication, is predominantly material, rather than conscious or mental, as Dante believed. What matters to us is mainly just matter as such, for we have learned to see reality as merely a physical system—a material aggregate governed by laws that science sternly exposes.

In following this line of thought we also come to see that the dissolution of geocentric astronomy signaled a total revision of even the very idea and meaning of 'truth'. For the medieval ideal of a Truth that God, the sovereign *Subject*, reveals is here giving way to an *objective* truth that human reason infers from observation. To be sure, the groundwork for this great epistemological shift was laid already much earlier by the Scholastics, and here in particular, by Albert the Great and Thomas Aquinas (p.273). But it was only when Copernicus tried to establish—with perfectly pious intent—that his heliocentric design was a superior match for the facts that there arose the possibility, for the very first time in Christian history, that objective truths uncovered by reason could have the power to fashion a world of their own. Aquinas had added *"intellege, ut credas"* to Augustine's more orthodox *"crede, ut intellegas"* (p.273). But the advance of Copernicus seems to suggest, wholly unintendedly, that the actual, more adequate motto may be a statement more trivial by far: *"intellege, ut intellegas."* The modern scientist, whom Copernicus typified, albeit still vaguely and largely unconsciously, seeks knowledge and truth not to believe, but rather more simply, in order to know. The purpose of science in modern perception no longer is to reveal the glory of God but merely to show the world as it is.

An indication for how deeply this pertinent shift has penetrated our contemporary consciousness is the near synonymity of the words 'objective' and 'true' in present-day usage. 'Objective' to us is the golden attribute that sets apart a genuine truth from a mere subjective opinion or statement of faith. The true, to us, is the objective and the objective the true. By implication, we moderns are prone to accept the rule of the 'facts' with a sort of habitual readiness that borders on slavish submission. Whatever so happens to carry the label 'objective' may rightly demand that we meekly defer to it. We are conditioned to operate in an objective, factual world of scientific theories, technological systems, economic realities, political structures, educational strategies, psychological mechanisms, and instinctual drives—the list goes on—which in their sum define for us the very essence of human existence. Moreover, when faced with these unyielding constraints we are called upon to simply accept whatever is given—and, more often than not, we willingly do. Rarely indeed do we ask what meaning there is—instead, we commonly only inquire "what is?" Experience shows what reality is, and meaning has nothing whatever to do with it. And hence the Copernican turn: from a world of total integration to one of utter disconnect.

In a sense, of course, the problem may simply have been that the integration was far too close and far too confident to ever be lasting. The *Comedy* is here a case in point. For while it certainly is true that Dante did *not* compose this masterpiece of his chiefly to establish that Aristotle and Aquinas had been right, it certainly is *also true* that he assumed them to be right when he composed it (mostly, that is[IV]). The Aristotelian spheres of the heavens, according to Dante, were actual spheres, the circles of hell were actual circles, and the Earth's absolute center was really the devil's abode. As a matter of course, there is nothing inherently inconsistent in the idea that the "kingdom dolorous" is carried about at the heart of a planet. Somewhere in this universe in one of a hundred billion galaxies there is a star that humans call Sun; it is one of a hundred billion other stars in this one galaxy alone, and about it there travel some planets of which a certain one—not the smallest and not the biggest—so happens to harbor the cosmic master of evil. There is no logical contradiction, just plenty of silliness.

Is it not plain obvious then, in light of all this, that John Lennon was right to *imagine* that there is "no hell below us" and "above us only sky"? Quoting a pop-song may seem to trivialize the matter unduly, but that is, of course, precisely the point. For as far as meaning is concerned the modern universe is

---

[IV] Dante was vitally inspired by Aristotle and Aquinas in his cosmological and metaphysical views but he also differed from them in some important respects. A case in point here is Dante's conception of the empyrean as an entirely immaterial realm which put him in conflict with Aquinas's opposing belief according to which the empyrean was part of the corporeal world (see [Moe], p.21, for further discussion).

trivial indeed—totally, utterly trivial.

Sophie: That song, though, was not a lament. Lennon envisioned a world without transcendent ballast because he genuinely yearned for it.

Philonous: I understand: no transcendence, no religion, no belief, and thus, we all live in peace—perfectly tolerant, highly enlightened, relaxed, and wholly at ease.

Sophie: Perhaps the point is well taken. Perhaps there is a lesson that Copernicus inadvertently taught us that we would do well to absorb.[V]

Philonous: Such as?

Sophie: The lesson of the "Pale Blue Dot."

Philonous: The image that Carl Sagan made popular?

Sophie: That's the one. I have a copy of it (Figure 5.7). Can you see the Earth in it?

Figure 5.7: the Pale Blue Dot.

[V] If the lesson in question is construed to be the realization of how humble a place in the universe mankind occupies by being confined to Planet Earth, then Copernicus was actually not the first to teach it to us—consciously or not. For as C.S. Lewis points out (in [Lew2], p.26) many medieval writers and thinkers, who took their inspiration from Cicero's *Republic*, pointed to the Earth's diminutive size when their intent was "to mortify human ambition." On the other hand, though, the reference to Copernicus seems justified in that the cosmological revolution that Copernicus started not only resulted in a further vast reduction of the Earth's relative size but also made its position in the cosmos appear to be entirely random.

Philonous: It's right there, that single blue pixel, right in that sunbeam.
Sophie: It's amazing, isn't it? The Earth reduced to a dot. The picture, by the way, was taken by Voyager 1, in 1990, at a distance from the Earth of about 3.8 billion miles (which is roughly the average distance to Pluto).
Philonous: So what about the lesson then? What do you take it to be?
Sophie: Well, speaking of Carl Sagan, he answered that question as follows:

> Consider again that dot. That's here, that's home, that's us. On it everyone you love, everyone you know, everyone you ever heard of, every human being who ever was, lived out their lives. The aggregate of our joy and suffering, thousands of confident religions, ideologies, and economic doctrines, every hunter and forager, every hero and coward, every creator and destroyer of civilization, every king and peasant, every young couple in love, every mother and father, hopeful child, inventor and explorer, every teacher of morals, every corrupt politician, every "superstar," every "supreme leader," every saint and sinner in the history of our species lived there—on a mote of dust suspended in a sunbeam.
>
> The Earth is a very small stage in a vast cosmic arena. Think of the rivers of blood spilled by all those generals and emperors so that, in glory and triumph, they could become the momentary masters of a fraction of a dot. Think of the endless cruelties visited by the inhabitants of one corner of this pixel on the scarcely distinguishable inhabitants of some other corner, how frequent their misunderstandings, how eager they are to kill one another, how fervent their hatreds.
>
> Our posturings, our imagined self-importance, the delusion that we have some privileged position in the Universe, are challenged by this point of pale light. Our planet is a lonely speck in the great enveloping cosmic dark. In our obscurity, in all this vastness, there is no hint that help will come from elsewhere to save us from ourselves.
>
> The Earth is the only world known so far to harbor life. There is nowhere else, at least in the near future, to which our species could migrate. Visit, yes. Settle, not yet. Like it or not, for the moment the Earth is where we make our stand.
>
> It has been said that astronomy is a humbling and character-building experience. There is perhaps no better demonstration of the folly of human conceits than this distant image of our tiny world. To me, it underscores our responsibility to deal more kindly with one another, and to preserve and cherish the pale blue dot, the only home we've ever known.[46]

Philonous: I like it.

Sophie: You do?

Philonous: Yes, I find his viewpoint appealing. Unmasking "the folly of human conceits"—preferably, of course, in other people not myself—is a worthy objective; and a keener awareness of how humble a place in the universe we happen to occupy may very well help us to reach it. So, yes, Carl Sagan is right—to an extent.

Sophie: Why do you qualify?

Philonous: Because his argument appears to be based on the spurious hunch that smallness somehow implies lack in importance: the Earth is small and thus irrelevant.

Sophie: Not the Earth itself—only the foolish obsessions of some of its inhabitants.

Philonous: Unfortunately, though, if our obsessions are made ridiculous, as Sagan suggests, by being confined to a dot, then so are our greatest virtues too. That is to say, it doesn't matter how we act or what we are—foolish or wise, kind or unkind—if either way we are equally small. A "mote of dust" is a mote no matter its conduct.

Sophie: And that may be the truth of it: we are hapless dwarves of quantum size—irrelevant, stupid, and fleeting, and without a reason for being other than happenstance.

Philonous: That *is* a possibility, I fully agree.

Sophie: It is?

Philonous: Of course.

Sophie: Coming from you, that's very unexpected.

Philonous: It depends on the view that I pick. If I choose to adopt a modern scientific perspective, then clearly this little blue planet of ours, with all that exists on it, is likely a product of chance and nothing but chance. There are some people, of course, who fabricate dubious arguments designed to establish—from a scientific perspective—that our presence in this world is somehow intended, but...

Sophie: You mean people like you who try to convince others, let's say, that quantum mechanics links matter to consciousness in a purposeful, intentional manner?

Philonous: No, that's not what I mean. Because when *I* do it, it's I who does it, and when *others* do it, it's others who do it.

Sophie: And so?

Philonous: And so the logic is sound in the former case and deeply confused in the latter.

Sophie: Why did I ask?

Philonous: I don't know—but back to my point: some people argue, as I said, that science quite strongly suggests that human life—or life in general, at least—is somehow intended. For supposedly, the constants of nature—such as the gravitational constant or Planck's quantum of action—are intricately fine-tuned so as to make the universe a potentially bio-friendly place. Even a very slight relative change in the magnitudes of these various constants, so the pertinent analysis apparently shows, would alter the make-up of physical reality so decidedly that highly complex biological systems, including us humans, could never evolve. In other words, the laws of nature were set up with homo sapiens in mind.

Sophie: It's the *anthropic principle,* if I'm not mistaken.[VI]

Philonous: You have heard of it?

Sophie: I have indeed, but why do you object to it?

Philonous: Truth be told, I don't object to it because I do in fact believe in it. But for the sake of honesty, I also must admit that there exists a plausible alternative; namely the idea that our own 'little' world—the known universe—is part of a larger assemblage of parallel worlds that exhaustively cover, one by one, all the possible random paths that this one universe, in which we exist, could have potentially taken.

Sophie: I don't understand.

Philonous: What I have here in mind (inspired by the exposition in [Den]) is something akin to an image that the Argentinian writer Jorge Luis Borges describes in one of his metaphysical fictions. In *The Library of Babel*[47] Borges envisions a universe composed of a vast and potentially infinite number of hexagonal galleries that are lined by shelves and connected by hallways. On each shelf there are 35 books with 410 pages each. The librarians who inhabit this world conjecture that it contains all the possible books—of this particular format—that can be produced by randomly arranging the letters of the alphabet. So every such letter arrangement, on 410 standard-sized pages, can be found in one of the books on one of the shelves somewhere in the Library.

Sophie: A universal library—the image is intriguing.

Philonous: Intriguing indeed: a total, cosmic collection of possible texts—of every story and every account, every theory, future or past, every historical fact and every distortion of it, every valid prediction and every false prophecy, every translation with every mistake, every truth and every lie in every language, known or unknown—and, most importantly, every piece of gibberish that can be produced by lining up letters by chance.

Sophie: With the point being, I suppose, that even the seemingly sensible works are ultimately gibberish too. For the meaning they seem to convey was never intended but merely arose, as you said, "by lining up letters by

---

[VI]There are weaker versions of the anthropic principle that merely assert the tautological truism that the existence of human life and consciousness requires that the universe have a physical structure in which such life and consciousness can in fact exist. But the stronger version referred to above is more interesting to contemplate and therefore our version of choice.

chance."

Philonous: So is it not possible then that this world we live in, which seems
to have been so carefully tuned to bring about life, is also at bottom mere
gibberish? Is it not possible that we are at home in a world that merely is
a book on a shelf, so to speak, in a universal library of worlds?

Sophie: Possible, yes—plausible, probably not.

Philonous: You may be surprised, but this notion of a universe of parallel
worlds has in fact been proposed as a possible *and plausible* way to interpret
quantum mechanics.

Sophie: It has? On what grounds?

Philonous: Do you recall what we said about the central quantum enigma—the
mystery of measurement?

Sophie: Of course, I do. The problem we discussed was how continuously evolving quantum clouds of superimposed alternatives contract, at the point of
measurement, into well-defined observable events.

Philonous: Well, according to the so-called *many-worlds hypothesis*, this riddle can be solved if we suppose that quantum clouds quite simply don't
contract. That is, instead of assuming that quantum waves collapse randomly into specific follow-up states, we may as well postulate that every
such collapse is a dispersive event in which all the possible follow-up states
are realized and are each giving rise to a parallel world. An electron, for
instance, in a double-slit experiment does not materialize at one random
point on the detector screen but rather at all possible points simultaneously
in as many parallel worlds as there are points on that screen.[VII]

Sophie: So the world is constantly splitting—one world for every quantum
alternative.

Philonous: And you yourself are splitting as well. For just as there are books
in Borges's Library that tell of all the possible lives you could have been
fated to live, so there are parallel quantum worlds in which all of these lives
did in fact happen. In some of these worlds you never were born, in some
you died as a baby, in some others you died in an accident while crossing
a road at age 26, and in some others still you are going die on your 100th
birthday, on May 31st, 2065.

Sophie: But in none of them, and that is important, will I continue to live for
10,000 years, because in all of them the laws of nature are equally valid.
And in particular, the constants of nature that condition these laws must
still be set up just right. For otherwise neither I nor any of my quantum
split images could ever exist. So quite in spite of any of your deconstructive
reasonings, the anthropic principle remains fully intact.

Philonous: Your view is too narrow, but let me explain...

[VII]To be precise, the distribution of these worlds would have to correspond to the probability
distribution that is given by the wave function and observed in experiments. But a detailed
discussion of this issue would definitely lead us too far.

Sophie: Please do.

Philonous: To begin with, it is helpful to realize that even if we did assume that all of these parallel worlds are globally governed by the same set of natural laws, it wouldn't follow necessarily that all of them will show coherently lawful behavior.[VIII] Afterall, some of these worlds would represent quantum paths that are made up of nothing but the most unlikely quantum alternatives. In a world like ours, which presumably is close to the statistical mean, a double-slit experiment, say, tends to produce predictable outcomes, as certain regions on the detector screen are consistently more frequently hit than others. Significant deviations from this statistical pattern are extremely unlikely, but since they are not altogether impossible, there must be some worlds in which they do in fact happen. By implication, there also are worlds in which *no* double-slit experiment and even no physical process whatever will ever be lawfully patterned.

Sophie: Put differently, in some of these worlds anything goes.

Philonous: Precisely.

Sophie: In that case, it seems, there also would be some really capricious, odd-looking worlds in which I will in fact celebrate 10,000 birthdays.

Philonous: In principle, yes, for insofar as we consider your reaching that age a highly unlikely, yet still remotely possible quantum alternative, the many-worlds hypothesis does indeed imply that it will come about in some freakishly random parallel world. Furthermore, inspired by this thought, we even can go further and assume that lawlessness is the norm and lawfulness, by contrast, an aberrant exception. For just as a book in the Library of Babel may give a false appearance of intelligent authorship, so a universe like ours that seems to be governed by rational laws may conceivably be a random singularity in a universal library of inherently lawless physical worlds.

Sophie: So each of these worlds, in this way of thinking, is a random account of physical processes that sometimes so happen to align themselves in a seemingly orderly fashion and even bring forth intelligent life.

Philonous: That is correct—and hence we behold the Copernican vision in its most radical, desolate form: a universe of utter randomness—no meaning, no purpose, no design, and also no designer. Copernicus, of course, never intended it, but by reducing the Earth to a planet he surely did initiate its later advent. For it was only in consequence of this initial reduction that we moderns came to perceive our little blue world as a traveling dot—aimless,

---

[VIII]In recent years the notion of a so-called *megaverse* has been put forth to account for the fact that the number of coherent cosmic structures appears to be exceedingly large. According to the latest estimates of superstring-cosmology, there may be as many as 10^{500} of them (which is amazing in light of the fact that the total number of atoms in the universe is estimated to be less than 10^{80}). So it is indeed conceivable that there are parallel worlds, numerous almost beyond measure, whose natural laws are distinct from the set of laws that the universe we live in happens to be constituted upon.

obscure, and alone. And it was due as well to this initial advance that modern science could flourish and ultimately bring forth, in quantum mechanics, a random description that wholly dissolves the traditional notion of a divinely ordered universe to which Copernicus himself still strongly adhered.

Sophie: You mustn't forget, however, that the many-worlds hypothesis, as you yourself said, is merely an interpretation. Consequently, that hypothesis, along with its stronger Borgian variant, must not be confused with serious science.

Philonous: Certainly, what we are dealing here with is not a scientific theory that can be tested in experiments. But it is a viable metaphysical notion that science inspires and, more importantly, that logic admits.

Sophie: It is viable but also distinctly depressing.

Philonous: On the contrary, I find it uplifting.

Sophie: Because it warmly goes to show that meaning, purpose, and design are logically dispensable?

Philonous: Of course. For what is the alternative? That there is some empirical fact or rational argument—scientific or otherwise—from which a design and therefore a designer can be inferred with logical necessity? If that were the case then faith in God or purpose or meaning or whatever we happen to cherish would no longer be a genuine choice. We wouldn't be *free* to believe or reject but simply be forced to admit.

Sophie: So the Borgian creed—the creed of Babel—is to you a welcome alternative that guarantees your actual, personal faith in meaning and God to be a true act of choosing.

Philonous: Indeed, without some other valid alternative, my will wouldn't be free and my faith wouldn't be faith. You see, when you suggested previously that we might be mere "hapless dwarves of quantum size," I fully agreed because I can indeed decide to consider this sort of belief a viable option. I can *choose* to follow Sagan's argument to its final logical consequence—a step that Sagan himself quite clearly rejected—and measure the value of human life solely by the size of the planet to which it is bound. "The Earth is small and thus *we* are irrelevant" is logically a possible view which I am perfectly free to adopt.

Sophie: ...but which, in fact, you don't adopt.

Philonous: That is correct, because, as I see it, there are human acts that are not only not completely irrelevant but are instead highly significant. To me the vastest expanse of empty space is truly as nothing compared to, let's say, an act of compassion, love, or self-sacrifice. Even an entire universe, if totally lifeless, is to me of no import next to the deeds of a woman like Corrie ten Boom or a man like Mahatma Gandhi. That is to say, the image of "The Pale Blue Dot" can teach us humility, as Sagan, rightly suggested, but it cannot negate the value of human life and action by some kind of factual or logical compulsion.

Sophie: Perhaps then this is the ultimate lesson that Copernicus taught us—
that meaning in the modern universe is entirely a matter of choice.

Philonous: Perhaps you are right.

What Makes a Falling Body Fall?

The juxtaposition of the world of the *Comedy* and the universal Library that Borges describes forms a thematic contrast of the most extreme harshness: total integration on the one hand and utter nihilistic randomness on the other. This is all the more remarkable as Borges was, in fact, one of Dante's most fervent modern-day admirers. He used the *Comedy* as a source of inspiration for a number of his own fictions and parodies, and he is quoted as saying that "as soon as I open [the *Comedy*] tomorrow, I will discover things I did not see before. I know this book will go on, beyond my waking life, and beyond ours."[48]

In the light of this acknowledged deep impress that Dante's poem left on Borges's highly sensitive, literary mind, it is fascinating to see how distinctly post-Copernican a spirit *The Library of Babel* conveys to its readers. The story of this library is narrated by a seeker of knowledge who spent his life traveling its hexagons in search of a book—a "catalogue of catalogues"[49]—that would explain and justify the universe. Speaking of historical events, the narrator recounts a heady time—"[f]ive hundred years ago"[50]—of great discoveries, optimism, and hope. At the dawn of this luminous era, a book was found containing almost two full pages of continuously sensible text. When the language of this passage had been identified—"[w]ithin a century"—its content turned out to pertain to "some notions of combinative analysis, illustrated with examples of variation with unlimited repetition."[51] In consequence, "a librarian of genius"[52] was able to discover the Library's most fundamental law: all of its books are composed of the same finite set of symbols—the letters of the alphabet, the space, the comma, and the period. Asserting further, that there are no two books that are the same, this librarian also "deduced that the Library is total"[53]—or 'universal', as *Philonous* explained.

Evidently, what Borges here describes, fairly overtly, is the inception of the modern age of science. His mention of a time "five hundred years ago" directly points to the Renaissance period,[54] and the "examples of variation with unlimited repetition" are a thinly veiled allusion to the discovery of the calculus—a discovery, as one should add, that Newton brilliantly authored and also employed in his groundbreaking work on theoretical physics.

By implication, it is in direct reference to the West's actual historical development when Borges has his narrator explain how the expectant, hopeful mood that these initial advances produced "was followed by an excessive depression."[55] Faced with the unbearable realization that the Library, by being total, was far too vast for any of its treasures of knowledge to ever be found, men began to despair, and, before long, their morals eroded. Eventually, as gloom gave way to aggression, obscene acts of blasphemy and wanton destruction became common phenomena. In this latter-day world of decay, violence, and "heretical conflicts"[56] the narrator himself, having reached the end of his journey, finds his only consolation in the thought that the Library, while infinite, might also be cyclic. The chaos it harbors, so he speculates, repeats itself interminably in an overall orderly fashion. Dying in solitude, he "is gladdened by this elegant hope."[57]

The Library of Babel is a haunting tale of a disillusioned, weary world in which the quest for knowledge has collapsed. Indeed, the image of the modern era that Borges here depicts is no less somber to behold than the flock of wide-eyed monsters that assail the sleeper in Francisco Goya's visual metaphor of modern man's rational nightmare (Figure 1.1, p.2). Here as there, the promise of reason disintegrates, and a sense of foredoom is all that is left.

But how did it all come about? How did a hope, so bright and alluring, turn out so sullen and bleak? This is the question we ought to address, and in order to approach it properly we must start at the start and mentally return to that initial time when the hope was arising. In *The Library of Babel* that time was reached, as noted above, when a book was found containing a sizable portion of sensible text. In actual history, the book in question was the Book of Nature, and the man who first deciphered it was an Italian mathematician whose name we all recognize as a symbol for progress in science as well as for the human struggle for freedom of thought: *Galileo Galilei.*

Galileo was born near Pisa on February 15th, 1564.[58] While little is known about his mother Giulia Ammannati, his father, Vincenzio, is reputed to have been a professional musician of considerable originality whose high regard for mathematics especially inclined him toward the study and creative pursuit of musical theory.

At the age of thirteen Galileo was sent to the monastery of Vallombrosa, where he studied Latin and Greek and became a novice. Soon, however, his father told him to come home again, most likely for reasons of financial distress. Vincenzio's artistic career was far from lucrative, and he therefore wished for his son to contribute to the family's income by becoming a doctor. In consequence, Galileo enrolled at the University of Pisa, in 1581, as a student of medicine.

His father, meanwhile, became embroiled in a controversy after openly challenging his former teacher, Gioseffo Zarlino, in one of his recently published theoretical writings. In the *Dialogue of Ancient and Modern Music* he wrote:

> It appears to me that they who in proof of any assertion rely simply on the weight of authority, without adducing any argument in support of it, act very absurdly. I, on the contrary, wish to be allowed freely to question and freely to answer you without any sort

of adulation, as well becomes those who are in search of truth.[59]

To Vincenzio's likely regret, his son all too eagerly embraced the rebellious spirit of these words when, against his father's wishes, he abandoned the study of medicine in favor of a less prestigious career in mathematics. In 1585, Galileo returned to his father's house in Florence, without a degree, and embraced his mathematical studies with vigor, proving theorems and writing papers on geometry, including one on the conical shape of hell in Dante's *Inferno* (the first part of the *Comedy*).

When his work began to be recognized by professional mathematicians, he was offered a teaching post at the University of Pisa which he gladly accepted. True to character, however, Galileo did not settle down into a quiet, scholarly life but directly headed for conflict as his disputatious nature quickly asserted itself. Most notably, he made himself unpopular with the local establishment by engaging the professors of philosophy in arguments concerning their claim that objects fall at rates proportional to their weight. It was to settle this dispute that Galileo supposedly climbed the Leaning Tower of Pisa and publicly dropped his cannon balls. In the light of our earlier remarks concerning this scene (p.150), his failure to sway the philosophers' minds by his demonstrations may be considered a case in point regarding the elusiveness of objective human judgment. But the episode also testifies to Galileo's inherent great readiness to break with convention in seeking the truth.

Galileo left Pisa, in 1592, for the chair of mathematics at the University of Padua where he entered upon what he would later describe as "the happiest period of his life."[60] At Padua he became recognized as a captivating lecturer, acquired social status, invented new technologies, and, above all, produced that highly influential scientific work for which we best remember him: his studies of the mechanics of motion. Concerning these studies, however, it is by no means easy to discern to what extent the results that they produced were truly distinctive and novel. In popular perception Galileo commonly looms as a Promethean great pioneer who single-handedly forged the modern new age of science and reason. But upon closer inspection, the case is notably less obvious. For even those particularly famous deeds that everyone assigns to him, such as the discovery of the principle of inertia or the quantitative formulation of the law of falling bodies, did not in fact originate with him. The former of these had been known to some extent already to medieval theorists of impetus, and the latter dates back to the work of certain Scholastics in Oxford and Paris in the 14th and early 15th centuries.[61]

On the other hand, though, the directly opposing opinion that Galileo merely revived and perhaps slightly enriched a pre-existing tradition is equally untenable. For as regards the law of falling bodies, for example, his medieval predecessors never established that critical link to direct observation that played so decisive a role in much of Galileo's pertinent research. In *The Two New Sciences* Galileo describes a number of experiments concerning balls descending on inclined planes which he asserts to have repeated "many, many times"[62]—but no such accounts can be found in any of the relevant medieval expositions. In fact, according to the historian of science, Ernan McMullin, the Scholastics arrived at their quantitative description from a purely speculative, mathematical analysis of a uniformly accelerated motion without providing any evidence that natural free fall was indeed such a motion.[63]

Furthermore, Galileo also conjoins the separate conceptions of a constant-speed inertial motion and a uniformly accelerated, vertical fall to give a mathematical description of projectile motion that far surpasses in its cogency any treatment of this topic given either in medieval times or in antiquity. Using contemporary terminology, we may say that the problem here in question is to determine the path of an object in a constant gravitational field in absence of air resistance. And as it turns out, Galileo *correctly* states the solution as follows:

> A projectile which is carried by a uniform horizontal motion compounded with a naturally accelerated vertical motion describes a path which is a semi-parabola.[64]

In the dialogue in *The Two New Sciences* from which this conclusion emerges, one of the three interlocutors, Sagredo by name, assesses the pertinent argument as "new, subtle and conclusive." And indeed, Galileo's analysis is not only new and conclusive, but also extremely important. For on the one hand, the idea of a motion composed of accelerated and non-accelerated parts directly foreshadows Newton's very similar description of the Moon's (or the planets') orbital travel; and on the other hand, it completely does away with the woefully inadequate treatment of projectile motion in Aristotle's *Physics*. According to Aristotle, motions can never be independently superimposed[65] and also require for their maintenance the continuous action of an agent of motion whom he refers to as 'movent'. In the case of a projectile, this agent supposedly is the surrounding volume of air. For the original movent—the sling catapulting a stone, let's say—imparts to the air a dynamic agency, so Aristotle conjectures, that propels the projectile along its trajectory. By implication, motion in Aristotelian physics can never occur in a vacuum. And hence we come to see how radical a departure from traditional modes of thought was signified by Galileo's brilliant advance.

Interestingly, though, Galileo never abstracted from his own lucid analysis of projectile motion an equally lucid formulation of the principle of inertia upon which that analysis was partially based. In particular, he never arrived at the Newtonian conception of a force-free motion that proceeds at a constant rate along a straight line in space. For instead of taking his own insight at face value and proposing that in absence of an accelerating gravitational force a projectile would float through the air at uniform velocity, he only envisioned a motion that was tied to a specific material support, in this case a horizontal plane:[1]

> Imagine any particle projected along a horizontal plane without friction; then we know... that this particle will move along this same plane with a motion which is uniform and perpetual, provided the plane has no limits.[66]

Moreover, his attendant assertion to have derived this principle conclusively turns out to be false. In one instance he infers the perpetuity of frictionless motion on a horizontal plane—erroneously and rather obscurely—from the observation that motions on sloping planes are either accelerating or decelerating,[68] and in another he discusses an experiment from which the principle can indeed be derived but then makes no attempt to do so.[69]

In spite of these various reservations, however, we also need to acknowledge of course that Galileo quite keenly perceived the deeper implications that the law of inertia entails. And to see what here the larger context is, it is helpful to recall that Copernicus tried to counter Ptolemy's assertion concerning the violent turbulence that a rotating Earth supposedly would cause among the objects on its surface by shrewdly observing that "sailors on a ship that floats over a tranquil sea will find the objects on that ship to remain completely at rest" (p.346). In other words, according to Copernicus, an inertial motion has no discernible effects on objects that participate in it—or, in more sophisticated, current-day lingo: the laws of nature are the same in all frames of reference that are non-accelerating (which is a special case of the more general principle of Einstein's discussed on p.340f). Galileo, of course, did not exactly put it thus, but in his *Dialogue on the Great World Systems*—which he wrote to defend the Copernican scheme—he astutely discusses this issue as follows:

> Shut yourself up with some friend in the largest room below decks of some large ship, and there procure gnats, flies, and such other small winged creatures. Also get a great tub full of water and within it put certain fishes; let also a certain bottle be hung up, which drop by drop lets forth its water into another narrow-necked bottle placed underneath. Then, the ship lying still, observe how those small winged animals fly with like velocity towards all parts of the room; how the fishes swim indifferently towards all sides; and how the distilling drops all fall into the bottle placed underneath. And casting anything towards your friend, you need not throw it with more force one way than another, provided the distances be equal; and jumping broad, you will reach as far one way as another.

---

[1]Ernan McMullin points out in this context that Galileo offers an alternative formulation of the principle of inertia in his *Dialogue Concerning the Two Chief Systems of the World* that more closely resembles Newton's first law. However, even here the appeal to a force free motion is somewhat veiled, and the assertion that Galileo never formulated the principle of inertia with final clarity therefore appears to be justified.[67]

Having observed all these particulars, though no man doubts that, so long as the vessel stands still, they ought to take place in this manner, make the ship move with what velocity you please, so long as the motion is uniform and not fluctuating this way and that. You shall not be able to discern the least alteration in all the aforementioned effects, nor can you gather by any of them whether the ship moves or stands still. Of this correspondence of effects the cause is that the ship's motion is common to all things contained in it and to the air also; I mean if those things be shut up in the room; but in the case those things were above in the open air, and not obliged to follow the course of the ship, differences more or less notable would be observed in some of the forenamed effects, and there is no doubt but that smoke would stay behind as much as the air itself; the flies also and the gnats, being hindered by the air, would not be able to follow the motion of the ship if they were separated at any distance from it; but keeping near thereto, because the ship itself... carries along with it part of the nearest air, they would follow the ship without any pains or difficulty.[70]

It may be true that the medieval theorists of impetus had a conception of the principle of inertia that wasn't much inferior to Galileo's. But true is as well that they never employed it to support the Copernican system because in their day that system just didn't exist. In other words, Galileo occupies so prominent a place in history not only because of his very considerable objective accomplishments but also because he so happened to live in a time when these accomplishments could strike at tradition with maximal force.

This latter assessment is valid as well and in particular in respect of Galileo's seminal contributions to observational astronomy. For here again we see how the impact of his work was powerfully amplified by the larger Copernican historical context. Galileo's involvement with astronomy began in 1609, when he was distracted from his inquiries into the laws of motion by rumors spreading from the Netherlands concerning the invention of a spyglass that reportedly magnified faraway objects and brought them into closer view.[71] Inspired by the news, he immediately set out to build his own, vastly improved version of the instrument and presented it to the Venetian Senate for its potential in military applications. Later the same year, he pointed his telescope at the night sky and there made discoveries that were to attract the attention of all of Europe. On the Moon he saw a surface scarred by craters rather than the smooth heavenly perfection predicted by Aristotle. Looking at Jupiter, he was most amazed to find the giant planet circled by four smaller ones—the moons of Jupiter—in blatant contradiction to the traditional view that all celestial bodies must revolve about the Earth. On the Sun he detected moving spots that indicated a rotational motion seemingly akin to that which Copernicus had imparted to the Earth. And the Planet Venus he found to alter its appearance through a crescent cycle in ways that could not be accounted for under the assumption of a central Earth, thus providing further strong support for the Copernican system.

When Galileo published his spectacular discoveries in the *Starry Messenger*, in 1610, the issue of Copernicanism suddenly attracted greater public interest and was no longer confined to esoteric debates among astronomers. It was at this point also that opposing voices in the Catholic Church were raised with greater frequency and determination. To bolster their case the critics quoted from the *Book of Joshua*, wherein God intervenes to halt a moving sun, and also from the *Psalms:* "He set the earth on its foundation so that it can never be moved."[72] In 1614, a particularly vicious attack was led by a young Florentine priest, Tommaso Caccini by name, who denounced Galileo and his followers from his pulpit as "practitioners of diabolical arts" and "enemies of true religion."[73] As a faithful Catholic, Galileo was deeply troubled by these accusations, for he considered heresy a crime "more abhorrent than death itself."[74] In a letter to a former student of his he asserted the absolute veracity of biblical revelation and "added that, though Scripture cannot err, its expounders are liable to err in many ways... when they would base themselves always on the literal meaning of the words."[75]

The causes of the Catholic opposition to Copernicanism are not easily identified. In individual cases an overly zealous insistence on biblical literalism and suspicion of secular learning certainly played a role, but such intellectual poverty is not inherently a Catholic tradition. Afterall, in her long scholarly history, the Roman Church had been flexible enough to accommodate the theological systems of such authentic great thinkers as St. Augustine and St. Thomas Aquinas—and the latter in particular can hardly be accused of anti-intellectualism in matters of science. Furthermore, in speaking of biblical literalism, it is instructive to note that Aquinas, much like Galileo, was willing to adjust his exegetical methods whenever he found the literal meaning of biblical texts to be at variance with reason. In the *Summa Theologica*, for instance, he states that a "theory [which] can be shown to be false by true reasons... cannot be held to be the sense of Holy Scripture."[II] And further on he observes that biblical authors like Moses were speaking to "ignorant persons" and had to be careful not to set before them "something beyond their knowledge."[76] Consequently, a scholar who probed a biblical passage at a deeper, non-literal level could well expect to find a deeper truth in it.

If at all, the charge of anti-intellectualism could be leveled against, not the Catholic establishment, but certain Protestant leaders who felt themselves

---

[II]The grammatical form in which this quote is here given makes it appear somewhat more general than in the original text. For the "theory" that Aquinas speaks of is a specific theory relating to a specific passage in the Book of Genesis. But since the quote in the given form appears to correctly represent Aquinas's exegetical attitude, the grammatical modification in question seems permissible.

called to defend the Christian faith against various forms of Catholic corruption, including all metaphorical or allegorical modes of Scripture interpretation. Martin Luther spoke of reason as the "devil's whore"[77] and accused Copernicus of foolishly contradicting Holy Writ;[78] and his fellow reformer and close associate, Philipp Melanchthon, is quoted as saying that

> [t]he eyes are witnesses that the heavens revolve in the space of twenty-four hours. But certain men, either from the love of novelty, or to make a display of ingenuity, have concluded that the earth moves; and they maintain that neither the eighth sphere nor the sun revolves... Now, it is a want of honesty and decency to assert such notions publicly, and the example is pernicious. It is the part of a good mind to accept the truth as revealed by God and acquiesce in it.[79]

By contrast, the initial Catholic reaction was rather restrained or even conducive. For as we saw previously (p.345), Pope Gregory XIII actually helped the new ideas gain respectability by basing his calendar reform on the Copernican system. However, in a time when Catholic authority was already challenged severely by the Protestant Reformation, the conservative forces within the Church eventually gained a stronger voice in opposing the revolutionary spirit of the new cosmology. A low point in this drive towards intolerance was reached during the reign of Pope Paul V (1605–1621) who set up a panel of expert consultors to determine once and for all whether the Copernican teaching could be reconciled with Catholic doctrine.

Galileo was present in Rome, in February 1616, when the cardinals of the Holy Office denounced the idea of a central Sun as not only "formally heretical"[80] in direct contradiction to Holy Scripture but also as "foolish and absurd."[81] The notion that the Earth is not immobile and not the center of the world was equally rejected as philosophically unsound and "erroneous in faith."[82] Having thus re-established by decree the order of the universe, the panel communicated its conclusions to the Holy Office of the Inquisition. On February 26, Galileo was taken to the Vatican where it was announced that the heliocentric doctrine could no longer be proclaimed a fact but only a hypothesis. Further on it was decided that Copernicus's treatise *On the Revolutions of the Heavenly Spheres* was to be placed on the Index of Prohibited Books.

Fate appeared to take a turn for the better when, in 1623, Galileo's longtime friend and admirer, Maffeo Cardinal Barberini, ascended to the See of Peter as Pope Urban VIII. Ironically though, it was under Urban's rule that Galileo was eventually tried and found guilty of heresy. In 1632, when Urban was involved in a struggle with Spain over the Thirty Years' War in Germany, Galileo attracted the pope's anger with the publication of his *Dialogue on the Great World Systems*, wherein he allowed the Aristotelian ignoramus, *Simplicio*, to expound Urban's philosophy of science. At the age of 68, with his health failing, Galileo was once again summoned to Rome—this time, however, not to be admonished but to face trial at the threat of death. After four hearings before the commissary general of the Holy Office of the Inquisition, the cardinal inquisitors announced the results of their deliberations on Wednesday, June 22, 1633:

> We say, pronounce, sentence, and declare that you, Galileo, by reason of the matters which have been detailed in the trial and which you have confessed already, have rendered yourself in the judgment of this Holy Office vehemently suspected of heresy, namely of having held and believed the doctrine which is false and contrary to the Sacred and Divine Scriptures, that the Sun is the center of the world and does not move from east to west and that the Earth moves and is not the center of the world; and that one may hold and defend as probable an opinion after it has been declared and defined contrary to Holy Scripture. Consequently, you have incurred all censures and penalties enjoined and promulgated by the sacred Canons and all particular and general laws against such delinquents. We are willing to absolve you from them provided that first, with a sincere and unfeigned faith, in our presence you abjure, curse and detest the said errors and heresies, and every other error and heresy contrary to the Catholic and Apostolic Church in the manner and form we will prescribe to you...[83]

Only seven of the ten inquisitors had signed this sentence when Galileo knelt before the tribunal in the "white robe of the penitent"[84] to abjure as required.

Within days of the verdict, a clemency request by the pope's nephew Francesco Cardinal Barberini was granted and Galileo was transferred "from the dungeons of the Holy Office to the Tuscan embassy in Rome."[85] Later the same year he was first entrusted "to the custody of the archbishop of Siena"[86] and then allowed to return to his home in Arcetri where he stayed under house arrest until his death on January 8, 1642.

Sophie: At least he wasn't burned at the stake like Bruno before him.
Philonous: You mean *Giordano* Bruno, I assume.
Sophie: Yes, he was publicly burned in Rome, in 1600, for being a Copernican.
Philonous: ...among other, more important 'heresies'. For the central 'crime' that Bruno was found guilty of was not his unflagging support for heliocentric astronomy but rather his deviant view concerning the sacraments and also his unsparing criticism of the Church's habitual and wholly un-Christian reliance on violence in suppressing opposing beliefs. His cosmological teachings were considered suspect but not so much because he endorsed the Copernican system but rather because he envisioned the universe to be infinite and home to a vast multitude of independent worlds.[87] In fact, the most offensive part in this regard was his attendant conclusion

that God was not strictly transcendent. For if the universe was infinite, so Bruno thought, then nothing could exist outside of it, not even God.

Sophie: I have heard this assessment before. But whatever the truth in this matter may be, the cruel inhumanity of Bruno's murderous inquisitors is bound to remain what it is: a hideous testament to religious perversity. Afterall, he was not only burned at the stake but also previously tortured.

Philonous: ...in the name of Jesus, the loving Redeemer.

Sophie: Which makes me wonder, I must say, how anyone today can still be a Catholic, or how for that matter the Catholic Church could ever have survived for as long as it did. There is no organization on the face of the earth that rivals that church in terms of longevity. But the two thousand years of her uninterrupted history are unfortunately, when looked at properly, two thousand years of continuous crimes.

Philonous: ...crimes that are too numerous to count and mostly too cruel to speak of. Just think of all the crusades, witch hunts, torture chambers, and also more recently, the child abuse scandals.

Sophie: I know—the record is grim.

Philonous: It's truly horrendous.

Sophie: Then let me ask again: why would anyone today still want to be Catholic?

Philonous: That's a legitimate question, but equally well you could ask why anyone today would still want to be British or French or Russian or Chinese. There is no human social entity—no church, no country, no state—that has been on the one hand large enough and old enough to encompass a sizable portion of human history and has been on the other not completely corrupt. Everywhere you look, human beings have treated their fellows with such exquisite brutality that I wouldn't even be able to imagine it, if it weren't for the fact that I am perfectly able to do just that.

Sophie: ...imagine it?

Philonous: That's right—I am not any better.

Sophie: Meaning, I suppose, that the image of the Church in history is more or less the image you see when you look in the mirror: good and evil are entwined.

Philonous: And thus, the question is not "why would anyone today still want to be Catholic or Russian or French?" but rather, somewhat redundantly, "why would anyone ever want to be human?"

Sophie: So what do you think?

Philonous: Well, consider the Church: on the one hand there is the Grand Inquisitor and on the other there is St. Francis of Assisi. By implication, the answer may be that, by being human, we are given a choice that may be worth making.

Sophie: That's the answer that Pico gave too (p.306).

Philonous: In essence it is.

Sophie: But does it really satisfy?

Philonous: Why would it not?

Sophie: Because what you are basically saying is this: the Catholic Church has an evil history, and since I am evil myself, I might as well join it. In other words and by the same token, I might as well join the Sicilian mafia.

Philonous: Except that St. Francis was not a mafiosi.

Sophie: You cling to St. Francis, let's speak of the Church.

Philonous: I am speaking of her, and I fully admit to all of her failings. The Church has always had profoundly disturbing tendencies—but so have you and so have I. Do I find in myself the intolerance, cruelty, and hate that it takes to be a venomous inquisitor? Absolutely! Could I in principle be Galileo's spiteful accuser and Bruno's merciless judge? The answer is "yes." But in admitting all that I merely acknowledge the obvious—and hardly do I thereby do justice to Catholic history in all its varied dimensions. St. Francis and Mother Teresa did not belong to a criminal syndicate, but they did belong to a church that was large enough and old enough to have witnessed among its numerous members numerous criminal acts. Moreover, you may have observed that burning witches and cardinal torturers are a little less common today than five hundred years ago, say. In other words, some progress has here been achieved.

Sophie: But that's because of secular influence. The Church has been civilized, not by the teachings of Christ, but by scientific Enlightenment forces. If it weren't for the fact that science destroyed the Church's worldview monopoly, we would still live in fear of Roman tribunals and papal despotic decrees.

Philonous: I cannot argue with that. The lessons of modern science have been for Christians in general and Catholics in particular a wholesome reminder that humility is a heavenly virtue that helps us guard against dogmatic overconfidence. But, having admitted as much, we also need to ask, for reasons of fairness, whether and to what extent modern scientists themselves have taken to heart the lessons they taught. Advances in cosmology, physics, and also in biology have all but swept away ancient doctrinal positions, and Scholastic appeals to Aristotle's time-honored writings have been superseded by systematic empirical inquiry. But have we thereby really gained freedom from dogma, or have we merely replaced the dogmas of the faith by the dogmas of science? It would be nice to think that the philosophers' stubborn refusal to recognize the synchronous fall of Galileo's cannon balls has served succeeding generations of scientists as a stern warning against the follies of prejudice. But I'm afraid that such is not the case.

Sophie: You made that point before.

Philonous: I did indeed.

Sophie: ...as for example when you commented that scientists today, who do not acknowledge the NDE body of evidence, act, as it were, no less absurdly than Galileo's Aristotelian detractors (p.150f).

Philonous: That's a typical case, but there are others besides.

Sophie: Such as?

Philonous: A striking one that comes to mind—and that even has to do with falling bodies—concerns a long-term study at Princeton University that was intended to assess the influence of consciousness on physical reality.

Sophie: In the realm of quantum mechanics?

Philonous: Not necessarily.

Sophie: Please elaborate.

Philonous: The Princeton Engineering Anomalies Research (PEAR) program was established in the spring of 1979 and remained in operation for twenty-eight years until February 2007. In order to understand its purpose and founding idea, it is helpful to look at some prior developments. The field of parapsychology, to which this program loosely belonged, traces its origins as an academic discipline to the late 1920s when J.B. and Louisa Rhine joined the Duke University Department of Psychology to undertake a rigorous empirical study of such purported psychic phenomena as extrasensory perception and psychokinesis. In some of their typical experiments the Rhines' asked selected individuals to identify sequences of geometric symbols on randomized cards or to influence mentally the roll of a die.[88] In assessing their work many years later, J.B. Rhine concluded that the outcomes obtained had been unmistakably positive:

> The phenomena that were being studied began to show lawful interrelations and even a degree of unity. One by one the major claims, based originally only on spontaneous human experiences, were subjected to laboratory test and experimentally verified.[89]

Sophie: Exactly what are those "claims" and what are the methods of testing?

Philonous: Concerning the experiments with dice, the basic claim would simply be that a person's willful intent can have an effect on how a die falls.

Sophie: So if I will a die to show a six, then a six it will show?

Philonous: Not every time, but on occasion it will.

Sophie: But that's a trivial assertion. Every die will show "on occasion" a six.

Philonous: Of course, but that's not the point. To see what I mean, consider the following simple example: suppose that a die is rolled 100 times and that it shows a 1, a 2, or a 3 fifty-two times. Would that be surprising?

Sophie: Given that the *expected* number of such outcomes evidently is $100 \cdot 3/6 = 50$, I will say "no, not one bit."

Philonous: And in that you are perfectly justified because the chance that the deviation from the expected value 50 is greater than or equal to 2 is larger than 75%. But how would you react if the number of rolls were increased from 100 to 10,000 and the corresponding number of outcomes equal to 1, 2, or 3 turned out to be 5,200?

Sophie: How would I react? I don't know. What about you?

Philonous: I would be very astonished indeed because the chance for that to happen (i.e., for the deviation from the expected number $10,000 \cdot 3/6 = 5000$ to be greater than or equal to 200) is significantly less than one in ten thousand.

Sophie: And, I assume, if the total number of rolls were increased even further from 10,000 to 1,000,000, let's say, the corresponding chance for getting 520,000 outcomes between 1 and 3 (i.e., a deviation from the mean of at least 20,000) would be smaller still.

Philonous: It would be almost nil. Furthermore, if only we increase that total number far enough, any bias that a person's conscious effort might induce, no matter how slight, will ultimately become detectable. That is to say, any systematic deviation from chance expectation will eventually become apparent with high probability.[III]

Sophie: Is that how the Rhines derived their conclusion? They had their subjects roll a die millions of times and then determined whether the outcomes obtained differed significantly, in statistical terms, from the outcomes expected?

Philonous: In principle, yes, but the problem evidently is that millions of rolls, in practical terms, are scarcely a feasible option. Moreover, the Rhines' experimental procedure was not only slow but also lacking in rigor. One obvious flaw was due to the fact that no die can be assumed to be perfectly unbiased, and another arose from the possibility that the counting of outcomes by hand was naturally error prone. The resulting data distortions were likely minute, but nonetheless potentially significant as the expected effects of conscious intent were thought to be tiny as well. A partial solution to these problems was found by a theoretical physicist, named Helmut Schmidt, who had been inspired by the Rhines' research to conduct his own psychokinetic experiments. Schmidt began his pertinent studies as a research fellow at Boeing in the mid nineteen-sixties and then joined the Rhines' laboratory at Duke, in 1970. The central thrust of his work was to improve the Rhines' protocol by objectifying the underlying random process. Instead of a die rolled by a human operator he employed a random number generator (RNG) that utilized the inherent quantum-mechanical randomness of radioactive decay. Furthermore, to run his experiments, Schmidt enlisted the help of prominent psychics whom he asked to either predict or consciously influence the output that his RNGs yielded.[90]

Sophie: So did he succeed?

Philonous: Indeed, his results were statistically highly significant, and he went on to publish them in various scientific and parapsychological journals.[91] However, the rate of data production, even in Schmidt's improved exper-

---

[III]The precise mathematical theorem from which this conclusion derives is known as the weak law of large numbers.

iments, was still very low, and his reliance on psychics could be criticized as being bizarre.

Sophie: In other words, the setup had to be further improved.

Philonous: And this is where our story returns to the program at Princeton and here in particular to a gifted young sophomore in the school of engineering who had recently chanced upon some of Schmidt's papers. Feeling deeply intrigued by the adventurous notion that human consciousness could perhaps directly affect a machine, this student decided to approach Robert Jahn, then dean of engineering at Princeton, with a proposal to independently verify the validity of Schmidt's empirical claims. After some initial hesitation, Jahn agreed to supervise a two-year undergraduate project but only on condition that the student would first conduct a thorough bibliographical search and manage to convince him that the topic at hand had sufficient provisional credibility to warrant its further pursuit. When the student completed this task, to Jahn's satisfaction, she was given permission to proceed and began to develop her own experimental designs. As the project progressed and was starting to yield some compelling results, Jahn found himself getting ever more deeply involved, making suggestions and giving advice.[92] At the end of two years of fruitful exploration the student concluded that the phenomena under investigation were real, but then moved on to graduate and abandoned her psychic research. Jahn, however, was left with a set of empirical data that had not only piqued his curiosity but also given him a growing sense of concern that modern technology's increasingly sensitive information processing systems might be vulnerable to the "effects suggested by [his student's] pilot experiments."[93]

Sophie: And thus he founded the program at Princeton.

Philonous: That is correct and sounds rather simple, but given the nature of the research involved, the problems that Jahn encountered in getting his program established were rather pronounced. In his book *Margins of Reality*,[94] which he co-authored with his principal PEAR collaborator, Brenda Dunne, he politely understates these problems as follows:

> The historical details of the genesis and evolution of this program, and of its interactions with the academic, industrial, and federal communities, could provide the material for yet another volume, but we cannot afford this excursion here. Let us simply note that the substance and style of this work have severely tested the sacred tenets of freedom of inquiry and humility in the face of experimental evidence that the scientific and academic communities have long espoused.

To give you an impression of the sort of resistance to novelty that Jahn and Dunne had to contend with, especially in academic circles, I should perhaps add that an editor of a "prominent science magazine" once agreed to publish a PEAR research report but then went on to insist that the manuscript be transmitted to him via telepathy.[95]

Sophie: What was the report concerning?

Philonous: The details I don't know, but I can say that PEAR research in general was meant to make more rigorous the prior work by Schmidt and the Rhines. One of the most prominent experiments that Jahn and Dunne conducted involved a type of RNG that may be best described as a microelectronic coin-tossing device. This machine randomly produced zeros and ones at such a high a rate[IV] that more data could be amassed in the PEAR laboratory during a single afternoon than the Rhines had collected in a lifetime.[97] It is this vastly superior rate of data acquisition that gave the Princeton study a statistcal base sufficiently solid for the certain detection of even the most delicate of anomalous phenomena. By the mid nineteen-eighties the RNGs at PEAR had recorded a total of nearly 700 million electronic coin flips[98]—with highly intriguing results.

Sophie: More intriguing than Schmidt's?

Philonous: More elaborate and also more broadly inclusive. For the greater volume of data generated at Princeton supported a far more discerning statistical analysis, and also made unnecessary Schmidt's controversial reliance on psychics. That is to say, the operators chosen by Jahn and Dunne were ordinary men and women without any claims to unusual paranormal abilities.

Sophie: So they placed these people one by one in front of some machine and then told them to affect it by their consciousness alone?

Philonous: I know it sounds ridiculous but that's exactly right. Each operator was instructed to affect the RNG output in accordance with three different forms of pre-recorded volition: increasing the number of ones (positive intent), increasing the number of zeros (negative intent), or leaving the output unchanged (neutral intent). Amazingly, these choices of intent did really make a difference. Again and again it was found that an RNG's average output would shift as operators changed their volitional attitude. Moreover, individual operators were found to have distinct effectual signatures: some achieved large shifts, others only small ones; some exerted symmetric effects,[V] others did not; for some the direction of the shift was opposite to their intent, for others it was in agreement; some achieved better results when choosing their intent freely, others did better when being instructed.[99] In fact, it even was observed that operator effects were dependent on gender[VI] and that pairs of operators could exert compound effects

---

[IV]To be precise, Jahn and Dunne refer to these machines as 'random event generators' and use the acronym REG rather than RNG.[96]

[V]By this it is meant that the effects for positive and negative intents were approximately equal.

[VI]According to Dunne, the effects exerted by males are more strongly correlated with pre-recorded intentions and also show a smaller statistical spread.[100]

that differed considerably from those produced by operators individually.[VII]
And finally, the supposedly neutral intent, which frequently did leave the
mean output invariant, turned out to be not entirely neutral afterall. For
the corresponding data set had a smaller than usual statistical spread. In
other words, the neutral intent somehow had a constraining influence in
that it lowered the output values' propensity to fluctuate.[102]

Sophie: In summary, what you are saying is that psychokinesis really is a well
established scientific fact. The human mind, by means of conscious intent,
can have a measurable influence on external physical systems.

Philonous: Indeed, this claim is very well supported by the data that the PEAR
program produced. Moreover, when considering the overall results of all the
various studies that have been conducted independently in different places
throughout the years, the evidence is truly overwhelming. Dean Radin, one
of the leading parapsychologists of our time, assesses the matter as follows:

> As decades passed, and as improvements in experimental design
> addressed testable criticisms, replications continued to show small
> but persistently successful outcomes. More sophisticated criticisms
> arose, and were resolved in subsequent studies, until today virtu-
> ally no serious criticisms remain for the best RNG experiments.
> Informed skeptics agree that something interesting is going on.[103]

Sophie: But given the resistance that the PEAR team had to face, this view is
very likely quite unpopular.

Philonous: Very likely, yes it is.

Sophie: And the reason is, as you might say, that scientists today are just as
stubbornly inflexible in the face of incontrovertible empirical evidence as
Galileo's Aristotelian opponents.

Philonous: There is no doubt that people are and always have been intensely
biased in favor of the status quo. In current-day scientific communities, this
bias takes the form of a very unfortunate reluctance to acknowledge any
kind of new phenomenon that cannot be neatly reduced to purely material
concepts. Any empirical fact or novel idea that threatens to dissolve or even
just to slightly indent the time-honored modern consensus that reality at
bottom is a black-and-white extract from sternly objective natural laws is
bound to be rejected and despised.

Sophie: But what about you? You're saying that people are biased in favor of
the scientific status quo. But aren't you perhaps equally biased *against* it?

Philonous: Of course I am biased, everyone is. But does it therefore follow
that everyone will try to suppress dissenting opinions?

Sophie: 'Suppress' is a strong word to use. Afterall, no one has put the PEAR

[VII]Here again, the operator's gender did play a role. Opposite-sex pairs achieved greater
effects than same-sex pairs, and in the former group the effects were greatest for pairs with
deep emotional bonds.[101]

team under house arrest or forced them to recant before a Roman tribunal.

Philonous: But in an academic environment in which non-private funding is largely conditional upon publication in mainstream peer-reviewed journals, the deliberate withholding of peer support is in effect a covert form of censorship. Brenda Dunne poignantly comments on this problem as follows:

> We have submitted our data for review to very good journals but no one would review it. We have been very open with our data. But how do you get peer review when you don't have peers?[104]

To me this is a travesty. I mean, here you have a group of highly qualified scientists doing excellent work with potentially profound implications, and no one is paying any attention. My point is not that specialized work in established fields is inherently inferior to grand new ideas. But there surely must be some room for exciting new data that puts into question some of our most cherished and most fundamental scientific beliefs.

Sophie: It sounds a little overstated, doesn't it? For even if it were the case that conscious intent can somehow exert a mysterious influence on RNG output, it wouldn't follow necessarily that science as a whole is therefore in need of revision. Afterall, the influence is marginal at best.

Philonous: It is marginal in absolute magnitude but conceivably vast in conceptual significance.

Sophie: What do you mean by "vast" when outputs shift by one in ten thousand bits?

Philonous: What is at issue here is not a minor abnormality or isolated oddity but rather a question of ultimate reality. Galileo and Newton taught us to think that the world as such is constituted upon objective external dependencies, called 'natural laws', that are mathematical in form and thus inherently completely unexcepting. But maybe this view is merely a plausible fiction—a useful approximation but not a final truth. Perhaps there are no absolute laws that govern the external because nothing is ever entirely external. According Jahn and Dunne, reality arises solely at the interface between a perceiving consciousness and its physical environment[105] (see also p.89). And they may have a point, for their studies affirm that the unlawful subjective particular of a consciously chosen volition is actively exerting an effect on that which we would commonly believe to be external and truly objective.

Sophie: But none of this is really all that surprising and novel. For didn't we already previously agree—in our discussion of quantum mechanics—that the notion of a discontinuous wave collapse requires for its coherent conceptual description an actively engaged, observing consciousness (p.89ff).

Philonous: We certainly did, but the PEAR results suggest a far more pervasive mind/matter connection that even extends to macroscopic everyday phenomena.

Sophie: But inasmuch as the random devices at PEAR were micro-electronic in nature, the distance to the quantum realm may not be as large as it seems.

Philonous: So your contention apparently is that conscious intent here comes to bear on individual electrons in RNG circuits because electrons, as quantum entities, are subject to the sort of wave collapse that consciousness supposedly effects.

Sophie: It vaguely makes sense, doesn't it?

Philonous: Very vaguely at best, because there is a twofold problem here: firstly, all currently known quantum formalisms are far too reductionistic for such an extravagant notion of mind/machine interaction to be plausibly modeled by any one of them;[VIII] and secondly, the PEAR research corroborates the claim that mental influence not only bears on microelectronic circuitry but also on genuinely macroscopic physical systems.

Sophie: ...such as a rolling die?

Philonous: ...or maybe a random mechanical cascade (RMC).

Sophie: A cascade?

Philonous: The specific RMC employed by Jahn and Dunne is a flat, box-shaped apparatus mounted vertically, in which 9000 polystyrene balls are funneled into an array of 330 nylon pegs (Figure 5.8). As the balls descend, they are randomly reflected off the pegs and off each other and are then collected into 19 parallel bins. Typically, the distribution that the balls produce approximates a bell-shaped Gaussian curve with a central peak right underneath the funnel. Operators watching the RMC from a comfortable couch in front of it try to mentally influence the descending balls so as to shift the distribution to the right (positive intent), to the left (negative intent), or to leave it unchanged (neutral intent).

Sophie: With positive results?[106]

Philonous: Indeed, the balls are found to be conditioned in their random descent not only by collisions and gravitational forces but also by an operator's inner mental attitude. By implication, we may rightly conjecture that even so simple a physical process as the falling of an object when we drop it, may not be truly independent and external afterall. For conceivably, no

---

[VIII] As a qualifying remark we wish to add to this assertion that there is in fact a mathematically well described quantum effect that conceivably allows for a concrete physical influence to be exerted by an observing consciousness upon subatomic quantum processes. In a paper entitled "The Zeno's Paradox in quantum theory" (see [MS]) B. Misra and C.G. Sudarshan argue that continuous observation of a potentially radioactive particle can prevent that particle from ever actually decaying. In applying this insight to the well known paradox of Schrödinger's cat the authors further suggest that the continuous conscious observation of that cat could be viewed as an observation of a given particle's state of decay and thus in turn prevent a decay from ever occurring. In order not to cause any misunderstandings, however, we need to emphasize that this latter suggestion is really just that, a suggestion, and that its presently proposed explanatory extension to the phenomena described by Jahn and Dunne has to be viewed as highly speculative.

Figure 5.8: the RMC at Princeton.

full account can wholly disregard all conscious interference.

Sophie: In other words, what makes a falling body fall—or at least, what slightly affects it—is not only gravity and frictional force (i.e., air resistance) but also subjective intent.

Philonous: And what is more, the law of gravitation may not be truly a law because it may not be truly objective.

Sophie: You raised that possibility before (p.129f).

Philonous: But this time I add some genuine empirical evidence. For it is the Princeton research that lends credibility to my former comment that natural laws may be at times "responsive to subjective conscious influence" (p.129).

Sophie: That credibility, though, is probably not very widely recognized.

Philonous: Certainly, the views that I have here put forth are bound to seem ridiculous in the eyes of many a mainstream natural scientist. However, as regards the related idea that the laws of nature are at bottom human mental constructs for which a true analogue in the so-called 'external' world does not exist, it is instructive to note that Max Planck, for instance, addressed this issue as follows:

> All ideas we form of the outer world are ultimately only reflections of our own perceptions. Can we logically set up against our self-consciousness a 'Nature' independent of it? Are not all so-called natural laws really nothing more or less than expedient rules with which we associate the run of our perceptions as exactly and conveniently as possible?[108]

Sophie: But even if the answer should be "yes," it doesn't follow at all that Planck would ever have believed that prayers to machines can be effective.

Philonous: Yet here again it is surprising to realize that some of the early pioneers of quantum mechanics were actually not as hard-headed as many of their less accomplished successors. Jahn and Dunne, for instance, comment on this issue as follows:

> Wolfgang Pauli's interest in mysticism and the occult led him to explore the influence of archetypal concepts in the development of physical theories.[109] Erwin Schrödinger's study of Eastern and Western philosophy prompted him to write extensively on mystical and metaphysical issues.[110] Werner Heisenberg developed new thrusts in the philosophy of science and its ethical and social applications.[111] Pascual Jordan speculated on the implications of modern physics for the comprehension of various psychic phenomena.[112] Eugene Wigner explicitly acknowledged the need to incorporate consciousness in physical theory.[113] Carl Friedrich von Weizsäcker proposed information as the fundamental currency of physics, and pondered the relationship between Eastern metaphysics and Western science.[114] And Albert Einstein frequently alluded to the bond between science and religion.[115] Beyond these varied personal interests, it is also notable that many of this group maintained cognizance of the contemporary parapsychological research then in progress at the Rhines' laboratory and commented upon it.

Sophie: Which goes to contradict, it seems, your earlier assertion that scientists today are just as stubbornly prejudiced as those notorious philosophers who couldn't be swayed by Galileo's cannon balls.

Philonous: Partly I agree, but I would like to qualify that openness to alternative patterns of thought appears to be more common among the truly innovative creators of a field than among those who later usurp it. Copernicus and Kepler, as we saw, were strongly influenced by Renaissance humanism and neo-Pythagorean mysticism; Newton considered his theological writings to be of greater import than his physical theories; and the case of the quantum pioneers has just been examined.

Sophie: So I suppose your own non-standard tendencies, when seen in this light, are really a mark of distinction—a badge of honor which you share with scientific giants of the past.

Philonous: You always find a way to accuse me of immodesty. But presently I really am just trying to suggest to you a less sterile, more colorful ontology. As I see it, the research at Princeton can help us mend the rift between the inner and the outer world by which the modern mind appears to be so heavily burdened. I understand, of course, that minimal mental effects on random electric devices are not emotionally stirring. But the related, broader idea that human consciousness is not a passive observer but rather an active "participant in the process of reality creation" (p.96) may well be said to be central to many a mystical experience and religious belief. In fact, you yourself once said, in this particular context, that "the loss of meaning that [you] suffer from could easily be overcome" if only you could make yourself believe that prayer for instance can be effective (p.127).

Sophie: It would make a difference, no doubt. But as you said yourself, your "minimal mental effects" are not exactly "stirring" and certainly do not impel me to infer that there exists a God who listens to my prayers and responds to them.

Philonous: Of course not, but the existence of rigorous statistical evidence in support of the claim that mind can influence matter may give a person's faith in the efficacy of meditation or prayer an admittedly limited but nonetheless valid empirical grounding. To me at least it matters quite a bit whether I imagine the world to be wholly conditioned by impersonal absolute laws or whether I instead believe that conscious experience, including my own, is somehow vitally a part of the reality equation. I find it fascinating to think that even the fall of a body in a gravitational field, this prototype of an objective physical process, may not be completely disjoint from me the conscious participant. Somehow my mind and the world are deeply connected. I don't understand it and I don't know how strong the link really is, but that it exists I do indeed believe.

The Dream of Perfect Clarity

Depending on a person's intellectual attitude or metaphysical taste, the phenomena discussed in the preceding dialogue may alternately appear to be intensely absorbing or totally irrelevant. The latter characterization can easily be justified by pointing to the minuscule absolute magnitude of the anomalous effects that Jahn and Dunne claim to have detected. And we also can argue, of course, that Philonous's attendant assertion, according to which tiny effects such as these are somehow indicative of a deeper mind/matter connection with concrete spiritual significance, is wholly unconvincing. Afterall, among religious believers, the efficacy of prayer is commonly ascribed, not to a tentative structural bond between material reality and consciousness, but to the purposeful action of God.

On the other hand, though, the seemingly miraculous nature of paranormal phenomena in general and psychokinesis in particular generates a distinct attentional pull that is hard to evade. The promise of mystery is strongly alluring. Yet why is that so, and wherein exactly lies the allure? At first sight it is tempting to think that the action at a distance of an elusive consciousness on 'solid' material objects—like balls in a random cascade—is so profoundly counterintuitive a notion that it cannot but leave us deeply intrigued. But the trouble here is that many a standard scientific conception, as gravity, say, or electricity, is ultimately no less perplexing. For there is nothing whatsoever obvious about the classical view that masses or charges attract or repel one another at a distance instantaneously,[1] and the competing relativistic or quantum-mechanical schemes of present-day physics are equally weird. That is to say, a gravitational force that objects *somehow* exert or a four-dimensional curvature effect that they *somehow* induce by virtue of having *some* inscrutable quality, that people call 'mass', is *a priori* just as odd as a volitional, macroscopic influence of mind upon matter.

A skeptic, of course, will likely object that it is one thing for matter to act upon matter in Newton's theory of gravity or Einstein's general relativity but that it is an altogether different thing for consciousness to do the same. For how in the world is an internal, subjective state of intent ever going to impose itself on that which is objective and external? The notion is silly in the extreme. And silly indeed it would be if it weren't so perfectly common. Afterall, in our modern age of science and technology we are surrounded by the wondrous *material* byproducts of human mental activity everywhere and always. A car, for instance, is first and foremost a secretion of human intelligence, and so is a phone, a computer, a fridge, a moon rocket, an atom bomb, and a large hadron collider. The common, almost by definition, is that which we deem unworthy of note or attention. But upon more careful reflection it is not only worthy of note but truly amazing to think that the ultimate outcome of the conscious mental activity of men like Copernicus, Kepler, Galileo, and Newton was the creation of a scientific civilization which, for better or worse, completely transformed the face of the earth. Copernicus envisioned a rearrangement of orbital circles, Kepler employed ellipses instead, Galileo proposed that projectiles move on parabolas, and Newton explained, by means of his calculus, why Galileo and Kepler had both been correct—and thus there was laid the mental foundation for an historical shift of global proportions. What better illustration for the efficacy of consciousness in physical reality could there be than such a sweeping real-world success?

Furthermore and quite apart from any atom bombs or hadron colliders, even the simplest bodily motion—the intentional movement of a hand, a leg, or a foot—gives evidence that conscious volition can very directly influence matter. It is true, of course, that the anomalies described by Jahn and Dunne are not compatible—at least not currently—with the prevailing reductionistic

---

[1]In the classical theory of electrostatics, the Coulomb force has, qualitatively, the same mathematical form as Newton's universal force of gravitation, and both are therefore descriptive of an instantaneous action at a distance. However, the more elaborate electrodynamical theory of Maxwell's also incorporates the concept of an electromagnetic wave that communicates electromagnetic effects, not instantaneously, but rather at the finite speed of light. In the present context, though, a discussion of such fine-point distinctions is completely unnecessary as all of the various concepts in question are ultimately equally counterintuitive.

paradigm of contemporary science.[II] But just the same is true as well of even the most ordinary willful locomotion. How does an act of volition trigger a flow of neuronal electricity that in the end brings forth a muscular contraction? No one knows.

As usual, one way to bypass this embarrassing fact is to deny consciousness its independent willful agency by willfully reducing it to a physical epiphenomenon. In other words, we can beat a retreat from dualism to materialistic monism and declare the conscious human self to be nothing but an animate discharge of cranial chemistry. Unfortunately, however, the cogency of such a crudely paradoxical view, according to which the animate is merely matter and hence inanimate, can hardly be said to be very impressive. This is not to say, of course, that such a crude belief is necessarily false but merely that it is crude.

Up to this point then, our various attempts to answer the question "wherein exactly lies the allure?" have come to very little: paranormal phenomena are counterintuitive, but so are scientific conceptions; actions of consciousness on matter are strange, but nonetheless common; and psychokinesis is impossible to reconcile with a reductionistic scientific perspective, but so too is any bodily motion that the human will initiates in everyday living. So why then are claims to psychic effects so routinely and so strongly divisive? How is it they are predictably met, among the scientific minded, with scorn and derision or total neglect, and among the spirit minded, equally predictably, with fervent approval? Is it really so much more silly or so much more amazing to think— depending on attitude—that the roll of a die could be subject to a conscious interference than that a moment of conscious inspiration, for example, could become physically manifest in a great work of art or a brilliant technological invention? Perhaps the answer is "yes" because the latter phenomenon, by a habit of perception, is construed to be consistent with the laws of nature whereas the former is not. But what law of nature is a moment of inspiration really consistent with? How do we propose to model it? What mathematical formula do we write down to capture it? Conceivably, consciousness interacts in such a moment of creative unrest with physical reality—as represented by an artist's or an innovator's brain—via a quantum wave collapse (see also p.89). But such a description would only pertain to the influence that a sudden inspiration can have upon matter—it would not in any way elucidate how the inspiration itself can be understood to be derivative of known physical laws.

And yet, we may be on to something here because a consciousness whose lawless action is confined to the inside of a skull may still seem rather handy. From a scientific point of view it can be comforting to think that the unspeak-

---

[II]Concerning this issue of compatibility with present-day scientific theories Jahn and Dunne have argued that quantum mechanics may serve as a blueprint for a model of consciousness that can accommodate anomalous phenomena.[107] But their pertinent conceptions are largely metaphorical in nature and therefore have little to no predictive potential.

able—the mind/matter interaction—happens in that one specific, well defined location—the material brain—and nowhere else outside. Somewhere deep inside the cranial circuitry the conscious mind asserts itself by causing myriads of quantum jumps. But other than that the physical world is truly external and truly self-contained. It is a world that smoothly evolves in strict accordance to natural laws and that therefore can be *fully comprehended*. At bottom, then, the vision that a scientist is eager to defend is one in which reality is split between a conscious inner world and an external realm of energy and matter.

A materialistic monist, of course, may argue in reply that this reality split is not actual but only an appearance as consciousness—in a monist's *mind*—is merely a chemical excretion. But even the most ardent proponent of such a mechanistic philosophy will not be able to explain, truly conclusively, how an aggregate of atoms, composing a brain and represented by symbols, can ever experience a vivid emotion or be inspired to create a great work of art. Monism can be asserted but never established and lived, and a solid core of voluntary or *involuntary* dualistic thinking is therefore bound to remain fully intact. In other words, the lawless domain of conscious volition is a stubborn, inordinate presence that no feat of scientific abstraction will ever remove.

By implication, the central modern dogma of the comprehensive reach of human reason can only be upheld if mind and matter are kept neatly distinct. For given the inherent rational opacity of consciousness, the word 'comprehensive' here can evidently only mean 'comprehensive in respect of the exterior, material world'. Put differently, we may say that the defining creed of modern natural science—the complete rational transparency of the realm of sensory perception—requires for its plausible assertion that the essential otherness and separateness of consciousness be antecedently affirmed. Only if the world of personal volition and experience is radically set apart can we ever hope to give a description of physical reality solely in terms of universal laws, that is, a description excluding all freakishly conscious particulars. And it is precisely this all-important assumption of the total otherness of consciousness that is violated in a queer paranormal world in which rudimentary prayers to a machine can be effective and in which gravitational forces can be compromised, no matter how slightly, by volitional influences which even may depend upon an operator's gender.

As long as consciousness exerts its unruly effects in a mediate and strictly localized fashion, via the human nervous system, the traditional worldview of science can be maintained. But once the lawless individuality of volition, intent, and emotion becomes *de*localized and begins to suffuse a supposedly lawful external domain with irreducible subjective disturbance, problems are bound to arise. For the scientific belief in the rational integrity and transparency of physical reality is seriously undermined if the physical is also the mental.[116]

In order for science as we know it to work, human consciousness must encounter the physical source of its own experience—the realm of sensory perception—as an alien land of universal laws that are wholly disjoint from the law-defying individuality that this consciousness in turn is constituted upon. The world of science therefore is a world that we can know but that cannot know us because its rules have nothing to do with us. Consequently, the allure of the miraculous or paranormal lies in the promise that the sharp dividing line between the inner and the outer world, along which the scientific world-view has been erected, can somehow be softened or partially pierced. What is at stake here is the earnest hope that rigorous empirical knowledge can be knowledge of a world to which we humans can be deeply connected—a world that isn't just sternly abiding by absolute laws, like a machine, but rather is open to manifold subject/object interconnections.

Once again we therefore see that the critical issue upon which our thoughts are converging is the modern disconnect between experience and meaning: sensory experience reveals to us by way of scientific analysis a lawful material universe to which a meaning relevant to human spiritual needs cannot be affixed—or so at least we come to think if the strict dualism of mind against matter is an axiom we accept. Historically, this dualistic vision—so evident in Plato's thought—was strongly reasserted and revitalized in the heyday of the Scientific Revolution by *René Descartes*, the rationalist par excellence who is widely considered the founder of modern philosophy.

Descartes was born on March 31st, 1596, into an old distinguished family at La Haye, in west-central France. His mother died within days of his birth, thus leaving the boy to the care of his father. Due to his fragile health, the young René spent most of his time in his father's home until, at the age of eight, he was sent to the Jesuit college of La Flèche. In the years that followed, he pursued his education eagerly, seeking "a clear and certain knowledge" of "all that is useful in life."[117] Yet by the time of graduation, he had grown disillusioned with the obscurity of traditional Scholastic learning[III] and found himself "embarrassed with so many doubts and errors that it seemed to [him] that the effort to instruct [himself] had no effect other than the increasing discovery of [his] own ignorance."[118] Among the various disciplines only mathematics could satisfy his longing for clarity and logical necessity. In his *Discourse on Method* he later wrote concerning this point:

> Most of all I was delighted with Mathematics because of the certainty of its demonstrations and the evidence of its reasoning; but I did not yet understand its true use, and, believing that it was of service only in the mechanical arts, I was astonished that, seeing how firm and solid was its basis, no loftier edifice had been reared thereupon.[119]

[III]The curriculum at La Flèche was aimed at integrating medieval Scholasticism with the classical learning of the Renaissance.

After completing his education at La Flèche, Descartes obtained a degree in law from the University of Poitiers, in 1616, and thereafter briefly immersed himself in the pleasures of social life. But with boredom setting in, he soon retired for another two years of study, this time dedicating himself to mathematics exclusively. At the end of this period he determined that a more thorough reading of "the great book of the world"[120] was needed to advance his understanding of the practical affairs of men; and thus he made up his mind to join the military and experience life as a soldier. In 1618, at the outbreak of the Thirty Years' War in Germany, he enlisted in the army of Prince Maurice of Nassau and a year later transferred his allegiance to the Duke of Bavaria. As an unpaid volunteer he was not exposed to the full rigors of military life and was able to set aside some time for reading and reflection. And so it happened, on a night in November, when his regiment was detained by the onset of winter in the small town of Ulm, that a nightly vision announced to him his destiny. In his diary we read:

> 10 Nov. 1619: I was filled with enthusiasm, discovered the foundation of a marvelous science, and at the same time my vocation was revealed to me.[121]

His vocation, it turned out, was to create a pristinely rational philosophy that would enable human reason to attain to perfect clarity and certainty of knowledge. Henceforth, he aspired to build a system of thought so solid and sure that no doubt could ever undo it. And since doubt could only be defeated, so he thought, if it was faced head-on, he resolved to do just that right at the outset: he imagined that his entire conscious experience—his perception, his thought, his memory—was nothing but an evil deception—a wicked display of trickery that a "malignant demon"[122] had slyly induced. But as he was thus toying with the thought "that there was nothing in all the world, that there was no heaven, no earth, that there were no minds, nor any bodies,"[123] he also came to realize that in the very act of doubting he had affirmed his own conscious existence: *cogito ergo sum*—I think therefore I am. It was this proclamation of self-awareness of the thinking subject that Descartes chose as his point of departure and ultimate anchor of truth. In radically isolating and setting apart his rational self he established the base from which the larger, surrounding reality could be rediscovered and reclaimed with rigorous certainty.

In his *Meditations*, the first step he takes in this process of deductive reconquest is to rationally ascertain the existence of God. To do so he notes to begin with that apart from his "clear and distinct" idea of his having his being in thought he also is equally clearly aware of a notion of Being that "is absolutely perfect, and infinite."[124] But whence did this notion arise? Did it arise in his mind? No it did not, Descartes concludes, because his mind is *finite* and thus cannot beget the infinite—not even as a conception. Similarly, it also did not arise from the exterior world that the senses portray—faithfully or falsely—for that world is finite as well. Consequently, the only option left open to him is to assume that the notion in question has its source in an actual, external Being that really is perfect and infinite. That is to say, it must have its source in a God who really is there.

Turning from the Creator to His creation, Descartes observes next that intrinsic to the idea of divine perfection is the virtue of absolute truthfulness. By implication, the created material world is not an illusion because God is not a deceiver. In other words, from the existence of God Descartes directly infers the objective existence of the exterior world.

It is doubtful, to say the least, whether 'demonstrations' such as these can really force belief. But what matters far more than the adequacy—or *in*adequacy—of the pertinent reasonings is the spirit that fostered them. For the Cartesian philosophical system is not so much convincing as a system in its own right as it is significant as a powerful vision that boldly announced the birth of a vibrant new era. Descartes's proof of the existence of God, for instance, had been given already in similar form by St. Anselm of Canterbury in the 11th century, and even his celebrated *cogito* was merely a rehash of Augustine's equally poignant *"si fallor, sum"* (p.258). But the fact that Descartes cleaned the slate, started from doubt, and then attempted to recover reality— including its divine creative source—in a lucidly rigorous, self-contained fashion was profoundly symbolic of the break with tradition and the proud assertion of human autonomy that the Scientific Revolution so saliently signified.

Descartes was a great philosopher whose greatest accomplishment was to author a dream. His desire was to clear away the rubble of stagnant tradition and groundless dogmatic opinion and thus to set the mind free to discover those authentic truths that self-imposed ignorance hitherto had obscured. If only the axioms are properly chosen and the method of discourse is sound, so he believed, the human mind will come to solve the ultimate riddles reality poses. If only we assume nothing false and break down a problem into its parts— methodically, carefully, precisely—so as to uncover its essence and mathematical base, then we really *can* know. True understanding *can* be achieved. This is the creed of modern reductionistic analysis, the high road of reason that leads to genuine insight and truth.

And indeed, can we not just abandon for once the folly of prejudice, purify our minds, clear our vision, and finally see what all of it is really all about? Can we not just break free from unreason at last and let in the light of rigorous, rational thought? We can, says Descartes, as long as we truly believe that the world that we see is a mathematical, mechanical system—a lawful machine whose workings are strictly reflexive. That is to say, we need to agree that black-and-white mathematical thinking really can grasp and capture the world as it is—except of course for that part of the world that really does the thinking: the rational mind of man. If we divide reality up into a substance that thinks and another, called 'matter', which we presume to be ruled by the mathematical laws that the former invents, then the former can know the latter by logical default.

It was thus that Descartes ventured to suppose "that the mind or soul of man is entirely different from the body"[125] and that only man's rational spirit can ever be truly alive. For in order for the body to be comprehensible it had to be a mere "machine"[126] by definition. It simply had to be if the Cartesian dream of perfect rational transparency was to be more than a wishful fantasy. Ultimately, then, what Descartes achieved was not to establish a method of rational conduct by means of which reality could be revealed, but rather to redefine reality so as to ensure that his reductive rational method could in fact reveal it.

Sophie: So the question he answered was not what the world, at bottom, is like—rational or irrational, normal or paranormal—but rather what it ought to be and must be like if the human mind is to be able to conquer it.

Philonous: That's not how Descartes would have put it, but yes, I agree. Descartes willfully cut the world in half in order to guarantee that the law-bound matter in one half is fully transparent to the minds that inhabit the other half. In consequence, he became the principal architect of the modern clockwork universe in which only reason is free and matter is wholly conditioned.

Sophie: If I'm not mistaken, he even went so far as to declare that animals— due to their lack of rational faculties—are wholly conditioned as well and are thus in essence are automata.

Philonous: Indeed, Descartes was rather unrelenting in his dualistic thinking. In his *Discourse on Method*, for instance, he claims that if there existed "machines, possessing the organs and outward form of a monkey or some other animal without reason, we should not have any means of ascertaining that they were not of the same nature as those animals."[127] And a little further on in the same work he notes that "natural movements which betray passions... may be imitated by machines as well as be manifested by animals."[128]

Sophie: In other words, a pig that's viciously beaten and therefore squeals is not to be pitied because its apparent expression of suffering is merely a mechanical reflex.

Philonous: I'm afraid you are right.

Sophie: The view is repulsive.

Philonous: ...but hardly surprising in light of current-day global realities. Afterall, in a time of widespread ecological destruction it surely behooves us not to consider coincidental the fact that modern philosophy traces its roots to a thinker who crudely mechanized and devitalized the natural world. This is not to say that Descartes was altogether an unpleasant character—he reportedly had "a kindly disposition" and treated his servants with generosity[129]—but merely that his overbearing desire for systematic consistency seriously impaired his judgment in this essential regard.

Sophie: But in tracing the roots of our present ecological plight, we mustn't forget that Christianity as well exerted—and exerts—a distinctly negative influence.[130] For it clearly doesn't help the environmental cause when the Christian God, in *Genesis*, calls upon His human offspring to "subdue"[131] the earth and to "rule" over animal life.[132]

Philonous: The wording, though, depends on the passage you look at. In the second creation account, for example, man is not to "subdue" but rather to "take care."[133] And in another verse in *Genesis* we read that "all the beasts of the earth" have "the breath of life"[135] in them—which evidently means they aren't mere machines. Moreover, the biblical notion of a divinely created natural world quite readily inspires the sort of universal respect for creaturely being that men like St. Francis and Schweitzer,[IV] for instance, so famously personified. But unfortunately, it also must be admitted, of course, that the religion called 'Christianity', in the minds of far too many of its misguided adherents, fostered an anthropocentric arrogance that proved to be environmentally extremely injurious. Dante for instance betrays this damaging attitude when he speaks of animals as being "detestable."[136]

Sophie: Which is ironic in light of Christ's teaching that any judgment you pass falls back on yourself.

Philonous: That point, I think, is very well taken. For instinctively, I always felt that people's strenuous efforts to widen the gulf that separates them from the animal kingdom only serve to reveal how close they sense themselves subconsciously to be to it. Just consider, for instance, how visitors in a zoo routinely devote especial attention to the animals that are biologically closest to them, like apes or baboons. The perceived behavioral crudities that these creatures display are laughed at precisely because they resemble so strikingly some of the visitors' own unflattering penchants.

Sophie: Such scenes I always found embarrassing. I remember well how even as a child the apes in particular struck me as stunningly man-like. A chimpanzee to me looked more akin to a severely retarded human being than an ordinary animal—and the laughter of the on-lookers seemed therefore downright disgraceful to me.

Philonous: My sentiments are similar. On the one hand I recognize, of course, that the differences between humans and apes are very pronounced, but on the other I also am awed by the astounding depth and breadth of anatomical and behavioral overlaps. In fact, when I look at myself in the mirror I easily get that strangely insistent impression that my 'distant' relations up in the trees are really close cousins.

Sophie: It's sobering, isn't it? Scientists say we descended from monkeys, but when you observe how humans behave, you have to wonder at times whether

---

[IV] In Schweitzer's ethic of the "reverence for life," as expounded in [Schw2], the extension of compassion from humans to animals plays a central role.

we ever descended. Worse still, the supposed descent may really have been what we call it—a descent—rather than an ascent, as we commonly fantasize. Afterall, consciousness, more often than not, does not alleviate our behavioral indignities but only makes them more glaring. And the pet-like indeterminacy of our human phenotype is scarcely what I call 'attractive'. That is to say, a civilized human, weakened by comfort and bloated by chronic indiscipline, had better think twice before he pokes fun at animal life.

Philonous: No doubt, the human condition is frequently deeply depraved. And even our highest good, the rational mind, serves often just, as Goethe wrote, to make us "beastlier than any beast."[134] But then again, it is precisely this specter of decadence, degeneracy, and self-inflicted lowliness that may on occasion impel us to try to transcend—to rise above all limiting circumstance and reach out for brighter horizons. In the final analysis, it was this desire to better the human lot that drove a man like Descartes, and other philosophers like him, to seek for salvation in reason. For it is one thing to crawl about in the mud, like a pig, but it is an altogether different thing to do so while being fully conscious of it.

Sophie: ...like some of us humans.

Philonous: That's right.

Sophie: But given your earlier, eager approval there really is no reason to transcend.

Philonous: My approval?

Sophie: ...of the crawling about. You advertised it recently as a welcome stage in your overall journey (p.328).

Philonous: But that view I came to adopt much later in life. It took me many years to see that my muddy stupidity was given to me with wholesome intent.

Sophie: Are you saying you weren't always as wise?

Philonous: Believe it or not, but as a young man, I still had that hope that somehow someday I would figure it out, get past my mental limitations, and master my life with rational certitude. The Cartesian dream of perfect clarity was still a promise I savored. And much like Descartes, I was deeply impressed with that ideal consistency and rationality that mathematics so brightly exemplifies. Originally, my leanings had been to theoretical physics, but when I encountered that subliminal, mathematical world of axioms, definitions, theorems, and necessary reasonings, I just couldn't resist—abstract mathematics had to be it. To those who never entered that realm of purified thought and absolute rigor, its alien austerity may seem forbidding and even revolting. But to the devotee who gets absorbed in it, there is revealed a beautiful mental domain, untouched by corruption and free of decay—a pristine intellectual landscape that no force of nature will ever erode.

Sophie: You speak with genuine passion of it.

Philonous: I do, but nowadays mainly in retrospect. I remember distinctly how powerfully affected I felt when the beauty of the axiomatic method was initially brought home to me. It was in my very first university course—an introduction for physicists to higher mathematics—that, starting from logic and sets, we built up the system of numbers from nothing but a handful of basic assumptions: the axioms of Peano. Proceeding with utmost precision, we first constructed the integers, then the rationals, the reals, the complex numbers, and finally even the entire analytic machine referred to as 'the calculus'. It was astonishing and deeply gratifying to see how so far-flung a scheme could be erected upon so tiny a base if only the method of inference was perfectly flawless and sound. At last, so it seemed, I had been presented with a system of thought that really made sense, was fully comprehensible, and truly transparent. Nothing was left unexplained, nothing was unclear, nothing uncertain. The axioms themselves, of course, were statements of faith, but the rest was necessity pure.

Sophie: It sounds appealing but also quite odd. Most people consider mathematics a subject that is unpleasantly impersonal, tediously technical, and confusingly abstract. You, on the other hand, attach to it attributes that are mostly aesthetic in kind and cheerful in tone: pristine, subliminal, pure.

Philonous: Mathematics is *im*personal as much as it is *super*personal and thus devoid of all the faults and defects that individual, material being so often is beset with. It is an anti-world to the actual world—a superbly ordered universe of elegant designs and harmonious relations that sharply contrasts with the inherent randomness and brokenness of our actual physical lives.

Sophie: It's just, I don't find that world that easy to enter. Its beauty may be alluring to those who can see it, but sadly, I can't.

Philonous: Actually, you *can*.

Sophie: See it?

Philonous: Yes, because there is a style in modern art that models that beauty in visual form. Are you familiar by any chance with the movement known as *De Stijl*?

Sophie: The one that *Piet Mondrian* led?

Philonous: "Co-led" is slightly more accurate.

Sophie: Well, I have seen some paintings of his, but I must say, I found them bizarre. For why would an artist of talent and skill, paint nothing but rectangles in primary colors enclosed by black lines? I don't understand it.

Philonous: The most fascinating part of his art was really the development it took. Mondrian started out as a fairly conventional painter of Dutch landscapes with alternatingly naturalistic and impressionistic leanings. But following his encounter with the art of the cubists—which prompted him to move to Paris in 1911—he began to pursue an ever more rigid form of abstraction. His painting of *The Red Tree*[V] of 1908–10 (which, according to the reproduction rules of the Mondrian/Holtzman trust, cannot be displayed in this book, but which can easily be viewed on the Internet) was still distinctly concrete in subject and style. But the topical restriction from a landscape to a single tree and the attendant emphasis on an elementary red/blue contrast (between the tree and its background) already signal that prominent drive to reduce—to simplify, and purify—that was to become Mondrian's trademark obsession. Furthermore, the densely worked sky between the tree's branches suggests a merging of foreground and background that in effect eliminates the illusion of space.

Sophie: ...which is a typical element in all cubist art.

Philonous: ...and some fauvistic art too. For at this stage in Mondrian's work, the influence most evident is the pure coloration and compositional flatness in the works of the fauvist Henri Matisse—rather than the analytic cubist reduction of Picasso and Braques. The latter theme, however, comes to the fore in *The Grey Tree* of 1911, and even more plainly in the painting of the *Flowering Apple Tree* of 1912 (see the Internet for both of these paintings). Here, the original three-dimensional object that provides the motif is completely merged with the background and thereby dissolved into a two-dimensional, cubist array of interlocking segments that are notably austere in color and shape.

Sophie: And in the *Composition No. II* of 1913 you can't even tell that there once was a tree (see the Internet again).

Philonous: That's because there probably wasn't one. The painting suggests "a cross motif"[137] by means of an uneven distribution of horizontal and vertical rectangles, but a representation of a concrete material object is no longer discernible. And it was precisely this path away from the particular, physical object that Mondrian followed with utmost resolve until the reduction was truly complete. What was left in the end was a perfectly purified world of geometric austerity that consisted of nothing but rectangular color fields enclosed by rigid straight lines—where 'color', of course, exclusively meant 'primary color'—red, yellow, and blue—or 'noncolor'—grey, white, and black. Ultimately, what Mondrian created was a minimalist universe of total abstraction and total mental repose. 'By abstracting one achieves," so he contended, "pure abstract plastic expression."[138] Thus he came to refer to his art as 'neo-plasticism'—a self-contained manifestation of human 'visual reason' without any reference point in external, material forms. In fact, as Mondrian astutely observed, there were no forms whatsoever, only relations:

The colored planes, as much by their position and dimension as by

---

[V]The correct full title is, *Avond: The Red Tree*, with 'avond' being the Dutch word for 'evening'.

the greater value given to color, plastically express only relationships and not forms.[139]

Sophie: But can there be content in absence of form? Exactly what is this 'art' supposed to accomplish?

Philonous: It is intended to make visible on canvas a rational absolute—a universal harmony of pure relatedness that nothing particular or individual soils.

Sophie: In other words, it is painted philosophy.

Philonous: Indeed, Mondrian was a philosopher who happened to paint.[VI] He was a prophet of modernity and a utopian pioneer whose ultimate goal was not to spread out colors on canvas but rather to fashion a completely new world.[140] Inspired by his theosophic belief in encompassing unity and lawfulness, Mondrian envisioned a future geometric "Eden"[141] in which man will be liberated from the burden of his unruly individuality by becoming a part of a resolutely purified environmental whole. Being "[n]othing in himself,"[142] man will be the glad inhabitant of neo-plastic cityscapes, buildings, and rooms, and he will find his happiness by being absorbed into these perfectly balanced exterior spaces.

Sophie: Is this supposed to be some kind of stoic world in red, yellow, and blue? A geometric paradise inhabited by denaturalized, square-shaped personas?

Philonous: I don't know, but Mondrian was certainly in earnest about it— and he certainly tried to live what he preached. His Paris apartment, for instance, he transformed, as it were, into a neo-plastic oasis (Figure 5.9). True to his own philosophy, he designed it with rigid, unyielding precision: every object—utensil, appliance, or piece of furniture—he painted in one of the primary colors or noncolors, and on the walls he arranged colored cards to directly match the rectangles in his signature paintings. A visitor to his studio once described her impressions as follows:

> The staircase was terrible; it looked awfully shabby. As was usual there, each landing had a toilet, and everyone made use of it. The front door was nothing special; just a wooden door. Between the front door and the studio there was a little vestibule and a dark corridor. Then you went through his door and suddenly there was a marvelous white studio with a color plane here and there. It was like stepping into a paradise. It made a deep impression on me. In my own house too, everything was suddenly white with stripes and planes.[143]

[VI]Most likely, Mondrian himself would not have agreed with this statement as he explicitly asserts in one of his essays that "Neo-Plastic was not born of calculation or philosophic reflection" (see [Mon1], p.238). However, the character of his art and especially also of his voluminous writings about his art is so distinctly cerebral and deeply reflective in kind that the description here given of him as "a philosopher who happened to paint" may rightly appear to be fitting.

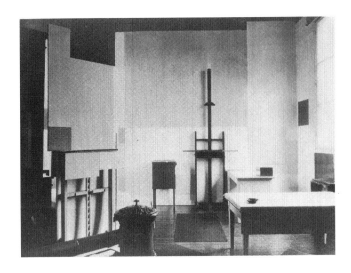

Figure 5.9: Studio of Piet Mondrian, 26 Rue du Départ, Paris. (Photograph by Paul Delbo, 1926, Original Gelatin Silverprint, Archive of Cesar Domela, RKD - Netherlands Institute for Art History, The Hague.)

Sophie: I cannot imagine to live like that.

Philonous: Like what?

Sophie: Like a square in a box.

Philonous: To be honest I can because I once did.

Sophie: You did? How so?

Philonous: It was during my student days, back in Berlin. I don't remember the details exactly, but it must have been in my second or third year that I somehow conceived the idea to treat my little apartment—or better, one room of it—to a minimalistic refurbishing. In fact, I wasn't so much inspired by Mondrian's studio design as by the Bauhaus concept of the *Gesamtkunstwerk*.[VII] But in essence the game was the same: I painted geometric compositions on the walls, built Bauhaus blinds for the windows, encased the furniture with colored paper, and even constructed a geometric lampshade.

Sophie: How did you like it?

Philonous: It was nice to look at for a while, but on the whole I found it a little too sterile to really get used to it. In this regard, by the way, my experience was fairly similar to that of César Domela, a friend of Modrian's, who couldn't quite handle it either. Here is how he recalls it:

[VII]This German word signifies a work of art that integrates into a whole various components from various fields of creative expressions, including most prominently, painting, sculpture, design, and architecture.

I met Mondrian by chance. Montparnasse was the neighborhood of
Paris where most of the artists lived at that time. In the evenings
they often went to Le Dôme and talked with each other about
the possibilities of getting exhibitions and so forth. Mondrian was
sitting there with some people and someone I knew introduced
me. He immediately invited me to come to his studio. From that
moment on we were friends. ...

You came directly through the door into the studio. There was a
little vestibule where you could hang your jacket. There were no
violent colors in the studio. Red, yellow, and blue were hardly to
be seen, only black and greys. ...

You couldn't imagine any woman and child in a Mondrian studio,
it wouldn't be possible. I made various Neo-Plastic interiors myself
in Berlin. They've all disappeared. I'd made my own apartment in
Berlin Neo-Plastic as well, but it's not a place to live in. We used
to meet each other in the café downstairs, as we couldn't stand it
there. You cannot live *in* a painting, only *with* a painting. When I
saw that it didn't work, I gave it up.[144]

Sophie: You couldn't imagine a woman in it?
Philonous: Mondrian never got married—just like Descartes.
Sophie: That's a point worth exploring, isn't it?
Philonous: Worth exploring? Why?
Sophie: Because it raises the question, "what about you?" Afterall, you also had
   once a neo-plastic room, and hence it is fitting to ask how many women—if
   any—inhabited *it*.
Philonous: My room?
Sophie: Or your apartment.
Philonous: I had some visitors from time to time, if that's what you mean.
Sophie: Not quite.
Philonous: It's not?
Sophie: No.
Philonous: So what you mean, more narrowly, is not visitors *per se*, but rather
   female companions in a more concrete, empirical sense.
Sophie: What I mean is women in the woman-sense—w-o-m-e-n.
Philonous: In that very sense?
Sophie: Pretty much.
Philonous: Let's see, if I add them all up, then—strictly speaking—there were...
Sophie: ...none.
Philonous: That's it—no women, no children, no pets.
Sophie: Do you think it possible that this had something to do with your
   eventual aversion to it?
Philonous: Aversion to my neo-plastic room?

Sophie: Yes.

Philonous: Let's say, I realized I'd made a mistake—philosophically and also reproductively. On the philosophical side...

Sophie: The reproductive side is more entertaining. Let's examine that first.

Philonous: But the two are closely entwined.

Sophie: First things first.

Philonous: Very well then on that latter side the problem I encountered was a palpable incongruence: reason and instinct don't match.

Sophie: In other words, the neo-plastic purity of your Bauhaus designs just didn't accommodate the earthy intents of your animal drives.

Philonous: It sounds a bit blunt—but yes, you are right.

Sophie: I can be more subtle if you wish, that is, if you wish to submit to some further revealing analysis.

Philonous: ...in the Cartesian tradition?

Sophie: Of course.

Philonous: In that case, I wish to say first that, in spite of your evident glee at my reproductive *past* predicaments, the issue at hand is only partly a matter for joking. For as I said before, against the backdrop of present-day ecological pathologies, we cannot consider trivial the fact that modern Western Civilization was founded upon a system of thought that aimed to mechanize nature and thus, in effect, to alienate man from his natural roots. Nor is it irrelevant from this point of view that modern architecture and design were heavily influenced by an artist like Mondrian who made denaturalization his foremost thematic concern. To be sure, mastery over animal instincts is something that all human beings need to achieve—to a certain extent; and there is also nothing inherently wrong, of course, with choosing to forego the pleasures and burdens of family life. But such mastery need not lead, as it did in Mondrian's case, to an active disdain for the animal-like,[145] and abstinence from marriage doesn't necessarily have to be justified with cynical views of spousal relations. That is to say, it is more than a little disturbing when Descartes, in this context, is quoted as saying that "a husband [who] weeps over a dead wife" still feels "in his innermost soul... a secret joy."[146]

Sophie: Did he really say that?

Philonous: So far as I know.

Sophie: And Mondrian? Did he also put forth such endearing opinions?

Philonous: Mondrian was described by those who knew him as a very decent man, very chaste and very modest—but also quite lonesome.[147] I am not aware of any hostile remarks of his concerning marriage. But he never had a family of his own, and on the whole, it seems, he was a city-life ascetic whose only personal indulgence was his interest in dancing. However, the point here is not to evaluate Mondrian's personal life, but rather to honestly investigate why reason and nature appear to be so often so difficult to reconcile. Why is it that reason seems to unfold such life-denying tendencies when reason is really a product of life? I myself have often felt that prolonged engagement in mathematical, problem-solving thinking has a strangely disorienting effect. It is as though there is induced an inner disconnect. As abstract reason begins to dominate, one suffers a loss of emotional grip. And, very tellingly, a like effect I also experienced while dwelling in my Bauhaus apartment. For here as well I had that same disquieting sense of becoming inwardly unhinged.

Sophie: But if the effects are akin, then so may be the causes.

Philonous: Indeed, Cartesian mathematical reason and neo-plastic artistic expression are structurally closely entwined. And the key to insight here is Mondrian's statement, according to which "the colored planes" in his works "express only relationships and not forms" (p.394). You see, in mathematics as well we don't define 'objects' by what they are but merely by how they relate to one another.

Sophie: We said as much before on various occasions (pp.55,170f,289ff).

Philonous: ...in various respects—I know. But the point is really crucial yet again. To see what I mean let's take a quick look at the concept of a counting number as established by the axioms of Peano. Surprisingly, the purpose of these axioms is not to define what a counting number is, in and of itself, but rather to abstractly assert the existence of a set—the set of counting numbers—the assumed properties of which characterize its elements only as parts of a whole—the whole of the set. We can try to picture a number, of course, as a point on a line. But what is a point? An infinitely small dot that really is a nothing-at-all.

Sophie: So a number is a 'no-thing' that is a something because it somehow relates to other 'no-things'.

Philonous: ...and the same may be said of the visual elements in Mondrian's paintings: they are 'no-things', defined only by how they relate to other 'no-things'. In fact, in such a denuded reality space, even man is "nothing in himself," as Mondrian explicitly states (p.395). For he as well assumes his significance only in relation to a whole. To my mind, Mondrian's utopian conception of a rationally reduced visual environment in which men can shed their "petty" individuality aims at nothing less than the rigorous aesthetic realization of the Cartesian intellectual dream. For where Descartes defined external reality to be mathematically representable—that is, to be in a one-to-one correspondence with a symbolic, relational void—Mondrian set out to actually transform that external domain into an image of precisely that void. In his studio Mondrian went so far as to paint even ashtrays and boxes of matches in either the primary colors or noncolors. Every object was thus denaturalized and deprived of its original individual identity. Descartes did not hesitate to reduce animals to mere machines in order to guarantee their representability, in principle, by wholly devitalized mathe-

matical symbols—and Mondrian, in following suit, tried to make that utter
devitalization directly apparent in visual form. The painted 'objects' in his
studio were really not objects at all but rather patches of color that derived
their existence from being related to other such patches.

Sophie: I wonder how he would have treated a pet. Painted it blue?

Philonous: The obvious answer here is that pets—painted or not—just cannot
be allowed to exist in a purified space in which every object is assigned a
stable compositional function.

Sophie: Which raises the further question as to why anyone would find such
rigid conditions appealing to live in.

Philonous: Ultimately, I think, the appeal lies in the promise of control. For
when I ask myself exactly what it was that made—and sometimes still
makes—mathematics and neo-plasticism so strongly attractive to me, it is
not only the aesthetic experience of absolute clarity that comes to mind
but also the sense that both of these worlds appear to be coherent wholes
that human reason can fully contain. It is this possibility of being rationally in control that Descartes boldly asserted in respect of the physical
world and that Mondrian, in turn, purposed to make directly apparent
by visual means. Reality in both of these systems is compressed into a
handy scheme that human beings can imagine themselves to be completely
in charge of. The entire material world, from a Cartesian reductive perspective, is a mathematical system that reason can penetrate, and the neo-
plastic universe, by virtue of its structural kinship, really looks as though
this perspective were true. As a matter of course, the desire for control as a
motivating force underlies not only neo-plasticism and Cartesian rationalism but also, for instance, positivistic empiricism, historical materialism,
religious fundamentalism, and a whole host of other such 'isms' that are all
equally narrow and dull. In the end, it really makes no difference whether
the illusion of knowledge and of being-in-charge is rational, aesthetic, or
religious in kind. For an illusion is an illusion regardless.

Sophie: A possible difference, though, could be that the rational illusion of
Descartes had some distinctly non-illusional side effects—such as the astounding vast success of the modern scientific quest.

Philonous: It could be indeed—as we will see in a moment.

Miraculous Insights

There is an anecdote told about Mondrian according to which he once spent
an entire afternoon sitting in front of a virgin white canvas unable to make
a single mark on it. Overwhelmed by the ideal purity of absolute whiteness
he could not bring himself to introduce the disturbing individuality of even
just a single stroke of his brush.[148] The story may or may not be true, but
that it could be true is readily apparent. For any fully consistent pursuit of

perfect clarity must needs arrive at utterly nondescript blankness. That is to say, the cleanest, most rarefied form of expression is always the absence of any expression whatever. Thus, we feel reminded here of Wittgenstein's assertion that "what can be said at all can be said clearly, and what cannot be talked about we must pass over in silence" (p.293)—because ultimately, *nothing* can be said clearly, and *nothing* is therefore worth being said.

Mathematics and neo-plasticism, as well as Wittgenstein's terminal philosophy, they all stop short of that absolute void to which they all inherently point. But they all get so very close to it that the human spirit instinctively senses in them the frightening pull of vacuum suction. The austere beauty that these domains so strikingly display is paid for with a life-negating loss of abundance from which the human soul cannot but shrink and recoil.

However, the fact that it recoils means very little from a modern 'objective' perspective. For in the modern mind, external reality is what it is and therefore is wholly detached from any emotions we like to project on it. Mathematics may be at bottom vacuous, but that does not imply its necessary incompleteness—it only implies that the reality it describes is probably vacuous too.

It is easy enough to criticize the mathematical reductionistic methods of present-day science for being philosophically crude, psychologically harmful, and spiritually destructive—much harder is to reconcile these supposed inadequacies with the splendid advances and triumphs to which these methods gave rise ever since they were devised in the 17th century. If science were merely a scholarly fancy—a natural philosophy, say, according to which the world is made up of fire or water or air or some other 'ultimate' stuff—we could confidently cast it aside and put in its place whatever belief we happen to find a little more cozy or pleasing. But such is not the case. Nor is it the case that modern science was embraced by its European creators solely because it suited their pride. To be sure, the fulfillment of the promise of control that modern science achieved entails the reality of power as a necessary consequence and thus invites arrogant, prideful abuse. But Copernicus was not so much arrogant as he was mostly correct in his thinking—and so were Kepler, Galileo, and Newton who followed him suit.

From our contemporary vantage point, from which the spiritual and ecological devastations wreaked by modern science and technology are all but blatantly apparent, it may be attractive to think that all these disturbances are due to a simple disconnect: reality and our scientific model of it are poorly matched. Hubris, as it were, has misled us to believe that science describes the world as it is, when in truth even our most advanced theoretical schemes are but a pitiful groping about in the dark. All we need to do, therefore, for our planet and our souls to regain their natural balance is to give up our epistemological presumption and sincerely repent of our rational overreach. If only we humbly admit how utterly empty all our knowledge finally is, harmony will be restored—without and within. Unfortunately, it isn't quite that simple. For while it is certainly true that in this world no one and nothing is perfect and that science in particular is fallible as well, it very probably is also true that the victims of the Black Death pandemic, for instance, would have been glad of a bit of that 'empty' and 'arrogant' knowledge that science comprises. It really might have made a difference for them if they had known that the bacterial agents causing the pestilence were spread by fleas that lived on rats. How many prayers were uselessly offered to God by those nameless millions that the bubonic plague randomly devoured? And how many lives could have been saved by simple hygenic measures if only the relevant scientific knowledge had been available and had been applied?

Similarly, the geometric austerity of Mondrian's art may readily appear emotionally chilling. But against the backdrop of the European witch hunts, for instance, *which truly came to an end only in the late 18th century*,[I] it also may appear to be a luminous symbol of hope—a visual statement of faith in the power of reason to conquer the darkness of blatant unreason and vile superstition. This is obviously not to say that Mondrian ever made reference in any of his writings to either the Inquisition or to its victims, but it is to say that he believed his neo-plastic art to be a beneficial force supporting human freedom.[II] According to Mondrian, art "enlighten[s] mankind" and aims to establish "complete life" in unity and equilibrium and "free from all oppression."[149] In other words and in summary, no matter how deep the hole may be that we are currently stuck in, the revealing light of history makes it easy to see why we dug it.

As a matter of course, none of this is to deny that there is a problem and that there has been loss. Alienation, spiritual emptiness, and utter absence of purpose are real phenomena with real-world effects. In our present age, even the most devout religious believers will find it difficult to muster the same sense of awe that the ancient Israelites probably felt at the sight of a rainbow. For even they cannot deny that rainbows are expressive of well known physical laws and that these laws in turn can also explain why the same phenomenon of spectral decomposition can be observed, for example, when sunlight strikes water that's sprayed by a garden hose. The sign of God's covenant, thus analyzed and reproduced, appears mundane and no longer inspires true reverence—and, yes, that may be considered a loss. But the fact simply is that the laws of refraction and reflection do indeed allow us to correctly predict, by way of the calculus, how rainbows are formed. It really works. It is not a delusion.

Hence it is time to finally give science its due and to recognize its power

---

[I]In fact, the last execution in Europe occurred in 1811, and in some non-Western countries, the practice continues to this day.

[II]In his essay *Liberation from Oppression in Art and Life* Mondrian writes concerning this point that "[a]rt is the expression of truth" (see [Mon2], p.328), and in another passage of the same essay we read that art "can invoke in us the conviction of existent truth" (see [Mon2], p.323).

and astonishing victories. And to do so, we will now go back in history and look at the developments that truly made apparent for the very first time the potential of science to capture reality in mathematical form. That is to say, we will examine next the miraculous insights that the greatest of all modern scientists, *Isaac Newton*, produced.

The beginnings of Newton's life were humble indeed.[150] The women who assisted at his birth, on Christmas Day 1642 (the year of Galileo's death), had little hope to see him live. He had been born prematurely and was so tiny as to fit "inside a quart pot."[151] Adding to the odds against survival was the poor health of his mother who still suffered from the shock of her husband's death three months prior. Further uncertainties loomed as the year 1642 had witnessed the outbreak of the English civil war. Some of the early battles between the armies of Charles I and the Roundheads under Oliver Cromwell were fought within a few miles of Woolsthorpe where the Newtons had their home. In the face of such adversities the little infant clung to life with a tenacity that bespoke a physical constitution on par with the future power of his intellect.

When Isaac was four his mother Hannah moved to the nearby town of Grantham where she married the Reverend Barnabas Smith. Soon thereafter, her son was left to the care of his grandmother, Margery Ayscough. But in the marriage agreement he was assured of a parcel of land that together with the inheritance from the paternal estate yielded an annual income of about £80. Upon the Reverend's death, in 1653, Hannah returned to Woolsthorpe, taking with her the three children she had borne her second husband.

In 1655, Isaac was sent off to attend King's School at Grantham where Henry Stokes was the headmaster. At first he showed little interest in his academic work and ranked second to last in his class. Instead of studying Latin and Greek, he preferred to amuse himself with mechanical contraptions of his own design. Dr. William Stukeley, a friend of Newton's in his later years, describes these early creative endeavors as follows:

> Every one that knew Sir Isaac, or have heard of him, recount the pregnancy of his parts when a boy, his strange inventions and extraordinary inclination for mechanics. That instead of playing among the other boys, when from school, he always busyed himself in making knicknacks and models of wood in many kinds: for which purpose he had got little saws, hatchets, hammers and a whole shop of tools, which he would use with great dexterity.[152]

The list of his inventions is long: "kites with lanterns to scare the credulous villagers,"[153] a water clock, a sundial, work boxes and toys, and, most intriguingly, a mill in which he placed a mouse to turn the wheels. "To pay a visit to Isaac's mouse miller"[154] quickly became popular among the townsfolk and the peasants from the surrounding countryside.

As for the boy's lamentable study habits, it may be said that it took a kick in the stomach to cure him of his laziness. For when a classmate once attacked him thus, he did not content himself with physical revenge, which he inflicted skillfully, but resolved as well to get the better of the bully academically. As it turned out, the feat was easily accomplished. For Isaac quickly left behind not only his attacker but all the other students too.[155] Impressed by the deed, Henry Stokes took note and recognized the lad to be endowed with talents far beyond the common.

At about the age of fifteen his mother called him back to Woolsthorpe to manage her estate, but, absentminded as he was, Isaac proved ill suited for the task. Stukeley notes:

> When at home if his mother ordered him into the fields to look after the sheep, the corn, or upon any rural employment, it went on very heavily through his manage. His chief delight was to sit under a tree, with a book in his hands, or to busy himself with his knife in cutting wood for models of somewhat or other that struck his fancy, or he would go to a running stream, and make little millwheels to put into the water... The dams, sluices and other hydrostatic experiments were his care without regarding the sheep, corn, or such matters under his charge, or even remembering dinnertime.[156]

All the same, however, his mother refused to listen at first when her brother, the Reverend William Ayscough, and Henry Stokes entreated her to send her son back to school in preparation for the university. In time, however, she relented and admitted that her son apparently was not cut out to live as a yeoman in Lincolnshire. Thus, in June 1662, after some additional work at Grantham and with his mother's consent, Isaac Newton was on his way to Cambridge.

During his first year at Trinity College he was tutored by Benjamin Pulleyn, a Regius Professor of Greek. True to the Scholastic tradition, the curriculum was largely aimed at the study of classical literature and Aristotelian philosophy. However, Newton's thirst for knowledge soon inspired him to independently explore the more recent, pioneering works of Copernicus, Brahe, Kepler, Galileo, and Descartes. In 1663, he stopped taking notes on Aristotle's *Organon* in his commonplace book and opened a new section which he chose to entitle *Quaestiones quaedam Philosophicae (Certain Questions Concerning Philosophy)*. On the top of the first page we find the following, momentous remark:

> Amicus Plato amicus Aristoteles magis amica veritas. (I am a friend of Plato, I am a friend of Aristotle, but truth is my greater friend.)[157]

His notebook shows that, by 1664, he had internalized the essence of the scientific method—the synthetical merging of rational analysis with experimental, empirical inquiry. Reason and observation, so he realized, must closely cooperate if the laws of nature are to be unlocked.

Moreover, since reason in science is predominantly pertaining to quantity, Newton now began to immerse himself more deeply in the study of mathematics. His forays into the field, however, were not as effortless as the magnitude of his genius might lead us to suspect. Starting with a book on trigonometry, he failed to understand the demonstrations and turned instead to Euclidean geometry. He covered the whole of Euclid's *Elements*, but it took a second reading before he really grasped the text's didactic purpose. Next on his list was Oughtred's *Clavis Mathematica*, "which he understood, though not entirely."[158] Upon taking up Descartes's *La Géométrie*, he only progressed in stages while repeatedly rereading the initial sections. Eventually, though, "he made himself master of the whole,"[159] and, in 1665, when the outbreak of the plague forced him to return to Woolsthorpe, his tireless efforts resulted in the creation of that universal computation scheme referred to as *the calculus*.

The plague years 1665–66 are known as Newton's *anni mirabiles*. In this short span of time, the better part of which he spent in isolation at his home,[III] he laid the foundations for all his major discoveries in optics, mathematics, physics, and celestial mechanics. Some fifty years later he recalled this period of frenzied mental activity in a memoir:

> In the beginning of the year 1665 I found the Method of approximating series and the Rule for reducing any dignity of any Binomial into such a series. The same year in May I found the method of Tangents of Gregory and Slusius, and in November had the direct method of fluxions and the next year in January had the Theory of Colours and in May following I had entrance to the inverse method of fluxions. And the same year I began to think of gravity extending to the orb of the Moon and having found out how to estimate the force with which [a] globe revolving within a sphere presses the surface of the sphere from Kepler's rule of the periodical times of the Planets being in sesquialterate proportion of their distances from the centres of their Orbs, I deduced that the forces which keep the Planets in their Orbs must [be] reciprocally as the squares of their distances from the centres about which they revolve: and thereby compared the force requisite to keep the Moon in her Orb with the force of gravity at the surface of the earth, and found them answer pretty nearly. All this was in the two plague years of 1665 and 1666. For in those days I was in the prime of my age of invention

---

[III]Newton apparently did not spend the full two years at his home in Lincolnshire, but returned to Cambridge between March 20 and late June 1666.

and minded Mathematics and Philosophy more than at any time since.[160]

Newton's mention of binomials in the first sentence refers to his derivation of the binomial theorem according to which, an expression of the form $(1+x)^{\alpha}$ can be written as an infinite sum of integer powers of x—an accomplishment, as one should add, that proved to be of utmost importance for the furture development of analytical theory and its application to problems in science. Furthermore, the "direct method of fluxions" that Newton alludes to next is the differential calculus, and the "inverse method" is the integral calculus.

As for the remaining, non-mathematical discoveries, the first among these is the "Theory of Colors," concerning which Newton performed his own independent experiments. In the process of his investigations he was led to conclude that a light ray's color is directly correlated with its refractivity, that is, its tendency to bend when entering a medium of greater optical density. In other words, what Newton here achieved was to establish the foundations of the science of spectroscopy.

Turning now from optics to the theory of gravity, there comes to mind to begin with that famous little tale of his regarding the apple that dropped from a tree.[IV] Supposedly, it was this humble event—the fall of an apple in his mother's backyard—that prompted his seminal pertinent thought that the force of gravity is not a local effect, confined to the Earth, but rather a *universal* attraction. When Newton saw the apple descend he somehow came to perceive that the force which pulled it to the ground could also be made to account for keeping the Moon on its orbit. And indeed, here as there the relevant motion is governed by an attractive force in the direction from the object in question to the Earth's center. At first, of course, this claim will seem implausible because the linear fall of an apple seems to have little to nothing in common with the Moon's revolving motion. But the puzzle can be solved if we recall how Galileo shrewdly dissected the movements of projectiles close to the Earth (p.366). For just as the parabolic path of a ball, let's say, that rolls off a platform, is traced out in the air as a constant-speed horizontal motion is overlaid with a uniformly accelerated, vertical fall, so the Moon's nearly circular orbit results as a radial gravitational acceleration, at any given moment in time, is superimposed upon a uniform linear motion along the orbital tangent line. That is to say, in either case the apparent bending of the trajectory away from either the horizontal or the tangential direction is caused by exactly the same kind of force—the Earth's gravitation.

Having thus understood the general nature of orbital motion, Newton went on to deduce, as he writes, "that the forces which keep the Planets in their

---

[IV]The variant tale according to which, the apple fell on his head is almost certainly a later invention. In fact, even the less striking account, given above, may not have truly a basis in fact—but then again it may, as a remark of Stukeley's suggests. A detailed discussion of this question can be found in [Chr], pp.77–83.

Orbs must [be] reciprocally as the squares of their distances from the centres about which they revolve." This law, which describes the force of gravitation quantitatively, can be obtained, as Newton indicates (in the quote on p.405), by combining Kepler's third law (p.46) with a general formula for the centripetal force that needs to be exerted in order to keep an object of a given mass revolving on a circular path at a given constant speed (see also the discussion on p.47). The details of his argument need not concern us here, but it is crucial for us to appreciate how enormous a shift this novel teaching signified, away from the ancient, Aristotelian conception. For the notion of a *universal* force that equally applies to all the motions in the cosmos completely eliminates the traditional distinction between celestial mechanics on the one hand and earth-bound physics on the other. This shift, of course, was strongly hinted at already earlier by Galileo's astronomical discoveries. But it is Newton and only Newton who stamps it with the seal of rigorous mathematical lawfulness—and it is he, thereby, who truly merges physics with astronomy and thus demystifies the heavens.

This move toward a unifying mathematical description of physical reality is further reinforced by Newton's formulation of the three fundamental laws of classical mechanics. The first of these is the law of inertia according to which, any force-free motion proceeds along a straight line in space at constant velocity;[V] the second asserts that force equals mass times acceleration;[VI] and the third one states that the force exerted by one object upon another is always countered by a directly opposing force of equal magnitude that the latter exerts on the former. Any object anywhere in the universe is subject to these laws— according to Newton. Whether we analyze the trajectories of stars in distant galaxies or the fall of an apple close to the Earth, it is always these laws to which we appeal.

In order to highlight the astonishing greatness of Newton's achievement, we also need to emphasize, yet again (pp.45f,114), that Newton actually applied the universal law of gravitation in conjunction with the second fundamental law of mechanics to theoretically establish the validity of Kepler's laws by means of certain calculus deductions. Using nothing but a couple of postulates, he managed to prove that the heavens were organized as Kepler had claimed. Never before in human history had such a feat been accomplished. Where Kepler had labored over table after table of observational data for more than twenty years, never certain where his next guess might lead him, Newton succeeded elegantly and brilliantly with the compelling force of rational inference alone.

In 1687 Newton's scientific career culminated in the publication of his mas-

---

[V] For the sake of accuracy we wish to mention that many historians of science assign authorship for this law to Descartes rather than Newton. And we also must not forget, of course, that Galileo had already stated this law in a more limited form for motions close to the earth.

[VI] More precisely, this law says that force equals the rate of change of momentum. The more familiar formulation given above is valid only if the mass of an object is constant.

terpiece, the *Philosophiae Naturalis Principia Mathematica*, also known more
simply as the *Principia*. In it he gave a detailed account of all his major discoveries in mathematics, physics, and astronomy and thus provided modern
science with a theoretical foundation of such unyielding solidity that even today the study of physics can never be divorced from it. The publication of the
Principia marked the apex of the Scientific Revolution and the mathematical
point of inception of the Age of Enlightenment.

In the light of this assessment it is more than a little surprising to learn
that Newton, in fact, did not consider the *Principia* to be his most important
accomplishment. Instead, he regarded more highly his voluminous writings on
theology and Church history. Newton was a man in search of the truth, but
he didn't limit that search to rational, empirical science. What he was after
was to uncover not only the mathematical laws that *govern* the cosmos but
also the soul that *indwells* it. Thus, strange as it may seem in retrospect, he
immersed himself deeply in the study of alchemy and obsessively searched "for
the philosopher's stone and the elixir of life."[161] When he moved to London,
in 1696, to assume a public office as Warden of the Mint, he stored many of
his writings on such matters in a chest that was passed on to his niece after his
death. In 1936, the renowned economist John Maynard Keynes reassembled
about half of the original contents and, having carefully studied them, arrived
at the following remarkable conclusion:

> In the eighteenth century and since, Newton came to be thought of
> as the first and greatest of the modern age of scientists, a rationalist,
> one who taught us to think on the lines of cold and untinctured
> reason.
>
> I do not see him in this light. I do not think that any one who has
> pored over the contents of that box which he packed up when he
> finally left Cambridge in 1696... can see him like that. Newton was
> not the first of the age of reason. He was the last of the magicians,
> the last of the Babylonians and Sumerians, the last great mind
> which looked out on the visible and intellectual world with the
> same eyes as those who began to build our intellectual inheritance
> rather less than 10,000 years ago. Isaac Newton, a posthumous
> child born with no father on Christmas Day, 1642, was the last
> wonder-child to whom the Magi could do sincere and appropriate
> homage.[162]

According to Keynes, Newton's interest in the occult receded when he began his administrative career upon moving to London. This move, in fact,
had been arranged by his friends who had become seriously concerned about
his mental condition. For in 1692, about three years after the death of his
mother, "to whom he was deeply attached," Newton had suffered "a severe
nervous breakdown."[163] Haunted by diffuse "fears of persecution"[164] and in-

cessant dark moods, his letters from the time testify to how disturbed his mind had become. Living in extreme inner isolation, fearful and deeply suspicious by temperament, his introspective quest for ultimate truth had finally exhausted his powers. The devil had tempted him to believe, as Keynes suggests, "that he could reach all the secrets of God and Nature by the pure"[165] strength of his intellect, and in failing to resist he came precariously close to losing his way in a mental abyss.

In the years that followed, however, he regained his inner balance as he dedicated himself wholeheartedly to his administrative duties and official functions. He was promoted from Warden to Master of the Mint in 1699, ascended to the presidency of the Royal Society in 1703, and was knighted by Queen Anne in 1705, at Trinity College. Regrettably, he also spent considerable time engaged in a "shameful squabble"[166] with Leibniz over priority regarding the discovery of the calculus. But on the whole his later years in London were a period when he presented the image that subsequent generations would remember of him: the patriarch of the Age of Reason, surpassing in fame every ruler and king and firmly enthroned in the great halls of genius.

In the early morning hours of March 20, 1727, the last of the magicians and foremost of modern scientists, the man who had lived a life of monastic abstinence committed to thought and duty alone, died at his home in Kensington at the age of eighty-four. On a tablet over the fireplace in the room where he was born, his miraculous insights into the workings of the cosmos are commemorated in the following words of Alexander Pope:

> Nature and Nature's laws lay hid in Night
> God said: Let Newton be! And all was Light.[167]

Philonous: The luminosity and brilliant elegance of Newton's conceptual designs have always left me profoundly astounded. Just picture how wondrously simple a world his system portrays: you set up three axes at pairwise right angles—one for each dimension of space—add in an axis for time, and then imagine all the world's material objects to be made up of pointlike components that carry each a certain mass and trace a certain path. As time progresses steadily on an absolute scale, the equally absolute spatial coordinates of any one masspoint undergo change in strict accordance with natural laws that fully describe the physical forces—future and past—to which that masspoint can be subjected due to the presence of other such masspoints.

Sophie: ...and hence the Newtonian rational world-machine.

Philonous: Indeed, what we here behold is a supremely ordered universe that humans, in principle, can perfectly know—a transparent material world that reason reveals to be totally causally closed.

Sophie: Strangely, though, the one place in which it wasn't quite closed was in Newton's own mind. For Newton thought, as I recall (p.235), that the actions of the force of gravity, which occur in his scheme at any distance instantaneously, are due to God and therefore caused *transcendently*.

Philonous: The context, though, is crucially important. For Newton's appeal to divine intervention was made in a time when Cartesian mechanist thinking was widely *en vogue*. In our day, in which quantum entanglement and the instantaneous action it implies are well established phenomena, Newton would likely not trouble himself with causal accounts. And in particular, he probably wouldn't invoke the action of God.

Sophie: Still, it strikes me as odd. And what is worse, there was another case where Newton called upon God for assistance: the solar system's structural stability. He didn't know how to argue mathematically why the mutually perturbing gravitational forces that the planets exert on one another did not compromise the long-term regularity of their orbital paths. And so he fancied yet again that God would kindly step in to directly effect the needed corrections.[VII]

Philonous: It is true, Newton was off in this case. But the more important point here is that, ultimately, the problem *could be* resolved within the system that Newton had built. He himself could not accomplish it, but the rapid improvement of analytic techniques in the 18th century—driven by men like Leonhard Euler (1707–1783) and Joseph Lagrange (1736–1813)—eventually supplied the tools to tackle the problem successfully. In the end, it fell to Pierre Simon Laplace (1749–1827)—the French Newton—to unravel the mystery. Using a method of variations devised by Lagrange, he managed to demonstrate that a planet's mean distance from the Sun will not change appreciably even as the other planets pull on it continuously over very long stretches of time. That is to say, the laws of motion even out the very disturbances that these laws in turn are the cause of.[169]

Sophie: Which goes to show how truly misguided Newton's appeal to divine intervention had been. In fact, there is a poignant anecdote according to which Laplace presented once a work of his to Napoleon, then ruler of France. When the latter had closely examined it, he reportedly said: "Newton in his works speaks of God. I have gone through yours, but find no mention of God." To this Laplace retorted: "Citizen First Consul, I found no need for that hypothesis."[170]

Philonous: It's a popular story, but so far as I know, the evidence supporting it is somewhat uncertain. Moreover, when Laplace was informed, near the end of his life, that the alleged interchange was to appear in print in a biographical encyclopedia he demanded its removal.[171]

Sophie: But his reply—given or not—was right on target regardless. Afterall, the planets do indeed remain on track for purely mathematical reasons. So why appeal to God?

[VII]According to Newton, "[t]his most beautiful system of the sun, planets, and comets, could only proceed by the counsel and domination of an intelligent and powerful Being."[168]

Philonous: In essence, I agree. Newton's God was a god of the gaps, and Laplace did well to discard him. Whether he did so pridefully or with pious regret may be uncertain but hardly is all that important. In respect of the larger history, the critical issue is not what personal attitude he chose to adopt but whether his theoretical insights were valid.

Sophie: ...and valid they certainly were.

Philonous: No doubt, Laplace's demonstration of the solar system's stability has stood the test of time.[VIII] It was a solid accomplishment that illustrated vividly, to Europeans at the time, how vast a progress in science was being achieved. Thanks to the work of exceptional thinkers like Euler, Lagrange, and Laplace, the power inherent in Newton's ideas was finally fully uncovered. What emerged in consequence was the specter of a singular, intellectual sea change—a radical reshaping of man's view of the cosmos and his own place therein. The rigorous application of pure mathematical reason to the description of observable, material reality—made possible and splendidly exemplified by Newtonian theoretical physics—had finally opened the door to dependable knowledge and genuine truth.

Sophie: And more was still to come.

Philonous: ...much more—the list of brilliant successes is long.

Sophie: ...and surely includes, close to the top, the case of *Le Verrier* and the discovery of Neptune.

Philonous: A perfect example, please elaborate.

Sophie: Late in the 18th century, astronomers noticed that the Planet Uranus did not adhere to its predicted trajectory—observation and theory were not in harmony. Attempts to explain the anomaly were quickly engaged in, but when progress could not be achieved, interest soon subsided. In the second and third decades of the 19th century, however, the problem re-emerged as new computations of Uranus's path revealed its distortion even more starkly. Speculations regarding the cause included an invisible Uranian satellite, a collision with a comet, an impeding interplanetary fluid, and even a bold suggestion that Newton's law of gravity might have to be modified for very large distances.[173] Apart from these, it seemed, there was but one other option: the perturbing attraction of an unknown planet in trans-Uranian space.

Philonous: Enter Monsieur Le Verrier.

Sophie: Indeed it fell to him, Urbain Jean Joseph Le Verrier (1811–1877), the great French astronomer, to accomplish the astonishing feat of computing indirectly the position and size of that conjectured new planet by carefully analyzing Uranus's deviant path.

Philonous: "Astonishing" is not the right word to use. The feat was *outrageous:* equipped with nothing but a handful of tables of anomalous data and a

---

[VIII]Later generations of astronomers modified and enriched Laplace's analysis, but the core of his achievement remains intact.[172]

theoretical system to bring to bear on them—the Newtonian scheme—Le Verrier was able to deduce the size and position of a solar satellite—the Planet Neptune—which until then had been but a phantom in thought. All he did in essence was to manipulate mathematical symbols on paper, and from among these encryptions there suddenly somehow emerged an actual material object that no one till then had ever observed.

Sophie: But observed it duly was when, on September 23, 1846, Johann Gottfried Galle, at the observatory in Berlin, directed his telescope at the precise position in the sky that Le Verrier had identified.[IX]

Philonous: "It was a discovery which almost took men's breath away for the moment in astonishment and admiration and showed that the age of intellectual giants cast in the mould of Newton and Laplace was not yet closed."[174] Those are the words by which the Scottish astronomer Charles Piazzi Smyth chose to commemorate Le Verrier's seminal deed at the occasion of the latter's death, in 1877. But the story doesn't end there. For even Le Verrier could not account for all the orbital anomalies that astronomers, in his day, had been aware of. The one stubborn problem that seemingly no one could solve was to explain the perihelion drift of Mercury's path. In fact, it was Le Verrier himself who was the first to conclude, in 1859, that the slow advance of Mercury's perihelion position was not consistent with Newtonian physics. And—not surprisingly—he came to think that here again the cause might be an undiscovered planet.[X]

Sophie: But this time, I suppose, his guess was mistaken.

Philonous: ...and so were a number of competing ideas put forth to explain the disturbance—such as for instance a deformity in the Sun's apparently spherical shape, a retarding influence of zodiacal light (or better of the particles from which that light is reflected), and again a potential defect in Newton's law of gravitation.[175]

Sophie: So how was the issue resolved?

Philonous: To answer that question, we need to change gears and enter the world of electrodynamics.

Sophie: Are you saying that Mercury is subject to fields that are electromagnetic in kind?

Philonous: Incidentally, that was another proposal made at the time,[176] but what I have in mind is something quite different: a fundamental shift in physical, conceptual thought.

Sophie: Please proceed, it sounds inviting.

[IX] The British astronomer John Couch Adams simultaneously worked on the same problem as Le Verrier, and claims have been made that, due to his efforts, that Neptune was discovered at the Cambridge Observatory about six weeks earlier than in Berlin. However, exactly what the truth in this matter may be is a question that we don't presume to be able to decide conclusively in this exposition.

[X] Alternatively, Le Verrier also proposed that the disturbance was perhaps caused by an inner asteroid belt close to the Sun.

Philonous: The story begins with one of history's great scientific pioneers: the British physicist Michael Faraday (1791–1867). Gifted with a keen intuition and prodigious experimental abilities, Faraday greatly advanced the study of electromagnetic phenomena in almost all its various aspects. But most significant in respect of our present train of thought is his work concerning magnetic induction and the theory of fields. In 1831, Faraday in essence discovered that a changing magnetic field causes a current to flow in an electric conductor[XI]—a fact, as we should add, upon which all electric engines and generators depend for their functioning.[XII] Years later, he attempted to ground this observation of his—along with other, related phenomena—in a larger unifying description. To do so he envisioned lines of flux that emanated from magnets and electric charges and extended into the space surrounding them. These lines are nowadays referred to as 'flow lines' and are commonly associated with magnetic or electric field vectors to which they run parallel. Furthermore, the law of induction— thus conceived more abstractly—asserts that any magnetic field vector at any point in space generates, by changing in time, a corresponding electric one.[XIII] Initially, this notion of a field of vectors existing in space was widely rejected. But in time, the skeptics relented.

Sophie: What caused them to retreat?

Philonous: The most important catalyst in this regard was the work of James Clerk Maxwell (1831–1879) concerning the foundations of electrodynamical theory. Relying heavily on Faraday's field concept, Maxwell was able to formulate, in 1861, four fundamental equations that together established this theory with perfect mathematical rigor. The first of them described Faraday's law of induction, the second Ampère's law, and the third and fourth are known as the electric and magnetic laws of Gauss, respectively. Without undue exaggeration we may say that these four equations, taken in conjunction, stand out as one of the most prominent landmarks in the entire world of science. They are as foundational to electromagnetism as Newton's laws to classical mechanics, and our knowledge of physics is centrally defined by them. In principle, every classical electromagnetic phenomenon can be deduced from these elemental equations.

[XI]In his pertinent experiment, Faraday found that a current flowing through an insulated wire that is wrapped around an iron ring briefly induces—at the moment when it starts to flow—a current in a second wire which is wrapped around the same ring at a different position. Incidentally, the same observation was made independently and slightly earlier, by Joseph Henry, but Faraday was the first to publish his results.

[XII]In the case of an engine the principle is in a sense reversed as the magnetic field is constant and the change in magnetic flux is produced as a loop-shaped conductor within that field starts to spin as an externally generated alternating current flows through it.

[XIII]More precisely, the law of induction asserts that the negative time derivative of the magnetic field vector equals the so-called curl of the electric field vector, the components of which are certain differences of products of the spatial derivatives of the electric field vector in turn.

Sophie: In other words, their scope is vast.

Philonous: ...as vast as their beauty is compelling. For the form that Maxwell's equations assume when describing a field in a vacuum is almost ideally symmetric. To be precise, though, it was only when Maxwell inserted a previously unknown term into the second of them—the one describing Ampère's law—that this near perfect symmetry became truly apparent. But here is the crux: when Maxwell combined this modified second equation with the first and then used the third and fourth to simplify the resulting expression, he was led to conclude that the components of the electric and magnetic field vectors individually satisfy a type of equation that mathematicians commonly use to model wave-like phenomena. Furthermore—as any such equation—Maxwell's *wave equation* specifies a certain speed at which the waves that it describes propagate through space—and, most amazingly, this speed turned out to be *the speed of light.* Put differently, what Maxwell here discovered is the fact that light is an electromagnetic phenomenon.

Sophie: The deed is impressive no doubt. But how does it follow from any of this that Mercury traces a deviant path?

Philonous: It doesn't follow yet.

Sophie: So what then are you getting at?

Philonous: Well, as we contemplate the fact that Maxwell's wave equation prescribes a certain propagation speed, we may feel prompted to inquire "*relative* to whom or what?" The equation itself simply asserts that electromagnetic waves move through vacuum space at the speed of light universally. But this is perplexing because the ordinary waves of our everyday experience always move in a medium, like water or air. And it is relative to this supporting medium that we determine their speed.

Sophie: So are you saying that the medium in this case is the vacuum?

Philonous: No, because the vacuum isn't much of a medium. Consequently, physicists came to believe that there was a mysterious massless substrate, called 'ether', that empty space was actually filled with.

Sophie: ...thereby rendering it nonempty.

Philonous: ...and thereby providing an absolute point of reference relative to which the speed of light was really the speed of light—and really assumed its specific numerical value of 300,000 kilometers per second.

Sophie: It seems to be a sensible idea.

Philonous: ...but it is not, for as it turned out, reality did not comply.

Sophie: Why not?

Philonous: To understand the issue properly, it is helpful to assume—for the sake of argument—that the ether substance does in fact exist. For then it evidently follows that the speed of light in the vacuum will be found to be 300,000 kilometers per second only by those observers who are at rest relative to that vacuum and to the ether therewith. All other observers will measure a greater or a smaller speed depending on their own state of motion. Afterall and by analogy, if I am in a moving train and throw a stone, then the velocity of the stone relative to a non-moving observer outside will equal the sum, or so it seems, of the velocities of the train and of the stone relative to the train.

Sophie: I certainly would think so.

Philonous: ...and so would I. But unfortunately, the story took an unexpected turn. For in 1887, the American physicists Albert Michelson and Robert Morely performed an experiment that was intended to demonstrate that measurements of the speed of light are indeed observer dependent. As their moving vehicle they used, not a train, but the Earth itself, and instead of a stone they used a beam of light. Remarkably, however, the variation in speed that they detected was so small as to very nearly fall within their experiment's margin of error.

Sophie: In other words, there really was no variation.

Philonous: That is correct, and later experiments confirmed this result with ever increasing precision.

Sophie: So what are we to make of it?

Philonous: Given the empirical evidence, we are forced to admit that speed-of-light measurements are observer invariant. No matter how I move, I always find the same constant value of 300,000 kilometers per second.

Sophie: The logic is sound but the physics is less than convincing.

Philonous: ...to put it very mildly, I would say. For in its consequence the claim that I just made is very confounding indeed: if I move relative to you, let's say, at a speed of 30 kilometers per second (which approximately equals the orbital speed of the Earth relative to the Sun) and send out a signal of light in the direction in which I am moving, then I will see the light advancing at a speed of 300,000 kilometers per second and so will you. Common sense, of course, suggests that if I measure 300,000 kilometers per second, then you will measure 300,030 kilometers per seconds.

Sophie: That is to say, the speeds are added.

Philonous: ...but they are not—and even worse, imagine now that my speed relative to you was very large or was in fact the speed of light.[XIV]

Sophie: So you are moving at the speed of light and so is the signal you send.

Philonous: ...relative to both of us.

Sophie: The signal?

Philonous: Indeed, the signal that I send is moving at the speed of light relative to both you *and* me.

Sophie: If that's the case, then relative to me, the signal and you are equally fast.

Philonous: ...and therefore, the distance between us will never increase.

[XIV] According to the laws of physics, any material object with a positive restmass, always moves at a rate strictly smaller than the speed of light. All the same, however, we have here chosen to consider this limiting case because it entails a more poignant conclusion.

Sophie: Between you and the signal?

Philonous: That's right, because if two objects—the signal and I—travel relative to you at equal velocities in equal directions then the distance between them, from your point of view, must remain constant.

Sophie: More precisely, it must remain zero because a constant distance that is zero at one time—when the signal is sent—can only be zero throughout.

Philonous: So how can this be? How can a signal move away from me at the speed of light and at the same time stay in place and not move at all?

Sophie: I don't know.

Philonous: ...but Einstein knew. For he concluded correctly that the only option left open here is to assume that in my world no time is passing. Once I reach the speed of light, time ceases to elapse, and where there is no time elapsing no distance can be ever be traveled even if the rate of travel is as large as the speed of light.

Sophie: There is no time?

Philonous: None whatsoever. From your point of view, my world has come to a temporal standstill. There is no conscious experience left that still connects me to this universe because I simply have reached the end of all being in time.

Sophie: In other words, you have reached eternity.

Philonous: ...from your point of view.

Sophie: But that's an amazing conclusion!

Philonous: ...and it leads us right into the heart of special relativity—the theory that Einstein created in 1905. What Einstein realized was that the observer invariance of the speed of light, as evidenced by the Michelson-Morely experiment, requires for its conceptual coherence a radical rethinking of the essential nature of time and space. Neither time nor space are absolute, as Newton thought, but radically relative to an observer's state of motion.

Sophie: ...and thus it really is the case that your watch stands still when relative to me you reach the speed of light?

Philonous: Not only that because—by symmetry—it also is the case that your watch stands still from my point of view!

Sophie: But my watch always keeps moving.

Philonous: ...from your point of view but not from mine.

Sophie: It's a bit perplexing, isn't it?

Philonous: Intuitively, "yes, it is," but mathematically, "no, not at all." There is no simpler theory in mathematical terms than special relativity. But even so I cannot here provide a detailed technical account. Instead, I'd like to highlight an intriguing consequence that comes about whenever that "perplexing" symmetry so happens to be broken.

Sophie: It can break?

Philonous: Very easily, for all that is required is that one of us does not maintain a constant-speed motion. For instance, if I fly off in a rocket ship, turn around, and then come back to Earth, then, in the process of turning around, I undergo a change in velocity and an element of absolute asymmetry is thereby introduced. In consequence we will find, upon my return, that more time has elapsed on your watch than on mine. In fact, the faster a rocket I choose, the greater that difference in time will turn out to be.

Sophie: How great is 'great'?

Philonous: As great as you please, if only the speed of the rocket is sufficiently close to 300,000 kilometers per second—the speed of light.

Sophie: So the difference in time could turn out to be two seconds, two days, or two million years?

Philonous: In principle, yes, it certainly could.

Sophie: By implication then, upon your arrival, it could be the case that I have grown grey hair while you are still as youthful as ever.

Philonous: That is correct. For temporal travel, according to physics, is a real world possibility that does in fact occur with almost every move we make in everyday life. For whenever two observers travel through space and time in an asymmetric fashion—as for instance when I walk about and you are at rest in your chair—their respective temporal paths are bound to be slightly unequal in length. As a matter of course, in everyday life the velocities involved are commonly so small compared to the speed of light that the corresponding time travel effects lie far below the threshold of detectability. But from all that we know they must be assumed to be real nonetheless.

Sophie: These are astonishing thoughts, I willingly admit, but the link to Mercury's orbital anomaly is still not anywhere apparent.

Philonous: But isn't it fascinating to see how strange a detour we have taken? From experiments with magnets and wires, conducted by Faraday, we moved to introduce the field concept, then came to realize—by way of Maxwell's equations—that light is an electromagnetic phenomenon, and from there we were led to conclude that temporal travel can be achieved by doing nothing more than walking about.

Sophie: The detour is strange, I agree. But what about Mercury?

Philonous: Well, since Mercury traces its orbital path in space and time, in accordance with the law of gravity, and since space and time were reconstrued in relativity to be observer dependent, it clearly behooves us to ask how this observer dependence in turn can be consistent with the action at a distance of Newton's gravitational force. The details here again we have to leave aside, but in the light of the fact that Newton's force of gravity is inversely proportional to the square of an absolute distance in absolute space (p.46) and that no distance in Einstein's relativity is ever absolute (because if time is relative then so is distance too), it may not be all that surprising to learn that a relativistic theory of Newtonian gravity is rather difficult to formulate.[XV]

[XV] One specific problem that here arises pertains to Einstein's photon concept, according to

Sophie: Meaning, I suppose, it simply doesn't work: gravity and relativity are not in harmony.

Philonous: ...and therefore Einstein decided—very courageously—that gravity must be revised. He believed in relativity and therefore could not believe in Newton's time honored system.

Sophie: Please proceed, it's getting quite absorbing.

Philonous: Glad to hear that, here we go: as Einstein began to address in earnest the problem of integrating gravity with relativity, there occurred to him, in the fall of 1907, an all-important thought concerning the relative nature of gravitational forces. In one of his manuscripts, Einstein describes this critical moment as follows:

> Then there occurred to me the 'glücklichste Gedanke meines Lebens,' the happiest thought of my life, in the following form. The gravitational field has only a relative existence in a way similar to the electric field generated by magnetoelectric induction. *Because for an observer falling freely from the roof of a house there exists*—at least in his immediate surroundings—*no gravitational field.* Indeed, if the observer drops some bodies then these remain relative to him in a state of rest or of uniform motion, independent of their particular chemical or physical nature (in this consideration the air resistance is, of course, ignored). The observer therefore has the right to interpret his state as 'at rest.'
>
> Because of this idea, the uncommonly peculiar experimental law that in the gravitational field all bodies fall with the same acceleration attained at once a deep physical meaning. Namely, if there were to exist just one single object that falls in the gravitational field in a way different from all others, then with its help the observer could realize that he is in a gravitational field and is falling in it. If such an object does not exist, however—as experience has shown with great accuracy—then the observer lacks any objective means of perceiving himself as falling in a gravitational field. Rather he has the right to consider his state as one of rest and his environment as field-free relative to gravitation.[178]

Sophie: Am I right in assuming that "the uncommonly peculiar experimental law" that Einstein here invokes is none other than the law of falling bodies?

Philonous: You are very right indeed.

---

which, radiation energy is broken up into discrete quanta that are proportional in magnitude to the radiation frequency. For since the frequency equals the number of wave oscillations per unit of time, and since time, as we saw, is observer dependent, it follows that radiation energy as well is relative rather than absolute. This observation taken by itself is not problematic, but when one attempts to integrate a special relativitic perspective with Newtonian gravity one readily finds that the sensitivity of radiation energy to relativistic transformation effects causes the law of the preservation of energy to be violated.

Sophie: Then what about this law is really so peculiar?

Philonous: ...the fact that our world depends on it for its overall spatiotemporal structure. If it weren't for this humble law—which Galileo discovered some four hundred years ago and which experience consistently confirms—the universe would not be shaped as it is.

Sophie: It sounds mysterious.

Philonous: ...because it really *is*. Just think how utterly weird it is that the mass in Newton's equation for force—$F = ma$—is also the mass that produces gravitation and reacts to it.

Sophie: I don't understand. Mass is mass—it's plain common sense.

Philonous: Are you familiar by any chance with Coulomb's law?

Sophie: The law that quantifies the force between two stationary charges?

Philonous: Indeed—the one that claims the force between two charges q and Q, separated by a distance R, to be proportional to the product qQ and inversely proportional to the square of R, that is, $F \sim qQ/R^2$.

Sophie: It's covered in physics in high school. But why do you mention it?

Philonous: Because its mathematical form very closely resembles the form of Newton's law describing gravitation: $F \sim mM/R^2$ (p.46). That is to say, in this law of Newton's, mass—or better *gravitational* mass—is akin to electrical charge. Material objects so happen to have a charge-like quality, called 'mass', that causes them to attract one another. By contrast, the *inertial* mass in the equation $F = ma$ has nothing charge-like about it at all. It is a quality that specifies how much an object will resist a change in its velocity. Put differently, the gravitational mass gives objects their weight. We feel it as a downward pull that keeps us on the ground as the mass of the earth attracts the mass of our body. But inertia on the other hand has nothing to do with any attraction whatever. It is descriptive of a type of mass that we encounter, for instance, when sitting in a car that presently accelerates. The backward push we sense as the car's velocity increases is not produced by gravity but rather by our body's natural resistance to changes in its state of motion.

Sophie: But your point precisely is that this distinction really is irrelevant as weight equals inertia, and inertia equals weight [XVI]

Philonous: That is correct[XVII] but in itself entirely non-obvious. For why would

---

[XVI]Strictly speaking, we can only say that the gravitational mass and the inertial mass are proportional. But the constant of proportionality depends on the units of measurement we choose and thus is basically irrelevant.

[XVII]The principle that every weight is or can be construed to be an intertia is, as we will see, absolutely central to the mathematical structure of Einstein's general theory of relativity. For without this principle it would be impossible to describe spacetime as a composite of segments that are each gravity-free and therefore special relativistic in nature. By contrast, the reverse assertion that every inertia is also a weight is essentially equivalent to the more speculative principle of Mach's to which Steven Weinberg for instance refers in his explanation that centrifugal forces can be viewed to be gravitational effects induced by the rotational motion of distant stars (see the quote on p.341 and also the footnote on the same page).

anyone expect a body's resistance to changes in velocity to be expressive
of a material quality that also generates a gravitational attraction like a
charge?

Sophie: I must admit, the way you put it, it seems odd.

Philonous: ...very odd—and very significant. For it is due entirely to this
identity of weight and inertia that falling bodies fall at equal rates. Afterall,
if the inertial m in the equation $F = ma$ equals the gravitational m in
Newton's pertinent law—$F \sim mM/R^2$—then, in replacing the F in the
latter relation by ma, we find that $ma \sim mM/R^2$, and therefore, $a \sim M/R^2$
after canceling m. In other words, the acceleration a is independent of m
and thus assumes the same value universally for all falling objects.

Sophie: ...and hence we find, as Einstein says, that an observer falling freely
in a gravitational field "lacks any objective means of perceiving himself as
falling."

Philonous: We do indeed. For imagine, for instance, a freely falling box to
which you are confined. How would you ever know that you in fact are
falling? Within the box you would experience absolute weightlessness as
you and the box—according to the law of falling bodies—would equally
accelerate (if air resistance can be strictly disregarded). And just the same
of course would be the case as well for any object in the box that you so
happen to observe. That is to say, in the total absence of any relative
motion within your box environment you really wouldn't know that free
fall is occurring.

Sophie: So for all practical purposes I would be gravity-free.

Philonous: That's right and that's the key: the free-fall motion from the point
of view of someone who is falling is inherently force-free. To be precise
we need to add that this conclusion only holds, as Einstein wrote, in an
observer's "immediate surroundings"—or, alternatively, in a gravitational
field that happens to be *constant*. To see why this restriction can't be
dropped, we only need to look, for instance, at the straight-line trajectories
of two freely falling observers in the globally non-constant field of the earth.
Since these trajectories, when fully extended, will intersect at the earth's
center, it is clear that the distance between the observers who travel on
them will steadily decrease. That is to say, the presence of a field will here
become manifest in a relative motion that draws the two observers closer to
each other. By contrast, in a constant field, the two trajectories will simply
run parallel, the two observers will remain at relative rest, and neither will
detect a gravitational effect.

Sophie: But why is this the key—the key to what?

Philonous: ...to giving the universe its geometric structure. Here is how it
works: a freely falling observer in a constant gravitational field experiences
a world that is completely gravity-free and thus completely described by
special relativity.

Sophie: I understand: where gravity is not perceived there also is no point in trying to describe it.

Philonous: But now consider an observer in this constant field who is not falling but at rest. Would he as well conclude that gravity does not exist?

Sophie: Of course not. For he would feel his body's weight.

Philonous: ...his weight or his inertia?

Sophie: His weight because it's gravity that acts on him.

Philonous: But how exactly does he know that? If he were in a box, could he not just as well believe that his apparent weight is an inertia that he feels because the box so happens to accelerate?

Sophie: In view of what we said, the answer is, "he could."

Philonous: By implication then, instead of asking how a constant gravitational field is to be modeled relativistically, we may simply get rid of the field and ask how an observer who undergoes a constant acceleration would experience space and time in a relativistic world in which gravity does not exist—and how, in particular, he would perceive the falling of an object.

Sophie: From what you have explained, it seems to me, the tables would be turned. For what we commonly consider to be an accelerated fall relative to a stationary observer in a gravitational field would here be re-construed to be a force-free motion that's observed by an accelerated observer in total absence of any gravitational forces.

Philonous: And since the latter case, as it turns out, can be quite easily described within the *special* theory of relativity, we really have now found the key to fashioning a *general* theory of relativity with which Newtonian gravity is properly revised. All we have left to do in essence is to account for the fact that fields of gravity in actuality are not constant globally but only locally and only approximately. Close to the surface of the earth, for instance, the gravitational acceleration is approximately constant and so is the field that causes it. But as we go up higher into space the field diminishes, and the acceleration accordingly grows weaker. Consequently, we are led to think of space and time in general as a patchwork, as it were, of individual gravitational pieces. Each piece represents a locally constant field and thus can be regarded, as we saw, as a segment in a gravity-free world that is perceived by an observer who accelerates at a corresponding constant rate. Mathematically speaking, this patchwork of pieces creates an encompassing geometric entity—a so-called manifold—that can be described by means of the concepts that Riemann devised in his groundbreaking work on the foundations of geometry (p.17). In adapting Riemann's computational tools to his own relativistic spacetime descriptions, Einstein was able to reinterpret the traditional notion of a gravitational force as a local geometric effect that the curvature of spacetime induces. The cosmos, according to Einstein, is a giant spacetime web that curves into higher dimensions. That is to say, where Newton envisioned a world in which masses generate attractions and respond to them, Einstein beheld a geometric universe in which masses produce curvature and curvature in turn produces the dynamic effects by which masses are guided along their spacetime trajectories. Furthermore, the gravitational field equations that Einstein derived in order to specify how masses induce the overall curvature structure are mathematically of such a kind that their essential form remains invariant under changes in the frame of reference or coordinate system that an observer uses to describe them. In fact, more globally it is the case, as we discussed (p.340), that not only the field equations themselves but all the laws of nature remain invariant in this specific mathematical sense. That is to say, *general* relativity is truly general in that it guarantees the observer invariance of all the laws of nature universally. In special relativity, this same invariance is valid only for observers whose velocity is constant. But in general relativity there is a deeper symmetry and uniformity that makes the laws of nature truly absolute by making spacetime truly relative and thus truly subjective.[179]

Sophie: The vision is astounding.

Philonous: Absolutely, yes it is. And who would ever have believed that we could get to it from Galileo's humble law by way of Faraday's experiments?

Sophie: No one, I assume, except for Albert Einstein.

Philonous: But even Einstein was more than a little amazed when he finally saw, after some ten years of labor, that his theory could be empirically verified. For in the late fall of 1915, Einstein was able to demonstrate that his revolutionary theory of gravity was sufficiently distinct in predictive terms from Newton's classical scheme to bring the perihelion drift of Mercury within the reach of theoretical explication. In the very strong gravitational field close to the Sun, where Mercury traces its path, the spacetime curvature effects of general relativity produce a planetary orbit that very nearly agrees with the one that astronomers actually observe in the sky. "For a few days" following this discovery Einstein "was beside [himself] with joyous excitement" and even experienced "palpitations of the heart."[180]

Sophie: I'm glad he survived it.

Philonous: ...and he was probably too. For otherwise he would have missed how another great test of his theory was carried out and completed successfully.

Sophie: What was the test concerning?

Philonous: The bending of light.

Sophie: The notion sounds familiar.

Philonous: It's a very well known but surprising effect: just imagine yet again an observer in a box which presently accelerates.

Sophie: So the box is an elevator simulating a field?

Philonous: Yes it is, but this time there is a window at the side through which there enters in a horizontal ray of light. What do you think the observer would see?

Sophie: A ray of light.

Philonous: Of course, but how would he perceive the ray to travel in the box? What path would it describe relative to him?

Sophie: It would go down because the box is moving upwards.

Philonous: That is correct, but more than that, it would go down and in the process *bend*. If the box were moving upwards at a *constant* rate, the light would simply travel downwards at an angle that is fixed. But as the box accelerates, the rate at which the ray appears to be descending would steadily increase. By implication then, the same will happen too within a box that is at rest in some surrounding field. For as we know, the latter and the former case are perfectly equivalent.

Sophie: In other words, the field will cause the light to fall like any other object.

Philonous: It is amazing, isn't it? An initially horizontal ray of light, when exposed to gravity, will drop to the ground like a waterfall—assuming that the distance it travels is long enough and gravity is strong enough. Naturally, the Earth's gravitational field is far too weak for this effect to manifest. But light from distant stars that passes close to the Sun may very well be sufficiently affected for measurements on Earth to reveal its gravitational deflection. In fact, it was precisely such a measurement, conducted in 1919 during a solar eclipse on the West African island of Principe, that gave another piece of evidence for the correctness of Einstein's revolutionary theory. The expedition to Principe was led by Sir Arthur Eddington, and when the results were announced to be positive, Einstein became an international celebrity and popular science phenomenon of the very first rank—a living legend of utmost, Newtonian acclaim.

Sophie: ...and all because he understood the law of falling bodies.

Philonous: That's right, only he had truly understood it, and only he had truly had the vision and the courage to elaborate its deepest implications. In the brilliance of Einstein's achievement science ascended to lofty new heights and thereby established itself—once and for all—as a powerful worldview that no one should ever attempt to push aside lightly. By implication, the lesson for us can only be this: if ever we are to integrate the scientific account of reality into a larger, more wholesome perspective, we really need to leave completely untouched the solid core of truth that science undoubtedly harbors.

A World Without Substance

The success of modern physical science, to which the preceding discussion so amply testifies, rests on two central pillars: mathematical rational analysis and experimental empirical inquiry. In order for knowledge to properly flourish, reason must be brought to bear on the facts of observation, and observation in turn must be inspired by the concepts and insights that reason supplies. A case in point here is the succession of advances that led from Faraday's empirical studies by way of the field concept and Maxwell's wave equation to the invariance experiments of Michelson and Morely and on from there to Einstein's theory of relativity. It is this critical interplay of conceptual thought and controlled observation that defines the essence of the scientific method.

By implication, it is little surprising to learn that a corresponding dual thrust was prominently evident in late Renaissance and early modern epistemological thought. On the Continent, it was René Descartes who, as we saw, endeavored to establish modern science on rational mathematical grounds; and some decades prior, in England, the empirical component of scientific knowledge had been eloquently emphasized by *Francis Bacon* (1561–1626), an ambitious politician and prominent statesman for whom science and philosophy were mostly and merely sparetime pursuits.

The works of Bacon, much like those of Descartes, exhude the spirit of a fresh new beginning—an original quest for true understanding that promises to bring about a better, more prosperous age of science and reason.[181] The procurement of knowledge and the promotion of learning, according to Bacon, are the two most vital means by which the human race progresses. But both of these must be extensively refashioned and improved before they can bestow their fullest benefit. Grandiose conjecturings and "specious meditations"[182] have to be abandoned and supplanted with a careful method of "genuine induction"[183] which step by step ascends from observational particulars to higher-order conceptual constructs.

Thus we find that Bacon, as Descartes, was filled with a nagging discontent at the rational sterility of the late Scholastic tradition. In his treatise on the *Advancement of Learning* he accuses the "schoolmen" of "unprofitable subtility,"[184] narrow-mindedness, and intellectual degeneracy.[185] Moreover, his comments upon the ancient Greek authorities are almost equally scathing. Plato and Aristotle, for instance, he criticizes severely for corrupting philosophy[186] by favoring logical argument and theological abstraction over a careful and unprejudiced appraisal of the facts. These leaders of the past, while speculating groundlessly on first principles and final causations, neglected woefully the systematic search for those "real and physical causes"[187] which alone can be of practical importance.

Against the obstructing influence of ancient and medieval traditions, Bacon sets up a novel epistemological doctrine whose purpose is to free the human mind from its inherent tendency to indulge "false notions" and to cling to cognitive "idols."[188] Human reason by nature is weak and easily succumbs to fallacy. Thus it must be guided by a *method* that is so designed that the very act of faithfully adhering to it produces dependable knowledge of needs.

Most famously and most effectively Bacon develops his pertinent thoughts in the first book of the *New Organon*, or *Novum Organum*—so titled to allude to the Aristotelian *Organon* which Bacon sought to supplant. On the second page we read:

There are and can exist but two ways of investigating and discovering truth. The one hurries on rapidly from the senses and particulars to the most general axioms, and from them, as principles and their supposed indisputable truth, derives and discovers the intermediate axioms. This is the way now in use. The other constructs its axioms from the senses and particulars, by ascending continually and gradually, till it finally arrives at the most general axioms, which is the true but unattempted way.[189]

And some sections further down we find the notable demand to shun "the whirl and confusion of argument"[190] and to pursue instead "a regulated and digested... course of experiment."[191] Axioms, according to Bacon, are to be introduced incrementally in response to experiments, and experiments in turn are to be suggested by axioms.[192]

In view of these remarks, it may be rightly said that the rapid rise of modern science, in consequence of Newton's seminal advance, marked the fulfillment of a dual epistemological prophecy that Bacon and Descartes had independently authored. For both of these two pioneers had acutely foreseen the stunning powers that unfold when reason is guided by *method*. However, we also must not overlook the differences that here exist between the deductive rationalism of Descartes and the more pragmatic, empirical outlook of Bacon. Knowledge in this latter view is less axiomatic and also less abstract. It serves the practical end to expand the human dominion[193] and never strays far from observable facts.

Interestingly, this focus on the facts—which always tends to undermine traditional beliefs—reveals a striking parallel to Bacon's medieval namesake, Roger Bacon, whom we encountered previously as a decided critic of blind adherence to authority and an early promoter of the free application of man's rational and sensory faculties (p.300). In fact, a similarly practical and independent attitude is characteristic of much or most of the British tradition of thought. We noticed it as well, for example, in the radical nominalism of William of Ockham (p.301); and, following Bacon, it led to that great flowering of empiricist philosophy in the late 17th and early 18th century that constituted the British contribution to the Age of Enlightenment. The most prominent thinkers of this later period were John Locke, George Berkeley, and David Hume.

Of these three, *John Locke* (1632–1704), perhaps, is most deserving of attention in the sense that he came first and thus was most original. However, given our larger integrative theme, it seems expedient to treat his system rather briefly and tangentially and also to highlight its faults more than its merits.

The argumentative starting point in Locke's *Essay concerning Human Understanding*—his most important work—is the assertion that there are no principles or "primary notions"[194] with which the human mind is innately equipped or imprinted. Consequently, all understanding—be it speculative or moral in

kind—is grounded in original *experience*. All bits of knowledge and all the
contents of the consciousness are derivative of observations "about external
sensible objects, or about the internal operations" that the intellect performs
on them.[195] There are no ideas or states of awareness that do not spring from
either one of these two sources: the direct perception of external phenomena
or the subsequent internal reflection on cognition itself. By implication, the
human mind at birth is a *tabula rasa* waiting for experience to activate its
powers of reception.[196]

Since Locke's intent, in taking this approach, was to elucidate the nature
of knowledge, we may here feel compelled to ask how knowledge grounded
in experience can ever be truly objective. What do we really come to know
when we rely, primarily, on sensory perception—the object in itself or merely
our own subjective image of it? In response Locke introduces two fundamental divisions: one between simple and complex ideas and another between
primary and secondary qualities. Simple ideas, according to Locke, are the uncompounded primitives or elemental building blocks of every perception and
thought. They can be neither created nor destroyed but are, instead, immediately given to us as irreducible particulars. The specific form they take may
be, for instance, a visual impression, a scent, a taste, an instance of thinking,
or an act of volition.

However, among these various primitives, and more especially, among those
that are rooted in sense, it is only certain ones that directly correspond to objective material qualities as only certain qualities are indeed truly objective.
Those that are, Locke refers to as 'primary qualities' and lists exhaustively
as number, solidity, extension, figure, and mobility.[197] Thus we may say, for
example, with Locke that objects are perceived to be solid and extended because these properties they really do possess—they really are solid and really
are extended. The perception and its source, in this case, directly resemble
each other. By contrast, an idea that a secondary quality produces in us—such
as for instance an awareness of a taste, a color, or a scent—has no objective
analogue whatever. There is something in an object, it is true, that causes the
sensation, say, of whiteness or sweetness, but that something is neither white
nor sweet. That is to say, no object ever has color or taste when unperceived,
but all objects have extension and solidity regardless of whether we so happen
to observe them.

It goes without saying that this latter conclusion is far from obvious. Extension is perceived by sight and so is color. So why then are we to infer that
objects are extended objectively but colored only in the mind? Is such a view
not starkly inconsistent? Moreover, a similar problem is evident as well in
Locke's treatment of ideas that are not simple but complex. Such compound
ideas, as Locke explains, can always be categorized as belonging to one of three
essential types: ideas of modes, of substances, and of relations. The details
of this classification scheme need not concern us here, but what is worth ob-

serving is that only the ideas of substances are thought "to represent distinct particular things subsisting by themselves."[198] For modes, by definition, are "dependences on, or affections of substances"[199] that precisely do *not* subsist in objects independently, and relations merely are pertaining to comparisons of ideas with one another. In other words and in summary, the link from knowledge to external physical reality in Locke's empiricist philosophy is more than a little confusing.

The task of thinking through these issues more coherently was taken on in the first decade of the 18th century by the young *George Berkeley* (1685–1753) at Trinity College in Dublin. Upon completion of his bachelor's degree, in 1704, Berkeley had become increasingly engrossed in studying the new philosophies of Newton and Locke, but what he found left him, in part at least, bewildered and dissatisfied. Before long therefore, he ventured forth to formulate responses and solutions of his own. Faced with Locke's distinction, for example, between primary and secondary qualities, he proposed to overcome the difficulties it implied by blatantly rejecting it outright. Solidity, extension, and the like were no more independent or objective, so he thought, than color, sound, or taste, and hence there could not be a meaningful distinction.

At first acquaintance, this idea may strike us as simplistic to the point of being crude. But once we pause a moment to reflect, we quickly feel more puzzled than dismissive. For what is here asserted is in essence nothing less than that *all being is perception.* Material objects in themselves do not have any primary qualities that really do belong to them, and therefore, material objects as such are really nonexistent. Objects do not consist of some occult external 'stuff', referred to as 'matter', but rather of perceptions in the mind. All that we can ever be aware of in respect of a given 'material thing' is the aggregate of sensory impressions or ideas that our mind associates with it. By implication then, it is this aggregate that really forms the thing. In his treatise concerning the *Principles of Human Knowledge*, published in 1710, Berkeley expresses his pertinent insights as follows:

> The table I write on, I say, exists, that is, I see and feel it; and if I were out of my study I should say it existed, meaning thereby that if I was in my study I might perceive it, or that some other spirit actually does perceive it. There was an odour, that is, it was smelled; there was a sound, that is to say, it was heard; a colour or figure, and it was perceived by sight or touch. This is all that I can understand by these and the like expressions. For as to what is said of the absolute existence of unthinking things without any relation to their being perceived, that seems perfectly unintelligible. Their *esse* is *percipi*, nor is it possible they should have any existence, out of the minds or thinking things which perceive them.[200]

Sophie: It sounds like quantum physics, doesn't it?

428 *Science and Spirit*

Philonous: The similarities are hard to overlook.

Sophie: Especially if we recall that Heisenberg initially gave up all particle ontologies and chose to concentrate instead on the actual data that physicists *perceive* (p.69).

Philonous: But there is more to it, because when Berkeley here insists that being is perception by a mind, I feel reminded most immediately of how we formerly attempted to resolve the mystery of measurement.

Sophie: I do remember it: in choosing to adopt "an encompassingly systemic view" (p.88), we traced the locus of a quantum wave collapse all the way back to what appeared to be a mind-and-matter interface. And hence we came to realize that conscious observation is the all-important agent that transforms a cloud of quantum possibility into an actual material event.

Philonous: Furthermore, in order to guarantee, in view of this conclusion, the continuity and permanence in existence of physical reality, we chose to postulate a universal mind (p.90) who can perceive and thus create events when no one else is watching.

Sophie: That is correct. The mind of God, we said, produces physical existence.

Philonous: ...and Berkeley would agree. For he as well was led to introduce that very same postulate for that very same reason. He hints at it when he invokes "some other spirit" in the quote above and also states it with explicitness in one of his didactic dialogues. Here is how he puts it:

> To me it is evident... that sensible things cannot exist otherwise than in a mind or spirit. Whence I conclude, not that they have no real existence, but that seeing they depend not on my thought, and have an existence distinct from being perceived by me, *there must be some other mind wherein they exist.* As sure therefore as the sensible world really exists, so sure is there an infinite omnipresent Spirit who contains and supports it.
>
> ...
>
> Men commonly believe that all things are known or perceived by God, because they believe the being of a God, whereas I on the other side, immediately and necessarily conclude the being of a God, because all sensible things must be perceived by him.[201]

Sophie: The reasoning indeed is perfectly analogous.

Philonous: Moreover, the details of the pertinent ontologies are also matching closely. According to Berkeley, reality consists of ideas that spirits perceive, and according to quantum mechanics, the universe is made of information 'stuff' that conscious minds beget (p.84). In other words, in either view reality is immaterial and spirit-based. What ultimately constitutes the world in both of these descriptions is not a harsh Cartesian opposition between a passive mental realm and an autonomous material domain, but rather a more natural and less conflicted interplay of spirits and ideas.

Sophie: The view is readily coherent.

Philonous: ...but nonetheless still dual in kind. And Berkeley is emphatic on this latter point when he declares that words as 'will', 'soul', or 'spirit', "do not stand for different ideas, or in truth, for any idea at all, but for something which is very different from ideas, and which being an agent cannot be like, or represented by, any idea whatsoever."[202] A spirit, according to Berkeley, is a being that is "simple, undivided, [and] active" whereas ideas are "passive and inert."[203] By implication, a spirit can perceive but never be perceived.

Sophie: Put differently, the mind can know but not be known.

Philonous: Indeed, the mind or spirit is entirely off limits. For in contrast to an ordinary 'thing', it derives its existence, not from being perceived, but from the act of perceiving. Using more familiar quantum talk, we also may here say—and have said previously (p.89)—that an observing consciousness is not a physical entity described by Schrödinger's equation. Instead, it is an extra-physical fact that can never be captured by the ideas or mathematical formalisms with which the physical, by definition, is identified.

Sophie: It seems we keep returning to this point: we came to it by way of quantum physics first (p.89), then rediscovered it in Wittgenstein's philosophy (p.292), and now we find that Berkeley too did independently arrive at it.

Philonous: ...and so did Dante in the *Comedy*.

Sophie: ...because he too believed that only God sustains material existence (p.353)?

Philonous: That is undoubtedly a valid indication. But more directly to the point, the Dante scholar, Christian Moevs, makes this astonishing assertion:

> [T]he essential insight that underlies the [redemptive] principle [on which the *Comedy* is built] is that the individual subject of experience, though it may be "in" the world, is ultimately not part of the world: it is not simply a thing.[204]

Sophie: So that's the lesson we should learn? The conscious self is not a thing.

Philonous: It's one of the lessons that Berkeley was trying to teach us. In fact, there was a strong didactic streak in him. For Berkeley developed his philosophy from a distinctly Christian perspective. He was an ordained Anglican clergyman and even spent the last two decades of his life in an elevated ecclesiastical function as the Bishop of Cloyne. To Berkeley it was entirely a matter of course that all his philosophical thought had to openly support or be at least consistent with the doctrines of the Faith. In particular, the necessary transcendence of the subject, of which we just treated, corroborated in his mind the essential Christian belief that human souls are not destroyed in bodily death:

> We have shown that the soul is indivisible, incorporeal, unextended, and it is consequently incorruptible. Nothing can be plainer, than

that the motions, changes, decays, and dissolutions which we hourly
see befall natural bodies... cannot possibly affect an active, simple,
uncompounded substance: such a being therefore is indissoluble
by the force of nature, that is to say, *the soul of man is naturally
immortal.*[205]

Sophie: Was Berkeley then a theologian more than a philosopher?

Philonous: Definitely not. Berkeley was a man of faith who aimed to instill
in his readers "a sense of the presence of God."[206] But in his major works
he proved himself to be an authentic philosophical thinker of uncommon
rational acuity. His arguments were highly original, difficult to refute, and
pleasantly eccentric.

Sophie: 'Eccentric' is the word to use. Afterall, he did away with matter.

Philonous: He replaced it with ideas that are perceived. But what he really
did was to positively overcome that sullen sense of lifeless reduction that all
materialistic conceptions are inherently beset with. You see, Berkeley was
blessed with a rather jovial temperament and therefore eager to embrace
the joy that life's *experiences* offer. He reveled in his writings more than
once in sensory delights as he immediately encountered them, unsoiled by
tiresome abstractions. The "purple sky," the "sweet notes of birds," the
"fragrant blooms upon the trees and flowers,"[207] they all inspired him to
fervently believe—and rationally argue—that the so-called 'physical world'
is not mediate and material but rather concrete and fully coincident with
sensory perception. The beauty of a rainbow, say, is not an epiphenomal
attachment to an abstract realm of particles of matter but plainly and
simply the beauty that we see.

Sophie: I grant the vision is attractive.

Philonous: ...and persuasive.

Sophie: ...not so much, for even if I take a fuzzy quantum view, I find it difficult
to see how matter made of particles can be entirely fictitious. It may be
true that matter becomes actual only when a consciousness becomes aware
of it, but actual it still becomes.

Philonous: What physics tells us is that particles are useful *theories* by means
of which we organize the flow of our sensory perceptions—and Berkeley
would accept that. But what he would deny is that we have good reasons
to assume that particles, as theories, exist extra-mentally in some obscure
abstracted world that no one can perceive.

Sophie: ...but common sense suggests we can—we can perceive that world
because it's there, immediately before us. And you can see it too.

Philonous: Not at all. What I can see are visual perceptions—which Berkeley
calls ideas. But as for matter that supposedly exists apart from any sensory
awareness that I have of it, I must confess, that I am wholly unaware of it.

Sophie: So you perceive perceptions?

Philonous: Of course.

Sophie: It doesn't sound profound.

Philonous: ...but makes good sense and even common sense—unlike, as I would say, the standard matter-based account.

Sophie: You mean, the matter-based ontology.

Philonous: That's right. This standard view is wholly incoherent. Just take for instance the perception of a sound.[208] What science here explains is how a vibrating string, let's say, produces density fluctuations in the air surrounding it, how these fluctuations in turn spread out as waves, and how a human ear is thereby caused to generate a flow of nervous pulses to the brain. All along we are here given physical descriptions of phenomena in terms of particles in motion: the atoms that compose the string, the molecules of air that form the waves, and finally the electrons that flow in currents to the brain. But how does motion ever sound like anything? There is no plausible connection. Some particles are moving in a void and suddenly we hear a sound and even judge its quality to be harmonious or displeasing—the thought is utterly preposterous.

Sophie: But don't you think the reasoning is accurate? Do not indeed the sound waves propagate and bring about effects as your account suggests?

Philonous: Of course—the science is correct. But what we learn from it is not how motion turns by way of magic into sound, but rather how the flow of sensory particulars that we perceive can be conceptually organized. The laws of nature governing the 'physical processes' with which we commonly associate the flow of sensory experience are simply mental rules that specify how basic sensations like sounds or tastes or smells are predictably conditioned and connected. In other words, as Berkeley writes, "the set rules or established methods, wherein the mind we depend on excites in us the ideas of sense, are called *the laws of nature*."[209]

Sophie: So in a quantum setting we would say that the transformation of a cloud-like possibility into an actual occurrence by way of conscious perception is constrained by probabilities that quantum rules define.[I]

Philonous: ...and that's what makes reality objective. The world is more than mere subjective consciousness because—and only because—it places limits on perception. It is not the postulated existence of particles of matter that allows us to speak coherently of an objective outside world but rather the lawful coordination and channelling of the sensations that conscious agents from that world receive. That which we are used to calling 'the external world' is nothing but a principle which guarantees that your perceptions are reliable and regular and—even more importantly—*compatible with mine.* When I drop a stone and you are standing next to me, we both will see

---

[I]Eugene Wigner points out in this context that quantum mechanics in its standard linear form is not suitable for describing the interactions between two or more conscious observers. However, the description of the laws of nature here given does clearly not depend for its basic validity on the technical adequacy or inadequacy of current-day quantum descriptions.[210]

it fall in ways that are inherently consistent—you from your position and I from mine. Our respective experiences will not be randomly subjective and disjoint but synchronous and shared.

Sophie: I think, I understand it now—in Berkeley's renegade philosophy the facts remain unchanged but not the words: things become ideas, objective attributes become perceptions, and laws are re-construed as principles that tell us how ideas are synchronized and patterned.

Philonous: In essence, that's correct.

Sophie: But then, it seems, his matter-free reality is nothing but a verbal readjustment—which even is quite trivial in the sense that Berkeley is correct *by definition*. He changes the ontology by choosing different words but leaves the facts entirely untouched. By implication then, as far as science is concerned, he never can be wrong.

Philonous: Notwithstanding, though, he does provide a fresh alternative perspective. For he eliminates the artificial layer of abstraction that matter represents and thereby makes the world immediate and real. Put differently, in taking reality at face value and declaring the 'material' to be congruent with our perception of it, he counters our modern sin to constantly say 'just'.

Sophie: I beg your pardon.

Philonous: What I am here referring to is that according to the standard view—the matter-based ontology—a rainbow, for example, or some other pleasant sight is *just* a purposeless material phenomenon that somehow happens to look nice. It's *just* a physical fact to which we foolishly attach some odd aesthetic sentiments. But Berkeley on the contrary would say that pleasant sights are pleasant in the very act of being so perceived. What is real about a sight is not its postulated source in material substance but only the state of consciousness that it induces in us. That is to say, what Berkeley doesn't do is to declare that the neutral mathematical abstractions and material descriptors with which sights in general and pleasant sights in particular can be effectively modeled are somehow more real, in some obscure sense, than the actual experience of becoming aware of such sights by means of perception.

Sophie: In summary, his purpose is to bring reality to life.

Philonous: ...and it is thus that Berkeley finds himself compelled to contemplate why thinkers commonly are so intent to do the very opposite—to quench the eager flow of life and cling instead to colorless abstractions. Why is it that the universal and abstract is so much more alluring a terrain than the abundant world of sensory particulars that our minds immediately perceive? As it turns out, the answer is not difficult to find: the culprit is the *word*. It is the power of language that causes scholars and philosophers to seek in vain for actual realities, existing independently, behind the names and universal terms that human thought produces. 'Matter', for instance, is an abstract notion whose actual reality materialists posit and certain "Schoolmen"[211] speculate upon without ever reflecting that there does not exist any particular sensory data that truly corresponds to it. In letting their imaginations be captured by words that merely are names and thus signify nothing, such thinkers become confused and deceived and wholly lose sight of the real as it is—the real that is immediate, commonsensical, and fully concrete. In other words, what Berkeley does in essence is to forcefully reject the devil's advice: "On *words* let your attention centre" (p.280). He uncovers the devil's deception and thereby clears the path to genuine insight and truth. According to Berkeley, "we need only draw the curtain of words, to behold the fairest tree of knowledge, whose fruit is excellent, and within the reach of our hand."[212]

Sophie: But all that Berkeley *really* does, as we agreed, is to exchange one set of words for another. He attaches to the same phenomena that scientists describe a different verbal frame so as to create a more inviting, lively picture. But in so doing so, it seems, he also centers on the *word*.

Philonous: It is true, of course, that Berkeley must express himself by using words, but what his mind is focused on is not the word but the *particular* idea to which the word applies.

Sophie: Yet even so, the problem still remains: Berkeley opposes the misuse and abuse of words by using words.

Philonous: The issue is inherently perplexing—and Berkeley frankly confesses that "an entire deliverance from the deception of words"[213] is too lofty a goal for anyone to truly attain to. For it would require that the bond between words and ideas be broken, not by falsely postulating the existence of 'abstract ideas' and linking them to names, but rather by stripping genuine particular ideas of all the names that we will commonly tag on to them. Somehow the mind would have to enter a state of purified awareness in which particulars can be received without being tied in the process to any universal, verbal descriptors.

Sophie: Unfortunately, though, if Berkeley ever were to reach this higher mental state, he wouldn't be able to communicate its benefits without in the process abandoning it, that is, without using words.

Philonous: ...and that is why he finds himself appealing to his readers to perceive the meaning of his words by trying to directly re-experience the thoughts from which he derived them:

> Unless we take care to clear the first principles of knowledge, from the embarrass and delusion of words, we may make infinite reasonings upon them to no purpose; we may draw consequences from consequences, and never be the wiser. The further we go, we shall only lose ourselves the more irrecoverably, and be the deeper entangled in difficulties and mistakes. Whoever therefore designs to read the following sheets, I beg him to make my words the occa-

sion of his own thinking, and endeavour to attain the same train of
thoughts in reading, that I had in writing them. By this means it
will be easy for him to discover the truth or falsity of what I say.
He will be out of all danger of being deceived by my words, and I
do not see how he can be led into an error by considering his own
naked, undisguised ideas.[214]

Sophie: So understanding Berkeley's works requires more than simply reading
them. One needs to form some parallel world in the mind that mirrors the
thoughts of their author.

Philonous: Another way to put it is to say that one must somehow transcend—
in Wittgenstein's sense—the level of mere words and reach beyond it to
that genuine first-person experience which precisely cannot be captured by
words. According to Wittgenstein, those who understand his propositions
will come to recognize "them as nonsensical" and thereby be enabled to
surpass them. They will cast aside the ladder of words and thus perceive
"the world aright" (p.298).

Sophie: Would it then be fair to say that Berkeley, just as Wittgenstein, construes philosophy to be essentially a verbal misunderstanding?

Philonous: It would be mostly fair but not entirely. For Berkeley is in this
regard a little less consistent.

Sophie: And that is so because...?

Philonous: ...because when Berkeley speaks of God and souls that are immortal
(p.428), he openly displays the sort of traditional metaphysical confidence
that Wittgenstein would surely have rejected.

Sophie: But other than that, philosophy in either view is largely a collection
of problems that become non-problems as soon as the tangle of words is
properly cleared.

Philonous: Largely—yes, it is.

Sophie: And what is more, the views may both be equally unpopular. For
Wittgenstein, as I recall, was not exactly optimistic in regards to the extent
of his imagined audience. A single kindred soul that truly understood his
cryptic pronouncements was all he dared to hope for (p.293). And I must
say, it seems to me, that Berkeley's followers as well may be quite limited
in number. Afterall, apart from you, I haven't met a single person yet who
thought that matter is a thought.

Philonous: The fact, however, is that Berkeley was explicitly inclusive in his
attitude and general intent. His purpose was to reinstate the rule of common sense and thus to do away with all the learned subtleties and foolish
arguments that Schoolmen and philosophers are prone to entertain.

Sophie: So he believed that common people in the streets would eagerly agree
with him and choose to inhabit a matter-free world?

Philonous: He thought they did inhabit it already and only had to be aided
a bit to properly acknowledge it. But be that as it may, I don't consider

popularity a particularly cogent criterion for judging the truth of a philosophical doctrine. It may be accurate to say that people in general and scientists in particular strongly believe that matter exists extra-mentally and independently, but so what? Instead of trying to settle the issue by taking a vote, I may as well try, as Berkeley aptly counsels, to form my own thoughts.

Sophie: ...and as you do that Berkeley's arguments are going to impel you to assent?

Philonous: Let's say, the materialists' counterclaims are going to appear highly obscure: the universe, according to science, consists of particles like electrons and quarks that are afloat in a vacuum and interact by way of fundamental forces.[II] Furthermore, the vacuum in turn is thought to be a cauldron of quantum activity in which particles are constantly created and destroyed. But strange as it may seem, none of all these various elementary entities—in transit or in permanence—have any discernible attributes at all. An electron does not have color, taste, or tangible solidity—and neither has a photon or a muon or a quark. (Afterall, what people call the 'color' of a quark is really just an abstract quality that might as well be said to be a 'roloc'—a 'color' spelled backwards.)

Sophie: But electrons have charge and energy and mass (and spin and whatever), as physicists will readily point out.

Philonous: But what is the appearance of a charge, its color or its taste? The answer is, "the question makes no sense because a charge is not a quality that humans can perceive."

Sophie: Yet it is real in that it clearly has effects on how an object or a particle will move.

Philonous: Except that electrons don't move in any ordinary sense because, as we have learned, they do not trace observable paths. In other words, an electron that moves cannot be said to even have a well defined position. So how then can we speak of it as being a genuine thing? Or how can we so speak of any other 'object' in the universe apart from how we perceive it? The universe, when unobserved, is a perfectly elusive non-entity that is entirely attribute-free—it is a nothing, a no-thing, a void—indefinable, vacant, and utterly faceless.

Sophie: So much then for the notion of a charge—but what about the other two? Please don't forget to slaughter mass and energy as well.

Philonous: That's easy to do. Just notice to begin with that, conceptually, these two imagined qualities are perfectly equivalent. Mass is energy and energy is mass because, by relativity, $E = mc^2$ (see also p.43). Consequently, to do away with only one of them, with energy, let's say, is logically

---

[II]In quantum field theory the forces as well are represented by particles. The electromagnetic force between two electrons for instance is thought to be transmitted by way of photon exchange.

sufficient.

Sophie: One will do, as long as the killing is properly juicy.

Philonous: Very well, I'll do my best: according to the standard science lore, the stuff we label 'energy' is that which everything is ultimately made of. Consequently, it surely ought to be possible to go to a library, take a book on physics from a shelf, consult the index, and look up a statement that reads: "The energy of a given physical system is defined to be..." Sadly, though, there is no definition as this because energy—far from being an objective material entity—is nothing but a useful conceptual tool that makes our physical theories look elegant and highly efficient.

Sophie: But physics does assert that energy is universally preserved.

Philonous: Certainly, in any physical system that people so far have explored it has been possible to introduce a mathematical input/output scheme—or energy-accounting scheme—that strictly obeys this universal law of conservation. Energy is not an absolute that can be globally described, but in any given case we can define it as a quantity whose value is preserved. A planet, for instance, that orbits the Sun in absolute space, has a well defined kinetic energy that increases in proportion to the square of its speed. And at every point along its orbit it possesses as well a so-called potential energy whose local variation prescribes, by way of the calculus, the force of gravity exerted by the Sun.

Sophie: ...and the total is *preserved* because the sum of the kinetic and potential parts is constant over time.

Philonous: That is correct, but as it is, a closer look is somewhat disconcerting. For not only is the total energy typically negative,[III] and therefore *less than nothing,* but the potential energy even tends to evaporate whenever we switch from a classical Newtonian to a contemporary relativistic perspective.

Sophie: The energy evaporates?

Philonous: Only the potential part—but, yes, it does completely disappear. Potential energy is like a magic phantasy—a jolly balloon that pops and reinflates depending on which theory we happen to apply. You see, in relativity, as both of us discussed, the existence of a gravitational force is locally always a matter of perspective. Locally, we can always choose a point of view that makes the gravitation disappear. Consequently, it doesn't make much sense—or any sense at all—to try to define an absolute potential energy that locally generates a gravitational force. So while it is true

---

[III]Strictly speaking, this depends on how the potential energy is normalized. But if we make a standard choice and set the potential energy equal to zero at infinity, then the total energy of a material object tracing a closed orbit about the Sun will indeed be less than zero. Furthermore, if we work with Newton's simplest model in which the Sun and the planets are pointlike, then the potential energy will tend to negative infinity as a planet's position approaches the Sun, and in particular, close to the Sun it will be negative no matter how the normalization is handled.

that potential energy is a wonderful mathematical concept that efficiently describes the Newtonian gravitational force, it also is equally true—for reasons of principle—that no such concept can exist in Einstein's relativistic description. In general relativity fields contain a well defined *global* energy but the notion of a *local* potential energy is necessarily meaningless.[215]

Sophie: That is to say, the conclusion here must be that Berkeley was correct: matter doesn't exist because the jolliness of energy balloons is necessarily a matter of *perception*.

Philonous: He was correct because the universe that modern physicists depict is so notoriously devoid of anything resembling an objective independent substance that his idea-based mental world looks very substantive by contrast. Afterall, what sort of genuine solidity can be ascribed to a world wherein elementary particles semi-exist, wherein spacetime curvatures exert dynamic effects, and quantum entanglements cause miracle reactions? Is this a world that truly is material in kind or can we not as well construe it to be mental?

Sophie: Your answer is, "we can."

Philonous: Indeed, I do believe that we are free to choose. There are no logical arguments and no scientific facts that contradict the views that Berkeley so delightfully espouses. By implication then, we really are at liberty to follow where he leads and paint the world in tones that are more colorful and brighter. It is up to us to decide whether the world that we see is a mere material machine or whether instead it is a freely flowing mental stream that God Himself sustains by His awareness and His thought. Do we inhabit a physical void detached from human consciousness or rather a more friendly place of spirits and ideas?

Sophie: I don't know.

Chapter 6

The Death of God

Only Seeing Is Believing

When we ask ourselves what kind of a tenor or mood the philosophical vision of Berkeley most notably conveys, we readily find that attributes like 'joyous', 'lively', or 'spontaneous' are forcefully coming to mind. The spirit that pervades his thought is strongly life-affirming, embraces the concrete, and cheerfully avoids all barren abstractions. Physical reality, according to Berkeley, is not an alien aggregate of 'particles of matter' or 'quanta of energy', but rather is a vibrant flux of sensory particulars that directly imprint themselves upon the human consciousness.

Indeed, what Berkeley aims to achieve, in the final analysis, is nothing less than a spiritual renewal—a healing of the modern rift between the inner and the outer world. For in proposing a consistently idealistic ontology and thereby bridging the Cartesian mind/matter divide, he naturally sets the stage for meaning and experience to be re-linked. Afterall, in a world in which there only are ideas and spirits who perceive them, no inner sentiment of personal significance is any more unreal inherently than any 'physical' phenomenon that sensory *experience* portrays. The feeling of awe and reverence, for instance, that a mountainous landscape inspires in us may here appear to be of equal firmness and solidity as the initiating perception of colors and shapes that represents *and constitutes* the landscape's 'physical' outline. And so, as the alienating influence of materialistic abstractions is fully exposed and thus overcome, the human soul recovers its ability to resonate freely and gladly with life's abundant flow of information.

Moreover, this information flow in turn is patterned and designed to directly reflect the presence and magnificence of God. For according to Berkeley, the "wisdom and benevolence"[1] of the Author of the universe are plainly evident in the order and beauty that Nature displays:

> If we follow the light of reason, we shall, from the constant uniform method of our sensations, collect the goodness and wisdom of the *Spirit* who excites them in our minds.[2]

In other words, meaning is truly and fully recovered as the Creator Himself becomes apparent to us in the lawful structures that our sense perceptions exhibit.

So far then, the doctrine that Berkeley offers to us seems edifying and pleasantly appealing. But unfortunately, there also are some critical questions that need to be asked. Berkeley correctly uncovered the flaws in Locke's philosophical system, but does he not himself commit some equally obvious blunders? He vigorously attacks the evils of abstraction, but whence does he get his notion of God? Previously we saw that Berkeley deduces the being of God from the requirement that physical reality be permanent and properly objective (p.428). Yet even if we view this argument as sound, we still may rightly feel confused when Berkeley first refuses to infer that everyday objects, as tables or chairs, are made of some actual, 'material' stuff, and then goes on to confidently establish the benevolent nature of a supreme Being that no human organ of sense has ever perceived.

Furthermore, in arguing against the abuses of words, Berkeley observes—very astutely—that language is inherently deceitful. Our linguistic conventions suggest to us, as it were, that 'matter' is real independently when in truth it merely is a name whose meaning, we might say, is nothing but its use. But how then does he manage to detect the *actual* "goodness and wisdom" of a transcendent being behind such names as 'Creator', 'God', or 'Spirit'. What manner of reasoning does he employ? Surely, it cannot be abstraction from the concrete, for abstract ideas, in Berkeley's mind, are perfectly illusory. So what is the method he uses? Judging from his writings we must say, he really uses none. Berkeley *asserts* that God's loving kindness is plainly evident in sensory experience, but a cogent explanation he never provides.

In the light of these remarks, it is instructive to note that a thinker like Wittgenstein, whose powers of linguistic analysis were clearly not in short supply, opted in this context for a very different view. For in the *Tractatus* we read that the way "things are in the world is a matter of complete indifference for what is higher" and that therefore "God does not reveal himself *in* the world."[3] We may agree or disagree, but either way we probably do well to admit that 'goodness' is not an attribute that we can easily assign to the world as it is—or, by implication, to the One who supposedly created it. The world may be good because it is free, but other than that it doesn't look all that inviting. In fact, a sober-minded observer might well consider it an unrelenting, bloody death machine and not seem unintelligent thereby.

Worse still, Berkeley's most salient advice, namely to shun all verbal abstractions so as to behold an uncorrupted flux of naked particulars, is not exactly easy to heed. Language, it seems, is so vitally a part of human mental activity that it is virtually impossible to meaningfully think the notion of a human consciousness without appeal to its employment. To be sure, it is simple enough to imagine a being that can competently manage this feat of wholly disconnecting sensations from words. But the sort of ceature that here comes to mind is not a woman or a man but rather, more likely, a cat or a dog. Put differently, the misuse of words can be avoided most easily where words are absent altogether. Similarly, the re-integration of meaning and experience that Berkeley's philosophy implicitly aims at is best achieved when there is nothing to re-integrate, that is, when animal experience is all that there is.

Consequently and in the light of these various problems and perplexities, it may be best to take a step back, assume a realistic attitude, and really try to see the world for what it really is, apart from any odd notions of spirits or gods. In other words, it may be time for us to turn to *David Hume* (1771–1776)—the Scotsman from Edinburgh who was the last and most radical in the great British troika of Enlightenment empiricists. In fact, in respect of Hume, the latter label is inaccurate in that he really was an empiricist far more than an Enlightenment figure. For his philosophy, as we will see, effectively demolished all the epistemic certainties and ontologic verities to which the optimistic mainstream thought of 18th century Europe was prone to assent.

In order to familiarize ourselves with Hume's irreverent views, we need to pose to start with the basic dual inquiry from which all philosophical thinking ultimately departs: "what is there and how do we know it?" According to Hume, the first of these questions—construed objectively—is unanswerable, and the second needs to be rewritten with the personal pronoun emphasized: "how do *we* know it?" *We* as humans do not know what is there—externally and independently—but *we* do have elementary sensations and inward sentiments which Hume calls *impressions*. And what we also have are certain thoughts or ideas—less vivid but typically more complex—that these impressions give rise to. A pain that we feel or a color that we see, for instance, is an original datum of experience which our thought may come to operate upon by way of recollection and reflection. Underlying this distinction between basic sentiments and higher mental constructs there is the fundamental assumption that impressions, not ideas, are the bottommost atomic building blocks of the contents of the consciousness. That is to say, the immediate sensory imprint or inner experience—rather than the derivative thought—is that original, irreducible primitive in which any piece of human knowledge or awareness always has its source.

So far one might assume that Berkeley would agree. Hume employs a slightly different terminology by speaking of simple ideas as 'impressions', but other than that, the tune is more or less the same: knowledge is grounded in perception. However, as we earlier discussed, Berkeley was not content to leave it at that, for he proclaimed that being, too, was grounded thus: *esse est percipi.* In other words, Berkeley makes an ontological assertion where Hume merely delimits what humans can know. Consequently, we are not surprised to find that Hume, in his most famous work—his *Enquiry Concerning Human Understanding*—replaces Berkeley's programmatic assertion, that matter does not exist, with his own, equally programmatic confession of ignorance:

> It is a question of fact, whether the perceptions of the senses be produced by external objects, resembling them: how shall this question be determined? By experience surely; as all other questions of a like nature. But here experience is, and must be entirely silent. The mind has never anything present to it but the perceptions, and cannot possibly reach any experience of their connexion with objects. The supposition of such a connexion is, therefore, without any foundation in reasoning.[4]

That is to say, according to Hume, we cannot rationally affirm or deny the existence of genuine exterior objects because the word 'exterior' essentially means 'beyond the reach of sensory perception'.

Berkeley believed that his philosophy was an antidote to skepticism because it freed the human mind from any nagging mistrust concerning the faculties of sense. Afterall, there is no need to question whether we can ever truly know that independent, material realm that lies concealed behind the flow of our sensory perceptions if we in fact suppose, *a priori*, that no such realm can possibly exist.[5] But Hume strikes here a very different note, less optimistic and assured. His attitude is evident, for instance, when he writes that the recognition "of human blindness and weakness is the result of all philosophy"[6] and that the "ultimate springs and principles" of phenomenal reality "are totally shut up from human curiosity and enquiry."[7] Reason must cling to experience if it is not to lose itself in speculative labyrinths because reason, by its very nature, is feeble and narrowly bounded.[8]

Indeed, Hume's philosophy is a call to intellectual modesty that barely stops short of being nihilistic. We have ideas composed of impressions, but other than that, we really have nothing at all:

> When we entertain... any suspicion that a philosophical term is employed without any meaning or idea (as is but too frequent), we need but enquire, *from what impression is that supposed idea derived?* And if it be impossible to assign any, this will serve to confirm our suspicion.

Naturally, anyone who strictly abode by this rule would thereby unavoidably establish that just about any traditional ontological concept is nothing but a random invention. Souls, spirits, and gods—they all would be immediately cast out and land on the scrap heap of worthless philosophical fantasies. To be sure, what Hume insists upon is not so much that entities as these do not exist, but merely that thinkers like Berkeley or Descartes, who argue at length that they do, have nothing of worth to show for their efforts. Spirits, according to Berkeley, are not ideas and therefore cannot be dissected into elementary, atomic impressions. By implication, as Hume would readily point out, we really know nothing about them at all. Nothing can be said regarding them to which a meaning can be plausibly attached.

In taking this approach, all common concepts of reality are bound to dissolve in skeptical doubting, and even the human subject itself must needs appear to be of uncertain status. Impressions are received, it is true, but is there really a receiver—a person with a self, a soul, a well-defined essence? The answer once again can only be that we don't know. We cannot perceive that "inner man" (p.152) that Plato wrote about, and thus we had better be silent about him.

A famous case in point is Hume's analysis of "liberty and necessity"[9]—the problem of free will. Do humans choose their actions voluntarily or are they merely driven to act by physical cause and effect? Having posed the question thus, it is advisable for us to first explore how Hume construes the notion of a *cause*. A simple case of an apparent causal dependency that Hume endeavors to elucidate is the transferral of motive energy between two billiard balls in consequence of their elastic collision: as one ball hits the other, both are found to alter their velocities. Nothing, it seems, could ever be more obvious than the idea that this resulting change is brought about by the anterior impact. That is to say, there is a *necessary* link by which these two phenomena are causally connected.

Yet where in the events that we observe is this necessity conclusively revealed? Exactly how do we discern its evidential markings? By rational deduction? To frame these questions properly, Hume asks us to imagine that we had been "brought... into this world" all of "a sudden"[10] and had never before experienced any of its physical workings. Would we then be able to predict that the perceived motion of two billiard balls toward each other is bound to result in a bouncing effect which rigidly obeys a rule that physicists refer to as the law of the preservation of momentum? There is no doubt that we would not. As totally unprejudiced observers we might as well expect that the balls, upon 'impact', will shatter to pieces, disappear, pass through each other, or continue to move in any one of a million fanciful fashions. In other words, there is nothing *a priori* necessary whatever about the particular arrangement of sensory imprints that represents to us the motions of the balls before and after their collision.

So why then does our common sense so strongly suggest the presence of a necessary causal connection? Why is it that we are so very much inclined to think that one event here brings about another with perfect lawful certainty? Because we have formed, says Hume, a habit of perception. Experience has taught us over and again that things occur the way they do with law-like regularity. But genuine necessity in an absolute sense there really is none—so far as we know. We are *subjectively* disposed to assume that our sensations are derivative of an objective material world in which certain phenomenal recurrences bespeak the sovereign authority of absolute natural laws. But any further claim that this disposition of ours somehow conforms to the world as it is can only be a statement of belief.

In order to understand how such a radically deconstructive view of causal dependency in physical reality might inform our understanding of liberty and necessity in human behavior, it is helpful to notice that in human life as well we encounter numerous law-like regularities. People have customs and cultural conventions that make their interactions in many a case seem scarcely less predictable than the rigid collision reflexes of billiard balls. In greeting rituals, for instance, hands will be shaken, smiles exchanged, and welcome phrases will be adequately uttered. In other words, an unprejudiced observer would here have valid reasons to conclude that human life is governed by absolute behavioral laws in much the same way as a mechanical system.

As a matter of course, to this idea one may immediately object that in the former case the regularities are far less uniform and stable. Afterall, two people who have never met will not at all times honor the accepted etiquette. On occasion their expression will appear indifferent or displeased or even openly aggressive. But then again two billiard balls as well may sometimes be diverted from their ordinary, well ingrained behavior. An airflow may deter them, a spinning motion bend their paths, and changes in temperature may alter their elastic properties. Naturally, in classical physics at least, all these variations and effects could also be construed to be expressive of dependencies that laws condition and prescribe—but so could be, conceivably, the deviations from the norm in human social conduct. By implication and by inversion, it seems permissible to claim that if the human will is free then free as well are motions in mechanics.

In response we may here feel compelled to interject that there appears to be a fundamental difference in kind between a billiard ball, which blindly reacts to random physical forces, and a living person who consciously chooses a certain manner of conduct. But unfortunately, in a world in which knowledge is based exclusively upon irreducible atomic impressions we really cannot tell wherein that difference objectively consist. Judging from the evidence of sense, the existence of a metaphysical person with genuine volition and intent is just as spurious a proposition as the independent reality of an external, material substrate that absolute physical laws supposedly govern. Here as there the notion of an actual, ontological core beneath the flow of sensory particulars is altogether groundless.

In order not to cause any misunderstandings, it is advisable to add that Hume was not a dogmatist and thus was fairly well content to let the human mind indulge its natural propensities and cognitive instincts. He acknowledged, for example, that "Nature is always too strong for principle"[11] and that excessive skepticism always capitulates before the presence of those concrete objects and realities "which actuate our passions and sentiments."[12] However, when faced with pompous claims to rational or moral certainties that no experience could possibly support, Hume was rather unrelenting in his deconstructive attitude. In consequence, he created a shallow, impressionistic portrait of a world that merely was an insubstantial flux—a hollow composite of sensations and sentiments to which no genuine essence—material or personal—could ever be attached.

Sophie: "Impressionistic" is the proper word to use. For I really feel reminded here of paintings by *Monet* in which a cityscape, for instance, or some other outdoor scene is decomposed into its elementary luminal parts. Just look, for instance, how he renders the Cathedral at Rouen (Figure 6.1). Instead

Figure 6.1: *Rouen Cathedral* by Claude Monet (1893).

of a solid building in stone we only see a hazy profusion of sensory, visual imprints. What do we really see? A physical object with genuine substance and well defined shape or merely a fleeting, colorized flux?

Philonous: We see an object which as such is nothing but a flux—according to Berkeley and Hume (where Hume of course would add the skeptical caution "so far as we know"). In other words, the painting by Monet is what I call 'empiricism on canvas'. However, when it comes to the idea of decomposing things into impressions à la Hume, I find the pointillistic works of *Georges Seurat* to be an even better, more befitting illustration. For as Seurat dissects a given image or motif into separate dots of pure spectral colors (as for instance in the painting shown in Figure 6.2), he very lucidly conveys the fact that complex wholes can be made up of basic building blocks that in themselves are structureless and plain.

Figure 6.2: *A Sunday Afternoon on the Island of La Grande Jatte* (Seurat, 1884–6).

Sophie: I understand, but on the other hand I sense that this more intellectual approach is based upon a type of rational analysis that any true empiricist would probably reject. It almost seems as though Seurat depicts a theoretical description. Scientific insight, as it were, suggests that matter and light consist of particles and quanta, and thus he paints the world as though that insight were correct.

Philonous: It may be better here to speak—in a more classical fashion—of spectral decomposition rather than quanta of light. Afterall, the quantum world was still unknown when Seurat invented his style in the late eighteen hundreds.

Sophie: But either way, the rational demand that light be shown in discretized, atomic form appears to lend his works an air of tightly disciplined composure. That is to say, the pointillistic style is more cerebral and controlled in kind than the unhindered spontaneity and generous fluidity that typify the paintings of Monet—as well as those of other true impressionists, like Degas, Pissarro, or Renoir. In fact, in taking Berkeley's point of view, one may be led to diagnose that there is evident in paintings by Seurat an oddly stultifying rigidness that is induced by the *abstractness* of his analytic view.

Philonous: Certainly, the artists whom you call the "true impressionists" were animated by a life-affirming, optimistic mood that was averse to what is barren and abstract. And yes, we may discover in this style that same appeal to uncorrupted, pure experience that we detected too in Berkeley's spirit-based philosophy.

Sophie: So you are willing then to grant that this more fluid style is more empirical in kind than the atomic coloration of Seurat?

Philonous: Perhaps I am, but as it is, I do not think that question that important. Afterall, we surely cannot finally decide which manner of artistic expression truly aligns with which empiricist tradition. The matter clearly is too vague for that. But as we contemplate how art and philosophy in this case interlink, there is a chance that we attain a more complete and vivid understanding. You see, it may be true that some of Berkeley's philosophic sentiments are rather well expressed in paintings by Monet. But then again, we also mustn't overlook that Berkeley, relative to Hume, was less consistent an empiricist. What we perceive as positive and cheerful in the former's thought is closely tied to his embedding ontological assumptions—namely his belief that spirits do exist. That is to say, what Berkeley does is to enlarge the world in order then to joyfully affirm it.

Sophie: And therefore your suggestion is that these additional dimensions are amiss in Hume's philosophy as much as in the pointilism of Seurat.

Philonous: Here again we mustn't be too strict in our art/philosophy comparisons. But I admit that I find Hume's description of the world to be quite well portrayed in the idea that any image that we see is nothing but an aggregate of spectral-colored parts. Furthermore, that stultifying abstract sense that you perceived in paintings by Seurat reminds me in its psychological effect of Hume's near-nihilistic ontological assumptions. In either case reality is but a fragmentary surface play with nothing but a vacuum beneath. There is nothing behind the color points of Georges Seurat, and nothing whatever supports a Humean impression. That said, we also need to see, of course, that paintings by Monet—while certainly more fluid in style—are structurally just as superficial. In fact, they may be even more so as they lack that deeper rational side that underlies, as you observed, the pointillists' dissections of light. Ultimately, what Monet presents to us are nothing but visual imprints frozen in paint.

Sophie: The mood, though, as we earlier agreed, is in this latter case more lively and less soberly cerebral.

Philonous: But as for the reality we see, it may be equally as void.

Sophie: ...in your subjective, personal opinion.

Philonous: ...in mine and also in Renoir's.

Sophie: You mean *Auguste Renoir*, the great impressionist?

Philonous: ...the '*true* impressionist'—as you proposed to label him.

Sophie: The label isn't merely mine. In any book on painting and its history he will be so described.

Philonous: Certainly, in any such account there will be properly discussed some famous work of his such as his painting of *The Dance at the Moulin de la Galette* (Figure 6.3). And yes, a work as this convincingly displays the vital traits that we expect of it: a carefree gaiety of manner and motif, an easygoing unconcern for tedious details, and a playful fascination with brilliant random light effects. However, on the other hand, these traits con-

Figure 6.3: *Le Moulin de la Galette* (1876) by Renoir.

spire to induce in us a feeling of frivolity and shallowness to which Renoir himself became progressively alerted. That is to say, he came to sense, very acutely, that impressionism had headlong abandoned a venerable artistic tradition and foolishly become engrossed in superficial, visual sensation. In consequence, he altered course and gave his later works a far more solid and deliberate appearance. In his depiction of *The Artist's Family* (Figure 6.4), for instance, of 1896, there is far less of that conspicuous looseness in col-

Figure 6.4: *La famille de l'artiste* (1896) by Renoir.

oration and compositional structure that is so emblematic of his earlier, impressionistic phase.

Sophie: In other words, these later works essentially were meant to fill the Humean void—the vacuum of radical empiricist philosophy.

Philonous: By analogy they were indeed. Renoir had seen reality disintegrate and it unsettled him—and not only him. For Hume as well was rather ill affected by the products of his own mutinous mind. In one of his letters he relates how in the early fall of 1729—after having conceived an exciting "new Scene of Thought"[13]—he experienced a sudden bout of distemper that utterly wasted his "Spirits."[14]

Sophie: ...despite the fact, as one might add, that "Spirits," by his own account, he really didn't have.

Philonous: One might indeed, because in reading Hume's description of his nervous sufferings, it really does appear quite evident that there was more involved than his empiricist ontology could plausibly accommodate. He speaks of spirits frequently and even argues that his *soul* would benefit if he gave up his contemplative solitude in favor of a less obsessive active life.[15] On the whole one simply cannot help but feel that in his letter Hume depicts, not some impressionistic vacuum, but rather a genuine person with inner essence and a self. In fact, it almost seems as though he underwent a veritable existential crisis. There is a passage, for example, where he recollects his continual attempts to fortify himself, by means of philosophical reflection, "against Death, Poverty, Shame, Pain, [and] all the other Calamities of Life."[16]

Sophie: I have a hunch his struggle was quite similar to mine. Afterall, the loss of meaning in the face of death is certainly a plight that I am also well familiar with.

Philonous: I must admit there was a time when I as well was similarly suffering from mental strain induced by metaphysical confusion.

Sophie: There was? How so? You never mentioned that before.

Philonous: Because it is quite long ago—some twenty years perhaps. But it is true: I know firsthand that haunting sense of nothingness that certain types of mental attitudes are liable to generate.

Sophie: ...attitudes such as the nearly nihilistic one of Hume?

Philonous: That would be an example. But more generally I would say that any system of philosophy or scientific thought which doesn't recognize a supersensory dimension is bound to leave us utterly dissatisfied. As for myself, I still remember well my frantic veering back and forth between a number of such disembodied theories and modern worldview offerings. In my attempts to grasp the nature of my personhood I ventured to explore a whole gamut of Freudian, behavioral, or otherwise reductive schemes that all contained some fragments of the truth but in themselves were all entirely godless and hollow. In essence, all these schemes, including Hume's, present us with a world that nowhere has an outlet to transcendence—so far as we know. And in the end we always find that such a world—no matter how we paint it—can only be a nothing-at-all—a lightless void that totally depresses us.

Sophie: ...unless, of course, we should decide to look at it through Berkeley's eyes and fancy it a dwelling place of spirits, souls, and gods.

Philonous: ...unless we so decide—you put it right.

Sophie: Then let me say that I am glad to learn that your experience and mine, to some extent, appear to overlap. Perhaps we should reclaim that common "godless" ground to better understand where both of us are coming from.

Philonous: Re-entering these empty desert lands will hardly be an edifying trip. But I agree, it may bestow some benefit.

Charles Versus Darwin

In the late 1950's, the behavioral physiologist, Erich von Holst, conducted a series of empirical studies at the Max Planck Institute in Seewiesen, Germany, concerning *Electrically Controlled Behavior*[17] in vertebrates. Building upon the pioneering work of Walter Hess of Zurich, he demonstrated experimentally that animals become inclined to carry out specific patterns of instinctual behavior when certain regions of their brains are artificially energized by electrodes.

In one such study, for example, the skull of an anesthetized rooster was surgically equipped with threaded plastic fittings through which electrodes could be inserted and linked to specific target areas in the rooster's brain stem. To conduct an experiment, the animal would be placed on a small round table on which it was accustomed to freely move about. Initially, when all the electrodes were passive, the bird would be observed to placidly pursue its ordinary business, pecking here and there and gently clucking in the process.[18] But once a current was externally induced, there would occur a sudden change of 'mood' resulting in displays of complex sequential behaviors for which no adequate external stimulus was discernibly present. Depending on the brain locale that the experimenters chose to energize, the rooster would, for instance, act increasingly aggressive, try to escape from an imaginary predator, be put on high alert, or settle down and go to sleep. In fact, according to von Holst, "almost all the forms of activity and vocalization familiar to those acquainted with chickens"[19] could be evoked by properly positioning the stimulating electrodes.

Furthermore and as a matter of course, the rigid physiological conditioning of certain kinds of animal behavior to which experiments as these so strongly testify is commonly genetic. Animals are born with certain programs in their brains in order to be able to take on the challenge of survival. A chicken that is threatened by a weasel, say, or by a fox must know at once how to react because a second chance to learn from its mistakes it probably won't get. In

other words and in direct reference to Locke's empiricist philosophy, we may
here say that a chicken's brain at birth is definitely *not* a tabula rasa—it is not
a blank sheet that only life's experience is competent to write upon (p.426).

In the light of this latter remark we probably should hasten to add that
humans are not chickens and that therefore von Holst's experiments do not
disprove Locke's pertinent claim that *human* intellects are *not* equipped with
knowledge and ideas that are innate. But even so it ought to be permissible
to ask whether this dictum of Locke's—in respect of humans—can really be
persuasively maintained. Is it really true that human minds, initially, are
content-free and wholly neutral in their world-depicting attitudes?[1]

To find an answer with authoritative weight it is expedient for us to once
again consult the great book history and this time turn the page to the philosophical writings of *Immanuel Kant* (1724–1804). For it was he, the eminent
thinker from Königsberg, who took the question we just posed and boldly ventured to reply to it by creating in effect one of the great original works of the
Western philosophical canon. Indeed, already on the very first page of the Introduction to his *Critique of Pure Reason* Kant defines his fundamental stance
concerning that question as follows:

> But, though all our knowledge begins with experience, it by no
> means follows, that all arises out of experience. For, on the con-
> trary, it is quite possible that our empirical knowledge is a com-
> pound of that which we receive through impressions, and that which
> the faculty of cognition supplies from itself...[20]

According to Kant, "the faculty of cognition [cannot] be awakened into exercise
otherwise than by means of objects which affect our senses."[21] But cognition
also contains an *a priori* component that precedes and even vitally conditions
any experience that human consciousness can ever reflect or produce. And it is
precisely this *a priori* component, this knowledge that the mind itself supplies,
that Locke had famously denied and that von Holst had saliently identified—at
least in a chicken.

Having thus announced the maxim of his thought, Kant resolutely set about
to argue exhaustively for its correctness. In the process he partly undid the
metaphysical damage that empiricist philosophy, in his eyes, had wreaked—
yet not by setting up a novel dogma of his own, but rather by examining
the human mind itself—"the pure faculty of reason."[22] Committed to utmost
logical care and "methodic precision,"[23] he endeavored thereby to determine,
once and for all, the conditions under which metaphysics—as a science—could
possibly exist.

---

[1]For the sake of precision, we need to mention in this context that Locke denied innate
ideas but not innate powers. Human minds, according to Locke, have certain fundamental
abilities, and therefore, they are "neutral in their world-depicting attitudes" only insofar as
they initially do not and cannot rely on any inherited knowledge.

To Kant it was a matter of course that the great existential questions to which this pivotal discipline attempts to reply—questions concerning, for instance, the nature of liberty, the grounds of morality, and the being of God—could never be declined. Man cannot help but inquire about the ultimate verities that underlie his own conscious existence. Consequently, the challenge posed by the empiricists—and here especially by Hume—could not go unanswered. Kant understood that Hume in essence had declared metaphysics to be null and void.[24] But he also granted readily that Hume had been an authentic "great thinker"[25] whose attack had rendered a most valuable service—not only by awaking Kant himself from his "dogmatic slumber"[26]—but more importantly, by bringing into sharp relief the principal problem to which any metaphysical doctrine must antecedently address itself—namely the question of whether and in what sense a given metaphysical concept or claim can be construed to possess "an inner [*a priori*] truth, independent of all experience."[27]

In order to approach this latter question properly, it is helpful to widen it and to ask more generally whether there are any truths whatever—metaphysical or not—that human reason can establish independently with perfect necessary certainty. Fortunately, says Kant, there is "a wonderfully large domain"[28] in which this certainty is manifestly realized: the world of *mathematics*. In this context, it is important and somewhat surprising to note that Hume in essence did agree. For unlike Berkeley, who outright rejected abstraction *per se*, Hume fully acknowledged that abstract quantitative reasoning was a valid means of gaining knowledge. In fact, he even chose to strongly emphasize this conviction of his by closing his *Enquiry* with the following, caustic advice:

> If we take in our hand any volume; of divinity or school metaphysics, for instance; let us ask, *Does it contain any abstract reasoning concerning quantity or number?* No. *Does it contain any experimental reasoning concerning matter of fact and existence?* No. Commit it then to the flames: for it can contain nothing but sophistry and illusion.[29]

However, as Kant now proceeds to explore the nature and possibility of pure mathematical judgments—in preparation for his general critique—he comes to detect a fatal flaw in Hume's pertinent thought. According to Kant, Hume's writings implicitly show that he considered mathematical propositions to be in essence tautological.[II] In other words, Hume falsely assumed that mathematical truths are arrived at by merely elaborating concepts self-referentially rather than by *synthetically* connecting disparate concepts with one another.[30] If we judge, for instance, in geometry that a straight line is the shortest connection between two given points in space, we do not merely dissect the purely

---

[II] The term that Kant uses is 'analytical' rather than 'tautological' which is stronger. But in respect of mathematics at least the latter term expresses well the meaning that Kant intended to give to the former.

qualitative notion of straightness into its constituent parts but rather join it to the quantitative and therefore very different notion of a (minimal) length.[31] To a contemporary mathematician this view of Kant's will likely seem diffuse and lacking in precision. Yet what is relevant for us to contemplate is not so much what Kant exactly meant or whether he was right, but why he considered Hume's supposed mistake to be so corruptive.

And as regards this latter point, we need to first appreciate that Hume— again according to Kant—had correctly perceived that metaphysical judgments are inherently *a priori* and synthetical. The proposition, for example, that "the world must have a beginning,"[32] is *a priori* because the necessity implied by "must" can never be deduced from empirical facts, and it is synthetical because the notion of a temporal beginning is not in any way intrinsic to the concept of a world. That is to say, in Kant's analysis, Hume's denial of the possibility of metaphysics was rooted in a broader, more fundamental rejection of a certain type of judgment: human reason is incapable of establishing truth synthetically from *a priori* principles, and therefore all metaphysical judgments are inherently illusory. But how could Hume have drawn this skeptical inference if he had judged correctly that mathematical truths are not only *a priori* but synthetical as well? Can any consequent be ever proven true from a false antecedent? Obviously not. So if only Hume had duly recognized that mathematical thought is vitally synthetical, he would have been graciously prevented from casting metaphysics so rashly aside.[33]

A first approach, then, to undoing Hume's undoing of traditional philosophy should be a careful taking stock of truth in mathematics. How is it possible, say, that in geometry or in arithmetic we can assert with certainty that theorems are valid *universally* and true *necessarily* if neither of these attributes can ever be observed? Afterall, we cannot perceive, by way of the senses, that the shortest path between two points is a straight line segment of needs. So how then do we know it? In a sense, Kant's answer is that straight line segments are never observed to satisfy this property because they are never observed to begin with. They are not empirical objects but rather are rational constructs that derive the possibility of their existence from the internal constitution of the human mind. In other words, a proposition in geometry is true only insofar as it faithfully reflects the spatial intuition that the human cognitive apparatus is innately equipped with.

As a matter of course, a staunch empiricist will here object that the intuition in question is not at all innate but rather derived from sensory particulars. In fact, Hume explicitly states in this context that "every idea with which the imagination is furnished first makes its appearance in a correspondent impression."[34] Ultimately, he concludes, the idea of extension and thereby of space originates in the individual "impressions of colored points"[35] that compose a person's field of vision.

But Kant does not agree. For he observes rather compellingly that space can never be imagined not to exist.[36] What we can do quite easily is to remove in our thought the objects that a given space contains. But to 'envision' a genuinely spaceless reality is utterly beyond us. Space therefore is not an abstraction from sensory particulars but rather an inbuilt cognitive structure which our mind is designed to employ in representing to us the data of perception. To see an image always means to see an image in space because space is the indispensable cognitive precondition of any act of seeing. Similarly Kant asserts that time as well is not an empirical concept but rather "a necessary representation" that lies "at the foundation of all our"[37] conscious experience. We cannot think away time any more than we can mentally eliminate space, and both time and space "are therefore given *a priori*."[38]

Having reached this conclusion, Kant goes on to assert, somewhat unexpectedly, that time, construed in this way as an *a priori* pure intuition, also is the basis of arithmetic. For the concept of a number supposedly arises from "the successive addition of units in time."[39] Consequently and in summary, pure mathematics is possible, not as an abstraction from the concrete, but rather as a study of the human mental equipment. That is to say, the truths of mathematics are discovered as the human mind explores the spatio-temporal framework to which its own internal operation is inherently confined. Furthermore, the natural extension of this thought is the idea that metaphysics, too, can lead to knowledge that is genuine and true only insofar as it can be conceived as a science of reason itself. If we are to establish metaphysical truths with that same absolute certainty that mathematics so appealingly offers, we must use the structure of the understanding itself as our epistemological source. In particular, it is this internal cognitive faculty that we must antecedently analyze—and it is this faculty as well that Kant indeed *did* analyze in his *Critique of Pure Reason*.

In Kant's own words, the purpose of this major work of his was to make "inquiries into pure reason itself, and... to determine the elements as well as the laws of its use according to principles."[40] This determination, so Kant asserts, "was the most difficult task ever undertaken in the service of metaphysics;"— and in that, one is tempted to add, he almost was correct. For the only task more difficult than writing the *Critique of Pure Reason* is trying to read it. In fact, Kant himself admits that the product of his labors "is dry, obscure, opposed to all ordinary notions, and moreover long-winded."[41] Naturally then, we may here readily concede that a comprehensive treatment of Kant's critical, epistemological thought is clearly not a feasible objective. All we can hope to accomplish is to sketch a few broad outlines that are particularly relevant for the discussions that follow.

To properly approach this task, it is helpful to recall how Hume deconstructed the notion of causality: there is no sensory experience that rigorously implies the idea of a necessary connection between two events, and our stubborn insistence upon it is therefore based on nothing more substantive than a habit of perception. Kant could not accept this position of Hume's anymore than he could assent to the competing view of Locke's, according to which the notion of cause and effect is validly derivative of our observation of "the operations of bodies on one another."[42] The former opinion Kant believed to be implausibly skeptical and the latter rationally untenable. In consequence, he sought out an epistemological middle ground and ventured to proclaim that causality—like space and time—is an *a priori* conception that the human mind is designed to impose on the data that the senses provide. That is to say, a so-called 'cause' or 'causal link' can never be discernibly objective. There is no observation or sensory particular from which its existence can ever be validly inferred because, by its very nature, it is an innate subjective component of thought.

So what we see emerging here is an idealistic philosophy in which reality is vitally a human mental construct. It is not the external empirical world that imposes itself on the human mind by supplying its notions and concepts. But rather it is the reason of man that brings to bear its representational categories upon the empirical world and thereby, in essence, creates it. This inversion in the relation between the world and the subject that indwells it is the great Copernican turn of modern philosophy that Kant himself comments upon as follows:

> We here propose to do just what Copernicus did in attempting to explain the celestial movements. When he found that he could make no progress by assuming that all the heavenly bodies revolved round the spectator, he reversed the process, and tried the experiment of assuming that the spectator revolved, while the stars remained at rest. We may make the same experiment with regard to the intuition of objects. If the intuition must conform to the nature of the object, I do not see how we can know anything of them *a priori*. If, on the other hand, the object conforms to the nature of our faculty of intuition, I can then easily conceive the possibility of such an *a priori* knowledge.[43]

It is important to appreciate that the allusion to Copernicus is more than merely formal. For the Kantian subject/object inversion strikingly parallels the Copernican cosmological shift in its attendant psychological effects. When the Earth was discovered to be a tiny solar satellite, man was forced to realize that his physical station in the larger universe was utterly forlorn and insular. Where the geocentric world provided strong reassurance that man's existence had a well defined purpose intended by God, the modern scientific view merely evokes a sense of disconnect and total isolation. And it is precisely this modern loss of all connectedness that Kant's epistemology quite strongly reinforces. For when we ask exactly how the actual external world might be related to that inner, *a priori* world that the human cognitive apparatus produces, Kant only says that we don't know. The noumenon—the thing in itself—the world as it is—according to Kant, is unknowable by definition. Man depicts reality from within his own, solitary consciousness, and he can never hope to discover how that depiction of his corresponds to the real as it is.

In the light of these thoughts it is highly instructive to notice how very different in character the Kantian idealism is from the immaterialism of Berkeley. Kant does not deny the existence of an external material world apart from perception. But in order not to overstep the bounds of human cognition, he has to radically insulate human knowledge from its exterior material source. "[A]ll our knowledge begins with experience," but how faithfully that experience reflects the outside world from which it partly arises we simply cannot judge. We do not know if space and time are real objectively because subjectively we are not at liberty to imagine objective existence without them.

Berkeley by contrast believed that time was merely a name and as such inherently meaningless apart from the concrete everyday circumstances to which we apply it. We can ask what *time* it is and consult the hands on a watch for a perfectly well defined answer; or, perhaps, we can agree to meet with someone somewhere at a certain *time* without being in any way perplexed by the meaning of 'time' in this context. "But if time be taken," says Berkeley, "exclusive of all those particular actions and ideas that diversify the day, merely for the continuation of existence, or duration in abstract, then it will perhaps gravel even a philosopher to comprehend it."[44] That is to say, time is a convenient linguistic convention but an independent essence or existence in itself it really is entirely devoid of.

Berkeley's world is smaller than Kant's in that it is bereft of an extramental, noumenal dimension, but it also is more well defined and ontologically certain. Afterall, one of Berkeley's chief concerns was to defeat skepticism and to positively embrace the world as human perception directly portrays it (p.441). His goal was precisely to bridge that notorious philosophical chasm between the knowledge of the subject and the being of the object by grounding the latter in the former. In fact, Berkeley explicitly anticipates Kant's pertinent thoughts when he observes that, in "supposing a difference between *things* and *ideas*,"[45] we are forced to admit that knowledge of things in themselves is unattainable. For given this supposition, so he argues, it is indeed conceivable that "anything we know, all we see, hear, and feel, may only be a phantom and vain chimera, and not at all agree with the real things, existing in *rerum natura*."[46] But unlike Kant, Berkeley did not resign himself to this state of unknowing but rather declared the ideas that knowledge comprises to be congruent with the actual world that they pertain to.

Kant, of course, had also been reacting in his thought against a certain form of skeptical denial—the nihilism of Hume. But he did so with a far more detached philosophical attitude. He never ventured to assert an ontological doctrine and therefore had to content himself with a critical analysis of how the world that is there, whatever it may be, is represented to him internally by his own cognitive faculties. Indeed, it is astonishing and almost shocking to see how open-ended his answer to Hume ultimately turned out to be. Kant initially set out to demonstrate that Hume's denial of the possibility of metaphysics was premature. But when he had completed his painstaking analysis, deduced all the categories of the pure understanding, determined the nature of every conceivable judgment, and comprehensively discussed the inner contradictions that pure reason is inherently beset with, he still had surprisingly little to show for his efforts. He had accomplished an astonishing intellectual feat without being able to truly harvest its fruit.

It is true of course that Kant never intended to create a novel metaphysic. His goal was merely to establish the conceptual base upon which a scientific system of metaphysical thought could one day perhaps be solidly erected. But the fact remains that in all his works we do not find "a single synthetical proposition belonging to metaphysics"[47] which he had rigorously proven from *a priori* principles.

Kant duly acknowledged the questions concerning the reality of God and of life after death to be of ultimate existential importance. And he also did consider an affirmative answer to either of them not only an inescapable moral demand but also an eminently plausible rational choice. Yet strictly speaking, in making this choice, he had to leave behind, as he himself admitted, the domain of genuine knowledge and enter the realm of "doctrinal belief."[48] Thus when he contemplates, near the end of his work, the hypothetical charge that pure reason appears to be of very limited utility "in opening up prospects beyond the limits of experience"[49] and beyond the reach of common sense, he only offers us a starkly anticlimactic apology:

> I shall not here eulogize philosophy for the benefits which the laborious efforts of its criticism have conferred on human reason—even granting that its merit should turn out in the end to be only negative... But I ask, do you require that that knowledge which concerns all men, should transcend the common understanding, and should only be revealed to you by philosophers? The very circumstance which has called forth your censure, is the best confirmation of the correctness of our previous assertions, since it discloses, what could not have been foreseen, that Nature is not chargeable with any partial distribution of her gifts in those matters which concern all men without distinction, and that in respect to the essential ends of human nature, we cannot advance further with the help of the highest philosophy, than under the guidance which nature has vouchsafed to the meanest understanding.[50]

Sophie: I like the democratic spirit of these words—but goodness what a letdown: hundreds of pages of rarefied critical thought and in the end "the meanest understanding" cannot be surpassed.

Philonous: It's curious but otherwise not bothersome. For insofar as we interpret Kant's philosophy to be a call to epistemological modesty, I can
quite easily embrace it. In fact, I find it very much commendable for Kant
to recognize his human limitations—even if thereby he merely states the
obvious.

Sophie: ...in convoluted form.

Philonous: That is correct but also not especially offensive. I do not mind
Kant's infamous abstrusity, and I can tolerate his lack of elegance in style.
But what I do find troublesome is that distinctly arid sense of insular
autonomy (p.455) that all his works appear to be so thoroughly suffused
with. The human image in Kantian thought is always one of self-sufficient
isolation. Man creates his own cognitive and moral universe by drawing
exclusively upon his own internal sources (see also p.204 for some earlier
discussion of this point). He is not embedded but rather stands apart. I
am aware, of course, that this autonomy, for Kant, was closely tied to his
ideas of freedom and enlightenment. But here I always feel compelled to
ask: freedom from what? Freedom from life?

Sophie: As I see it, the problem is that all of Kant's philosophy is too cerebral and removed. It stays aloof and never intersects with anything that's
tangibly organic and alive.

Philonous: Indeed, Kant always keeps his distance, remains detached, and
never quite commits himself. He doesn't create a genuine worldview but
only writes critiques. Where Berkeley develops his thoughts to rationally
underpin his life-affirming attitudes, Kant, by contrast, seems to be content
to catalogue what attitudes his reason might permit him to coherently
assume. Moreover, the kind of reason he calls 'pure' or 'transcendental' is
an artificial absolute that is inherently lifeless and static. It is ahistorical
and never engaged in a truly dynamic give-and-take relationship with the
exterior empirical world. Reason imposes itself on the empirical data that
the senses provide. But as far as its *a priori* structure is concerned, it is not
conditioned or shaped by that data in any way whatever. In other words,
what Kant was sorely lacking was a proper evolutionary view.

Sophie: Meaning, I suppose, he should have been more mindful of the fact that
the structures that he found were really akin to those in a chicken, observed
by von Holst.

Philonous: Or perhaps he should have reflected, as *Darwin* famously did,
that one of his more distant relations most likely had been "a hairy...
quadruped" with pointed ears and a tail and "probably arboreal... habits."[51]

Sophie: A 'monkey' is more to the point.

Philonous: ...but doesn't sound nearly as fancy.

Sophie: Yet either way we mustn't forget that Darwin published his pertinent theory only in 1859[III]—more than fifty years after Kant's death, in 1804.

Philonous: I understand, we cannot fault Kant for failing to adopt an evolutionary view, if that view just didn't exist in his time. But as for us, it
surely behooves us to closely consider that evident link.

Sophie: ...from evolution to the human mind?

Philonous: Indeed, we need to realize, as Konrad Lorenz, for example, writes
in this context, that man is "a creature who owes his qualities and functions, including his highly developed powers of cognition, to evolution, that
age-long process of genesis in the course of which all organisms have come
to terms with external reality and, as we say, 'adapt' to it."[52] Furthermore,
we should take note when Lorenz here goes on to criticize the total disconnect that Kant perceived between the thing in itself and the subject
who perceives it. According to Lorenz, Kant "saw clearly that the forms of
apprehension available to us are determined by pre-existing structures of
the experiencing subject and not by those of the object apprehended, but
he did not see that the structure of our perceiving apparatus had anything
to do with reality."[53]

Sophie: In other words, the theory of evolution effectively closes the Kantian
gap.

Philonous: No, the gap remains, but a conceptual bridge is plausibly established. For by no means does Lorenz believe, as Berkeley did, that matter
is congruent with our subjective perception of it. Instead, he merely adds
to Kant's ideas the cogent suggestion that the external world imprinted its
structures and laws upon the human brain within the course of evolutionary
history.

Sophie: And thus we have a genuinely dual relation: mind creates empirical
reality by the act of representing sensory perceptions and empirical reality in turn creates mind by lawfully conditioning the brain's phylogenetic
development.

Philonous: Put differently, man's rational mind is Nature's mental mirror.
Nature created the brain, and the brain, in turn, recreates Nature in the
manner of its functioning.

Sophie: So space and time, in this way of thinking, are not just mental constructs that reason so happens to impose, but rather are derivative of something external—something that objectively exists.

Philonous: The answer is "yes" as long as we add that even in this evolutionary
view we still don't know that something *in itself.*

Sophie: No, but neither do we think that our perception of it is wholly unrelated
to it because our faculties of perception and cognition were genetically
molded by precisely that 'it'—that "something in itself."

[III]1859 is the year when Darwin published *The Origin of Species.* The quote above concerning the "hairy quadruped" was taken from Darwin's work on *The Descent of Man* which
he published in 1871.

Philonous: They were indeed.

Sophie: So in particular, that something really exists.

Philonous: Of course.

Sophie: But then, it seems, that Berkeley's view would have to be discarded. For he did not agree. He didn't think that there exists a world outside the mind, and thus he couldn't have maintained that reason somehow mirrors it.

Philonous: Your premise is mistaken. For as I previously explained (p.431), Berkeley never denied the existence of an objective exterior world. He rejected the notion of matter, but otherwise he left reality entirely untouched. His goal was not to make the human mind an island in nowhere but rather to re-link the mind to that which is external by making the physical universe an immediate mental domain supported by God.

Sophie: This reconnection, though, can also be achieved by following the logic of your evolutionary view. Afterall, if the Kantian thing-in-itself is really the natural architect of the Kantian reason, then it clearly follows that the two are closely entwined. In other words, the human mind is not as insular as Kant considered it potentially to be.

Philonous: In essence you are right. But we also need to be careful not to misjudge the nature of the worldview to which this logic is commonly thought to give rise.

Sophie: You're changing the subject.

Philonous: Not at all, I'm trying to get to its meaning. Let's take a look at one of Lorenz's pertinent remarks:

> Implied in the basic assumption that both the cognitive subject and the object of perception share the same kind of reality is a further equally important assumption, of the truth of which we are convinced. This is that everything reflected in our subjective experience is intimately bound up with, based on, and in some mysterious way identical with, physiological processes that can be objectively analyzed.[54]

You see, I don't deny that my subjective experience is intimately linked to nervous processes that happen in my brain. But when I further read that it is based on them, I start to hesitate, and Lorenz's final claim of actual identity I utterly reject.

Sophie: ...and that is so because, in your opinion, I assume, this final claim reduces your experience to nothing but a physical phenomenon. In other words, what you object to is the underlying view that matter is all that there is.

Philonous: That is my main concern—you put it right.

Sophie: It always is, as I would say.

Philonous: Perhaps, but given our present theme of evolutionary theory, there are some novel aspects to consider.

Sophie: Such as?

Philonous: The theory itself.

Sophie: In that regard, I think, I can be of assistance. For basically, that theory is simple to describe: organisms in natural environments produce more offspring than the resources available to them are able to support. By implication, there ensues a competitive struggle for survival in which the specimen that are genetically most well equipped are also the ones most likely to succeed and thus to reproduce. So as selective pressures come to bear in this manner on populations that are not genetically uniform, there is created an evolutionary genetic drift in the direction of optimal environmental adaptation.

Philonous: And it is this genetic drift which, starting from abiogenesis, has led to the eventual emergence of modern human beings—including you and me.

Sophie: That is correct.

Philonous: No, it is not! There is not a single paper, book, or treatise on evolutionary theory that has ever established that I as a person, in all my dimensions, have been produced by what is at bottom a chemical process. What has been argued by biologists is merely that my *body* has been so produced. But I am not my body. I am a spirit or soul that has become manifest—temporarily—in a certain physical form. And it is only this form—this outer material shell—that natural selection has ever come to bear upon.

Sophie: But bodies don't have souls in biological textbooks.

Philonous: But insofar as the authors of these books appeal to our rational capacities, we may as well with equal right appeal to theirs.

Sophie: I have a hunch you may have overlooked that souls are only believed in whereas fossil remains and DNA molecules can really be examined and observed—directly or indirectly.

Philonous: What has been overlooked very frequently—especially by scientists—is the astonishing fact that there are millions of people in this world who have experienced that at the point of death the human consciousness assumes a disembodied, immaterial form. The evidence is clear, compelling, verifiable, and thus incontrovertible.

Sophie: You made that point before (p.139ff).

Philonous: ...for very good reasons. Because if scientists ask us to accept that the evidence in favor of their evolutionary theory is clear, compelling, verfiable, and thus incontrovertible, then we may rightly ask them in turn to live up to their own rational standards. Did evolution occur? Sure it did. Did it extend over vast stretches of time? Certainly. Does it bear all the hallmarks of a contingent natural process rather than a one-time design event? Of course.[55] But why, if I may ask, should any such admission prevent me from acknowledging that many people close to death were able to perceive and later accurately recollect events that happened while their minds apparently were totally unconscious? What principle or fact should cause me to conclude that evolutionary biologists are intrinsically more honest and worthy of trust than thousands or millions of ordinary people who credibly report such near-death encounters?

Sophie: I don't know, but what I hear you saying is essentially that evolutionary theory is not *per se* erroneous but likely incomplete.

Philonous: It is incomplete *by definition.* It is the one theory that modern science has produced that necessarily negates itself. For included in the notion of an evolution of life there is a fundamental open-endedness. That is to say, the human plane is likely not the highest plane that life can ultimately reach.

Sophie: So we are back to your favorite topic: weak evolutionary transcendence.

Philonous: That's where my argument is headed, it is true.

Sophie: Then do I guess correctly if I say that your contention here will be that evolutionary theory is incomplete in that it's bound to evolve along with its authors?

Philonous: In principle, you do. But more specifically, what I should like to argue is that there is something woefully absurd in the idea that there could ever be a lower form of life that can explain, in causal terms, the forming of a higher. Exactly how would we, as human beings, plausibly describe the evolutionary emergence of a higher form of consciousness if that consciousness in turn will be of needs outside the range of our human comprehension?

Sophie: There is a problem here, I must admit.

Philonous: Worse still, we cannot even so describe the emergence of any consciousness whatever—be it higher or lower or merely our own. All we can say with reasonable certainty is that there has occurred a process of development in the course of which ever higher forms of consciousness—from animals to humans—became manifest. But insofar as we construe this process to be at bottom chemical in nature, we really cannot fathom in the least how consciousness could ever have been linked to it. Afterall, no chemist so far has been able to explain how molecules, when bunched together, can *experience* the world that they supposedly make up.

Sophie: Yet what is here the larger implication? It seems to me that if we take this thought concerning the material elusiveness of consciousness and combine it with your attendant conviction that souls depart from bodies in physical death, we are suddenly forced to admit that life—and evolution therewith—possesses a transcendent, non-material component. And thus it cannot be true that evolutionary development is entirely a matter of DNA mutations. Instead, there somehow must occur a matter/spirit parallel development. It really looks as though what happens on the physical

plane—the evolutionary process—must somehow be mirrored or matched
by a synchronous unfolding of consciousness in some parallel, extra-sensory
world.

Philonous: I don't know, but your idea that matter and consciousness are
moving in tandem is certainly attractive. To be sure, most scientists will
find such thoughts grotesque, bizarre, or totally ridiculous, but...

Sophie: ...but you don't care.

Philonous: Let's say I find some other, more accepted views no less deserving
of such labels. For imagine, for example, that somewhere in the distant
past—perhaps a billion years ago—there arose in our galaxy an intelligent life form that still exists today. And let's suppose as well, for the
sake of argument, that this alien race has undergone—for the past one
billion years—a steady evolutionary development to ever higher forms of
consciousness and civilizational competence. Do you think that beings so
advanced and so immeasurably far above the human plane would be impressed to learn that human evolutionary biologists believe themselves to
have created a complete and causally sufficient account of the formation of
life in the universe or even just of life on their own miniature planet? Is
it not perfectly ludicrous to assume that such a superior race would ever
pay heed to any human theories whatever? In our silly self-absorption we
may think that in meeting an alien form of intelligence we would see eye
to eye and somehow be treated as equals at least. But what if such beings
would regard our world with the same attitude as we would regard a prairie
dog town or a pond full of frogs—an interesting object of study but not an
occasion for exchanging notes or having a talk?

Sophie: But even *human* science, so far as it goes, is solidly grounded in truth.
It's imperfect and flawed but not entirely invalid.

Philonous: Of course not. Human cognition, so far as it goes, is very adequate
indeed—and so is a frog's cognition as well, so far as it goes. Furthermore
and in particular, Darwin's theory of evolution by way of selection and
random mutation also has a solid core of genuine validity. But that does
not at all imply that for some inscrutable reason I must assent when people
claim that these two forces—mutation and selection—are causally sufficient
to explain the genesis of life. Afterall, causal sufficiency can never be observed no matter how many fossils or DNA molecules we might happen to
analyze.

Sophie: I understand, but what I'm losing sight of is the link to my prior
suggestion. That is to say, I don't see how this question of causal sufficiency
relates to the idea that life traverses a dual matter/spirit trajectory.

Philonous: The problem simply is that the common causal reduction of life
to DNA-chemistry cannot be plausibly maintained if life involves an extra-
chemical dimension. For if it is the case that conscious experience is inherently non-physical, then there cannot exists an exclusively physical theory

that fully explains the evolution of life.

Sophie: So spirit is the cause of DNA designs?

Philonous: The word 'design' may here be easily misleading. The point is not that evolution is externally intended but merely that a full account of it must needs extend beyond the plane of human sense experience.

Sophie: ...because within that plane—that physical realm—there cannot be contained the being of a consciousness that any such experience implies.

Philonous: So to speak.

Sophie: Well then, my further question here is this: if spirits don't design the bodies they indwell, then how are they involved?

Philonous: The likely answer is that we will never know—at least not in this present life. As long as we are tied to physical existence, we cannot see or otherwise discern how souls and matter interact. In particular, when people speak of evolution by design, they also stay confined to human comprehension. There is no difference in this sense between a common evolutionist and a person who conjectures that a superhuman mastermind or god has given life its complex inner structure. For both attempt to make accessible to human thought a process or phenomenon that utterly transcends it. You see, I don't deny that God may here be vitally involved. On the contrary, I heartily embrace this thought. But this is not to say that I must limit God's reality to what my puny human mind can fathom and contain. There may be so much more to life than I can ever hope to grasp. What laws come into play when souls and bodies are evolving? What structures would we find if our senses could perceive that larger world that near-death travelers so frequently encounter? What words, if any, can we use to even hint at these exterior dimensions? I don't know.

Sophie: ...and neither do I.

The Madman and the Horse

The notion just discussed of a matter/spirit parallel development creates for us a view of evolutionary theory that seems to be quite readily compatible with common religious beliefs and faith-based convictions. Afterall, where souls are real and spirits are involved as life arises and unfolds, there is no reason to perceive that science and religion are intrinsically in conflict. Unfortunately, though, the indirect deduction of this purely speculative view from the available NDE body of evidence is less than satisfactory scientifically—to say the least. For the inherent inaccessibility of near-death states of consciousness to ordinary human awareness is liable to frustrate all attempts to understand how any such a parallel development might really be working in practice. That is to say, the recognition here proposed that consciousness, as an independent, *transcendent* reality, can never be divorced from evolutionary genesis is strictly philosophical in kind—it does not intersect with rigorous empirical science.

That said, there is but little hope that speculations such as these will ever help to pacify the battle fronts in current evolution wars. Scientists will go on to insist that consciousness must always and of needs be matter-bound, and orthodox religious folk will stubbornly continue to proclaim that evolutionary theory can only be a heresy.

Given this peculiar and very much lamentable predicament, it surely is advisable for us to try to carefully identify its probable causes. Exactly why is it the case that among the various branches of science it is evolutionary biology—first and foremost—that sets the agenda in present-day debates on science and religion? If the Bible declares that man was "formed" by God "from the dust on the ground,"[56] then why should it seem so strongly offensive to certain religious believers when modern adherents of Darwin assert that man arose from some primordial molecule by way of a monkey? If anything, the former tale seems even more deflating in its bluntness. The obvious reply that in the Bible we can also read how God ennobled man by imprinting His image upon him is certainly poignant—to an extent. But what it fails to justify is the especial rage that evolutionists so frequently attract. In other words, we may here readily admit that it is more appealing, psychologically, to feel oneself the product of divine intent instead of purposeless material developments. But inasmuch as that which is material is fundamentally and finally the province of the physicists, we should perhaps complain to them and view Darwinian biologists as merely secondary culprits.

The story of evolution, as commonly told, is ultimately quantum-chemical and therefore mathematical in nature. Consequently, what evolutionary reductionists in essence maintain is that reality in its entirety—including human life—is faithfully representable by the symbolic mathematical systems that physicists employ in modeling material phenomena. Reality in this sort of view is nothing but a sequence of symbols—a string of zeros and ones—that is acted upon by certain abstract rules called 'natural laws'. It is this assertion of the total equivalence of the real and the formal—this *zero-one hypothesis*—that ultimately constitutes the materialistic worldview—and it is this assertion too that hard-core evolutionists at bottom uphold.

Yet is this really all there is to it? Is it really this implicit embrace of zero-one reduction schemes that is the reason why the Darwinists especially are singled out for blame by Biblical literalists and other like-minded dogmatists? If the answer were "yes," then we would have to ask again, "Why not attack the physicists as well?" Afterall, it is the physicists and not biologists that are by far the most astute reductionists. In Newton's mechanistic world machine, for instance, there hardly is much room for anything that could be called 'a meaningful human existence'. For in a world where matter is governed inescapably by forces and laws that are rigidly deterministic in kind, no human act of will can ever control a human bodily motion. Consequently, the image of man in classical physics is the image of a robot who so happens to be conscious.

Darwin published his *Descent of Man* in 1871, but the work *Man a Machine*, by the French physician and philosopher Julien Offray de La Mettrie, dates back to 1747. What is the reason that it took more than a century, between these publication dates, for Christian fundamentalists to really get upset at scientistic godlessness?

In trying to find a plausible reply, it is instructive to observe that in the history of thought it was not La Mettrie but rather René Descartes to whom it fell to define the modern worldview at its inception. In consequence, the native modern ontology—the dualism of Descartes—left open a loophole for free-willed consciousness and also for God. Animals *are* machines, and matter *is* deterministically conditioned, but the mind of man is not material and therefore is at genuine liberty to exercise its independent, God-given agency. In the Cartesian philosophical system, the human faculty of reason is the one critical focal point at which the merely physical encounters its limit and through which transcendence is linked to the immanent material world.

Naturally, in his necessary ignorance of quantum mechanics, Descartes never managed to convincingly explain how human free will can really be free while being confined to a bodily shell which is material and therefore robotic. How can the rigidly determinate be subject to the free and thus be indeterminate? Descartes didn't know because he couldn't know, in his day, that in the quantum world the physical is *not* determinate and also *not* divorced from conscious volition.

But be that as it may. What matters here is not that the Cartesian ontology was lacking in cogency but that it was dualistic in kind—that it was designed to let the physical exist side-by-side with the mental and the transcendent. For it is thus that we can now more clearly see why Darwin's later theory appeared to be so scandalous. Prior to Darwin's momentous advance it was still possible to somehow believe that science had left untouched that image of sanctified personhood that God had imparted to Adam on the day of creation. But with the arrival of the evolutionary paradigm and the attendant compilation of vast amounts of evidence in favor of it this possibility quite simply ceased to exist. Suddenly and unexpectedly the figure of Adam receded from sight, and biblical mythology became zoological prehistory.

To be sure and as we just explained, a more acute perception of the ontological character of the classical Newtonian universe would have made it blatantly obvious that mankind had been stripped of its humanity long ago in early modern physics. But perhaps this earlier idea of human beings as automata was simply too remote and too directly contrary to common intuition to ever be met with wider acceptance. For it is one thing to ponder, in the abstract, how that which seemingly is free—the human volition—might really be conditioned and controlled by physical natural laws, and it is quite another thing to stare a monkey in the face and come to see oneself in it.

In summary then we may here conclude that Newton began what Darwin would finish—namely to render the world a system of matter that symbols can faithfully model. Darwin closed the circle that Newton had started to draw. When man was transformed from a creation of God to a fluke of natural history, the last piece of the puzzle fell into place, and the zero-one hypothesis was given a solidly factual status. Materialism had won the day, and, far from being a mere philosophical option, it now could be declared to be, or so it appeared, an integral part of rigorous, empirical science.

In consequence of this dramatic intellectual shift, the very core of the Western civilizational covenant—the Christian metaphysic—was suddenly facing a lethal attack. For in a Darwinian universe of random chemical genesis there isn't much room for spirits or gods or silly beliefs in purposeful acts of creation. Where matter is all that there is, being has no transcendent component to it, and man is but a naked ape whom natural selection mindlessly fashioned. Man in this modern scientific mythology no longer is the handiwork of some benevolent creator God, but rather is a soulless physical entity whose only purpose in living is living itself. He is not meant to be but only so happens to be because evolution so happened to produce him.

This ominous specter of a comprehensive metaphysical calamity has nowhere been captured more disturbingly, in Western philosophical literature, than in the parable of *The Madman* by *Friedrich Wilhelm Nietzsche* (1844–1900):

> Have you not heard of that madman who lit a lantern in the bright morning hours, ran to the market place, and cried incessantly, "I seek God! I seek God!" As many of those who do not believe in God were standing around just then, he provoked much laughter. Why, did he get lost? said one. Did he lose his way like a child? said another. Or is he hiding? Is he afraid of us? Has he gone on a voyage? or emigrated? Thus they yelled and laughed. The madman jumped into their midst and pierced them with his glances.
>
> "Whither is God" he cried. "I shall tell you. *We have killed him*—you and I. All of us are his murderers. But how have we done this? How were we able to drink up the sea? Who gave us the sponge to wipe away the entire horizon? What did we do when we unchained this earth from its sun? Whither is it moving now? Away from all suns? Are we not plunging continually? Backward, sideward, forward, in all directions? Is there any up or down left? Are we not straying as through an infinite nothing? Do we not feel the breath of empty space? Has it not become colder? Is not night and more night coming on all the while? Must not lanterns be lit in the morning? Do we not hear anything yet of the noise of the gravediggers who are burying God? Do we not smell anything yet of God's decomposition? Gods too decompose. God is dead. God

remains dead. And we have killed him. How shall we, the murderers of all murderers, comfort ourselves? What was holiest and most powerful of all that the world has yet owned has bled to death under our knives. Who will wipe this blood off us? What water is there for us to clean ourselves? What festivals of atonement, what sacred games shall we have to invent? Is not the greatness of this deed too great for us? Must not we ourselves become gods simply to seem worthy of it? There has never been a greater deed; and whoever will be born after us—for the sake of this deed he will be part of a higher history than all history hitherto."

Here the madman fell silent and looked again at his listeners; and they too were silent and stared at him in astonishment. At last he threw his lantern on the ground, and it broke and went out. "I come too early," he said then; "my time has not come yet. This tremendous event is still on its way, still wandering—it has not yet reached the ears of man. Lightning and thunder require time, deeds require time, the light of the stars requires time, deeds require time even after they are done, before they can be seen and heard. This deed is still more distant from them than the most distant stars—*and yet they have done it themselves.*"

It has been related further that on that same day the madman entered divers churches and there sang his *requiem aeternam deo.* Led out and called to account, he is said to have replied each time, "What are these churches now if they are not the tombs and sepulchers of God?" [57]

Sophie: The imagery and language, I must say, are powerful indeed.

Philonous: I totally agree, and I would add that Nietzsche as a writer was an artist of extraordinary aptitude. His German prose has never been surpassed in terms of quality of style and power of expression. But quite apart from brilliant artistry, we also can discover in his works a sumptuous variety of deeply passionate, intensely absorbing, and strangely bewildering thoughts. Nietzsche never was a systematic thinker, but he acutely understood the spirit of his times and he was driven to respond to it with radical resolve.

Sophie: He knew that God was dead, and he was not afraid to say so.

Philonous: ...and thus he painted in his works the image of a world that was entirely devoid of otherworldly elements.

Sophie: That is correct, for Nietzsche thought that God's demise could only mean the total abolition of transcendence. He argued and he wished that all reality was immanent of needs.

Philonous: Are you then familiar with his thought?

Sophie: To some extent, I am.

Philonous: What sparked your interest, may I ask?

Sophie: The fact that Nietzsche was so passionate an atheist. I felt attracted to his views because I sensed in them that urgent thirst for truth—for brutal honesty—that seeks to show the world for what it really is: a godless fight to dominate, a bloody struggle to survive, a battle of the will to conquer and possess.

Philonous: I understand, the world, as human rationality encounters it, is *"will to power* and nothing else"[58]—according to Nietzsche. Yet what exactly does he mean by this? What is that 'will' to which he grants so prominent a world-sustaining function? Is it an ontological absolute? A thing in itself? The real as it is? The answer is "no," for Nietzsche says explicitly that "'immediate certainty'... 'absolute knowledge' and 'thing in itself' are all contradictions in terms."[59] They are verbal "seductions"[60] to which we succumb simply because we are used to adhere to certain linguistic conventions. This negative reply, so we might think, is bound to be accompanied by some more positive, compelling explication. But unfortunately, what we are given merely is the very weird hypothesis that all 'effects' that human beings recognize are universally effects "of will upon will" and "that all mechanical happenings, insofar as they are activated by some energy, are will-power, will-effects."[61] What in the world am I to make of this? How would I ever use this sweeping claim to better comprehend, in causal terms, a typical mechanical occurrence, such as the motion of two billiard balls before and after their collision?

Sophie: It sounds bizarre, I must admit. But then again, if we deny that billiard balls are wills that act on other wills, we can with equal justice put to doubt the common claim that they are bodies with a mass that act by way of 'force'. In fact, as I recall, you argued once at length that forces in mechanics merely are notational conveniences that are as such entirely dispensable (pp.43–49).

Philonous: Certainly, the notion of a 'will-effect'—or 'ill-effect' or 'skill-effect'—is not inherently inferior to a more traditional conception like 'mass', 'momentum', or 'force'. But that's exactly why there is no profit in employing it. Nothing whatsoever is achieved by substituting words for other words.

Sophie: In essence I concur. But what I find a little odd is that you clearly were more tolerant, not long ago, when I remarked—and you agreed—that Berkeley more or less had done the same. He left the facts of science totally untouched and merely changed the verbiage (p.432). Where others speak of matter, energy, and actual objects, he only spoke of sense perceptions and ideas. So why then do you now complain when Nietzsche follows suit and offers us his own competing verbal scheme?

Philonous: Because it seems to me that Nietzsche, unlike Berkeley, failed to fully recognize that his interpretive alternative was really just interpretive. For he apparently believed that there are ways to found its truth more solidly upon a rigorous empirical—or quasi-empirical—analysis. Thus he writes in this context that we are "[n]ot to assume several types of causality until the *experiment* of getting along with a single one has been followed to its utmost conclusion"[62] (emphasis added). Moreover, so we are told, if "we really acknowledge the will as *effective*," then "we must *experiment* with taking will-causality as our only hypothesis"[63] (emphasis added in the second quote). It may sound harsh but nonetheless is fair to say that the notion of performing an experiment—or thought experiment—in order to validly infer the effective causal agency of will in physical or, as Nietzsche might say, 'volitional' reality is utterly absurd. No physicist has ever established the causal agency of any conception whatever. What physicists *can* do, of course, is to describe the world by means of mathematical systems in which certain letters like F for 'force', E for 'energy', or conceivably even W for 'will' are given certain roles to play. And what they also *can* do is to make these roles appear more tangible and easier to grasp by suggesting, for example, that forces are the *causes* of certain physical happenings. But what it might mean to properly deduce, by way of some mental or physical experiment, that such a choice of a manner of speaking is really more than merely a choice, I cannot even begin to conceive. If Nietzsche wishes to argue, say, that causes are forces and forces are wills—fine. But if he means to assert some deeper principle or truth—as he apparently does—then I will say his writings on this point are woefully inadequate.

Sophie: Apparently, you're trying to construe the will to power as a novel ontology that needs to be aligned with existing scientific descriptions. But in the overall context of Nietzsche's pertinent ideas, it is more accurate to say that his conception of this will is relevant mainly to our understanding of life in general and human behavior in particular rather than to ontological discussions of inanimate material phenomena. It is true that Nietzsche tries to close the gap between these two domains by suggesting, somewhat obscurely, that it may be possible "to understand the material world as a *preform* of life."[64] And it is also true that he thereby attempts to extend the potential range of validity of his hypothesis concerning the centrality of will to being as a whole. But all the same it seems to me your current emphasis on Nietzsche's relatively few remarks on purely physical phenomena is very much misguided.

Philonous: To that my answer is that Nietzsche's volitional monism may very well be more important to the overall scheme of his thought than you are willing to acknowledge.[1] For given his paradigmatic denial of any form of genuine transcendence, Nietzsche must be careful to avoid any suggestion

---

[1]Walter Kaufmann points out in [Kau1] regarding this point that Nietzsche initially embraced a dualistic view in which the will to power was opposed by the forces of reason and that his move toward a more consistently monistic position occurred only later in his most important work, in *Thus Spoke Zarathustra*.

that volition may be rooted in some otherworldly realm that differs fundamentally from the immanent physical realm of energy and matter. It is thus that Nietzsche speaks of matter, as you said, "as a preform of life" because it is thus that he can draw the following vital conclusion: if the inanimate is, in fact, *pre*animate and if life is governed by volition, then everything is life or *pre*life, and volition therefore governs everything.

Sophie: There is no doubt that Nietzsche's "volitional monism," as you just christened it, was intended to directly support his prior philosophical loyalties, including very importantly his rejection of transcendence. So, yes, Nietzsche did indeed propose his pertinent ontological views with a definite purpose in mind—but so did Berkeley too. The latter aimed to glorify God and the former to undo Him. The purpose was different but the method of argument—the choosing of a suitable ontology—was very much the same.

Philonous: It was the same in kind but not in quality and clarity of thought.

Sophie: But even so I wonder if that deficit in quality in Nietzsche's case was really as pronounced as you appear to be asserting. Do you really disapprove of Nietzsche's thought because it lacks conceptual concision or just because you happen to dislike it? Perhaps what you resent in his philosophy is not so much its insufficient rigor but rather its conspicuous irreverence. You believe in God but Nietzsche did not, and thus you are keen to uncover the flaws his thinking.

Philonous: In that you may be right. For I admit that I am loath to be reminded of that awful time, some twenty years ago, when Nietzsche's world of thought was similar to mine.

Sophie: ...that time you mentioned recently (p.448) when you were steeped in "metaphysical confusion"?

Philonous: ...that time when I did not believe in God and really had no proper frame of reference at all. My mind, back then, was aimlessly afloat in what appears to me in retrospect a highly chaotic, scientistic worldview mix. With no firm ground to stand upon I was entangled in a web of modernist philosophies and reductionistic theories that I found all to be equally pale and depressing. In consequence, my image of myself became precariously tenuous and volatile. Depending on my mood or current mode of functioning, I would regard myself to be a zero-one volitionless automaton, a higher form of animal life, a molecular aggregate, or an unruly Freudian compound of illicit desires and unconscious wishes—to name just a few of the relevant options.

Sophie: It sounds more interesting than "awful," I would say—especially the Freudian "unruly" part. But what about that link to "Nietzsche's world of thought"?

Philonous: Well, if you had told me in those days that all I do and think is fueled by an underlying power drive, I would have gladly taken that idea and put it in my mix.

Sophie: ...and then stirred it a bit?

Philonous: ...stirred it, while adding in some spice according to Darwin's favorite recipe. That is to say, I would have dressed that power drive most likely as an instinct to survive—to procreate, to pass on my genes, and thus to fulfill my evolutionary chemical function.

Sophie: And in that you would have been quite right—*partly*, that is, to be precise. For Nietzsche says that "[s]elf-preservation is only one of the *consequences*" of a still more fundamental urge that inheres in every "living thing"—the desire "to *discharge* its energy."[65]

Philonous: It makes good sense because, by definition, we may say that Nietzsche's will-to-power scheme—or energy-discharging scheme—is global in its reach and thus as fundamental as it possibly could be. For as it is, you can consider any aspect of my life, anything I do or say or think, any wish or impulse that I harbor, and cast it into any mold you like. You can squeeze me into a Freudian box, a Darwinian box, a chemical box, a physical box, and also, of course, a will-to-power box, and I will always fit in regardless. In fact, as long as you're not totally incompetent in rhetoric, the squeezing will be effortless.

Sophie: Put differently, the thing that you call 'I' can always be completely deconstructed.

Philonous: Completely, yes it can. And I myself have done it countless times with dedication and abandon.

Sophie: Deconstruct yourself?

Philonous: Myself and everything I do.

Sophie: What would be an example?

Philonous: An instance of this sort occurred one day when I was walking home to my apartment in Berlin. While on my way, I met an elderly neighbor of mine who had been out to shop for groceries. As she was evidently lacking in strength, I offered to carry her bags to her door (so far as I recall—see the footnote)[II] which she gladly accepted. Later that night, when I reflected back on this experience, it somehow struck me that I couldn't quite make sense of it. It was an act of kindness, sure enough, but why had I done it? What meaning did it have? Had I done it out of habit to satisfy an etiquette? Did I want to leave a positive impression? Or was I afraid that if I failed to help, I would appear uncaring and uncivilized? And what about my motivating impulse? Did genuine unselfishness inspire me or did I merely wish to make myself feel good? And why feel anything at all? Afterall, a hundred years from now, when both my neighbor and myself will

---

[II]The instance that *Philonous* here recalls may not be factual because it happened more than 20 years ago, and the present author's memory of it is therefore somewhat uncertain. Perhaps the good deed here recalled was only intended and not carried out or perhaps—more probably—it was preceded by a similar encounter in which the present author had actually failed to perform it. That is to say, the act of kindness here in question may have been motivated by feelings of guilt following this earlier failure.

long be dead and decomposed, all memory of my philanthropy will equally
have vanished. So why invest in it a positive—or negative—emotion?

Sophie: That's quite a bunch of questions to address. How did you sort the
matter out?

Philonous: My exact train of thought I cannot quite remember. But at the
most basic level I likely would have said, "It really doesn't mattter." For
insofar as I agree with Nietzsche when he says that all that I am is "body...
entirely and nothing else,"[66] I simply cannot fail to realize that as a body
who is bound to totally disintegrate in death, I cannot possibly assign any
lasting significance to any answer I might give to any of the questions that
I posed. However, if for some foolish reason I should decide to search for
answers notwithstanding, my first line of approach might be to try to trace
my act to certain forms of pseudo-altruistic animal behavior. In other
words, my human inclination to be kind may here be found to have its
origin in its utility in evolutionary history.

Sophie: And it is fair enough, for helpful deeds in monkey clans or prehistoric
human tribes can clearly be important for survival.

Philonous: They clearly can, and Nietzsche even is quite right when he remarks
in this regard that "the entire phenomenon of morality" is ultimately "animal" in nature.[67]

Sophie: He is quite right? So you agree?

Philonous: Certainly. For how could I ever deny that my animal ancestry is
plainly evident in much of what I do and say and think? Is it not perfectly
obvious that many of my social interactions in particular are patterned
upon structures that are animal in kind?

Sophie: Nietzsche would say "yes," for he observes that

> [t]he practices demanded in polite society: careful avoidance of the
> ridiculous, the offensive, the presumptuous; the suppression of one's
> virtues as well as of one's strongest inclinations; self-adaptation,
> self-deprecation, submission to orders of rank—all this is to be
> found as social morality in a crude form even in the depths of the
> animal world..."[68]

Philonous: So can I then construe my little act of helpfulness to be a high-end
form of animal behavior?

Sophie: It seems to me you can.

Philonous: And just as well, with equal ease, I can construe it in whatever
terms I like. I can construe it in psychological terms by following Freud or
Jung or Adler perhaps, in rational Platonic, Cartesian, or Kantian terms, in
British empiricist terms, French existentialist terms, American pragmatist
terms, Hegelian historicist terms, Newtonian physical terms, Nietzschean
will-to-power terms...

Sophie: ...or, more generally, in whosoever's however-whatever terms.

Philonous: Absolutely—anything goes.

Sophie: ...if that's the view you happen to adopt.

Philonous: But since I can adopt it if I wish, I may agree with Nietzsche's *madman* when he says that our modern or *post*modern world is really just a void—"an infinite nothing" through which we stray with no sense at all of any distinctive direction.

Sophie: So that's the lesson that your "awful" period has taught you?

Philonous: It is indeed, but I should add that I was taught that lesson too— directly and indirectly—when I encountered Nietzsche's deviant writings. For Nietzsche was notorious, not only for revaluing all values with programmatic purpose and intent, but also for revising constantly whatever purposes and views he somehow chose to be committed to. He was a devoutly pious Christian in his youth, then came to be an atheist, and ended up the spiteful author of *The Anti-Christ*; he eagerly admired Richard Wagner as a genius of the very highest rank but later 'recovered' from him as "one of [his] sicknesses;"[69] he was deeply impressed at first by Arthur Schopenhauer's *World as Will and Idea* but then detected in this work a life-denying decadence of which he wanted to be purged;[70] he was a German anti-German, a "saint of immorality,"[71] a nihilist who believed in seeking the truth,[72] and a truth-seeker who considered the will to truth to be inherently pernicious and destructive;[73] a conformist in personal etiquette, he utterly despised the human herd for its slavish adherence to customs of thought; and as a philosopher who aimed to unmask everyone and everything, he adopted numerous conflicting views and argumentative stances that really were nothing but "so many masks."[74] In fact, among the various philosophies that I have tried to make myself familiar with it was Nietzsche's thought undoubtedly that struck me as the most amorphous and ambiguous by far.

Sophie: And yet, from what I understand, you are unwilling to entirely reject it. Afterall, if "anything goes," then Nietzsche's thought as well may be regarded to be valid.

Philonous: It is not easy, as I said, to figure out exactly what it was that Nietzsche thought on any given issue. But once this question is decided in my mind, I always can convince myself *verbally* that he was fully justified. And the same, of course, may here be said as well of all the other authors and philosophies I mentioned. They all are right or wrong depending on my attitude.

Sophie: But then it seems that when you disagree with Nietzsche's claim that "God is dead" you merely offer me another pointless view—a view that is correct if I so wish. And hence, you only deepen my confusion.

Philonous: At the level of mere arguments my claim that God exists is just as true or false as Nietzsche's pertinent negation—and also just as meaningless. So, yes, in this sense you are right. But the problem here may be that the reality of near-death states of consciousness does not in any way depend on any arguments that you or I, or Nietzsche perhaps, may happen to field. To us the question of whether God is dead or is alive may be a matter of dispute, but to those who have beheld His brilliant light and joyfully experienced His overwhelming love there really is no question to be asked. These people *know* that God is real because they have seen Him and met Him and felt Him. For them He is a fact that cannot be denied.

Sophie: Roughly, then, what you are saying is that the great metaphysical problems of mankind—the deepest riddles of philosophy—can finally be solved as NDEs reveal to us what all of it is really all about. Twenty-five centuries of laborious intellectual inquiry are made obsolete as near-death survivors enlighten us with esoteric tales of otherworldly spirit realms.

Philonous: I know it sounds ridiculous, but as it is, I really do believe that those who have experienced in death a higher form of consciousness have much to share that we do well to carefully examine and absorb. This is not say, as you implied, that our human quest for rational knowledge and insight will thus be rendered "obsolete." But it is to say that there can be set up a very solid base from which that quest can be more fruitfully pursued.

Sophie: ...and from which, I suppose, the chaos of your "worldview mix" can also be effectively cleared up.

Philonous: To some extent it can. For the recognition of the factual reality of near-death encounters created in me a feeling of embeddedness in a larger transcendent world that restored to my life a sense of wholeness and inner cohesion. Reality to me recovered its integrity once I acknowledged and fully understood that there is more to it all than matter, energy, and natural science—much more. Ultimately, human life is not a metabolic zero-one phenomenon but a journey of the soul that serves a definite, God-given purpose. Those who have seen the Beyond will tell us very consistently that our existence in this world is meant to be a learning phase that aids the growth of our spirit. We are here to loosen the bonds of selfishness and sin, and to reach out to others in empathy, compassion, and love.

Sophie: By carrying their bags?

Philonous: That's one of many possibilities.

Sophie: So all those questions that you asked concerning the why and what-for of helping your elderly neighbor can now be finally settled as follows: we are to help each other out because that is what life in this world at bottom is about.

Philonous: ...*objectively* about, as I would say. You see, what matters here is not for me to piously pronounce that life is all about kindness and love but rather to suggest that this is what it *is* about—objectively and undeniably. I understand, of course, that there is nothing more offensive to our modern sense of personal autonomy and our postmodern faith in total subjectivity than the idea that we may not have a choice, that things may be what they are regardless of how we happen to view them. But even postmodernists will one day experience physical death and even they will have to face that otherworldly realm that lies *objectively* beyond it. So even they will probably be told one day—like many others before them—that human life indeed is most effectively lived in faithful adherence to the two great commandments: "[l]ove the Lord your God" and "[l]ove your neighbor as yourself."[75] We may not be able to perceive it thus, in our present material state, but seen from the spirit realm this law of human life may be as binding and as firm as any law of physics.

Sophie: In other words, as bodies fall to the ground when we drop them, so the purpose of life is most fully realized as we learn to obey this golden rule that Jesus once set up.

Philonous: There may be other rules besides, but yes, I like the way you put it.

Sophie: Then let me say that I can easily agree that taking stock in what near-death accounts reveal to us may very well be useful and important. But we mustn't forget, of course, that useful information can be gleaned, not only through the 'disembodied eyes' of near-death travelers, but also through the regular material eyes that you and I possess. And when I use the latter sort, as I currently must, I really cannot see that kindness and love are the dominant themes of human existence. Indeed, a Darwinian view may here appear more accurate by far: life is a struggle of all against all in which the strong will succeed and the weak will be vanquished. And Nietzsche's will-to-power scheme may also be more viable empirically than your transcendent loving fantasies.

Philonous: I don't have a problem with that. I don't contend that Darwin was entirely mistaken, that science is irrelevant, and all philosophy a fluke. On the contrary, my point precisely is that we should take as broad a view as possible and never willfully reject important information. But unfortunately, most current-day philosophers and scientists will do exactly that. They will deny what cannot be denied—the reality of near-death encounters—and thus create descriptions of the world that are hopelessly stunted and twisted. It is not wrong to explore the material world—the world of sensory perception. Nor is it unwise to contemplate the philosophical implications of the knowledge that we thus procure. But it is very wrong indeed to insist that matter is all that there is. For given the NDE record, we really can *know*—with high-level certainty—that there is a Beyond and that transcendence is not an illusion.

Sophie: I think you missed the point that I was getting at. I am not contesting your assertion that modern scientists may have unduly restricted their vision. Instead, my claim at present is that your vision, too, is far too narrow and selective. It seems to me you don't appreciate to what extent your law of love directly contradicts the facts of life as we consistently observe them. For not only are unselfishness and love far rarer than they ought to be, but what is worse, we never can be sure that they are present where we think they are. Indeed, you were quite right to ask in this regard if your 'unselfish' act was meant, perhaps, to only make yourself feel good.

Philonous: As I see it, what truly matters here is not whether there is such a thing as absolute, ideal unselfishness but whether I choose to act as though there is. Put differently, we certainly can try to figure out exactly what my motivations were in picking up my neighbor's bags. But in the end the fact that counts is that I really picked them up. One day, when I have entered the Beyond, so I believe, I will review that little scene and will be glad to see that I had chosen to be helpful.

Sophie: You will be glad and thereby reap your benefit—so much for your 'unselfishness.'

Philonous: You overlooked that at the time, back in Berlin, I didn't believe in any Beyond and thus did not expect to be transcendently rewarded. Yet either way, I don't see what is wrong with helping out my neighbor and increasing my own happiness thereby. As I see it, the law of life is so designed that *everyone* will benefit whenever anyone adheres to it.

Sophie: In that case, though, we must conclude that those who do 'good', while believing in this law, are actually *more* selfish than those who do good while being unaware of it. For the latter likely won't expect to be given one day a heavenly blessing in retrospect.

Philonous: In following this logic it would seem that those belonging to the former group can prove their own unselfishness only by abstaining from doing good, that is, by abstaining from unselfish acts—which is absurd.

Sophie: All the same, though, and in light of these perplexities, I wonder if the view that Nietzsche took was not perhaps more plausible than yours. It has been said of him that "he suspect[ed] all 'good' urges of originating from bad ones" and that he "proclaim[ed] the 'evil' ones as those which ennoble and exalt life."[76] Given your evident inability to explain to me coherently what constitutes a truly unselfish act, we may as well suspect that Nietzsche was correct.

Philonous: In response to this, I only can reiterate that I wholeheartedly support all honest exploration. Should we search for the origins of human moral behavior, as Nietzsche did, even if the results that we find may not be flattering? By all means! If we acknowledge, for instance, that absolutely pure and loving motivations do not exist and that, in particular, there is no such thing as genuine unselfishness, we may feel positively humbled thereby. But *objectively* and quite in spite of any such acknowledgments, reality is still what it is. That is to say, my decision to carry those bags may not have been free of ulterior motives, but the effects that it produced were beneficial no less. Furthermore, when Nietzsche searches for goodness in that which we tend to regard as 'evil' or 'bad', I am in principle again quite open to his findings. Aggression in nature, for instance, is 'good' in the sense that it fulfills a vital regulatory function.[77] But the problem here is that Nietzsche, of course, is not content to stay scientifically detached. His main intent is not to state an ethological fact but rather to frontally attack his favorite enemy: "the religion of *pity*"[78]—the Christian moral code. Here is how he puts it:

> Pity on the whole thwarts the law of evolution, which is the law of *selection*. It preserves what is ripe for destruction; it defends life's disinherited and condemned; through the abundance of the ill-constituted of all kinds which it *retains* in life it gives life itself a gloomy and questionable aspect. ...To say it again, this depressive and contagious instinct thwarts those instincts bent on preserving and enhancing the value of life: both as a multiplier of misery and as a conservator of everything miserable it is one of the chief instruments for the advancement of *décadence*—pity persuades to *nothingness*![79]

And what is worse, these kinds of quotes can be readily multiplied. In another passage, for instance, we read that the "first principle of" Nietzschse's will-to-power "philanthropy" is that "[t]he weak and ill-constituted shall perish" and that one ought to "help them to do so."[80] Moreover, so we are told, Christianity "is more harmful than any vice" in that it encourages "[a]ctive sympathy for the ill-consituted and weak."[81]

Sophie: I grant these quotes are deeply disconcerting.

Philonous: Yet even more disturbing is the fact that Nietzsche would be right to view these matters thus, if he were right in his prior conviction that human life is bodily life "and nothing else" (p.472). For given this premise of his, it could be argued easily—and plausibly—that the law of life is the law of evolutionary, *bodily selection* and that, by implication, humans whose bodies are weak are unclean elements that ought to be removed.

Sophie: But fortunately, as you will certainly insist, humans are not mere physical systems but rather are beings with souls that are sensitive to higher laws of the spirit—laws that make room for kindness and love, and sympathy and pity.

Philonous: ...laws that are, if I may add again, inherently *objective*. We can use our free will to overrule them temporarily, but we can never erase them, and sooner or later they always resurface and assert themselves—somewhere, somehow. A case in point here is the story of Nietzsche's ultimate breakdown. You see, Nietzsche lived in many ways a very tortured life. He suffered from syphilis, was tormented by terrible migraine headaches, experienced often extreme isolation, and actually spent the last eleven years of his life in a state of apathetic madness. Perhaps his last act of sanity occurred on the 3rd of January, 1889, when he spontaneously took *pity* on a helplessly suffering horse:

> As he was leaving his lodgings [that day]... Nietzsche saw a cabman beating his horse at the cab rank in the piazza Carlo Alberto [in Turin]. With a cry he flung himself across the square and threw his arms about the animal's neck. Then he lost consciousness and slid to the ground, still clasping the tormented horse. A crowd gathered and his landlord, attracted to the scene, recognized his lodger and had him carried back to his room. For a long time he lay unconscious. When he awoke he was no longer himself...[82] (R.J. Hollingdale)

Sophie: He had lost his mind.

Philonous: ...and he had lost it at that very moment when he could not help but obey that ultimate law of kindness and love that he had tried to overturn for so many years with so much resolve and intellectual passion. He had waged a war of words against the good as it is, revalued all values on page after page, but in the end reality did not comply. In the end, a suffering horse was still what it was—a hapless, frightened creature that irresistibly called forth his human compassion. Men can do horrible things, but no one can make the horrible non-horrible, not even Nietzsche.

Existence Stripped Bare

The fundamental assumption that matter is all that there is—or more to the point—that reality does not extend beyond the reach of sense-based human cognition has come our way in various guises. It was stated by Nietzsche with programmatic explicitness, it was implied by the constitution of the Newtonian world machine, had an early progenitor in the atomism of Leucippus,[I] and was evident as well in the agnostic nihilism of Hume, in the traditional Darwinian account of evolutionary genesis, in the *Astonishing Hypothesis* of Francis Crick (p.156), and also in the closely related assertion by Lorenz that subjective human experience must somehow be identical with objective physiological processes that happen in the brain (p.459).

Taking the latter claim as our current point of departure, we need to emphasize—yet again—that physiological processes, by definition, are processes governed by physics which are as such faithfully representable by symbolic mathematical means. In other words, Lorenz—as any true materialist—in essence upholds the zero-one hypothesis: physical reality exists; it can be

---

[I]As we pointed out earlier (p.51), Leucippus's fellow atomist, Democritus, taught that human beings have a soul. However, this postulate does not compromise the strict materialism of the atomist system because, according to Democritus, souls are composed of atoms and are not immortal.

experienced; the experience of it is itself a physical phenomenon; and since the physical is congruent with the symbolic, it follows that reality cannot be distinguished objectively from a purely formal zero-one system. The real is nothing but a digital stream—a binary flux of information bits that is generated by quantum randomness and that evolves in time in strict accordance to the mathematical rules that physicists refer to as 'natural laws'.

Nietzsche did not appeal in his writings to this digital imagery, but it is hard to deny that his chilling appeals to assist the "weak and ill-constituted" in perishing are fully compatible with it. Afterall, a person, for example, who is physically or mentally handicapped—which is the same—may here be rightly viewed to be a binary string that has been corrupted and therefore is useless. He or she—or *it*—is nothing but a faulty piece of software code that ought to be deleted. The program that we call 'reality' runs more smoothly without it. Seen in this light, the cleaning-up of the unfit that Nietzsche promotes is a positive hygienic measure that enhances life by ensuring its flawless logical functioning.

At this point one may readily object that neither Lorenz nor Crick nor Hume ever endorsed such horrific ideas as the intentional removal of 'useless' human life. We may be willing to admit that the selective destruction of life has an important health-promoting role to play in natural habitats. But surely no one, apart from Nietzsche—or Hitler, perhaps—would ever wish to actively encourage it in respect of humans.

That may indeed be so, but our current concern is not what people endorse or wish for, but rather what conclusions we can draw from the worldview they adhere to. In other words, the question here is not whether the personal attitude of any one philosopher or scientist is consistent with the precepts of materialism but whether the precepts of materialism are compatible with the utter inhumanity of certain of Nietzsche's opinions. And here it seems there is but one way to reply: "yes, absolutely!"

There is nothing wrong whatsoever with eliminating dysfunctional human entities because humans, as molecular aggregates, are nothing but zero-one strings. They are digital compounds that are wholly devoid of a metaphysical essence and thus are totally bereft of any inherent right to exist. Indeed, since the very notion of 'morally wrong' is also just a binary construct, secreted by the neurons in a brain, we may even say more globally that there is nothing wrong with *anything* because nothing can possibly matter, if matter is all that there is.

A materialist, of course, could argue against this view that symbolic representations—as representations—are not the real thing. Evidently, the world is more than a sequence of zeroes and ones; it is an actual world in which real people live real lives that ought to be valued and protected. But when we further inquire what the word 'actual' might here be assumed to signify, the materialist will be forced to admit that that which is 'actual' is that which is 'material' and thus congruent, by definition, with the formal mathematical systems of contemporary physics. It is tiresome to restate this point again and again, but given the overwhelming ideological influence that materialism exerts in current-day Western societies in general, and Western academic circles in particular, the repetition may well be worth the fatigue that it causes.

Incredible as it may seem, the Western *mind* has somehow begotten and endorsed the *mind-denying* philosophical doctrine that the world in its entirety is but a digital skeleton that has no metaphysical quality other than existence itself. Zeroes and ones exist and that's it. Instead of acknowledging the limits of human reason and perception, Western man has limited reality to human rationality and thereby reduced the world to a binary shell that surrounds an absolute nothing (see also the discussion on pp.116–124). By implication, human life within that shell is wholly essence-free and wholly superficial of needs.

In this context it is revealing to realize that Nietzsche, on the one hand, forcefully asserted the inherent value of a certain type of life—a strong and healthy instinctual life—but on the other never managed to explain wherein that value precisely consists.[83] He revalued all values by depriving the very notion of a value of its metaphysical depth, but he completely failed to establish convincingly how that which has no depth can ever be of value. In *Thus Spoke Zarathustra* Nietzsche holds out to his readers the evolutionary ideal[II] of the "overman"[84] as a saint of the earth who knows but the law of courage and might and proudly affirms his own, superior type of existence. Yet why does he affirm it? Because he does? Because he is the overman? Nietzsche never says. The overman affirms what he affirms because he is his own self-contained end. He lives in the here and now, despises all "heavenly things,"[85] calls evil his highest and best,[86] and "creates a meaning for the earth"[87] from nothing but his will to meaning itself. Hence we read how Zarathustra challenges his listeners as follows:

> All beings so far have created something beyond themselves; and do you want to be the ebb of this great flood and even go back to the beasts rather than overcome man? What is the ape to man? A laughing stock or a painful embarrassment. And man shall be just that for the overman: a laughingstock and a painful embarrassment. You have made your way from worm to man, and much in you is still worm. Once you were apes, and even now, too, man is more ape than any ape. ...
> Behold, I teach you the overman. The overman is the meaning

---

[II]The word 'evolutionary' is here meant to be understood more broadly than in strictly biological, Darwinian terms. Nietzsche fully acknowledged the reality of evolution as a biological process, but the overman is not so much a member of a higher future species as he is a developmental goal that humans can reach by means of a process that Nietzsche refers to as 'self-overcoming'.

of the earth. Let your will say: the overman *shall* be the meaning of the earth! I beseech you my brothers, *remain faithful to the earth*, and do not believe those who speak to you of otherworldly hopes! Poison-mixers are they, whether they know it or not. Despisers of life are they, decaying and poisoned themselves, of whom the earth is weary: so let them go.[88]

Elsewhere, in an autobiographical aside, Nietzsche has Zarathustra recall the pious yearnings of his youth—those visions of love and divine apparitions that once enchanted his soul. Zarathustra remembers them "like dead friends"[89] that he once possessed and that still possess him, even now that the light of their happiness has been stolen from him. He shakes his fist at the evil enemies of his who "assaulted [him] with filthy ghosts"[90] and cruelly thwarted the joy of his passion. They robbed him with their treachery of the heavenly springs of his soulful delights and thus inflicted on him an irrevocable, heartrending loss.

However, it was precisely at this very moment of total despair, when fate had pushed him to the limits of endurance, that Zarathustra discovered the path to true overcoming—the path that led him to a higher form of life. "[I]n me," so he realized then, "there is something invulnerable and unburiable, something that explodes rock: that is *my* will."[91] In consequence, Zarathustra boldly went forth to exercise that will of his in an elemental act of self-reassertion. In doing so he made himself the master of his own chosen destiny, and hence he became his own creator and god, his own source values and morals. His will was the force that wholly set him free—free to be what he was destined to be and free to decide what life is about and who is worthy to live it.

Naturally, the question that arises here is whether indeed the exercise of the will to life is in itself sufficient to furnish life with a genuine purpose or goal. Exactly why should a purely physical entity—called 'woman' or 'man'— that happens to have an active volition be interested in willfully maintaining its functional material integrity? Afterall, all bodies and things are congruent to digital strings, the dead no less than the living. So why affirm the one and not the other? Why choose life rather than death? Perhaps *Albert Camus* was right to insist in this context that "[t]here is but one serious philosophical problem, and that is suicide."[92] Did Nietzsche fail to realize that this is the ultimate problem that man must address? Did he never feel the utter absurdity of willing life for the sake of willing? And did he never wish to put an end to it? The answer is, "yes and no." It is, "yes" because Nietzsche does admit that "the thought of suicide is a strong consolation" that can help a person "to get through many a bad night,"[93] and it is, "no" because the overman is not suicidal—not in the ordinary sense, that is. The overman likes to live dangerously and is not afraid to die. He knows when his time for parting has come, and he is willing to return to the earth in freedom and strength.[94]

But contemplating the absurdity of human existence and seeking a premature escape from it is a form of decadence that he cannot but strongly reject.

Moreover, the very idea that life can be ended for good by means of suicide is directly in conflict with Nietzsche's famous doctrine of the *eternal recurrence*. In the *Gay Science* Nietzsche asks us to imagine that a demon "sneak[s] after" us, into our "loneliest loneliness," and says to us, "This life as you now live it and have lived it, you will have to live once more and innumerable times more; and there will be nothing new in it, but every pain and every joy and every thought and sigh and everything immeasurably small or great in your life must return to you—all in the same succession and sequence—even this spider and this moonlight between the trees, and even this moment and I myself. The eternal hourglass of existence is turned over and over, and you with it, a dust grain of dust."[97] Thus Nietzsche's affirmation of life for life's sake only is put to its ultimate radical test: he is asked to say "yes" unendingly, for now and for all the infinite future. Nietzsche refers to this test as the *"greatest stress"*[98]—a stress that threatens to "crush"[99] him. But true to himself he makes his will the master of it and fervently answers the demon as follows: "You are a god, and never have I heard anything more godly."[100]

Thus Nietzsche unwittingly settles the problem posed by Camus by denying its premise. Life can never be ended in suicide because there simply is no end to it—no final escape from its clutches. For existence, as it were, is a giant cosmic wheel that spins about in perfectly monotonous, identical cycles. No matter how miserable, pointless, or cruel our present existence may be, we must relive it again and again and again—and if we were overmen, we even would welcome this harrowing prospect.

This then is Nietzsche's absurd solution to the problem of life in an absurd material universe: absurdity is overcome by absurdly willing its cyclic recurrence for all times to come. Thus speaks Nietzsche, and thus speaks only he. His views are his own and only his own—and so, of course, are ours as well. For in a skeletal zero-one information world there simply cannot exist a common metaphysical ground in which to anchor our views communally. We are all completely disconnected, and we all must create, like puny little gods, our own philosophical islands in nowhere. There is no transcendent center of gravity that jointly attracts us, but only a structureless sea of random information bits in which we all are adrift haplessly without a purpose or direction. We can fantasize about eternal recurrences, desire suicide, live healthy practical lives, or descend into madness. But no matter the choice that we favor, reality will always respond with the same flatly permissive reply: "suit yourself."

In the light of these sobering thoughts, it is interesting but scarcely surprising to learn that Camus was prompted to pursue his life-or-death inquiry because he perceived a fundamental disconnect between the world of matter outside and the conscious subject that indwells it. In *The Myth of Sisyphus* he writes:

A world that can be explained even with bad reasons is a familiar world. But, on the other hand, in a universe suddenly divested of illusions and lights, man feels an alien, a stranger. His exile is without remedy since he is deprived of the memory of a lost home or the hope of a promised land. This divorce between man and his life, the actor and his setting, is properly the feeling of absurdity.[101]

According to Camus, man desires the world to be human; he wants to see himself in it so as to be able to relate to it. If man could realize "that the universe like him can love and suffer, he would be reconciled."[102] But contemporary man has altogether lost that hope for a meaningful human connection. His vision cannot penetrate the surface of appearances and therefore leaves him wholly unaware of what lies underneath it. He is forced to see the world scientifically as that which it appears to be, and thus it utterly "evades"[103] him. "[T]he shimmering... phenomena"[104] that his senses portray are to him like pigments of paint on a canvas that his reason can methodically dissect but that his spirit cannot integrate into a coherent, familiar depiction:

And here are trees and I know their gnarled surface, water and I feel its taste. These scents of grass and stars at night, certain evenings when the heart relaxes—how shall I negate this world whose power and strength I feel? Yet all the knowledge on earth will give me nothing to assure me that this world is mine. You describe it to me and you teach me to classify it. You enumerate its laws and in my thirst for knowledge I admit that they are true. You take apart its mechanism and my hope increases. At the final stage you teach me that this wondrous and multicolored universe can be reduced to the atom and that the atom can be reduced to the electron. All this is good and I wait for you to continue. But you tell me of an invisible planetary system in which electrons gravitate around a nucleus. You explain this world to me with an image. I realize then that you have been reduced to poetry: I shall never know.[105]

Put differently, scientists use symbols to represent perceptions, and the meaning of these symbols in turn they purport to explain by means of the imagery—or "poetry"—that their perceptions suggest. There is no opening in this for genuine knowledge and truth. Nor is there any meaningful link to the one who perceives—the conscious human mind.

To be sure, in describing in this way the existential dilemma of man, Camus is not imagining himself to be original. For he explicitly acknowledges that others before him arrived at more or less the same dispiriting conclusions. His goal is not to show that the relation between man's inner and outer realities is absurd, but rather to decide what course of action he should follow because it *is* absurd. "Does the Absurd dictate death?"[106] so Camus asks. Or does it perhaps require, instead, that one takes flight into hopes that reason cannot justify—hopes for an afterlife or some other transcendent fulfillment?

In working out his answer, Camus observes that the latter route—the route of philosophical escape—had been chosen by various existential philosophers that went before him, men like Jaspers, Chestov, or Kierkegaard. Faced with the irrationality of existence and the impossibility of knowledge, these thinkers had performed sudden leaps into transcendence that amounted in effect to a "sacrifice of the intellect."[107] They had entered "the waterless deserts where thought reaches its confines"[108] but then hurried on to chase a mirage of palm trees in the distance. However, the "real effort," says Camus, "is to stay there... and to examine closely the odd vegetation"[109] that even deserts still provide. In other words, Camus does not want to leap. He wishes "to live *solely* with what he knows" eventhough he is fully aware that the only true knowledge available to him may be that, ultimately, true knowledge will always elude him.[110]

For Camus, absurdity is a fact that man must not escape from. He adamantly refuses to be swayed to lessen the tension between the world and his reason by any form of metaphysical trickery. And it is this refusal to surrender his intellect that is his act of defiance—"his only truth."[111] That is to say, in order to be true to himself he must remain suspended in his awareness that life is meaningless and not seek out an inauthentic exit. Thus he rejects hope as much as voluntary death.

Indeed, Camus positively welcomes this state of existential indecision because it is for him the indispensable prerequisite of true inner freedom. The absurdity of a finite life that must end in death is the principle upon which he stakes his claim to genuine liberty. He is free to do as he chooses because everything he does is destined to vanish in total oblivion. As a matter of course, when Camus speaks of 'liberty', he does not have in mind a metaphysical absolute but rather a concrete freedom of action "which a human heart can experience and live."[112] Afterall, his very purpose is to live without any wishful appeals. He desires to embrace the factual and concretely existent and thereby to shun the merely possible and hypothetical. Hence we read:

> The absurd man thus catches sight of a burning and frigid, transparent and limited universe in which nothing is possible but everything is given, and beyond which all is collapse and nothingness. He can then decide to accept such a universe and draw from it his strength, refusal to hope, and the unyielding evidence of a life without consolation.[113]

Finally, when Camus addresses the question as to what exactly it means to be alive in such a "limited universe," he offers us the rather startling assertion that the passion of the absurd man is to maximize the sum of his experiences—even though, or better, precisely *because* he knows full well that

all his experiences are utterly pointless. What matters to him above all is not
to live the best possible life but merely to somehow grab the *most* of it. For it
is thus that he is enabled to maintain his revolt against the revolting condition
that he finds himself in; and it is thus, says Camus, that the initial anguish
that he feels when confronted with a world without depth is transformed into
a fervent stance of existential self-assertion that gives him a reason for being
alive.

It is doubtful to say the least, whether this highly idiosyncratic 'solution'
to the problem of life in a physical vacuum is any more convincing than the
willing-of-life-for-the-sake-of-willing that Zarathustra so strangely exhorts. Is
anguish really overcome by maximizing a person's experiential exposure to a
meaningless state of existence? If reality is wholly indifferent to human life and
mindlessly threatens it with random suffering and certain death, then why not
feel afraid of it? In a hollow, digital cosmos humans are conscious functional
entities that simply so happen to be. They are at the whim of natural mathematical laws that have nothing to do with their personal longings and needs,
and they can never know if or when these laws will conspire with happenstance to hurt them or destroy them. So why should they not experience fear
at being exposed to such a distinctly inhumane world? Perhaps the absurd
man can conquer his dread in his stubborn revolt so long as fate assigns to
him a comfortable place from which to contemplate Camus's pertinent writings. But once he has to face reality head-on, he likely will succumb again to
that naked angst at being alive that *Edvard Munch*, for example, captures so
brilliantly in his 'existential paintings' (good examples are *The Scream* (1893)
and *Evening on Karl Johan Street* (1892), both of which can easily be viewed
on the Internet). He will know that he is lost and that will be the end of it.

Sophie: The reference to Munch is clearly out of place. For Munch was not an
existentialist. He did not rid the world of essence and transcendence, but
on the contrary, desired to express in his works that deeper realm that lies
beneath the surface of appearance. His paintings were meant to be visual
symbols that hinted at unseen, elusive dimensions.

Philonous: He aimed to create "soul-art"—rather than "soap-art," as the impressionists.[114] But he also made apparent in his works that fundamental
disconnect between the human and the world that is so typical of existentialist experience. Reality in his art is portrayed as an ominous irrational
presence—a looming threat that reason cannot subdue. What Munch discovers when he penetrates the surface of the familiar is highly disturbing,
fearsome, and dark. And he openly acknowledges this personal propensity
of his in one of his pertinent biographical remarks:

> The angels of fear, sorrow, and death stood by my side since the
> day I was born. They followed me when I played—followed me
> everywhere. Followed me in the spring sun and in the glory of

summer. They stood by my bedside when I shut my eyes, threatening me with death, hell, and eternal damnation. Often I awoke in
the middle of the night, gazing around the room in wild fear—was
I in Hell?[115]

Sophie: Which goes to show precisely what I said, namely that his outlook was
profoundly transcendental in nature.
Philonous: Yet later in his life, he turned agnostic and abandoned the faith
of his youth. Like Nietzsche and many other modern men before him, he
ventured forth into a world that was religiously foundationless.
Sophie: Speaking of Nietzsche, though, we may want to mention as well that
Munch never resented religion *per se.* He was a seeker of truth who believed
in souls and spoke of God.[116]
Philonous: But nonetheless, he also was deeply impressed by certain ideas that
Nietzsche conceived (so much so, in fact, that he painted the philosopher's
portrait in 1906 (see the Internet)).
Sophie: You are referring, I suppose, to Nietzsche's volition-based ontology.
Philonous: I am indeed, for Munch as well believed the will to be pervasive.
Sophie: But there are differences in this regard that we had better be aware of.
For Nietzsche's will to power was transformed in Munch's artistic view into
a less imperious, more integrative force—a universal animating energy that
suffused the whole of physical existence. The stars in the sky, the rocks
on the ground, the clouds in the air, the waves on the ocean, they all were
endowed in his mind with spirit and vivacity.[117]
Philonous: He saw a vital urge at work where Nietzsche perceived "a preform
of life" (p.469). The words are different but the meaning is the same.
Sophie: I don't agree because the latter was an atheist, whereas Munch may
be considered a mystic or a pantheist but definitely not an enemy of God.
In fact, he honored the teachings of the *New Testament* and even believed
that Christ was "very close to godlike."[118]
Philonous: Your labels may be accurate, but all the same I do insist that many
of Munch's works may rightly be considered existentialist. In a painting
like *The Scream*, for example, we clearly recognize that same disharmony
between the inner and the outer worlds that existentialists have been so
eager to assert. It is awareness that here turns an ordinary scene into
a nightmare scenario of alien objects and spaces. A bridge becomes a
knife that cuts into a landscape,[III] a clouded sky a symbol of oppression,
and common passers-by are suddenly perceived as faceless silhouettes that
haunt us with their lifelessness.
Sophie: So your concern is not what Munch *himself* believed but what his works
communicate *to you* regardless of his views.

[III]Apparently, what looks like a bridge in Munch's painting was actually a path with a
safety rail in the original motif that inspired his work (see [Prid], p.151). But the distinction
obviously is not very important.

Philonous: That would be fair to say. But more especially, my object is the link that I detect between the visual symbolisms of Munch on the one hand and certain literary themes on the other that prominently characterize the existentialist outlook. In *Jean Paul Sartre's* novel *Nausea*, for instance, we come across that same estrangement from the familiar that seems so evident as well in paintings like *The Scream*. Indeed, the 'Nausea' that Sartre depicts is a profoundly disquieting sense of worldview dislocation—a perceptual distortion that afflicts the novel's main protagonist, *Antoine Roquentin*, with feelings of vertigo and unexpected fear. In his diary Roquentin describes the onset of his ailment as follows:

> Something has happened to me, I can't doubt it any more. It came as an illness does, not like an ordinary certainty, not like anything evident. It came cunningly, little by little; I felt a little strange, a little put out, that's all. ...
>
> For instance there is something new about my hands, a certain way of picking up my pipe or fork. Or else it's the fork which now has a certain way of having itself picked up, I don't know. A little while ago, just as I was coming into my room, I stopped short because I felt in my hand a cold object which held my attention through a sort of personality. I opened my hand, looked: I was simply holding the door-knob. This morning in the library, when the Self-Taught Man came to say good morning to me, it took me ten seconds to recognize him. I saw an unknown face, barely a face. Then there was his hand like a fat white worm in my own hand. I dropped it almost immediately and the arm fell back flabbily. ...
>
> So a change *has* taken place during these last few weeks. But where? It is an abstract change without object. Am I the one who has changed? If not, then it is this room, this city and this nature; I must choose.[119]

Sophie: So what does he choose?

Philonous: At first he decides that he himself must be the cause—that the Nausea is in him. It is his own awareness, so he concludes, that is beginning to twist and transform the physical world that surrounds him. But later he finds that, on the contrary, he "is the one who is in *it*."[120] The Nausea is that which exists—contingently, without necessity—and thus he finds himself engulfed in it. But then again, he also possesses it because he understands it.[121]

Sophie: He understands it? I'd say he is entirely confused by it.

Philonous: Initially, he certainly is. In fact, he is falling apart. His social life already has and now he himself is following suit. Roquentin is a solitary urban individual who lives alone, has no friends, receives nothing, and gives nothing to anyone. He speaks to no one—except for the Self-Taught Man

who is nameless and therefore doesn't count—and his interpersonal contacts are limited to occasional sexual encounters that are conversation-free
and wholly perfunctory. Roquentin is inwardly dissolving, and the implo-
sion that shatters his self is the vacuum force that sucks up and distorts the
physical facts that surround him. A beer glass becomes inexplicable to him,
sunlight turns pale, clouds appear ridiculous, doors seem threatening and
ominous, and even his own face, reflected in a mirror, looks suddenly like
an alien lunar landscape that is lifeless and sullen. He sees the world as one
who is being reduced to nothing but his own naked awareness. Roquentin
is conscious, but conscious of what? He no longer knows. There are phenomena, but there is no coherent reality that rationally binds them. In
consequence, the entire realm of sensory experience becomes to him an
alien menagerie of random impressions and factoids. Names for objects
lose their meaning, thoughts accordingly disintegrate, and sensations, too,
turn hollow and void. Ronquetin exists—he thinks and is aware, and therefore he is there. But in 'truth' he only thinks that he is there because at
bottom the 'he' is a nothing—a symbolic vacuum that harbors no essence
at all. Roquentin stares into the abyss of his own inner emptiness and pulls
back in fright:

> I am. I am, I exist. I think, therefore I am; I am because I think,
> why do I think? I don't want to think anymore, I am because I
> think I don't want to be, I think that I...because...ugh! I flee.[122]

Sophie: Given the parallels you drew to the paintings by Munch, I would like
to submit that your description of Roquentin's existential troubles reminds
me very much of certain works by the modern British artist *Francis Bacon.* His unsightly rendering, for instance, of Velázquez's portrait of *Pope
Innocent X* is a haunting but truly poignant depiction of that state of total
inner dissolution that Roquentin apparently has fallen into (see the Internet
for Bacon's *Head VI* (1949) and Velàzquez's portrait of *Pope Innocent X*
(1650)). Bacon crudely disfigures and mutilates the reality that Velázquez
so carefully assembled. He takes a person full of life and turns him into
a tortured torso in a cage—a vacant material shell that delivers to itself a
soundless random scream, prompted by nothing.

Philonous: There are many such parallels to modern works of art. In fact,
the dazzling abundance of styles that modern artists have produced is in
itself an existentialist phenomenon. For it bespeaks the kind of radical
subjectivism that a world without structure is liable to foster. But more
specifically, the existentialist themes of alienation, fear, and absurdity, of
nothingness and death are powerfully evident in many modern paintings.
We discover them, for instance, in the bizarre artifacts and alien green skies
of *Giorgio de Chirico's Pittura Metafisica,* in the startling juxtapositions
of the surrealists, the grotesque nihilism of the dadaists, the bare present-

ness of *Marcel Duchamp's* ready-mades, the distorted human images in the works of *Pablo Picasso*, and also in the insular figures that are on display in *Edward Hopper's* modern urban sceneries (see the Internet, for instance, for Picasso's *Self-portrait* (1972), de Chirico's *Disquieting Muses* (1916), and Hopper's *Nighthawks* (1942)). But you are right, the paintings of Bacon as well are perfectly fitting examples.

Sophie: Especially when you consider how Bacon himself describes the 'purpose' of his art in the modern cultural context:

> Also, man now realizes that he is an accident, that he is a completely futile being, that he has to play out the game without reason. I think that even when Velázquez was painting, even when Rembrandt was painting, they were still, whatever their attitude to life, slightly conditioned by certain types of religious possibilities, which man now, you could say, has had cancelled out for him. Man now can only attempt to beguile himself, for a time, by prolonging his life—by buying a kind of immortality through the doctors. You see, painting has become, all art has become a game by which man distracts himself. And you may say that it always has been like that, but now it's entirely a game. What is fascinating is that it's going to become much more difficult for the artist, because he must really deepen the game to be any good at all, so that he can make life a bit more exciting.[123]

Philonous: It's right on target, isn't it? For when you trace the modern history of thought from Nicolaus Copernicus to Sartre and Camus, you cannot help but think that this is what it had to come down to. All along we moderns have endeavored to describe the world disinterestedly with mathematical precision, and what our analyses ultimately left us with was a disinterested mathematical world that really was a vacuum. Bacon understood the 'spirit' of his times, and in his works that spirit is extremely well reflected.

Sophie: Yet even so it would be nice if paintings that command this power of expression could somehow be less dark and somberly depressing.

Philonous: In that regard, so I believe, we'll have to wait for better times to come. A true improvement we will only see if there occurs a shift to some new period in history that is more hopeful and more spirit-filled—a period of "soul-art" perhaps and corresponding "soul-ontologies."

Sophie: "Soul-art" à la Munch?

Philonous: Not exactly, I'm afraid. His art was powerful, moving, and deep. But hope was nowhere to be found in it. Reality, according to Munch, is fearsome and oppressive, and the souls that indwell the figures in his works have nothing to look forward to beyond the physical grave that awaits them. Where Camus embraces the absurd and where Roquentin is cured of his illness—eventually—by entering a state of heightened awareness that reveals to him the raw presentness of uncreated existence, Munch announces to us, somewhat more compellingly, the finality of anxiety and death. But neither Camus nor Roquentin nor Munch has anything to offer to us that any being with a soul can truly draw upon for sustenance. There is no nourishment in nothingness.

Sophie: Your claims concerning Munch are once again decidedly inaccurate. For Munch explicitly asserts that "[i]t is necessary to believe in immortality, insofar as it can be demonstrated that the atoms of life or the spirit of life must continue to exists after the body's death."[124] Existence is eternal, says Munch, because in nature nothing perishes and everything always reenters the cycle of life.

Philonous: So what he really says is this: the chemical compounds of which his body consists will fertilize the plants that will grow on the soil in which he will be buried. I wouldn't call that a meaningful afterlife. But don't get me wrong—Munch was a wonderful artist whose concern for the deeper realities behind the veil of physical phenomena was truly exemplary. He rightly reached for the spirit in man, but he did so in an age when spirits had ceased to exist. In consequence, his vision was left incomplete, for it lacked that vital aspect of transcendence that genuine soul-art would have to express. I don't know, of course, what such a future 'soul art' will be like. But it will be the art of an age when people understand again—again and for the first time—that matter is not all that there is and that life on earth is part of a larger transcendental journey—a sojourn through the spirit realm.

Sophie: In other words, it will be the art of an era of wisdom when people have finally learned to see the world aright. The vision is attractive perhaps, but realistic it is not.

Philonous: Another possibility here is that, ultimately, we may not be given a choice. For if we fail to embrace the kind of spirit-friendly vision of the world that genuine soul-art would embody and arise from, we may not be able to make it. If we continue to cling to our materialistic and nihilistic ontologies, we will most likely not achieve that inner sense of balance which alone will allow us to restore the outward, ecological balance of Nature. That is to say, we cannot live on this planet continuously without destroying it, if we don't understand the purpose we are here for. Seen in this light, wisdom is not a lofty goal that cannot be reached but rather a naked demand of physical survival.

Sophie: Except for the fact, of course, that survival is guaranteed in life after death.

Philonous: That is correct—we will survive if only we can somehow understand that death can never be an option.

Infantile Illusions

Existentialism as a concrete first-person experience—an actual state of being in the world—is very appropriately and very effectively expressed in literary fictional form. Some of the great defining works that here come to mind are novels such as *Nausea* and *The Age of Reason* by Sartre and *The Plague* by Camus. However, apart from these fictional writings, we also find essays and treatises that attempt to elaborate the fundamental tenets of existentialist philosophy in a more systematic, methodical form. An example of the latter sort is Sartre's magnum opus, *Being and Nothingness.*

In the introduction to this work Sartre opens his discussion of ontology with a brief review of certain attempts by modern philosophers to overcome the Kantian dualism of essence and appearance. The gist of these attempts, according to Sartre, is to consider objects or "existents" as equivalent to the series of all the various appearances by which they become manifest in human consciousness. A force in physics, for example, is not a mysterious metaphysical something, but merely is a certain set of observable effects. Forces do not 'cause' changes in an object's state of motion but rather are identical with them. So in this way of thinking, the equation $F = ma$ defines the force F to be the infinite totality of all the sense-based measurement procedures that allow us to specify the numerical values of the mass m and the acceleration a in a given physical setup (see also the discussion on p.43ff). Similarly, the 'essence' of an object like a cup is not a Kantian thing-in-itself, beneath the surface of appearance, but rather is the principle that unites the infinite series of its manifestations in sensory perception.

In evaluating the success of this school of thought, Sartre observes that the reduction of being to series of appearances, when driven to its limit, amounts to little more than a reassertion of Berkeley's famous formula *"esse est percipi."* Empirical knowledge, in the form of perception, is declared to be all that there is, and the independent noumenal reality of matter is thereby denied. This view, though, is untenable, according to Sartre, because a table, for instance, cannot "be identified with the knowledge which we have of it" for "otherwise it would be consciousness... and it would disappear as table."[125] Furthermore, those who wish to reduce all being to knowledge had better be prepared to offer us "some kind of [prior] guarantee for the being of knowledge."[126] Afterall, how can we say that being is knowledge if we cannot explain how knowledge has being?

Faced with this question concerning the being of knowledge, Berkeley would have probably replied that knowledge is composed of ideas and that ideas have their being in a spirit that conceives them. But Sartre, of course, has to reject this view because, in his mind, spirits or souls or conscious essences do simply not exist. On the other hand, though, he does admit that knowledge—universally—is knowledge in reference to consciousness.[127] There are no spirits

that are conscious but there are basic acts of consciousness, and it is to these
that knowledge necessarily is tied.

As Sartre now expands on this thought, through a sequence of rather intricate philosophical arguments, he comes to conclude that the attempt to
ground being in knowledge leads to logical absurdities.[I] In consequence, he
is led to assert the primacy of consciousness over knowledge and discovers
the ground of existence in elemental acts of awareness and self-awareness that
simply are there, without a substrate to support them. Consciousness as such
is empty and void,[II] but the particular state of being conscious of an object
is that ultimate, raw instance of being (of being-for-itself) on which Sartre
bases his ontology—or better, bases one half of it. For an equally elemental
form of simply being there (of being-in-itself), Sartre also grants to the things
to which the consciousness refers. These things, like tables or cups, are not
in the consciousness but exist externally in space. They are not unknowable
noumena in the Kantian sense, but reveal themselves in appearance—albeit
incompletely—and their being merely *is*—it "is what it is."[132]

"To exist," says Roquentin, "is simply *to be there*."[133] Indeed, it is this realization that finally discloses to Roquentin the nature of his unnerving malaise.
Suddenly he understands that his intense uneasiness, was caused by a coming to the fore in his consciousness of the disturbing otherness of the thing
that simply is there—the thing that appears to him but otherwise has nothing
whatever to do with him. Here is how he describes it:

> ... I have understood all that has happened to me since January.
> The Nausea has not left me and I don't believe it will leave me so

---

[I]Roughly speaking, Sartre's argument proceeds as follows: consciousness is always consciousness of an object, but consciousness is also self-aware. That is to say, one cannot help
but be conscious of being conscious. Consequently, there is such a thing as "consciousness
of consciousness."[128] However, if we attempt to construe this latter type of consciousness in
epistemological terms as a knowledge of knowing, we are led to contemplate a corresponding
knower who is known, because knowledge always is the knowledge of a subject in respect
of an object. But what about this knower who is known? If he is known, then there must
be a knower—a knower of the knower who is known. As we pursue this argument to its
natural end, we are faced with an infinite regress to ever more remote knowers of knowers
that are known, which is absurd. In order to avoid this absurdity, "there must be," says
Sartre, "an immediate, non-cognitive relation of the self to itself,"[129] and this relation he
captures in his attendant, intentionally circular claim that "[e]very conscious existence exists
as consciousness of existing."[130] In other words, the state of being conscious of itself is the
very mode of existence of the consciousness and therefore is one with it. In asserting this
unity, Sartre avoids the problem of the infinite regress that the subject-object dichotomy of
knowledge forced him to pose.

[II]Due to this inherent emptiness, Sartre defines the being of the consciousness as "a being,
the nature of which is to be conscious of the nothingness of its being."[131] In fact, in Sartre's
ontology nothingness enters the world through consciousness. That is to say, to be conscious
is to be aware of lacks, doubts, and questions, of possibilities that are as yet unrealized, and
it is in these negative elements, these things that are not or not yet, that nothingness is
ultimately rooted.

soon; but I no longer have to bear it, it is no longer an illness or a passing fit: it is I.

So I was in the park just now. The roots of the chestnut tree were sunk in the ground just under my bench. I couldn't remember it was a root anymore. The words had vanished and with them the significance of things, their methods of use, and the feeble points of reference which men have traced on their surface. I was sitting, stooping forward, head bowed, alone in front of this black, knotty mass, entirely beastly, which frightened me. Then I had this vision.

It left me breathless. Never, until these last few days, had I understood the meaning of "existence." I was like the others, like the ones walking along the seashore, all dressed in their spring finery. I said like them, "The ocean is green; that white speck up there is a seagull," but I didn't feel that it existed or that the seagull was an "existing seagull"; usually existence hides itself. It is there, around us, in us, it is *us*, you can't say two words without mentioning it, but you can never touch it. ... And then all of a sudden, there it was, clear as day: existence had suddenly unveiled itself. It had lost the harmless look of an abstract category: it was the very paste of things, this root was kneaded into existence. Or rather the root, the park gates, the bench, the sparse grass, all that had vanished: the diversity of things, their individuality, were only an appearance, a veneer. This veneer had melted, leaving soft, monstrous masses, all in disorder—naked, in a frightful, obscene nakedness.[134]

In the light of this revealing account, we can now more clearly see how Sartre's system of philosophy is meant to be directly relevant to human life in actual experience. For the twofold grounding of existence in the being of the consciousness on the one hand and the being of the thing on the other, which Sartre's ontology posits, is felt to be by Roquentin a profoundly alienating, stark opposition. Up to his moment of insight, Roquentin had lived in a world whose bare reality his conscious mind had diversified, ordered, and verbally identified and thus effectively hidden from sight. He had painted the world in multiple colors but never stopped to think that it was he who was doing the painting and that the world in itself was altogether colorless and plain. But when his vision is transformed, suddenly, in the instant of his epiphany, he comes to behold—immediately and non-verbally—the absolute presence of being itself. Yet simultaneously he also comes to see that this being in turn—this undifferentiated mass of naked existence—is wholly indifferent to him. It does not know him and does not care, because ultimately it merely is there (see also the discussion on p.435ff).

Roquentin has learned to see reality anew, and he is no longer ill. But the price he has to pay for his 'health' is a total loss of any sense of rational relatedness. He is an absurd man now whose only relationship to the things and people around him is that of being *"In the way."*[135] They are in his way, and he is in theirs. As a random piece of existence—"soft, weak, obscene, digesting, juggling with dismal thoughts"[136]—Roquentin perceives himself to have no reason for being alive other than happenstance. In consequence, he vaguely considers suicide but then declines the thought because he sees no profit in replacing a superfluous life with an equally superfluous non-life. There simply is no point in becoming a decomposing chunk of flesh in the ground, if that chunk as well relates to nothing and no one except by being *"In the way."*

Given these sobering thoughts, there comes to mind again that image of hollowed-out personhood that Bacon depicts in his art. And yes, there is a close connection here, but there is too a critical distinction. For unlike Bacon's distorted humanoids, the absurd man is not enclosed in a cage. Indeed, he is not confined by anything, at least not in his consciousness. He stands apart in his utter unrelatedness and therefore is free in the most radical, absolute sense. The world has nothing to say to him, doesn't relate to him, doesn't restrain him, and thus he truly is at perfect liberty to think and to act as he chooses. The only limit that reality places on him is the inescapability of freedom itself. His freedom is his destiny. Man is "free and alone, without assistance and without excuse, condemned to decide without support from any quarter, condemned forever to be free."[137]

In this emphatic insistence on human free agency Sartre blatantly reveals himself to be a staunch anti-determinist. He perceives a radical difference between the being of the consciousness and the being of the thing,[138] and the causal determinism that conditions the latter can therefore not restrain in any way the former. The consciousness is sovereign and totally unfettered.

But is it really plausible to see it thus? Is human conscious choice indeed completely unconfined? Or is it not on the contrary quite obvious that any human act depends upon a multiplicity of factors and determinants that unavoidably compromise the freedom that Sartre proclaims?—factors that pertain to past experience, genetic inheritance, social environment, psychological complexes, instinctual drives—the list goes on. Sartre does not deny the existence of pressures such as these. But decisive in the end, so he asserts, is not the 'objective' situation that we find ourselves in but rather the meaning that we *choose* to assign to it. There may be desires or fears or memories of past events, yet the way in which we interpret these givens and then position ourselves vis-à-vis our future possibilities is really and truly for us to decide.[139]

To further elaborate this point, Sartre observes that every human act, "no matter how trivial,"[140] must be considered to be embedded in a larger psychic structure that ultimately extends to the whole of the person. At the local level of specific, individual acts there may be an appearance of behavioral determinism, but once we take a more global, encompassing view, the fact of free agency re-emerges to sight. For instance, a man who suffers from an inferiority complex may frequently display "patterns of failure behavior"[141] that are due to his complex and thus appear to be conditioned. But at a deeper level, his complex in its entirety "is a free and global project of [himself] as inferior before others"[142]—it is the way in which he *chooses* to be in the world.

To this one may readily object that the construal of an inferiority complex as a freely chosen "project" may fail to take into account that no such complex is ever fully disclosed in a person's awareness. Afterall, if *Freud* was right, then there is a vast unconscious region in the human psyche that wholly or partly contains the complexes we suffer from. By implication, our behavior may be driven by internal forces that we are mostly unaware of and therefore are unable to control.

Naturally, the type of psychological determinism that this Freudian postulate of the unconscious implies cannot be acceptable to a thinker like Sartre who strongly affirms the reality of human conscious liberty. Thus, Sartre must refute Freud in order to defend his own opposing proposition. To do so, he argues at the outset that Freud's conception of the psyche can be condensed to the following three essential elements: the conscious, the unconscious, and the 'censor.' The last of these is a mediator, as it were, that controls the flow of information between the conscious and the unconscious and thereby functions as the agent of repression. Its job is to make sure that harmful or unsuitable contents do not become manifest in a person's waking awareness. But exactly who or what is the censor and how does it do the censoring? Well, given that psychoanalytic patients appear to be actively resisting the becoming-aware of repressed psychic contents, we must conclude, says Sartre, "that the censor in order to apply its activity with discernment must know what it is repressing."[143] In other words, the censor is a knowing rational entity that acts with purposeful intent but somehow manages to conceal its existence and activity from the awareness of the person whose psyche it partially constitutes. But this is clearly humbug. There is no such rational entity, and belief in its existence is surely a case of very *bad faith.* It is an insincere attempt to blame one's own self-deception on a deceiver that really is wholly fictitious.

It may be readily admitted that Sartre has a point. For the nature of the censor does indeed seem highly obscure. But on the other hand, the counter-claim that an inferiority complex, for example, is a freely chosen project that defines the mode of a person's being-in-the-world is also not fully convincing. Do people really *choose*, directly or indirectly, to feel inferior to others? The notion seems contrived and somehow artificial. But be that as it may; we cannot here examine in detail the various arguments that Sartre and his interpreters have fielded for or against the Freudian paradigm. The work in which Sartre puts forth his pertinent views—*Being and Nothingness*—is very difficult and very dense, and we simply cannot do justice to it in this brief exposition. However, what we can perhaps assert with reasonable confidence is that the

apparent conflict between Sartre and Freud is not so much a head-on opposition as it is a fundamental, methodological disconnect. Sartre had no more use
for Freud's empirical approach than Freud had for Sartre's philosophical one.
In other words, their respective patterns of thought were altogether different.

That said, it is natural to ask what point there is in trying to link Sartre
to Freud if there really isn't a link. The proper answer is, "It isn't quite
that simple." For the images of man that these two thinkers present to us—
while different in texture and style—are nonetheless quite similar in some of
their most salient compositional elements, namely their inherent godlessness,
emptiness, and hopelessness. Using Bacon's art as a vehicle for our comparison,
we may say that Freud's brushwork suggests a somewhat more solid, scientific-
looking outline, but the human shell that it depicts is still a shell regardless.
It is a material vacuum that no spirit animates, no hope consoles, and no god
protects. Indeed, in one essential respect, Freudian psychoanalysis is markedly
more faithful to the Baconian imagery than existentialist philosophy because
Freud, like Bacon after him, confined the human being to a cage. Freud was a
scientific materialist and psychological determinist who couldn't be bothered
to speculate on how the ontological character of consciousness might entail a
radical notion of human free agency à la Sartre or Camus. The evidence of
psychoanalytic practice suggested otherwise, and that was all there was to it.

Indeed, in a later revision of his psychic topography, Freud described the
conscious part of the human *ego* as pitiful, weak, and embattled. Far from
being free, the ego is tossed about and constantly harassed. It is threatened by
the external world, pressured by the instincts and drives of the amoral *id*, and
heavily burdened with feelings of guilt and anxiety as the ever watchful *super-
ego* imposes its "hyper-moral"[144] and frequently cruel demands. According to
Freud, the ego is akin to a "dweller in a borderland that... tries to mediate
between the world and the id, to make the id comply with the world's demands
and... to accommodate the world to the id's desires."[145] "Whenever possible,"
the ego "tries to remain on good terms with the id; ... it pretends that the id is
showing obedience to the mandates of reality, even when in fact it is remaining
obdurate and immovable; it throws a disguise over the id's conflicts with reality
and, if possible, over its conflicts with the super-ego too. Its position midway
between the id and reality tempts it only too often to become sycophantic,
opportunist, and false, like a politician who sees the truth but wants to keep
his place in popular favour."[146] Moreover, concerning the ego's relation to the
super-ego, Freud has this to say:

> But since the ego's work of sublimation results in a defusion of the
> instincts and a liberation of the aggressive instincts in the super-
> ego, its struggle against the libido exposes it to the danger of mal-
> treatment and death. In suffering under the attacks of the super-
> ego or perhaps even succumbing to them, the ego is meeting with a
> fate like that of the protozoa which are destroyed by the products

of disintegration that they themselves have created. From the economic point of view, the morality that functions in the super-ego
seems to be a similar product of disintegration.[147]

In view of this assessment it scarcely surprises us when Freud further asserts
that the "ego is the true abode of anxiety."[148] Man's position in the world
is as frightfully precarious as his inner conflicts are oppressive, and fear is
therefore no less prominent a human reality in Freudian psychoanalysis than
in existentialist philosophical thought. The method of argument is strikingly
different, but the theme in essence is the same.

To find some other such thematic overlaps, it is instructive to examine
how Freud addresses the problem of the purpose of life. In *Civilization and
Its Discontents* he observes, in true existentialist fashion, that there really is
no rational reason at all to suppose that any such purpose could ever be objectively identified. Afterall, "[n]obody talks about the purpose of the life of
animals,"[149] and doing so in respect of humans is therefore inherently presump-
tuous. However, at the more modest, empirical level of actual human behavior
there can be little doubt that people strive to be happy. This quest for happiness, of course, may very well be meaningless, but the problem of whether and
how one can succeed in its pursuit can nonetheless be meaningfully posed.

As Freud now applies himself to this latter pair of questions, his scientific
realism compels him to assume, right from the start, a less than optimistic
attitude. Thus we read that "the programme of the pleasure principle" on the
one hand "dominates the operation of the mental apparatus" even from earliest infancy, but on the other hand is hopelessly "at loggerheads" with all the
regulations and laws that govern the cosmos.[150] There is no right to human
emotional fulfillment in God's plan of Creation, especially because—according
to Freud—there really is no God and also no plan. Man's inner constitution
and the world's outer reality do not intersect. And what is worse, the human
psychological makeup is such that happiness can never be maintained. For
enjoyment derives from contrast and change and rapidly fades in static conditions. Freud does not explicitly assert in this context that man's position in
the universe is alienated and absurd in the existentialist sense, but conducive
to this view his outlook clearly is. Moreover, when Freud goes on to lament
that among the various negative forces, opposing our happiness, there is none
that is quite so painful to endure as the discord we experience in our interpersonal relationships, we cannot help but feel reminded instantly of Sartre's
famous quip "L'enfer, c'est les autres"—"Hell is other people."[151]

Having thus set the tone of his inquiry, Freud proceeds to survey a number
of common strategies that people employ in their attempts to become and stay
happy. Beginning with unsustainable efforts to satisfy a person's every need
and want, he moves on to "the happiness of quietness"[152] experienced in social
isolation, to active community membership, to chemical intoxication, to self-
denial and control of the instincts, and on from there to the sublimation of the

instincts in higher artistic and scientific endeavors. The last of these may seem
to be the most wholesome and promising, but it requires gifts and dispositions
that only a few can command, and the satisfaction that it offers is weak compared to the gratification that derives from indulging the primary instincts.
The final two methods that Freud remarks upon are flight from reality by way
of religious belief and the pursuit of love and being loved. But once again his
assessment is bleak: religion is a vain delusion that leads nowhere, and love is
a high-risk strategy that ends in suffering and despair when the object of love
is lost or withdraws its love from us. In conclusion then, we may say that man,
in Freudian thought, has nothing much to hope for. He faces a hostile physical
and social environment that frustrates and oppresses him, and no matter what
path through life he is driven to trod, he never will be reconciled. Yet if he
is mature enough, he will not run away and not escape into fantasy. He will
accept the given as he finds it, endure his fate "with resignation,"[153] and live
his life soberly but also uprightly in the matter-of-fact awareness that civilized
discontent is inescapably his lot.

   Thus we have reached the end of the road. The death of God was proclaimed by Nietzsche, and the absurdity of human life was nervously experienced by the existentialists. But it is only with Freud that the acceptance
of godlessness and hopelessness becomes a simple demand of being grown-up.
Freud doesn't rant against God, as Nietzsche did, he doesn't embrace the absurd, as Camus, and also isn't nauseous or vertiginous as Roquentin; instead,
he simply tells it as it is. He is an unflinching realist who calmly dissects the human condition, presents us with the facts, and then calls us to be adult enough
to not take flight into silly delusions. Where Nietzsche posed as a Promethean
anti-moralist, and where the existentialists made a show of their purported
fear and gloominess, Freud simply says—far more compellingly—"let's not be
children anymore."

Philonous: And that's why *his* attack on faith and tradition was by far the
   most lethal. Freud may not have been a true empirical scientist, and his
   methods may have been rightly criticized for lack of rigor and concision,
   but it is clearly not by chance that his ideas have been so vastly influential.
   His writings can never be lightly pushed aside—they are great literature,
   and they absolutely command your attention. Indeed, in reading his works,
   I always get that disconcerting sense that I myself am partially revealed in
   them. I may not buy into his premises or final inferences, but in between
   there always is a lot to which I can assent. Freud makes sense, at least to
   me, and I admit it.

Sophie: Regarding his great influence, W.H. Auden put it well when he remarked that Freud is not a person anymore "but a whole climate of opinion."[154]

Philonous: I eagerly agree. Freud is not just another brilliant thinker, like
   Sartre or Kant—he is an outlook—a view of the world—a manner of feeling

and being and thinking. And in that he even is the truer existentialist. For his ideas and his mode of thought are more directly relevant to life—by far—than anything that I have ever read in *Being and Nothingness*.

Sophie: Your point is certainly well taken. Just consider, for example, all those mishaps and slips of the tongue and lapses of memory that Freud analyzes so lucidly in *The Psychopathology of Everyday Life*. There is no doubt that anyone who reads that work with honesty and openness will find its truth to be quite strikingly apparent.

Philonous: Speaking of lapses, there comes to mind a personal experience of mine that really is a fitting illustration. Some years ago I frequently had trouble to recall the name of a colleague of mine at the college where I teach. Each time I met him in the hallway, I would suddenly go blank. Try as I might, his name would escape me. The phenomenon struck me as curious because my colleague's name was really rather common and shouldn't have been difficult to recollect. When the problem persisted, I finally decided to get to the bottom of it. So I remembered Freud's association game and asked myself, "What is the first thing that comes to your mind when you think of that name?" And sure enough the first thing that popped up was a newspaper article that I had read a few years earlier about a man whose last name was identical with that of my colleague. Interestingly, it was the *first* name that I commonly forgot, but it was the *last* name that created the link.

Sophie: What did the paper say about the man?

Philonous: It listed his professional accomplishments—including certain shady ones that seemed to me decidedly illicit.

Sophie: Any details?

Philonous: It wouldn't be appropriate.

Sophie: I will be discreet.

Philonous: There is no way—I cannot be explicit.

Sophie: You mean you cannot be honest.

Philonous: I didn't tell a lie.

Sophie: Not openly, but you withheld the most revealing facts.

Philonous: The ones my censor tried to block?

Sophie: That's right.

Philonous: Well sorry, but I can't. Besides, what matters here is not my honesty or lack thereof, but rather how effectively my problem was resolved: I never lapsed again, not even once.

Sophie: If that's your final word on it, then let me ask you this: if Freud was commonly so right "in between," as you just chose to put it—and as your own example illustrates—then why was he globally wrong? Perhaps he made sense because he really made sense all the way, from beginning to end.

Philonous: As I see it, Freud made sense precisely because and only insofar as he was wholly unfaithful to his own basic assumptions. He was a scientific materialist who didn't believe in spirits or souls. But in his works he routinely acknowledged—albeit implicitly—the influence of spirit upon matter on page after page. And it is due entirely to this acknowledgment of his that his ideas will strike us as profound.

Sophie: Please elaborate.

Philonous: Just consider once again my story of my targeted forgetting, and ask yourself how you might plausibly account for it in purely material terms.

Sophie: I'd have to focus, so it seems, exclusively on how your brain was functioning. That is to say, I'd have to analyze exactly how your neurons made you read that newspaper article and how from there your nervous processing effected in the end your memory malfunction.

Philonous: In particular, my being conscious of illicitness and shadiness would really have no role to play.

Sophie: No role whatsoever, because if matter, indeed, were all that there is, then consciousness would be strictly epiphenomenal and therefore inherently totally passive. It would be an atmospheric aura, so to speak, that would accompany the physical but not in any way affect it.

Philonous: By implication, all causal connectedness would lie entirely on the physical side. My states of consciousness would match my brain's material activity, but they would not in any way be causing one another.[III] There would be causes and effects at the level of neuronal, physical processing, but not in the parallel realm of subjective awareness.

Sophie: Your consciousness, indeed, would never be involved.

Philonous: For if it were involved, we would have to concede that mind can rule over matter. Think about it: if my psyche had been the cause of my memory lapse, then it also would have been the cause thereby of the corresponding brain state to which that lapse presumably was tied. Put differently, if we accept Freud's psychological paradigm, according to which psychic processes are meaningfully linked and causally related to each other, and if we also accept that every psychic state is physically expressed in nervous correlates, then we essentially acknowledge in effect that the psyche can act upon matter.

Sophie: The logic seems correct: your psyche cannot cause you to forget a name unless it can persuade your brain to keep your memories locked up.

Philonous: And therefore we may rightly say that Freudian psychoanalysis is a science of the spirit more than the brain—whether Freud himself admitted it or not.

[III]William James points out in this context that the so-called 'conscious-automaton theory' would imply "that feelings, not causing nerve-actions, cannot even cause each other."[155] An awareness of good news, for instance, would not be the cause of attendant emotions of joy because any such feeling would only be a correlate "of some nerve-movements whose cause" would lie "wholly in a previous nerve-movement."[156]

Sophie: Yet even so his attitude was hostile. Freud may not have been a true-type materialist, but an atheist and psychological determinist he certainly was, and any form of genuine transcendence he actively dismissed. In his essay on *The Future of an Illusion,* for instance, he writes that all "religious doctrines... are illusions and insusceptible of proof"[157] and that

> [n]o one can be compelled to think them true, to believe in them. Some of them are so improbable, so incompatible with everything we have laboriously discovered about the reality of the world, that we may compare them—if we pay proper regard to psychological differences—to delusions.[158]

And in another passage he even speaks of religion as "the universal obsessional neurosis of humanity."[159] He views it as a psychological pathology that closely matches in its function the like pathologies that tend to accompany a child's "development to the civilized stage."[160] Worse still, he compares the teachings of religion to those by which children are made to believe "that new-born babies are brought by the stork."[161]

Philonous: And the ultimate cause of man's religious malaise he diagnoses to be the childish longing for protection by the father. Men fear God as they once feared the male head of the family, but they also desire to rely on Him for safety and provision.

Sophie: And he does have a point. For the great transcendent verities that religion proclaims do indeed seem strangely tailor-made for human needs and wishes: we hope for a life after death, and sure enough, so we are told, the faithful will be saved; we long for justice and peace, and the Messiah is coming soon to bestow them; we crave emotional support, and God is always there to love us; we struggle with adversity, illness, and pain, but gladly rest assured that in Him all things work together for good and that the devil will be vanquished.

Philonous: ...and every year at Christmas time the glow of the candles and lights warms our hearts with seasonal tidings of comfort and joy.

Sophie: It's really convenient—it works like a charm.

Philonous: But unfortunately, as Freud harshly reminds us, there is precious little evidence in favor of any of this. We are told to believe because propriety demands it, but when it comes to actual facts, no religious dogma has anything much to offer to us. Under the searching light of critical rational inquiry the so-called 'truths of the Faith' must needs appear contradictory, inauthentic, or blatantly false. Just notice for example, says Freud, how unfavorably the claims to truth made by religion compare to those made by geography. Anyone who doubts the veracity, for instance, of the assertion that "the town of Constance lies on the Bodensee"[162] can simply go there and see for himself. Similarly, there are well known ways of testing the claim that the Earth is spherical in shape. But no such verification of knowledge is available to the skeptic who questions the propositions of religion. For here all trust is blind and all assent inherently unjustified.

Sophie: And once again, Freud does have a point.

Philonous: But following his own advice, his point should certainly be scrutinized. It is by reason not by faith—if Freud is right—that we are to decide if any given point is adequately justified.

Sophie: So what do you propose?

Philonous: ...to entertain a little thought experiment: suppose for instance that you told me that there is a card in your pocket on which there is printed a triangle. If I said in reply, "I don't believe you," you would show me the card, and if I saw the triangle on it, my doubts would be erased. But now suppose that I was part of a larger group. Everyone in that group is shown your card and asked to reproduce the figure it displays.

Sophie: Then everyone would draw a triangle of roughly similar proportions.

Philonous: ...or so we might expect. But what if we were wrong in that? What if the drawings thus produced looked notably distinct?

Sophie: As for instance in the case...?

Philonous: ...where some of them showed 'triangles' with edges bending inwards or outwards or curving in loops?

Sophie: It would be odd and very much surprising.

Philonous: Not necessarily—not if discrepancies as these had been our everyday experience from early childhood on. For then we never would have formed that deeply rooted confidence that what we see is really what is there— externally, objectively. Perhaps we'd have some partial confidence if there were certain common elements like vertices arranged in similar positions. But that firm sense of assurance of the truth that Freud apparently derives from looking at a physical phenomenon would likely be unknown to us.

Sophie: Most likely, yes it would.

Philonous: In other words, it is not the experience of sight itself that compels us to believe that vision can be trusted, but rather our attendant conviction that any such experience, in principle, is universally shared (see also the discussion on p.431). Anyone who travels to the Bodensee will see the town of Constance lying on its shore, but he will trust that he is not deceived only because he is convinced that others will agree—that 'anyone' means 'everyone'.

Sophie: All the same, though, what remains here is the fact that religious beliefs, ordinarily, cannot be tested in this way. We can agree on what we see but not on whether God exists or whether life continues after death.

Philonous: I understand. But let's assume here for the sake of argument that we could prove that deep inside we all share certain needs and attitudes which are spiritual in kind. Freud says that men strive to be happy. Perhaps there are other such appetites that we all have in common. Perhaps we all, if we are honest, long to be appreciated, to find meaning in what we do, to receive kindness, be loved, and give love—you name it.

Sophie: There clearly are such common desires and wants. But that does not imply that there exists, corresponding to them, some actual transcendent realm of which they are reflective. For that, it seems, is what you are suggesting: the physical world around us exists because we all agree on its appearance in perception, and the transcendent world of the spirit exists because we all so happen to long for its blessings.

Philonous: The argument is not entirely implausible, is it?

Sophie: The problem is that in the latter case we only have a want. We may *want* our lives to have meaning, and we may find that others *want* the same. But to say that therefore there is a Beyond—objectively and undeniably— that offers what we crave is wholly unconvincing.

Philonous: But there is yet another way to look at it. For according to Freud, the human "mental apparatus" has been evolved "in the attempt to explore the external world and must therefore have realized in its structure some degree of expediency." [163]

Sophie: The view is well familiar—Lorenz took it too.

Philonous: Certainly, but now remember that we also said, in this very context, that spirit may be actively involved as evolution progresses (pp.463ff). Consequently, the very spirit that Freudian psychoanalysis implicitly endows with physical efficacy may be resultant—just as the body—of a long historical development that ever more closely adapted its structure to givens and facts that are external to it.

Sophie: So just as our cognitive facilities are mirror images of the exterior physical world, so the composition of our spirit needs is expressive of actual transcendent realities. Where animals strive to satisfy their basic metabolic wants and reproductive urges, we humans aspire as well to higher fulfillments in friendship and love and other such noble pursuits, and it is thus that the objectively existent Beyond is more correctly reflected in us.

Philonous: Precisely.

Sophie: It sounds appealing, it is true. But unfortunately, the monumental realism of a thinker like Freud cannot be undermined with any such eccentric speculations. Your argument is simply too remote and far too philosophical in kind to ever stand a chance against his level-headed call to genuine adulthood.

Philonous: No chance at all?

Sophie: None whatsoever.

Philonous: In that case, we'll have to do better.

Sophie: ...much better.

Philonous: ...and I can promise you we will.

Chapter 7

The Spirit Reasserted

In view of the emphasis, placed by Freud, on evidence derived from sensory perception, it may be useful to consider the following eyewitness account of an open-heart surgery. The person recalling the scene is the cardiac patient on whom the operation was performed—which is surprising in the sense that patients during surgery are commonly assumed to be entirely unconscious.

> They had finished draping me, the anesthesiologist had started his stuff, and all of a sudden I became aware of it...like I was in the room a couple of feet or so above my head, like I was another person in the room....I can remember parts of the conversation that went on in there and that surprised me....They had all kinds of instruments stuck in that aperture. I think they're called clamps, clamped all over the place. I was amazed that I had thought there would be blood all over the place, but there really wasn't that much blood....And the heart doesn't look like I thought it did. It's big. And this is after the doctor had taken little pieces of it off. It's not shaped like I thought it would be. My heart was shaped like the continent of Africa. Bean-shaped is another way you could describe it. Maybe mine is odd-shaped....[The surface was] pinkish and yellow. I thought the yellow part was fat tissue or something. Yucky, kind of. One general area to the right or left was darker than the rest instead of it all being the same color....I could draw you a picture of the saw they used and the thing they used to separate the ribs with. It was always there and I can remember the details of that probably better than the other things. It was draped all around, but you could see the metal part of it. I think all they used that for was to keep it constantly open.[1]

As it turned out, the patient's account perfectly matched the surgeon's report, "as if he had visually witnessed the procedure."[2]

Freud never experienced, so far as we know, an episode as this of extra-sensory perception, and he may not have known that there are people who do. But regardless of Freud's pertinent insight and knowledge, it certainly is fair to say that out-of-body visual impressions, apparently, are just as vivid as the sight of Constance at the Bodensee (p.501). Anyone who has seen his or her own body stretched out on an operating table, who has observed the doctors and nurses go about their work, has listened to them talk, and watched them use their instruments—anyone, that is, who has witnessed these things first-hand with his or her own spirit eyes while physically anesthetized, *knows* with unquestionable certainty that consciousness is not inherently matter-bound and that materialism therefore is a delusion. Materialism is a childish attempt to assert the comprehensive dominion of human reason and perception over that vast sea of existence that people call 'reality'. It is a silly habit of thought that we simply and finally have to give up. We really need to learn to act like true adults and lay aside, at last, our infantile fantasies of our own intellectual and technological grandeur. For if we don't grow up, so we may find, the planet will go to hell in a hurry and we along with it.

As a matter of course, the existence of this link, from out-of-body perceptions to saving the earth, may not seem obvious at first. But as we consider more broadly the fundamental worldview revolution which here is at stake, the plausibility of our pertinent contention becomes apparent quite readily. For the shift from strictly materialistic to spirit-filled ontologies that out-of-body perceptions and near-death travels impel us to embrace is liable to radically alter our whole way of being and feeling and thinking—and acting thereby. Those who understand that matter is only a surface display, veiling a deeper, transcendent Beyond, will wish to stop destroying the world by constantly saying 'just' to all of its aspects. To them it will be repugnant to say that humans are *just* material systems, that animals are *just* soulless automata, that consciousness is *just* an epiphenomenon, that meaning is *just* a presumption, that morality is *just* a convention, that religion is *just* a neurosis, that God is *just* an illusion, or ultimately, that everything is *just* a nothing. In refusing to play the foolish modern *just*-game, they will be forced to set a new course. They will acknowledge the truth of transcendence and thereby be led to reassign value where value belongs.

In response, a skeptic may here ask: "will all the world's problems be solved if only people come to understand that souls exist, that matter is not all that there is, and that life continues after death?" And the answer is: "of course not." Afterall, belief in spirits and transcendence has always been widespread, and the record of history as well as of current events has frequently not been in favor of those who professed it—to say the least. Everyone knows how much intolerance, hate, and brutality religious faith has bred in ages past and still breeds today. By implication then, there surely is no point in favoring religion over science unreservedly. Nor is there any meaning to be found in 'brilliant' utopian plans for a grand restructuring of human thought and social behavior. For plans as these notoriously falter when they face the true complexities and vagaries of life. In other words, the goal is not to force reality to fit some novel ideology but rather to understand it more fully.

For the past five hundred years Western man has been engaged in an intellectual quest, called 'natural science', that has taught him how his sensory perceptions are lawfully patterned and organized. This effort, no doubt, has been enormously successful, and nothing that has been achieved should ever be denied or abandoned. But a fundamental readjustment that broadens the view and thereby enlivens the climate of thought has now become a very urgent need.

When Galileo conducted his motion experiments and observed the heavens through his telescope, the European academic elites were still committed to Aristotle's *Organon* as their scholarly standard of truth. But the kinds of truths that Galileo was discovering were not to be contained by insistence on standards, because ultimately, they simply were truths. Similarly, we rightly may expect that the vast body of evidence, supporting the reality of NDE phenomena, will eventually assert itself with an equally irresistible force. The current generation of scientists and academicians may still be bound by a rigidly materialistic paradigm, but paradigms tend to shift, and even the most fundamental convictions do not remain static indefinitely.

Is it really altogether inconceivable that university students, in a not too distant future perhaps, will be taught in their courses that reality is not congruent with human cognition—that matter, force, and energy, described symbolically, are not sufficient to capture the world as it is? And is it all that silly to assume that there may come a time when students take courses that actually mean something to them—courses that deal with the soul, the laws of the spirit, the purpose of life? For many years, Elisabeth Kübler-Ross conducted a seminar on death and dying at the University of Chicago. Why should a course as this not one day be a common college offering? Why should we not let our students know what can in fact be known about the threshold we call 'death'? Or what is wrong in helping them thereby to see the world in ways that are more spirit-filled and therefore true to life?

What is at issue here is not the establishment of a novel religion that all must embrace, but the organic, step-by-step creation of a new intellectual scene. For just as the modern university curriculum replaced the traditional scholastic one in a natural process of accommodation and adjustment, so there may arise one day a new educational landscape as the mounting NDE evidence continues to erode the present Western worldview. Aristotle taught that falling bodies accelerate at a rate proportional to their weight and that projectiles are propelled forward by the air that closes in behind them. But as it is, it simply isn't so: the rate of fall is weight invariant, and motion can occur in a vacuum. Similarly and by analogy, the current-day belief that everything there is—including consciousness—must somehow be a physical phenomenon is equally objectively erroneous. If truth will once again assert itself, then there will come a time when we all will agree that human life is not and cannot be entirely a process of chemistry. We will *know* that there is more to reality than mathematical lawfulness, and we will teach that knowledge in our schools and universities as nowadays we teach biology or physics. The students in that future age, so we may hope, will look upon our modern obsession with quantitative symbolic reductions as students today regard the scholastics' adherence to Aristotle's *Organon*—an historical mistake that has been corrected.

As a matter of course, we cannot possibly foresee how these developments will finally unfold. How will society be influenced if our institutions of learning should alter their course in the manner just proposed? What avenues of exploration will open up as people begin to see the world in the light of a new, more spirit-friendly paradigm? How far will their exploits carry them? What new mistakes will they commit? Obviously, we don't know. But it stands to reason to expect that the changes resulting will likely be sweeping. Almost all existing fields of science and culture are bound to be reshaped and new ones to be added. In literature, music, and art—and architecture too—there may be conceived new forms of creative expression, new designs, and new interpretations of ancient traditions. In medicine the healing agency of spirit and mind may be explored and subsequently utilized;[1] psychologist will openly acknowledge the presence of the soul; biologists will tell the tale of life as a matter/spirit parallel development; and even physicists may find some novel means to understand how consciousness is linked to energy and matter. And most pronounced the shift will be presumably in philosophy, theology, and also in the practice of religion. Indeed, religion may become more scientific in the sense that many of its tenets may re-enter the mainstream university discourse. That is to say, religion and reality may truly be rejoined.

In the light of these thoughts there arises a vision of a new historical era in which people will be taught differently, think differently, perceive differently, and therefore live and act in ways that really will be different. In these days to come, so we may speculate, men will inhabit different cities and different private spaces, be organized in different social contracts, different political structures, and different economic systems. The world to them will have a new look to it, a new feel, a new ontological aura. Will all the change be positive? Probably not. But one may hope—and hope with reason—that a more accurate grasp of the world as it is will bring about attendant transformations that, on the whole, will be for the better.

Philonous: I surely hope they will. For I must say the status quo is burdensome to me. I am more tired than I can express of living in a world in which deplorable philosophy can masquarade as scientific insight, in which all

---

[1]In this area, much research is already being done at present. For a survey of results the reader is referred to [Ko1], [Ko2], and [MHLKT].

things of value are reduced, dissected, and destroyed, and plainest evidence is ridiculed and foolishly cast out. What is the point in arguing that matter is all that there is if thousands and millions of people around the world have witnessed firsthand, in near-death encounters, that such is not the case—that consciousness can very well be wholly disembodied? Why do the brightest minds of our time continue to profess the most transparent falsehoods? How is it possible that our schools and universities—across the board—endorse curricula that promulgate untruth? Or why for that matter can Nobel prize winners not finally and openly admit that even the simplest bodily motions—the movement of a leg, the bending of an arm, the turning of a wrist—are causally inscrutable to scientific insight? Can we not just state the obvious at last—the simple truth that any willful locomotion, in order to be willful, must needs originate in something like a consciousness, or soul, that really has a will? How much longer do we have to endure this modern legacy of mind-denying nonsense?

Sophie: I don't know, but I can see you are upset.

Philonous: I am exhausted.

Sophie: It's not surprising after almost forty dialogues on everything from stone age clans to quantum realms and entropy to Kantian philosophy.

Philonous: That's not exactly it.

Sophie: I know it's not. Your problem is, as I see it, a painful lack of meaningful companionship. You feel that you have seen a better world that is more real and more coherent, but what you sorely miss are kindred souls with whom you might in harmony inhabit it.

Philonous: There have been thinkers in the past and even in more recent times whose company I surely could enlist. Some names that come to mind are William James, Henri Bergson, and Albert Schweitzer. And presently there are the pioneers of NDE research.

Sophie: Anyone you personally know?

Philonous: I do know you.

Sophie: But you and I have struggled more than we agreed.

Philonous: But when we disagreed, we never did so viciously, and there has been much common ground as well. In fact, the notion that there may occur in future times a fundamental shift from matter-bound to spirit-filled ontologies may even further strengthen our ties.

Sophie: How so?

Philonous: You see, we both have felt at certain times in our lives the bleakness and the hopelessness that modern thought exudes. We both know what it's like when there is seemingly no link between the inner and the outer world—when meaning and exterior reality are largely disconnected. But where, apparently, your mental thrust has been to try to rediscover meaning in your sensory experience, my aspiration on the other hand has been to reach out for transcendence. It is not the immanent world of physical phenomena to which my hopes are tied but rather the Beyond—the realm that souls indwell and God is present in. Yet given our current train of thought, these different roads that we are on can plausibly be one day reconnected. For if indeed an era should arise in which the knowledge of the possibility of *experiencing* the Beyond directly, in extra-sensory perception, becomes an academic commonplace, then immanence, essentially, would be invaded by transcendence. In consequence, *you* would be enabled to perceive more meaning in experience, and *I* would benefit as well in that transcendence would appear to me more real and more immediate.

Sophie: ...because reality—as a social, educational construct—would vitally assume for you an otherworldly aspect.

Philonous: Precisely.

Sophie: But then again, that aspect isn't really new. Just think how very evident it was for instance in medieval times.

Philonous: ...and that is why, of course, the Middle Ages didn't know that telling modern loss of meaning and coherence.

Sophie: Yet hardly anyone would therefore want to resurrect them. The Middle Ages, probably, were not as dark as many moderns painted them, but very bright they weren't either.

Philonous: Look, the purpose cannot be to resurrect a bygone age that we have far surpassed in numerous respects. Instead, what I would hope to see is a positive merging of strengths—a novel synthesis that truly integrates medieval emphasis on spirit-life with modern competence in science and technology.

Sophie: You'd better mention, though, that spirit-life in this context means Christian life exclusively, because religion in medieval times was limited by force to Roman Catholic piety.

Philonous: I understand, but here again the goal is not to foolishly undo what modern times have laudably accomplished. There is no going back behind the liberties that the Enlightenment has won for us. But speaking of Christianity, let me submit, that in that postulated future age its grounding in reality will likely be perceived to be more evident and solid.

Sophie: Because belief in God and souls will be ubiquitous?

Philonous: ...more prevalent than nowadays. And what will change as well is that the members of that creed...

Sophie: ...members like yourself?

Philonous: Indeed, I am included here. For as I indicated previously, the Christian faith is dear to me.

Sophie: Sorry for interrupting.

Philonous: What I was saying is that probably the future members of that creed will live and think in ways that are more genuinely Christian. You see, whenever I observe how so-called Christians speak and act, in our present age, I cannot help but sense that underneath a thin veneer of weakly held beliefs there often looms a hardened core of unrelenting attitudes that science has induced. What seems to make these people function as they do is not their modicum of biblical beliefs but their much deeper loyalty to anti-Christian views.

Sophie: ...as for instance in the case...?

Philonous: ...when trust in God is eagerly replaced with engineering strategies; when physical illness is always and exclusively a physical problem; when mental imbalances are universally assumed to be in nature chemical; when new technologies are fervently embraced without concern for human implications; when solid evidence is only found in scientific facts—except, of course, in arguments involving evolution. I myself have grown up in a world in which the golden rule of practical philosophy was summed up in the claim that each and every happening is rooted in a cause that reason can detect. Already in my boyhood I believed, instinctively at least, that everything there is—by definition—is accessible to scientific insight. Indeed, the entire mode of being in the world that I adopted in my most impressionable years is very much at odds with all the Christian articles of faith that I supposedly am presently committed to.

Sophie: And it is this inherent lack of natural compatibility that would have been removed if you had grown up in that future world in which the immanent is partially invaded by transcendence.

Philonous: That is correct, but let me put it differently: if I said in that future age that my religion is Christianity, I would identify myself thereby as nothing but a follower of Christ.

Sophie: But so you would in our time as well. I don't see what the difference is.

Philonous: Not at all. What it means nowadays to make this claim is something more complex. Not only does it indicate that I adhere to Christ, but far more elementary, that I believe in God, in souls, in life after death. My faith in these transcendent elements must be asserted with explicitness because society, in our day, does not declare them to be real by general consent. We teach in our schools the law of gravity but not that God exists or that a soul indwells the human body. By implication, gravitation is objectively a fact whereas the presence of a soul is merely an opinion.

Sophie: I think I see your point: the future age that you are positing would make unquestionably real to you what presently is only a belief.

Philonous: It would transform my faith, in parts, into indubitable certainty. That is to say, in that anticipated future time, my choice to be a Christian by religion would naturally mesh with socially defined reality assumptions.

Sophie: ...and thus it would no longer be delusional in kind.

Philonous: Let's say it wouldn't be contrived and artificial. For that is how it feels to me when I profess a faith—the Christian faith—that flatly contradicts the scientific 'truth' that academia in this current age has chosen to endorse. Belief in God and worlds beyond must be asserted nowadays in blatant and defiant disregard for this accepted truth. And it's precisely this defiance that can strike us very easily—though very much mistakenly—as strangely immature and awkwardly pubescent.

Sophie: ...or infantile, as Freud would say.

Philonous: And once again, he does have a point.

Sophie: But in an age in which transcendence has become partially immanent and thus partially real, the roles would be reversed: the man of God would now appear to be the sensible adult and the skeptic the puerile detractor.

Philonous: The better option is to simply quit the labeling. There is no need to redefine who is superior to whom. For if indeed the new age here in question is a synthesis, then coexistence in a state of mutual respect will likely be quite natural in it.

Sophie: You mean, there will be harmony and peace?

Philonous: Perhaps a little more so than at present. As I see it—and as I hope—there really can be betterment if we can take to heart more thoroughly the lessons that near-death accounts contain. If we absorb these lessons carefully and teach them undogmatically, then change for the better can be achieved. I honestly believe that there is bound to be a notable, quite positive effect if all along we taught in our schools what NDEs consistently reveal to be the goal of human life.

Sophie: "Adherence to the two great commandments" (p.475)?

Philonous: In essence that is it.

Sophie: So what we ought to teach in summary is this: we are here for a purpose, and the purpose is love.

Philonous: Briefly stated, yes.

Sophie: Well then it seems we really could have said as much directly at the start. We didn't need to work through almost forty dialogues in order to collapse the whole of our argument in this concluding thought into a one-line law of love.

Philonous: In other words, the effort was a waste.

Sophie: ...a total waste.

Philonous: I think you are right.

Notes and Credits

Cover image: © Nicemonkey / Dreamstime.com.

Chapter 1. This chapter contains some material from Chapter 5 of [Bl2] in modified form (used with permission). Furthermore, the etching by Goya that is shown in Figure 1.1 is in the public domain, and the photograph shown in Figure 1.2 was provided by *Dreamstime* and was used with permission (© Manuel Alvarez Alonso / Dreamstime.com).

1. The claim that a Scientific Revolution never occurred is put forth, for example, by Steven Shapin in [Shap].

2. [Don], p.276, and [Kuh1], p.194.

3. Jung's account of his travels can be found in [Ju1], pp.238–88.

4. [Ju1], p.252.

5. The role of Cartesian philosophy in relation to the problem of alienation is very well discussed in [Tar] (in particular pp.416–45), and the specific image of a "modern trajectory" can be found in [Tar], p.223.

6. Genesis 3:6, *The New International Version of the Holy Bible.*

7. Recent examples of attempts to overcome the mind/matter dualism in the direction of matter are the expositions by Dennett in [Den] and by Lakoff and Johnson in [LJ]. An impassioned plea against the broader materialistic tendency in modern thought is offered by Jung in [Ju2], pp.173–95.

8. The exposition in [Gom], pp.39–42, was used as a reference for the few remarks here made on prehistoric art.

9. The word 'disenchantment' (or 'Entzauberung' in German) as a descriptor for modern man's spiritual condition was first introduced by Max Weber in his essay *Science as Vocation* (see [Web], pp.129–56).

10. Essentially the same sentiment was expressed by Steven Weinberg in [Wein], p.253, and he also quotes himself concerning this issue in the same source on p.255.

11. [Ju1], p.250.

12. More detailed accounts of how the presence of an observing conscious-ness may enter into the conceptual framework of quantum mechanics are given, for instance, in [Sta1], [Sta3], [Sta4], [Lockw], [Pen], and [Wig1].

13. A very similar thought experiment was proposed by Gottfried Wilhelm Leibniz in [Lei1], p.81.

Chapter 2. The expositions in [Copl1] and [Stö] served as standard references concerning the lives and ideas of the natural philosophers. Furthermore, this chapter contains some material from Chapter 18 of [Bl2] in modified form as well as copies of Figures 69.18 and 70.4 on pp.649 and 664 in [Bl2] (used with permission). The figures in question in the present work are Figures 2.10 and 2.12.

1. [Jas2], p.2.

2. [Jas2], pp.96–7.

3. A similar thought is expressed in [Copl1], p.23.

4. [Ari1], pp.501–2.

5. [Copl1], p.23.

6. [Th], p.141.

7. [Th], p.141.

8. insert direct reference to Copleston.

9. [Th], p.141.

10. [RobJ], p.26.

11. [Th], p.142.

12. [Th], p.142.

13. [Ari1], pp.503–4.

14. The relevant information is provided in [RobD] and [RobJ].

15. A more detailed discussion of this issue can be found in [Bu], pp.100–2.

16. This formulation of Euclid's parallel postulate is taken from [BM], p.106.

17. Some interesting ideas concerning the issue of comprehensibility can be found in [Mic] and in particular also in [Dav] and [Wig2].

18. A detailed discussion of this topic can be found in [Schaf1], pp.49–53.

19. [Copl1], p.39.

20. [Th], p.149.

21. [Th], p.149.

22. [RobJ], p.90.

23. The passage is from the Cratylus and is quoted in [RobJ], p.90–1.

24. [RobJ], p.93.

25. [Th], p.150.

26. [Th], p.150.

27. [Nei], p.100.

28. [Nei], p.100.

29. Genesis 3:22, *The New International Version of the Holy Bible.*

30. An interesting discussion of path-habits in water-shrews can be found in [Lor2], pp.108-27.

31. [Th], p.147.

32. In the form given, the quote can be found in [Feye2], p.134, and a slightly different version is stated in [Th], p.147.

33. [Th], p.146.

34. [Plat2], p.920.

35. [Th], p.157.

36. [Th], p.157.

37. [Th], p.157.

38. [Th], p.159.

39. [Gal2], pp.201–2.

40. [Th], p.180.

41. A detailed explanation of such a scheme that takes into account the relativity of time can be found in [Ba].

42. A non-temporal model of physical reality is developed in [Ba].

43. [Je], p.105.

44. [EI], p.31.

45. The word "nonsense" was used by Einstein in the context here referenced according to a recollected conversation that Heisenberg had with Einstein in 1926. The full account is given in [Hei1], pp.62–9.

46. A somewhat more detailed discussion of the problems inherent in a positivistic view of scientific conceptual knowledge can be found in [Wein], Chapter VII.

47. [Ein1], p.684.

48. This comment is partly inspired by the views expounded in [Feye1].

49. Here we are following the lead of Immanuel Kant who, in the preface to the second edition of his *Critique of Pure Reason*, proclaimed that "I must, therefore, abolish *knowledge*, to make room for *belief*" ([Kant2], p.18).

50. [Th], p.161–2.

51. [Th], p.162.

52. [Th], p.164.

53. In the original German, the treatise is entitled *Die Prinzipien der Mechanik* and constitutes the third volume of Hertz's collected works (see [Hert]).

54. [RobJ], p.197.

55. There are, of course, compatibilists who don't agree with this assessment (see, for instance, the chapter on "Compatibilist Perspectives on Freedom and Responsibility" in [KaneR]), but we prefer to side with what we consider to be the more convincing traditional view on free will and determinism expounded in [Wa] and [Wid].

56. [RobJ], p.212.

57. The footnote is inspired by Feynman's comment on the same issue in [Feyn2], p.57.

58. A more detailed discussion of present-day particle physics can be found in [KaneG].

59. Feynman speaks of electronns as theories in [Feyn2], p.57.

60. [Jas1], p.21.

61. This assessment of the trial of Anaxagoras is given in [Copl1], p.66.

62. This claim to primacy is supported by Copleston and Störig in [Copl1] and [Stö], but Aristotle in the *Metaphysics* cautions that similar views were expressed earlier already by Hermotimus of Clazomenae ([Ari1], p.502).

63. [Th], p.177.

64. [RobJ], p.184.

65. [Th], p.165.

66. This assessment of Anaxagoras' philosophy is loosely based upon the exposition in [Copl1], pp.69–71. A somewhat different view that de-emphasizes the contrast to Empedocles' philosophy is given in [RobJ], pp.181–2.

67. [Ari1], p.502.

68. The quote has been adopted from the exposition in [Copl1], p.71, but a differently worded version of it can also be found in [Ari1], p.502.

69. [Plat3], p.80.

70. [Ari1], p.503.

71. Max Planck first presented his improved formula for the energy distribution in black-body radiation on October 19, 1900, but only in a second report, dating from December 14 of the same year, did he offer a theoretical explanation in which he relied on his famous hypothesis concerning the quantization of energy. The relevant sources are [Plan1] and [Plan2].

72. A detailed discussion of the problem of black-body radiation within a quantum mechanical context can be found in [Boh3], pp.5–22.

73. A quote concerning this statement of Planck's can be found in [Crop], p.7.

74. The paper in question is [Ein3].

75. This evaluation of Einstein's paper on the quantization of radiation energy is based on the expositions in [Hei2], pp.32–3, and [Crop], pp.18–28.

76. The quote by Millikan is taken from [Crop], p.28 and so is the comment on the groundlessness of the photon concept (in its essential content).

77. The account of the circumstances of Heisenberg's discovery is based on the exposition in [Gr], pp.103–7, and Heisenberg's original technical publication is [Hei3].

78. [Wein], p.67.

79. [Wein], p.68.

80. [FLS], pp.1-4,1-5.

81. [Hei2], p.38.

82. The word "wavicle" is taken from a dialogue that Heisenberg records in [Hei1], p.95.

83. See again [Feyn2], p.57.

84. Here our argument follows the outline provided by Feynman in [FLS], pp.1-1–1-11.

85. This view is proposed by Bohr in a dialogue recorded by Heisenberg in [Hei1], p.105.

86. The passage can be found in [Hei2], p.48, and is also quoted in [Schaf1], p.38.

87. [Hei2], p.70.

88. A brief description of how an infinite variety of quantum mechanical pictures can be constructed can be found in [Shan], pp.147.

89. [Hei1], p.75.

90. [Hei1], p.71.

91. The image of a stopwatch was used by Feynman for essentially the same purpose in [Feyn1].

92. The statement of von Weizsäcker that we are here referring to can be found in [Weiz1], p.573. In the original German it reads as follows: "Der abstrakte Aufbau der Quantentheorie legt nahe, die Information als das Zugrundeliegende und insofern als die Substanz aufzufassen." Furthermore, the ontological view that information is "the sole currency of any reality" has also been proposed by Jahn and Dunne in [JD2], p.204.

93. The view in question was elaborated by von Neumann in Chapter VI of [Neu].

94. For more details see the exposition in [Shan] (in particular pp.175-6).

95. An account of such a low intensity experiment can be found in [Gh], pp.49-51.

96. This argument which leads to the path integral formulation of quantum physics can be found in [Ze], pp.7–10.

97. A rather comprehensive treatment of Feynman's formalism can be found in [Klei].

98. [Wig1], p.134.

99. Bohm outlined his theory in [Boh1] and [Boh2].

100. Our brief discussion of Bohm's theory here is based on the exposition in [Gh], Chapter 9.

101. A very similar view is endorsed by Klemm in [Klem], pp.361–3, and also by Jung in [Ju2], p.174.

102. [Hei1], p.101.

Chapter 3. The expositions in [Copl1], [Stö], [Lav], [All], and [KBW] served as general references concerning the lives and philosophies of Socrates, Plato, and Aristotle; and the remarks regarding the history of the Athenian Empire are mostly derived from [Horn]. Moreover, the discussion of certain aspects of evolutionary epistemology in the section on *The Frog at the Gate* is largely inspired by the exposition in [Lor1]. Finally, the image shown in Figure 3.2 is in the public domain.

1. [Plat6], p.572.

2. [Plat3], p.97.

3. [Plat3], p.98.

4. This assertion is made by Copleston in [Copl1], p.98.

5. There is no clear consensus in the literature concerning the extent of Plato's travels. Copleston is more skeptical than Störig regading the claim that Plato reached Egypt (see [Copl1], p.129), and the possibility that Plato even went as far as India is mentioned by Störig alone (see [Stö], p.172).

6. [Copl1], p.102.

7. [Aug1], p.303.

8. [Plat5], pp.747–50.

9. [Plat5], p.747.

10. The particular optical illusions shown in Figure 3.1 can be found in [Eib1], pp.54–5.

11. [Goeb], p.61.

12. A translation that takes the original meters into account is offered in [Goet], p.54: *The modest truth I speak to thee./If Man, that microcosmic fool, can see/Himself a whole so frequently,*

13. The argument that we are here beginning to develop is not new and can be found in fairly similar form for instance in [Di].

14. [Lor1], p.12.

15. The proposed division of reality into inorganic, organic, and consciously spiritual domains roughly follows Hartmann's theory of strata that Lorenz expounds in [Lor1].

16. [Kant2], p.29.

17. Accounts of such cognitive abilities in a chimpanzee can be found in [HN], p.64 and pp.107-8.

18. Following a very similar train of thought A.K. Dewdney asks in [Dew], p.161, whether it might not be the case "that most people have trouble understanding mathematics because it's too simple."

19. This remark, of course, is inspired by the famous saying of Protagoras, according to which "man is the measure of all things" (see, for instance, [Copl1], p.87).

20. A similar distinction was proposed by Ditfurth in [Di], p.189.

21. Richard Tarnas develops the notion of a "post-Copernican double bind" in the Epilogue of [Tar]. Our notion of a "contemporary double bind" is closely related but not entirely the same.

22. Here we are again following the lead of Richard Tarnas who expounds a very similar idea in [Tar], pp.418–9.

23. "Anything goes" is the motto that Paul Feyerabend espouses in [Feye1].

24. [Kant2], p.18.

25. Following a similar line of thought, Lothar Schäfer, in [Schaf2], introduces the idea that the Platonic forms can perhaps be interpreted as virtual cosmic quantum states.

26. [Aug2], p.28.

27. A quote attributed to James Jeans that expresses this thought-like quality of the universe can be found in [JD2], p.206, and a more exhaustive treatment is given in Chapter V of [Je].

28. Along similar lines, proponents of the newly popular idea of *emergence* have suggested that order in natural systems may be accounted for by process rather than law (see for instance [Ul]).

29. [Wh1], p.1.

30. [Wh1], p.24.

31. [Wh1], p.25.

32. Another reference, apart from [Wh1], where Wheeler discusses the notion of "law without law" is [Wh2].

33. [Wh1], p.15.

34. Perhaps the most well-known discussion of intra-specific aggression from an evolutionary point of view is the one provided by Konrad Lorenz in [Lor3].

35. A more detailed description of the function of the color patterns on coral fish is provided in [Lor3], Chapters 1 and 2.

36. The light/shadow analogy with respect to the problem of good and evil is frequently employed in the writings of Carl Jung. In [Ju2], p.35, for example, Jung first comments that "what is inferior or even worthless belongs to me as my shadow and gives me substance and mass," and then goes on to ask "How can I be substantial if I fail to cast a shadow?"

37. The notion that evil will try to conceal its nature by implicating its victims in its crimes is loosely based on ideas expressed in the very intriguing and highly enlightening exposition by Susan Neiman in [Nei].

38. [Ju3], p.234.

39. [To], pp.39–40.

40. This remark concerning our human need to perceive the future as a goal or hoped for possibility is in part inspired by Viktor Frankl's account of his experiences in a concentration camp ([Fra], pp.70–2).

41. The nurse's account can be found in [LW], p.2041, and it was also reported on in [Ve].

42. A similar suggestion was made by Shankar Vedantam in [Ve].

43. Further accounts of near-death experiences with specific verifiable details can be found for instance in [Gl], Chapter 4.

44. [Kub2], p.82 and [MP1], p.9.

45. The book in question is [Kub1], and its importance is indicated by the fact that the New York Public Library included it in a listing of the one hundred most influential literary works of the 20th century.

46. [Kub2], p.80.

47. [Kub2], pp.80–2.

48. The cases here referred to, of perceptions of events outside a patient's physical field of vision, are described in [Gl], pp.104-13, and [MP1] (pp.1-8 and pp.177–8). In fact, the literature on NDE's is full of such accounts.

49. The case of a woman who lost her vision as a premature baby in an incubator and then experienced sight during an NDE is described in [Lom], pp.23–26.

50. [Ari3], p.401.

51. [Dra1], pp.25–6.

52. Socrates's prayer in the given form can be found in [Copl1], p.207, and a slightly different translation is given in [Plat4], p.525.

53. This brief discussion of Plato's conception of the soul is based on the exposition in [Copl1], pp.207–208.

54. [Plat1], p.1452.

55. [Plat3], p.63.

56. Plato explicitly states this point for instance in [Plat1], p.1452.

57. [RuB], p.63.

58. The problem of determining whether another person indeed is conscious is a well known conundrum that is acknowledged to lie outside the explanatory reach of science even by a scientist like Christof Koch who otherwise propagates a reductionistic model of consciousness (see [Horg1], pp.181–2).

59. This assessment is based on the comments by Horgan and Crick in [Horg1], p.160, [Horg2], p.236, and [Cri], Chapter 2.

60. [Cri], p.3.

61. A general description of NDE's can be found in [Gl], pp.99–100, and [MP1], pp.10-1, and a very detailed personal account of a very deep NDE can be found in [Ale].

62. Examples of such studies can be found in [LW] and [MP2].

63. [Kub2], pp.95–8.

64. The technical data here provided can be found on the following website: http://en.wikipedia.org/wiki/Large_Hadron_Collider.

65. The information concerning the ATLAS detector can be found at http://www.sciencedaily.com/releases/2008/02/080229112216.htm

66. The headline in question was taken from the following website: http://www.sciencedaily.com/releases/2008/02/080229112216.htm

67. [Kant2], p.18.

68. [Kant2], p.469.

69. Copleston discusses this issue in [Copl1], pp.330–1.

70. This detail was taken from the Biographical Note in *Great Books of the Western World*, Volume 8, by Robert Maynard Hutchins (Editor in Chief), Encyclopedia Britannica, Inc., Chicago, 1952.

71. Copleston asserts that Aristotle himself established the branch of the Academy in Assos ([Copl1], p.267), but according to the more detailed account given by Allen in [All], pp.1–12, it was Hermias who did so.

72. [Copl1], p.272.

73. [Ari5], p.211–2.

74. [Ari1], p.499.

75. Lavine states this Aristotelian criticism of Plato's philosophy in a very similar form in [Lav], p.70.

76. [Stö], p.204.

77. The link between quantum theory and Aristotle's concept of *potentia* was pointed out by Heisenberg in [Hei2], p.53, and was further elaborated upon by Schäfer in [Schaf1], pp.44–7.

78. [Hei2], p.72.

79. The species here involved are the muscid fly *Philornis deceptivus* and the pearly-eyed thrasher of the Luquillo Rain Forest on Puerto Rico. A detailed description of the parasitic behavior here in question can be found in [UA].

80. See [Herl], Chapter 1, and [Coh] for further discussion of alternative models explanation for the Black Death phenomenon.

81. [Kel], p.113.

82. The quote by Boccaccio can be found in [Kel], p.106.

83. [Kel], p.186.

84. The quote can be found on the web at http://www.bbc.co.uk/history/british/middle_ages/black_08.shtml, and another version of the same quote can be found at http://en.wikipedia.org/wiki/Black_Death.

85. [Kel], p.229.

86. More detailed information on the means employed by *Yersinia pestis* in disabling a host's immune system is given in [MD].

87. These very brief remarks on Leibniz's views on the problem of evil are inspired by the expositions in [Copl4], pp.326–32, and [Jos], pp.177–88.

88. This questioning of motives is inspired by Susan Neiman's analysis of Kant's very similar concern ([Nei], p.69).

Chapter 4. The expositions in [Copl1], [Stö], [Tar], and [Pric] served as general references concerning the philosophical and historical developments of the long transitional period from the Golden Age of ancient Greece to the modern European era. In other words, the period here in question encompasses the Hellenistic era, the imperial Roman era, the Middle Ages, and the Renaissance. Furthermore the discusion of Kantian moral philosophy is based on Kant's original writings as well as the expositions in [Copl6], [Stö], and [Nei]. Finally, the images shown in Figures 4.1 and 4.2 are in the public domain.

1. [Ari2], p.101.

2. [Ari2], p.102.

3. [Ari2], p.92.

4. [Tar], p.74.

5. [Stö], p.221.

6. [Copl1], p.385.

7. This remark is based on the corresponding discussion in [Copl1], p.394.

8. [Aur], p.5.

9. [Aur], p.11.

10. [Aur], pp.49–50.

11. [Aur], p.71.

12. [Aur], p.47.

13. In this context D.A. Rees comments in [Aur], p.x, that "Stoicism has been frequently spoken of as the most modern of ancient ethical theories..."

14. Kant's discussion concerning the shortfalls of Stoicism can be found in [Kant1], p.346.

15. [Kant1], p.346.

16. [Aur], p.68.

17. [Aur], p.36.

18. [Aur], p.30.

19. [Aur], p.30.

20. [Aur], pp.89,91, and, in slightly different form, p.10.

21. [Aur], p.22.

22. [Aur], p.56.

23. [Aur], p.25.

24. [Aur], p.16.

25. [Aur], p.20.

26. [Aur], p.1.

27. The passage in question can be found in [Aur], p.2.

28. [Aur], p.13.

29. [Aur], pp.13–4.

30. [Kant1], p.361.

31. This reference to Konrad Lorenz is based on a remark of Ditfurth's in [Di], p.159.

32. [Kant3], p.151.

33. [Aur], p.29.

34. [Kant3], p.152.

35. [Kant3], pp.151-2.

36. [Kant1], p.345.

37. Susan Neiman very eloquently elaborates this point in [Nei], pp.57-84.

38. [Aur], p.16.

39. Susan Neiman carefully explains this point in [Nei], pp.57-84.

40. [Kant1], p.345.

41. [Kant1], p.346.

42. [Kant1], p.327.

43. [Kant1], p.346.

44. [Kant1], p.327.

45. "Love mankind" is a command stated by Aurelius in [Aur], p.47.

46. [Kant1], p.361.

47. [Kant1], p.344.

48. [Kant1], p.344.

49. In [Kant1], p.344.

50. [Kant1], p.344.

51. [Kant1], p.345.

52. [Aur], p.51.

53. [Kant1], p.344.

54. [Kant1], p.347.

55. Genesis 3:22, *The New International Version of the Holy Bible.*

56. Romans 7:15–25, *The New International Version of the Holy Bible.*

57. The quote here recorded is a free translation from the German original in [Schw2], p.34, that reads as follows: "Und diese Erkenntnis ist das große Ereignis in der Entwicklung des Seins. Hier erscheinen die Wahrheit und das Gute in der Welt; das Licht glänzt über dem Dunkel; der tiefste Begriff des Lebens ist erreicht, das Leben, das zugleich Miterleben ist, wo in einer Existenz der Wellenschlag der ganzen Welt gefühlt wird, in einer Existenz das Leben als solches zum Bewußtsein seiner selbst kommt...das Einzeldasein aufhört, das Dasein außer uns in das unsrige hereinflutet."

58. [Aur], p.47.

59. See the note #20 above.

60. Copleston uses the example of the commandment against adultery to illustrate the same point in [Copl6], p.311.

61. [Kant3], p.158.

62. The source in question is [Kant4].

63. [Boo], pp.90–1.

64. [Boo], pp.109–19.

65. [Boo], pp.111.

66. [Boo], pp.111.

67. [Nei], p.74.

68. Genesis 3:23–24, *The New International Version of the Holy Bible.*

69. [Boo], pp.224.

70. Matthew 6:10, *The New International Version of the Holy Bible.*

71. Romans 12:2, *The New International Version of the Holy Bible.*

72. Psalm 40:8, *The New International Version of the Holy Bible.*

73. Romans 12:2, *The New International Version of the Holy Bible.*

74. [Schw1], p.30.

75. [Bon2], p.55.

76. [Ju2], p.236.

77. [Bon2], p.18.

78. [Bon3], p.24.

79. Luke 18:19, *The New International Version of the Holy Bible.*

80. [Boo], p.180.

81. [Boo], p.180.

82. [Boo], p.180.

83. [Boo], p.180.

84. [Dos], p.266.

85. [Dos], p.275.

86. This assessment is based on Hannah Arendt's account in [Are], p.23.

87. [Are], p.253.

88. [Bon2], p.150.

89. [Bon2], p.151.

90. [Bon2], p.154.

91. [Bon2], p.151.

92. [Bon2], p.152.

93. [Bon2], p.154.

94. [Bon2], p.154.

95. Matthew 11:30, *The New International Version of the Holy Bible.*

96. [Pas], p.64.

97. 1 Corinthians 8:2–3, *The New International Version of the Holy Bible.*

98. The story of Maximilian Kolbe can be found in [Col].

99. The story of Helmuth James von Moltke is told in [Fri].

100. The verse here quoted is the last in Bonhoeffer's poem *Stations on the Road to Freedom* and can be found in [Bon3], p.23. The entire poem, in a different translation, is given in [Bon1], pp.516–7.

101. [Boo], p.219–20.

102. The quote is taken from [Col], p.808, and is a modification of the phrase "through the valley of the shadow of death" as given in Psalm 23:4 in *The New International Version of the Holy Bible.*

103. [Fri], p.395.

104. [Fri], p.396.

105. [Boo], p.67.

106. The theory of Freudian slips is elaborated in [Freu4].

107. [Ju5], p.22.

108. [Ju5], p.23.

109. [Ju6], p.511.

110. [Ju6], p.511-2.

111. [Pec2], p.254.

112. [Pec2], p.255.

113. [Lap], pp.3–4.

114. [Gh], p.136.

115. [Gh], p.136.

116. The paper in question is [EPR].

117. This claim concerning the entanglement of electrons after an interaction is based on the explanation given in [Gh], p.255.

118. This remark is based on the exposition in [Gh], pp.180–2.

119. [EPR], p.780.

120. [EPR], p.780.

121. [EPR], p.780.

122. This illustration is discussed in slightly modified form in [Gh], pp.184–5.

123. This remark is based on the exposition in [Chr], p.530.

124. [Chr], p.529.

125. [Chr], p.530.

126. [EPR], p.780.

127. [Gh], p.193.

128. [Gh], p.246.

129. [Gh], p.243.

130. This observation is inspired by Bonhoeffer's discussion in [Bon2], p.25–45.

131. For a far more penetrating analysis of the centrality of Jesus in Christian belief, the reader is referred to [Kün1].

132. [Gan], p.60.

133. [Kün1], p.52.

134. [Kün1], p.70.

135. [Lew1], p.56.

136. 1 Corinthians 1:20–25, *The New International Version of the Holy Bible*.

137. [Ju4], pp.12–3.

138. [Kün1], p.134.

139. [Kün1], p.164.

140. This remark on the work of St. Gregory is based on the discussion in [Copl2], pp.31–2.

141. That Augustine indeed was brought up by his mother as a Christian is mentioned in [Copl2], p.40, and Augustine himself confirms in [Aug2], p.32, that he had adopted Christian beliefs in his youth.

142. [Aug2], p.33.

143. [Copl2], p.40.

144. The particular aspects of the Manichean religion here mentioned are detailed by R.S. Pine-Coffin in [Aug2], p.13, and Augustine himself remarks on them in the same source on pp.67–8.

145. [Aug2], p.96.

146. [Aug2], p.47.

147. [Aug2], p.55.

148. [Aug2], p.114.

149. Augustine discusses this matter in [Aug2], pp.148–9.

150. [Aug2], p.165.

151. [Aug2], p.171.

152. [Aug2], pp.177–8.

153. [Stö], p.254.

154. According to the information provided in [Aug2], p.1, Augustine produced 113 books, over 200 letters, and more than 500 sermons.

155. The story of the meeting of the *Royal Society* has been adopted from the account given in [Di], p.191.

156. Paul provides an account of his hardships in 2nd Corinthians 6:3–10 and 11:23–33.

157. Our discussion of Augustine's epistemological outlook is based on the exposition in [Copl2], Chapter IV.

158. [Aug3], p.127.

159. This quote is taken from [Copl2], p.53, but the paragraph break follows the translation in [Aug3], p.128, and so do the quotation marks around the phrase 'But I am deceived, if I give my assent' as well as the quotation mark at the end of the phrase '...they see truly'.

160. [Aug1], p.460.

161. [Copl2], p.62.

162. [Aug2], p.181.

163. [Aug2], p.263.

164. [Aug2], p.263.

165. [Aug2], p.271.

166. [Aug2], p.264.

167. [Aug2], p.276.

168. [Aug2], p.216.

169. All three quotes are taken from [Aug2], p.242.

170. This question was posed and explored by Leibniz in his essay *On the Ultimate Origin of Things* ([Lei2], pp.136–44, and in particular, p.137), and also by Wheeler whom Horgan quotes in [Horg1], p.263.

171. [Aug2], p.279.

172. The very brief account of the decline of the Roman Empire in the west and the barbarian invasions is based largely on the exposition in [Can], pp.40–7 and pp.99–104.

173. The charges here referred to were presented to Augustine in a letter from an official named Marcellinus and specifically addressed the Christian teachings on "tolerating offences and submitting to injury" ([Aug1], pp.xiii-xiv).

174. Augustine comments on the destruction of the Roman commonwealth in [Aug1], p.75.

175. [Aug1], p.49.

176. [Aug1], p.429.

177. [Copl1], p.44.

178. This remark is based on the exposition in [Aug1], p.xii.

179. [Kün2], p.66.

180. [Aug1], p.1023.

181. [Aug1], p.831.

182. The phrases here quoted are excerpts from a statement by Jacob Meyer that is given in [Kee], p.12.

183. This assessment is based on the pertinent remark by Norman F. Cantor in [Can], p.78.

184. Our remarks on the subject of the contribution of Islam to the history of philosophy are based on the discussion in [Can], p.138.

185. [Copl2], p.114.

186. Copleston remarks on exactly this issue in [Copl2], p.140.

187. Abélard details the extend of this rivalry in [Ab], Chapter 2.

188. [Che], p.60.

189. This story of Aquinas and the temptress is based on the accounts given in [Che], pp.64–5, and [Stra2], pp.21–2.

190. [Free], p.145.

191. [Aq], p.9.

192. Küng makes a similar suggestion with respect to Pascal's thought in [Kün2], p.66.

193. Romans 1:20, *The New International Version of the Holy Bible*.

194. Richard Tarnas mentions this fact in [Tar], p.182, and as an example we can here give Aquinas's quote of that verse as well as of the directly preceding verse (Romans 1:19) in his *Treatise on God* in the *Summa Theologica* ([Aq], pp.6,12).

195. [Aq], p.12.

196. [Aq], p.9.

197. The image of 'two floors' is used by Küng in [Kün2] (see for instance p.35).

198. Richard Tarnas remarks on the influence of Albert the Great on Aquinas's views on universals in [Tar], p.187, and Anne Freemantle's discussion of Albert's pertinent doctrine in [Free], pp.146–7, is suggestive of this influence as well.

199. A brief account of that controversy can be found in [Ae], pp.24–6, and in [Chr], pp.92–3.

200. [Chr], p.141.

201. [Chr], p.141.

202. [Chr], p.142.

203. [Chr], p.143.

204. The dictionary in question is the third edition of the *American Heritage Dictionary of the English Language*, Houghton Mifflin, New York, 1992.

205. [Goet], p.77.

206. [Feye2], p.3.

207. [Wit], p.115.

208. [Aq], p.280.

209. [Aq], p.281.

210. [Aq], p.282.

211. [Aug1], p.465.

212. [Goet], p.20.

213. [New], p.403.

214. "Hypotheses non fingo" is the Latin version of Newton's comment "I do not feign hypotheses" in [New], p.943.

215. [Wit], p.115.

216. [Wit], p.117.

217. [Ken], p.60–1.

218. In the preface to the *Tractatus* Wittgenstein writes this: "I therefore believe myself to have found, on all essential points, the final solution of the problems" ([Wit], p.5).

219. The concluding sentence in the *Tractatus* is this: "What we cannot speak about we must pass over in silence" ([Wit], p.151).

220. [Wit], p.3.

221. [Wit], p.5.

222. [Wit], p.3.

223. [Che], p.59.

224. Christian Moevs comments on this point in [Moe], p.59, and Copleston quotes in this context one of Plato's letters in which Plato speaks of deeper things such as the nature of the Good that are "not communicable in words" ([Copl1], p.131).

225. [Moe], p.59.

226. [Moe], p.59.

227. [Moe], p.59.

228. [Aug1], p.304.

229. [Moe], p.63.

230. [Copl2], p.91.

231. [Moe], p.63.

232. [Wit], p.151.

233. Matthew 5:10, *The New International Version of the Holy Bible.*

234. Our account of the story of Héloise and Abelard follows the exposition in [Gi], but a very similar rendering of this story can also be found in [Stö].

235. [Gi], p.9.

236. The autobiography in questtion is [Ab].

237. [Can], pp.331–2.

238. [Eas], p.7.

239. This quote from Ockham's original writings is given by Philoteus Boehner in a footnote in [Oc], p.XX.

240. This description of Ockham's argument is based on the pertinent remarks in [Stö], p.307, and [Copl3], pp.50–1.

241. Störig remarks on this point in [Stö], p.308.

242. This apparent discrepancy between content and intent in Ockham's philosophy is emphasized by Tarnas in [Tar], pp.201–8.

243. [Herl], p.81.

244. [Zi], sp.1.

245. [Zi], p.2.

246. [Zi], p.1.

247. [Zi], p.3.

248. [Zi], p.3.

249. [Zi], p.3.

250. Matthew 5:42, *The New International Version of the Holy Bible.*

251. Acts 2:44, *The New International Version of the Holy Bible.*

252. Acts 2:45, *The New International Version of the Holy Bible.*

253. [Zi], pp.4–5.

254. [Jul], pp.247–8.

255. [Pi], pp.7–8 (an alternative translation is given in [Tar], pp.214–5).

256. [Lor2], p.196.

257. [Lor2], p.197.

258. [Schw2], pp.99–100.

259. [Rou1], p.3.

260. [Rou3], p.1.

261. [Rou3], p.5.

262. [Rou3], pp.5–6.

263. [Rou3], p.6.

264. [Rou3], p.6.

265. [Rou3], p.11.

266. [Rou4], p.339.

267. [Rou4], p.338.

268. This description is based on the exposition in [Sac], pp.76–80.

269. [Rou1], p.1.

270. [Rou1], p.1.

271. This quote is attributed to Heinrich Heine by Paul Strathern in [Stra1] ([Stra1], pp.23–4).

272. Paul Strathern comments on Kant's missing his walk in [Stra1], p.24.

273. Paul Strathern mentions that mutual grumpiness in [Stra1], p.39.

274. [Rou2], p.9.

275. [Rou2], p.9.

276. [Plat5], p.699.

277. Eibl-Eibesfeldt discusses this issue in [Eib2], p.189.

278. [Kem], p.27.

279. [Kem], p.144.

280. [Pi], pp.4–5.

281. Genesis 1:26, *The New International Version of the Holy Bible*.

282. [Ju2], p.235.

283. [Ju2], p.235.

284. The idea that Planet Earth is a "celestial boot camp" designed to foster spiritual growth is proposed by Scott Peck in [Pec1], p.226.

285. Matthew 8:20, *The New International Version of the Holy Bible*.

Chapter 5. The expositions in [Copl3], [Copl4], [Copl5], [Stö], [Tar], and [Pric] served as general references concerning the philosophical developments in the 16th, 17th, and 18th centuries. The discussion of the Copernican Revolution and subsequent developments has been crucially informed by the expositions in [Kuh1] and [Va], and many remarks concerning Dante's *Comedy* have been derived from [Moe]. Furthermore, this chapter contains some material from Chapters 5, 9, and 15 of [Bl2] in modified form (used with permission). Finally, concerning the images that are used in this chapter, the account is as follows: the image of *The Pale Blue Dot* in Figure 5.7 is a NASA image and is in the public domain; the photograph shown in Figure 5.8 of the RMC at Princeton University was provided by the International Consciousness Research Laboratories (ICRL) and was used with permission; the photograph of Mondrian's studio in Figure 5.9 was provided by the *Netherlands Institute for Art History* and was used with permission (Paul Delbo, Studio of Piet Mondrian, 26 Rue du Dpart, Paris, 1926, Original Gelatin Silverprint, Archive of Cesar Domela, RKD - Netherlands Institute for Art History, The Hague).

1. A more detailed discussion of the stars' relative motion can be found in [No], pp.394–8.

2. [Ari3], p.387–8.

3. [Ari3], p.377.

4. A more detailed discussion of eccentrics as well as more complicated eccentric-deferent constructions can be found in [Kuh1], pp.70–2.

5. [Pt], p.270.

6. The provision here referred to is remarked upon in a footnote to Ptolemy's *Almagest* ([Pt], p.291) and is also mentioned by Angus Armitage in [Arm], p.72.

7. [Arm], p.48.

8. This biographical sketch is based on the information provided in [Cope], pp.499-500.

9. [Cope], p.515.

10. John North comments on this issue in [No], p.281.

11. This remark, concerning the inferior accuracy of the Copernican system in its simplest form, is based on the pertinent discussion in [Kuh1], p.169.

12. Thomas Kuhn remarks in this context that "Copernicus did not solve the problem of the planets" ([Kuh1], p.169).

13. The distinction between major and minor epicycles is explained in more detail in [Kuh1], p.169.

14. A brief discussion of Mach's principle and of some of the difficulties pertaining to it can be found in [MTW], pp.543–9.

15. [Wein], pp.143–4.

16. Steven Weinberg argues this point at length in [Wein], Chapter VI.

17. [Wein], p.144.

18. [Cope], p.528.

19. [Cope], p.507.

20. [Cope], p.508.

21. [Cope], p.526–7.

22. [Kuh1], p.124.

23. [Kuh1], p.124.

24. [Kuh1], p.125.

25. [Kuh1], p.125.

26. [Cope], p.509.

27. These points are explained far more carefully in [Kuh1], Chapters 4, 5, and 6.

28. In the *Revolutions* Copernicus writes concerning this point that "rectilin-ear movement belongs only to bodies which are not in the right condition and are not perfectly conformed to their nature" ([Cope], p.520). Thus, according to Copernicus, the natural state of the Earth as a whole is not to be at rest a the center but rather to follow a circular motion.

29. [Pt], p.12.

30. [Cope], p.518.

31. [Cope], p.519.

32. [Cope], p.519.

33. [Pt], p.12.

34. [Pt], p.10.

35. See [Kuh1], pp.159–60, for a more detailed explanation.

36. In *The Revolutions* Copernicus mentions that certain of his predecessors had found the distance between the Earth and the Sun to be about 1160 times larger than the Earth's radius ([Cope], p.522), and Kuhn points out in [Kuh1], p.160, that Aristarchus had found the same factor to be about 1528.

37. [Kuh1], p.227.

38. [Arm], p.61.

39. This piece of information is derived from the introduction by Melinda Corey in [Dan2], p.xii.

40. [Dan2], p.255.

41. [Dan1], p.47.

42. This quote is taken from the introduction by Melinda Corey in [Dan2], p.xiii.

43. [Dan1], p.49.

44. Christian Moevs comments on this point in [Moe], p.5.

45. [Moe], p.10.

46. The quote is taken from a commencement address given by Carl Sagan and can be found at http://en.wikipedia.org/wiki/Pale_Blue_Dot. Sagan also wrote a book in which he used the image of the Pale Blue Dot as an inspiration for his personal vision for human space exploration (the book in question is [Sag]).

47. [Bor], p.51–8. The idea

48. [Dan2], p.xi.

49. [Bor], p.52.

50. [Bor], p.54.

51. [Bor], p.54.

52. [Bor], p.54.

53. [Bor], p.54.

54. Gene Bell-Villada makes this observation in similar form in [Bell-V], p.112.

55. [Bor], p.55.

56. [Bor], p.58.

57. [Bor], p.58.

58. The facts concerning Galileo's life that are here given are based mainly on the expositions in [Dra1], [Dra2], and [Sob].

59. [Sob], p.17.

60. [Sob], p.22.

61. A discussion of this issue can be found in [McM], pp.6–7 and p.27.

62. [Gal2], p.208.

63. [McM], pp.8–9.

64. [Gal2], p.238.

65. Ernan McMullin makes this point in [McM], p.21, and in the *Physics* Aristotle calls the idea "that a thing will have two motions at the same time" an "absurdity" ([Ari4], p.280).

66. [Gal2], p.238.

67. [McM], p.28.

68. In *The Two New Sciences* ([Gal2], p.224) Galileo states this 'inference' as follows: "Furthermore, we may remark that any velocity once imparted to a moving body will be rigidly maintained as long as the external causes of acceleration or retardation are removed, a condition which is found only on horizontal planes; for in the case of planes which slope downwards there is already present a cause of acceleration, while on planes sloping upward there is retardation; from this it follows that motion along a horizontal plane is perpetual; ..." Evidently, this conclusion is inadmissible (see also [McM], p.30).

69. The experiment in question concerns a ball that first rolls down along one inclined plane and then up another ([Gal2], p.225). Galileo observes that in absence of friction the ball will roll up the same height on the second plane from which it descended on the first, and that this is so even if the slopes of the two planes (in absolute value) are not the same. In the light of this observation it is possible to conclude that the distance

that the ball rolls along the second plane will tend to infinity as the slope of that plane tends to zero. Consequently, as the slope is made equal to zero, the motion will be perpetual.

70. [Gal1], pp.199-200.

71. The information concerning Galileo's invention of the telescope is derived from the exposition in [Sob], p.30.

72. Psalm 104:5, the *New International Version of the Bible*.

73. [Sob], p.66.

74. [Sob], p.60.

75. [Sob], p.63.

76. [Aq], p.357.

77. [Stö], p.327.

78. [Tar], p.252.

79. [Kuh1], p.191.

80. [Sob], p.78.

81. [Sob], p.78.

82. [Sob], p.78.

83. [Sob], p.274.

84. [Sob], p.275.

85. [Sob], p.278.

86. [Sob], p.278.

87. This assessment is mainly based on the exposition in [Wein], pp.122–3.

88. A brief account of the Rhines' work can be found in [JD2], pp.43–4, and in [McT], p.101.

89. This quote is taken from an address to the American Psychological Association given by J.B. Rhine in 1967 and can be found in [JD2], p.44.

90. A fairly detailed account of Schmidt's work can be found in [McT], pp.101–9.

91. See, for instance, [Schm1] and [Schm2].

92. [McT], p.110.

93. [JD2], p.89.

94. The book in question is [JD2].

95. This anecdote—along with some other, similar stories—is recalled in [JD1], p.361.

96. Some details on the construction and calibration of this REG are given in [JD2], pp.91–103.

97. This particular point is mentioned in [McT], p.113.

98. The figure given in [JD2], p.106, is "roughly 670 million."

99. See [JD2], pp.104–15 and also [JDN1].

100. A detailed analysis of this particular anomaly can be found in [Du1].

101. The relevant study is described in [Du2].

102. [JD2], pp.116–9.

103. [Ra], p.155.

104. http://imaginativeworlds.com/forum/showthread.php?
7176-Princeton-Engineering-Anomalies-Research-(PEAR)-closing

105. [JD2], pp.203-4.

106. Details concerning RMC experiments can be found in [JD2], pp.124-35 and in [JDN2].

107. A discussion of this quantum mechanical model of consciousness can be found in [JD3] and also in [JD2], pp.193–288.

108. [JD2], p.60.

109. [Pau].

110. [Schr] and [Schr].

111. [Hei1] and [Hei2].

112. [Jor].

113. [Wig1].

114. [Weiz1] and [Weiz2].

115. [Ein1] and [Ein2].

116. For further discussion of the larger implications of the PEAR research the reader is referred to the exposition in [JD2] and especially also in [JD1].

117. [Dec1], p.42.

118. [Dec1], p.42.

119. [Dec1], p.43.

120. [Dec1], p.44.

121. [Lav], p.87.

122. [Dec2], p.46.

123. [Dec3], p.78.

124. [Dec3], p.86.

125. [Dec3], p.101.

126. [Dec1], p.59 and also [Dec3], p.101.

127. [Dec1], p.59.

128. [Dec1], p.60.

129. [Copl4], p.66.

130. A detailed discussion of the link between the Christian Western world-view and the current ecological crisis can be found in [Dre].

131. Genesis 1:28, *The New International Version of the Holy Bible.*

132. Genesis 1:26, *The New International Version of the Holy Bible.*

133. Genesis 2:15, *The New International Version of the Holy Bible.*

134. [Goet], p.12.

135. Genesis 1:30, *The New International Version of the Holy Bible.*

136. [Dan1], p.57.

137. [Miln], p.109.

138. This quote was taken from Mondrian's essay on *Neo-Plasticism, the Home—the Street—the City* and can be found in [Pos], p.79.

139. [Mon3], p.137.

140. In [Mon2], p.327, Mondrian writes concerning this point that the "intention [of abstract art] is to create a new reality." Furthermore, Mondrian's vision of a neo-plastic world is developed in his essay on *Neo-Plasticism, the Home—the Street—the City* and can be found in [Pos], p.76.

141. [Pos], p.80.

142. [Pos], p.80.

143. The visitor in question was Maud van Loon, and her account can be found in [Pos], p.53.

144. This quote has been taken from [Pos], p.52, but in the original the passage in the third paragraph comes before the one in the second.

145. There is a specific comment concerning Mondrian's dislike of the "animal-based" in [Miln], p.166, and his concern for denaturalization is evident not only in his paintings and interior designs, but also in his writings (see, for instance, [Pos], pp.75–80).

146. [Lav], p.88.

147. This description of some of Modrian's personal habits and qualities is based on the testimonies by Arthur Lehning, César Domela, and Maud van Loon in [Pos], pp.51–3, as well as on a biographical note in [Ha], p.235.

148. [Roo], p.123–4.

149. [Mon2], p.323.

150. The subsequent biographical sketch is based on the expositions in [An], [Chr], and [Horn].

151. [Chr], p.1.

152. [Chr], p.13.

153. [Bell], p.37.

154. [An], p.23.

155. This anecdote is told by Bell in [Bell], p.37.

156. [Chr], p.19.

157. [Chr], p.54.

158. [Chr], p.62.

159. [Chr], p.62.

160. [Chr], pp.73–4.

161. [HollS], p.179.

162. [Key], p.277.

163. [Key], p.283.

164. [Key], p.283.

165. [Key], p.285.

166. [Bell], p.47.

167. [Neu], p.28.

168. [Chr], p.532.

169. The account of Laplace's demonstration is based on the exposition in [No], p.28.

170. The anecdote is recorded in [Kn], pp.69–70.

171. [Kn], p.70.

172. John North remarks on this point in [No], p.394.

173. These suggested causes are listed in [No], p.427.

174. [Kn], p.94.

175. [No], p.517–8.

176. [No], p.518.

177. Maxwell published his theory in a series of four papers in 1861 and 1862, the first of which is [Max].

178. This passage is taken from one of Einstein's unpublished manuscripts, the so-called Morgan manuscript. It is quoted in the given form in [Pai], p.178.

179. Einstein himself asserted in this context that by means of his field equations "space and time are deprived of the last trace of objective reality" (see [MTW], p.433).

180. [Pai], p.253.

181. In the *New Atlantis* Bacon develops a utopian vision of a society established upon rational scientific principles.

182. [Bac3], p.107.

183. [Bac3], p.108.

184. [Bac1], pp.12–3.

185. In respect of the Scholastics, Bacon speaks of "degenerate learning" and says that their "wits [were] shut up in the cells of a few authors (chiefly Aristotle their dictator)" ([Bac1], p.12).

186. Of Aristotle Bacon says that he "corrupted natural philosophy by logic" ([Bac3], p.113), and in reference to Plato he speaks of a "corruption of philosophy by the mixing it up with superstition and theology" ([Bac3], p.114).

187. [Bac1], p.45.

188. [Bac3], p.109.

189. [Bac3], p.108.

190. [Bac3], p.120.

191. [Bac3], p.121.

192. Bacon explicitly refers to this interplay between theory and observation in [Bac3], p.121.

193. The foundational purpose of the society described in the *New Atlantis* is to acquire genuine knowledge of physical causes and also to enlarge "the bounds of human empire" ([Bac2], p.210).

194. [Locke], p.95.

195. [Locke], p.121.

196. Locke explicitly recognizes that "the first capacity of the human intellect is... to receive the impressions made on it; either through the senses by outward objects, or by its own operations when it reflects on them" ([Locke], p.127).

197. [Locke], p.121.

198. [Locke], p.148.

199. [Locke], p.148.

200. [Ber1], p.54.

201. [Ber2], pp.160–1.

202. [Ber1], pp.62–3.

203. [Ber1], p.62.

204. [Moe], p.169.

205. [Ber1], pp.106–7.

206. [Ber1], p.113.

207. [Ber2], p.121.

208. Berkeley discusses this example in [Ber2], pp.131–2.

209. [Ber1], p.63.

210. A brief summary of Wigner's comments concerning the problems one encounters when describing interactions between two or more observers can be found in [Wig1], p.135.

211. [Ber1], p.46.

212. [Ber1], p.50.

213. [Ber1], p.50.

214. [Ber1], p.50–51.

215. The impossibility of *locally* defining the energy of a gravitational field in general relativity is discussed in [MTW], pp.466–8.

Chapter 6. The expositions in [Copl5], [Copl6], [Stö], [Tar], and [Lav] served as general references concerning the philosophical developments in the era extending from Hume and Kant to the early 20th century. Furthermore, the paintings shown in Figures 6.1, 6.2, 6.3, and 6.4 are in the public domain.

1. [Ber1], p.63.

2. [Ber1], p.79.

3. [Wig2], p.149.

4. [Hu1], p.410.

5. Berkeley discusses this point in [Ber1], p.85.

6. [Hu1], pp.310–1.

7. [Hu1], p.310.

8. Hume explicitly refers to the "narrow... bounds of human understanding" in [Hu1], p.291.

9. "Liberty and Necessity" is the title of Section VIII in [Hu1].

10. [Hu1], p.309.

11. [Hu1], p.416.

12. [Hu1], p.415.

13. [Hu3], p.13.

14. [Hu3], p.14.

15. [Hu3], p.14.

16. [Hu3], p.14.

17. Erich von Holst and Ursula von Saint Paul together published an article that carried this title in the *Scientific American* in 1962 (see [HS]).

18. This particular detail is derived from the description of von Holst's experiments that Ditfurth provides in [Di], pp.172–4.

19. [HS], p.53.

20. [Kant2], p.25.

21. [Kant2], p.25.

22. [Kant5], p.9.

23. [Kant5], p.8.

24. In [Kant5], p.4, Kant explains that "[i]n plain language" Hume's philosophy implies that "there is not, and cannot be, any such thing as metaphysics at all."

25. [Kant5], p.6.

26. [Kant5], p.7.

27. [Kant5], p.5.

28. [Kant5], p.32.

29. [Hu1], p.420.

30. In [Kant5], p.22, Kant asserts that Hume believed "that mathematics contains only analytical, but metaphysics synthetical, *a priori* judgments."

31. [Kant2], p.33.

32. [Kant2], p.34.

33. Kant makes this argument in [Kant5], p.22.

34. [Hu2], p.52.

35. [Hu2], p.53.

36. Kant uses this argument in [Kant2], pp.43–4.

37. [Kant2], pp.47–8.

38. [Kant2], p.48.

39. [Kant5], p.36.

40. [Kant5], p.24.

41. [Kant5], p.8.

42. [Locke], p.217.

43. [Kant2], p.12.

44. [Ber1], p.89.

45. [Ber1], p.85.

46. [Ber1], p.85.

47. [Kant5], p.143.

48. [Kant2], p.468.

49. [Kant2], p.470.

50. [Kant2], p.470.

51. [Dar], p.591.

52. [Lor1], p.6.

53. [Lor1], p.9.

54. [Lor1], p.4.

55. There are many books that convincingly establish the fact that life on earth emerged from an evolutionary process that extended over vast stretches of time. Some of these works are fiercely ideological in character while others are more restraint and objective. Two examples that belong to the latter category are [Coy] and [Mil2]. A somewhat deviant view of the nature of evolutionary developments can be found in [Gou], and an attempt to integrate evolutionary theory with a theistic perspective is provided in [Mil1].

56. Genesis 2:7, *The New International Version of the Holy Bible.*

57. [Kau2], pp.95–6.

58. [Ni1], p.44.

59. [Ni1], p.17.

60. [Ni1], p.17.

61. [Ni1], p.43.

62. [Ni1], p.43.

63. [Ni1], p.43.

64. [Ni1], p.43.

65. [Ni1], p.15.

66. [Ni4], p.34.

67. [HollR], p.161.

68. [HollR], p.161.

69. [Ni3], p.452.

70. [Ni3], p.451 and [Ni5], p.468.

71. [Man], p.365.

72. The question of whether Nietzsche was a nihilist is open to debate. Robert Schacht, for instance, acknowledges, in [Schac], pp.58–82, that Nietzsche is widely considered to have been an nihilist but then makes the case that he was not. In the process he discusses various quotes from Nietzsche's notebooks that apparently support the claim that Nietzsche *was* a nihilist, including one in which Nietzsche refers to himself as "the first perfect nihilist of Europe." Afterwards, however, Schacht goes on to argue that on the contrary Nietzsche believed "that there *are* positive general truths, both about the nature of reality and in the matter of value, which can be stated, and which ought to be recognized, at least by those who are strong enough to live with an awareness of them" ([Schac], p.65). In the light of these difficulties, it does seem plausible to assert that Nietzshe's position on nihilism was not free of inconsistencies. Indeed, Nietzsche explicitly emphasizes a fundamental duality of creation and destruction when he writes that anyone who "must be a creator of good and evil" must also "be an annihilator and break values" ([Ni4], p.116). That is to say, nihilistic deconstruction and positive creation may here go hand in hand.

73. [Kau2], pp.449–50.

74. [Copl7], p.394.

75. Matthew 22:37–39, *The New International Version of the Holy Bible*.

76. [Man], p.364.

77. Konrad Lorenz discusses this subject at length in [Lor3].

78. [Ni2], p.488.

79. [Ni2], p.488.

80. [Ni2], p.488.

81. [Ni2], p.488.

82. [HollR], p.282.

83. Thomas Mann writes in [Man], p.367, that Nietzsche "never said" why "[l]ife above all" was for him the highest value. According to Mann,

"[h]e never gave the reason why life should be something worthy of being adored unconditionally and preserved above all else..."

84. [Ni4], p.12.

85. [Ni4], p.32.

86. In [Ni4], p.188, Nietzsche writes that "[t]he greatest evil is necessary for the overman's best."

87. [Ni4], p.32.

88. [Ni4], pp.12–3.

89. [Ni4], p.110.

90. [Ni4], p.111.

91. [Ni4], p.112.

92. [Cam], p.3.

93. [Ni1], p.86.

94. Nietzsche discusses the issue of "free death" in [Ni4], pp.71–4.

95. [Cam], p.3.

96. [Ni4], p.71.

97. [Kau2], p.101.

98. [Kau2], p.101.

99. [Kau2], p.102.

100. [Kau2], p.102.

101. [Cam], p.6.

102. [Cam], p.17.

103. [Cam], p.14.

104. [Cam], p.17.

105. [Cam], pp.19–20.

106. [Cam], p.9.

107. [Cam], p.37.

108. [Cam], p.9.

109. [Cam], p.10.

110. [Cam], p.53.

111. [Cam], p.55.

112. [Cam], p.60.

113. [Cam], p.60.

114. [Prid], p.81.

115. [Prid], p.2.

116. Concerning his attitude toward religion, Munch wrote: "Through it all you might say I have been a doubter, but one who has never denied or mocked religion—my doubt was more an attack on the overpietism that dominated my upbringing" ([Boe], p.29).

117. This assessment is based on an account given by Munch's friend, Kristian Schreiner, as recorded in [Boe], pp.29–30. According to this account, Munch asserted this: "The world is one huge, living atom. It has thought-power and will-power, the clouds are its breath, the storms its mighty breathing, the glowing lava is its seething blood. Why shouldn't the sun have a will too, as it hurls its flow of light into space? There is life and will in everything, in stones and crystals as well as in the planets. The orbiting of the planets is evidence of will. And just as people's words can be sent in the form of waves through the ether, so can their thoughts travel in wave-like motion."

118. Late in his life, Munch summarized the nature of his faith as follows: "My declaration of faith: I bow down before something which, if you want, one might call God—the teaching of Christ seems to me the finest there is, and Christ himself is very close to godlike—if one can use that expression" ([Boe], p.29). In this context, however, we also need to mention that Munch, at earlier times of his life, had been strongly influenced by the death-of-God culture that was popular in the Bohemian circles to which he belonged.

119. [Sar2], p.4.

120. [Sar2], p.20, p.131.

121. [Sar2], pp.122–3, 130–1.

122. [Sar2], p.100-1.

123. [RuJ], p.1.

124. [Prid], p.119.

125. [Sar1a], p.lvii.

126. [Sar1a], p.l.

127. In [Sar1a], p.li, Sartre attributes this insight to Husserl.

128. [Sar1a], p.lii.

129. [Sar1a], p.liii.

130. [Sar1a], p.liv.

131. [Sar1b], p.47.

132. [Sar1a], p.lxvi.

133. [Sar2], p.131.

134. [Sar2], p.126–7.

135. [Sar2], p.128.

136. [Sar2], p.128. ·

137. [Sar3], p.320, and also [Sar1a], p.415.

138. In [Sar1a], p.lxiii, Sartre asserts "the being of the consciousness" to be "radically different" from the being of the phenomenon.

139. Sartre explains this issue, for example, in [Sar1a], p.426.

140. [Sar1a], p.435.

141. [Sar1a], p.435.

142. [Sar1a], p.435.

143. [Sar1b], p.52.

144. [El], p.516.

145. [Freu2], p.716.

146. [Freu2], p.716.

147. [Freu2], p.716.

148. [Freu2], p.716.

149. [Freu1], p.22.

150. [Freu1], p.23.

151. [Lav], p.376.

152. [Freu1], p.26.

153. [Freu3], p.50.

154. The quote by Auden can be found on the following website: blogs.scientificamerican.com/literally-psyched/2011/12/14/understanding-freuds-legacy-through-the-eyes-of-w-h-auden/

155. [Jam], p.87.

156. [Jam], p.87.

157. [Freu3], p.31.

158. [Freu3], p.31.

159. [Freu3], p.43.

160. [Freu3], p.42.

161. [Freu3], p.42.

162. [Freu3], p.25.

163. [Freu3], p.55.

Chapter 7.

1. [Sab], p.65-66.
2. [Sab], p.68.

Bibliography

[Ab] Abélard, Peter, *The Story of My Misfortunes*, translated by Henry Adams Bellows, The Free Press, Glencoe, Illinois, 1958.

[Ae] Aertsen, Jan A., Aquinas's philosophy in its historical setting, *The Cambridge Companion to Aquinas*, by Norman Kretzmann and Eleonore Stump (editors), Cambridge University Press, Cambridge, 1993.

[Ale] Alexander, Eben, M.D., *Proof of Heaven*, Simon & Schuster Paperbacks, New York, 2012.

[All] Allan, D.J., *The Philosophy of Aristotle*, Oxford University Press, Oxford, 1970.

[An] Anthony, H. D., *Sir Isaac Newton*, Collier Books, New York, 1961.

[Aq] Aquinas, Saint Thomas, *Summa Theologica*, Volume I, translated by the Fathers of the English Dominican Province, in *Great Books of the Western World*, Volume 19, by Robert Maynard Hutchins (Editor in Chief), Encyclopedia Britannica, Inc., Chicago, 1952.

[Are] Arendt, Hannah, *Eichmann in Jerusalem*, Viking Press, New York, 1963.

[Ari1] Aristotle, *Metaphysics*, translated by W.D. Ross, in *Great Books of the Western World*, Volume 8, by Robert Maynard Hutchins (Editor in Chief), Encyclopedia Britannica, Inc., Chicago, 1952.

[Ari2] Aristotle, *Nicomachean Ethics*, in *Aristotle on Man in the Universe*, by Louise Ropes Loomis (Editor), translated by James E.C. Welldon, Walter J. Black, New York, 1943.

[Ari3] Aristotle, *On the Heavens*, translated by J.A. Smith, in *Great Books of the Western World*, Volume 8, by Robert Maynard Hutchins (Editor in Chief), Encyclopedia Britannica, Inc., Chicago, 1952.

[Ari4] Aristotle, *Physics*, translated by R.P. Hardie and R.K. Gaye, in *Great Books of the Western World*, Volume 8, by Robert Maynard Hutchins (Editor in Chief), Encyclopedia Britannica, Inc., Chicago, 1952.

[Ari5] Aristotle, *Topics*, translated by W.A. Pickard-Cambridge, in *Great Books of the Western World*, Volume 8, by Robert Maynard Hutchins (Editor in Chief), Encyclopedia Britannica, Inc., Chicago, 1952.

[Arm] Armitage, Angus, *Copernicus and Modern Astronomy*, Dover Publications, Mineola, New York, 2004.

[Aug1] St. Augustine, *City of God*, translated by Henry Bettenson, Penguine Books, London, 1984.

[Aug2] St. Augustine, *Confessions*, translated by R.S. Pine-Coffin, Penguine Books, London, 1961.

[Aug3] St. Augustine, *Against the Academics*, translated by John J. O'Meara, in *Ancient Christian Writers* by Johannes Quasten and Joseph C. Plumpe (editors), Newman Press, New York, 1951.

[Aur] Aurelius, Marcus, *Meditations*, translated by A.S.L. Farquharson, Everyman's Library, New York, 1946.

[Bac1] Bacon, Francis, *Advancement of Learning*, in *Great Books of the Western World*, Volume 30, by Robert Maynard Hutchins (Editor in Chief), Encyclopedia Britannica, Inc., Chicago, 1952.

[Bac2] Bacon, Francis, *New Atlantis*, in *Great Books of the Western World*, Volume 30, by Robert Maynard Hutchins (Editor in Chief), Encyclopedia Britannica, Inc., Chicago, 1952.

[Bac3] Bacon, Francis, *Novum Organum*, in *Great Books of the Western World*, Volume 30, by Robert Maynard Hutchins (Editor in Chief), Encyclopedia Britannica, Inc., Chicago, 1952.

[Ba] Barbour, Julian, *The End of Time*, Oxford University Press, New York, 1999.

[Bell] Bell, Eric Temple, *On the Seashore*, in *Readings for Calculus* by Underwood Dudley (Editor), MAA Notes Number 31, The Mathematical Association of America, Washington, 1993.

[Bell-V] Bell-Villada, Gene H., *Borges and His Fiction*, The University of North Carolina Press, Chapel Hill, 1981.

[Ber1] Berkeley, George, *Principles of Human Understanding*, Penguine Books, London, 1988.

[Ber2] Berkeley, George, *Three Dialogues between Hylas and Philonous*, Penguin Books, London, 1988.

[BM] Boyer, Carl B., Merzbach, Uta C., *A History of Mathematics*, John Wiley & Sons, New York, 1991.

[Bl1] Blume, Frank, A derivation of the path-integral formalism of quantum mechanics from probability conservation along the velocity flows of classical particles, *Quantum Physics Letters* **2**, No. 2, pp.17–24, 2013.

[Bl2] Blume, Frank, *Applied Calculus for Scientists and Engineers*, Jones and Bartlett, Sudbury, 2005.

[Bl3] Blume, Frank, Minimal rates of entropy convergence for completely ergodic systems, *Israel Journal of Mathematics*, Vol. 108, pp.1–12, 1998.

[Bl4] Blume, Frank, Possible rates of entropy convergence, *Ergodic Theory and Dynamical Systems*, Vol. 17, pp.45–70, 1997.

[Boe] Boe, Alf, *Edvard Munch*, Rizzoli, New York, 1989.

[Boh1] Bohm, David, A Suggested Interpretation of the Quantum Theory in Terms of "Hidden Variables" I, *Physical Review* **85**, pp.166–79, 1952.

[Boh2] Bohm, David, A Suggested Interpretation of the Quantum Theory in Terms of "Hidden Variables" II, *Physical Review* **85**, pp.180–93, 1952.

[Boh3] Bohm, David, *Quantum Theory*, Dover Publications, New York, 1989.

[Bon1] Bonhoeffer, Dietrich, *A Testament to Freedom*, by Geffrey B. Kelly and E. Barton Nelson (editors), Harper Collins, New York, 1995.

[Bon2] Bonhoeffer, Dietrich, *Ethics*, translated by Neville Horton Smith, SCM Press Ltd., London, 1960.

[Bon3] Bonhoeffer, Dietrich, *The Cost of Discipleship*, with a Memoir by G. Leibholz, Collier Books, New York, 1963.

[Boo] ten Boom, Corrie, *The Hiding Place*, with John and Elizabeth Sherrill, Bantam Books, New York, 1974.

[Bor] Borges, Jorge Luis, *Labyrinths*, by Donald A. Yates and James E. Irby (editors and translators), New Directions, Norfolk, Connecticut, 1962.

[Bu]   Burton, David M., *The History of Mathematics*, McGraw-Hill, New
          York, 2003.

[Cam]   Camus, Albert, *The Myth of Sisyphus*, translated by Justin O'Brien,
          Alfred A. Knopf, New York, 1961.

[Can]   Cantor, Norman F., *The Civilization of the Middle Ages*, Harper-
          Perennial, New York, 1994.

[Che]   Chesterton, G.K., *Saint Thomas Aquinas*, Image Books, New York,
          1956.

[Chr]   Christianson, Gale E., *In the Presence of the Creator*, The Free Press,
          Macmillan, New York, 1984.

[Coh]   Cohn, Samuel K., The Black Death: End of a Paradigm, *The Amer-
          ican Historical Review*, Volume 107, 2002, pp.703–38.

[Col]   Colson, Chuck, *The Volunteer at Auschwitz*, in *The Book of Virtues*,
          by William J. Bennett, Simon & Schuster, New York, 1993, pp.803–8.

[Cope]   Copernicus, Nicolaus, *On the Revolutions of the Heavenly Spheres*,
          translated by Charles Glenn Wallis, in *Great Books of the Western
          World*, Volume 16, by Robert Maynard Hutchins (Editor in Chief),
          Encyclopedia Britannica, Inc., Chicago, 1952.

[Copl1]   Copleston, Frederick S.J., *A History of Philosophy*, Volume 1, Image
          Books, Doubleday, New York, 1993.

[Copl2]   Copleston, Frederick S.J., *A History of Philosophy*, Volume 2, Image
          Books, Doubleday, New York, 1994.

[Copl3]   Copleston, Frederick S.J., *A History of Philosophy*, Volume 3, Image
          Books, Doubleday, New York, 1994.

[Copl4]   Copleston, Frederick S.J., *A History of Philosophy*, Volume 4, Image
          Books, Doubleday, New York, 1994.

[Copl5]   Copleston, Frederick S.J., *A History of Philosophy*, Volume 5, Image
          Books, Doubleday, New York, 1994.

[Copl6]   Copleston, Frederick S.J., *A History of Philosophy*, Volume 6, Image
          Books, Doubleday, New York, 1994.

[Copl7]   Copleston, Frederick S.J., *A History of Philosophy*, Volume 7, Image
          Books, Doubleday, New York, 1994.

[Coy]   Coyne, Jerry A., *Why Evolution Is True*, Viking, New York, 2009.

[Cri]   Crick, Francis, *The Astonishing Hypothesis*, Charles Scribner's Sons, Macmillan Publishing, New York, 1994.

[Crop]   Cropper, William H., *The Quantum Physicists*, Oxford University Press, New York, 1970.

[Cros]   Crossan, John Dominique, *The Historical Jesus*, HarperSanFrancisco, 1991.

[Dan1]   Dante Alighieri, *Il Convivio (The Banquet)*, translated by Richard Lansing, Garland Publishing, New York, 1990.

[Dan2]   Dante Alighieri, *The Divine Comedy*, translated Henry Wadsworth Longfellow with an Introduction by Melinda Corey, Barnes & Noble, New York, 2008.

[Dar]   Darwin, Charles, *The Descent of Man and Selection in Relation to Sex*, in *Great Books of the Western World*, Volume 49 by Robert Maynard Hutchins (Editor in Chief), Encyclopedia Britannica, Inc., Chicago, 1952.

[Dav]   Davies, P.C.W., Why is the Universe Knowable?, in *Mathematics and Science*, by Ronald E. Mickens (editor), World Scientific, Princeton, Singapore, 1998.

[Dec1]   Descartes, René, *Discourse on the Method of Rightly Conducting the Reason and Seeking for Truth in the Sciences*, translated by Elizabeth S. Haldane and G.R.T. Ross, in *Great Books of the Western World*, Volume 31 by Robert Maynard Hutchins (Editor in Chief), Encyclopedia Britannica, Inc., Chicago, 1952.

[Dec2]   Descartes, René, *Meditations*, in *The Library of Original Sources*, Volume VI by Oliver J. Thatcher (Editor in Chief), University Research Extension Company, Milwaukee, 1915.

[Dec3]   Descartes, René, *Meditations on the First Philosophy*, translated by Elizabeth S. Haldane and G.R.T. Ross, in *Great Books of the Western World*, Volume 31 by Robert Maynard Hutchins (Editor in Chief), Encyclopedia Britannica, Inc., Chicago, 1952.

[Den]   Dennett, D.C., *Consciousness Explained*, Little, Brown, & Co., Boston, 1991.

[Dew]   Dewdney, A.K., *A Mathematical Mystery Tour*, John Wiley & Sons, New York, 1999.

[Di]   Ditfurth, Hoimar v., *Wir sind nicht nur von dieser Welt*, Deutscher Taschenbuch Verlag, München, 1981.

[Don]   Donne, John, *The Complete English Poems*, by A.J. Smith (editor), St. Martin's Press, New York, 1971.

[Dos]   Dostoevsky, Fyodor, *The Brothers Karamazov*, translated by Constance Garnett, Barnes & Noble Books, New York, 1995.

[Dra1]   Drake, Stillman, *Galileo*, Hill and Wang, New York, 1980.

[Dra2]   Drake, Stillman, *Galileo: A biographical Sketch*, in *Galileo*, by Ernan McMullin (editor), Basic Books, New York, 1967.

[Dre]   Drewermann, Eugen, *Der tödliche Fortschritt*, Herder Verlag, Freiburg, 1991.

[Du1]   Dunne, Brenda, Gender Differences in Human/Machine Anomalies, *Journal of Scientific Exploration*, Vol. 12, No. 1, pp.3–55, 1998.

[Du2]   Dunne, Brenda, Co-Operator Experiments with an REG Device, *PEAR Technical Note 91005*, December 1991.

[Eas]   Easton, Stewart C., *Roger Bacon and His Search for a Universal Science*, Greenwood Press, New York, 1970.

[Eib1]   Eibl-Eibesfeldt, Irenäus, *Der Mensch—das riskierte Wesen*, Piper, München, 1991.

[Eib2]   Eibl-Eibesfeldt, Irenäus, *Liebe und Hass*, Piper, München, 1991.

[EI]   Einstein, Albert and Infeld, Leopold, *The Evolution of Physics*, Simon and Schuster, New York, 1938.

[Ein1]   Einstein, Albert, *Albert Einstein: Philosopher Scientist*, Paul Arthur Schlipp (editor), MJF Books, New York, 1970.

[Ein2]   Einstein, Albert, *Out of My Later Years*, The Citadel Press, Secaucus, N.J., 1956.

[Ein3]   Einstein, Albert, Über einen die Erzeugung und Verwandlung des Lichtes betreffenden heuristischen Gesichtspunkt, *Annalen der Physik*, 17, pp.132–48, 1905.

[El]   Ellenberger, Henri F., *The Discovery of the Unconscious*, Basic Books, New York, 1970.

[EPR]   Einstein, A., Podolsky, B., Rosen, N., Can Quantum-Mechanical Description of Physical Reality Be Considered Complete?, *Physical Review*, Volume 47, 1935, pp.777–80.

[Feye1]   Feyerabend, Paul, *Against Method*, Verso, London, 2001.

[Feye2]   Feyerabend, Paul, *Conquest of Abundance*, The University of Chicago Press, Chicago, 1999.

[Feyn1]   Feynman, Richard P., *QED*, Princeton University Press, Princeton, 1988.

[Feyn2]   Feynman, Richard P., *Surely You're Joking Mr. Feynman!*, Bantam, New York, 1986.

[FLS]   Feynman, Richard P., Leighton, Robert B., Sands, Matthew, *The Feynman Lectures on Physics*, Volume III, Adison-Wesley, Palo Alto, 1965.

[Fra]   Frankl, Viktor E., *Man's Search for Meaning; an Introduction to Logotherapy*, Beacon Press, Boston, 1962.

[Free]   Freemantle, Anne, *The Age of Belief*, Houghton Mifflin, Boston, 1957.

[Freu1]   Freud, Sigmund, *Civilization and Its Discontents*, translated by James Strachey, W. W. Norton, New York, 1961.

[Freu2]   Freud, Sigmund, *The Ego and the Id*, translated by Joan Riviere, in *Great Books of the Western World*, Volume 54, by Robert Maynard Hutchins (Editor in Chief), Encyclopedia Britannica, Inc., Chicago, 1952.

[Freu3]   Freud, Sigmund, *The Future of an Illusion*, translated by James Strachey, W. W. Norton, New York, 1961.

[Freu4]   Freud, Sigmund, *The Psychopathology of Everyday Life*, translated by Alan Tyson, W. W. Norton, New York, 1960.

[Fri]   Friedrich, Otto, *Blood and Iron*, Harper Collins, New York, 1995.

[Gal1]   Galileo Galilei, *Dialogue on the Great World Systems*, in the Salusbury translation, The University of Chicago Press, Chicago, 1953.

[Gal2]   Galileo Galilei, *The Two New Sciences*, translated by Henry Crew and Alfonso de Salvio, in *Great Books of the Western World*, Volume 28 by Robert Maynard Hutchins (Editor in Chief), Encyclopedia Britannica, Inc., Chicago, 1952.

[Gan]   Gandhi, Mohandas K., *Autobiography*, Dover Publications, New York, 1983.

[Gh]   Ghirardi, Giancarlo, *Sneaking a Look at God's Cards*, Princeton University Press, Princeton, 2005.

[Gi]		Gilson, Étienne, *Héloise and Abélard*, Ann Arbor Paperbacks, The University of Michigan Press, 1960.

[Gl]		Glynn, Patrick, *God the Evidence*, Prima Publishing, Rocklin, 1997.

[Goeb]		Goebel, Julius, *Goethe's Faust Erster Teil*, Henry Holt, New York, 1946.

[Goet]		Goethe, Johann Wolfgang von, *Faust*, translated by Bayard Taylor, Macmillan, New York, 1946.

[Gom]		Gombrich, E.H., *The Story of Art*, Phaidon Press, London, 1995.

[Gou]		Gould, Stephen Jay, *The Structure of Evolutionary Theory*, Harvard University Press, Cambridge, Massachusetts, 2002.

[Gr]		Gribbin, John, *In Search of Schrödinger's Cat*, Bantam Books, New York, 1984.

[Ha]		Haftmann, Werner, *Malerei im 20. Jahrhundert*, Band 1, Prestel, München, 1980.

[Hee]		Heelan, Partick A., The Role of Consciousness as Meaning Maker in Science, Culture, and Religion, *Zygon*, Vol. 44, Number 2, 2009, pp.467–86.

[Hei1]		Heisenberg, Werner, *Physics and Beyond*, translated by Arnold J. Pomerans, Harper & Row, New York, 1971.

[Hei2]		Heisenberg, Werner, *Physics and Philosophy*, translated by F.F.C. Northrop, Prometheus Books, New York, 1999.

[Hei3]		Heisenberg, Werner, Über quantentheoretische Umdeutung kinematischer und mechanischer Beziehungen, *Zeitschrift für Physik*, Bd. XXXIII, pp.879–93, 1925.

[Herl]		Herlihy, David, *The Black Death and the Transformation of the West*, Harvard University Press, Cambridge, Massachusetts, 1997.

[Hert]		Hertz, Heinrich, *Prinzipien der Mechanik*, Gesammelte Werke, Band III, Herausgegeben von P. Lenard, Verlag von Johann Ambrosius Barth, Leipzig, 1910.

[HN]		Hayes, Keith J., Nissen, Catherine H., Higher mental functions of a home-raised chimpanzee, in *Behavior of Nonhuman Primates*, Volume 4, Allan M. Schrier, Fred Stollnitz ed., Academic Press, New York, 1971.

[HollR]   Hollingdale, R.J., *Nietzsche*, Louisiana State University Press, Baton Rouge, 1965.

[HollS]   Hollingdale, Stuart, *Makers of Mathematics*, Penguin Books, London, 1989.

[Horg1]   Horgan, John, *The End of Science*, Broadway Books, New York, 1997.

[Horg2]   Horgan, John, *The Undiscovered Mind*, The Free Press, New York, 1999.

[Horn]   Hornblower, Simon, *Greece: The History of the Classical Period*, in *The Oxford History of Greece and the Hellenistic World*, Boardman, J., Griffin, J., Murray, O., ed., Oxford University Press, Oxford, 1988.

[HS]   Holst, Erich von, Saint Paul, Ursula von, Electrically controlled behavior, *Scientific American*, **206**, No. 3, 1957, pp.50–9.

[Hu1]   Hume, David, *An Enquiry Concerning Human Understanding*, in *The Harvard Classics* by Charles W. Eliot (editor), Collier, New York, 1961.

[Hu2]   Hume, David, *A Treatise of Human Nature*, in *The Philosophy of David Hume* by V.C. Chappell (editor), The Modern Library, New York, 1963.

[Hu3]   Hume, David, *The Letters of David Hume* by J.Y.T. Greig (editor), Volume 1, Garland Publishing, New York, 1983.

[Jam]   James, William, *The Principles of Psychology*, in *Great Books of the Western World*, Volume 53, by Robert Maynard Hutchins (Editor in Chief), Encyclopedia Britannica, Inc., Chicago, 1952.

[Jas1]   Jaspers, Karl, *Philosophy of Existence*, translated by Richard F. Grabau, University of Pennsylvania Press, Philadelphia, 1971.

[Jas2]   Jaspers, Karl, *The Origin and Goal of History*, translated by Michael Bullock, Yale University Press, New Haven, 1953.

[JD1]   Jahn, R.G., Dunne, B.J., *Consciousness and the Source of Reality*, ICRL Press, Princeton, New Jersey, 2011.

[JD2]   Jahn, R.G., Dunne, B.J., *Margins of Reality*, Harvest Book, San Diego, 1987.

[JD3]   Jahn, R.G., Dunne, B.J., On the Quantum Mechanics of Consciousness with Application to Anomalous Phenomena, *Foundations of Physics*, Vol. 16, No. 8, August 1986, pp.721–72.

[JDN1]   Jahn, R.G., Dunne, B.J., Nelson, R.D., Dobyns, Y.H., Bradish, G.J., Correlations of Random Binary Sequences with Pre-Stated Operator Intention: A Review of a 12-Year Program, *Journal of Scientific Exploration*, Vol. 11, No. 3, pp.345–67, 1997.

[JDN2]   Jahn, R.G., Dunne, B.J., Nelson, R.D., Operator-Related Anomalies in a Random Mechanical Cascade, *Journal of Scientific Exploration*, Vol. 2, No. 2, pp.155–79, 1988.

[Je]   Jeans, James, *The Mysterious Universe*, Cambridge University Press, Cambridge, 1948.

[Jor]   Jordan, Pascual, Parapsychological implications of research in atomic physics, *International Journal of Parapsycholgy*, 2, no. 4, 1960, pp.5–16.

[Jos]   Joseph, H.W.B., *Lectures on the Philosophy of Leibniz*, Greenwood Press, Westport, Connecticut, 1973.

[Ju1]   Jung, C.G., *Memories, Dreams, Reflections*, translated by Richard and Clara Winston, Vintage Books, New York, 1989.

[Ju2]   Jung, C.G., *Modern Man in Search of a Soul*, translated by W.S. Dell and Cary F. Baynes, Harvest Book, San Diego, 1933.

[Ju3]   Jung, C.G., *C.G. Jung: Psychological Reflections*, by Jolande Jacobi and R.F.C. Hull (editors), Bollingen Series XXXI, Princeton University Press, Princeton, 1978.

[Ju4]   Jung, C.G., *Psychological Types*, translated by H.G. Baynes, Bollingen Series, Princeton University Press, Princeton, 1971.

[Ju5]   Jung, C.G., *Synchronicity*, translated by R.F.C. Hull, Bollingen Series, Princeton University Press, Princeton, 1973.

[Ju6]   Jung, C.G., *The Portable Jung*, translated by R.F.C. Hull, Joseph Campbell (editor), Viking Press, New York, 1971.

[KaneG] Kane, Gordon, *Supersymmetry*, Perseus Publishing, Cambridge, Massachusetts, 2000.

[KaneR] Kane, Robert, ed., *The Oxford Handbook of Free Will*, Oxford University Press, Oxford, 2002.

[Kant1] Kant, Immanuel, *Critique of Practical Reason*, translated by Thomas Kingsmill Abbott, in *Great Books of the Western World*, Volume 42, by Robert Maynard Hutchins (Editor in Chief), Encyclopedia Britannica, Inc., Chicago, 1952.

[Kant2]   Kant, Immanuel, *Critique of Pure Reason*, translated by J.M.D. Meiklejohn, Everyman's Library, London, 1991.

[Kant3]   Kant, Immanuel, *Fundamental Principles of the Metaphysics of Morals*, in *Basic Writings of Kant*, by Allen Wood (Editor), translated by Thomas K. Abbott, The Modern Library, New York, 2001.

[Kant4]   Kant, Immanuel, *On a Supposed Right to Lie from Altruistic Motives*, translated by Lewis White Beck, in *Ethics*, by Peter Singer (Editor), Oxford University Press, Oxford, 1994, pp.280–1.

[Kant5]   Kant, Immanuel, *Prolegomena*, translated by Paul Carus, Open Court, Chicago, 1997.

[Kau1]   Kaufmann, Walter, *The Discovery of the Will to Power*, in *Nietzsche* by Robert Solomon (editor), Anchor Books, New York, 1973.

[Kau2]   Kaufmann, Walter, *The Portable Nietzsche*, Penguin Books, New York, 1976.

[KBW]   Kunzmann, Peter, Burkard, Franz-Peter, Wiedmann, Franz, *dtv-Atlas Philosophie*, Deutscher Taschenbuch Verlag, München, 1991.

[Kee]   Keen, Maurice, *Medieval Europe*, Penguin Books, London, 1991.

[Kel]   Kelly, John, *The Great Mortality*, HarperCollins, New York, 2005.

[Kem]   Kempis, Thomas à, *The Imitation of Christ*, translated by Leo Sherley-Price, Penguin Books, London, 1952.

[Ken]   Kenny, Anthony, *The Wittgenstein Reader*, Blackwell Publishers, Oxford, 2001.

[Key]   Keynes, John Maynard, *Newton, the Man*, in *The World of Mathematics*, Volume 1, by James R. Newman, Simon and Schuster, New York, 1956.

[Klei]   Kleinert, Hagen, *Path Integrals in Quantum Mechanics, Statistics, Polymer Physics, and Financial Markets*, World Scientific, Singapore, 2006.

[Klem]   Klemm, David E., Religious Naturalism or Theological Humanism?, *Zygon*, Vol. 42, Number 2, 2007, pp.357–68.

[Kn]   Kneller, Karl A., *Christianity and the Leaders of Modern Science*, Real-View-Books, Fraser, Michigan, 1995.

[Ko1]   Koenig, Harold G., *Medicine, Religion, and Health*, Templeton Foundation Press, West Conshohocken, PA, 2008.

[Ko2]   Koenig, Harold G., *The Healing Power of Faith*, Touchstone, New York, 2001.

[Kub1]   Kübler-Ross, *On Death and Dying*, The Macmillan Company, New York, 1969.

[Kub2]   Kübler-Ross, *The Tunnel and the Light*, Marlowe & Company, New York, 1999.

[Kuh1]   Kuhn, Thomas S., *The Copernican Revolution*, Harvard University Press, Cambridge, Massachusetts, 1999.

[Kuh2]   Kuhn, Thomas S., *The Structure of Scientific Revolutions*, University of Chicago Press, Chicago, 1996.

[Kün1]   Küng, Hans, *Christianity*, translated John Bowden, Continuum, New York, 1998.

[Kün2]   Küng, Hans, *Does God Exist?*, translated by Edward Quinn, Crossroad, New York, 1994.

[Lap]   Laplace, Pierre-Simon, *A Philosophical Essay on Probability*, translated by Frederick Wilson Truscott and Frederick Lincoln Emory, Dover, New York, 1995.

[Lav]   Lavine, T.Z., *From Socrates to Sartre: the Philosophic Quest*, Bantam Books, New York, 1984.

[Leh]   Lehninger, Albert L., *Principles of Biochemistry*, Worth Publishers, New York, 1982.

[Lei1]   Leibniz, Gottfried Wilhelm, The Monadology, in *The Library of Original Sources*, Volume VI by Oliver J. Thatcher (Editor in Chief), University Research Extension Co., Milwaukee, 1915.

[Lei2]   Leibniz, Gottfried Wilhelm, *Philosophical Writings*, translated by Mary Morris and G.H.R. Parkinson, Everyman, London, 1997.

[Lew1]   Lewis, C.S., *Mere Christianity*, Macmillan Publishing Company, New York, 1960.

[Lew2]   Lewis, C.S., *The Discarded Image*, Cambridge University Press, Cambridge, 1994.

[LJ]   Lakoff, G., Johnson, M., *Philosophy in the Flesh*, Basic Books, New York, 1999.

[Locke]   Locke, John, *Concerning Human Understanding*, in *Great Books of the Western World*, Volume 35, by Robert Maynard Hutchins (Editor in Chief), Encyclopedia Britannica, Inc., Chicago, 1952.

[Lockw]   Lockwood, Michael, *Mind, Brain, and the Quantum: The Compound "I"*, Basil Blackwell, Cambridge MA, 1989.

[Lom]   Lommel, Pim van, *Consciousness Beyond Life: The Science of the Near-Death Experience*, HarperCollins, 2010.

[Lor1]   Lorenz, Konrad, *Behind the Mirror*, translated by Ronald Taylor, Harvest/HJB, New York, 1978.

[Lor2]   Lorenz, Konrad, *King Solomon's Ring*, translated by Marjorie Kerr Wilson, Mentor Books, New York, 1991.

[Lor3]   Lorenz, Konrad, *On Aggression*, translated by Marjorie Kerr Wilson, Bantam Books, New York, 1967.

[LW]   Lommel, Pim van, Wees, Ruud van, Meyers, Vincent, Elfferich, Ingrid, Near-death Experience in Survivors of Cardiac Arrest: a Prospective Study in the Netherlands, *The Lancet*, Dec. 15, 2001; 358, 9298; pp.2039–45.

[Man]   Mann, Thomas, *Nietzsche's Philosophy in the Light of Contemporary Events*, in *Nietzsche* by Robert Solomon (editor), Anchor Books, New York, 1973.

[Max]   Maxwell, James Clerk, On Physical Lines of Force, *The London, Edinburgh and Dublin Philosophical Magazine and Journal of Science*, Fourth Series, March 1861, pp.161–75.

[McM]   McMullin, Ernan, *Galileo, Man of Science*, Basic Books, Inc., New York, 1967.

[McT]   McTaggart, Lynne, *The Field*, HarperCollins Publishers, New York, 2002.

[MD]   Marketon, Melanie M., DePaolo, R. William, DeBoard, Kristin L., Jabri, Dana, Schneewind, Olaf, Plague Bacteria Target Immune Cells During Infection, *Science*, Vol. 309, no. 5741, pp.1739–41, September 2005.

[MHLKT]   McCullough, Micheal E., Hoyt, William T., Larson, David B., Koenig, Harold G., Thoresen, Carl, Religious Involvement and Mortality: A Meta-Analytic Review, *Health Psychology* 19, no. 3 (2000): 211–22.

[Mic]   Mickens, Ronald E. (editor), *Mathematics and Science*, World Scientific, Princeton, Singapore, 1998.

[Mil1]   Miller, Kenneth R., *Finding Darwin's God*, Harper Perennial, New York, 2007.

[Mil2]   Miller, Kenneth R., *Only a Theory*, Viking, New York, 2008.

[Miln]   Milner, John, *Mondrian*, Phaidon, Hong Kong, 2000.

[Moe]   Moevs, Christian, *The Metaphysics of Dante's Comedy*, Oxford University Press, New York, 2005.

[Mon1]   Mondrian, Piet, Cubism and Neo-Plastic, in *The New Art—The New Life*, by Harry Holtzmann and Martin S. James (editors and translators), G.K. Hall & Co, Boston, 1986.

[Mon2]   Mondrian, Piet, Liberation from Oppression in Art and Life, in *The New Art—The New Life*, by Harry Holtzmann and Martin S. James (editors and translators), G.K. Hall & Co, Boston, 1986.

[Mon3]   Mondrian, Piet, Neo-Plasticism: The General Principle of Plastic Equivalence, in *The New Art—The New Life* by Harry Holtzmann and Martin S. James (editors and tanslators), G.K. Hall & Co, Boston, 1986.

[MP1]   Morse, Melvin, with Perry, Paul, *Closer to the Light*, IVY Books, New York, 1990.

[MP2]   Morse, Melvin, Perry, Paul, *Transformed by the Light*, Ballantine/Fawcett, New York, 1994.

[MS]   Misra, B., Sudarshan, E., *The Zeno's paradox in quantum theory*, *Journal of Mathematical Physics*, Vol. 18, No. 4, April 1977, pp.756–63.

[MTW]   Misner, C.W., Thorne, K.S., Wheeler, J.A., *Gravitation*, Freeman, San Francisco, 1970.

[Nei]   Neiman, Susan, *Evil in Modern Thought*, Princeton University Press, Princeton, New Jersey, 2002.

[Neu]   von Neumann, John, *Mathematical Foundations of Quantum Theory*, Princeton University Press, Princeton, 1955.

[New]   Newton, Isaac, *The Principia*, University of California Press, Berkeley, 1999.

[Ni1]   Nietzsche, Friedrich, *Beyond Good and Evil*, translated by Marianne Cowan, Henry Regnery Company, Chicago, 1955.

[Ni2]   Nietzsche, Friedrich, *The Anti-Christ: Curse on Christianity*, in *The Nietzsche Reader* by Keith Ansell Pearson and Duncan Large (editors), Blackwell Publishing, Malden, MA, 2006.

[Ni3]   Nietzsche, Friedrich, *The Case of Wagner: A Musician's Problem*, in *The Nietzsche Reader* by Keith Ansell Pearson and Duncan Large (editors), Blackwell Publishing, Malden, MA, 2006.

[Ni4]   Nietzsche, Friedrich, *Thus Spoke Zarathustra*, translated by Walter Kaufmann, The Modern Library, New York, 1995.

[Ni5]   Nietzsche, Friedrich, *Twilight of the Idols; or, How to Philosophize with a Hammer*, in *The Nietzsche Reader* by Keith Ansell Pearson and Duncan Large (editors), Blackwell Publishing, Malden, MA, 2006.

[No]   North, John, *The Norton History of Astronomy and Cosmology*, Norton & Company, New York, 1994.

[Oc]   Ockham, William, *Philosophical Writings*, Bobbs-Merrill, New York, 1964.

[Pai]   Pais, Abraham, *'Subtle is the Lord...'*, Oxford University Press, Oxford, 1982.

[Pas]   Pascal, Blaise, *Pensées*, translated by A.J. Krailsheimer, Penguin Books, London, 1966.

[Pau]   Pauli, Wolfgang, The Influence of Archetypal Ideas on the Scientific Theories of Kepler, in *The Interpretation of Nature and the Psyche* by C.G. Jung and Wolfgang Pauli, Pantheon Books, Bollingen Series LI, New York, 1955, pp.149–240.

[Pec1]   Peck, M. Scott, *Further Along the Road Less Traveled*, Touchstone Book, New York, 1993.

[Pec2]   Peck, M. Scott, *The Road Less Traveled*, Touchstone Book, New York, 1978.

[Pen]   Penrose, Roger, *The Emperor's New Mind*, Oxford University Press, New York, 1989.

[Pi]   Pico della Mirandola, Giovanni, *Oration on the Dignity of Man*, translated by A. Robert Caponigri, Gateway Editions, Chicago, 1956.

[Plan1] Planck, Max, Ueber eine Verbesserung der Wienschen Spectralglei-
         chung, in *Planck's Original Papers in Quantum Physics*, annotated
         by Hans Kangro, Taylor & Francis Ltd., London, 1972.

[Plan2] Planck, Max, Zur Theorie des Gesetzes der Energieverteilung im Nor-
         malspectrum, in *Planck's Original Papers in Quantum Physics*, an-
         notated by Hans Kangro, Taylor & Francis, London, 1972.

[Plat1] Plato, *Laws*, in *The Collected Dialogues of Plato*, translated by A. E.
         Taylor, Edith Hamilton (Editor), Bollingen Series LXXI, Princeton
         University Press, 1961.

[Plat2] Plato, *Parmenides*, in *The Collected Dialogues of Plato*, translated
         by F. M. Cornford, Edith Hamilton (Editor), Bollingen Series LXXI,
         Princeton University Press, 1961.

[Plat3] Plato, *Phaedo*, in *The Collected Dialogues of Plato*, translated by
         Hugh Tredennick, Edith Hamilton (Editor), Bollingen Series LXXI,
         Princeton University Press, 1961.

[Plat4] Plato, *Phaedrus*, in *The Collected Dialogues of Plato*, translated by R.
         Hackforth, Edith Hamilton (Editor), Bollingen Series LXXI, Prince-
         ton University Press, 1961.

[Plat5] Plato, *Republic*, in *The Collected Dialogues of Plato*, translated by
         Paul Shorey, Edith Hamilton (Editor), Bollingen Series LXXI, Prince-
         ton University Press, 1961.

[Plat6] Plato, *Symposium*, in *The Collected Dialogues of Plato*, translated
         by Michael Joyce, Edith Hamilton (Editor), Bollingen Series LXXI,
         Princeton University Press, 1961.

[Pop]   Popper, Karl, *The Logic of Scientific Discovery*, Routledge Classics,
         London and New York, 2006.

[Pos]   Postma, Frans, *26, Rue du Départ*, by C. Boekraad (editor), with
         contributions by Luc Berger and Monique Suttrop, Ernst & Sohn,
         Berlin, 1995.

[Pric]   Price, Simon, *The History of the Hellenistic Period*, in *The Oxford
         History of Greece and the Hellenistic World*, J. Boardman, J. Griffin,
         O. Murray, ed., Oxford University Press, Oxford, 1988.

[Prid]   Prideaux, Sue, *Edvard Munch*, Yale University Press, New Haven,
         2005.

[Pt]   Ptolemy, *The Almagest*, translated by R. Catesby Taliaferro, in *Great Books of the Western World*, Volume 16, by Robert Maynard Hutchins (Editor in Chief), Encyclopedia Britannica, Inc., Chicago, 1952.

[Ra]   Radin, Dean I., *The Conscious Universe*, HarperCollins Publishers, New York, 1997.

[RobD]   Robinson, Daniel N., *The Great Ideas of Philosophy*, Part I, Lecture 3, in *The Great Courses on Tape* series, The Teaching Company, 1997.

[RobJ]   Robinson, John Mansley, *An Introduction to Early Greek Philosophy*, Houghton Mifflin Company, New York, 1968.

[Roo]   Rookmaaker, H.R., *Modern Art & the Death of a Culture*, Inter-Varsity Press, Leicester, 1970.

[RuB]   Russell, Bertrand, *The Problems of Philosophy*, Oxford University Press, London, 1964.

[RuJ]   Russell, J., *Francis Bacon*, Methuen, London, 1964.

[Rou1]   Rousseau, Jean Jacques, *Confessions*, Volume I, Everyman's Library, New York, 1971.

[Rou2]   Rousseau, Jean Jacques, *Confessions*, Volume II, Everyman's Library, New York, 1971.

[Rou3]   Rousseau, Jean Jacques, *Discourse on the Sciences and the Arts*, translated by Judith R. Bush, Roger D. Masters, and Christopher Kelly, in *The Collected Writings of Rousseau*, Volume 2, Roger D. Masters and Christopher Kelly (editors), Dartmouth College, University Press of New England, Hanover, 1992.

[Rou4]   Rousseau, Jean Jacques, *Discourse on the Origin of Inequality*, translated by G.D.H. Cole, in *Great Books of the Western World*, Volume 38, by Robert Maynard Hutchins (Editor in Chief), Encyclopedia Britannica, Inc., Chicago, 1952.

[Sab]   Sabom, Michael B., *Recollections of Death: A Medical Investigation*, Harper and Row, New York, 1982.

[Sac]   Sacks, Oliver, *The Man Who Mistook His Wife for a Hat*, Picador, London, 1986.

[Sag]   Sagan, Carl, *Pale Blue Dot: a Vision of the Human Future in Space*, Random House, New York, 1994.

[Sar1a]   Sartre, Jean-Paul, *Being and Nothingness* (abridged), translated by Hazel E. Barnes, Citadel Press, New York, 2001.

[Sar1b]   Sartre, Jean-Paul, *Being and Nothingness* (unabridged), translated by Hazel E. Barnes, Philosophical Library, New York, 1956.

[Sar2]   Sartre, Jean-Paul, *Nausea*, translated by Lloyd Alexander, Robert Bentley, Cambridge, Massachusetts, 1964.

[Sar3]   Sartre, Jean-Paul, *The Age of Reason*, translated by Eric Sutton, The Modern Library, New York, 1947.

[Schac]   Schacht, Robert, *Nietzsche and Nihilism*, in *Nietzsche* by Robert Solomon (editor), Anchor Books, New York, 1973.

[Schaf1] Schäfer, Lothar, *In Search of Divine Reality*, University of Arkansas Press, Fayetteville, 1997.

[Schaf2] Schäfer, Lothar, Quantum Reality and the Consciousness of the Universe, *Zygon*, Vol. 41, Number 3, 2006, pp.505–32.

[Schm1]   Schmidt, Helmut, Mental Influence on Random Events, *New Scientist and Science Journal*, June 24, 1971, pp.757–8.

[Schm2]   Schmidt, Helmut, Quantum Processes Predicted?, *New Scientist*, October 16, 1969, pp.114–5.

[Scho]   Schopenhauer, Arthur, *The Pessimist's Handbook*, translated by T. Bailey Saunders, University of Nebraska Press, Lincoln, 1964.

[Schr]   Schrödinger, Erwin, *My View of the World*, translated by C. Hastings, Cambridge University Press, Cambridge, 1964.

[Schr]   Schrödinger, Erwin, *Nature and the Greeks*, Cambridge University Press, Cambridge, 1954.

[Schw1]   Schweitzer, Albert, *Christianity and the Religions of the World*, translated by Joanna Powers, George Allen and Unwin, Ltd, London, 1955.

[Schw2]   Schweitzer, Albert, *Die Ehrfurcht vor dem Leben*, Verlag C.H. Beck, München, 1991.

[Shan]   Shankar, R., *Principles of Quantum Mechanics*, Plenum Press, New York, 1994.

[Shap]   Shapin, Steven, *The Scientific Revolution*, University of Chicago Press, 1996.

[Sob] Sobel, Dava, *Galileo's Daughter*, Penguin Books, New York, 2000.

[Som1] Sommerfeld, Arnold, *Elektrodynamik*, Vorlesungen über Theoretische Physik, Band 3, Verlag Harri Deutsch, Frankfurt/M., 1977.

[Som2] Sommerfeld, Arnold, *Mechanics*, Lectures on Theoretical Physics, Volume 1, Academic Press, New York, 1964.

[Sta1] Stapp, Henry P., Henry Stapp on Quantum Mechanics, Spirit, Mind, and Morality, *Zygon*, Vol. 41, Number 3, 2006, pp.599–615.

[Sta2] Stapp, Henry P., *Mindful Universe*, Springer-Verlag, Berlin, 2007.

[Sta3] Stapp, Henry P., *Mind, Matter, and Quantum Mechanics*, Springer-Verlag, Berlin, 1993.

[Sta4] Stapp, Henry P., Science's Conception of Human Beings as a Basis for Moral Theory, *Zygon*, Vol. 41, Number 3, 2006, pp.617–21.

[Stö] Störig, Hans Joachim, *Kleine Weltgeschichte der Philosophie*, Fischer Taschenbuch Verlag, Stuttgart, 1999.

[Stra1] Strathern, Paul, *Kant in 90 Minutes*, Ivan R. Dee, Chicago, 1996.

[Stra2] Strathern, Paul, *Thomas Aquinas in 90 Minutes*, Ivan R. Dee, Chicago, 1998.

[Stro] Strobel, Lee, *The Case for Christ*, Zondervan Publishing House, Grand Rapids, Michigan, 1998.

[Tar] Tarnas, Richard, *The Passion of the Western Mind*, Ballantine Books, New York, 1991.

[Te] Teilhard de Chardin, Pierre, *The Future of Man*, translated by Norman Denny, Harper & Row, New York, 1964.

[Th] Thatcher, Oliver J. (Editor in Chief), *The Library of Original Sources*, Volume II, University Research Extension Co., Milwaukee, 1915.

[To] Tolstoy, Leo, *A Confession and Other Religious Writings*, translated by Jane Kentish, Penguin Books, London, 1987.

[Tu] Turing, Alan, Computing machinery and intelligence, *Mind*, LIX (236), 1950, pp.433–60.

[UA] Uhazy, Leslie S., Arendt, Wayne J., Pathogenesis Associated with Philornid Myasis (Diptera: Muscidae) on Nestling Pearly-Eyed Thrashers (Aves: Mimidae) in the Luquillo Rain Forest, Puerto Rico, *Journal of Wildlidfe Diseases*, 22(2), 1986, pp.224–37.

[Ul]   Ulanowicz, Robert E., Emergence, Naturally!, *Zygon*, Vol. 42, Number 4, 2007.

[Va]   de Vacouleurs, Gérard, *Discovery of the Universe*, Macmillan, New York, 1957.

[Ve]   Vedantam, Shankar, Science Peers Closer at 'Near-Death' Experiences, *The International Herald Tribune Online*, Washington Post Service, Dec. 17, 2001, originally available at http://www.iht.com/articles/42139.html.

[Wa]   Waddell Ekstrom, Laura, Libertarianism and Frankfurt-Style Cases, in *The Oxford Handbook of Free Will*, by Robert Kane, ed., Oxford University Press, Oxford, 2002.

[Web]   Weber, Max, Science as Vocation, translated by H.H. Gerth and C. Wright Mills, in *From Max Weber: Essays in Sociology*, by H.H. Gerth (editor), pp.129–56, Oxford University Press, New York, 1946.

[Weh]   Wehr, Gerhard, *Giordano Bruno*, Deutscher Taschenbuch Verlag, München, 1999.

[Wein]   Weinberg, Steven, *Dreams of a Final Theory*, Pantheon Books, New York, 1992.

[Weiz1]   Weizsäcker, Carl Friedrich, *Aufbau der Physik*, Deutscher Taschenbuch Verlag, München, 1988.

[Weiz2]   Weizsäcker, Carl Friedrich, *The Unity of Nature*, translated by F.J. Zucker, Farrar, Straus, Giroux, New York, 1980.

[Wh1]   Wheeler, John Archibald, *Law without Law*, http://www.forizslaszlo.com/tudomany/wheeler_law_without_law.html

[Wh2]   Wheeler, John Archibald, On Recognizing 'Law Without Law', *American Journal of Physics*, 51, 1983.

[Wid]   Widerker, David, Responsibility and Frankfurt-Style Examples, in *The Oxford Handbook of Free Will*, by Robert Kane, ed., Oxford University Press, Oxford, 2002.

[Wig1]   Wigner, Eugene P., The Place of Consciousness in Modern Physics, in *Consciousness and Reality*, Musès, Charles, Young, Arthur M. eds., Avon Books, New York, 1972.

[Wig2]   Wigner, Eugene P., The Unreasonable Effectiveness of Mathematics, in *Mathematics and Science*, Mickens, Ronald E. ed., World Scientific, Singapore, 1998.

[Wit]   Wittgenstein, Ludwig, *Tractatus Logico-Philosophicus*, The Humanities Press, New York, 1974.

[Ze]   Zee, A., *Quantum Field Theory in a Nutshell*, Princeton University Press, Princeton, New Jersey, 2003.

[Zi]   Zinn, Howard, *A People's History of the United States*, Perennial Classics, New York, 2001.

76635350R10324

Made in the USA
San Bernardino, CA
16 May 2018